Praise for

daytripper

"From being ... world to comic con... ... lizing their life's w... ...young. ...utten and utterly gorgeous, *Daytripper* completely blew me away. Even more startling is the fact that for them this is truly just the beginning."
-Gerard Way
(*Umbrella Academy*, My Chemical Romance)

"Whimsical, professional,
and hauntingly charming in all the best ways."
-COMICS ALLIANCE

"The story is honest and arousing, and everything about Fábio Moon's artwork is sexy—even when it's dirty and lonely. Once I started reading *Daytripper*, I couldn't put it down!"
-Jeff Smith
(Bone)

"A story that lingers."
— THE COMICS JOURNAL

"Great. . . A cool, cool book."
-Blair Butler,
G4/Fresh Ink Pick of the Week

"*Daytripper* is the most engaging story I've read all year.
Fábio Moon and Gabriel Bá's tale of the life and deaths of a writer in Brazil is the creative love-child of Eisner and Fellini at their best; a love story grounded in stark reality, yet awash in the magic of circumstance. *Daytripper* is a fascinating puzzle I will be contemplating for the rest of my life."
-Terry Moore
(*Strangers in Paradise*, Echo)

"Every bit of this book was perfectly executed, from the way the story was presented to the art chores to Dave Stewart's ungodly coloring abilities and on and on... a rousing success."
-AIN'T IT COOL NEWS

"This latest from the Brazilian wonder twins is surely their best-looking work to date. In *Daytripper*, they give us a glimpse into an exotic yet believable world. It makes you want to be there with them...!"
-Paul Pope
(100%, BATMAN: YEAR 100)

"I couldn't be happier with how sad it made me feel... a believable, grounded celebration of life with just enough magical realism..."
-SAN ANTONIO EXPRESS-NEWS/Geek Speak

"Substantial."
-BOSTON HERALD

"Moon and Bá have crafted a frighteningly human story, winding together the moments that define who we are to weave a tapestry of life and death. Lyrical, poetic, and haunting, *Daytripper* is an experience that will resonate with you long after you have put the book down."
-Becky Cloonan
(DEMO, *East Coast Rising*)

"These Brazilian twins have the gift, the storyteller's gift. They so gracefully unwrap the tale of Brás de Oliva Domingos, an obit writer who dreams of more memorable prose, that you don't even recognize that their story has picked up speed before it carries you away."
-THE OREGONIAN

"Vertigo's newest book will be another fantastic addition to their illustrious library."
-CRAVE

"A book that forces you to slow down and think... A great book for those looking for something different in their comic book reading experience."
-IGN

"Beautifully written and illustrated... Will leave you panting for more."
-AM NEW YORK

"With its subtle but expert craftsmanship, its unique tale and innovative telling, its true-to-life characters and story beats, *Daytripper* doesn't just make a case for comics as literature or even comics as art: it makes an impassioned plea... Denying its brilliance is to deny life itself."
–POPMATTERS

daytripper

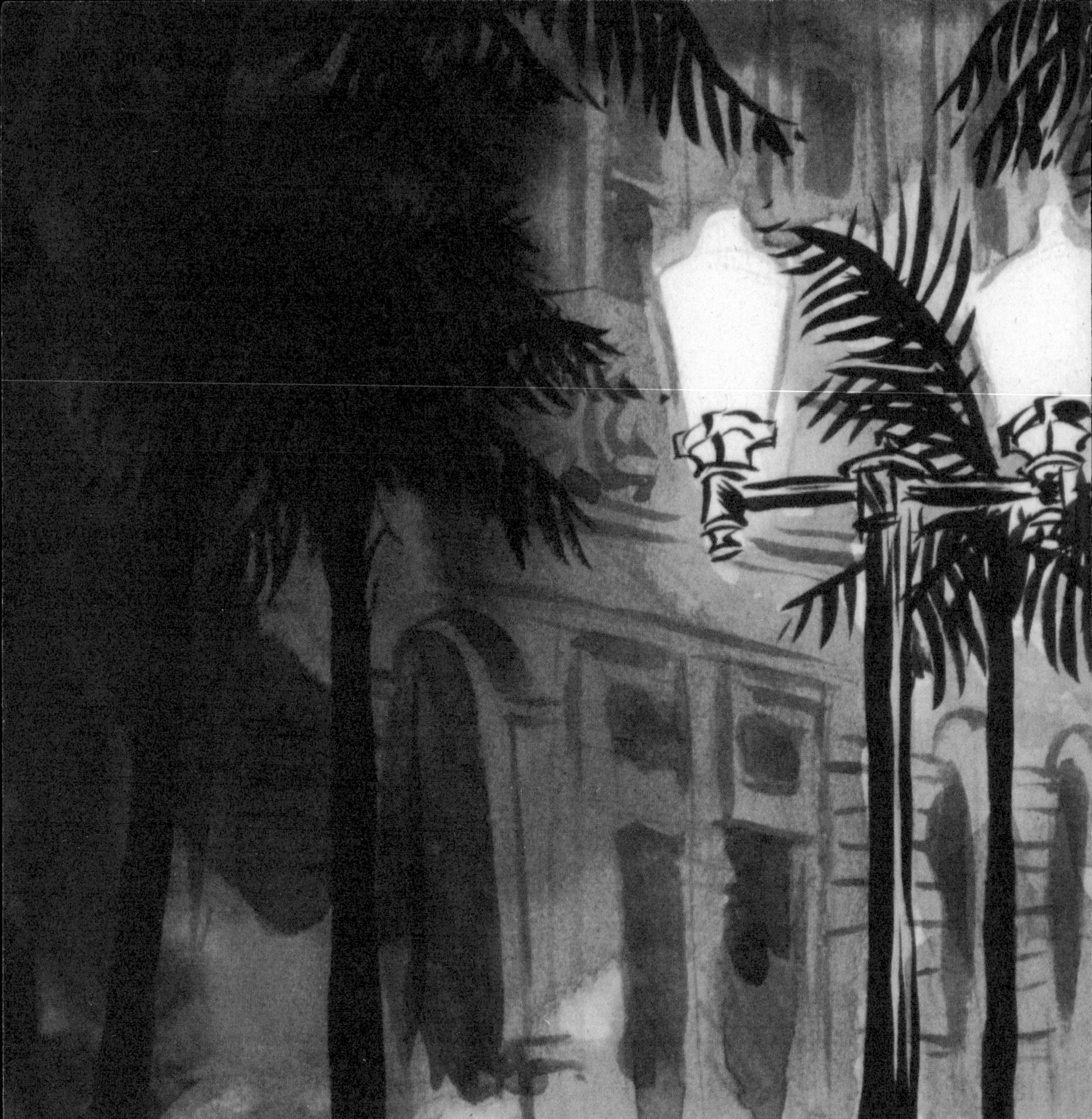

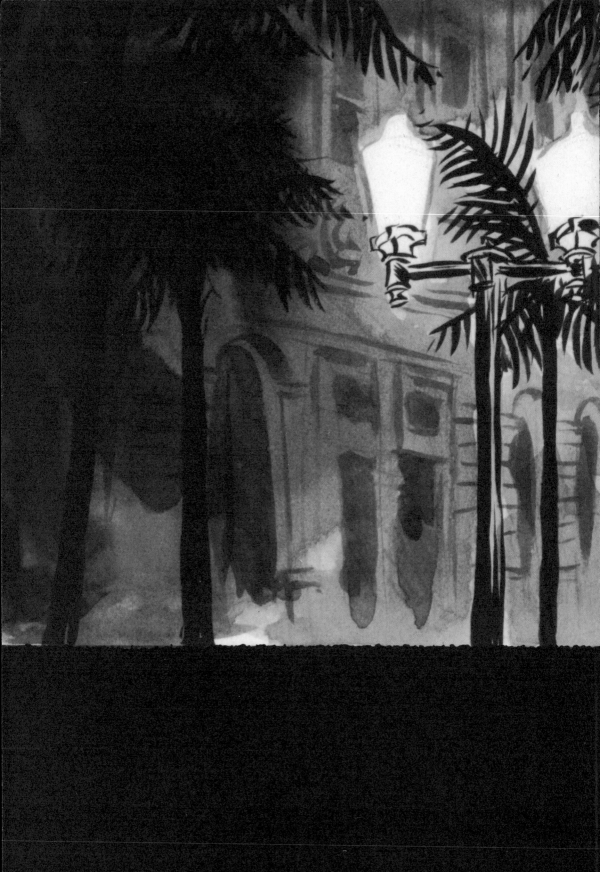

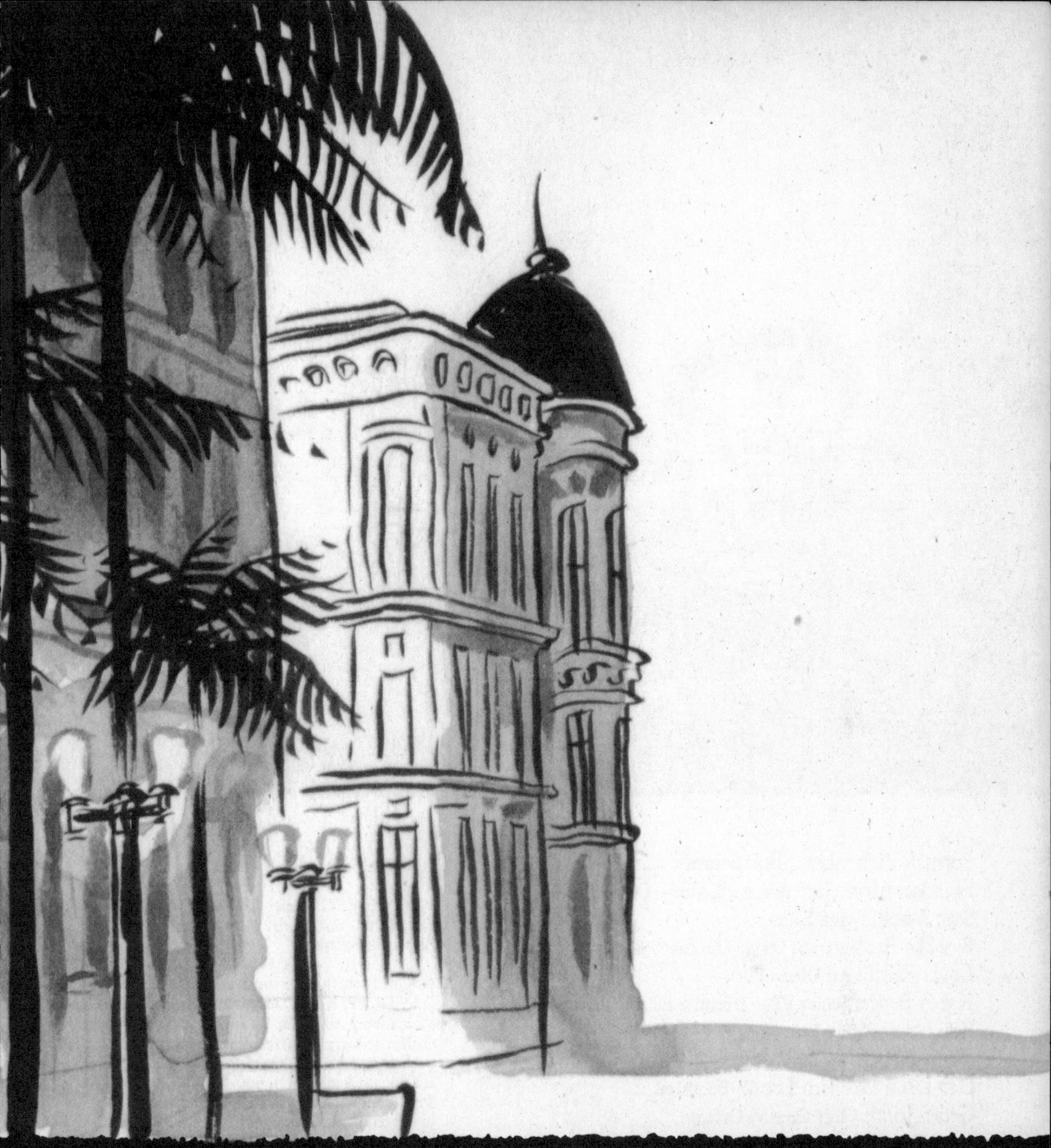

daytripper

By Fábio Moon & Gabriel Bá

with

coloring by Dave Stewart

lettering by Sean Konot

Pornsak Pichetshote, Bob Schreck Editors — Original Series
Brandon Montclare Assistant Editor — Original Series
Sean Mackiewicz Editor
Robbin Brosterman Design Director — Books
Louis Prandi Art Director
Karen Berger Senior VP — Executive Editor, Vertigo
Bob Harras VP — Editor-in-Chief
Diane Nelson President
Dan DiDio and Jim Lee Co-Publishers
Geoff Johns Chief Creative Officer
John Rood Executive VP — Sales, Marketing
and Business Development
Amy Genkins Senior VP — Business and Legal Affairs
Nairi Gardiner Senior VP — Finance
Jeff Boison VP — Publishing Operations
Mark Chiarello VP — Art Direction and Design
John Cunningham VP — Marketing
Terri Cunningham VP — Talent Relations and Services
Alison Gill Senior VP — Manufacturing and Operations
David Hyde VP — Publicity
Hank Kanalz Senior VP — Digital
Jay Kogan VP — Business and Legal Affairs, Publishing
Jack Mahan VP — Business Affairs, Talent
Nick Napolitano VP — Manufacturing Administration
Sue Pohja VP — Book Sales
Courtney Simmons Senior VP — Publicity
Bob Wayne Senior VP — Sales

DAYTRIPPER

Published by DC Comics. Cover, text and compilation
Copyright © 2011 Gabriel Bá and Fábio Moon.
All Rights Reserved.

Originally published in single magazine form as
DAYTRIPPER 1-10. Copyright © 2010 Gabriel Bá and
Fábio Moon. All Rights Reserved. All characters, their
distinctive likenesses and related elements featured in this
publication are trademarks of DC Comics. VERTIGO
is a trademark of DC Comics.
The stories, characters and incidents featured
in this publication are entirely fictional.
DC Comics does not read or accept unsolicited
submissions of ideas, stories or artwork.

DC Comics, 1700 Broadway,
New York, NY 10019
A Warner Bros. Entertainment Company
Printed in the USA. Fifth Printing.
ISBN:978-1-4012-2969-6

SUSTAINABLE
FORESTRY
INITIATIVE
Certified Sourcing
www.sfiprogram.org
SFI-01042
APPLIES TO TEXT STOCK ONLY

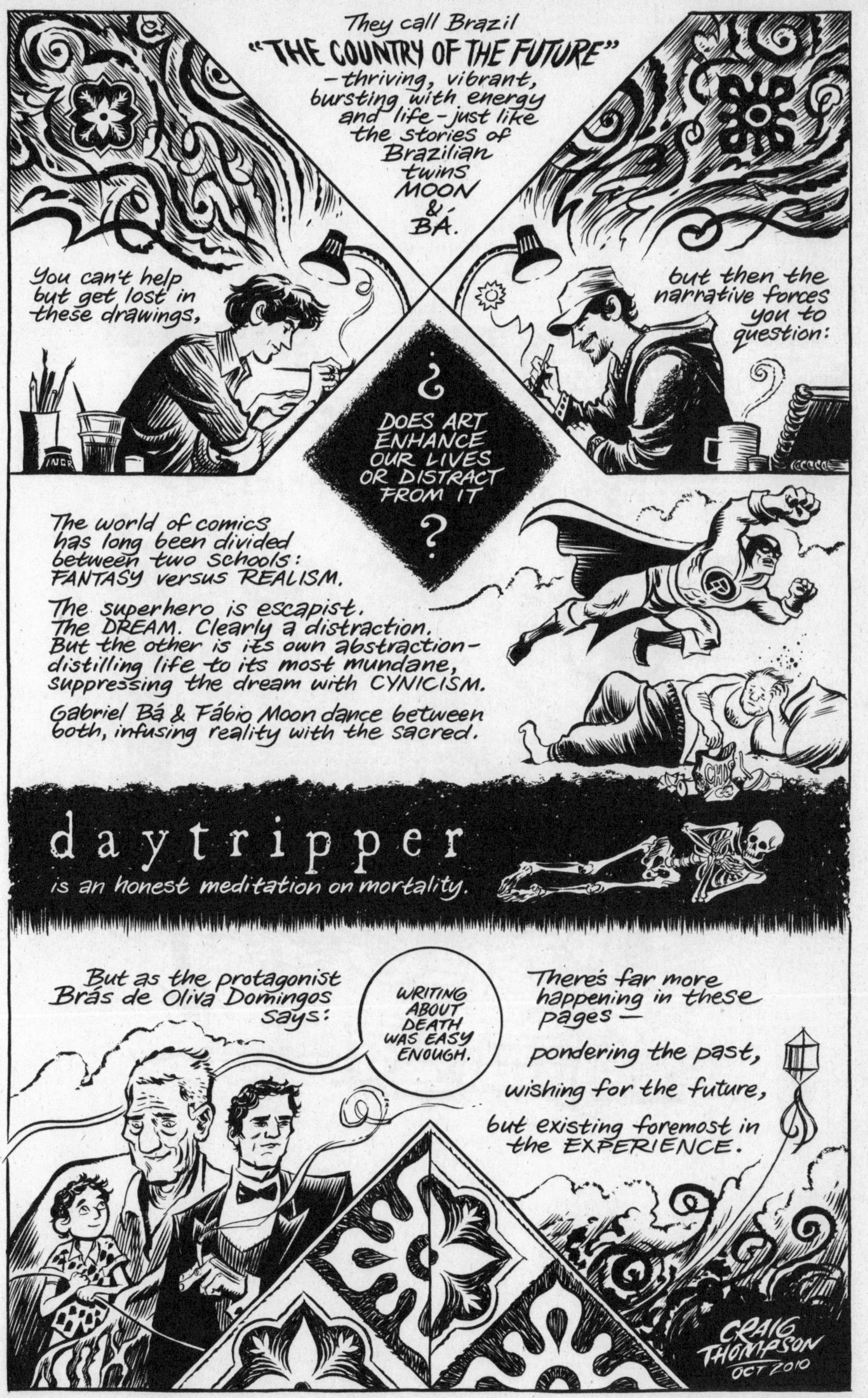
They call Brazil "THE COUNTRY OF THE FUTURE" —thriving, vibrant, bursting with energy and life—just like the stories of Brazilian twins MOON & BÁ.
You can't help but get lost in these drawings,
but then the narrative forces you to question:
¿ DOES ART ENHANCE OUR LIVES OR DISTRACT FROM IT ?
The world of comics has long been divided between two schools: FANTASY versus REALISM.
The superhero is escapist. The DREAM. Clearly a distraction. But the other is its own abstraction—distilling life to its most mundane, suppressing the dream with CYNICISM.
Gabriel Bá & Fábio Moon dance between both, infusing reality with the sacred.
CHIPS
daytripper
is an honest meditation on mortality.
But as the protagonist Brás de Oliva Domingos says:
WRITING ABOUT DEATH WAS EASY ENOUGH.
There's far more happening in these pages—
pondering the past,
wishing for the future,
but existing foremost in the EXPERIENCE.
CRAIG THOMPSON OCT 2010

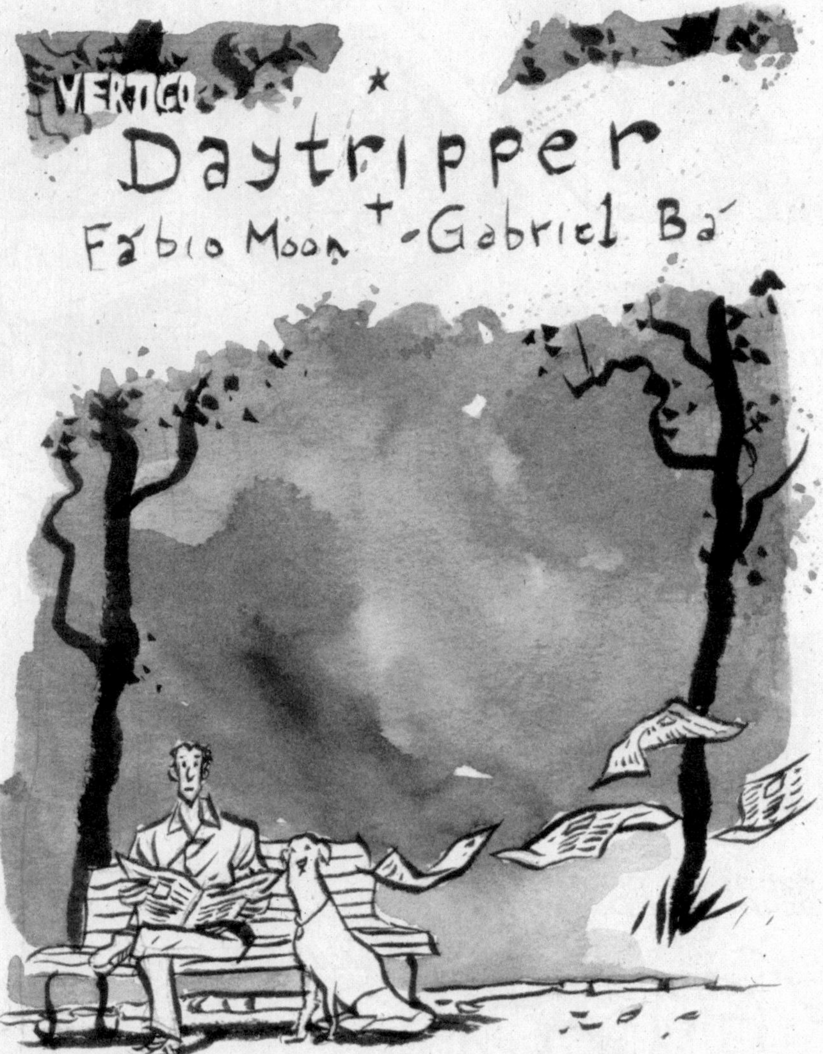
VERTIGO
Daytripper
Fábio Moon + Gabriel Bá

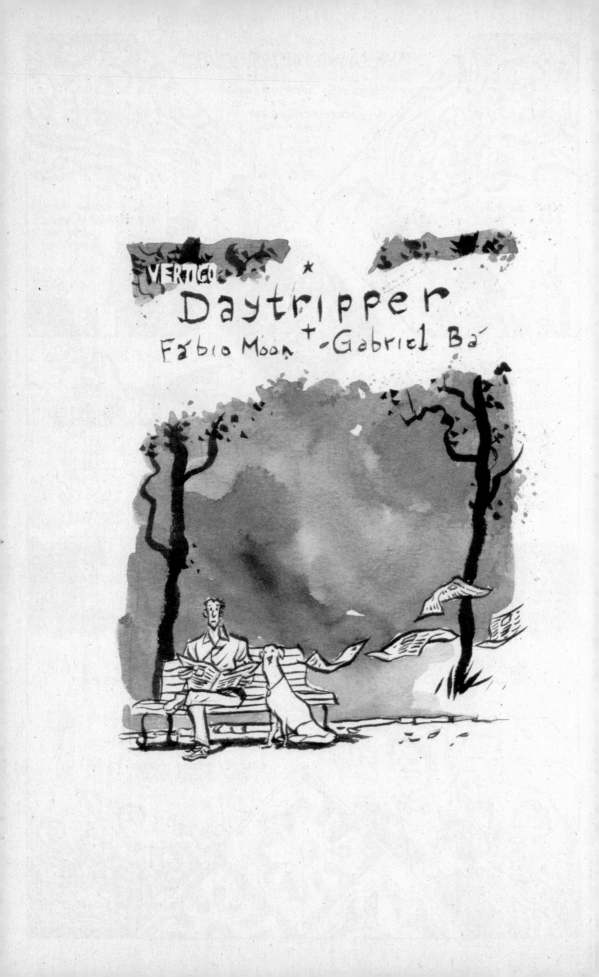

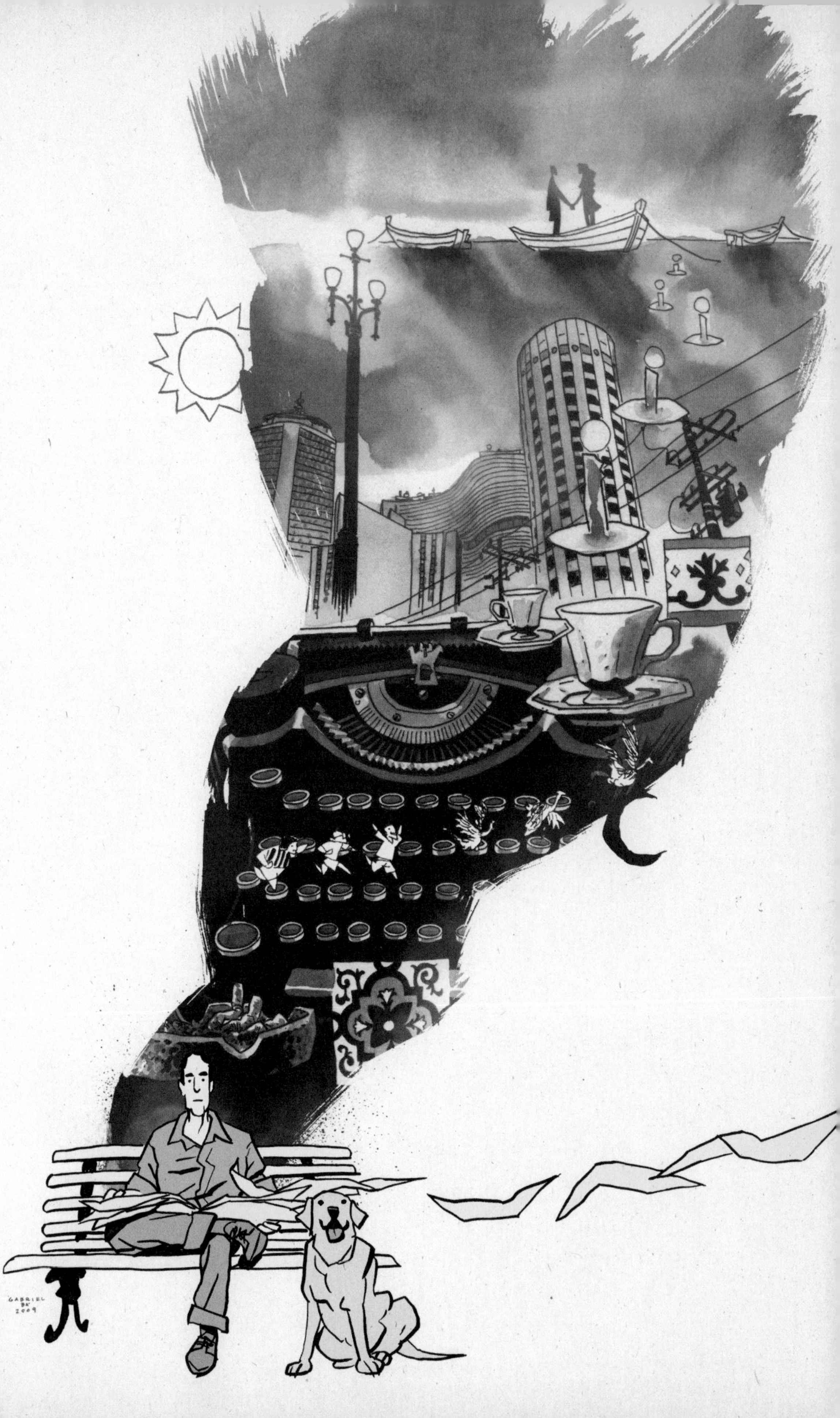
GABRIEL
BÁ
2009

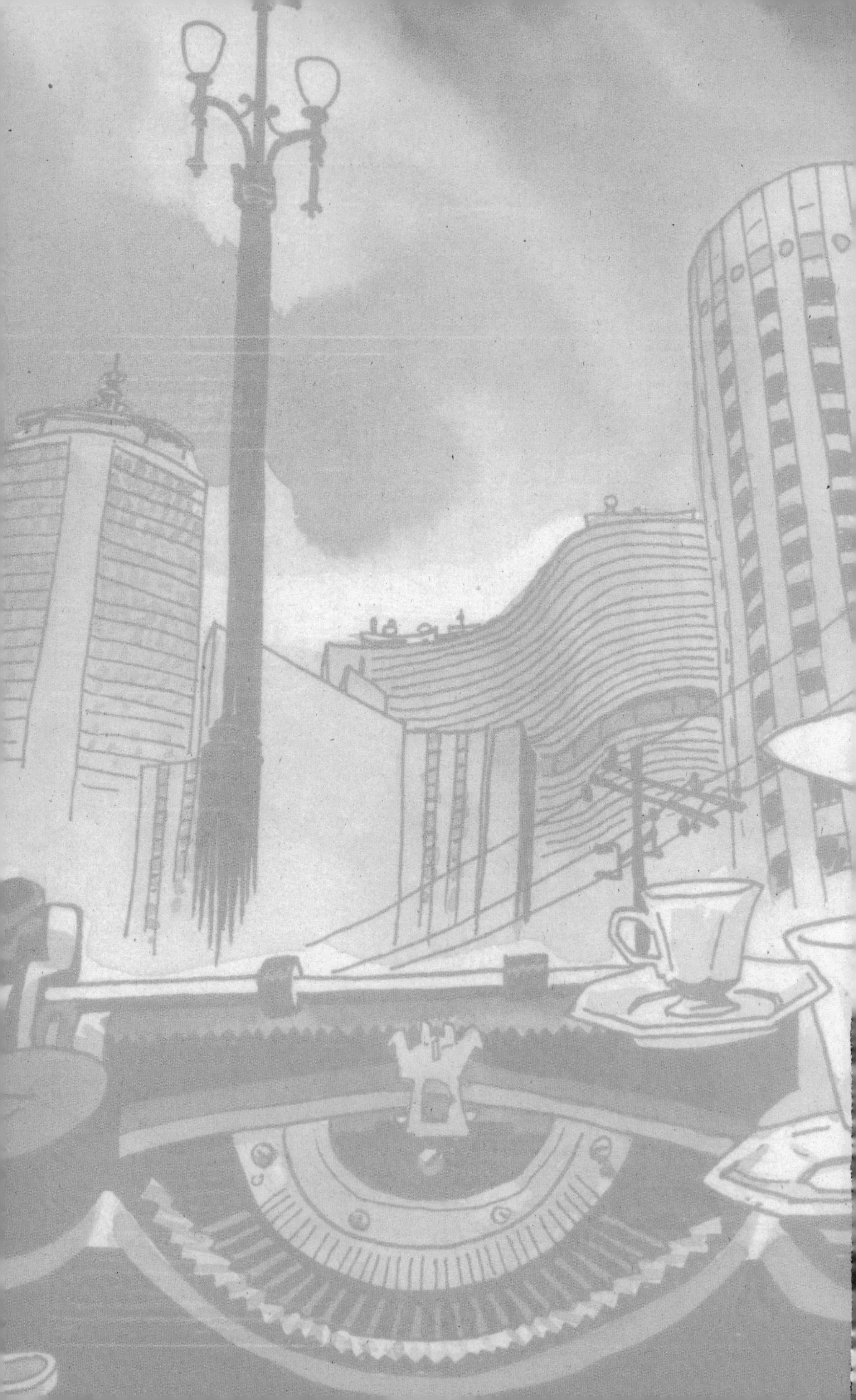

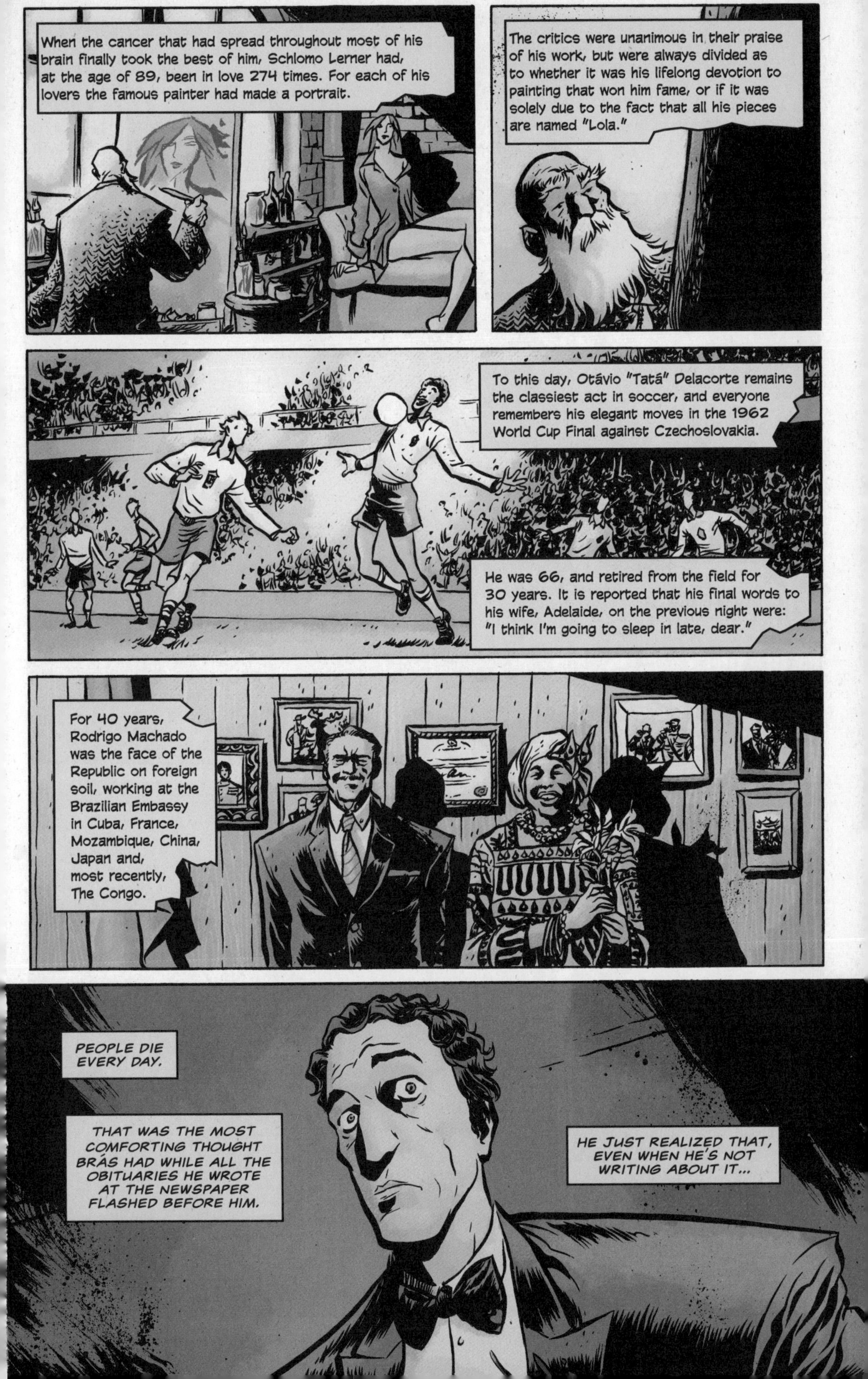
When the cancer that had spread throughout most of his brain finally took the best of him, Schlomo Lerner had, at the age of 89, been in love 274 times. For each of his lovers the famous painter had made a portrait.
The critics were unanimous in their praise of his work, but were always divided as to whether it was his lifelong devotion to painting that won him fame, or if it was solely due to the fact that all his pieces are named "Lola."
To this day, Otávio "Tatá" Delacorte remains the classiest act in soccer, and everyone remembers his elegant moves in the 1962 World Cup Final against Czechoslovakia.
He was 66, and retired from the field for 30 years. It is reported that his final words to his wife, Adelaide, on the previous night were: "I think I'm going to sleep in late, dear."
For 40 years, Rodrigo Machado was the face of the Republic on foreign soil, working at the Brazilian Embassy in Cuba, France, Mozambique, China, Japan and, most recently, The Congo.
PEOPLE DIE EVERY DAY.
THAT WAS THE MOST COMFORTING THOUGHT BRÁS HAD WHILE ALL THE OBITUARIES HE WROTE AT THE NEWSPAPER FLASHED BEFORE HIM.
HE JUST REALIZED THAT, EVEN WHEN HE'S NOT WRITING ABOUT IT...

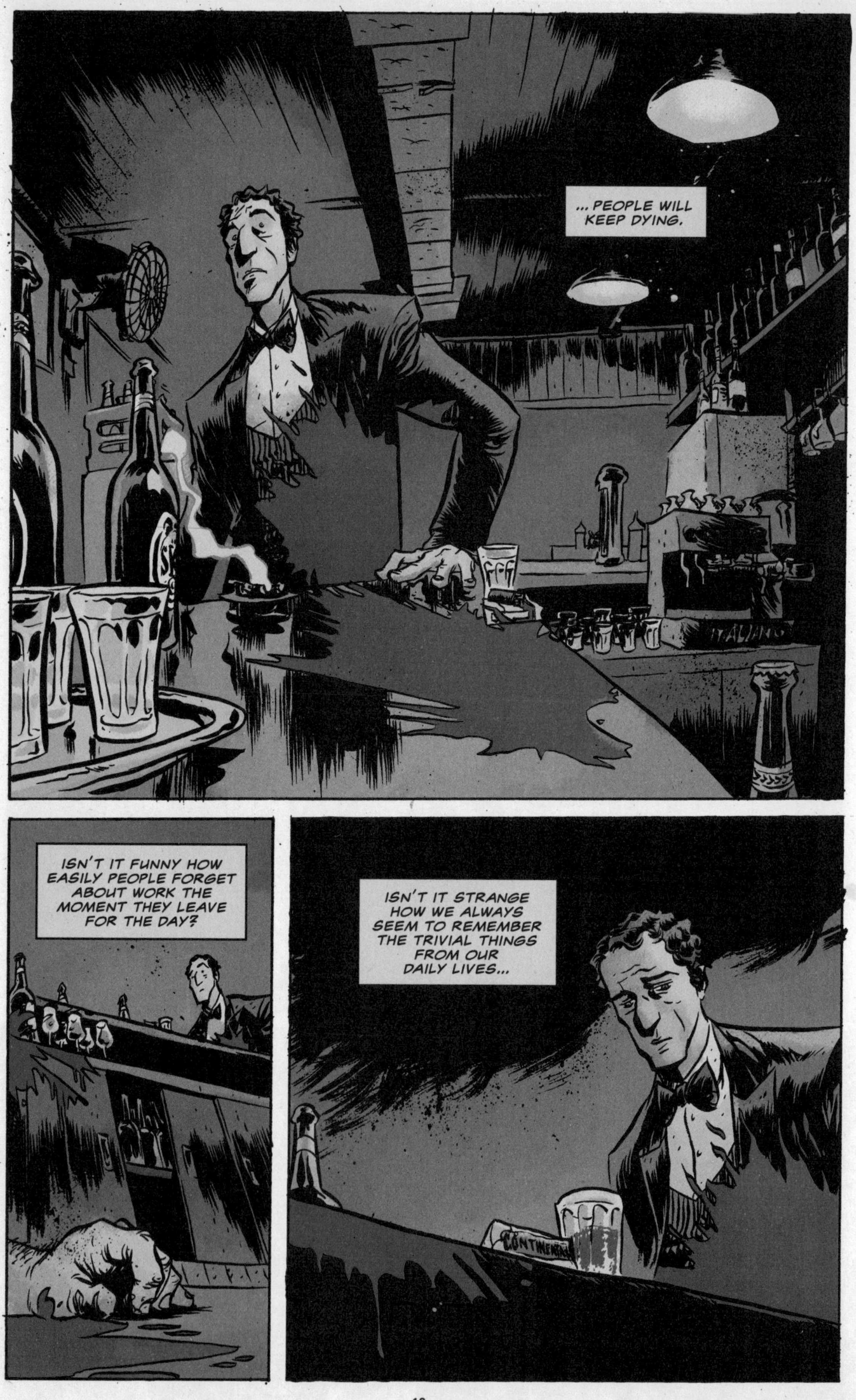
...PEOPLE WILL KEEP DYING.
ISN'T IT FUNNY HOW EASILY PEOPLE FORGET ABOUT WORK THE MOMENT THEY LEAVE FOR THE DAY?
ISN'T IT STRANGE HOW WE ALWAYS SEEM TO REMEMBER THE TRIVIAL THINGS FROM OUR DAILY LIVES...

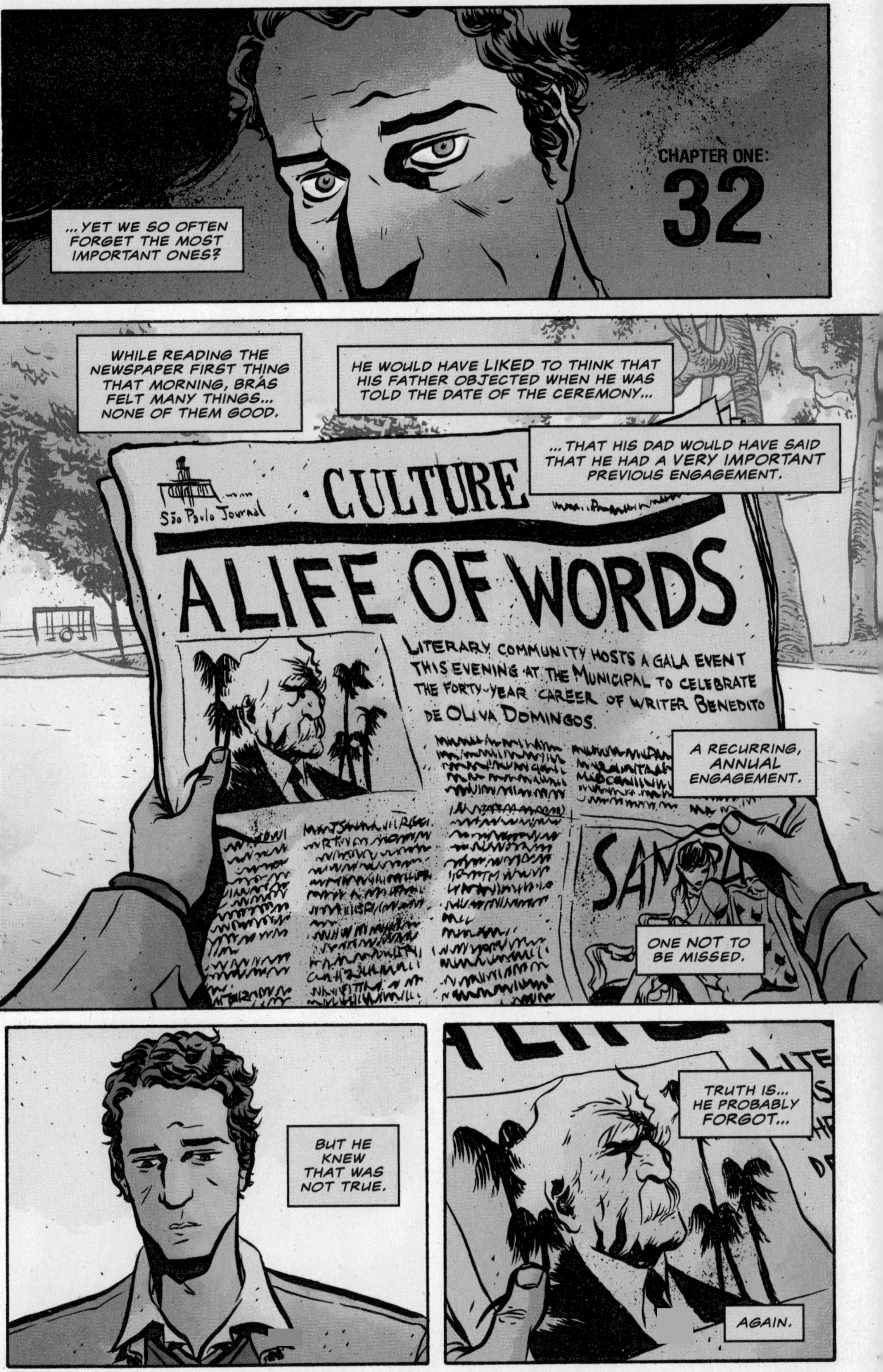
CHAPTER ONE:
32
...YET WE SO OFTEN FORGET THE MOST IMPORTANT ONES?
WHILE READING THE NEWSPAPER FIRST THING THAT MORNING, BRÁS FELT MANY THINGS... NONE OF THEM GOOD.
HE WOULD HAVE LIKED TO THINK THAT HIS FATHER OBJECTED WHEN HE WAS TOLD THE DATE OF THE CEREMONY...
...THAT HIS DAD WOULD HAVE SAID THAT HE HAD A VERY IMPORTANT PREVIOUS ENGAGEMENT.
São Paulo Journal
CULTURE
A LIFE OF WORDS
LITERARY COMMUNITY HOSTS A GALA EVENT THIS EVENING AT THE MUNICIPAL TO CELEBRATE THE FORTY-YEAR CAREER OF WRITER BENEDITO DE OLIVA DOMINGOS.
A RECURRING, ANNUAL ENGAGEMENT.
ONE NOT TO BE MISSED.
BUT HE KNEW THAT WAS NOT TRUE.
TRUTH IS... HE PROBABLY FORGOT...
AGAIN.

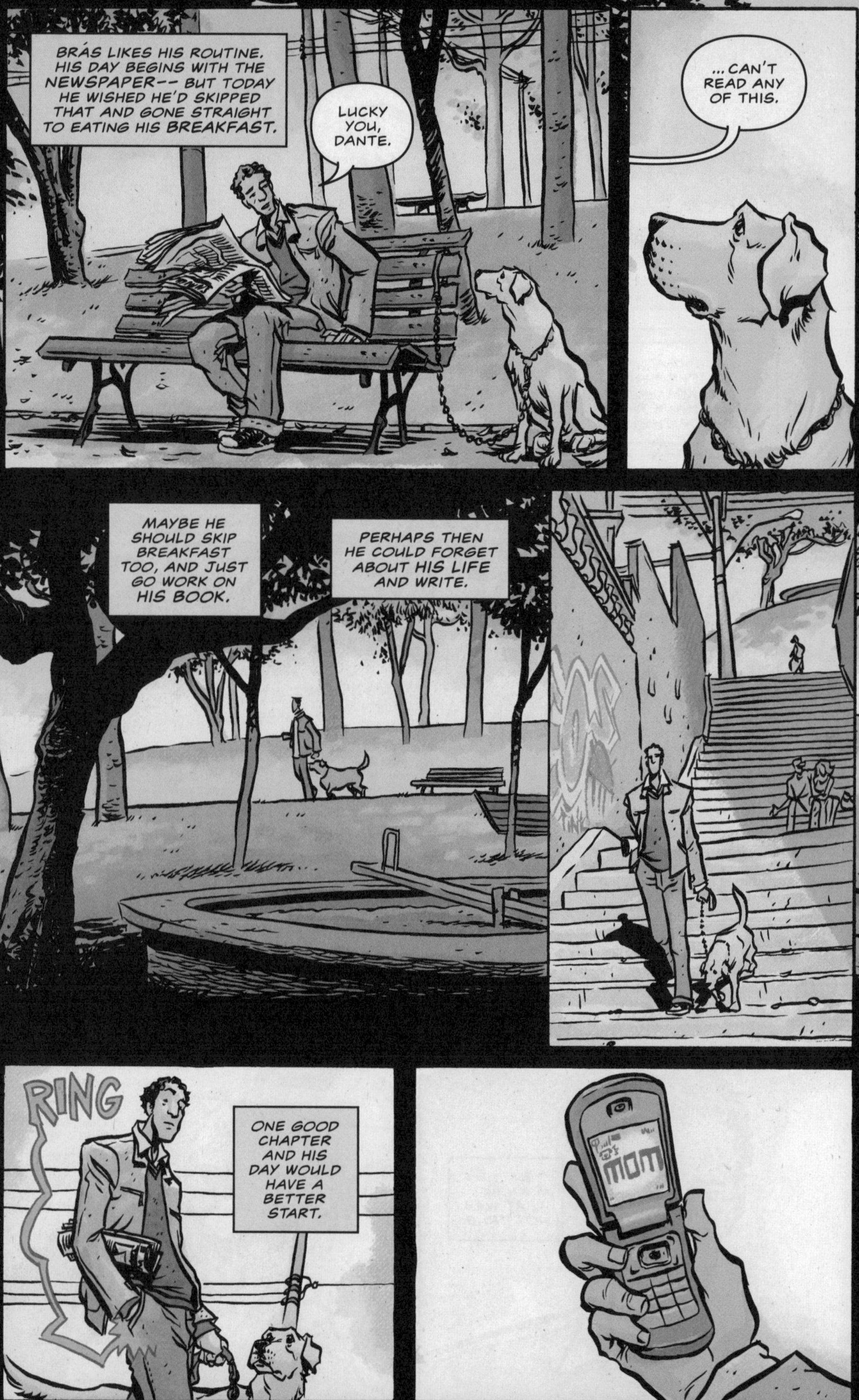
BRÁS LIKES HIS ROUTINE. HIS DAY BEGINS WITH THE NEWSPAPER-- BUT TODAY HE WISHED HE'D SKIPPED THAT AND GONE STRAIGHT TO EATING HIS BREAKFAST.
LUCKY YOU, DANTE.
...CAN'T READ ANY OF THIS.
MAYBE HE SHOULD SKIP BREAKFAST TOO, AND JUST GO WORK ON HIS BOOK.
PERHAPS THEN HE COULD FORGET ABOUT HIS LIFE AND WRITE.
RING
ONE GOOD CHAPTER AND HIS DAY WOULD HAVE A BETTER START.
MOM

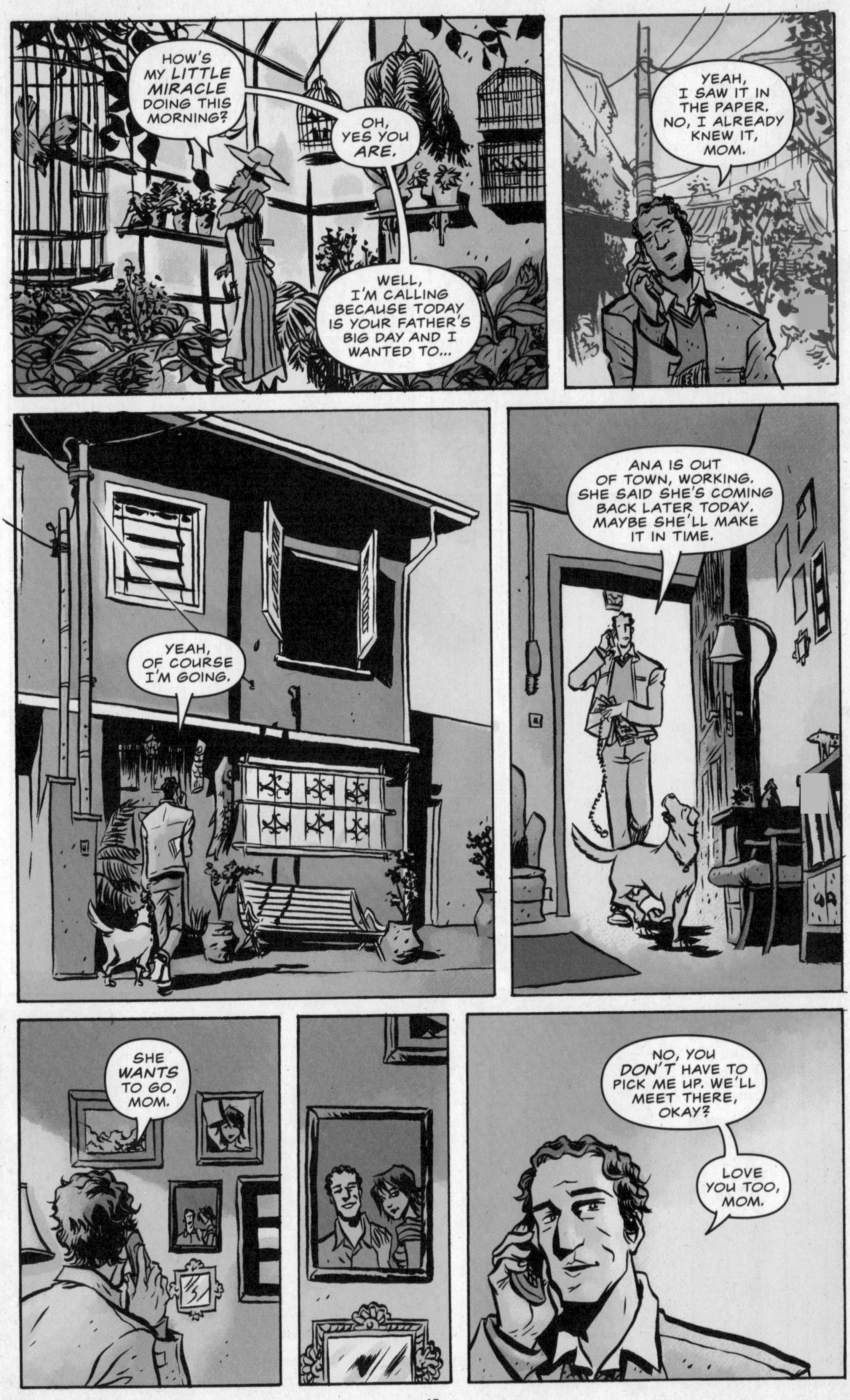
HOW'S MY LITTLE MIRACLE DOING THIS MORNING?
OH, YES YOU ARE.
WELL, I'M CALLING BECAUSE TODAY IS YOUR FATHER'S BIG DAY AND I WANTED TO...
YEAH, I SAW IT IN THE PAPER. NO, I ALREADY KNEW IT, MOM.
YEAH, OF COURSE I'M GOING.
ANA IS OUT OF TOWN, WORKING. SHE SAID SHE'S COMING BACK LATER TODAY. MAYBE SHE'LL MAKE IT IN TIME.
SHE WANTS TO GO, MOM.
NO, YOU DON'T HAVE TO PICK ME UP. WE'LL MEET THERE, OKAY?
LOVE YOU TOO, MOM.

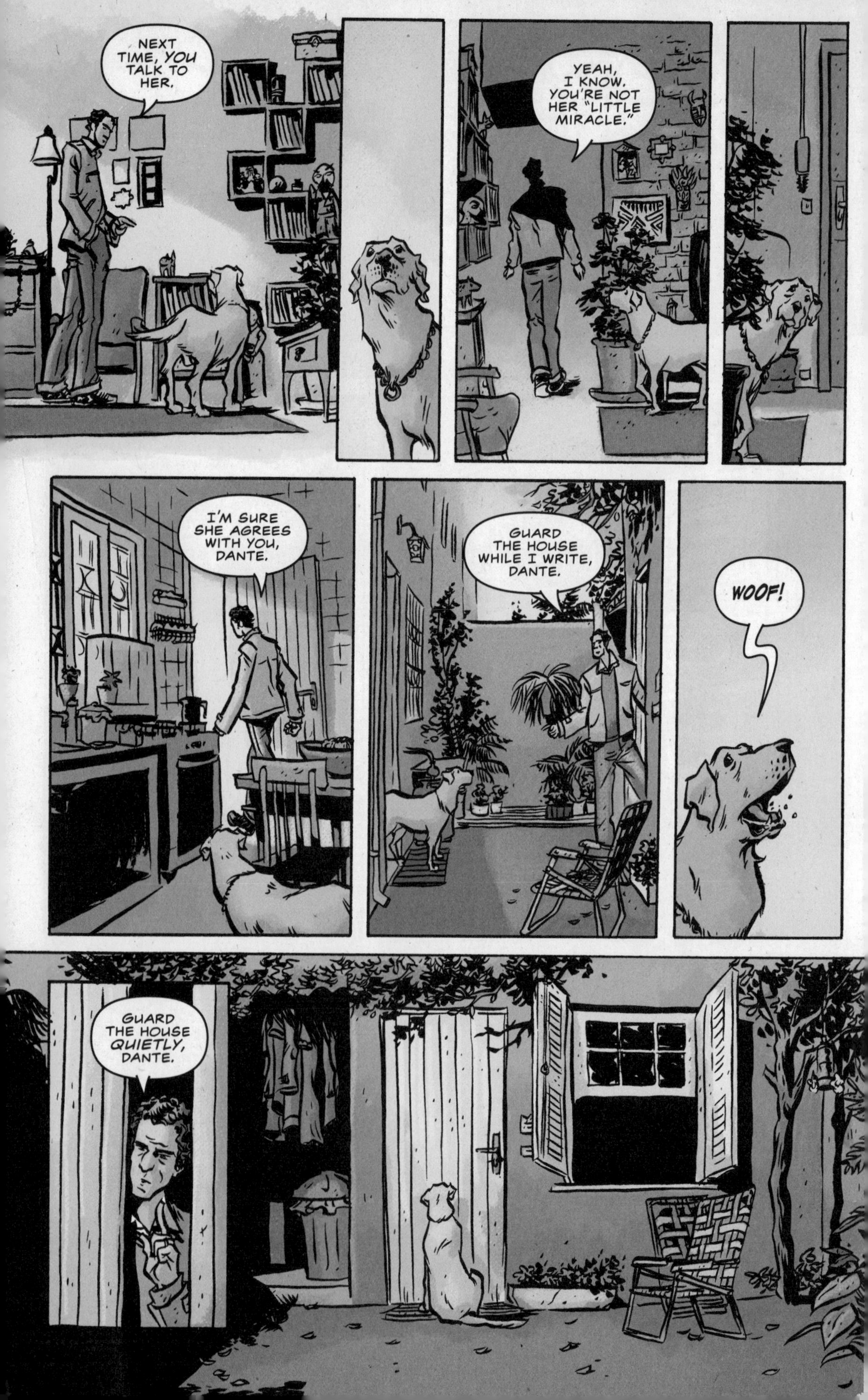
NEXT TIME, YOU TALK TO HER.
YEAH, I KNOW. YOU'RE NOT HER "LITTLE MIRACLE."
I'M SURE SHE AGREES WITH YOU, DANTE.
GUARD THE HOUSE WHILE I WRITE, DANTE.
WOOF!
GUARD THE HOUSE QUIETLY, DANTE.

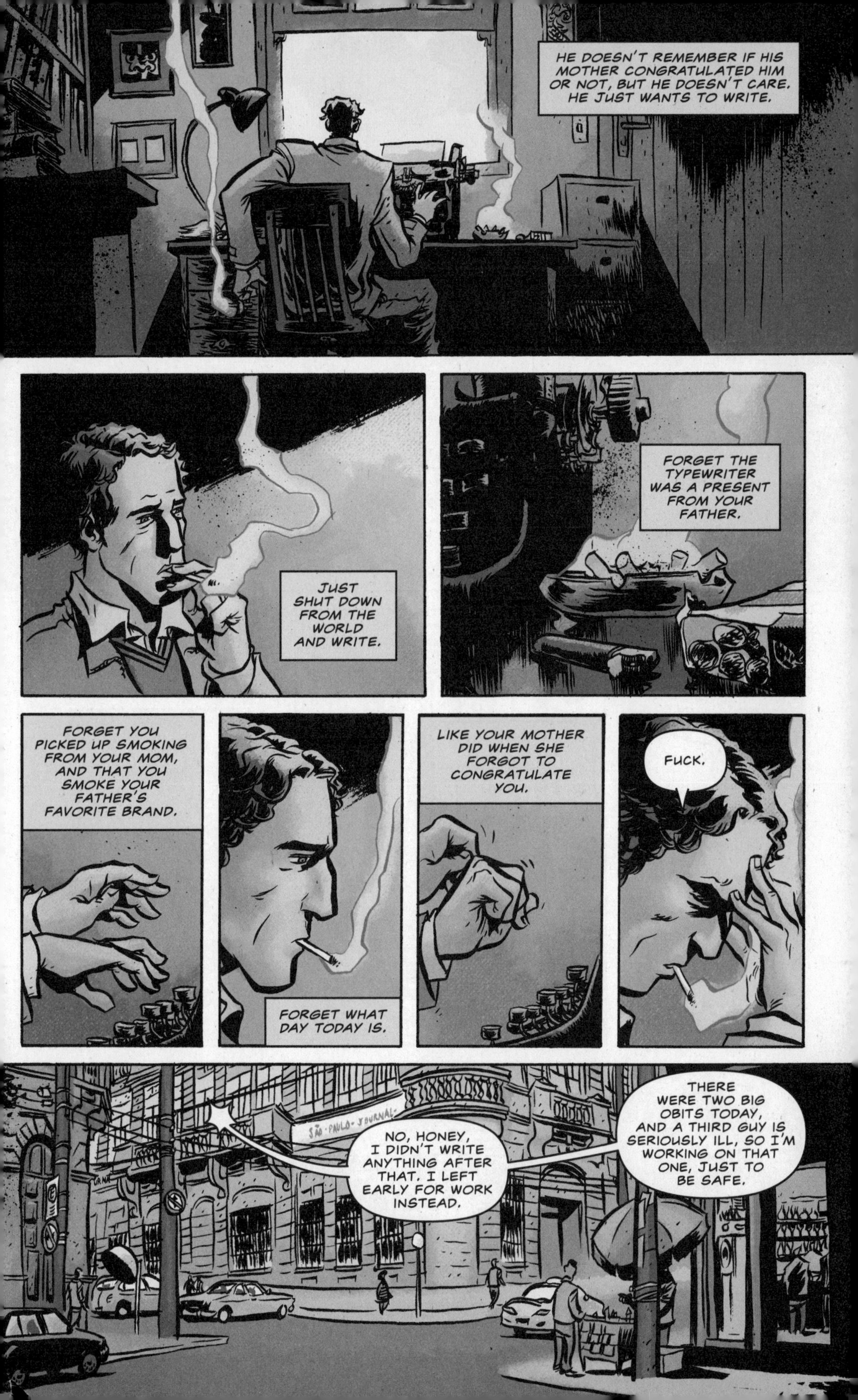
HE DOESN'T REMEMBER IF HIS MOTHER CONGRATULATED HIM OR NOT, BUT HE DOESN'T CARE. HE JUST WANTS TO WRITE.
JUST SHUT DOWN FROM THE WORLD AND WRITE.
FORGET THE TYPEWRITER WAS A PRESENT FROM YOUR FATHER.
FORGET YOU PICKED UP SMOKING FROM YOUR MOM, AND THAT YOU SMOKE YOUR FATHER'S FAVORITE BRAND.
FORGET WHAT DAY TODAY IS.
LIKE YOUR MOTHER DID WHEN SHE FORGOT TO CONGRATULATE YOU.
FUCK.
SÃO PAULO JOURNAL
NO, HONEY, I DIDN'T WRITE ANYTHING AFTER THAT. I LEFT EARLY FOR WORK INSTEAD.
THERE WERE TWO BIG OBITS TODAY, AND A THIRD GUY IS SERIOUSLY ILL, SO I'M WORKING ON THAT ONE, JUST TO BE SAFE.

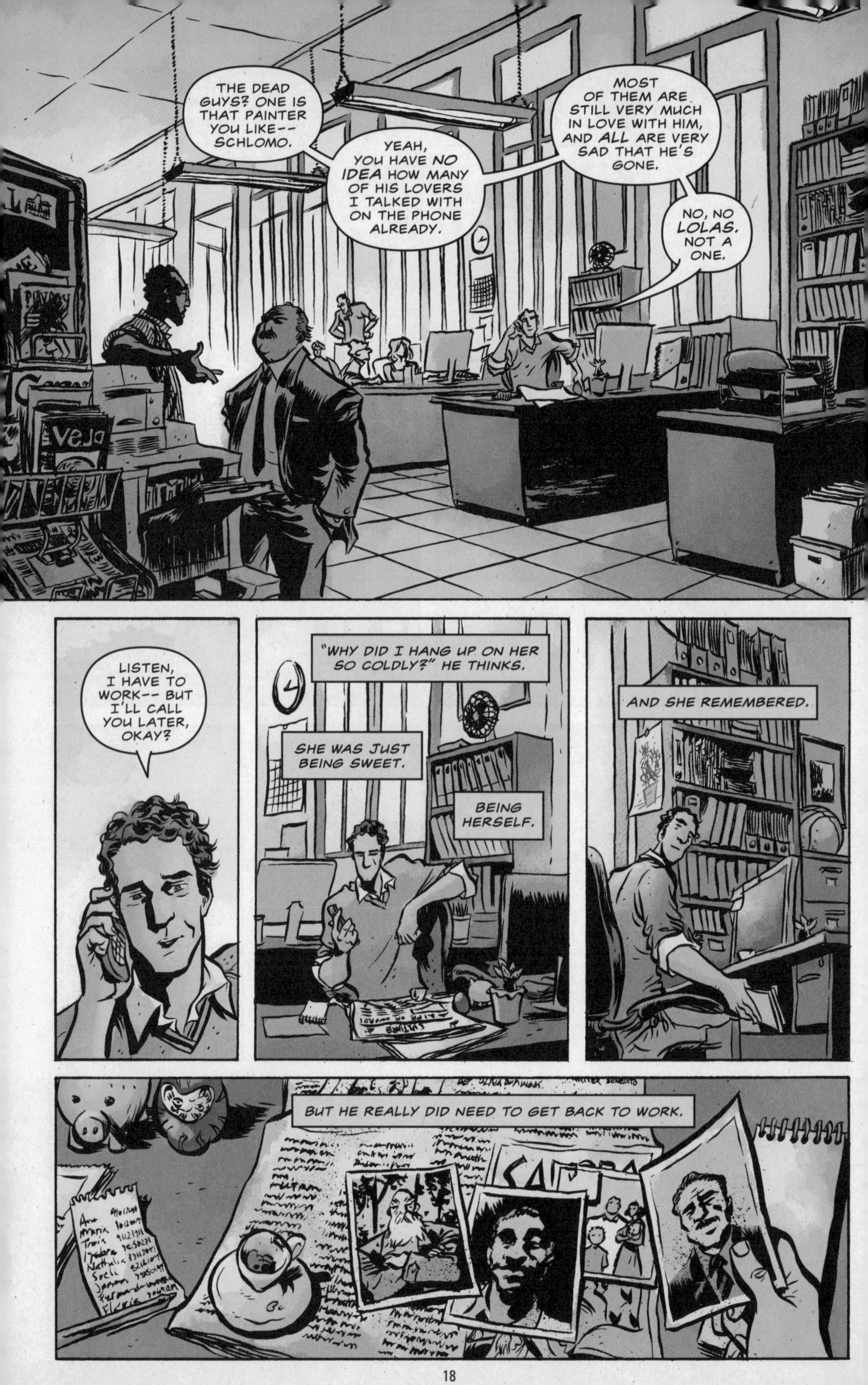

THE DEAD GUYS? ONE IS THAT PAINTER YOU LIKE-- SCHLOMO.
YEAH, YOU HAVE NO IDEA HOW MANY OF HIS LOVERS I TALKED WITH ON THE PHONE ALREADY.
MOST OF THEM ARE STILL VERY MUCH IN LOVE WITH HIM, AND ALL ARE VERY SAD THAT HE'S GONE.
NO, NO LOLAS. NOT A ONE.
LISTEN, I HAVE TO WORK-- BUT I'LL CALL YOU LATER, OKAY?
"WHY DID I HANG UP ON HER SO COLDLY?" HE THINKS.
SHE WAS JUST BEING SWEET.
BEING HERSELF.
AND SHE REMEMBERED.
BUT HE REALLY DID NEED TO GET BACK TO WORK.

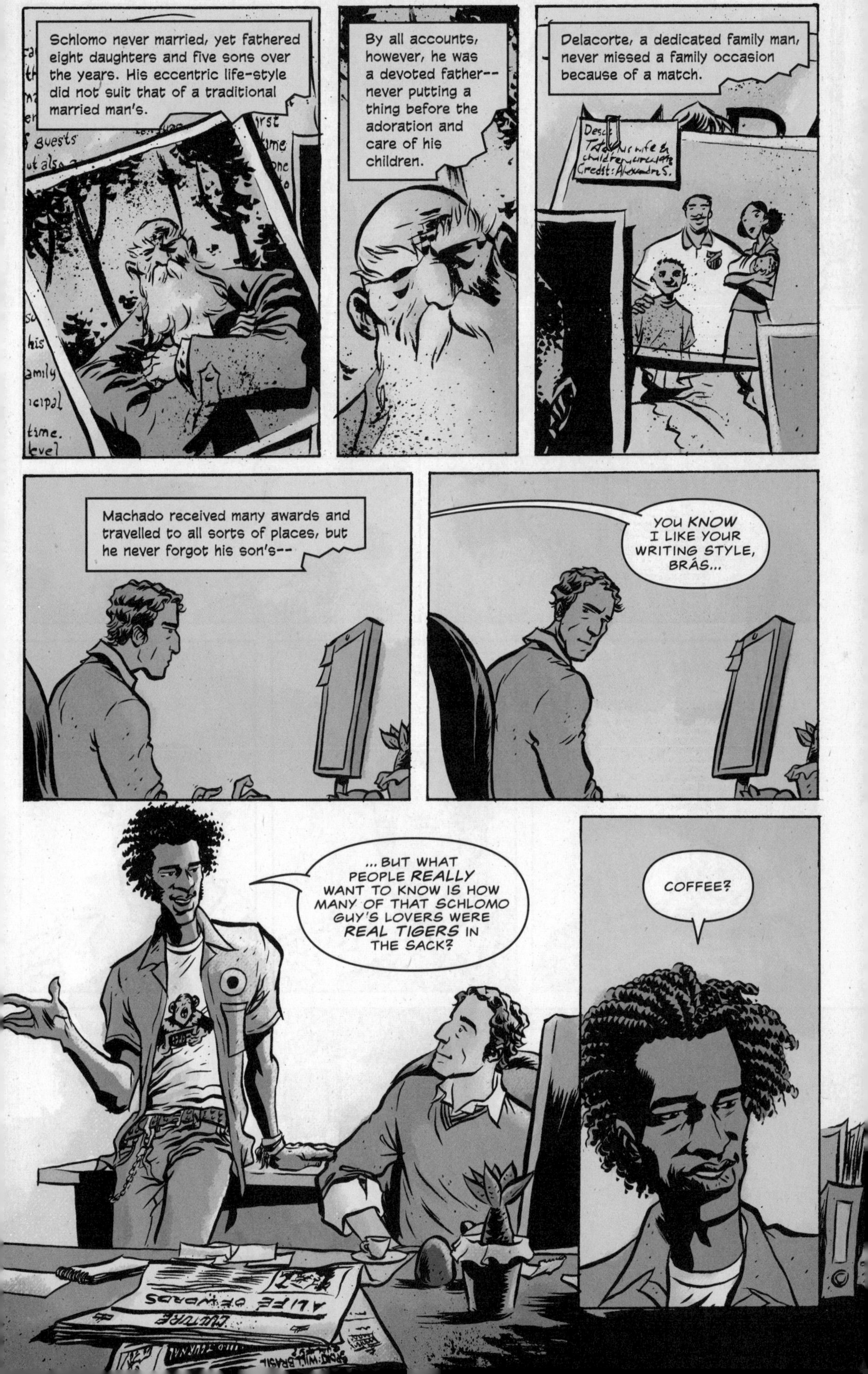
Schlomo never married, yet fathered eight daughters and five sons over the years. His eccentric life-style did not suit that of a traditional married man's.
By all accounts, however, he was a devoted father--never putting a thing before the adoration and care of his children.
Delacorte, a dedicated family man, never missed a family occasion because of a match.
Machado received many awards and travelled to all sorts of places, but he never forgot his son's--
YOU KNOW I LIKE YOUR WRITING STYLE, BRÁS...
...BUT WHAT PEOPLE REALLY WANT TO KNOW IS HOW MANY OF THAT SCHLOMO GUY'S LOVERS WERE REAL TIGERS IN THE SACK?
COFFEE?

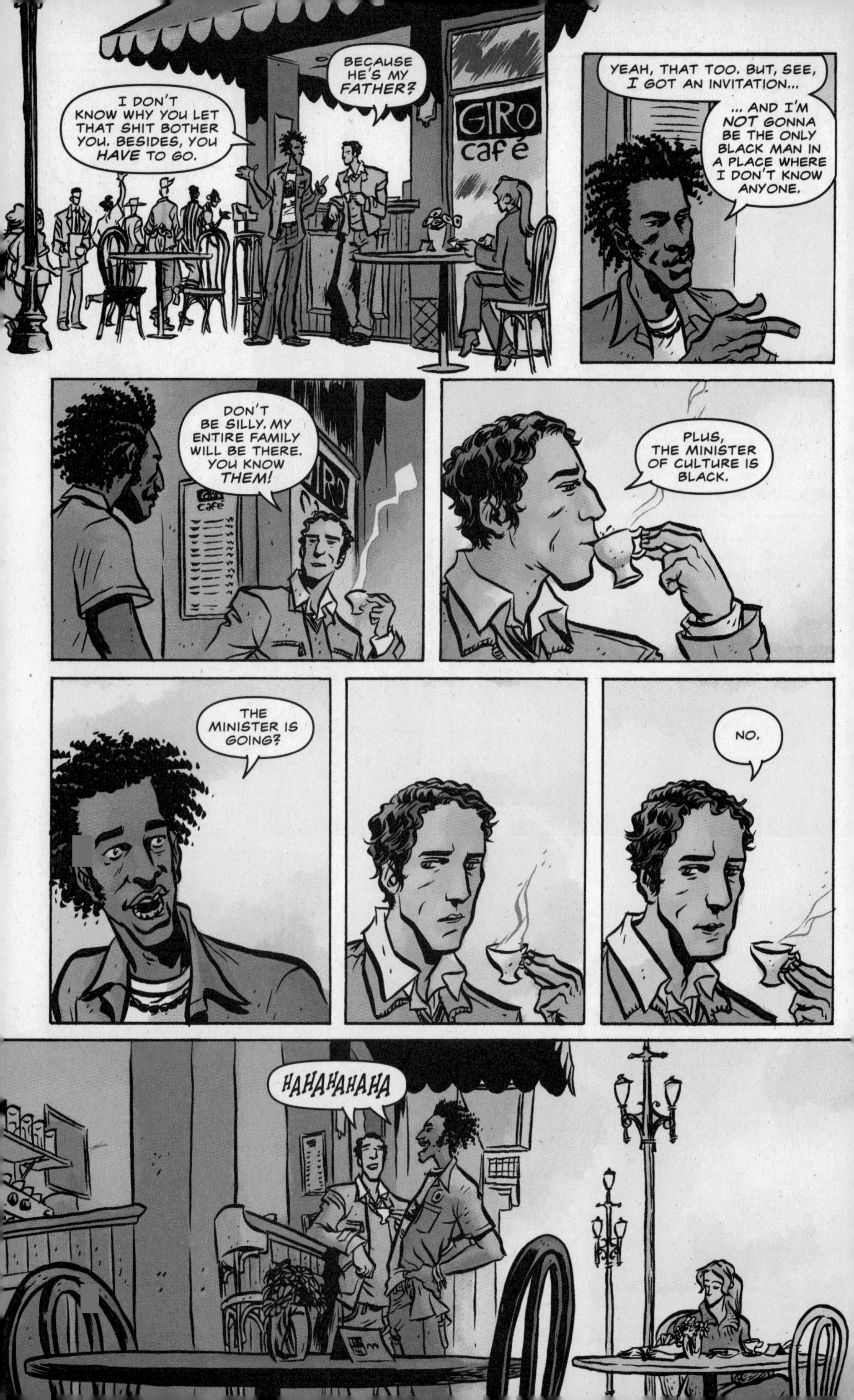
I DON'T KNOW WHY YOU LET THAT SHIT BOTHER YOU. BESIDES, YOU *HAVE* TO GO.
BECAUSE HE'S MY *FATHER*?
GIRO café
YEAH, THAT TOO. BUT, SEE, I GOT AN INVITATION...
... AND I'M *NOT* GONNA BE THE ONLY BLACK MAN IN A PLACE WHERE I DON'T KNOW ANYONE.
DON'T BE SILLY. MY ENTIRE FAMILY WILL BE THERE. YOU KNOW *THEM!*
PLUS, THE MINISTER OF CULTURE IS BLACK.
THE MINISTER IS GOING?
NO.
HAHAHAHAHA

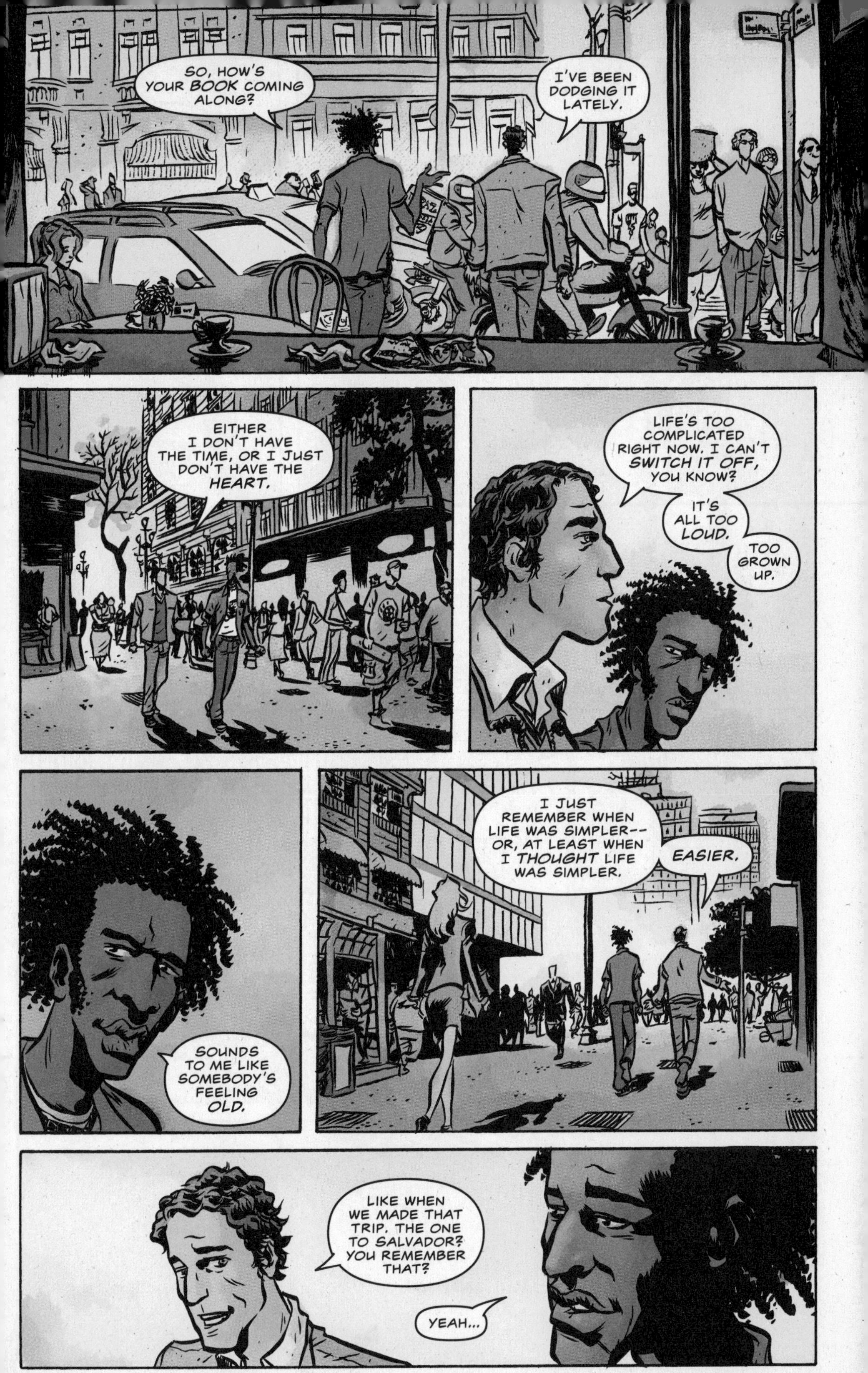
SO, HOW'S YOUR BOOK COMING ALONG?
I'VE BEEN DODGING IT LATELY.
EITHER I DON'T HAVE THE TIME, OR I JUST DON'T HAVE THE HEART.
LIFE'S TOO COMPLICATED RIGHT NOW. I CAN'T SWITCH IT OFF, YOU KNOW?
IT'S ALL TOO LOUD.
TOO GROWN UP.
SOUNDS TO ME LIKE SOMEBODY'S FEELING OLD.
I JUST REMEMBER WHEN LIFE WAS SIMPLER-- OR, AT LEAST WHEN I THOUGHT LIFE WAS SIMPLER.
EASIER.
LIKE WHEN WE MADE THAT TRIP. THE ONE TO SALVADOR? YOU REMEMBER THAT?
YEAH...

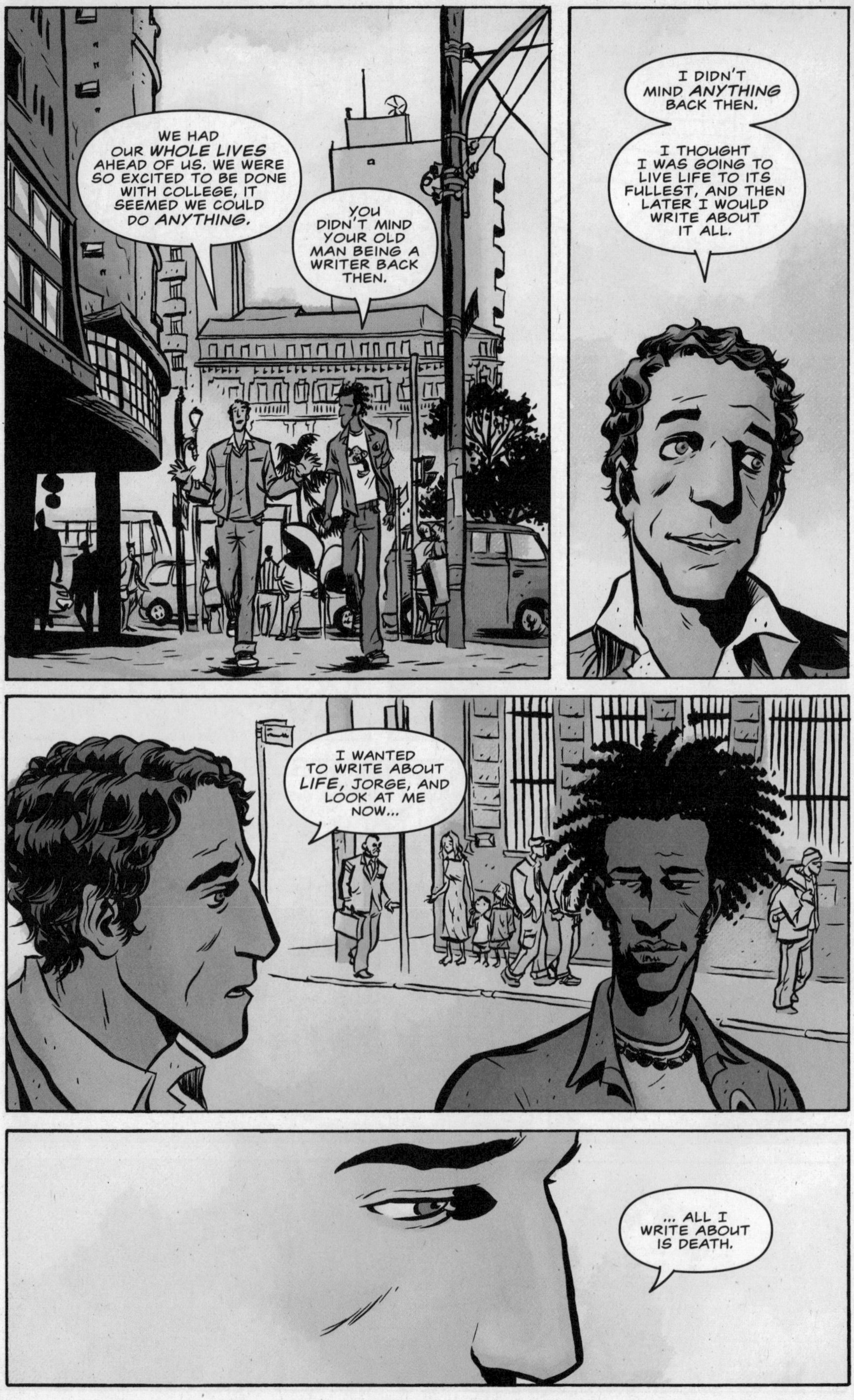
WE HAD OUR WHOLE LIVES AHEAD OF US. WE WERE SO EXCITED TO BE DONE WITH COLLEGE, IT SEEMED WE COULD DO ANYTHING.
YOU DIDN'T MIND YOUR OLD MAN BEING A WRITER BACK THEN.
I DIDN'T MIND ANYTHING BACK THEN.
I THOUGHT I WAS GOING TO LIVE LIFE TO ITS FULLEST, AND THEN LATER I WOULD WRITE ABOUT IT ALL.
I WANTED TO WRITE ABOUT LIFE, JORGE, AND LOOK AT ME NOW...
... ALL I WRITE ABOUT IS DEATH.

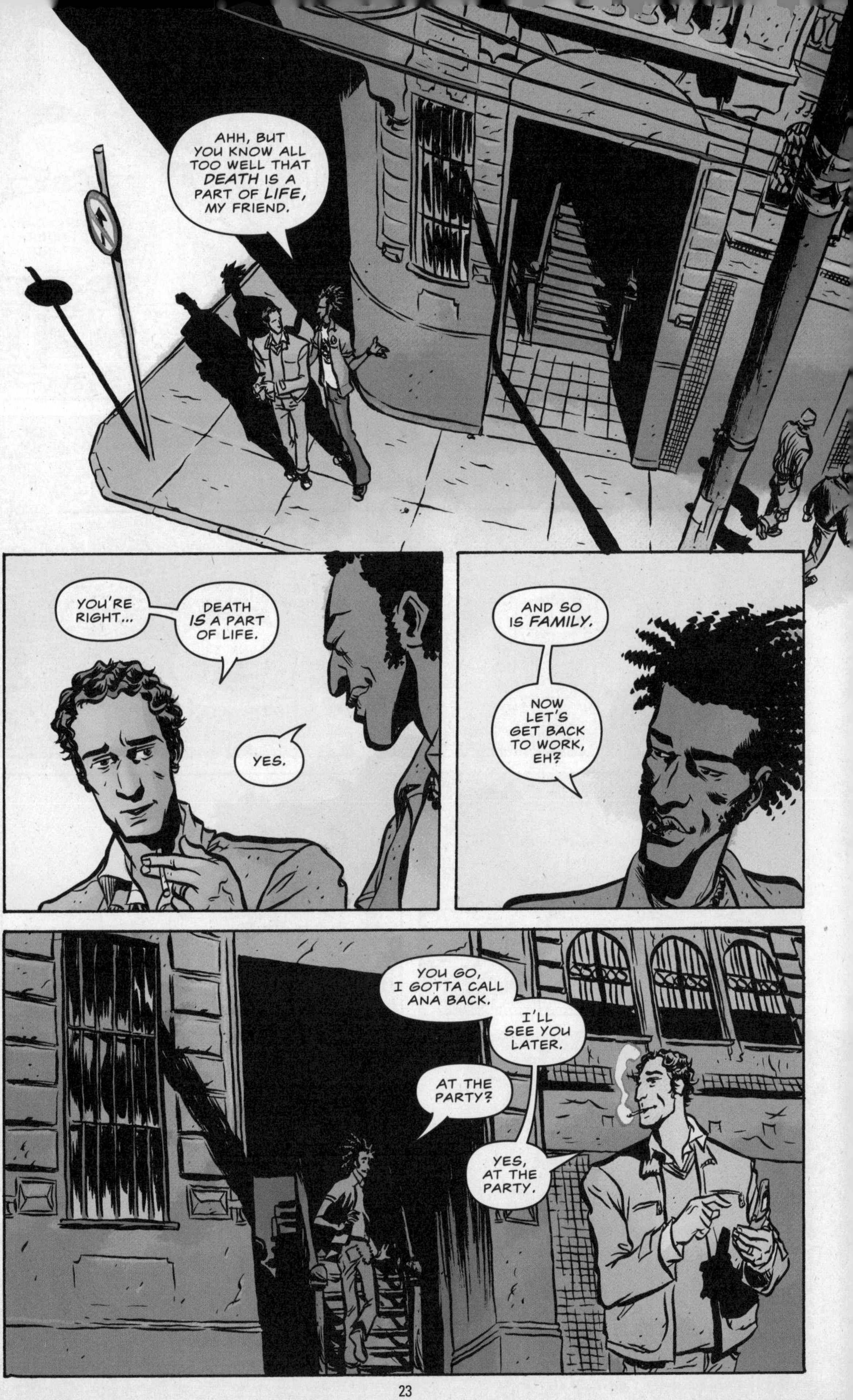
AHH, BUT YOU KNOW ALL TOO WELL THAT DEATH IS A PART OF LIFE, MY FRIEND.
YOU'RE RIGHT...
DEATH IS A PART OF LIFE.
YES.
AND SO IS FAMILY.
NOW LET'S GET BACK TO WORK, EH?
YOU GO, I GOTTA CALL ANA BACK.
I'LL SEE YOU LATER.
AT THE PARTY?
YES, AT THE PARTY.

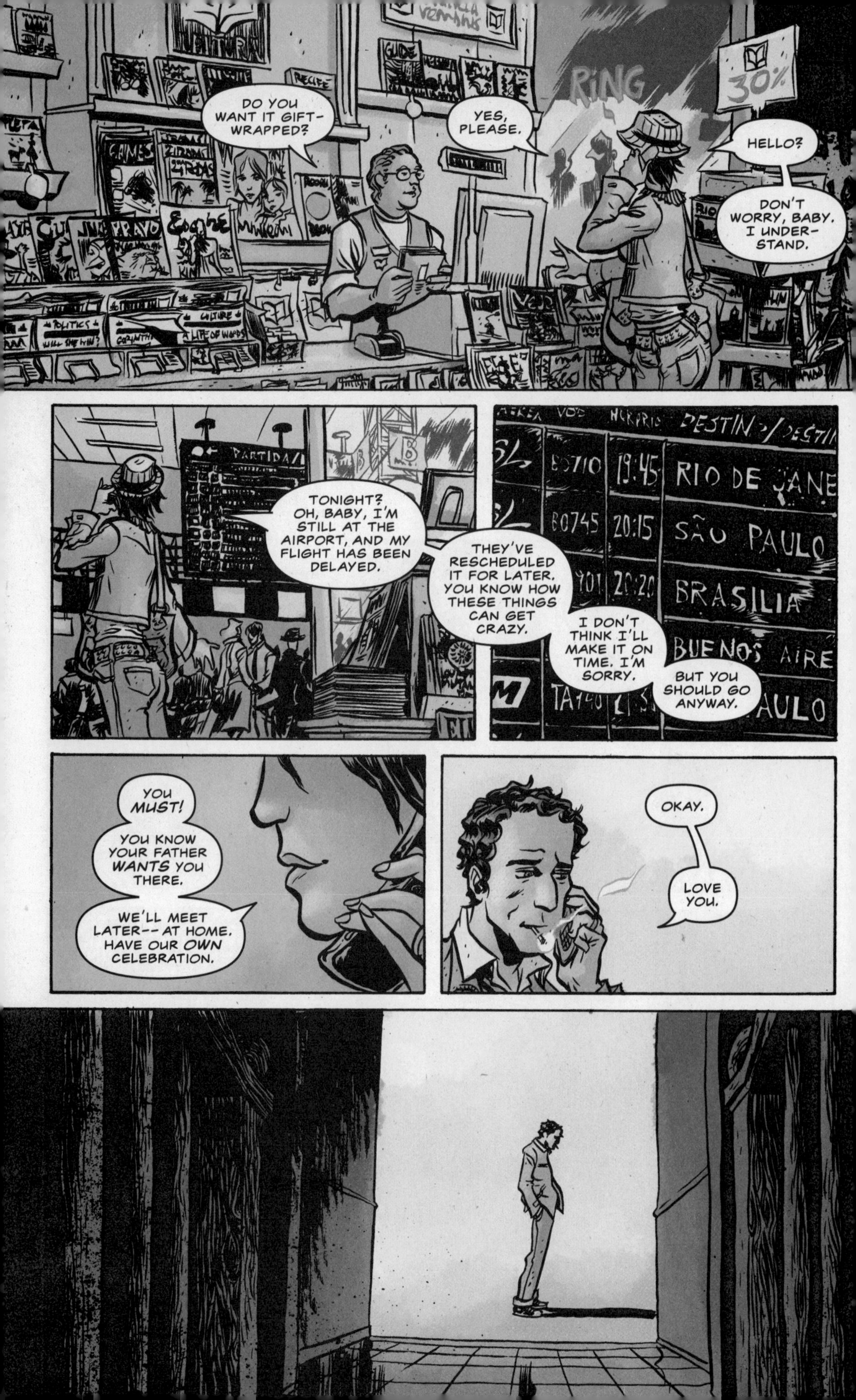
DO YOU WANT IT GIFT-WRAPPED?
YES, PLEASE.
RING
HELLO?
DON'T WORRY, BABY. I UNDERSTAND.
TONIGHT? OH, BABY, I'M STILL AT THE AIRPORT, AND MY FLIGHT HAS BEEN DELAYED.
THEY'VE RESCHEDULED IT FOR LATER. YOU KNOW HOW THESE THINGS CAN GET CRAZY.
I DON'T THINK I'LL MAKE IT ON TIME. I'M SORRY.
BUT YOU SHOULD GO ANYWAY.
YOU MUST!
YOU KNOW YOUR FATHER WANTS YOU THERE.
WE'LL MEET LATER-- AT HOME. HAVE OUR OWN CELEBRATION.
OKAY.
LOVE YOU.

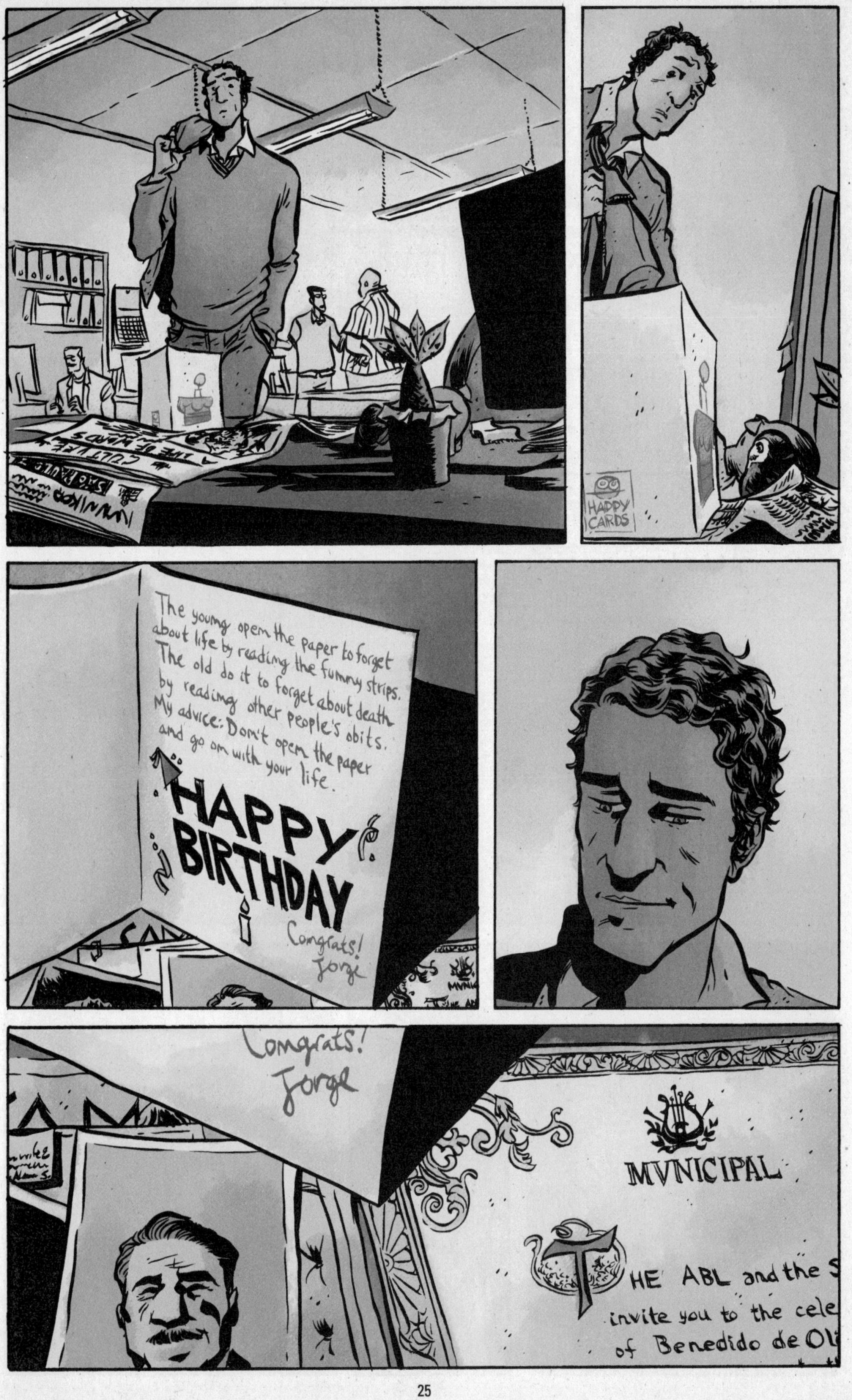
HAPPY CARDS
The young open the paper to forget about life by reading the funny strips. The old do it to forget about death by reading other people's obits. My advice: Don't open the paper and go on with your life.
HAPPY BIRTHDAY
Congrats! Jorge
Congrats! Jorge
MVNICIPAL
THE ABL and the S
invite you to the cele
of Benedido de Oli

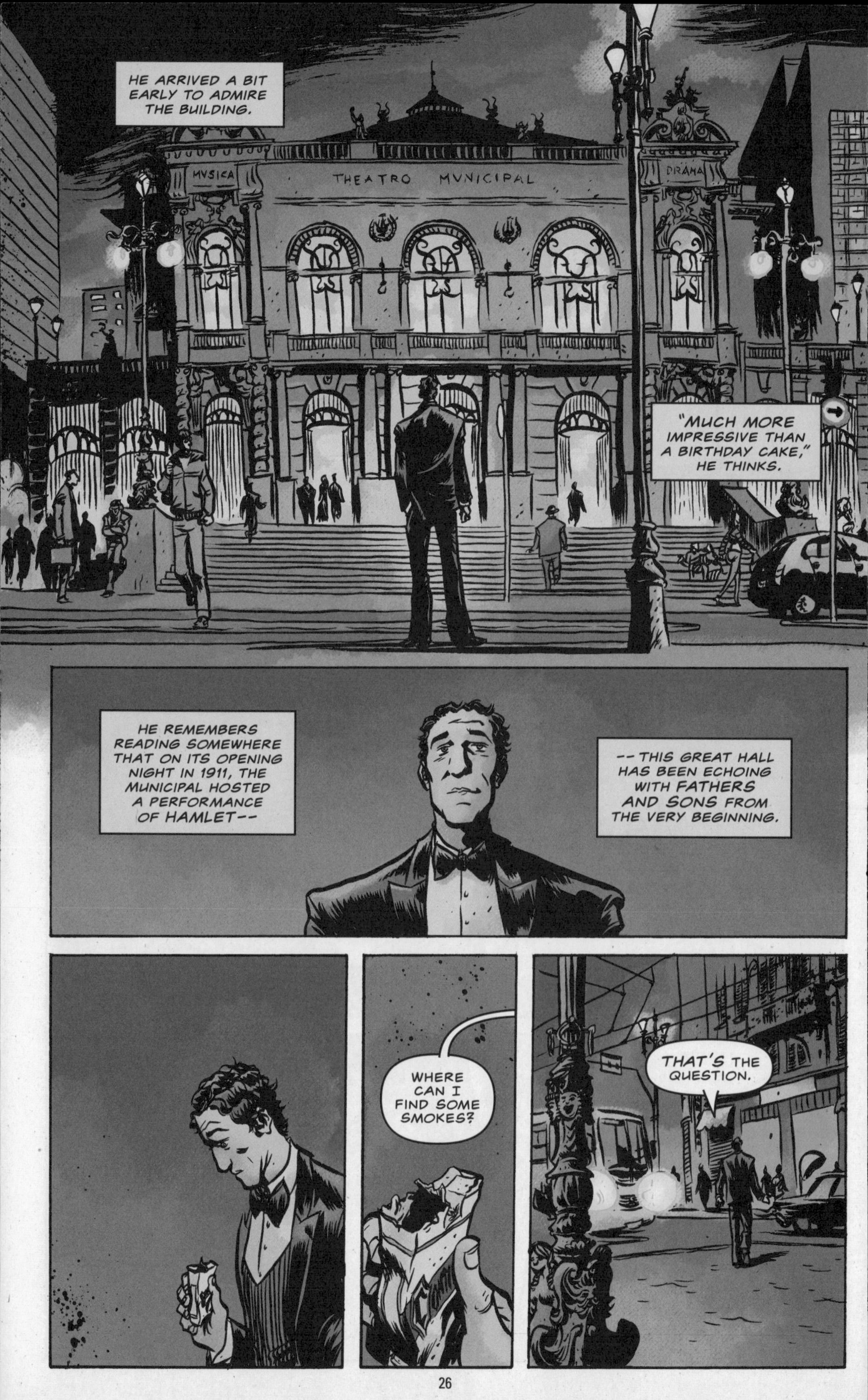
THEATRO MUNICIPAL
MUSICA
DRAMA
HE ARRIVED A BIT EARLY TO ADMIRE THE BUILDING.
"MUCH MORE IMPRESSIVE THAN A BIRTHDAY CAKE," HE THINKS.
HE REMEMBERS READING SOMEWHERE THAT ON ITS OPENING NIGHT IN 1911, THE MUNICIPAL HOSTED A PERFORMANCE OF HAMLET--
--THIS GREAT HALL HAS BEEN ECHOING WITH FATHERS AND SONS FROM THE VERY BEGINNING.
WHERE CAN I FIND SOME SMOKES?
THAT'S THE QUESTION.

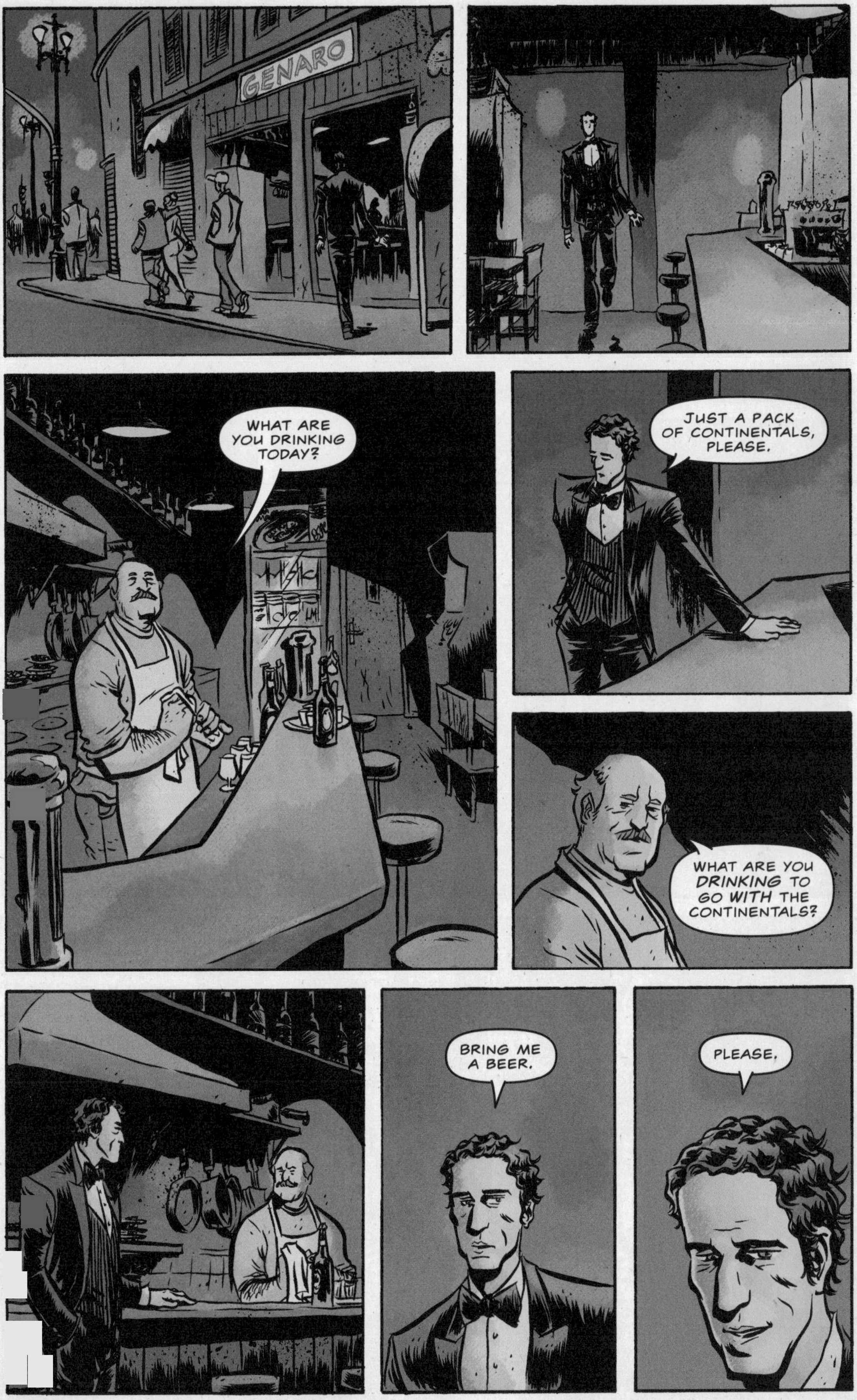
GENARO
WHAT ARE YOU DRINKING TODAY?
JUST A PACK OF CONTINENTALS, PLEASE.
WHAT ARE YOU DRINKING TO GO WITH THE CONTINENTALS?
BRING ME A BEER.
PLEASE.

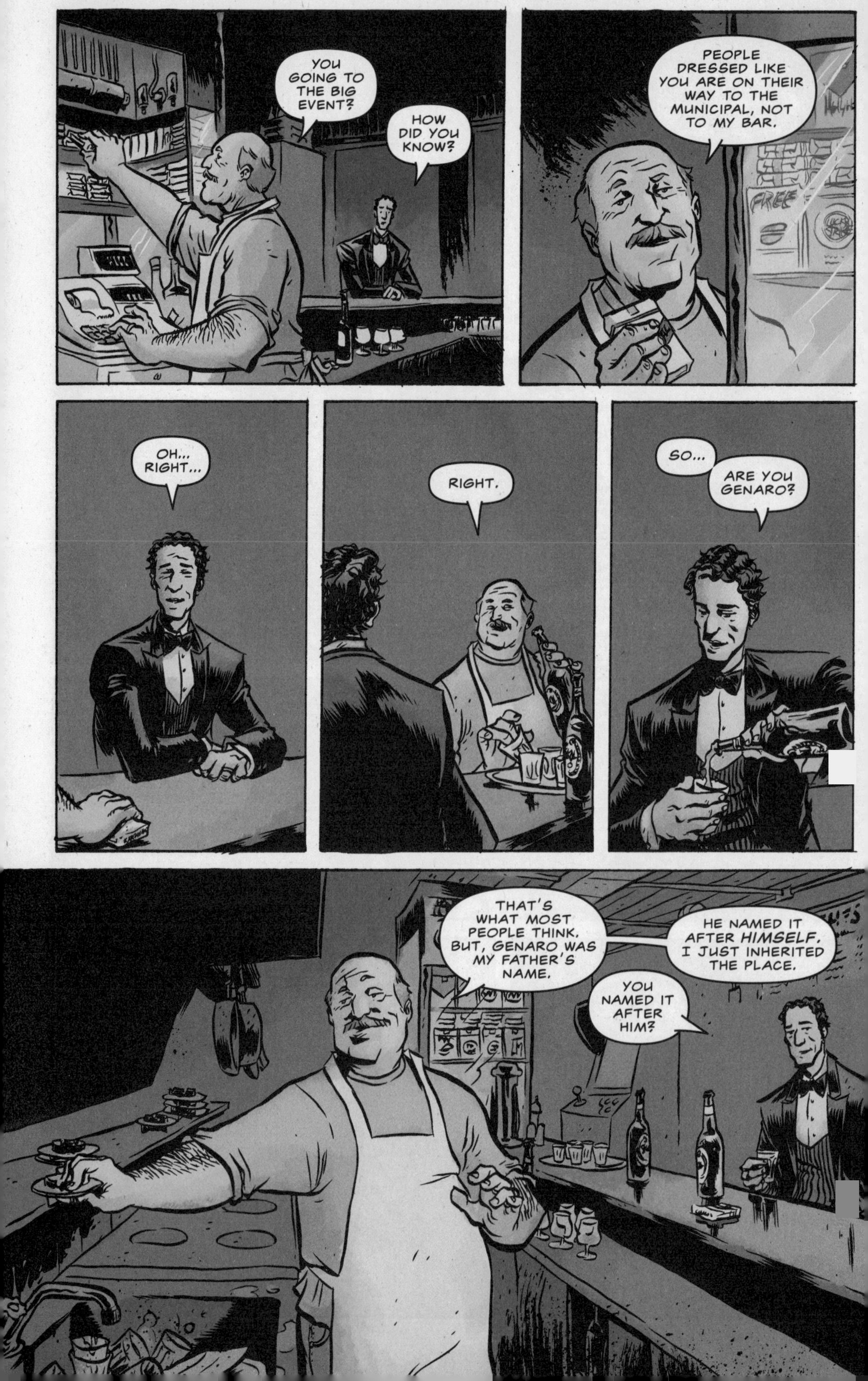
YOU GOING TO THE BIG EVENT?
HOW DID YOU KNOW?
PEOPLE DRESSED LIKE YOU ARE ON THEIR WAY TO THE MUNICIPAL, NOT TO MY BAR.
OH... RIGHT...
RIGHT.
SO...
ARE YOU GENARO?
THAT'S WHAT MOST PEOPLE THINK. BUT, GENARO WAS MY FATHER'S NAME.
HE NAMED IT AFTER *HIMSELF*. I JUST INHERITED THE PLACE.
YOU NAMED IT AFTER HIM?

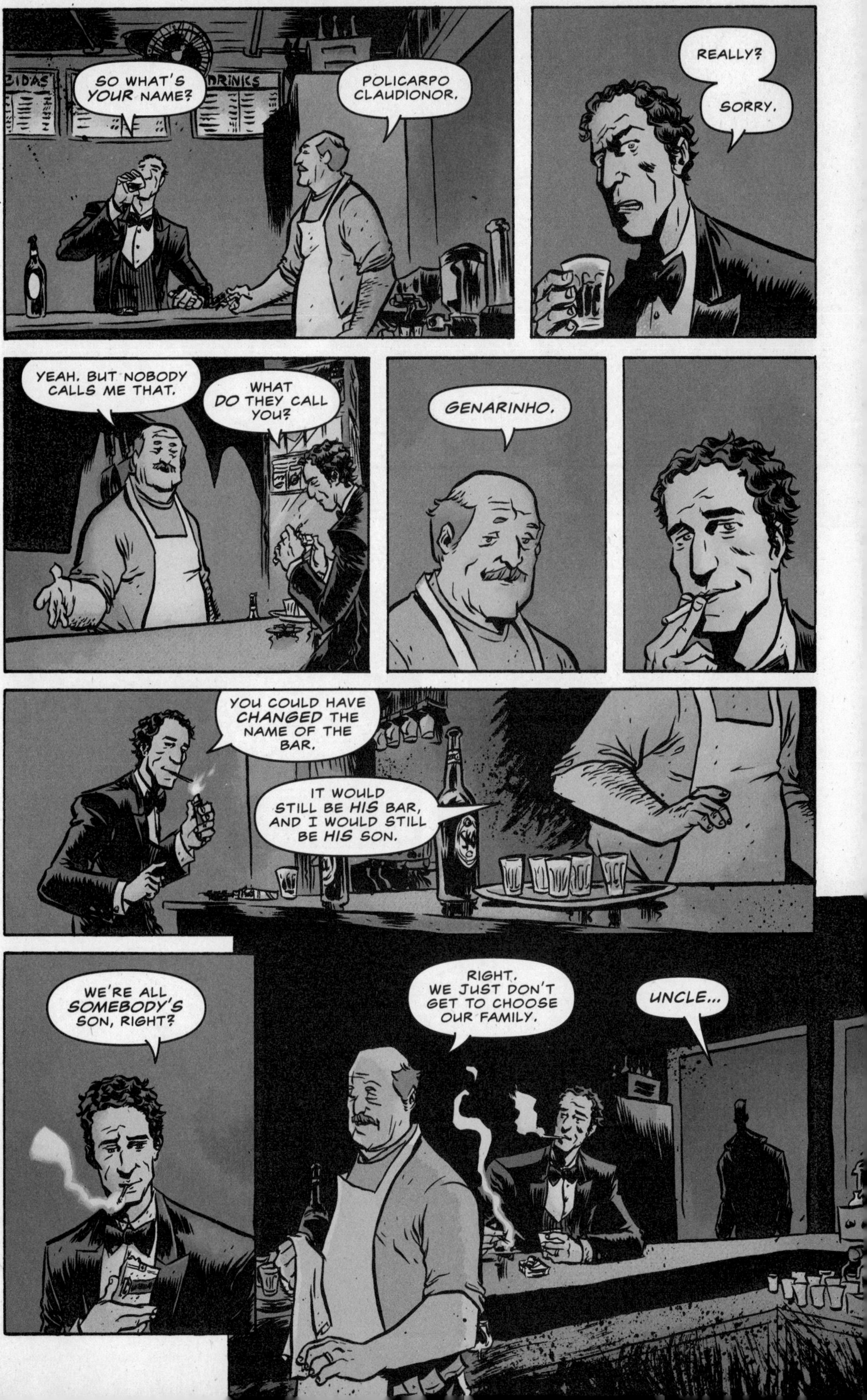
BIDAS
DRINKS
SO WHAT'S YOUR NAME?
POLICARPO CLAUDIONOR.
REALLY?
SORRY.
YEAH. BUT NOBODY CALLS ME THAT.
WHAT DO THEY CALL YOU?
GENARINHO.
YOU COULD HAVE CHANGED THE NAME OF THE BAR.
IT WOULD STILL BE HIS BAR, AND I WOULD STILL BE HIS SON.
WE'RE ALL SOMEBODY'S SON, RIGHT?
RIGHT. WE JUST DON'T GET TO CHOOSE OUR FAMILY.
UNCLE...

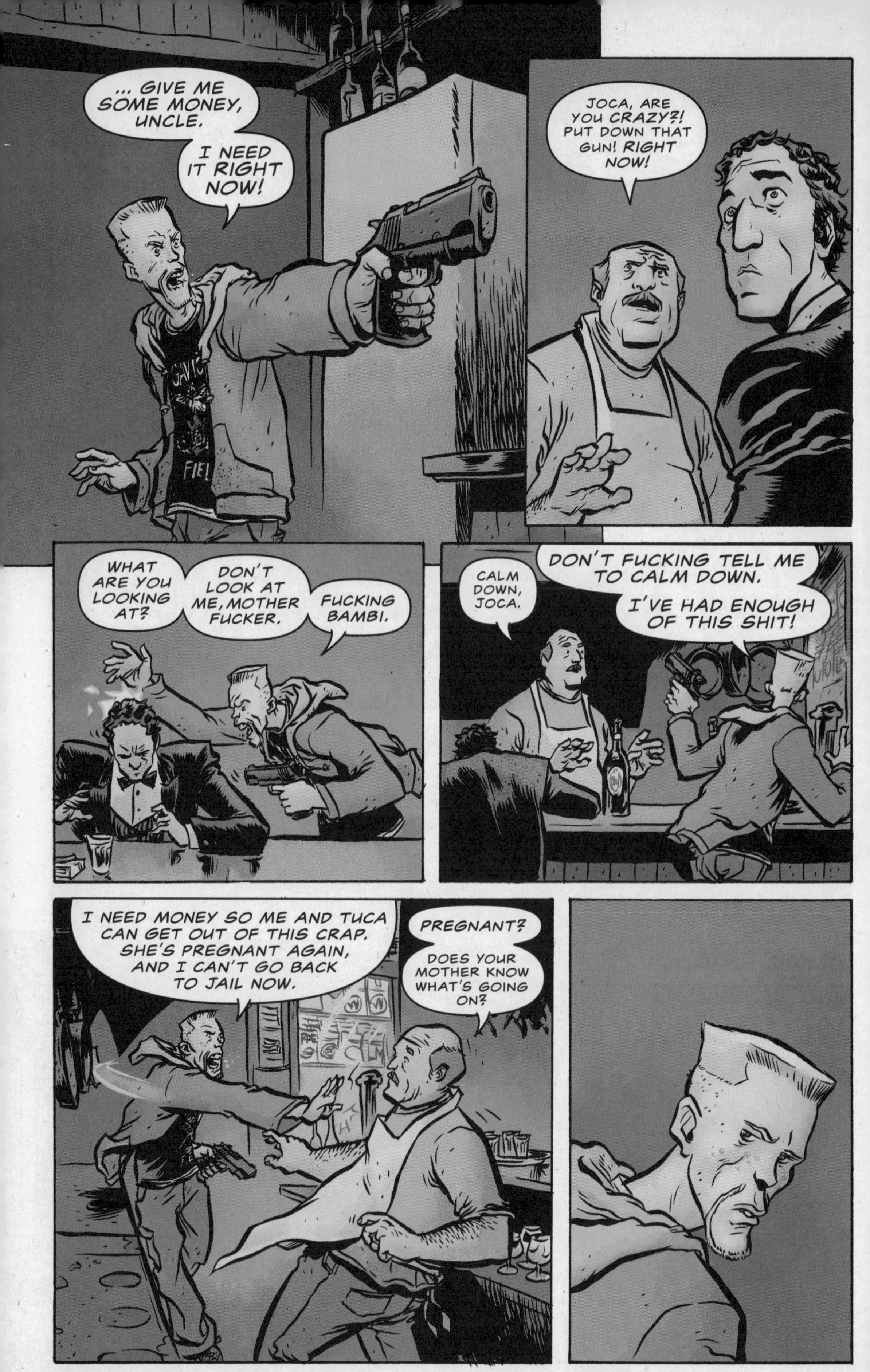
... GIVE ME SOME MONEY, UNCLE.
I NEED IT RIGHT NOW!
JOCA, ARE YOU CRAZY?! PUT DOWN THAT GUN! RIGHT NOW!
WHAT ARE YOU LOOKING AT?
DON'T LOOK AT ME, MOTHER FUCKER.
FUCKING BAMBI.
CALM DOWN, JOCA.
DON'T FUCKING TELL ME TO CALM DOWN.
I'VE HAD ENOUGH OF THIS SHIT!
I NEED MONEY SO ME AND TUCA CAN GET OUT OF THIS CRAP. SHE'S PREGNANT AGAIN, AND I CAN'T GO BACK TO JAIL NOW.
PREGNANT?
DOES YOUR MOTHER KNOW WHAT'S GOING ON?

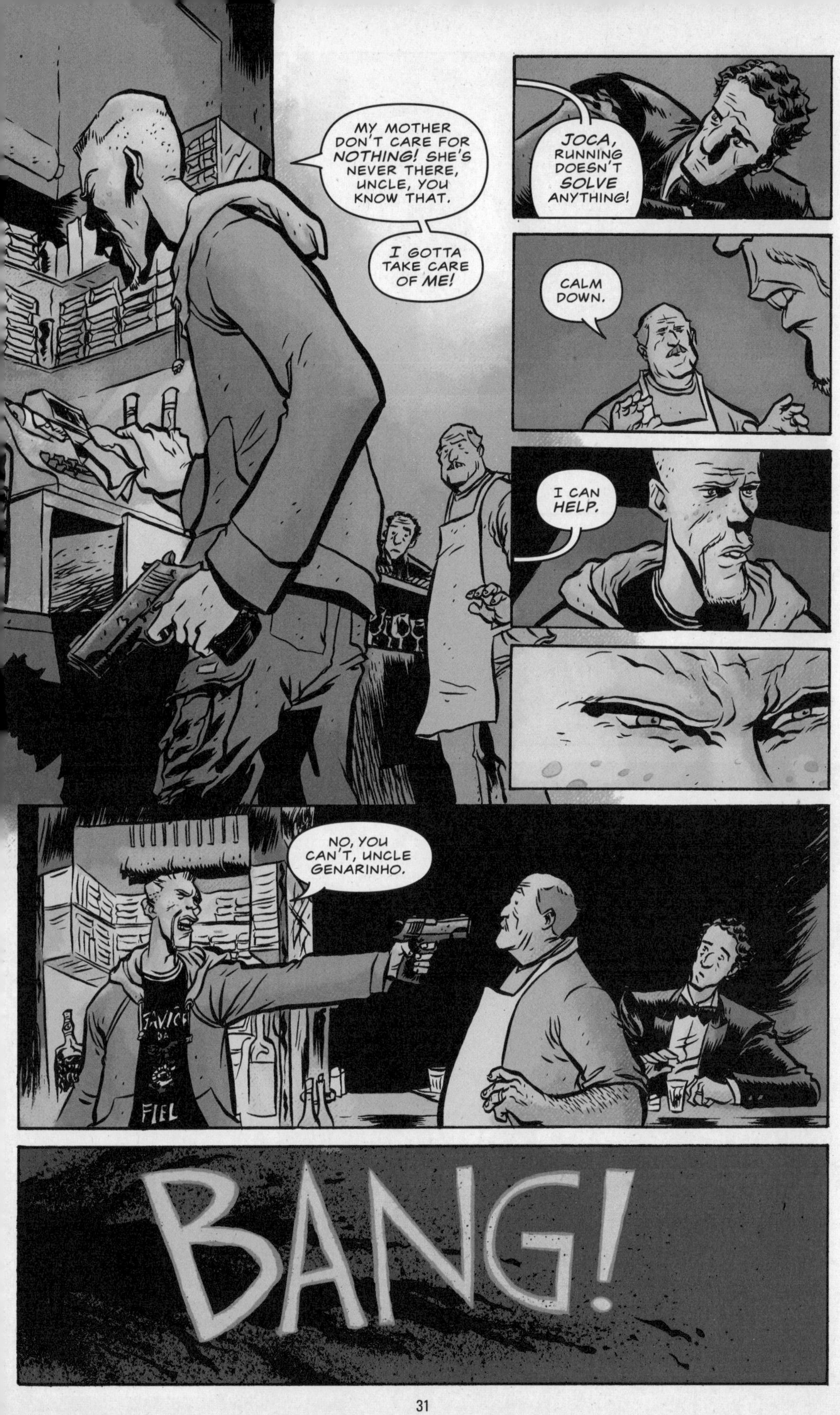

MY MOTHER DON'T CARE FOR NOTHING! SHE'S NEVER THERE, UNCLE, YOU KNOW THAT.
I GOTTA TAKE CARE OF ME!
JOCA, RUNNING DOESN'T SOLVE ANYTHING!
CALM DOWN.
I CAN HELP.
NO, YOU CAN'T, UNCLE GENARINHO.
FIEL
BANG!

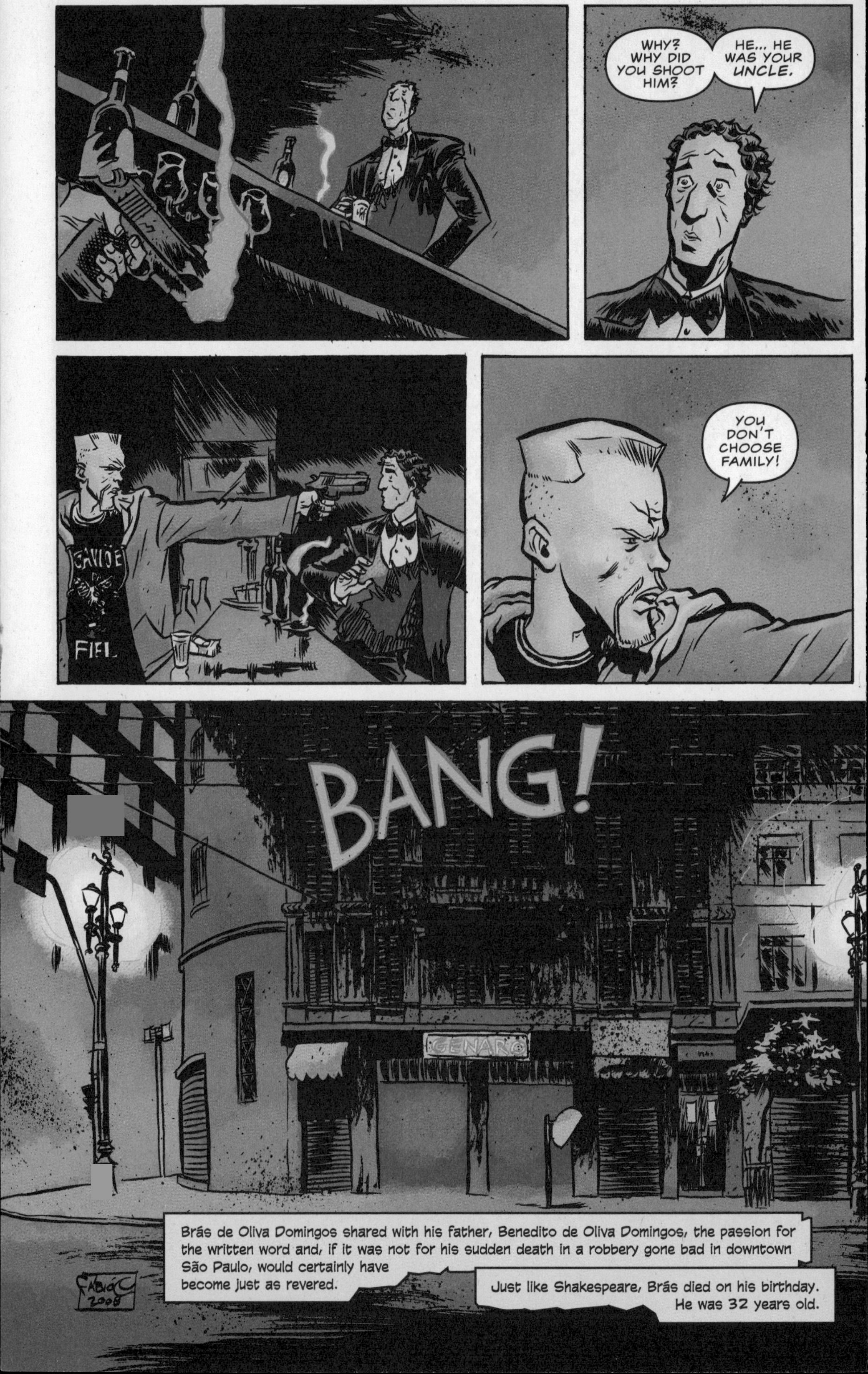

WHY? WHY DID YOU SHOOT HIM?
HE... HE WAS YOUR UNCLE.
YOU DON'T CHOOSE FAMILY!
BANG!
GENARO
FABIO C 2008
Brás de Oliva Domingos shared with his father, Benedito de Oliva Domingos, the passion for the written word and, if it was not for his sudden death in a robbery gone bad in downtown São Paulo, would certainly have become just as revered.
Just like Shakespeare, Brás died on his birthday. He was 32 years old.

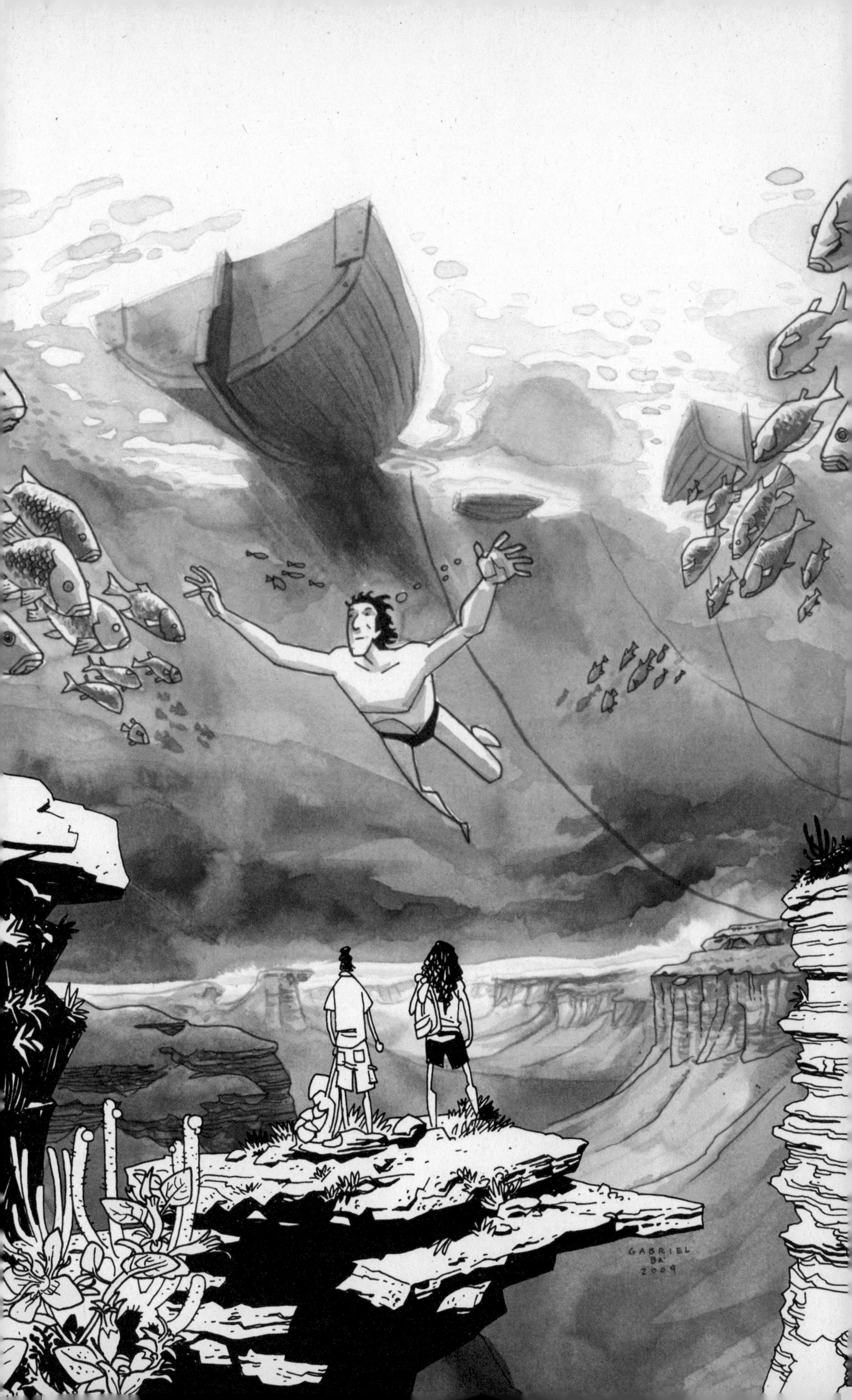
GABRIEL BÁ 2009

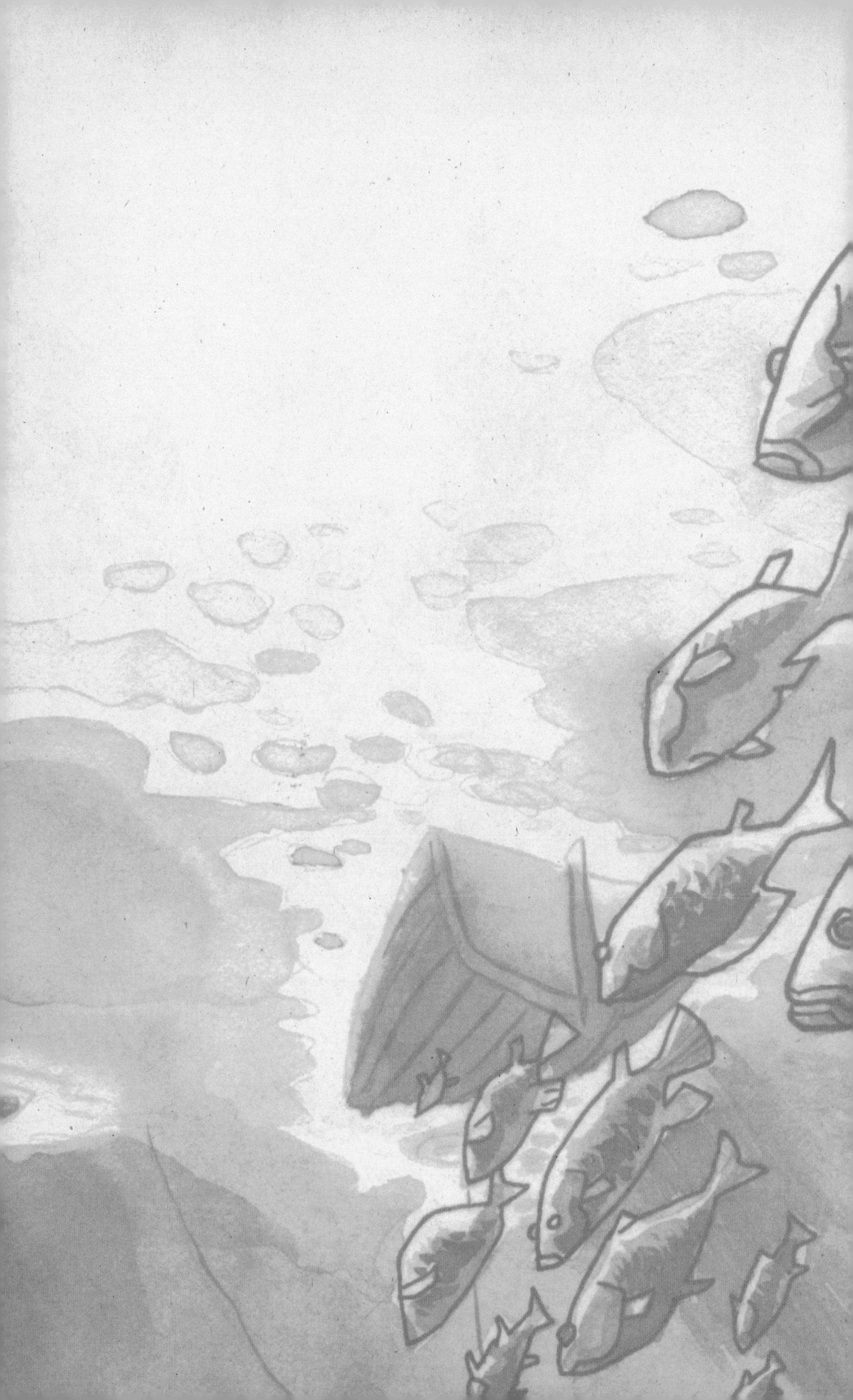

AND THERE HE WAS, DREAMING ABOUT THE FUTURE. IT LOOKED BRIGHT AND RIGHT AND READY FOR HIM. THERE WAS NO SCARY MYSTERY TO IT AND IT WAS RIGHT AROUND THE CORNER.

THEN BRÁS WOKE UP AND REALIZED THAT, WHEN YOU TURN THAT CORNER, THAT FUTURE YOU HAVE WRITTEN AND WISHED FOR IS NOT ALWAYS THERE WAITING FOR YOU. IN FACT, IT USUALLY ISN'T AT ALL WHAT YOU EXPECTED... AROUND THE CORNER THERE IS JUST ANOTHER BIG ANNOYING QUESTION MARK.

IT'S CALLED LIFE.

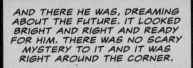

EVEN WHEN HE WAS AWAKE, HE WOULD CARRY HIS DREAMS WITH HIM. THEY REMINDED HIM OF WHO HE IS AND WHAT HE WANTED OUT OF LIFE.

HIS DREAMS WOULD TELL HIM WHAT TO DO. HOW TO NAVIGATE IN THIS WORLD.

YOU MUST COME AND SEE ME.

AND WHEN YOU DO, BRING ME SOMETHING PRETTY.

WAKE UP, NOW.

WAKE UP, DUDE.

YOU'RE MISSING IT.

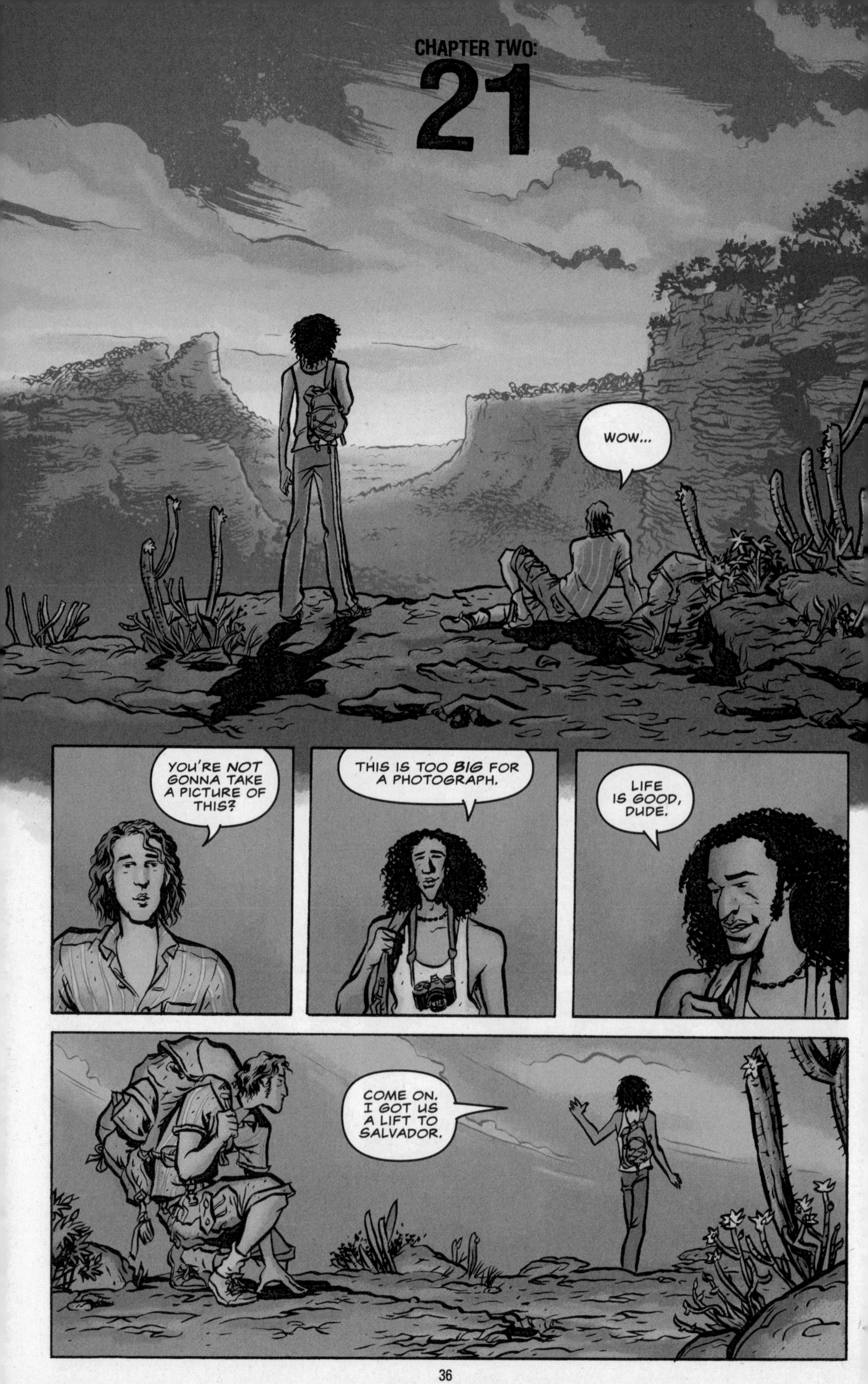
CHAPTER TWO:
21
WOW...
YOU'RE NOT GONNA TAKE A PICTURE OF THIS?
THIS IS TOO BIG FOR A PHOTOGRAPH.
LIFE IS GOOD, DUDE.
COME ON. I GOT US A LIFT TO SALVADOR.

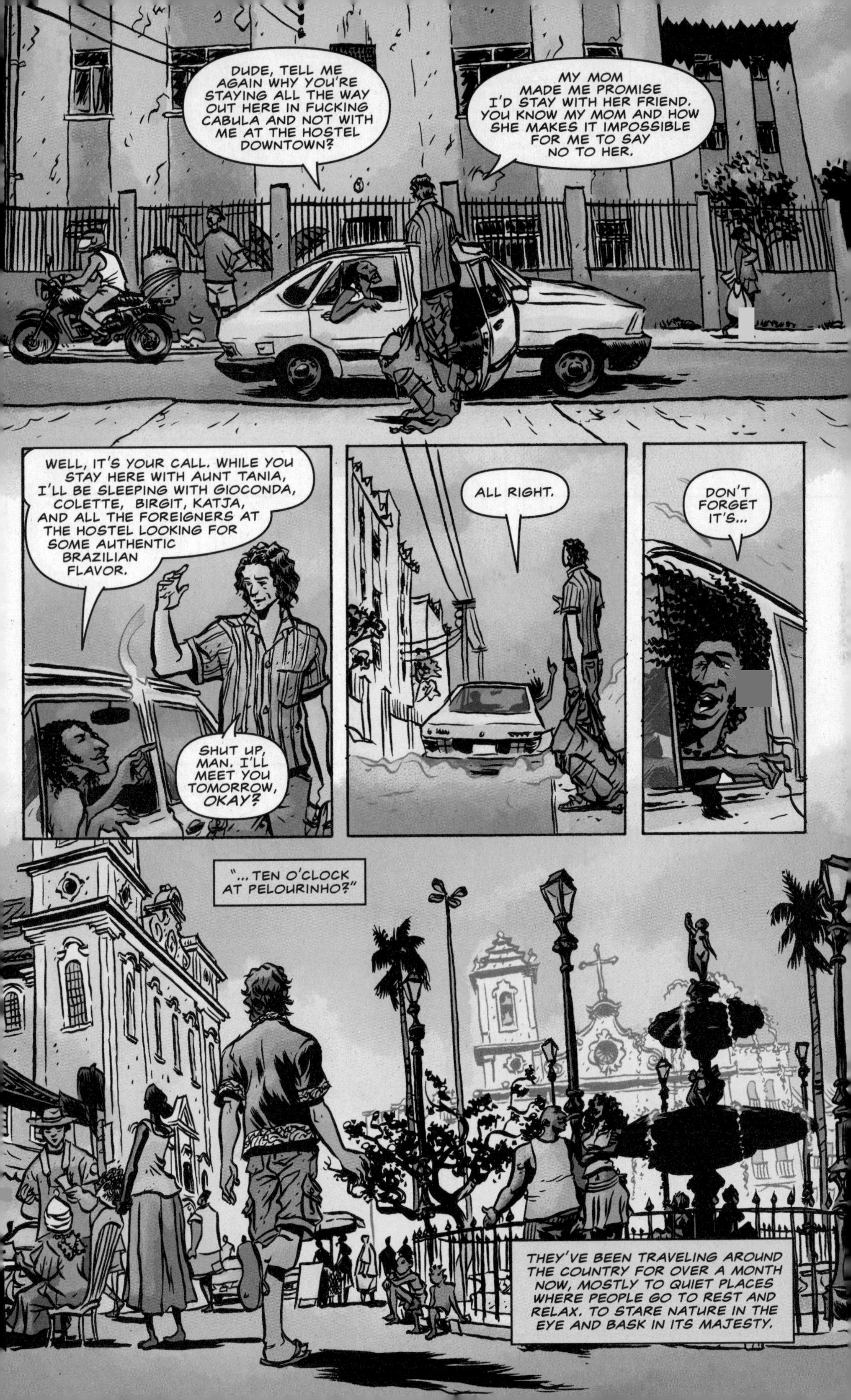
DUDE, TELL ME AGAIN WHY YOU'RE STAYING ALL THE WAY OUT HERE IN FUCKING CABULA AND NOT WITH ME AT THE HOSTEL DOWNTOWN?
MY MOM MADE ME PROMISE I'D STAY WITH HER FRIEND. YOU KNOW MY MOM AND HOW SHE MAKES IT IMPOSSIBLE FOR ME TO SAY NO TO HER.
WELL, IT'S YOUR CALL. WHILE YOU STAY HERE WITH AUNT TANIA, I'LL BE SLEEPING WITH GIOCONDA, COLETTE, BIRGIT, KATJA, AND ALL THE FOREIGNERS AT THE HOSTEL LOOKING FOR SOME AUTHENTIC BRAZILIAN FLAVOR.
SHUT UP, MAN. I'LL MEET YOU TOMORROW, OKAY?
ALL RIGHT.
DON'T FORGET IT'S...
"...TEN O'CLOCK AT PELOURINHO?"
THEY'VE BEEN TRAVELING AROUND THE COUNTRY FOR OVER A MONTH NOW, MOSTLY TO QUIET PLACES WHERE PEOPLE GO TO REST AND RELAX. TO STARE NATURE IN THE EYE AND BASK IN ITS MAJESTY.

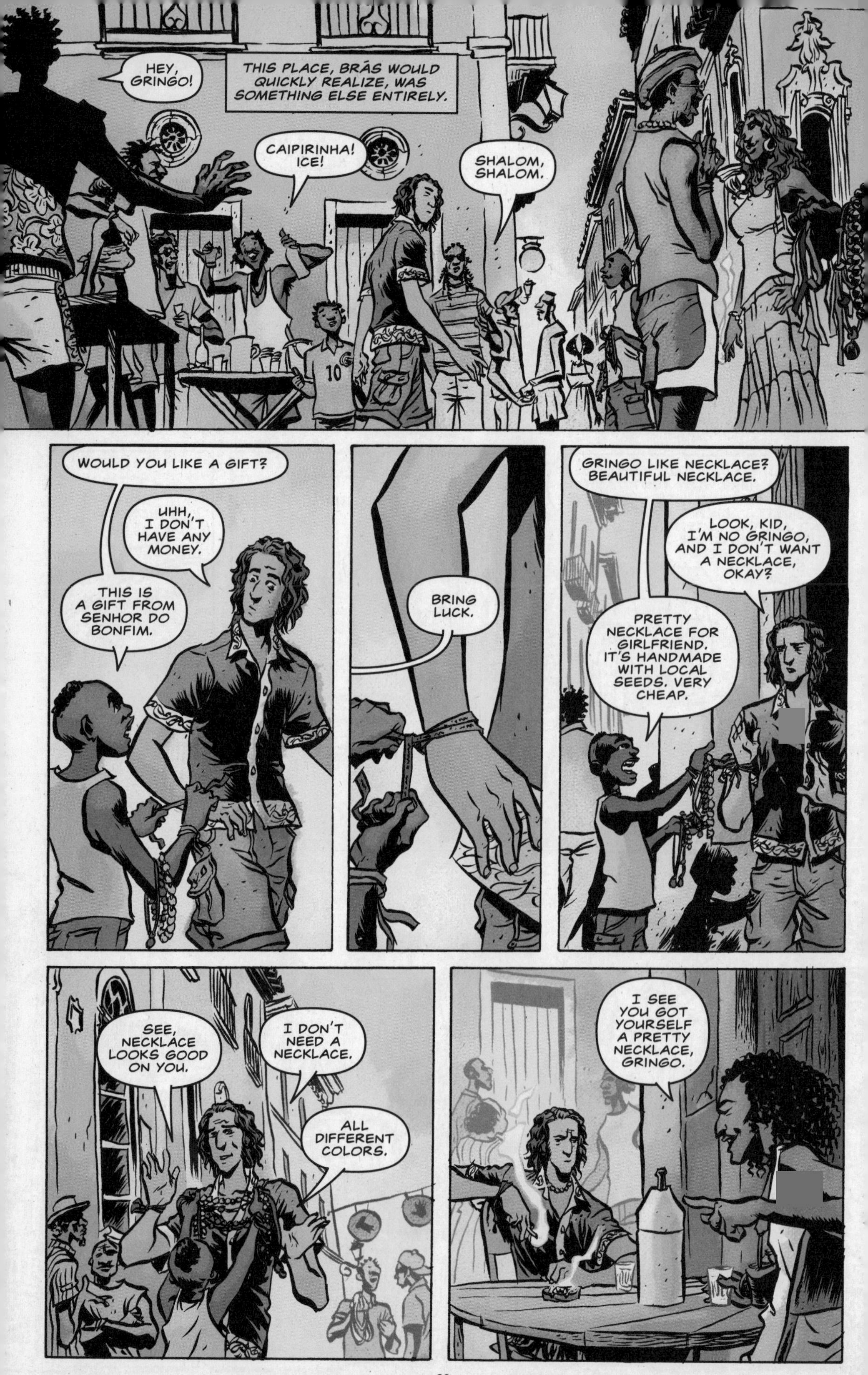
HEY, GRINGO!
THIS PLACE, BRÁS WOULD QUICKLY REALIZE, WAS SOMETHING ELSE ENTIRELY.
CAIPIRINHA! ICE!
SHALOM, SHALOM.
WOULD YOU LIKE A GIFT?
UHH, I DON'T HAVE ANY MONEY.
THIS IS A GIFT FROM SENHOR DO BONFIM.
BRING LUCK.
GRINGO LIKE NECKLACE? BEAUTIFUL NECKLACE.
LOOK, KID, I'M NO GRINGO, AND I DON'T WANT A NECKLACE, OKAY?
PRETTY NECKLACE FOR GIRLFRIEND. IT'S HANDMADE WITH LOCAL SEEDS. VERY CHEAP.
SEE, NECKLACE LOOKS GOOD ON YOU.
I DON'T NEED A NECKLACE.
ALL DIFFERENT COLORS.
I SEE YOU GOT YOURSELF A PRETTY NECKLACE, GRINGO.

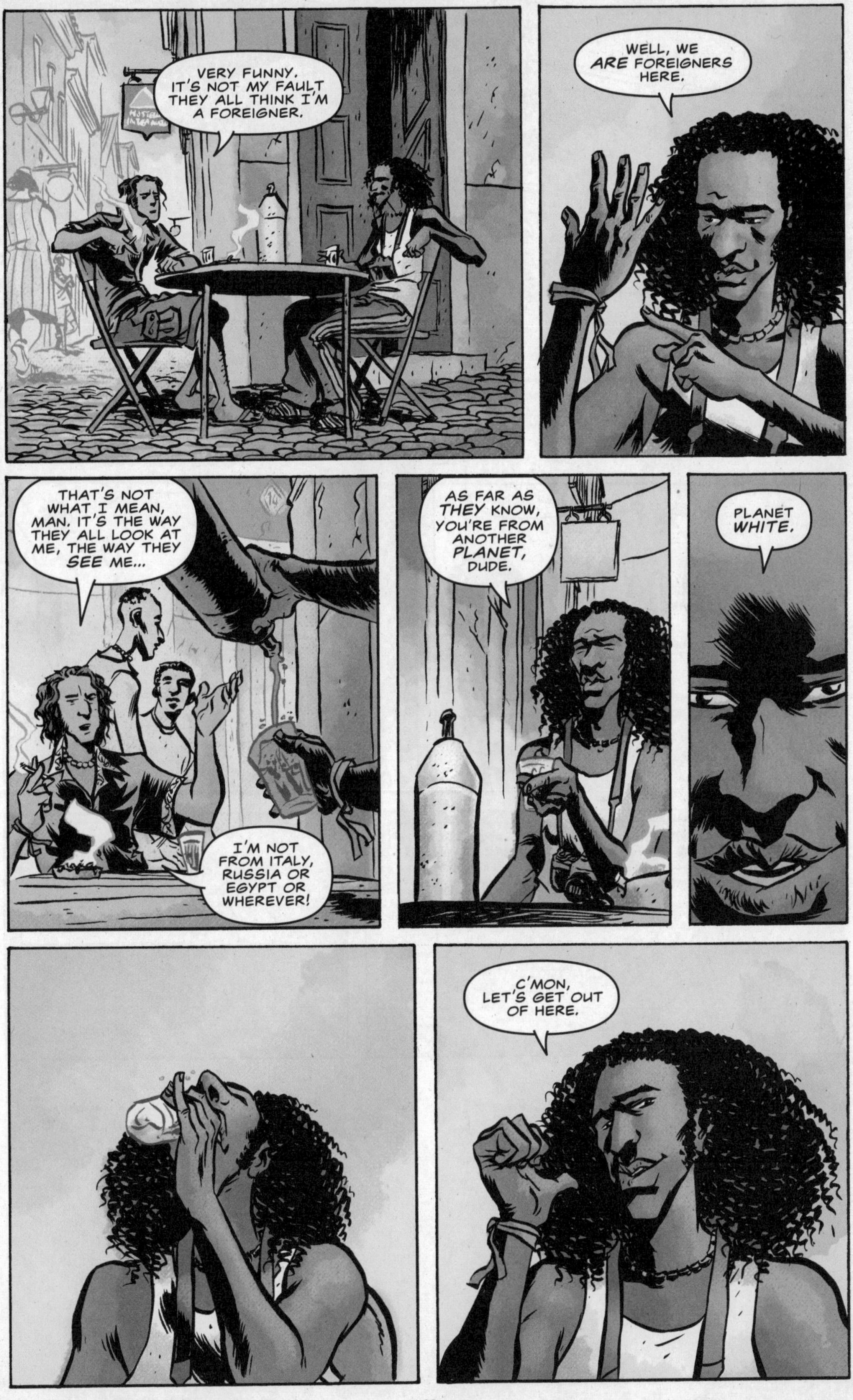
VERY FUNNY. IT'S NOT MY FAULT THEY ALL THINK I'M A FOREIGNER.
WELL, WE ARE FOREIGNERS HERE.
THAT'S NOT WHAT I MEAN, MAN. IT'S THE WAY THEY ALL LOOK AT ME, THE WAY THEY SEE ME...
I'M NOT FROM ITALY, RUSSIA OR EGYPT OR WHEREVER!
AS FAR AS THEY KNOW, YOU'RE FROM ANOTHER PLANET, DUDE.
PLANET WHITE.
C'MON, LET'S GET OUT OF HERE.

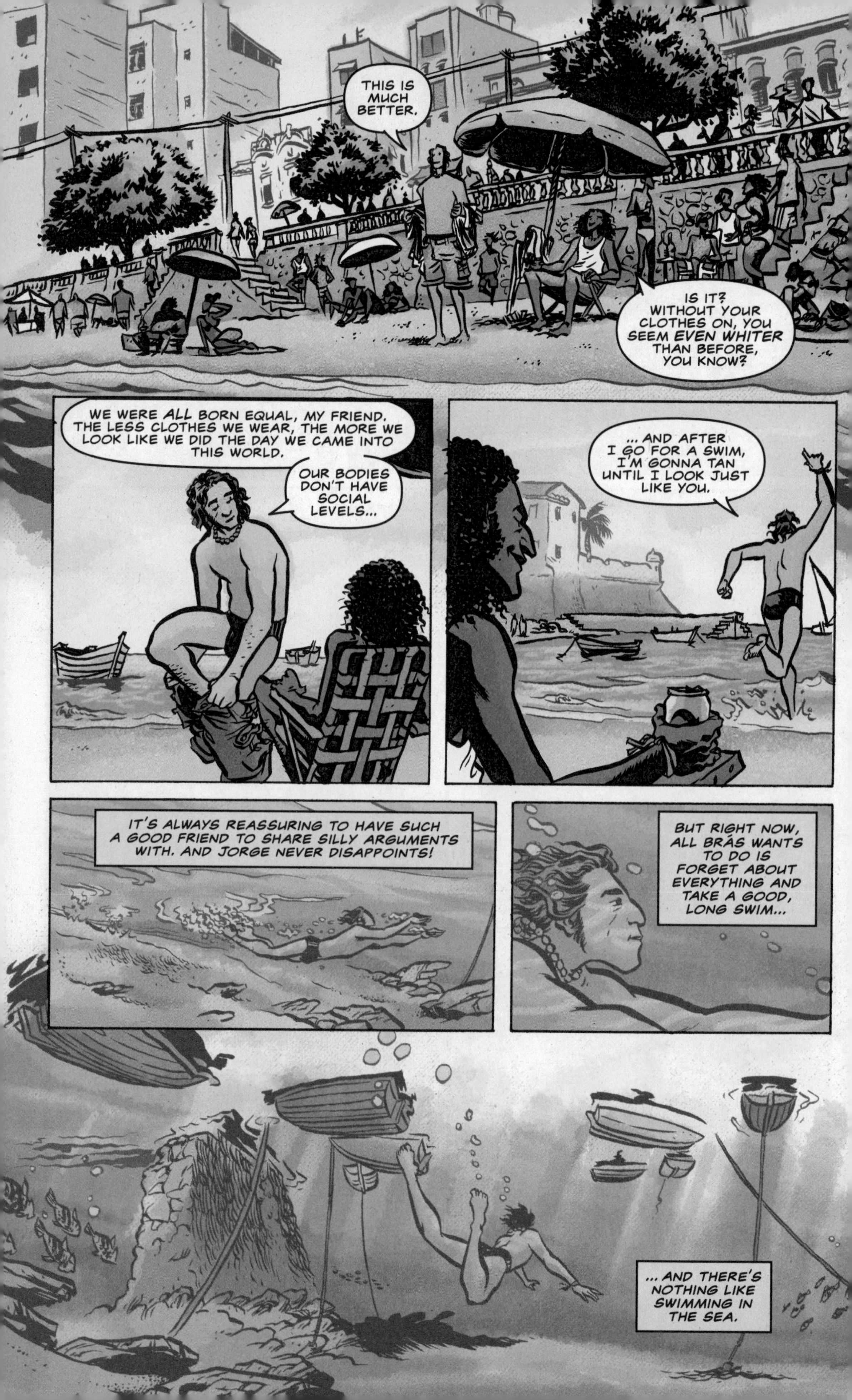
THIS IS MUCH BETTER.
IS IT? WITHOUT YOUR CLOTHES ON, YOU SEEM EVEN WHITER THAN BEFORE, YOU KNOW?
WE WERE ALL BORN EQUAL, MY FRIEND. THE LESS CLOTHES WE WEAR, THE MORE WE LOOK LIKE WE DID THE DAY WE CAME INTO THIS WORLD.
OUR BODIES DON'T HAVE SOCIAL LEVELS...
... AND AFTER I GO FOR A SWIM, I'M GONNA TAN UNTIL I LOOK JUST LIKE YOU.
IT'S ALWAYS REASSURING TO HAVE SUCH A GOOD FRIEND TO SHARE SILLY ARGUMENTS WITH. AND JORGE NEVER DISAPPOINTS!
BUT RIGHT NOW, ALL BRÁS WANTS TO DO IS FORGET ABOUT EVERYTHING AND TAKE A GOOD, LONG SWIM...
... AND THERE'S NOTHING LIKE SWIMMING IN THE SEA.

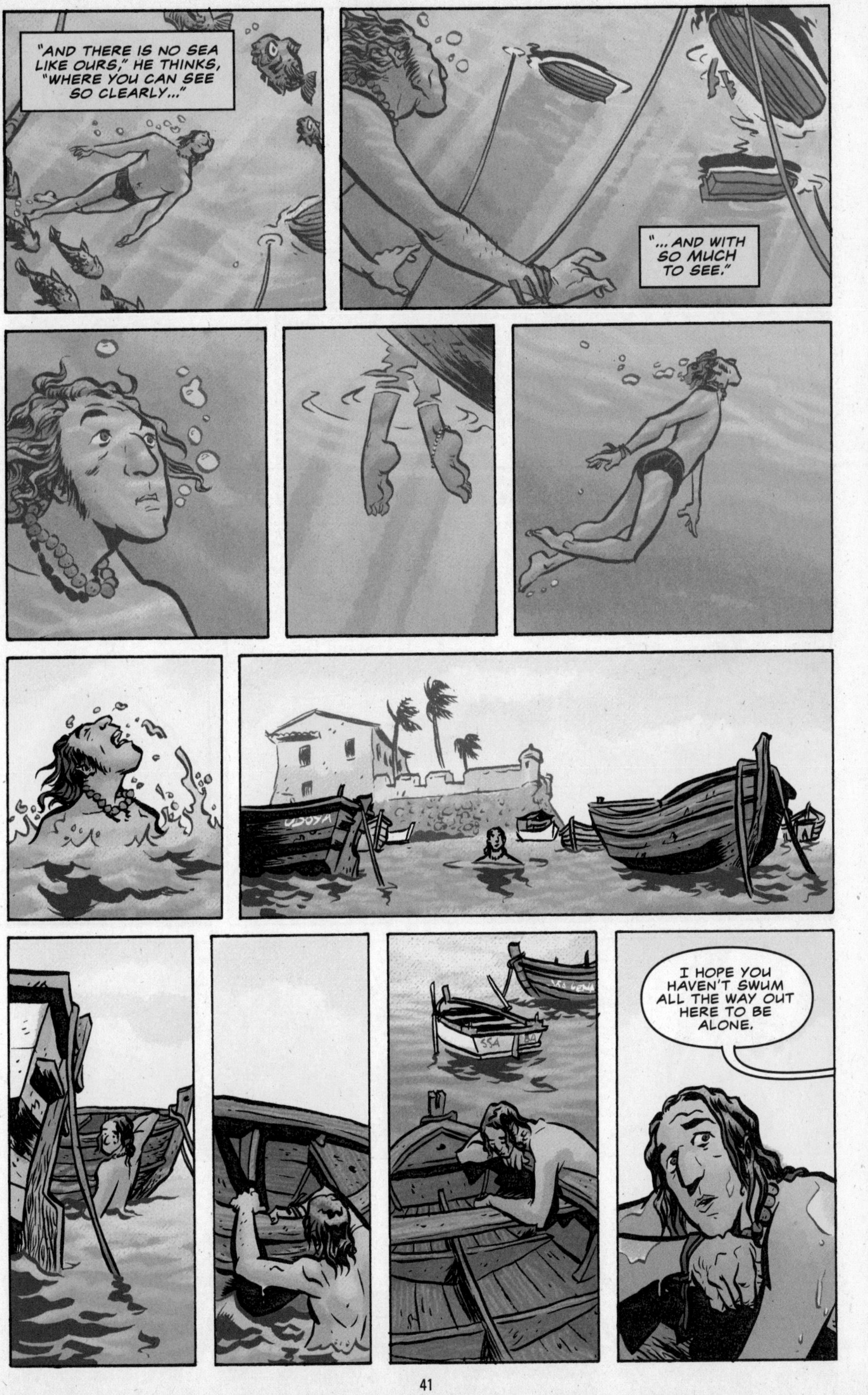
"AND THERE IS NO SEA LIKE OURS," HE THINKS, "WHERE YOU CAN SEE SO CLEARLY..."
"...AND WITH SO MUCH TO SEE."
I HOPE YOU HAVEN'T SWUM ALL THE WAY OUT HERE TO BE ALONE.

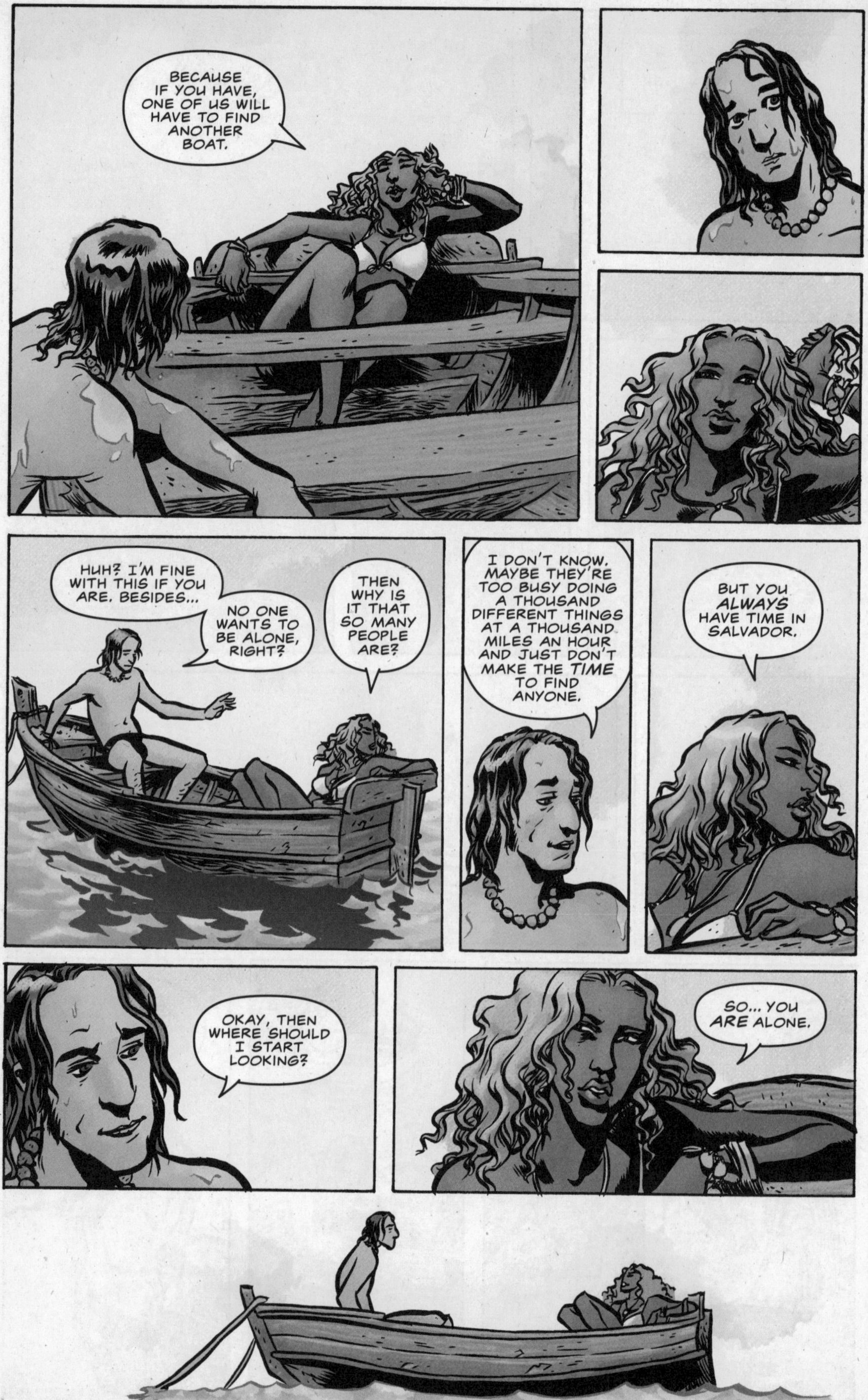
BECAUSE IF YOU HAVE, ONE OF US WILL HAVE TO FIND ANOTHER BOAT.
HUH? I'M FINE WITH THIS IF YOU ARE. BESIDES...
NO ONE WANTS TO BE ALONE, RIGHT?
THEN WHY IS IT THAT SO MANY PEOPLE ARE?
I DON'T KNOW. MAYBE THEY'RE TOO BUSY DOING A THOUSAND DIFFERENT THINGS AT A THOUSAND MILES AN HOUR AND JUST DON'T MAKE THE *TIME* TO FIND ANYONE.
BUT YOU *ALWAYS* HAVE TIME IN SALVADOR.
OKAY, THEN WHERE SHOULD I START LOOKING?
SO... YOU *ARE* ALONE.

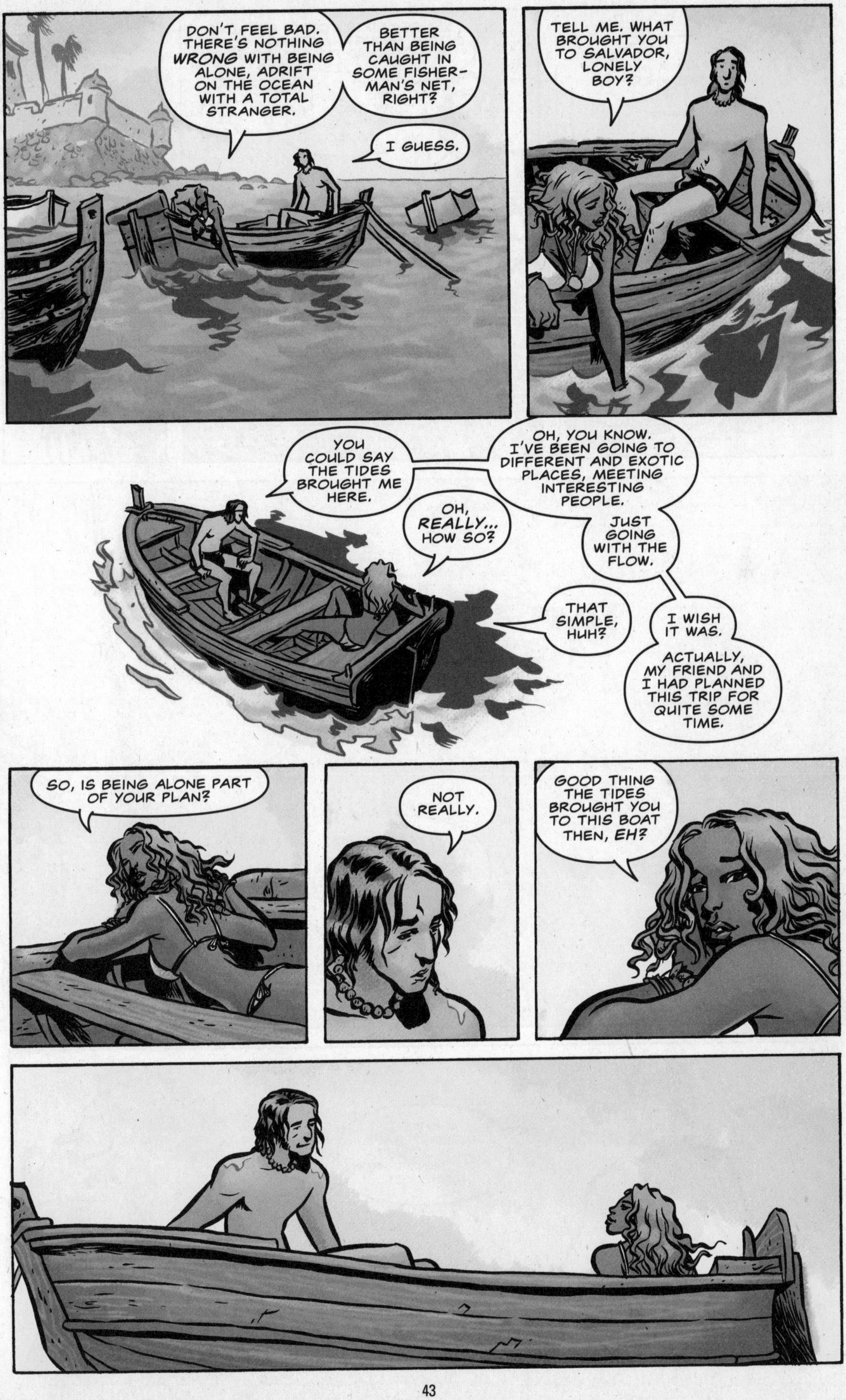
DON'T FEEL BAD. THERE'S NOTHING *WRONG* WITH BEING ALONE, ADRIFT ON THE OCEAN WITH A TOTAL STRANGER.
BETTER THAN BEING CAUGHT IN SOME FISHER-MAN'S NET, RIGHT?
I GUESS.
TELL ME. WHAT BROUGHT YOU TO SALVADOR, LONELY BOY?
YOU COULD SAY THE TIDES BROUGHT ME HERE.
OH, YOU KNOW. I'VE BEEN GOING TO DIFFERENT AND EXOTIC PLACES, MEETING INTERESTING PEOPLE.
JUST GOING WITH THE FLOW.
OH, *REALLY*... HOW SO?
THAT SIMPLE, HUH?
I WISH IT WAS.
ACTUALLY, MY FRIEND AND I HAD PLANNED THIS TRIP FOR QUITE SOME TIME.
SO, IS BEING ALONE PART OF YOUR PLAN?
NOT REALLY.
GOOD THING THE TIDES BROUGHT YOU TO THIS BOAT THEN, *EH*?

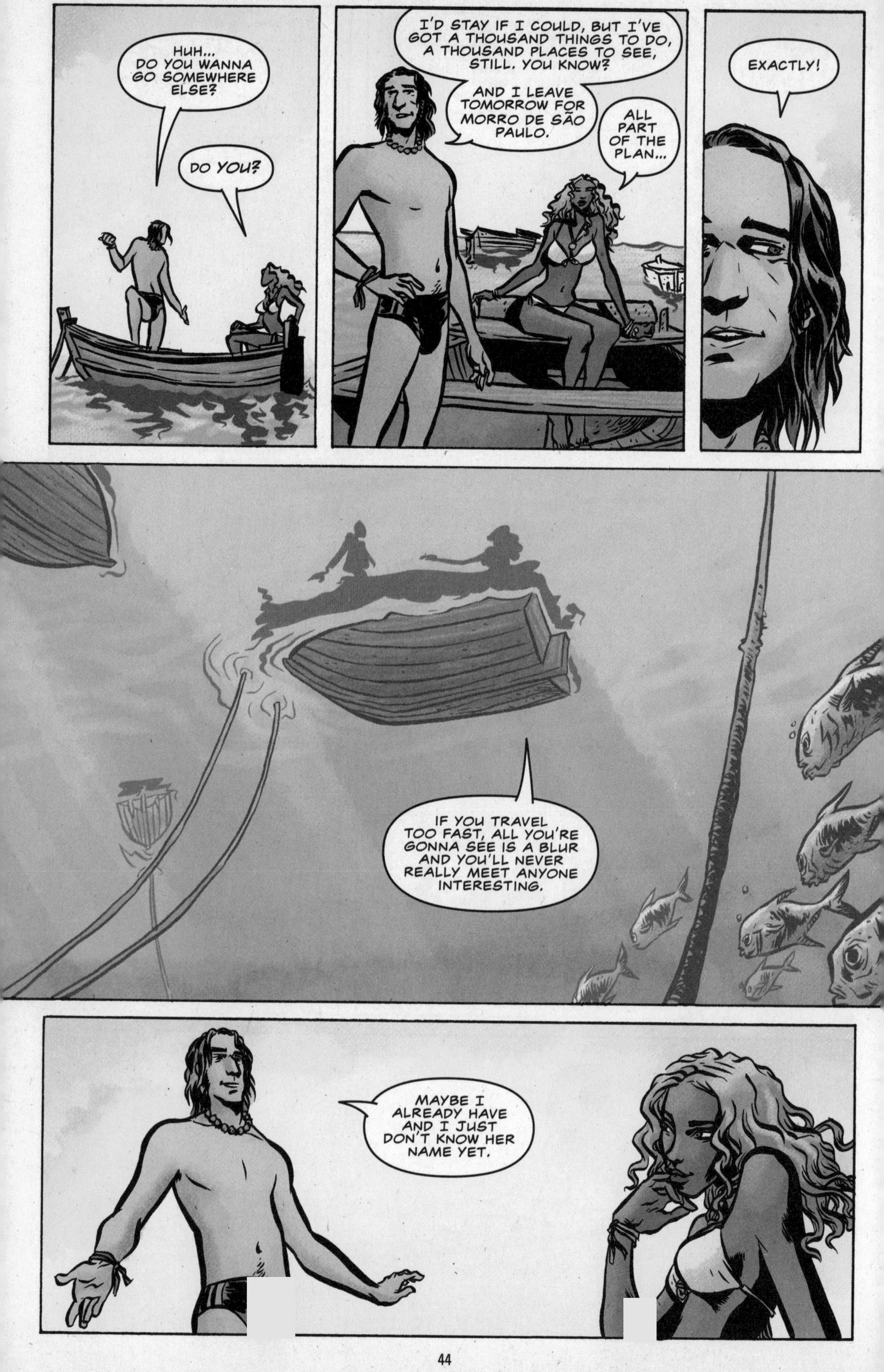
HUH... DO YOU WANNA GO SOMEWHERE ELSE?
DO YOU?
I'D STAY IF I COULD, BUT I'VE GOT A THOUSAND THINGS TO DO, A THOUSAND PLACES TO SEE, STILL. YOU KNOW?
AND I LEAVE TOMORROW FOR MORRO DE SÃO PAULO.
ALL PART OF THE PLAN...
EXACTLY!
IF YOU TRAVEL TOO FAST, ALL YOU'RE GONNA SEE IS A BLUR AND YOU'LL NEVER REALLY MEET ANYONE INTERESTING.
MAYBE I ALREADY HAVE AND I JUST DON'T KNOW HER NAME YET.

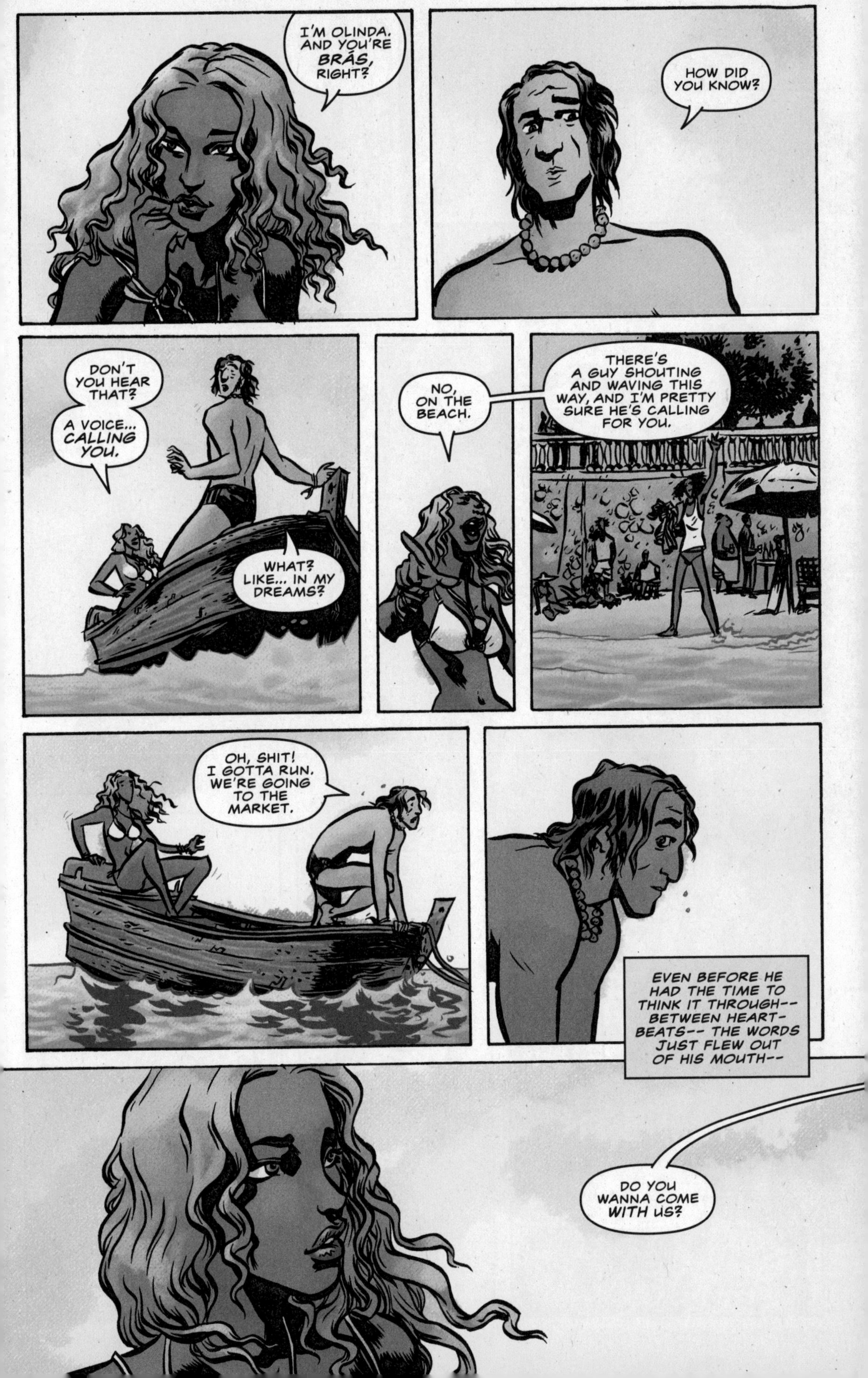
I'M OLINDA. AND YOU'RE BRÁS, RIGHT?
HOW DID YOU KNOW?
DON'T YOU HEAR THAT?
A VOICE... CALLING YOU.
WHAT? LIKE... IN MY DREAMS?
NO, ON THE BEACH.
THERE'S A GUY SHOUTING AND WAVING THIS WAY, AND I'M PRETTY SURE HE'S CALLING FOR YOU.
OH, SHIT! I GOTTA RUN. WE'RE GOING TO THE MARKET.
EVEN BEFORE HE HAD THE TIME TO THINK IT THROUGH-- BETWEEN HEART-BEATS-- THE WORDS JUST FLEW OUT OF HIS MOUTH--
DO YOU WANNA COME WITH US?

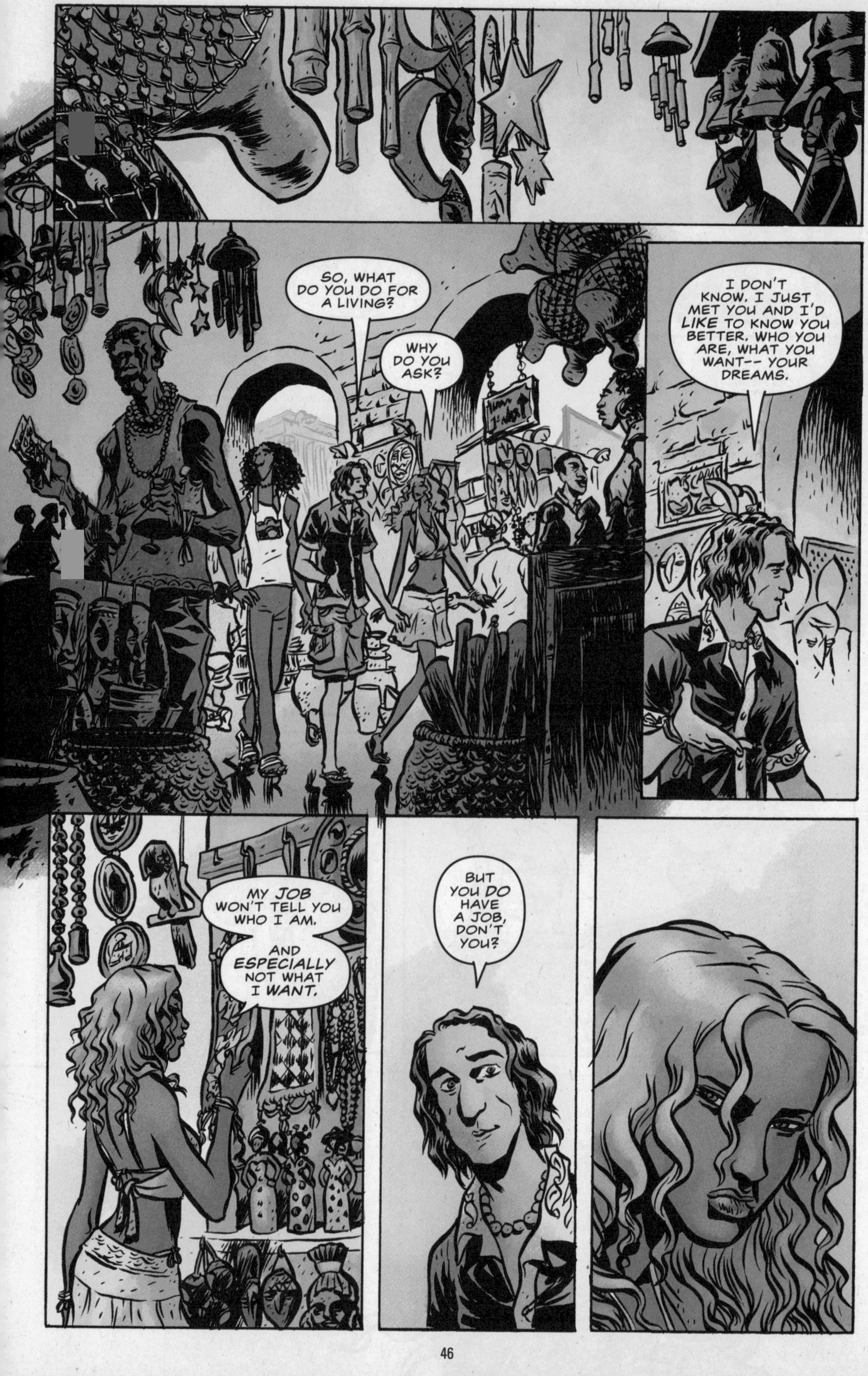
SO, WHAT DO YOU DO FOR A LIVING?
WHY DO YOU ASK?
I DON'T KNOW. I JUST MET YOU AND I'D LIKE TO KNOW YOU BETTER. WHO YOU ARE, WHAT YOU WANT-- YOUR DREAMS.
MY JOB WON'T TELL YOU WHO I AM.
AND ESPECIALLY NOT WHAT I WANT.
BUT YOU DO HAVE A JOB, DON'T YOU?

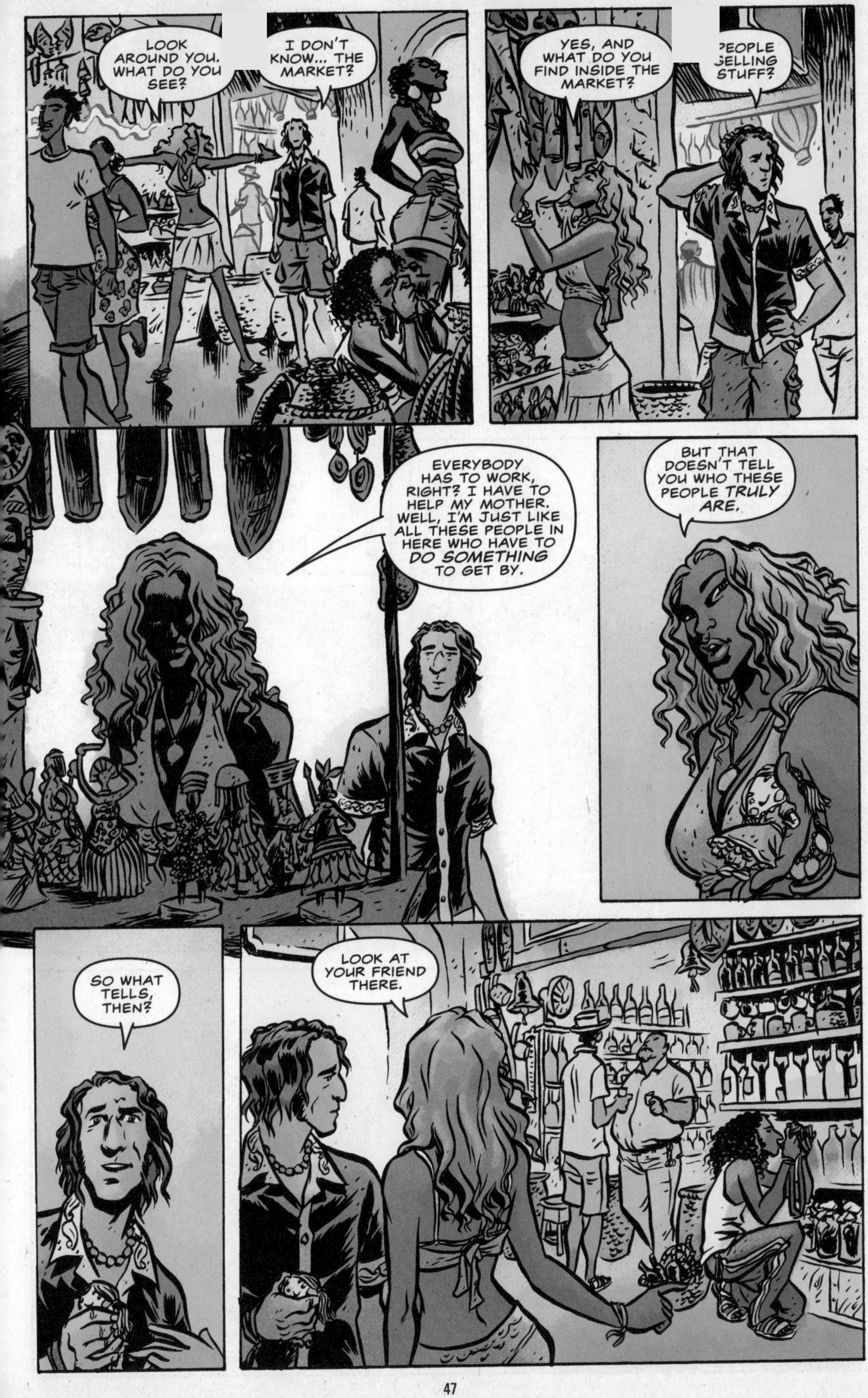
LOOK AROUND YOU. WHAT DO YOU SEE?
I DON'T KNOW... THE MARKET?
YES, AND WHAT DO YOU FIND INSIDE THE MARKET?
PEOPLE SELLING STUFF?
EVERYBODY HAS TO WORK, RIGHT? I HAVE TO HELP MY MOTHER. WELL, I'M JUST LIKE ALL THESE PEOPLE IN HERE WHO HAVE TO DO SOMETHING TO GET BY.
BUT THAT DOESN'T TELL YOU WHO THESE PEOPLE TRULY ARE.
SO WHAT TELLS, THEN?
LOOK AT YOUR FRIEND THERE.

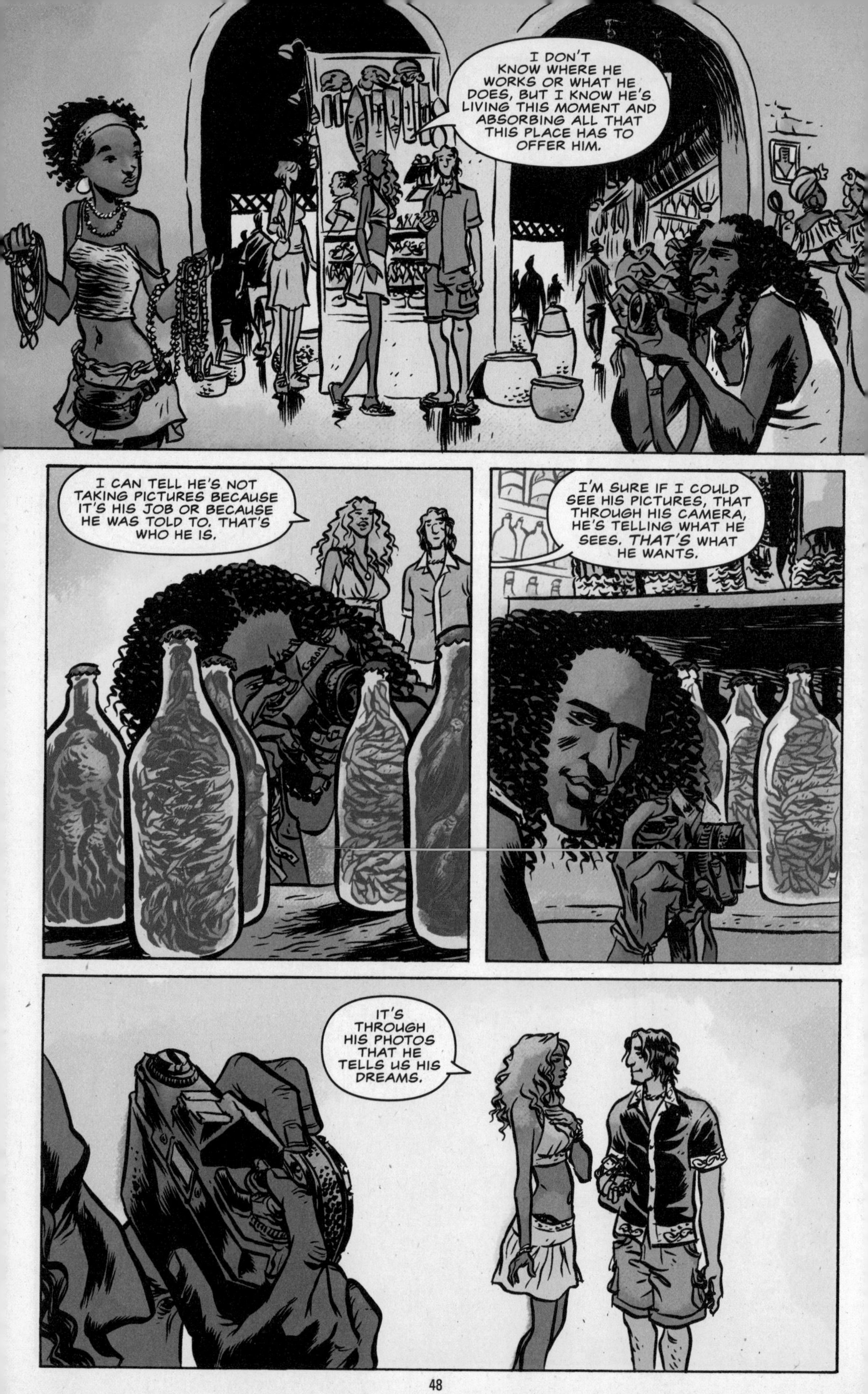
I DON'T KNOW WHERE HE WORKS OR WHAT HE DOES, BUT I KNOW HE'S LIVING THIS MOMENT AND ABSORBING ALL THAT THIS PLACE HAS TO OFFER HIM.
I CAN TELL HE'S NOT TAKING PICTURES BECAUSE IT'S HIS JOB OR BECAUSE HE WAS TOLD TO. THAT'S WHO HE IS.
I'M SURE IF I COULD SEE HIS PICTURES, THAT THROUGH HIS CAMERA, HE'S TELLING WHAT HE SEES. *THAT'S* WHAT HE WANTS.
IT'S THROUGH HIS PHOTOS THAT HE TELLS US HIS DREAMS.

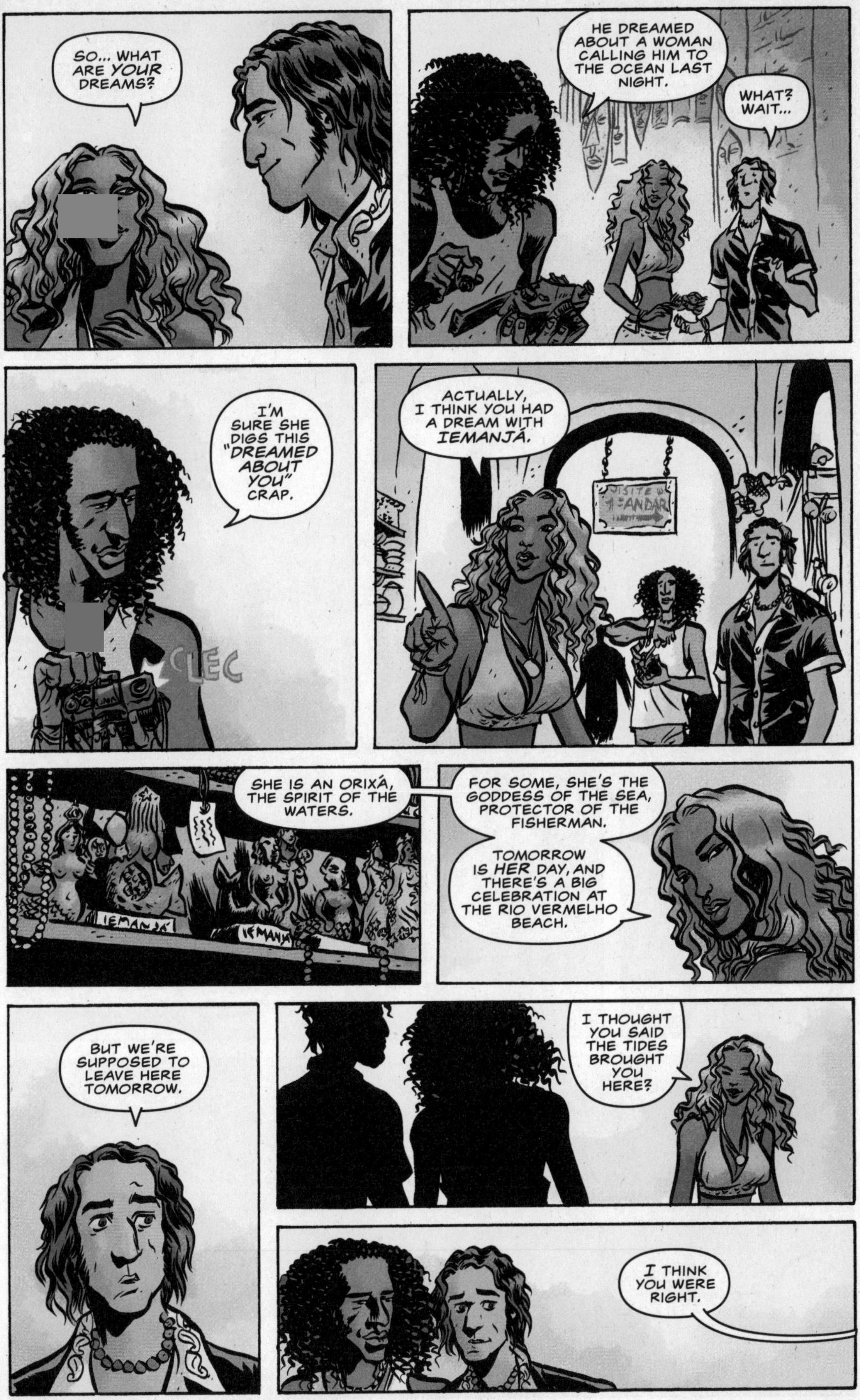
SO... WHAT ARE YOUR DREAMS?
HE DREAMED ABOUT A WOMAN CALLING HIM TO THE OCEAN LAST NIGHT.
WHAT? WAIT...
I'M SURE SHE DIGS THIS "DREAMED ABOUT YOU" CRAP.
CLEC
ACTUALLY, I THINK YOU HAD A DREAM WITH IEMANJÁ.
SHE IS AN ORIXÁ, THE SPIRIT OF THE WATERS.
IEMANJÁ
FOR SOME, SHE'S THE GODDESS OF THE SEA, PROTECTOR OF THE FISHERMAN.
TOMORROW IS HER DAY, AND THERE'S A BIG CELEBRATION AT THE RIO VERMELHO BEACH.
BUT WE'RE SUPPOSED TO LEAVE HERE TOMORROW.
I THOUGHT YOU SAID THE TIDES BROUGHT YOU HERE?
I THINK YOU WERE RIGHT.

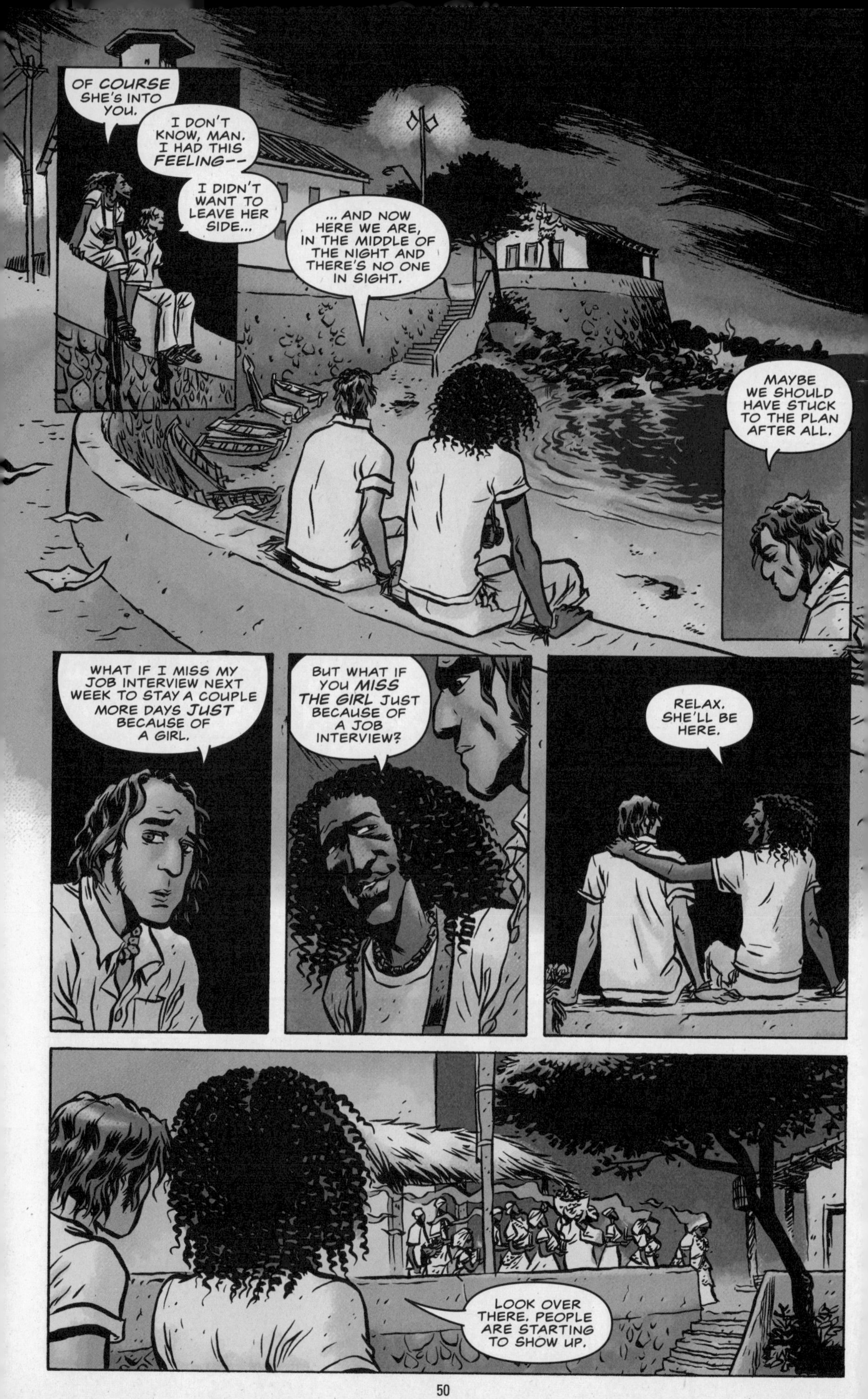
OF COURSE SHE'S INTO YOU.
I DON'T KNOW, MAN. I HAD THIS FEELING--
I DIDN'T WANT TO LEAVE HER SIDE...
... AND NOW HERE WE ARE, IN THE MIDDLE OF THE NIGHT AND THERE'S NO ONE IN SIGHT.
MAYBE WE SHOULD HAVE STUCK TO THE PLAN AFTER ALL.
WHAT IF I MISS MY JOB INTERVIEW NEXT WEEK TO STAY A COUPLE MORE DAYS JUST BECAUSE OF A GIRL.
BUT WHAT IF YOU MISS THE GIRL JUST BECAUSE OF A JOB INTERVIEW?
RELAX. SHE'LL BE HERE.
LOOK OVER THERE. PEOPLE ARE STARTING TO SHOW UP.

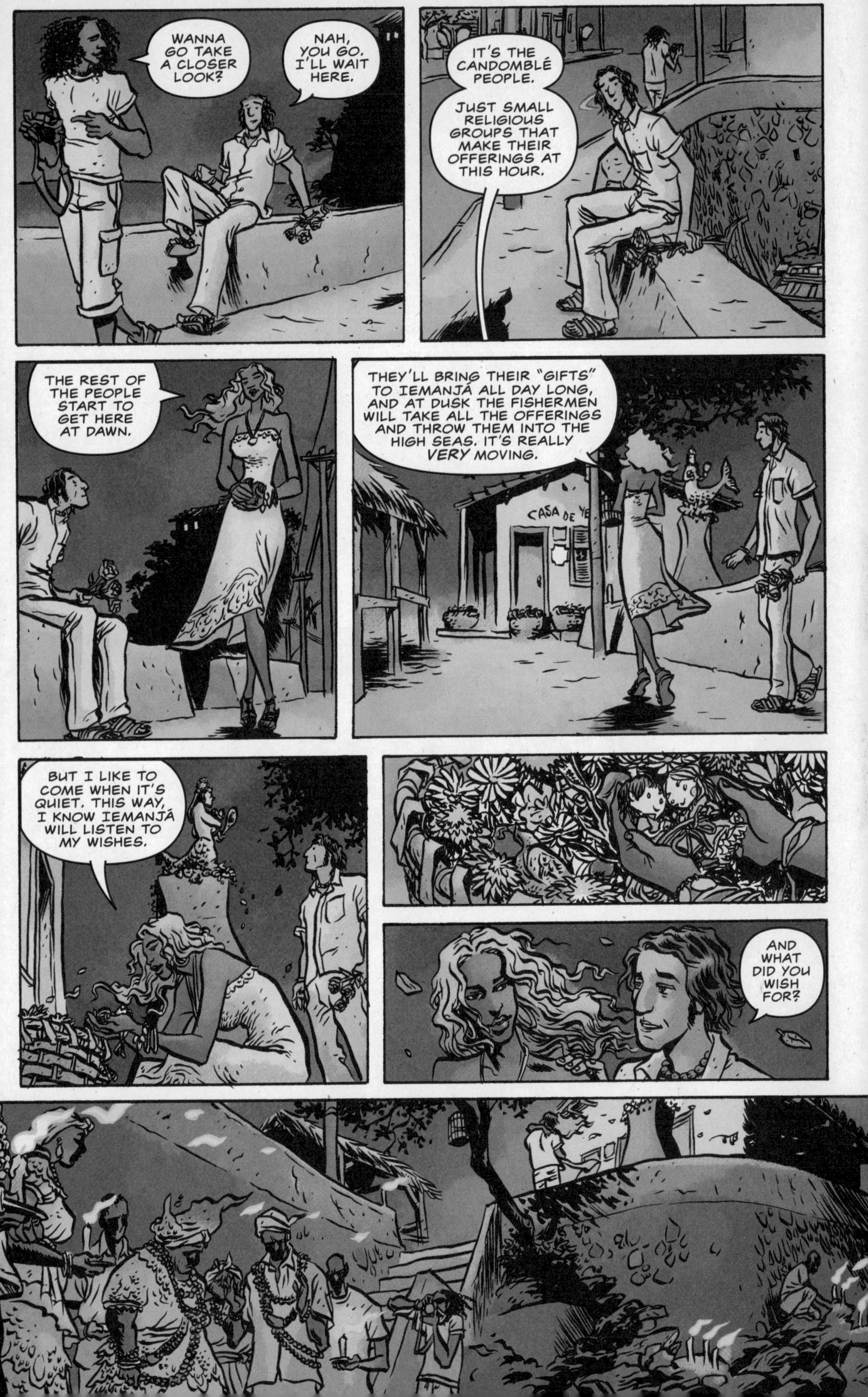
WANNA GO TAKE A CLOSER LOOK?
NAH, YOU GO. I'LL WAIT HERE.
IT'S THE CANDOMBLÉ PEOPLE.
JUST SMALL RELIGIOUS GROUPS THAT MAKE THEIR OFFERINGS AT THIS HOUR.
THE REST OF THE PEOPLE START TO GET HERE AT DAWN.
THEY'LL BRING THEIR "GIFTS" TO IEMANJÁ ALL DAY LONG, AND AT DUSK THE FISHERMEN WILL TAKE ALL THE OFFERINGS AND THROW THEM INTO THE HIGH SEAS. IT'S REALLY VERY MOVING.
CASA DE YE
BUT I LIKE TO COME WHEN IT'S QUIET. THIS WAY, I KNOW IEMANJÁ WILL LISTEN TO MY WISHES.
AND WHAT DID YOU WISH FOR?

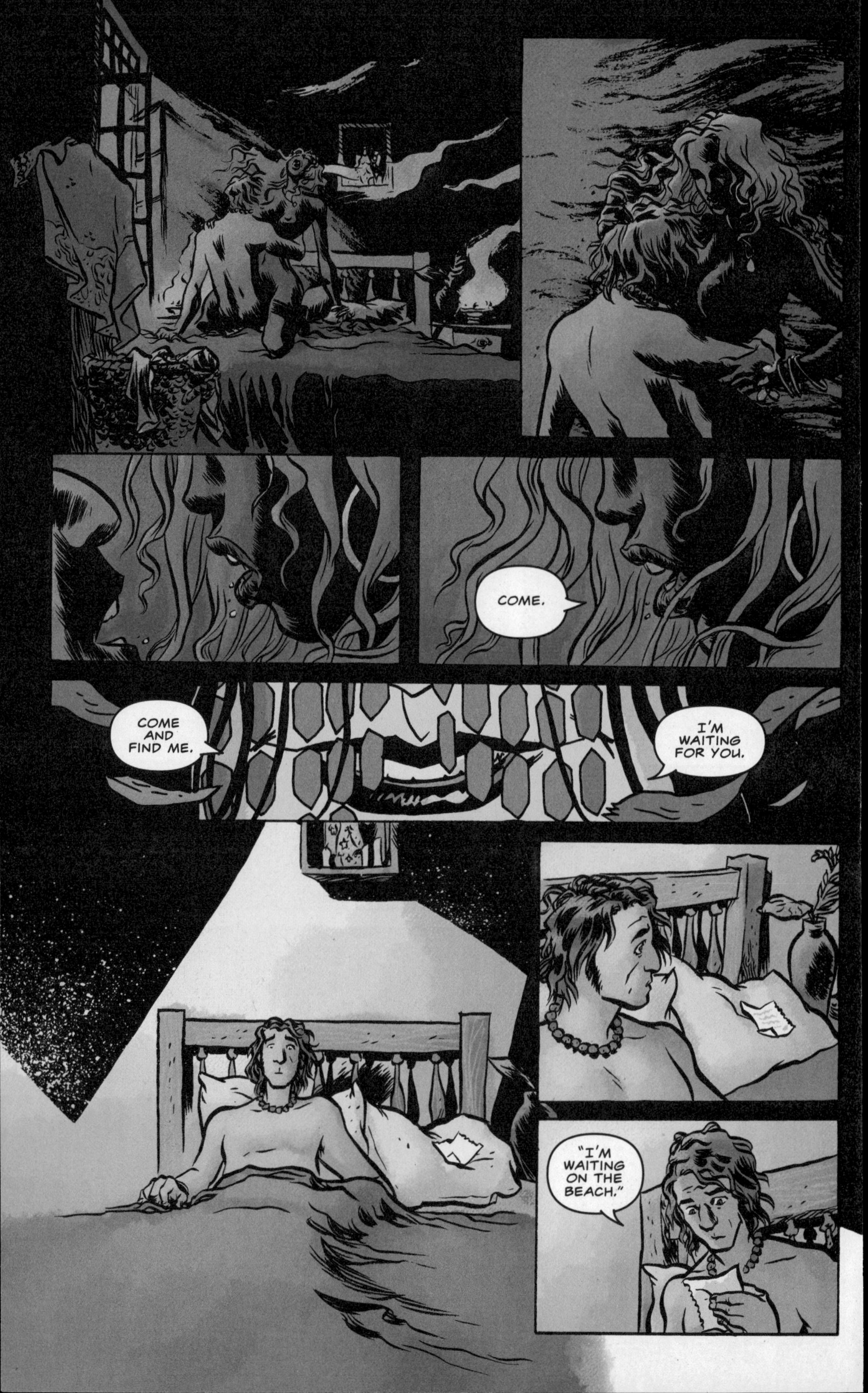
COME.
COME AND FIND ME.
I'M WAITING FOR YOU.
"I'M WAITING ON THE BEACH."

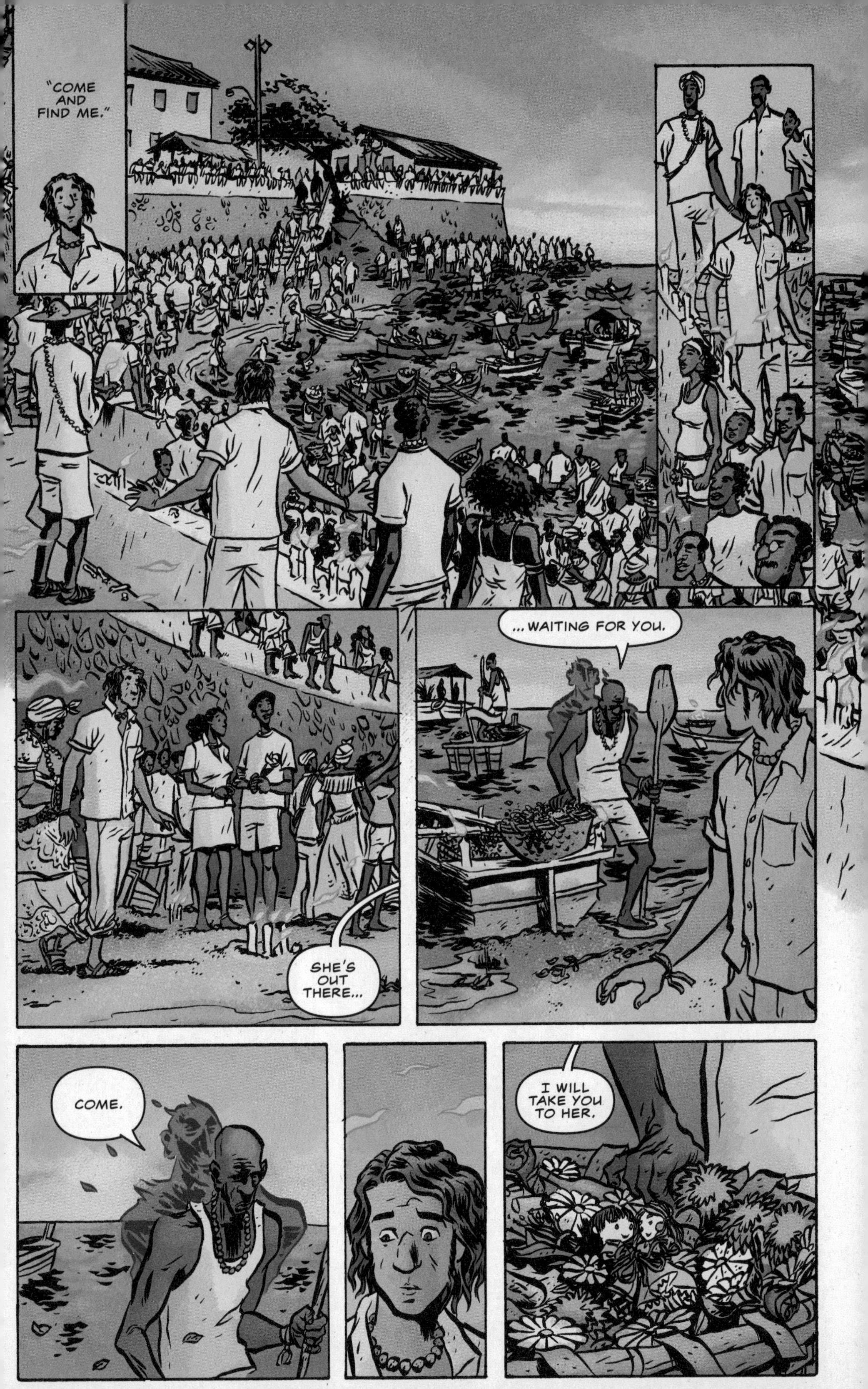
"COME AND FIND ME."
SHE'S OUT THERE...
...WAITING FOR YOU.
COME.
I WILL TAKE YOU TO HER.

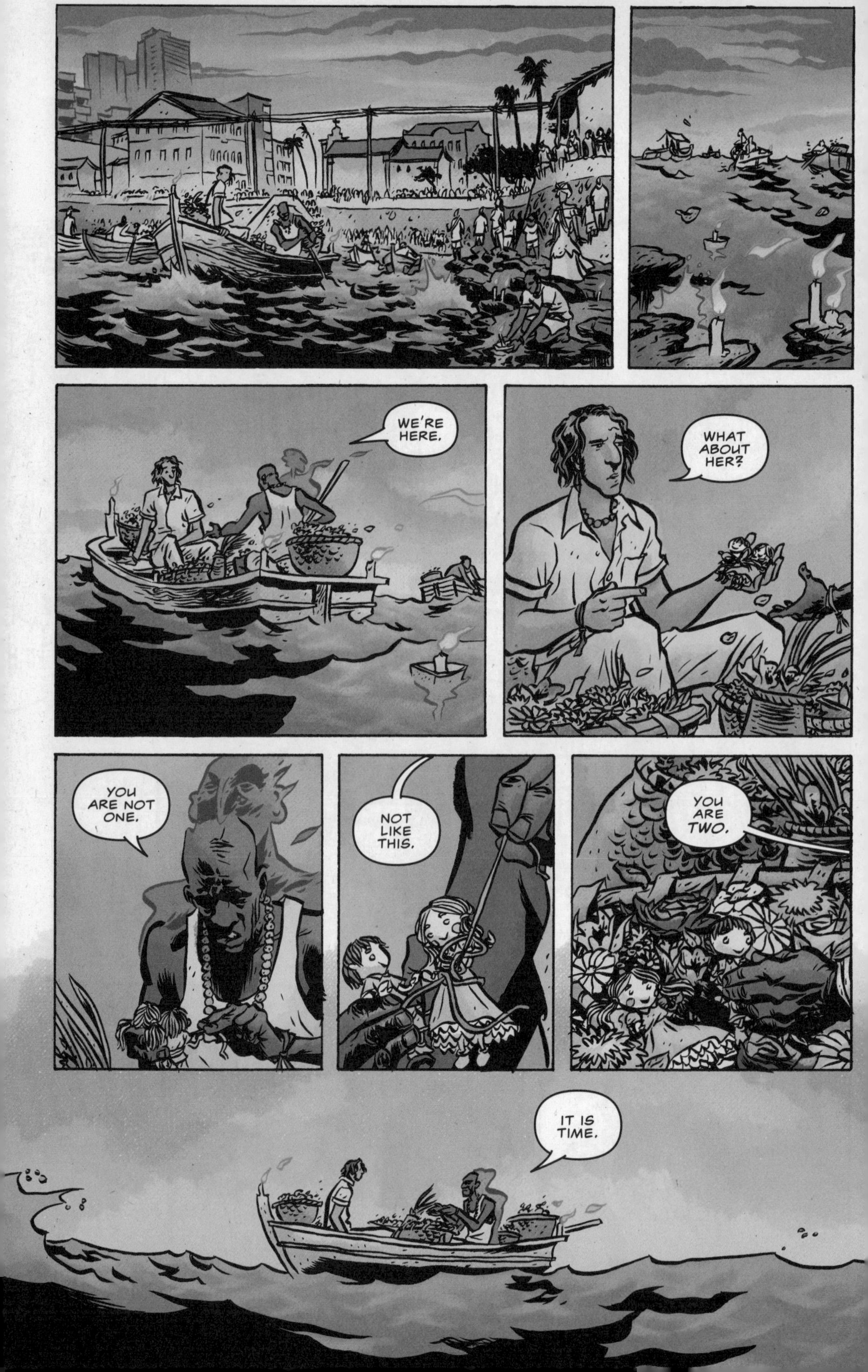
WE'RE HERE.
WHAT ABOUT HER?
YOU ARE NOT ONE.
NOT LIKE THIS.
YOU ARE TWO.
IT IS TIME.

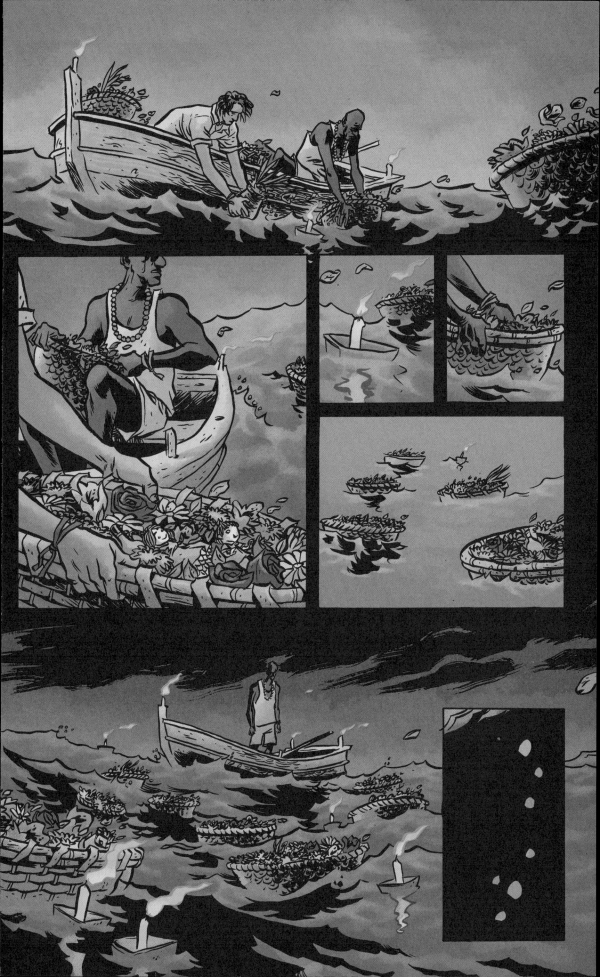

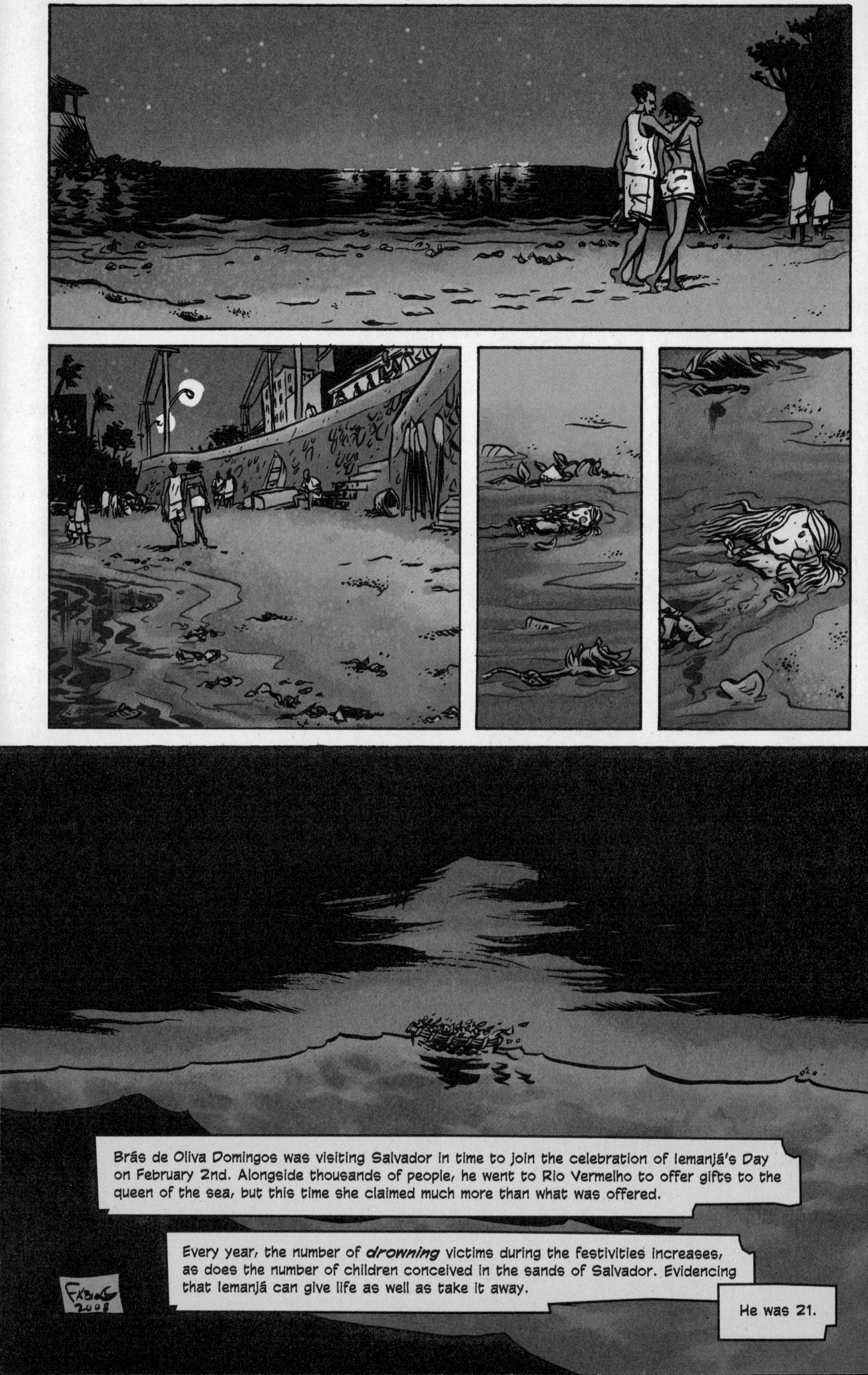
Brás de Oliva Domingos was visiting Salvador in time to join the celebration of Iemanjá's Day on February 2nd. Alongside thousands of people, he went to Rio Vermelho to offer gifts to the queen of the sea, but this time she claimed much more than what was offered.
Every year, the number of drowning victims during the festivities increases, as does the number of children conceived in the sands of Salvador. Evidencing that Iemanjá can give life as well as take it away.
He was 21.
FÁBIO 2008

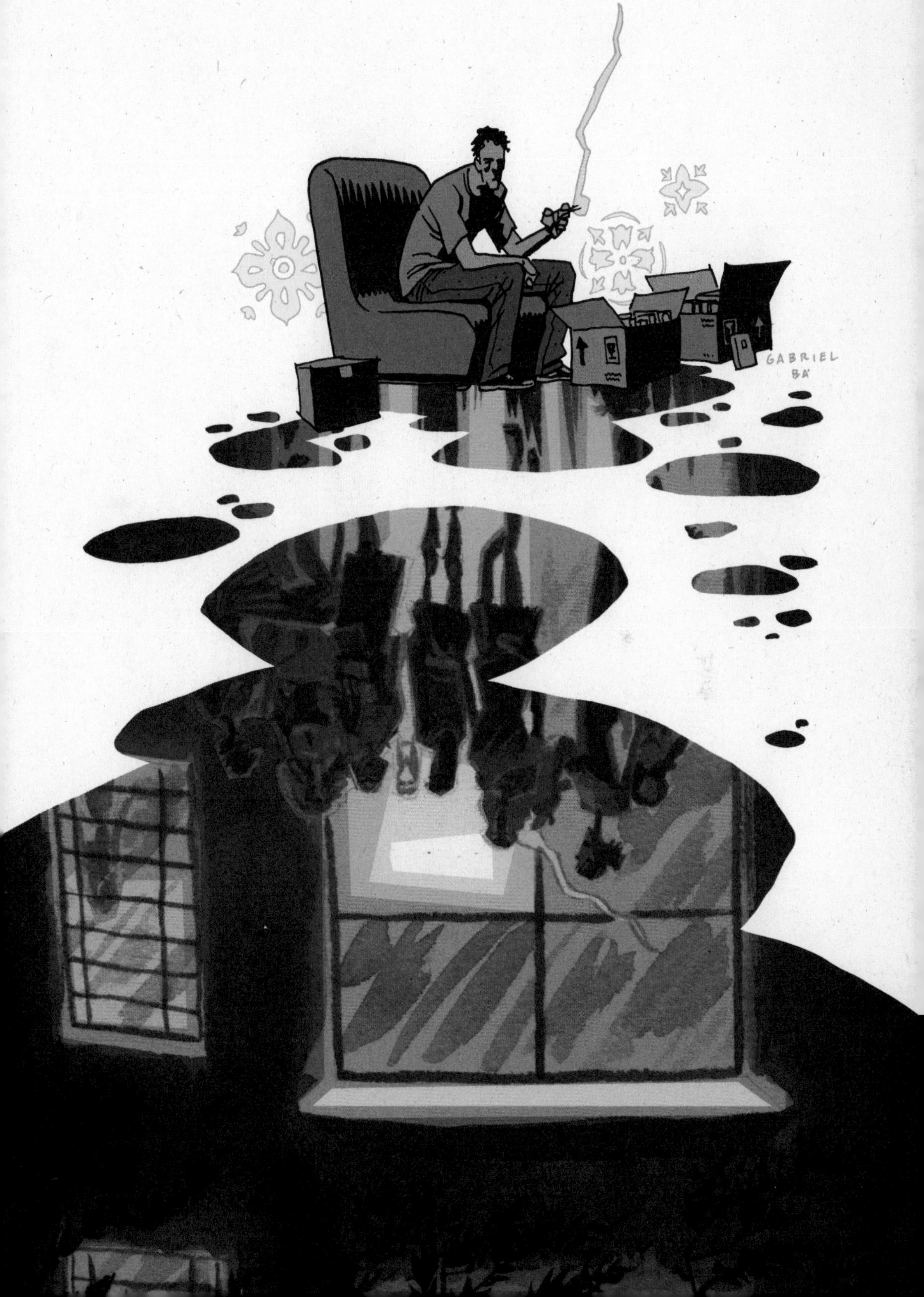
GABRIEL
BÁ

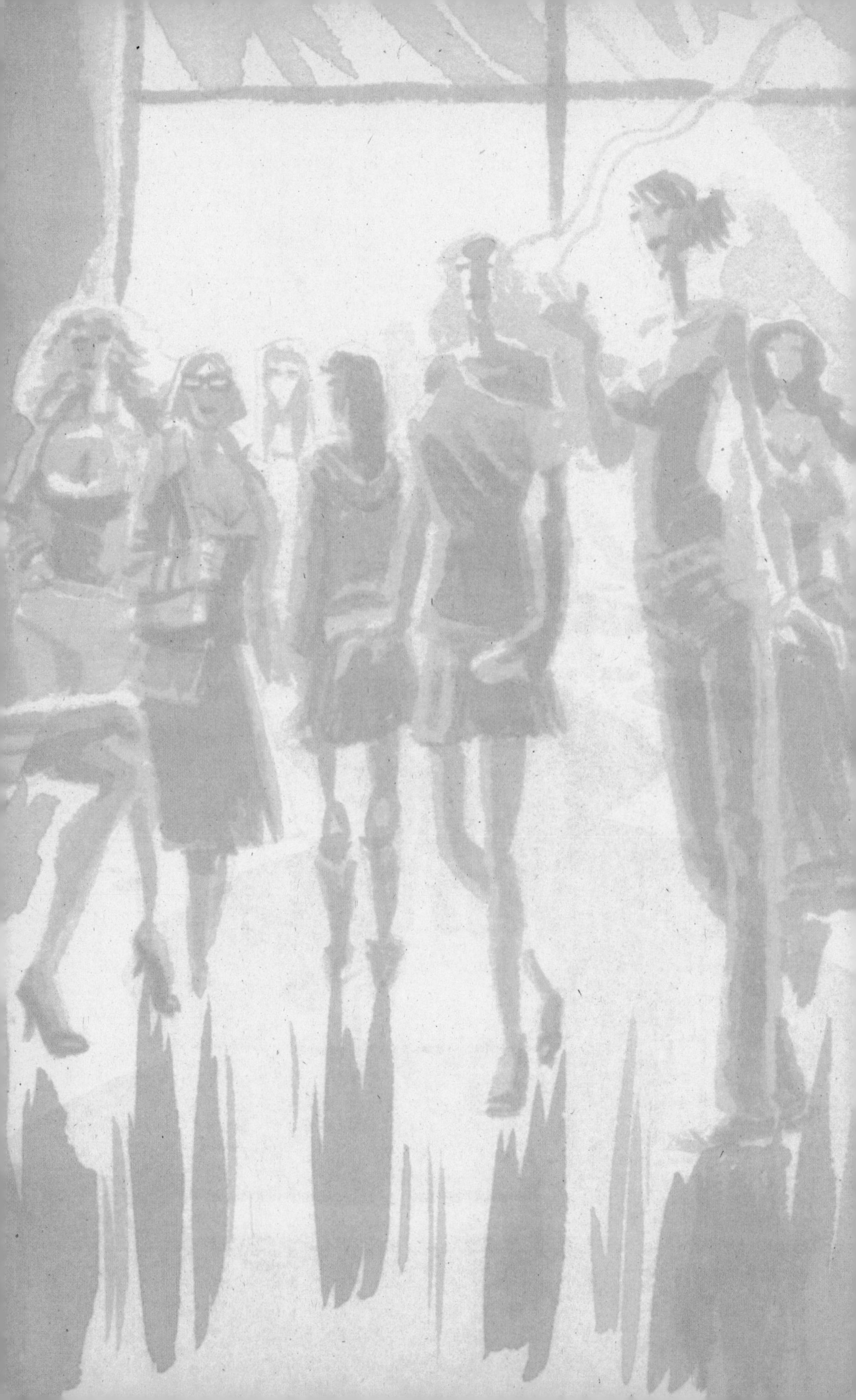

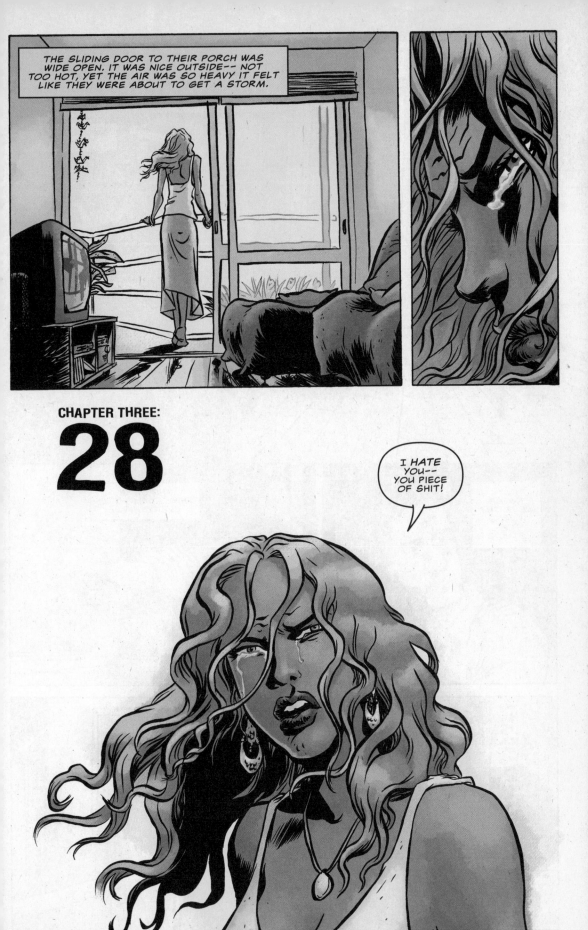

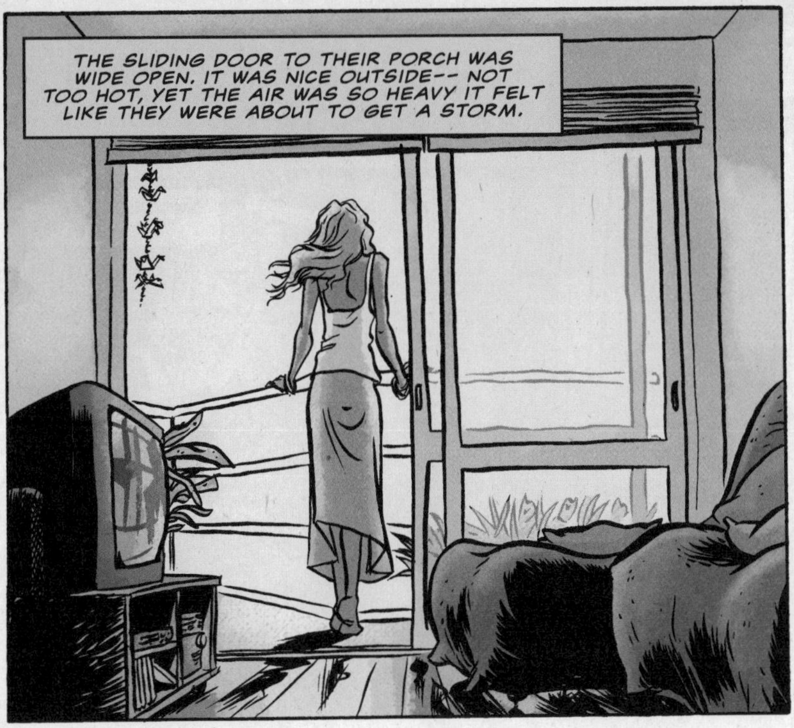
THE SLIDING DOOR TO THEIR PORCH WAS WIDE OPEN. IT WAS NICE OUTSIDE-- NOT TOO HOT, YET THE AIR WAS SO HEAVY IT FELT LIKE THEY WERE ABOUT TO GET A STORM.

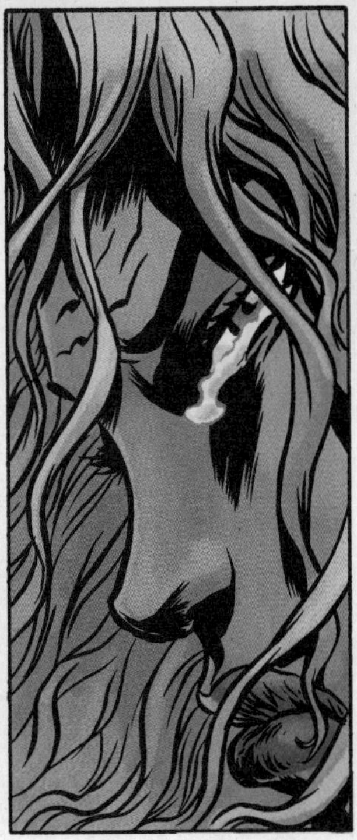

CHAPTER THREE:

28

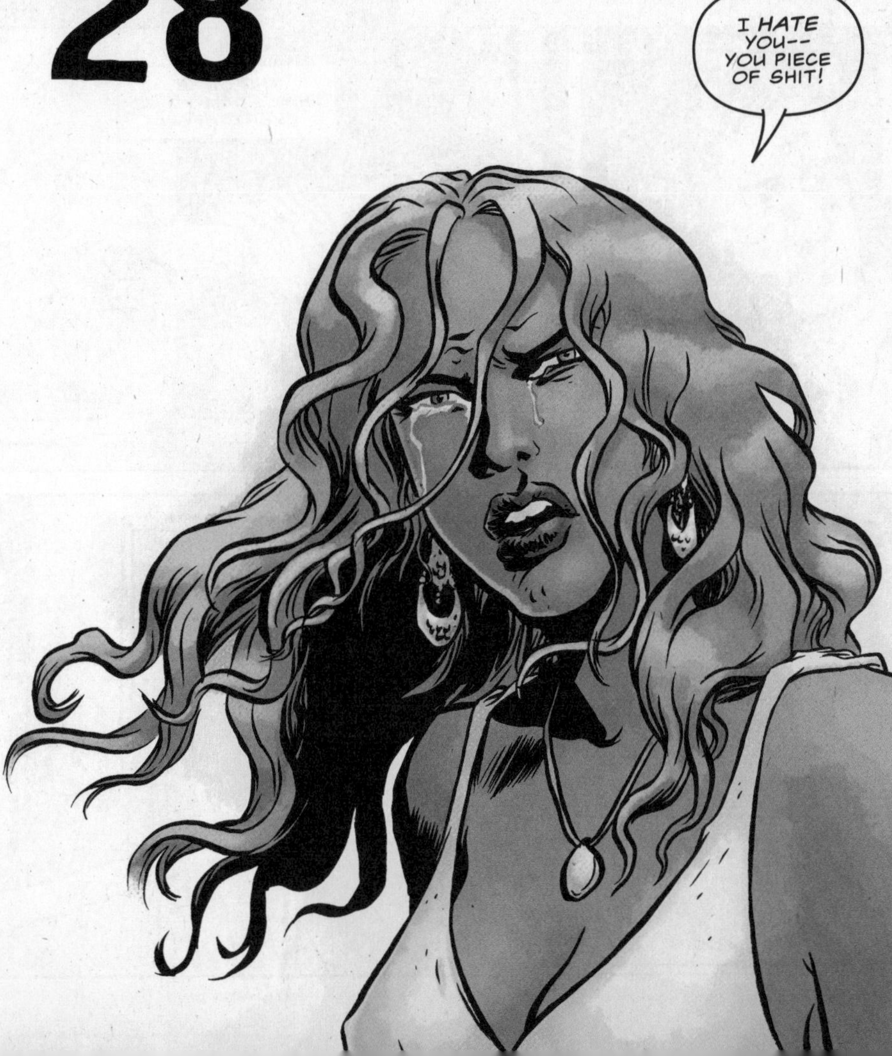
I HATE YOU-- YOU PIECE OF SHIT!

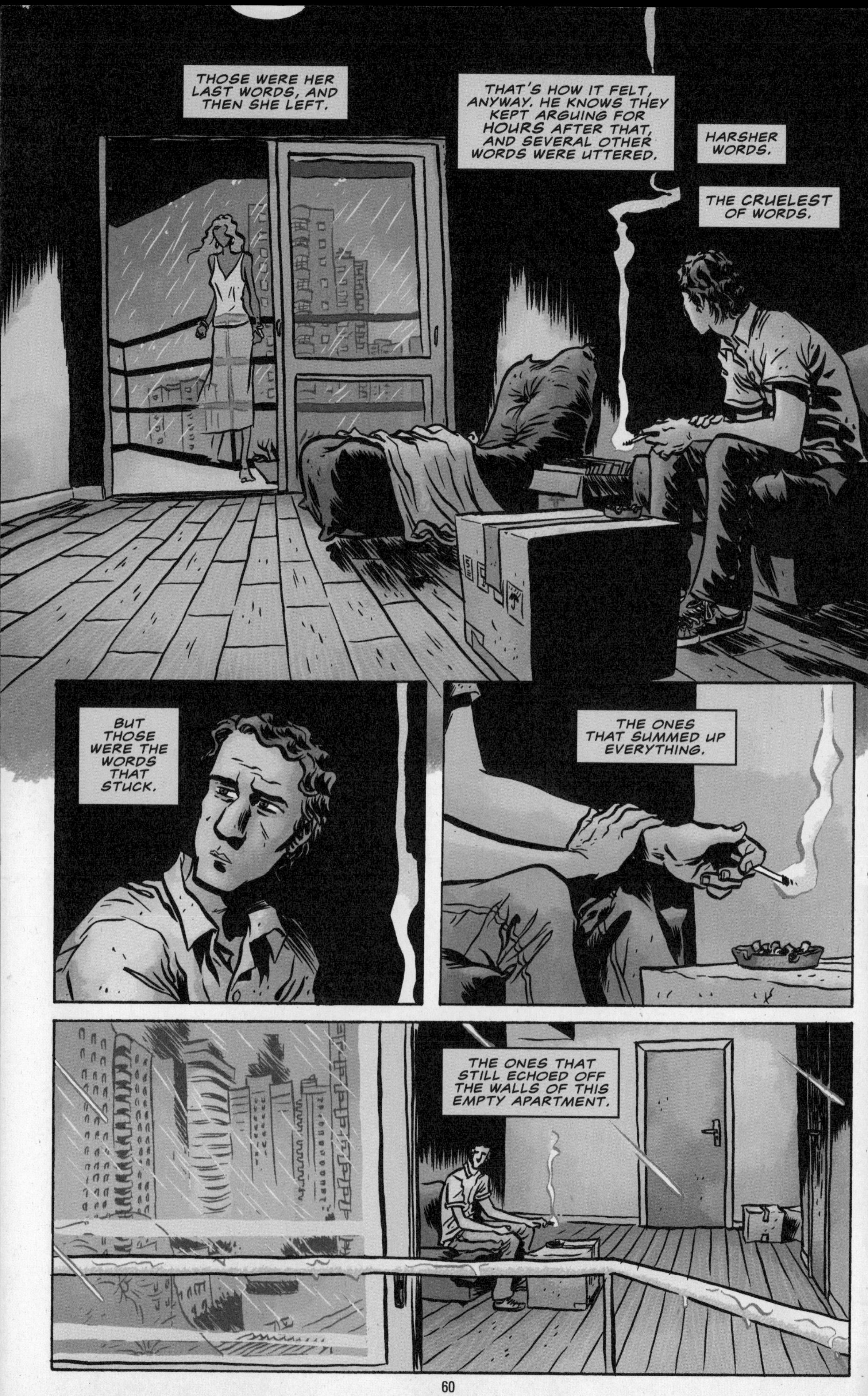
THOSE WERE HER LAST WORDS, AND THEN SHE LEFT.
THAT'S HOW IT FELT, ANYWAY. HE KNOWS THEY KEPT ARGUING FOR HOURS AFTER THAT, AND SEVERAL OTHER WORDS WERE UTTERED.
HARSHER WORDS.
THE CRUELEST OF WORDS.
BUT THOSE WERE THE WORDS THAT STUCK.
THE ONES THAT SUMMED UP EVERYTHING.
THE ONES THAT STILL ECHOED OFF THE WALLS OF THIS EMPTY APARTMENT.

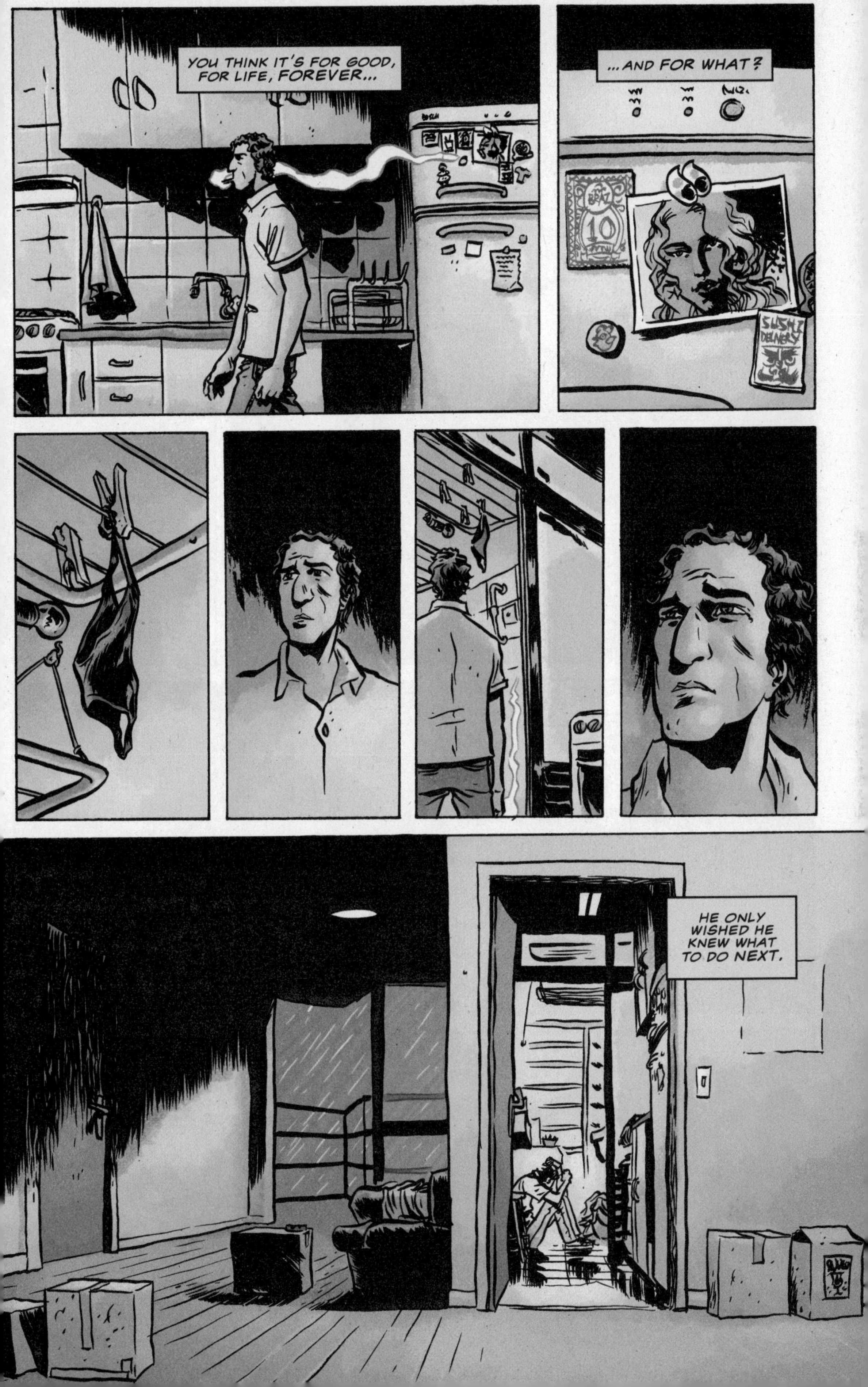
YOU THINK IT'S FOR GOOD, FOR LIFE, FOREVER...
...AND FOR WHAT?
HE ONLY WISHED HE KNEW WHAT TO DO NEXT.

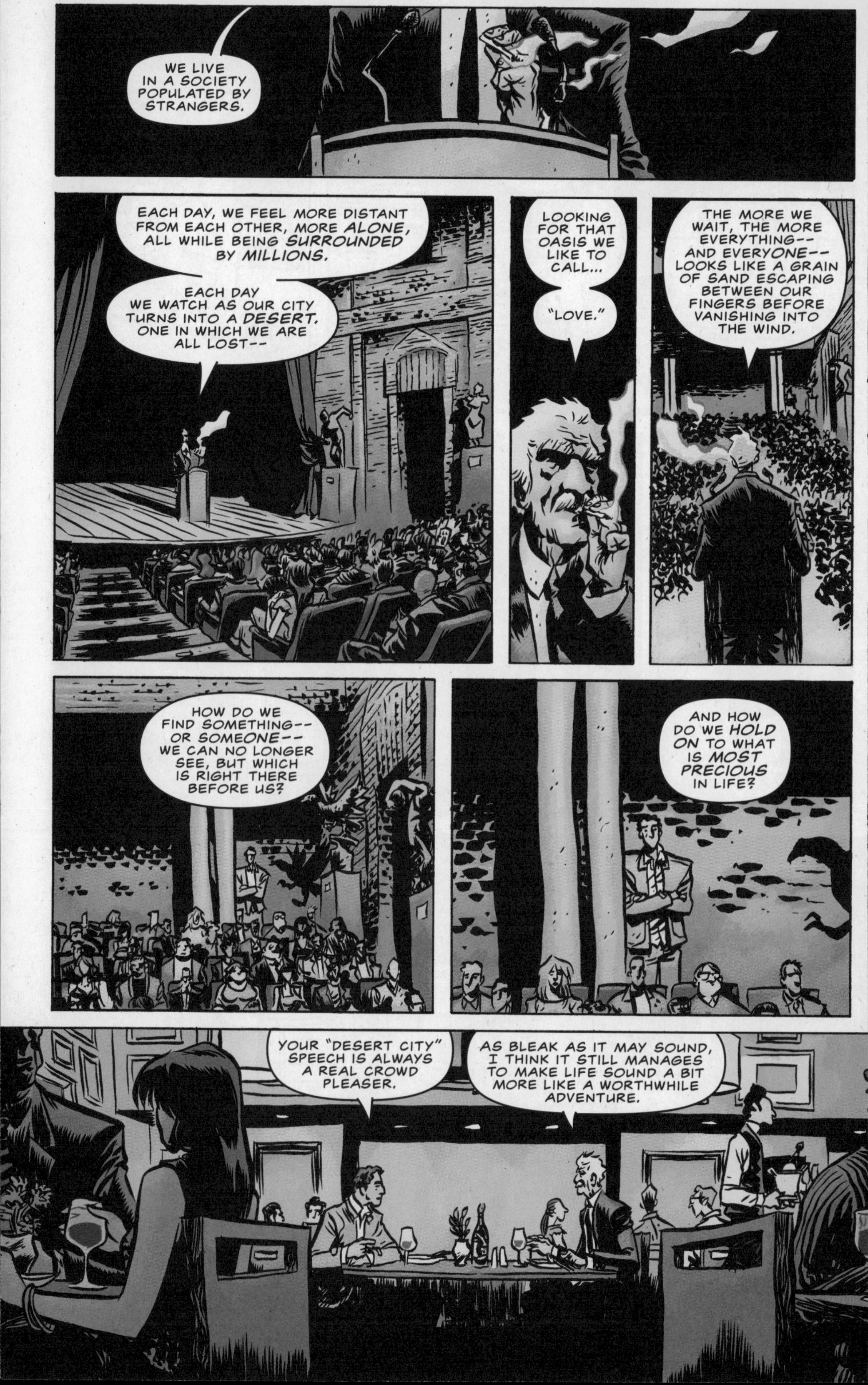
WE LIVE IN A SOCIETY POPULATED BY STRANGERS.
EACH DAY, WE FEEL MORE DISTANT FROM EACH OTHER, MORE ALONE, ALL WHILE BEING SURROUNDED BY MILLIONS.
EACH DAY WE WATCH AS OUR CITY TURNS INTO A DESERT. ONE IN WHICH WE ARE ALL LOST--
LOOKING FOR THAT OASIS WE LIKE TO CALL...
"LOVE."
THE MORE WE WAIT, THE MORE EVERYTHING-- AND EVERYONE-- LOOKS LIKE A GRAIN OF SAND ESCAPING BETWEEN OUR FINGERS BEFORE VANISHING INTO THE WIND.
HOW DO WE FIND SOMETHING-- OR SOMEONE-- WE CAN NO LONGER SEE, BUT WHICH IS RIGHT THERE BEFORE US?
AND HOW DO WE HOLD ON TO WHAT IS MOST PRECIOUS IN LIFE?
YOUR "DESERT CITY" SPEECH IS ALWAYS A REAL CROWD PLEASER.
AS BLEAK AS IT MAY SOUND, I THINK IT STILL MANAGES TO MAKE LIFE SOUND A BIT MORE LIKE A WORTHWHILE ADVENTURE.

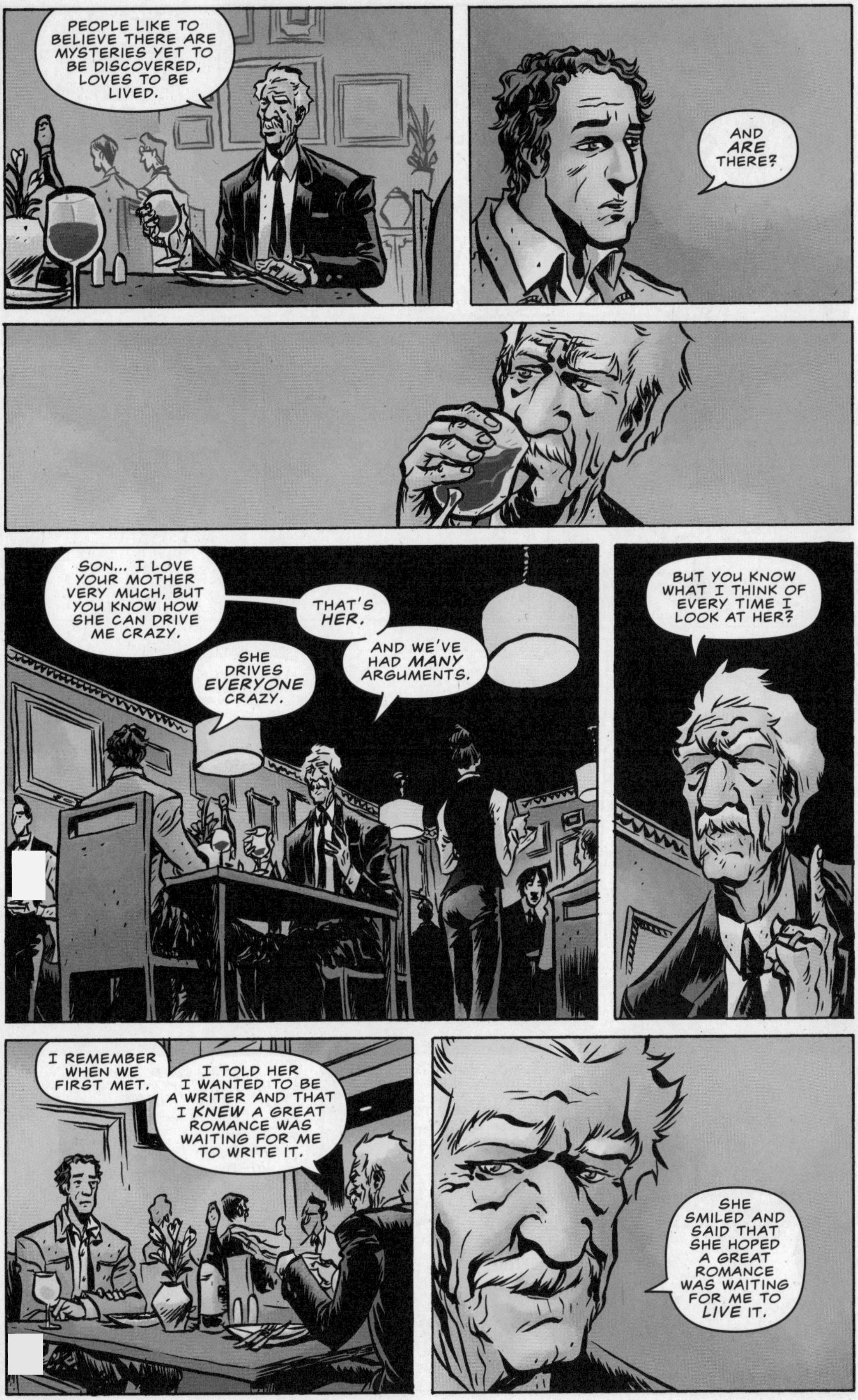
PEOPLE LIKE TO BELIEVE THERE ARE MYSTERIES YET TO BE DISCOVERED, LOVES TO BE LIVED.
AND ARE THERE?
SON... I LOVE YOUR MOTHER VERY MUCH, BUT YOU KNOW HOW SHE CAN DRIVE ME CRAZY.
SHE DRIVES EVERYONE CRAZY.
THAT'S HER.
AND WE'VE HAD MANY ARGUMENTS.
BUT YOU KNOW WHAT I THINK OF EVERY TIME I LOOK AT HER?
I REMEMBER WHEN WE FIRST MET.
I TOLD HER I WANTED TO BE A WRITER AND THAT I KNEW A GREAT ROMANCE WAS WAITING FOR ME TO WRITE IT.
SHE SMILED AND SAID THAT SHE HOPED A GREAT ROMANCE WAS WAITING FOR ME TO LIVE IT.

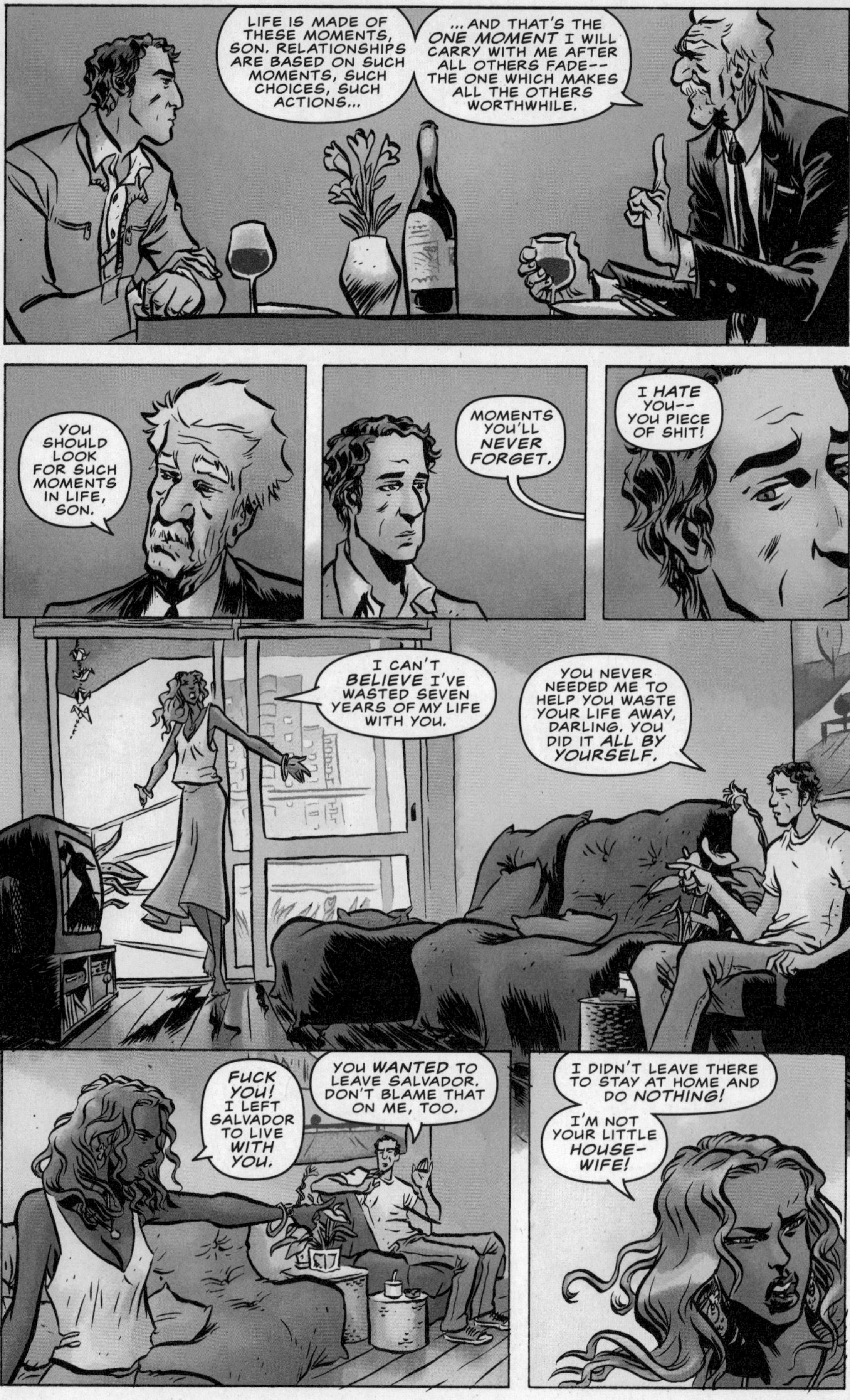
LIFE IS MADE OF THESE MOMENTS, SON. RELATIONSHIPS ARE BASED ON SUCH MOMENTS, SUCH CHOICES, SUCH ACTIONS...
...AND THAT'S THE ONE MOMENT I WILL CARRY WITH ME AFTER ALL OTHERS FADE-- THE ONE WHICH MAKES ALL THE OTHERS WORTHWHILE.
YOU SHOULD LOOK FOR SUCH MOMENTS IN LIFE, SON.
MOMENTS YOU'LL NEVER FORGET.
I HATE YOU-- YOU PIECE OF SHIT!
I CAN'T BELIEVE I'VE WASTED SEVEN YEARS OF MY LIFE WITH YOU.
YOU NEVER NEEDED ME TO HELP YOU WASTE YOUR LIFE AWAY, DARLING. YOU DID IT ALL BY YOURSELF.
FUCK YOU! I LEFT SALVADOR TO LIVE WITH YOU.
YOU WANTED TO LEAVE SALVADOR. DON'T BLAME THAT ON ME, TOO.
I DIDN'T LEAVE THERE TO STAY AT HOME AND DO NOTHING!
I'M NOT YOUR LITTLE HOUSE-WIFE!

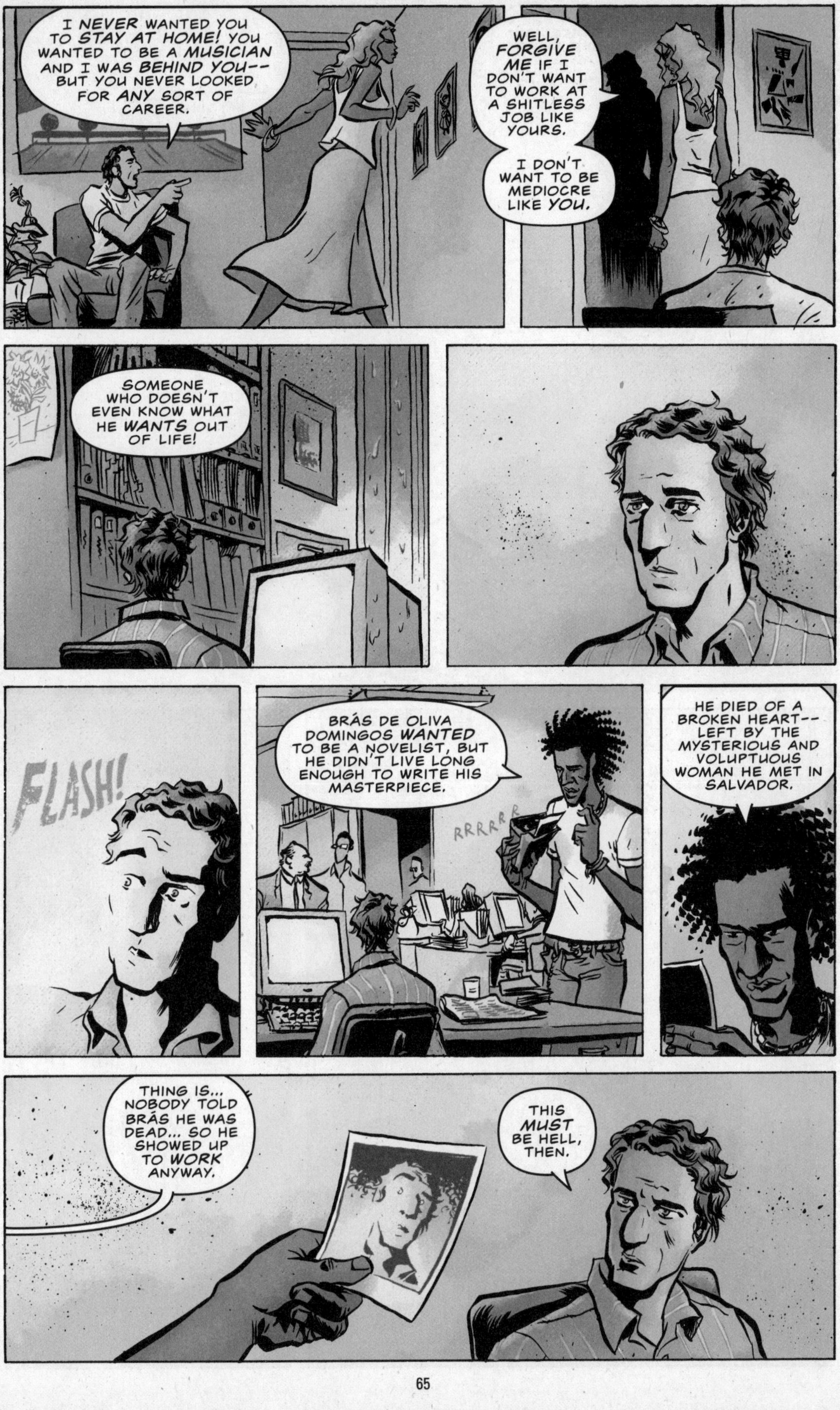
I NEVER WANTED YOU TO STAY AT HOME! YOU WANTED TO BE A MUSICIAN AND I WAS BEHIND YOU-- BUT YOU NEVER LOOKED FOR ANY SORT OF CAREER.
WELL, FORGIVE ME IF I DON'T WANT TO WORK AT A SHITLESS JOB LIKE YOURS.
I DON'T WANT TO BE MEDIOCRE LIKE YOU.
SOMEONE, WHO DOESN'T EVEN KNOW WHAT HE WANTS OUT OF LIFE!
FLASH!
BRÁS DE OLIVA DOMINGOS WANTED TO BE A NOVELIST, BUT HE DIDN'T LIVE LONG ENOUGH TO WRITE HIS MASTERPIECE.
RRRRRRR
HE DIED OF A BROKEN HEART-- LEFT BY THE MYSTERIOUS AND VOLUPTUOUS WOMAN HE MET IN SALVADOR.
THING IS... NOBODY TOLD BRÁS HE WAS DEAD... SO HE SHOWED UP TO WORK ANYWAY.
THIS MUST BE HELL, THEN.

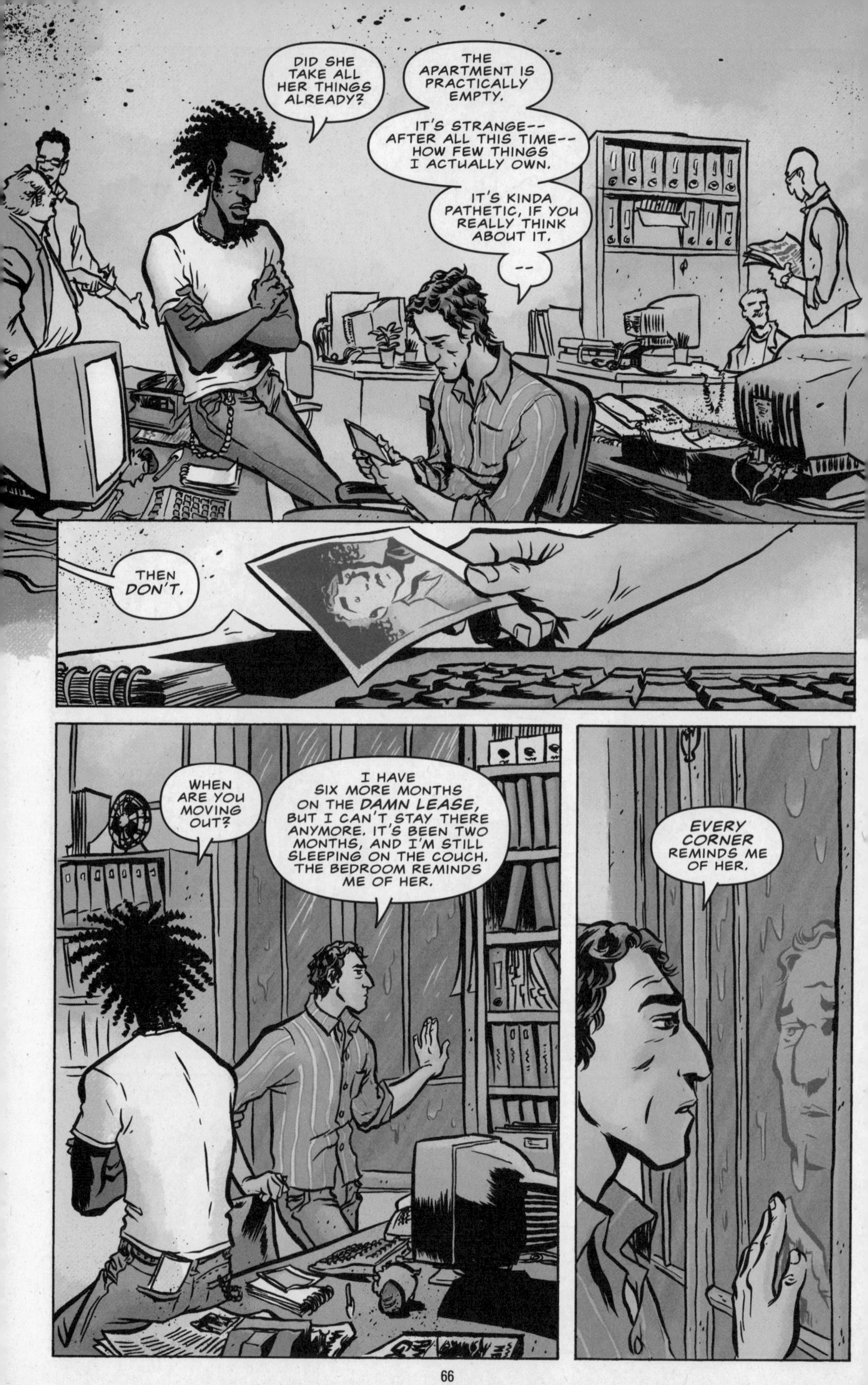
DID SHE TAKE ALL HER THINGS ALREADY?
THE APARTMENT IS PRACTICALLY EMPTY.
IT'S STRANGE-- AFTER ALL THIS TIME-- HOW FEW THINGS I ACTUALLY OWN.
IT'S KINDA PATHETIC, IF YOU REALLY THINK ABOUT IT.
--
THEN *DON'T.*
WHEN ARE YOU MOVING OUT?
I HAVE SIX MORE MONTHS ON THE *DAMN LEASE,* BUT I CAN'T STAY THERE ANYMORE. IT'S BEEN TWO MONTHS, AND I'M STILL SLEEPING ON THE COUCH. THE BEDROOM REMINDS ME OF HER.
EVERY CORNER REMINDS ME OF HER.

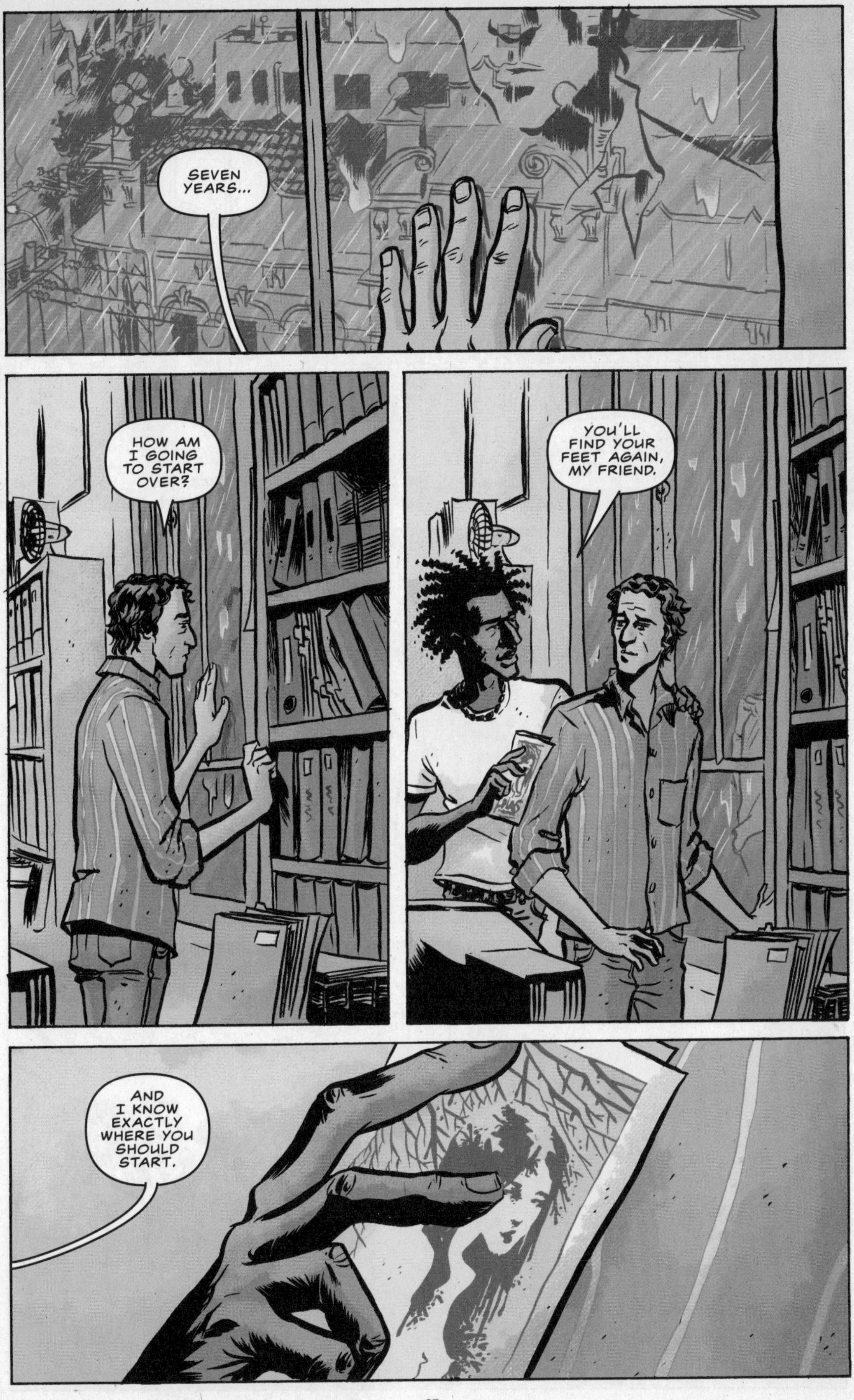
SEVEN YEARS...
HOW AM I GOING TO START OVER?
YOU'LL FIND YOUR FEET AGAIN, MY FRIEND.
AND I KNOW EXACTLY WHERE YOU SHOULD START.

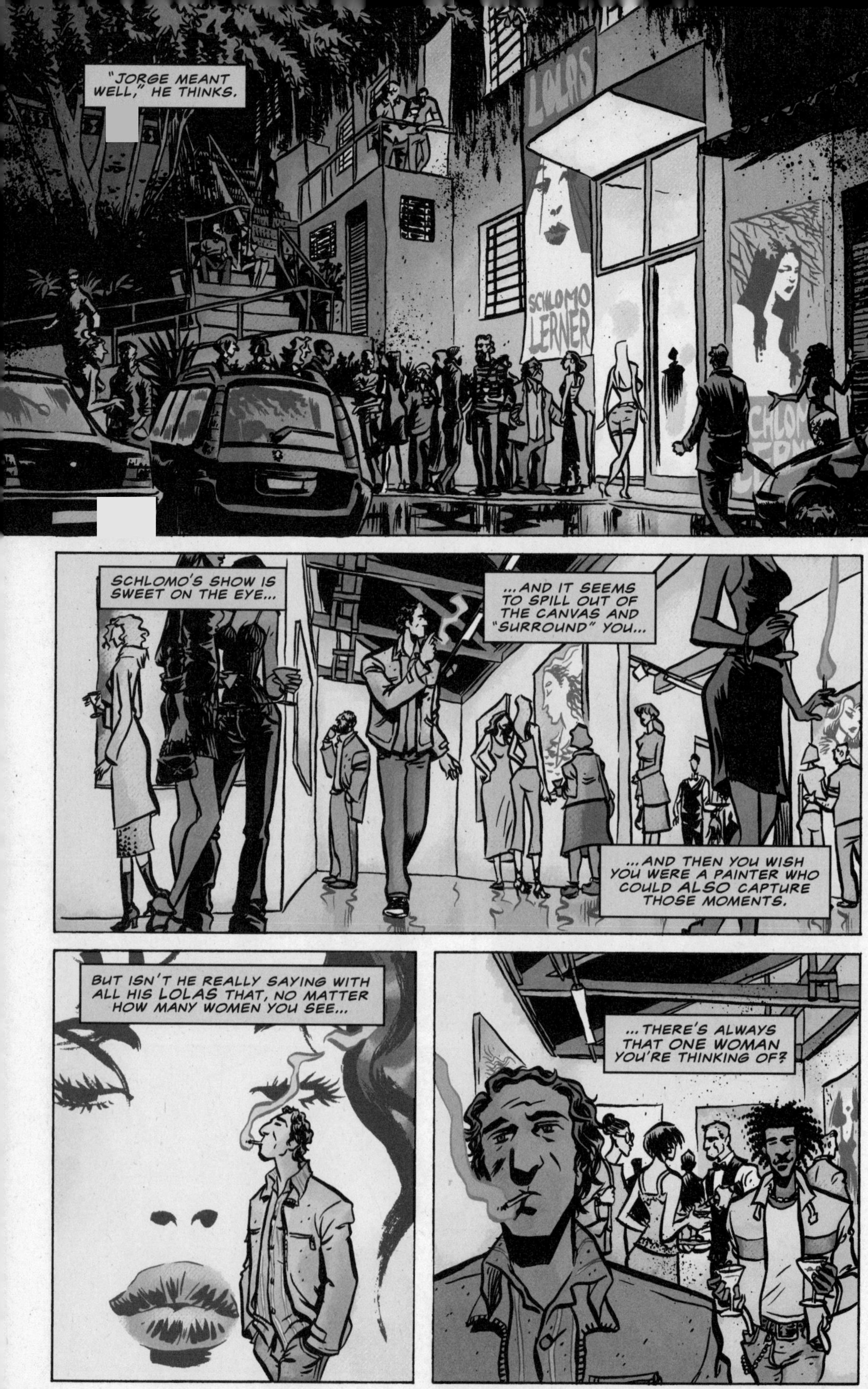
"JORGE MEANT WELL," HE THINKS.
LOLAS
SCHLOMO LERNER
SCHLOMO'S SHOW IS SWEET ON THE EYE...
...AND IT SEEMS TO SPILL OUT OF THE CANVAS AND "SURROUND" YOU...
...AND THEN YOU WISH YOU WERE A PAINTER WHO COULD ALSO CAPTURE THOSE MOMENTS.
BUT ISN'T HE REALLY SAYING WITH ALL HIS LOLAS THAT, NO MATTER HOW MANY WOMEN YOU SEE...
...THERE'S ALWAYS THAT ONE WOMAN YOU'RE THINKING OF?

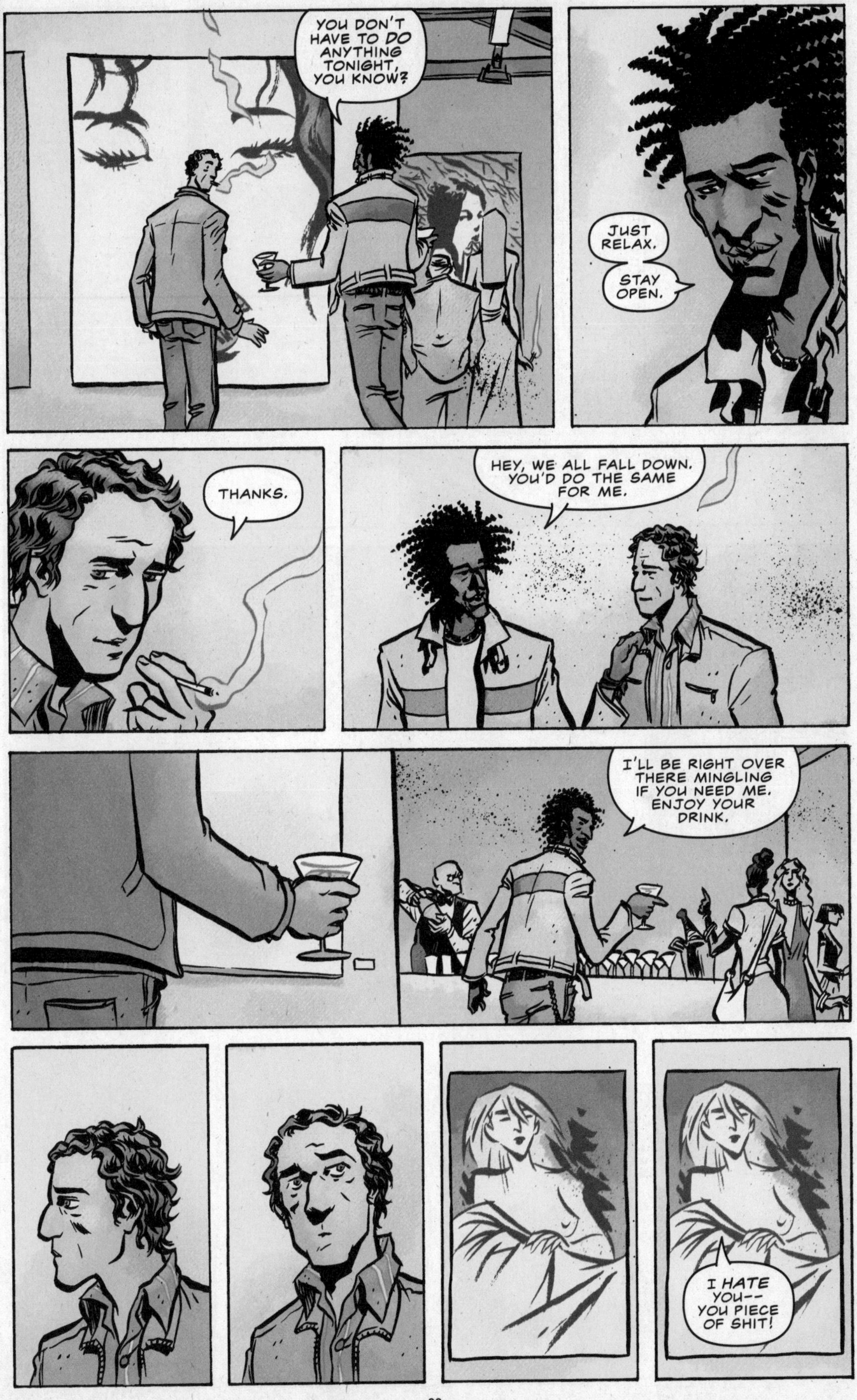
YOU DON'T HAVE TO DO ANYTHING TONIGHT, YOU KNOW?
JUST RELAX.
STAY OPEN.
THANKS.
HEY, WE ALL FALL DOWN. YOU'D DO THE SAME FOR ME.
I'LL BE RIGHT OVER THERE MINGLING IF YOU NEED ME. ENJOY YOUR DRINK.
I HATE YOU-- YOU PIECE OF SHIT!

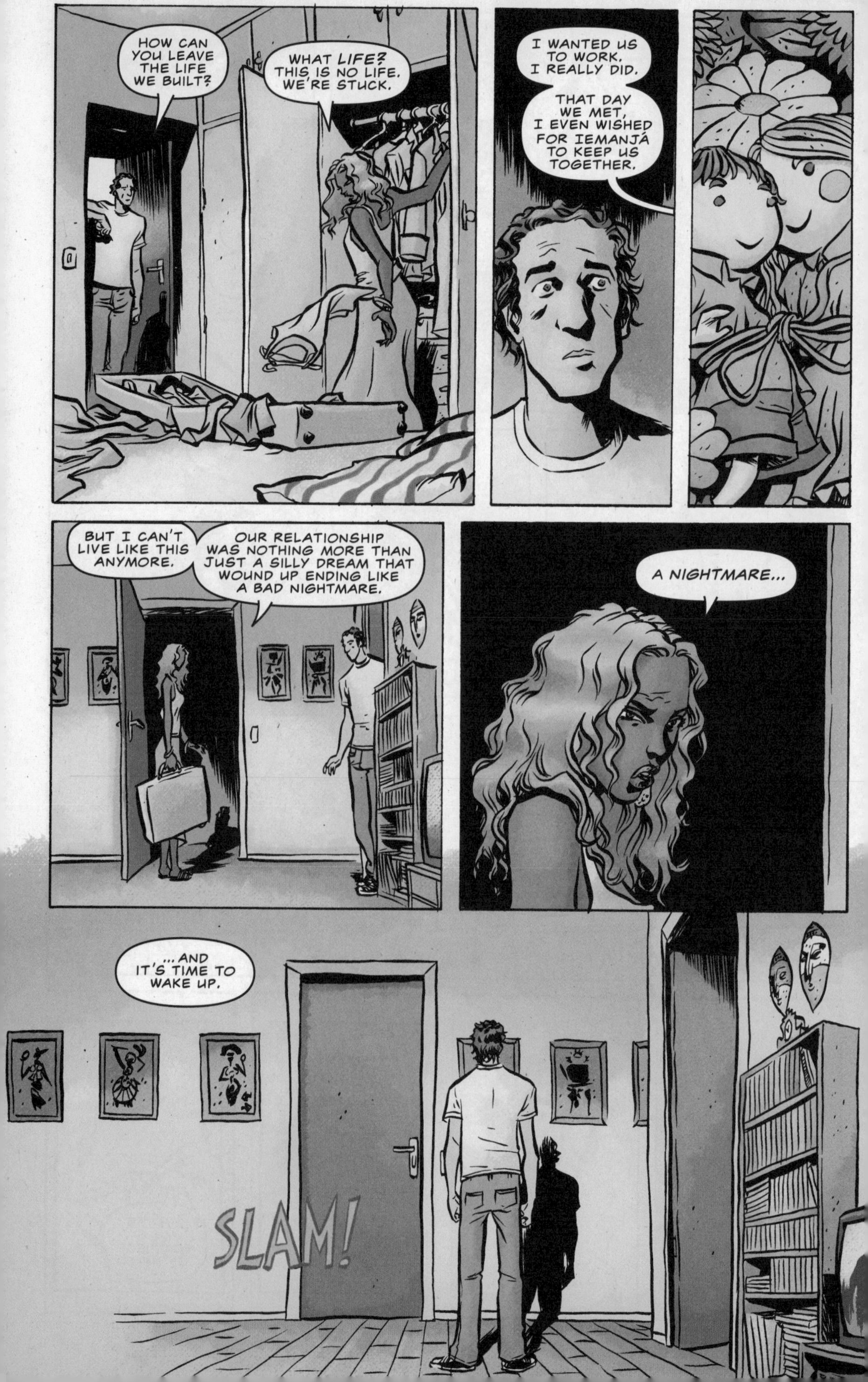
HOW CAN YOU LEAVE THE LIFE WE BUILT?
WHAT LIFE? THIS IS NO LIFE. WE'RE STUCK.
I WANTED US TO WORK. I REALLY DID.
THAT DAY WE MET, I EVEN WISHED FOR IEMANJÁ TO KEEP US TOGETHER.
BUT I CAN'T LIVE LIKE THIS ANYMORE.
OUR RELATIONSHIP WAS NOTHING MORE THAN JUST A SILLY DREAM THAT WOUND UP ENDING LIKE A BAD NIGHTMARE.
A NIGHTMARE...
...AND IT'S TIME TO WAKE UP.
SLAM!

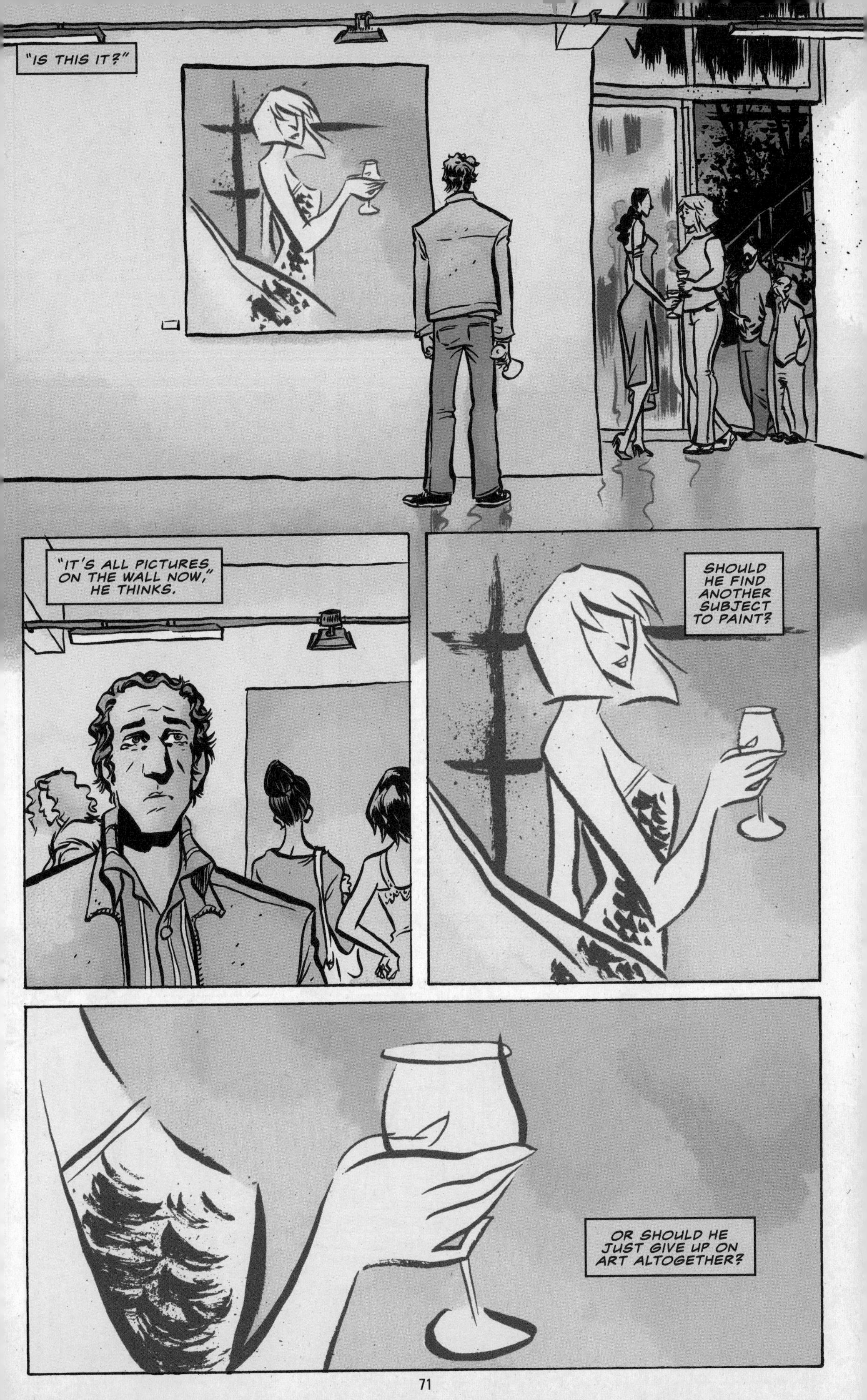
"IS THIS IT?"
"IT'S ALL PICTURES ON THE WALL NOW," HE THINKS.
SHOULD HE FIND ANOTHER SUBJECT TO PAINT?
OR SHOULD HE JUST GIVE UP ON ART ALTOGETHER?

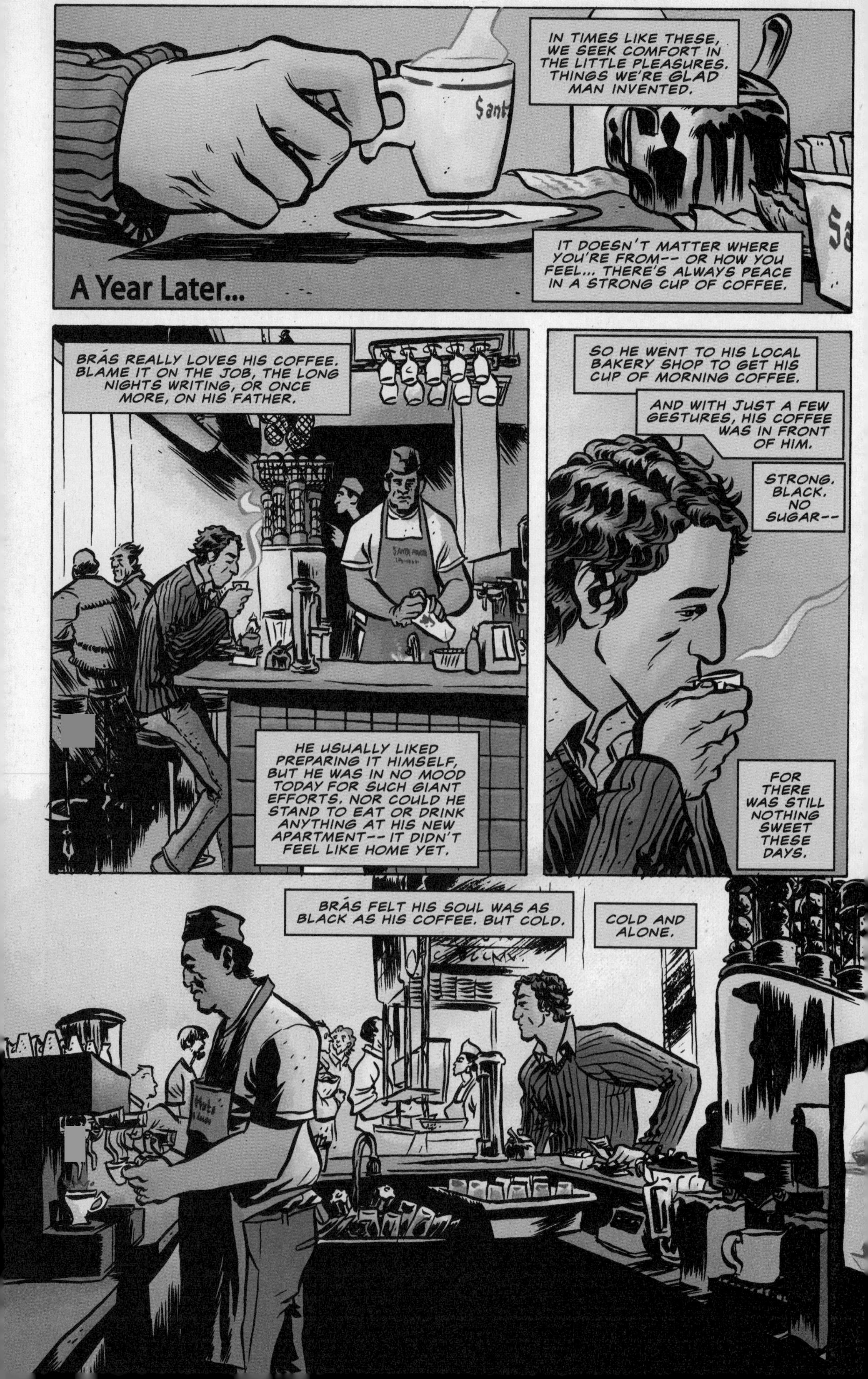
IN TIMES LIKE THESE, WE SEEK COMFORT IN THE LITTLE PLEASURES. THINGS WE'RE GLAD MAN INVENTED.
IT DOESN'T MATTER WHERE YOU'RE FROM-- OR HOW YOU FEEL... THERE'S ALWAYS PEACE IN A STRONG CUP OF COFFEE.
A Year Later...
BRÁS REALLY LOVES HIS COFFEE. BLAME IT ON THE JOB, THE LONG NIGHTS WRITING, OR ONCE MORE, ON HIS FATHER.
HE USUALLY LIKED PREPARING IT HIMSELF, BUT HE WAS IN NO MOOD TODAY FOR SUCH GIANT EFFORTS. NOR COULD HE STAND TO EAT OR DRINK ANYTHING AT HIS NEW APARTMENT-- IT DIDN'T FEEL LIKE HOME YET.
SO HE WENT TO HIS LOCAL BAKERY SHOP TO GET HIS CUP OF MORNING COFFEE.
AND WITH JUST A FEW GESTURES, HIS COFFEE WAS IN FRONT OF HIM.
STRONG. BLACK. NO SUGAR--
FOR THERE WAS STILL NOTHING SWEET THESE DAYS.
BRÁS FELT HIS SOUL WAS AS BLACK AS HIS COFFEE. BUT COLD.
COLD AND ALONE.

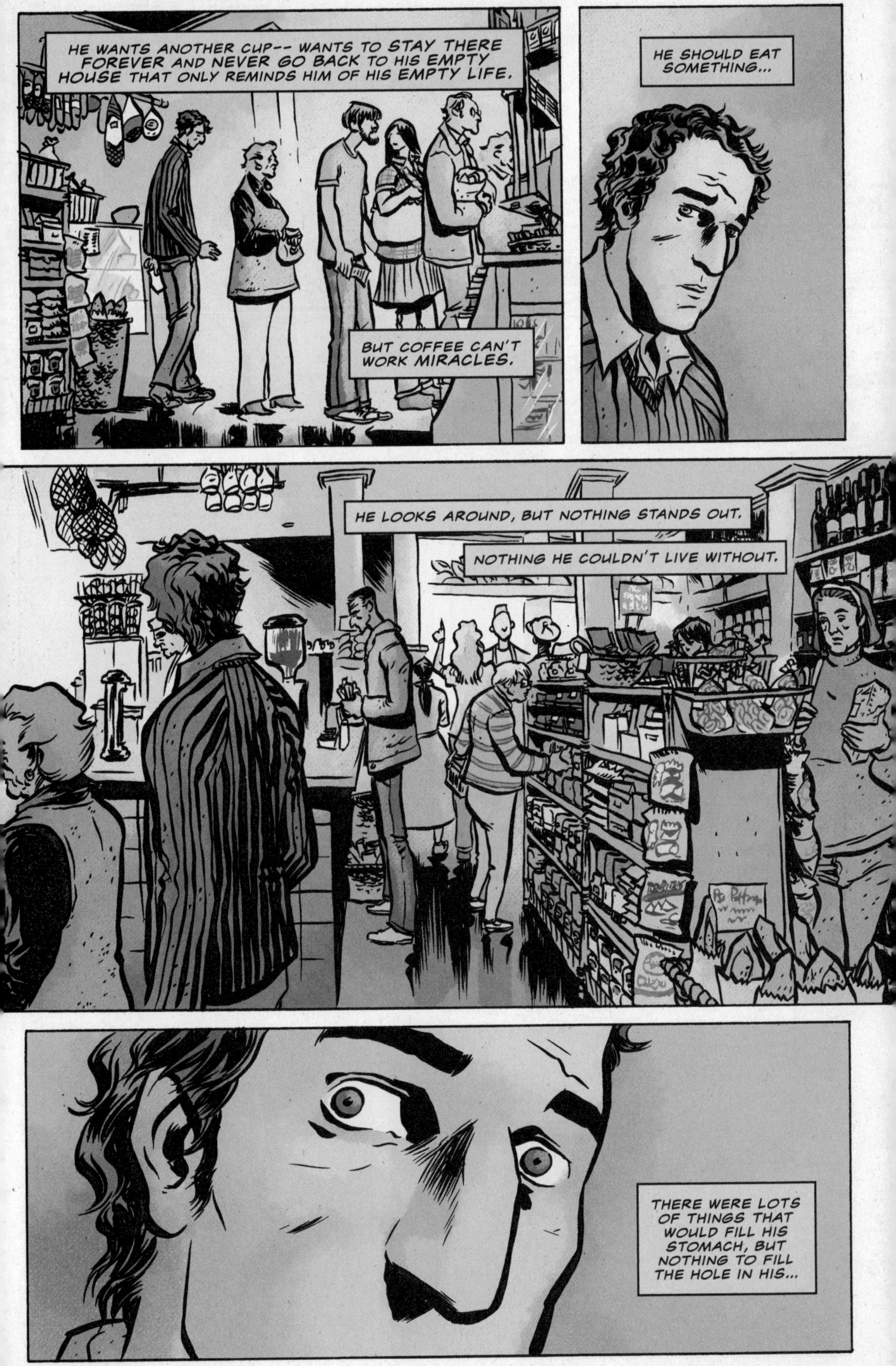
HE WANTS ANOTHER CUP-- WANTS TO STAY THERE FOREVER AND NEVER GO BACK TO HIS EMPTY HOUSE THAT ONLY REMINDS HIM OF HIS EMPTY LIFE.
BUT COFFEE CAN'T WORK MIRACLES.
HE SHOULD EAT SOMETHING...
HE LOOKS AROUND, BUT NOTHING STANDS OUT.
NOTHING HE COULDN'T LIVE WITHOUT.
THERE WERE LOTS OF THINGS THAT WOULD FILL HIS STOMACH, BUT NOTHING TO FILL THE HOLE IN HIS...

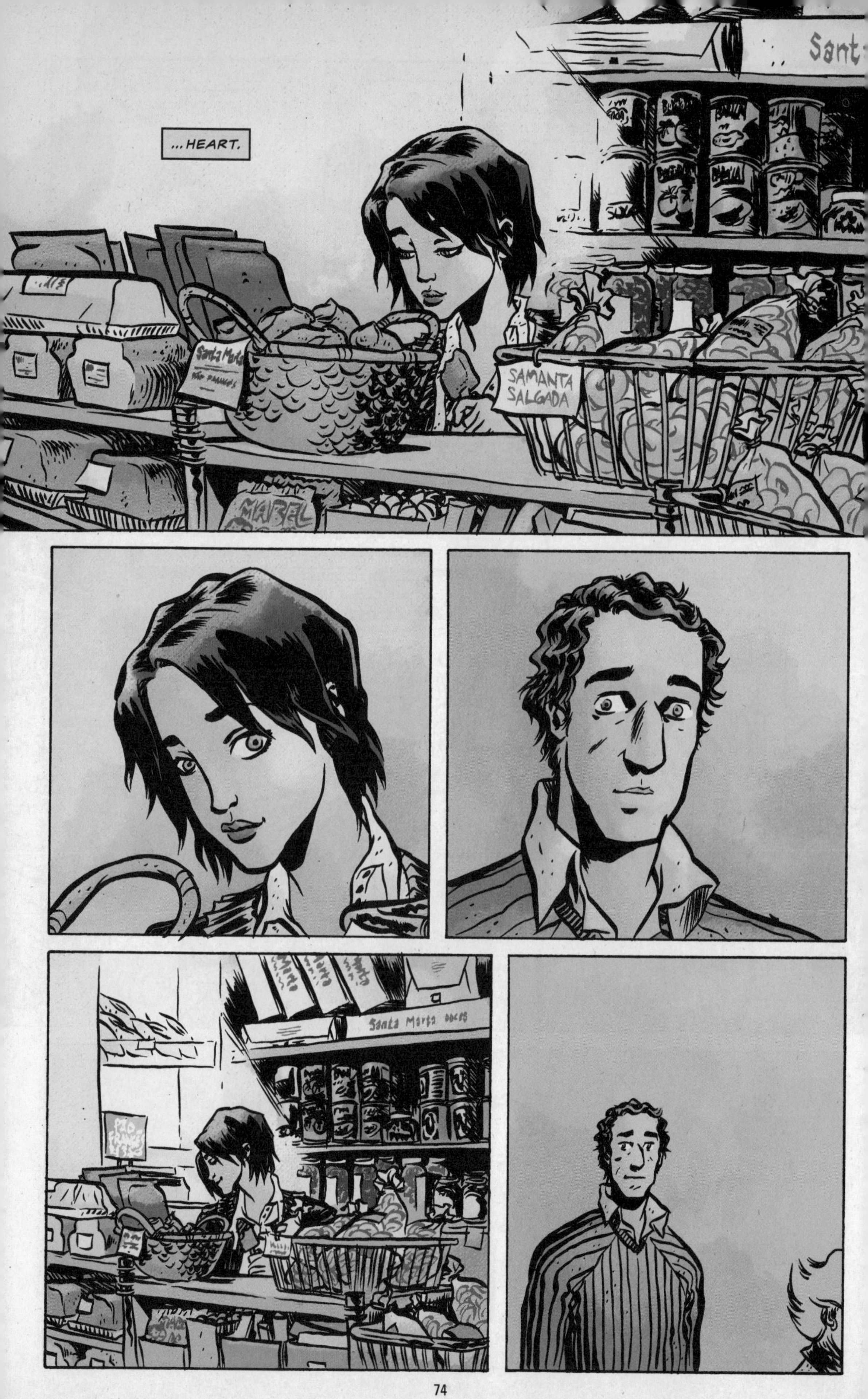
...HEART.
SAMANTA
SALGADA

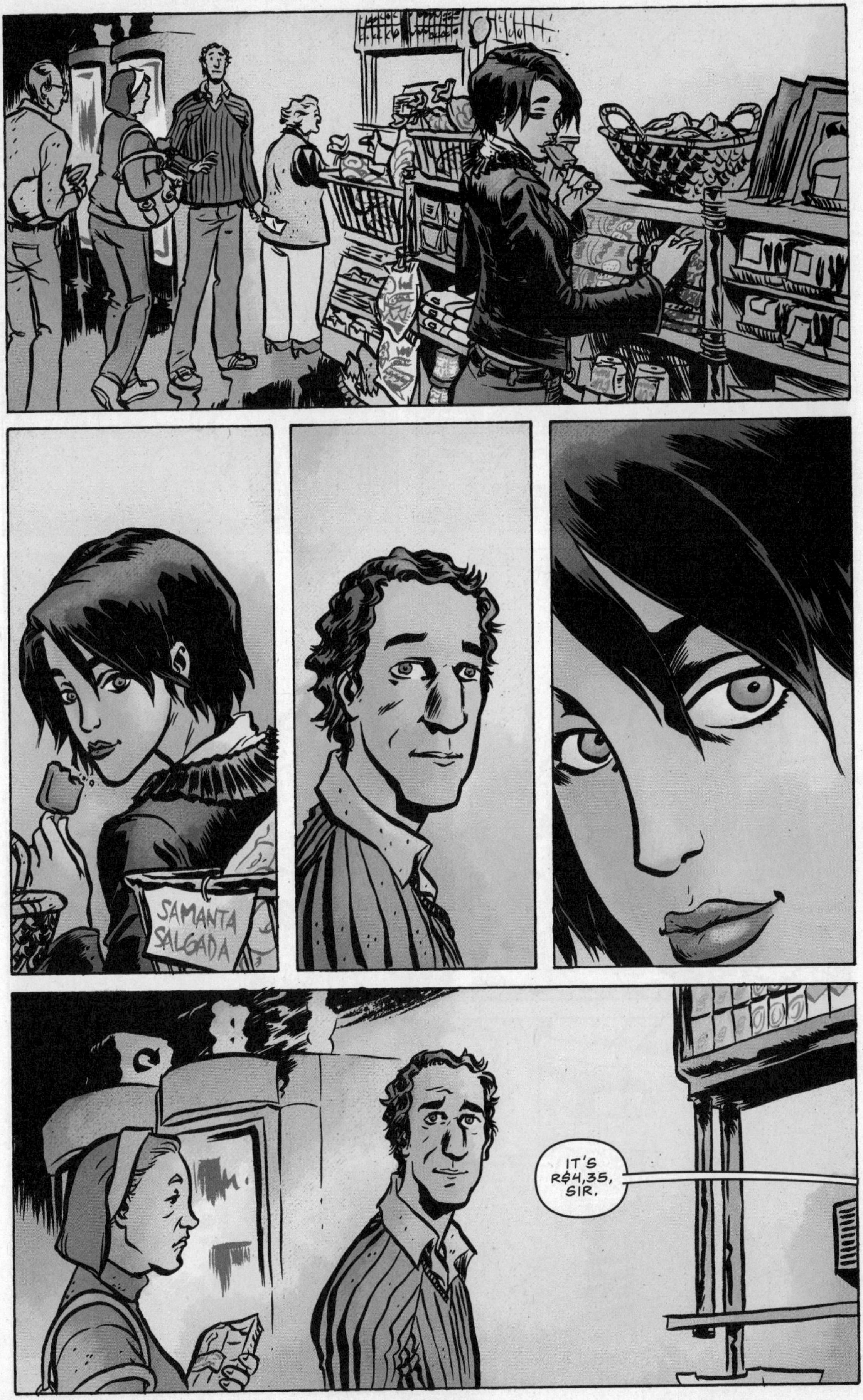
SAMANTA SALGADA
IT'S R$4,35, SIR.

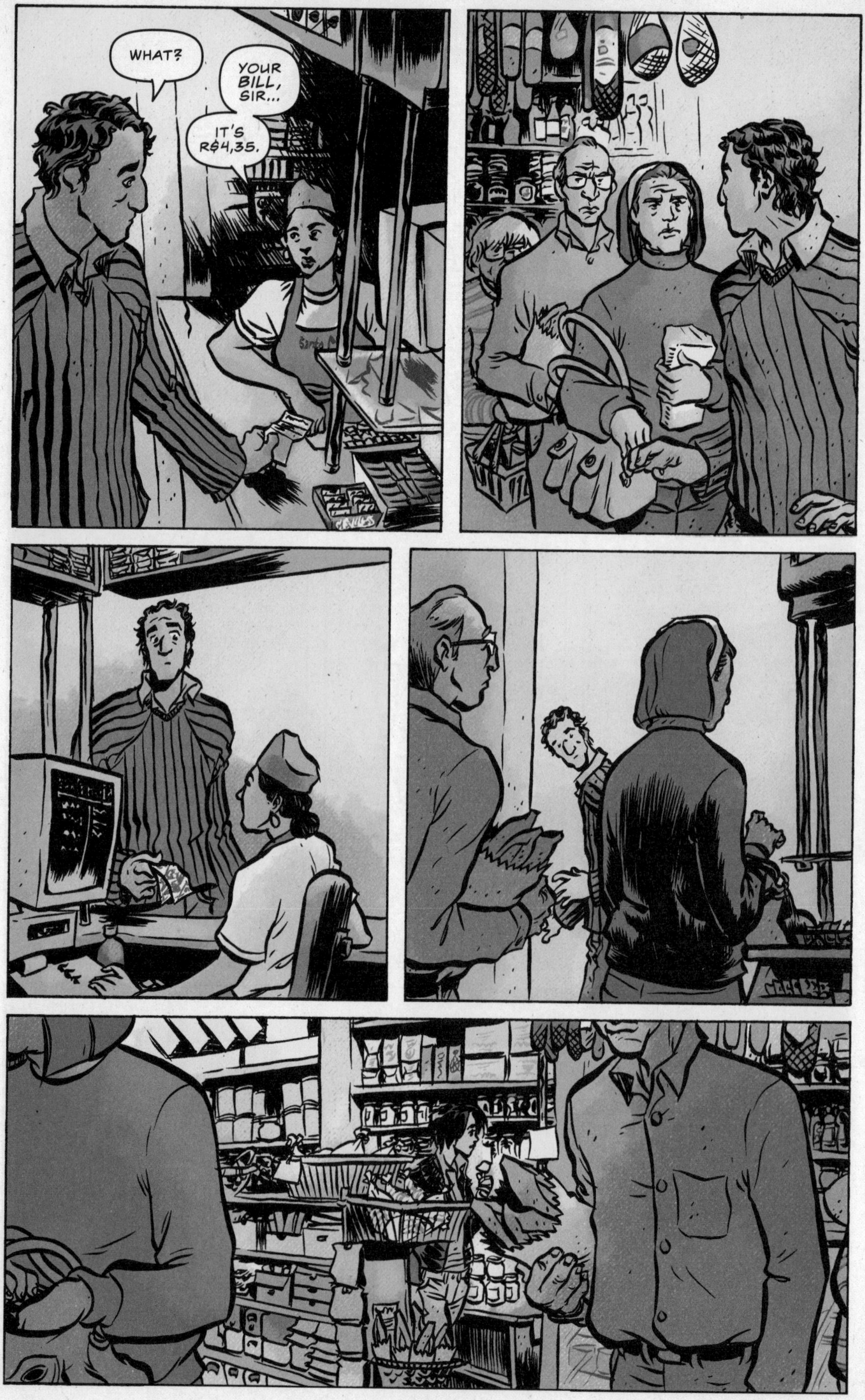
WHAT?
YOUR BILL, SIR...
IT'S R$4,35.

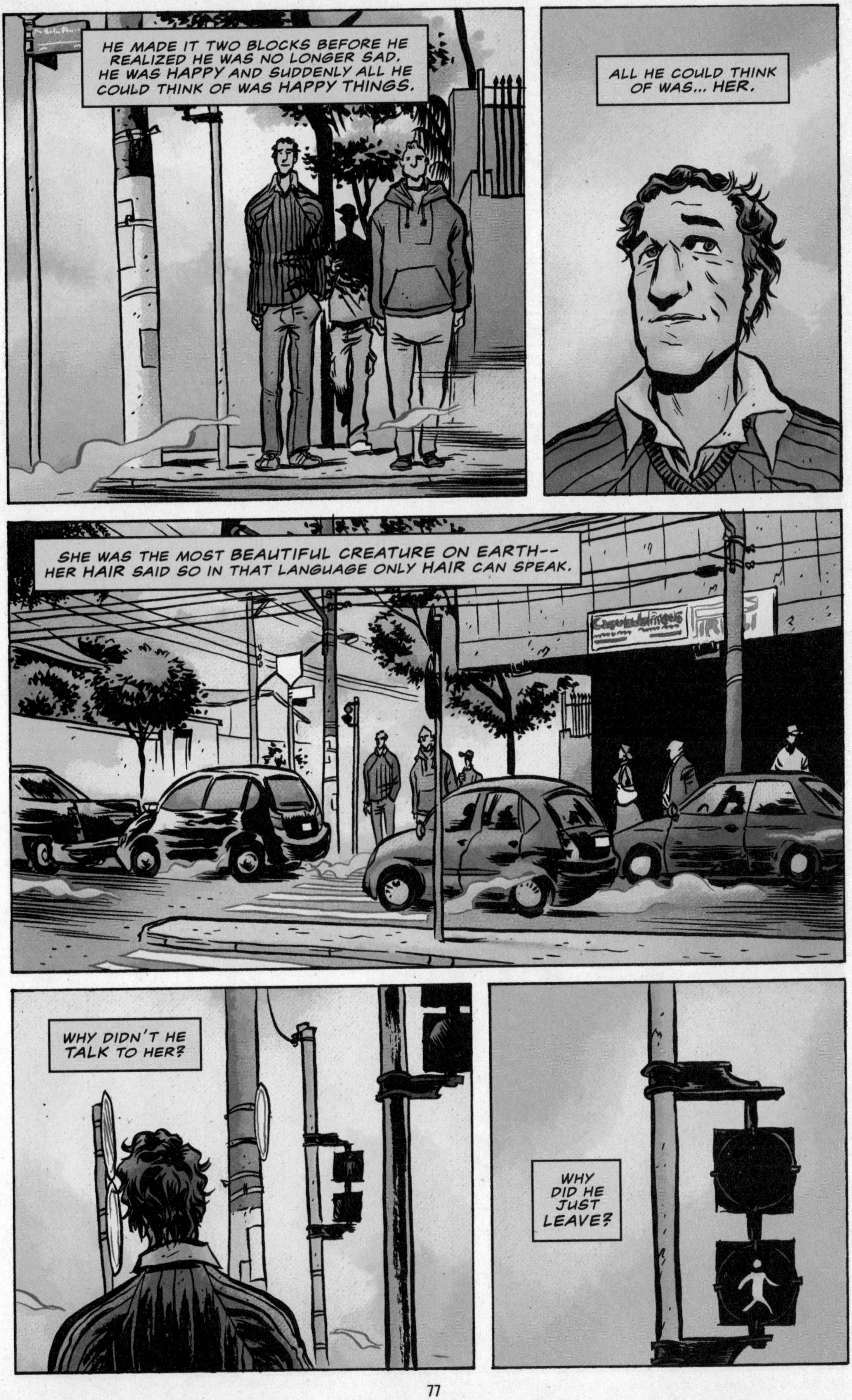
HE MADE IT TWO BLOCKS BEFORE HE REALIZED HE WAS NO LONGER SAD. HE WAS HAPPY AND SUDDENLY ALL HE COULD THINK OF WAS HAPPY THINGS.
ALL HE COULD THINK OF WAS... HER.
SHE WAS THE MOST BEAUTIFUL CREATURE ON EARTH-- HER HAIR SAID SO IN THAT LANGUAGE ONLY HAIR CAN SPEAK.
WHY DIDN'T HE TALK TO HER?
WHY DID HE JUST LEAVE?

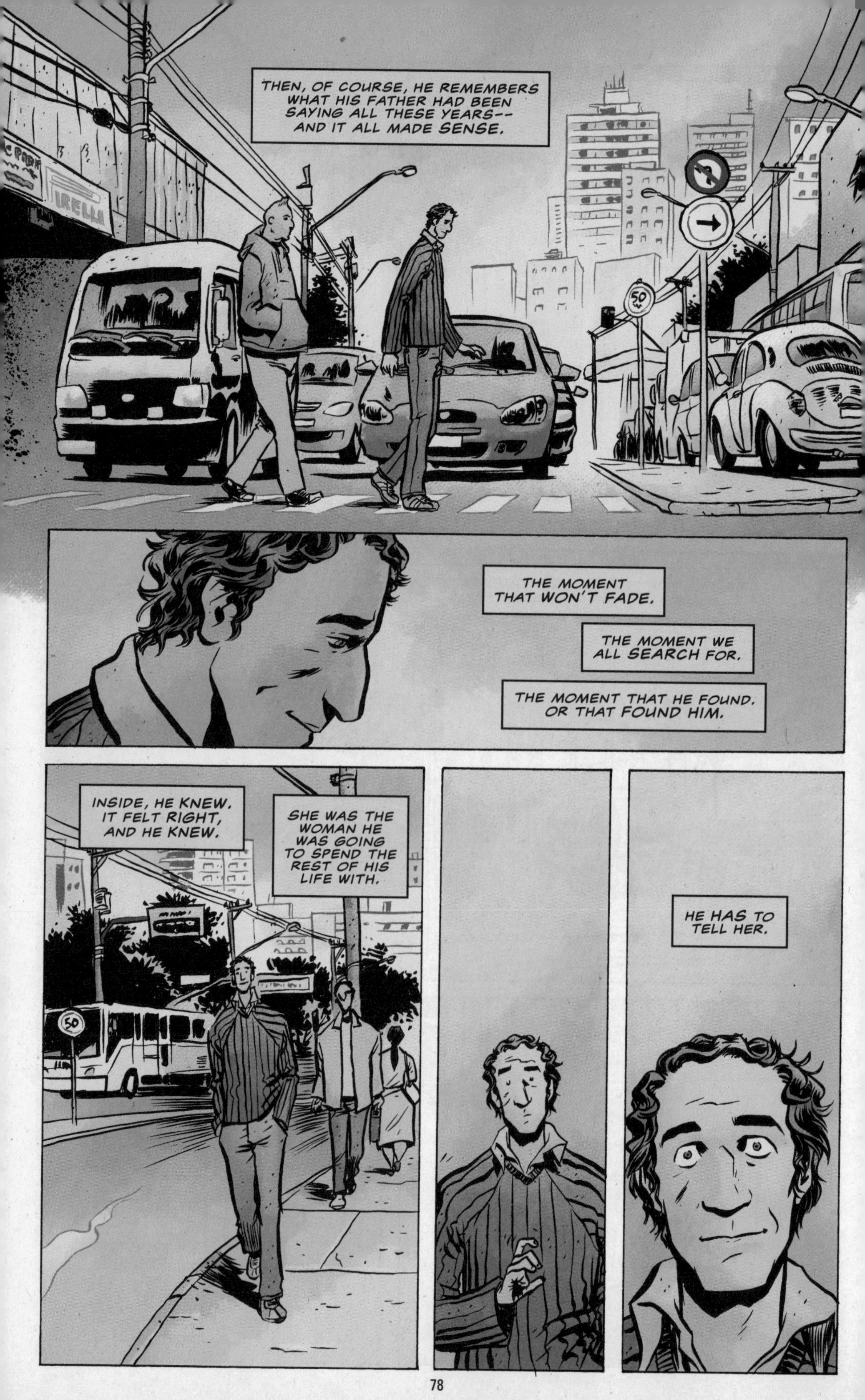
THEN, OF COURSE, HE REMEMBERS WHAT HIS FATHER HAD BEEN SAYING ALL THESE YEARS-- AND IT ALL MADE SENSE.
THE MOMENT THAT WON'T FADE.
THE MOMENT WE ALL SEARCH FOR.
THE MOMENT THAT HE FOUND. OR THAT FOUND HIM.
INSIDE, HE KNEW. IT FELT RIGHT, AND HE KNEW.
SHE WAS THE WOMAN HE WAS GOING TO SPEND THE REST OF HIS LIFE WITH.
HE HAS TO TELL HER.

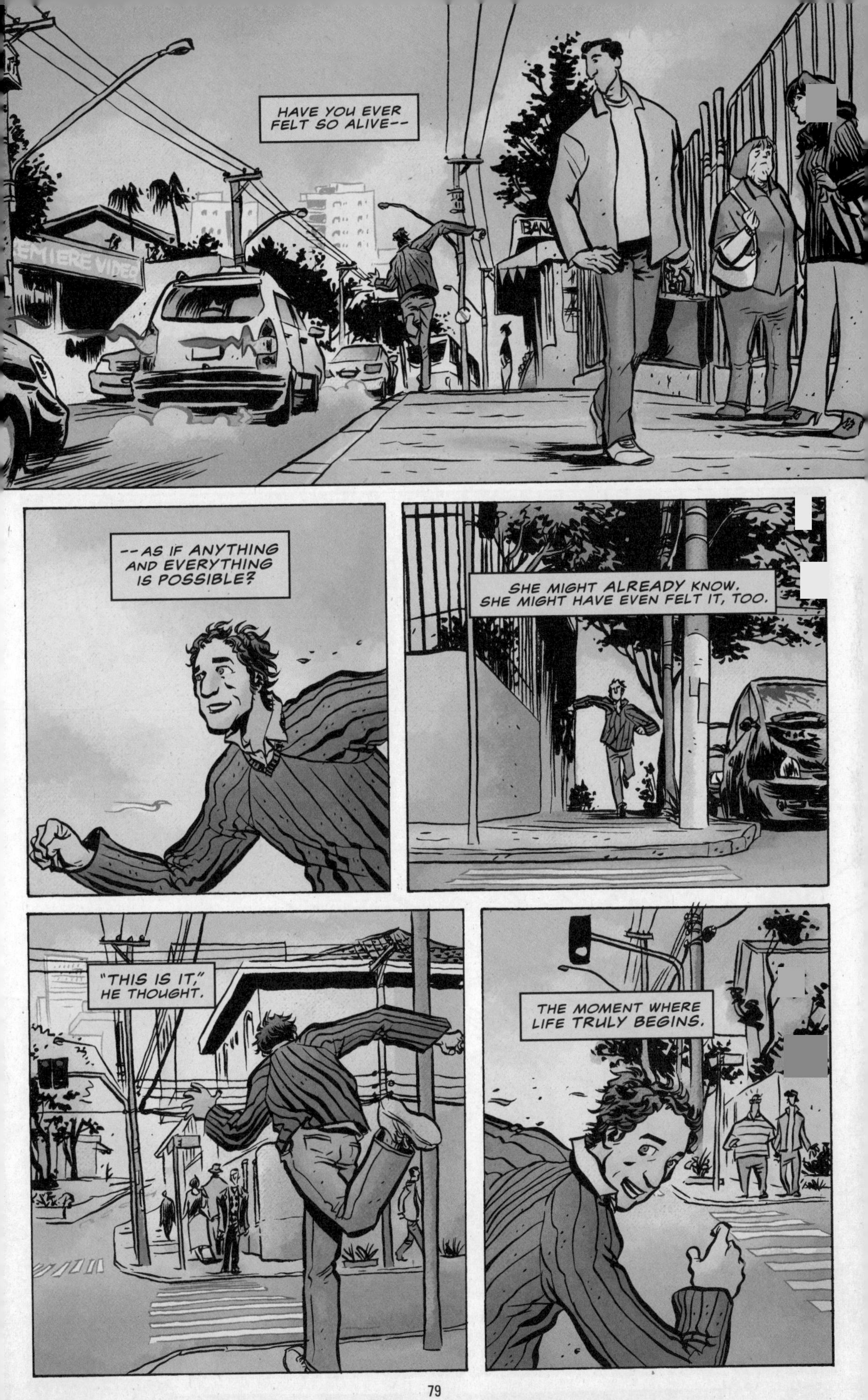
HAVE YOU EVER FELT SO ALIVE--
--AS IF ANYTHING AND EVERYTHING IS POSSIBLE?
SHE MIGHT ALREADY KNOW. SHE MIGHT HAVE EVEN FELT IT, TOO.
"THIS IS IT," HE THOUGHT.
THE MOMENT WHERE LIFE TRULY BEGINS.

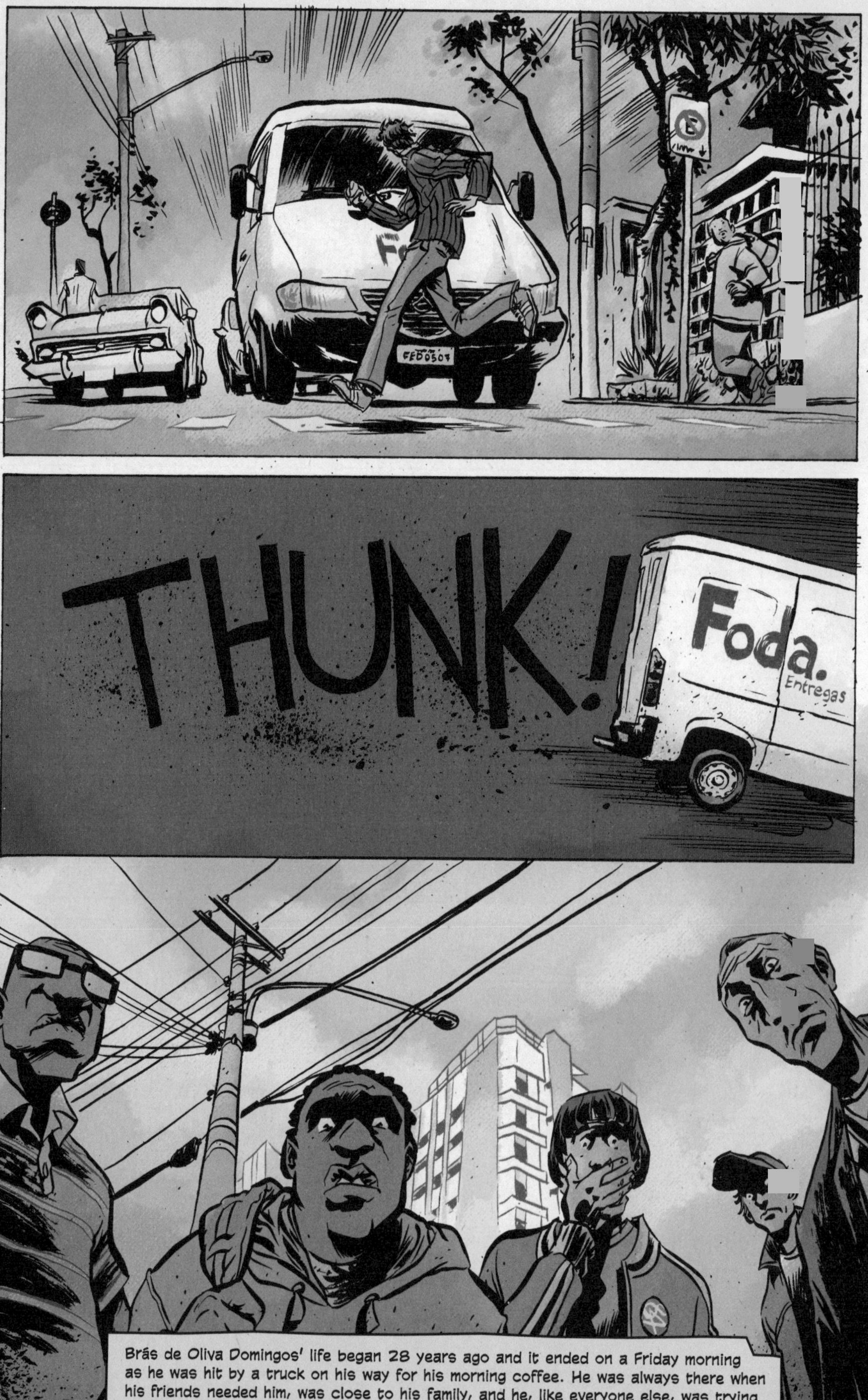
THUNK!
Foda.
Entregas
Brás de Oliva Domingos' life began 28 years ago and it ended on a Friday morning as he was hit by a truck on his way for his morning coffee. He was always there when his friends needed him, was close to his family, and he, like everyone else, was trying to find his way in the desert, looking for that oasis we like to call... "love."

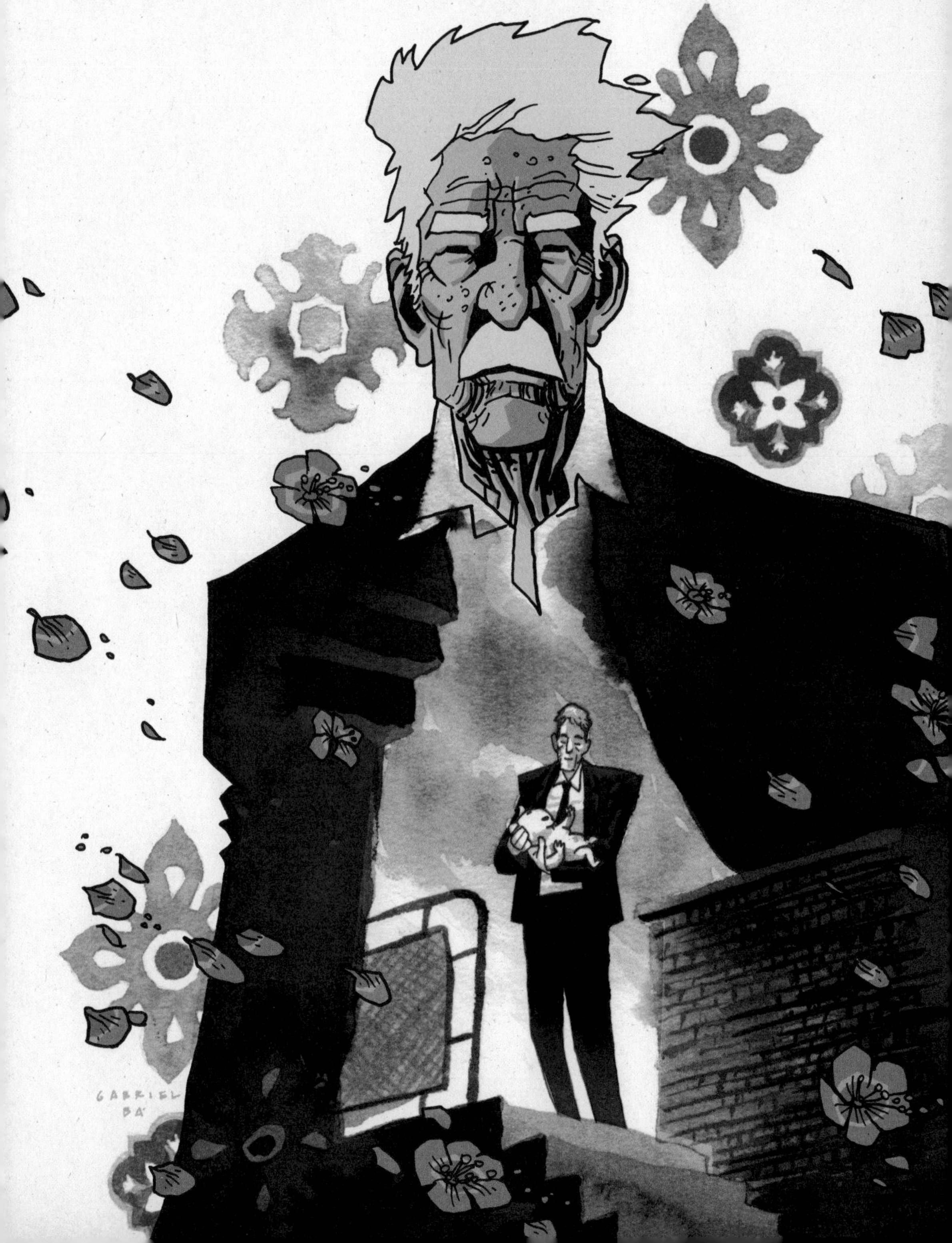
GABRIEL BÁ

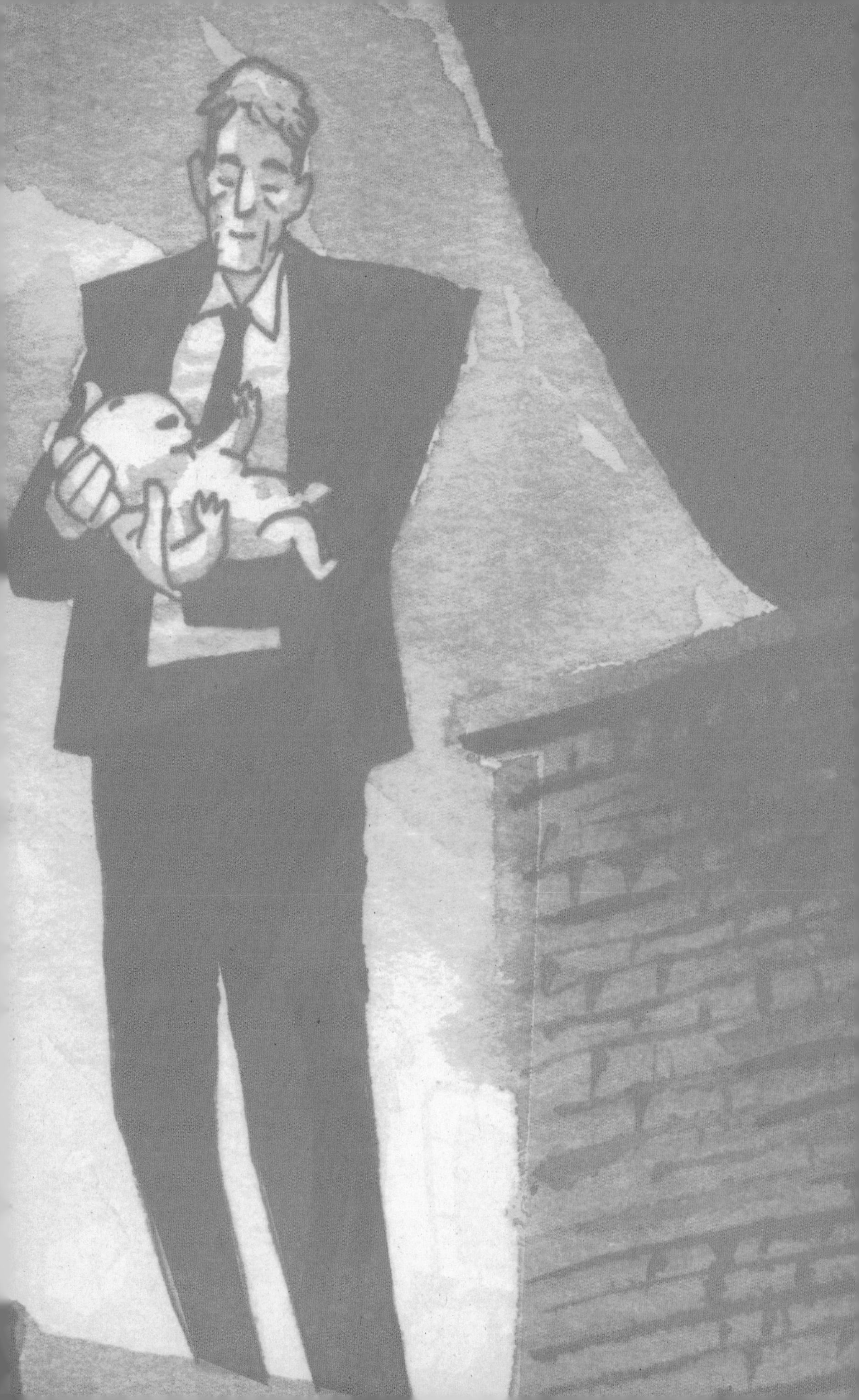

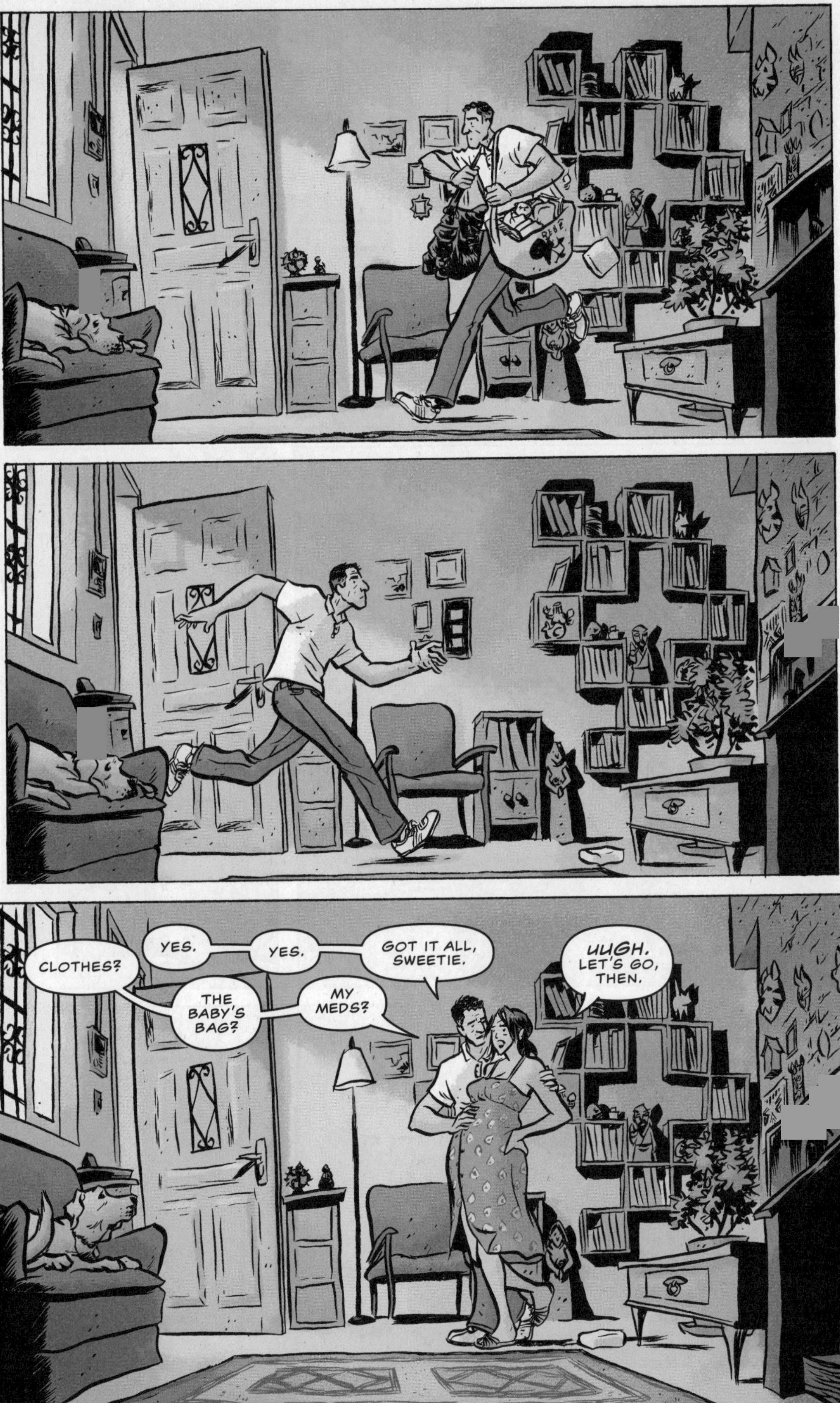
CLOTHES?
YES.
THE BABY'S BAG?
YES.
MY MEDS?
GOT IT ALL, SWEETIE.
UUGH. LET'S GO, THEN.

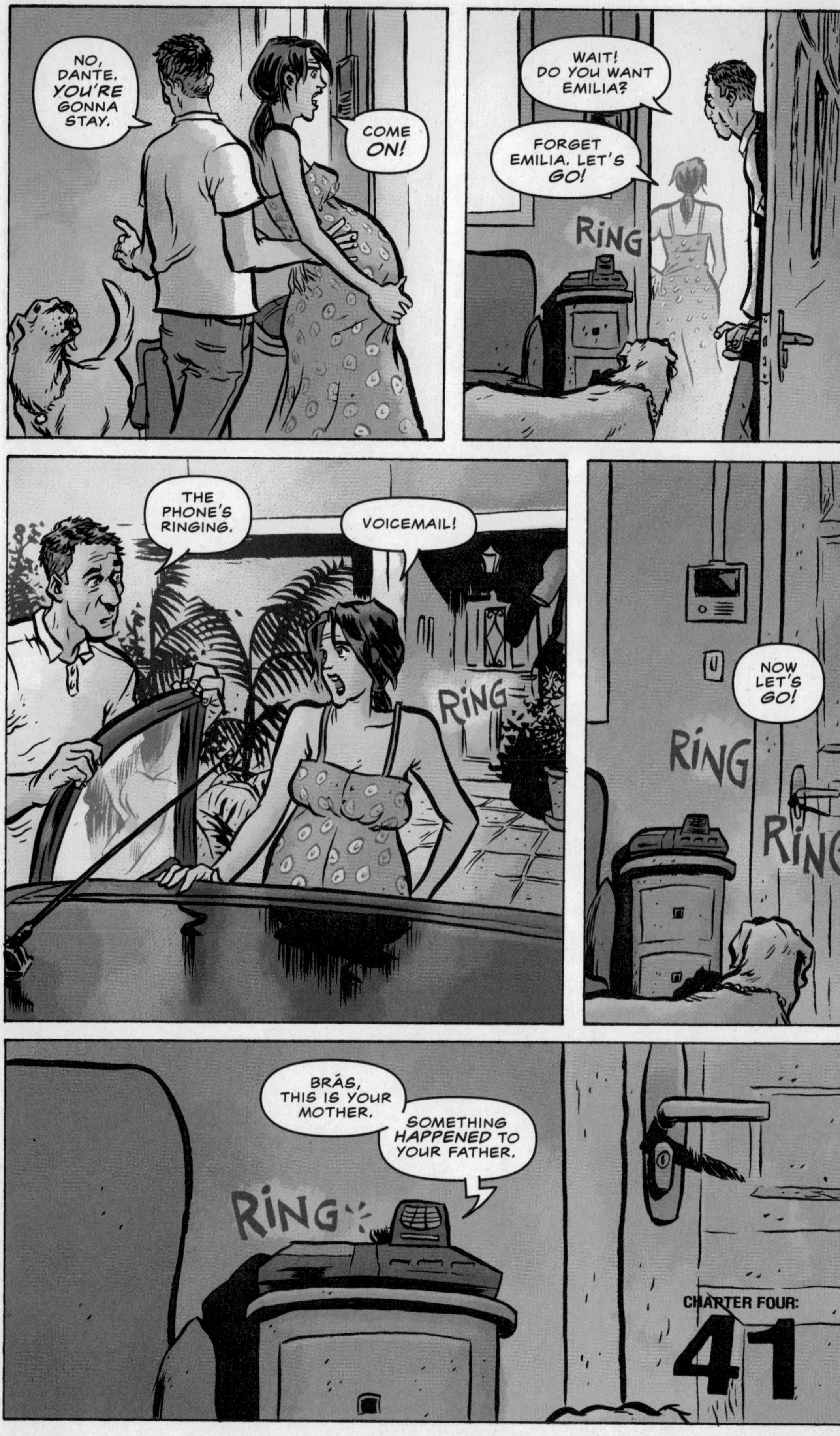
NO, DANTE. YOU'RE GONNA STAY.
COME ON!
WAIT! DO YOU WANT EMILIA?
FORGET EMILIA. LET'S GO!
RING
THE PHONE'S RINGING.
VOICEMAIL!
RING
NOW LET'S GO!
RING
RING
BRÁS, THIS IS YOUR MOTHER.
SOMETHING HAPPENED TO YOUR FATHER.
RING
CHAPTER FOUR:
41

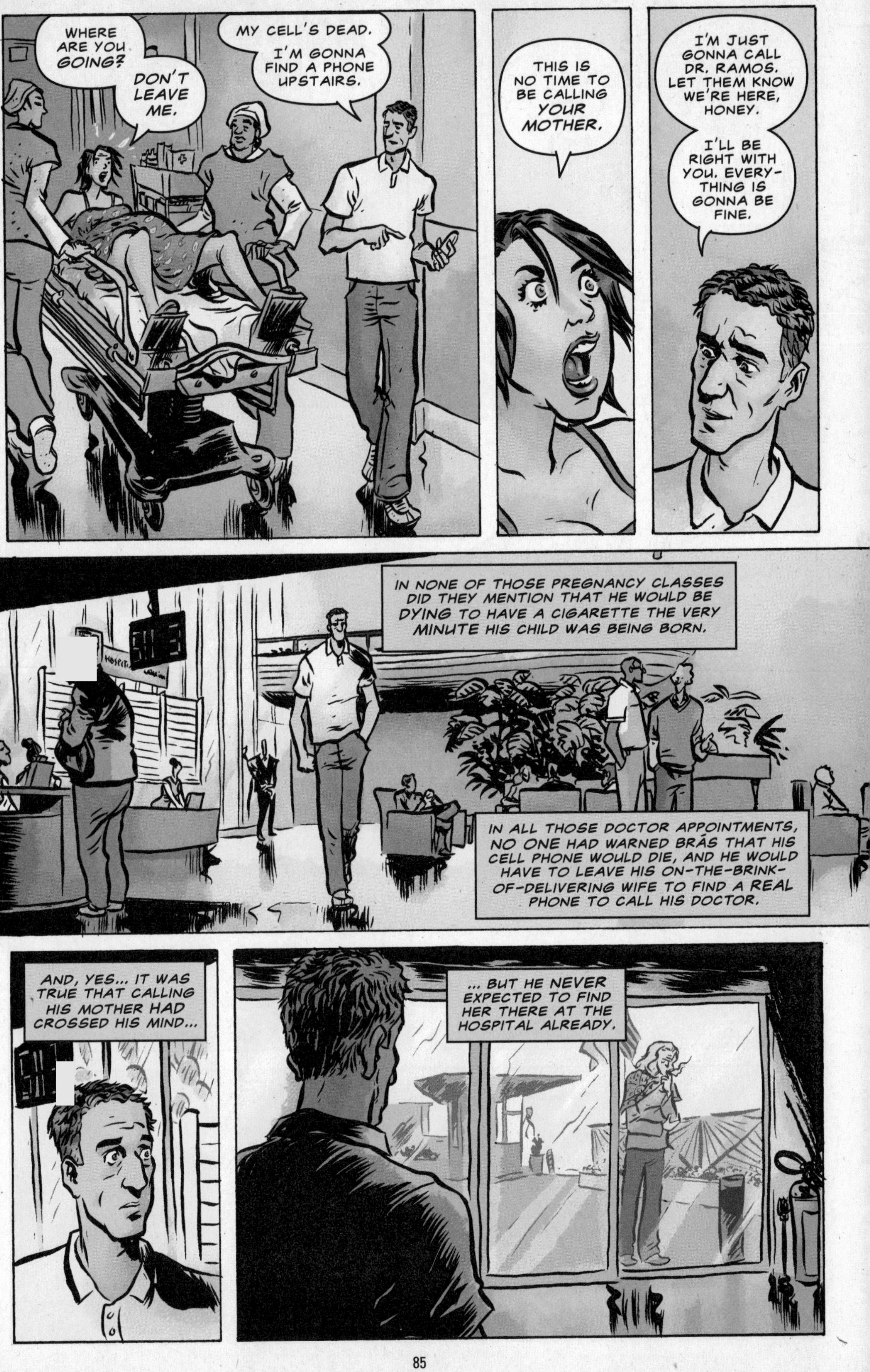
WHERE ARE YOU GOING? DON'T LEAVE ME.
MY CELL'S DEAD. I'M GONNA FIND A PHONE UPSTAIRS.
THIS IS NO TIME TO BE CALLING YOUR MOTHER.
I'M JUST GONNA CALL DR. RAMOS. LET THEM KNOW WE'RE HERE, HONEY.
I'LL BE RIGHT WITH YOU. EVERYTHING IS GONNA BE FINE.
IN NONE OF THOSE PREGNANCY CLASSES DID THEY MENTION THAT HE WOULD BE DYING TO HAVE A CIGARETTE THE VERY MINUTE HIS CHILD WAS BEING BORN.
IN ALL THOSE DOCTOR APPOINTMENTS, NO ONE HAD WARNED BRÁS THAT HIS CELL PHONE WOULD DIE, AND HE WOULD HAVE TO LEAVE HIS ON-THE-BRINK-OF-DELIVERING WIFE TO FIND A REAL PHONE TO CALL HIS DOCTOR.
AND, YES... IT WAS TRUE THAT CALLING HIS MOTHER HAD CROSSED HIS MIND...
... BUT HE NEVER EXPECTED TO FIND HER THERE AT THE HOSPITAL ALREADY.

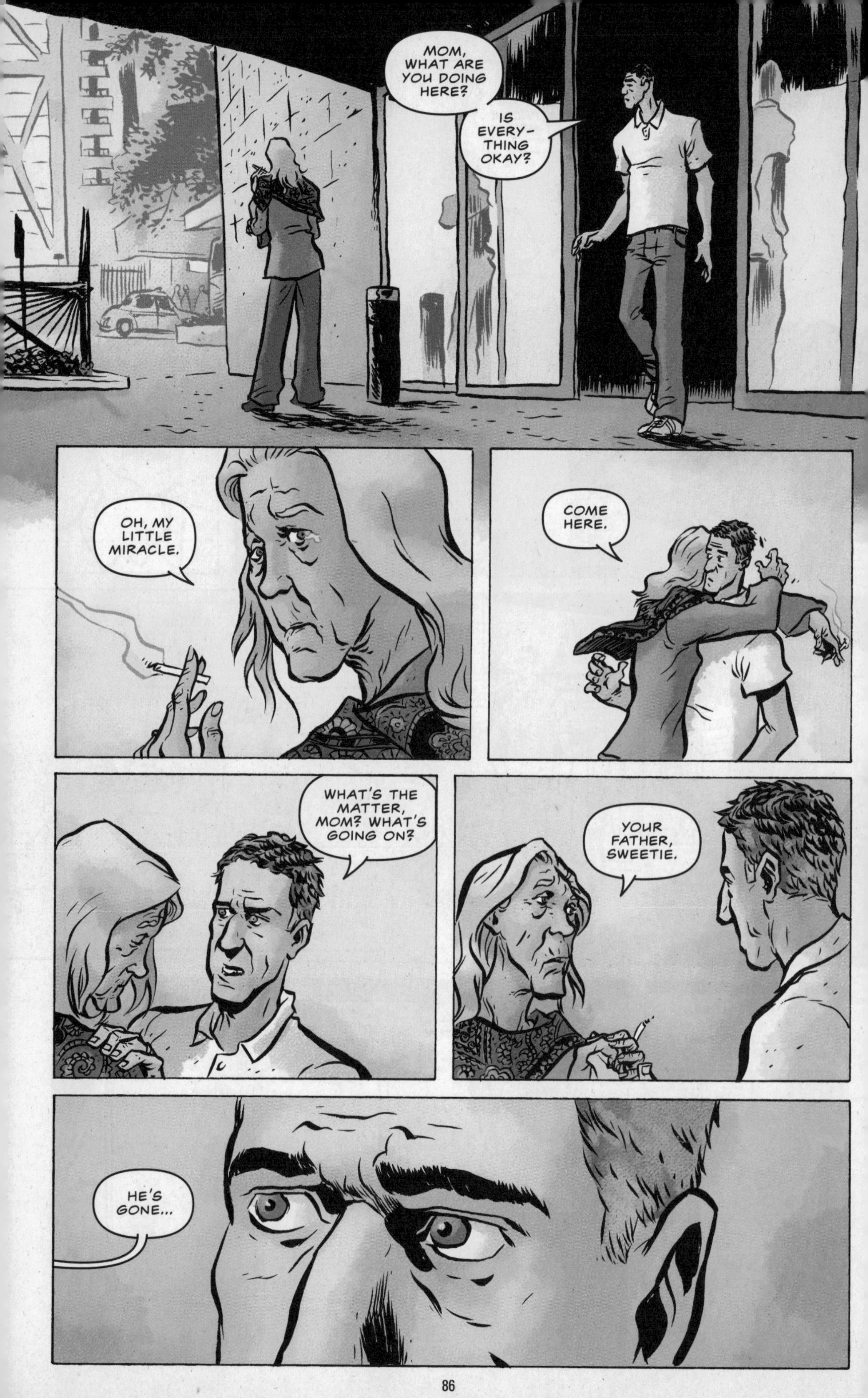
MOM, WHAT ARE YOU DOING HERE?
IS EVERYTHING OKAY?
OH, MY LITTLE MIRACLE.
COME HERE.
WHAT'S THE MATTER, MOM? WHAT'S GOING ON?
YOUR FATHER, SWEETIE.
HE'S GONE...

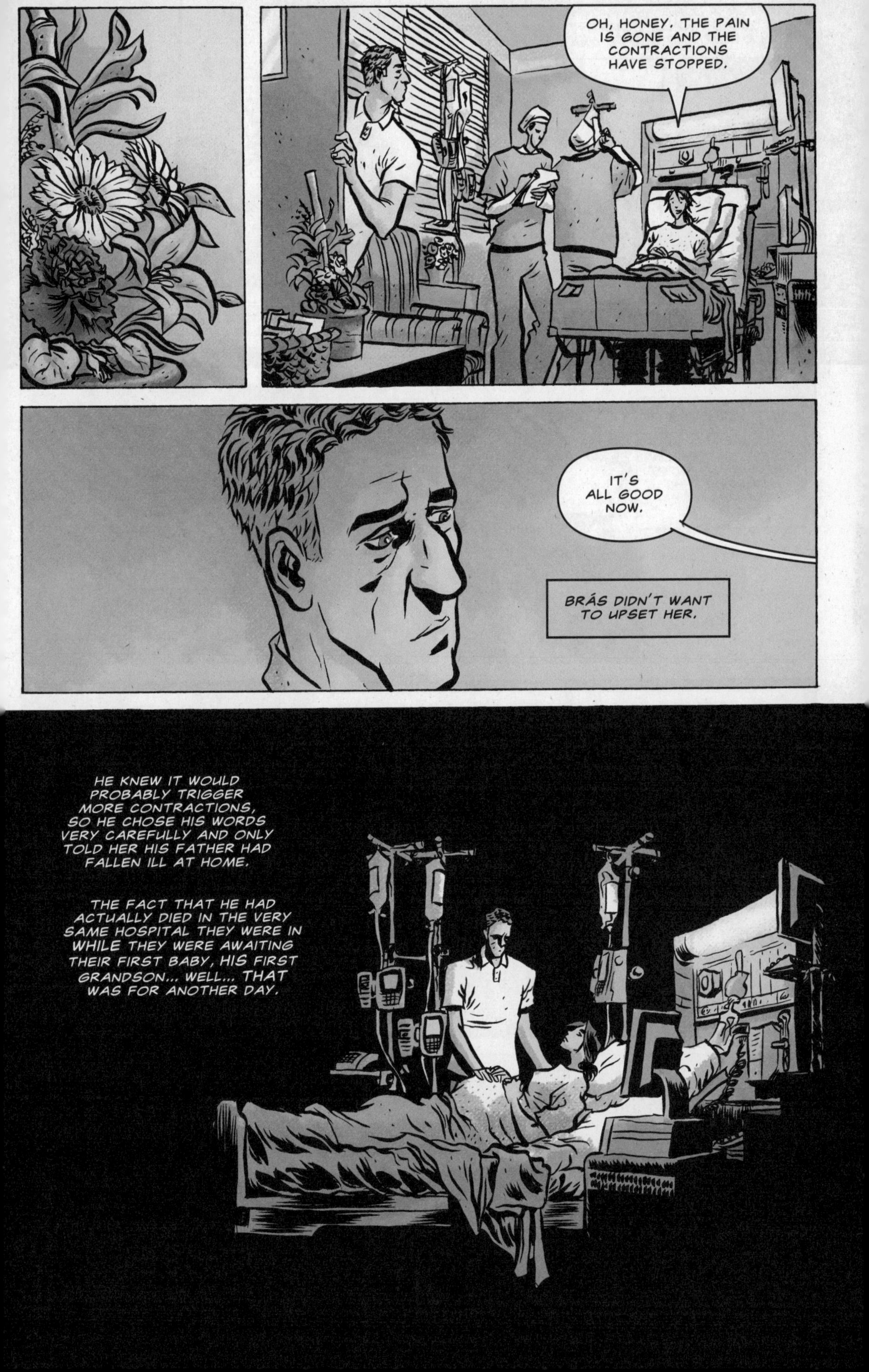

OH, HONEY. THE PAIN IS GONE AND THE CONTRACTIONS HAVE STOPPED.
IT'S ALL GOOD NOW.
BRÁS DIDN'T WANT TO UPSET HER.
HE KNEW IT WOULD PROBABLY TRIGGER MORE CONTRACTIONS, SO HE CHOSE HIS WORDS VERY CAREFULLY AND ONLY TOLD HER HIS FATHER HAD FALLEN ILL AT HOME.
THE FACT THAT HE HAD ACTUALLY DIED IN THE VERY SAME HOSPITAL THEY WERE IN WHILE THEY WERE AWAITING THEIR FIRST BABY, HIS FIRST GRANDSON... WELL... THAT WAS FOR ANOTHER DAY.

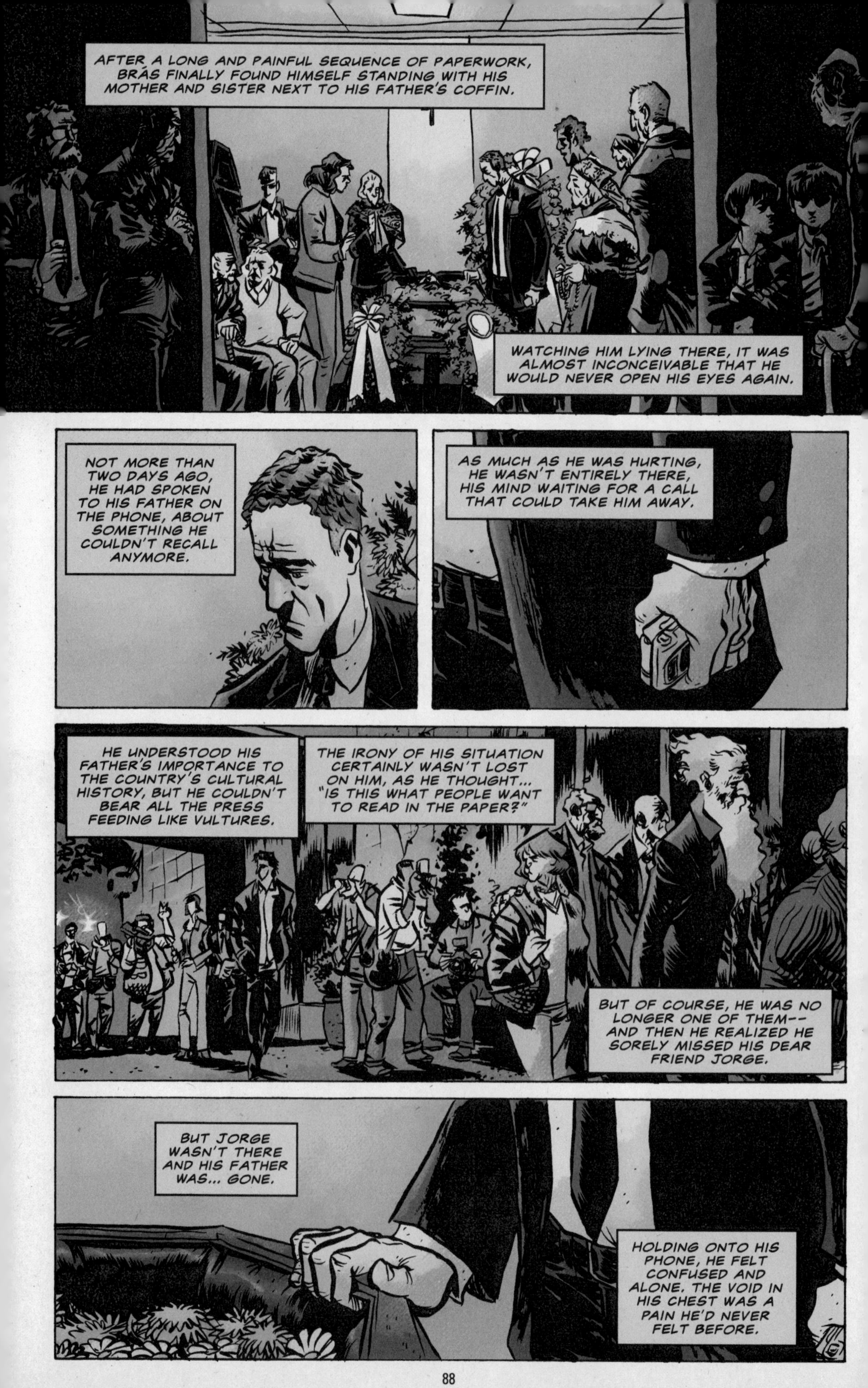
AFTER A LONG AND PAINFUL SEQUENCE OF PAPERWORK, BRÁS FINALLY FOUND HIMSELF STANDING WITH HIS MOTHER AND SISTER NEXT TO HIS FATHER'S COFFIN.
WATCHING HIM LYING THERE, IT WAS ALMOST INCONCEIVABLE THAT HE WOULD NEVER OPEN HIS EYES AGAIN.
NOT MORE THAN TWO DAYS AGO, HE HAD SPOKEN TO HIS FATHER ON THE PHONE, ABOUT SOMETHING HE COULDN'T RECALL ANYMORE.
AS MUCH AS HE WAS HURTING, HE WASN'T ENTIRELY THERE, HIS MIND WAITING FOR A CALL THAT COULD TAKE HIM AWAY.
HE UNDERSTOOD HIS FATHER'S IMPORTANCE TO THE COUNTRY'S CULTURAL HISTORY, BUT HE COULDN'T BEAR ALL THE PRESS FEEDING LIKE VULTURES.
THE IRONY OF HIS SITUATION CERTAINLY WASN'T LOST ON HIM, AS HE THOUGHT... "IS THIS WHAT PEOPLE WANT TO READ IN THE PAPER?"
BUT OF COURSE, HE WAS NO LONGER ONE OF THEM-- AND THEN HE REALIZED HE SORELY MISSED HIS DEAR FRIEND JORGE.
BUT JORGE WASN'T THERE AND HIS FATHER WAS... GONE.
HOLDING ONTO HIS PHONE, HE FELT CONFUSED AND ALONE. THE VOID IN HIS CHEST WAS A PAIN HE'D NEVER FELT BEFORE.

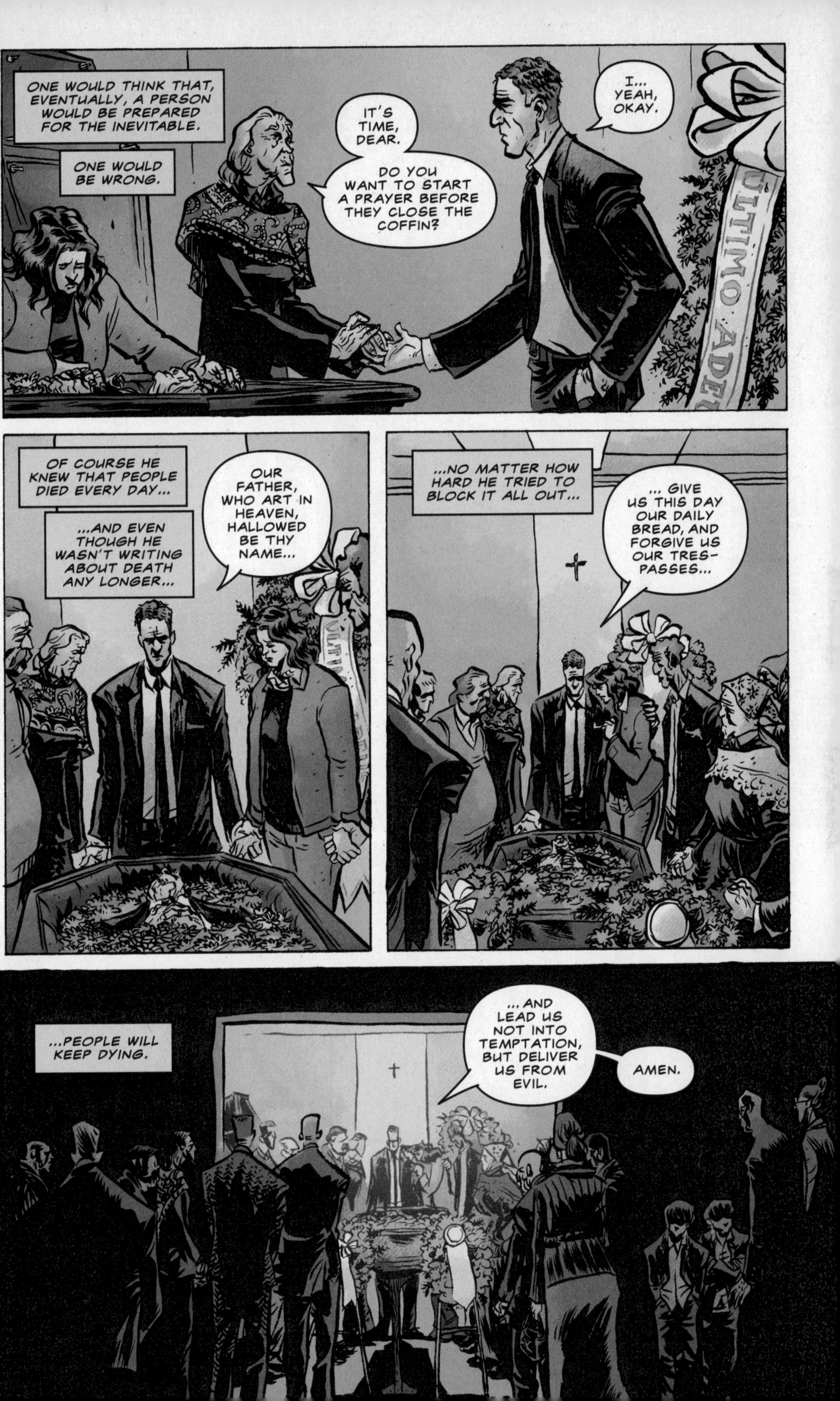

ONE WOULD THINK THAT, EVENTUALLY, A PERSON WOULD BE PREPARED FOR THE INEVITABLE.
ONE WOULD BE WRONG.
IT'S TIME, DEAR.
DO YOU WANT TO START A PRAYER BEFORE THEY CLOSE THE COFFIN?
I... YEAH, OKAY.
ULTIMO ADE
OF COURSE HE KNEW THAT PEOPLE DIED EVERY DAY...
...AND EVEN THOUGH HE WASN'T WRITING ABOUT DEATH ANY LONGER...
OUR FATHER, WHO ART IN HEAVEN, HALLOWED BE THY NAME...
...NO MATTER HOW HARD HE TRIED TO BLOCK IT ALL OUT...
... GIVE US THIS DAY OUR DAILY BREAD, AND FORGIVE US OUR TRES-PASSES...
...PEOPLE WILL KEEP DYING.
... AND LEAD US NOT INTO TEMPTATION, BUT DELIVER US FROM EVIL.
AMEN.

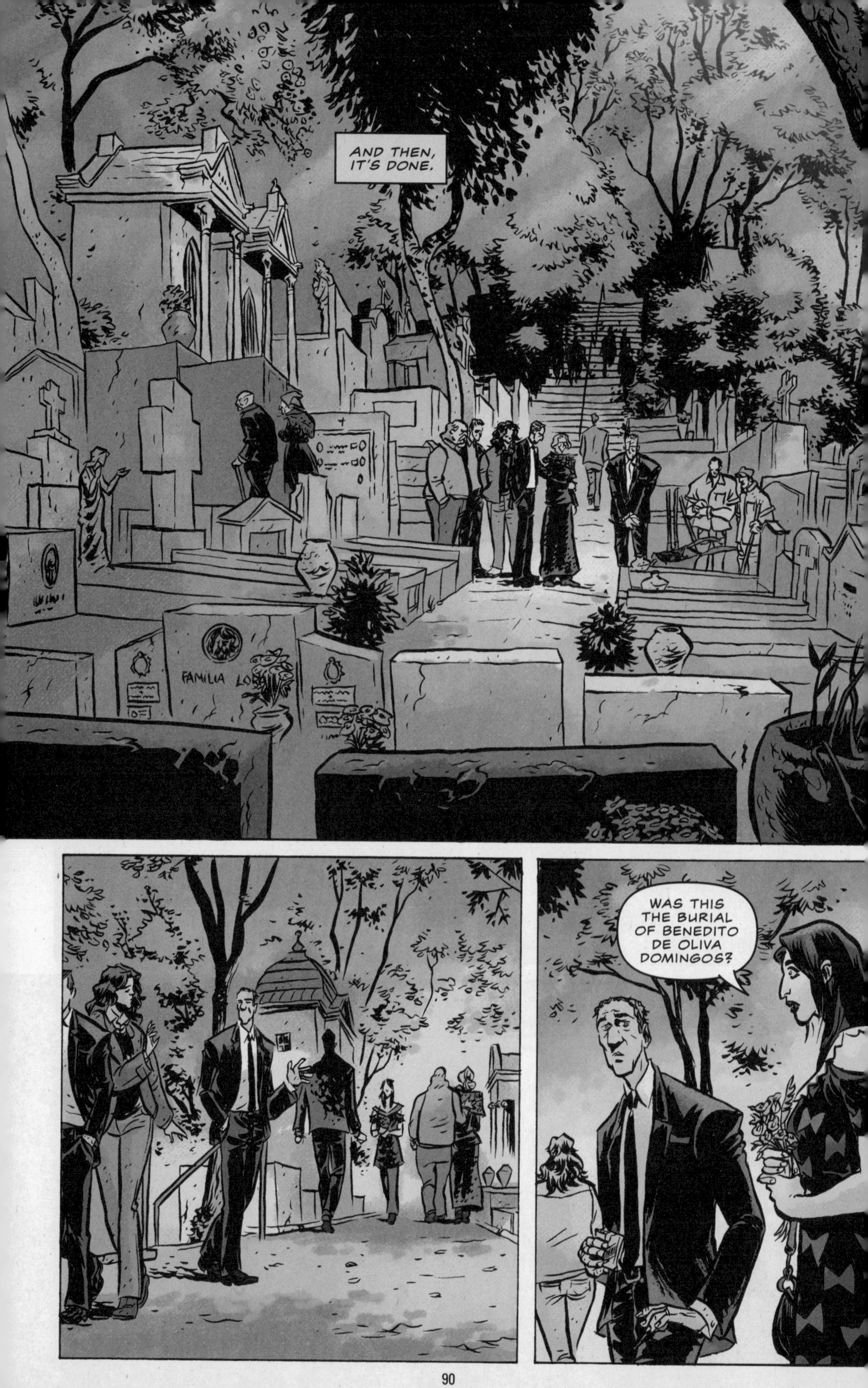
AND THEN, IT'S DONE.
WAS THIS THE BURIAL OF BENEDITO DE OLIVA DOMINGOS?

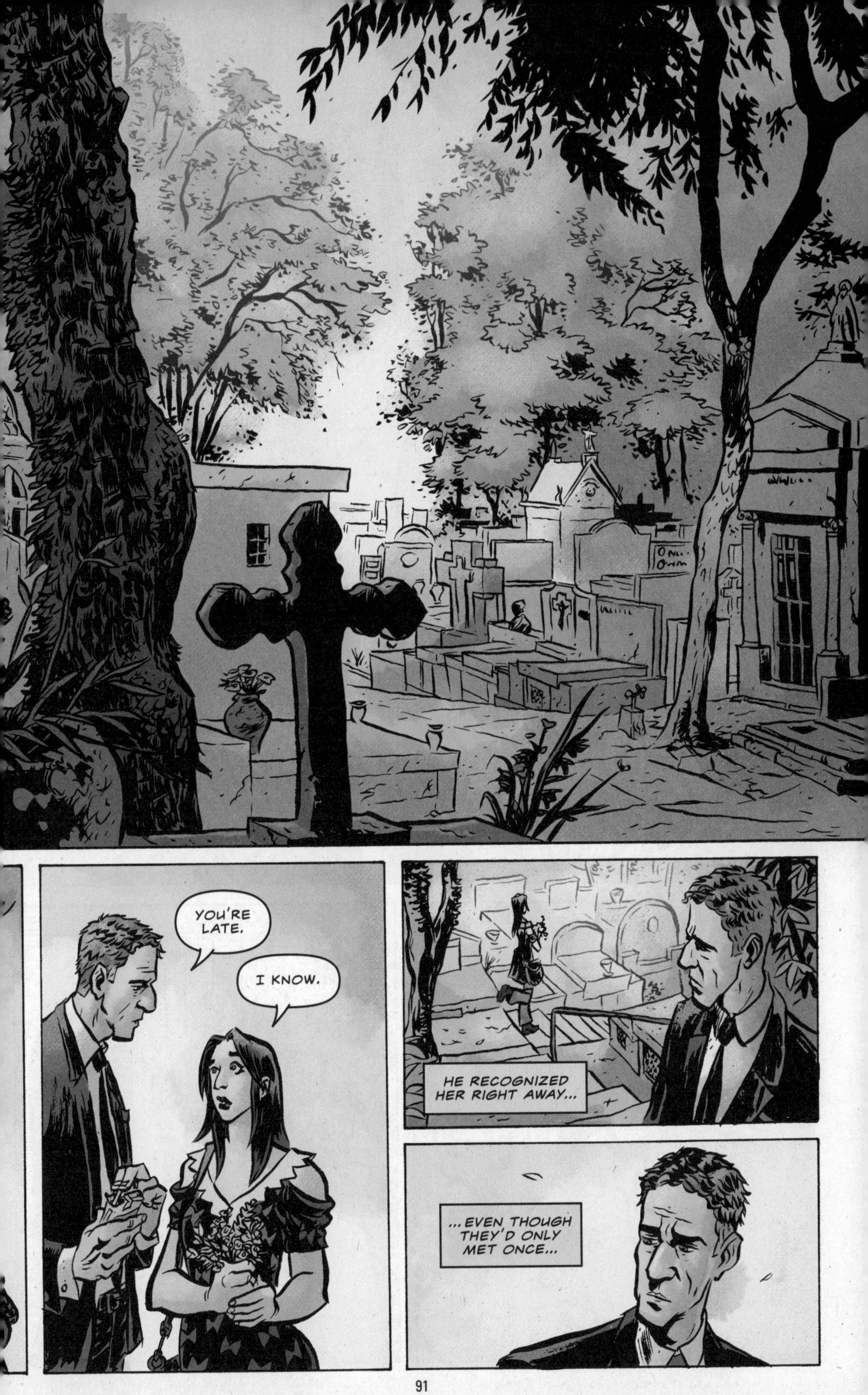
YOU'RE LATE.
I KNOW.
HE RECOGNIZED HER RIGHT AWAY...
...EVEN THOUGH THEY'D ONLY MET ONCE...

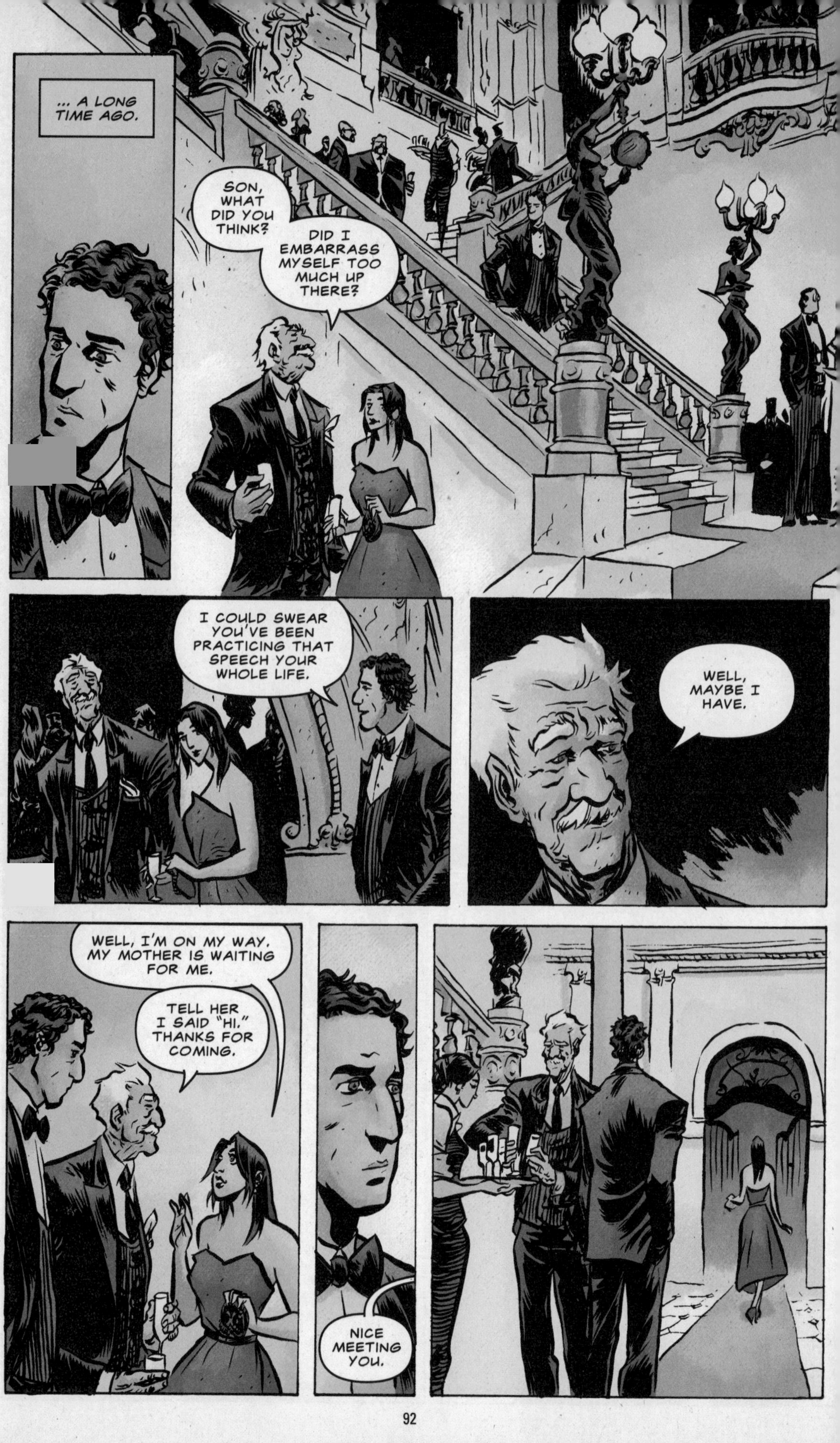

... A LONG TIME AGO.
SON, WHAT DID YOU THINK?
DID I EMBARRASS MYSELF TOO MUCH UP THERE?
I COULD SWEAR YOU'VE BEEN PRACTICING THAT SPEECH YOUR WHOLE LIFE.
WELL, MAYBE I HAVE.
WELL, I'M ON MY WAY. MY MOTHER IS WAITING FOR ME.
TELL HER I SAID "HI." THANKS FOR COMING.
NICE MEETING YOU.

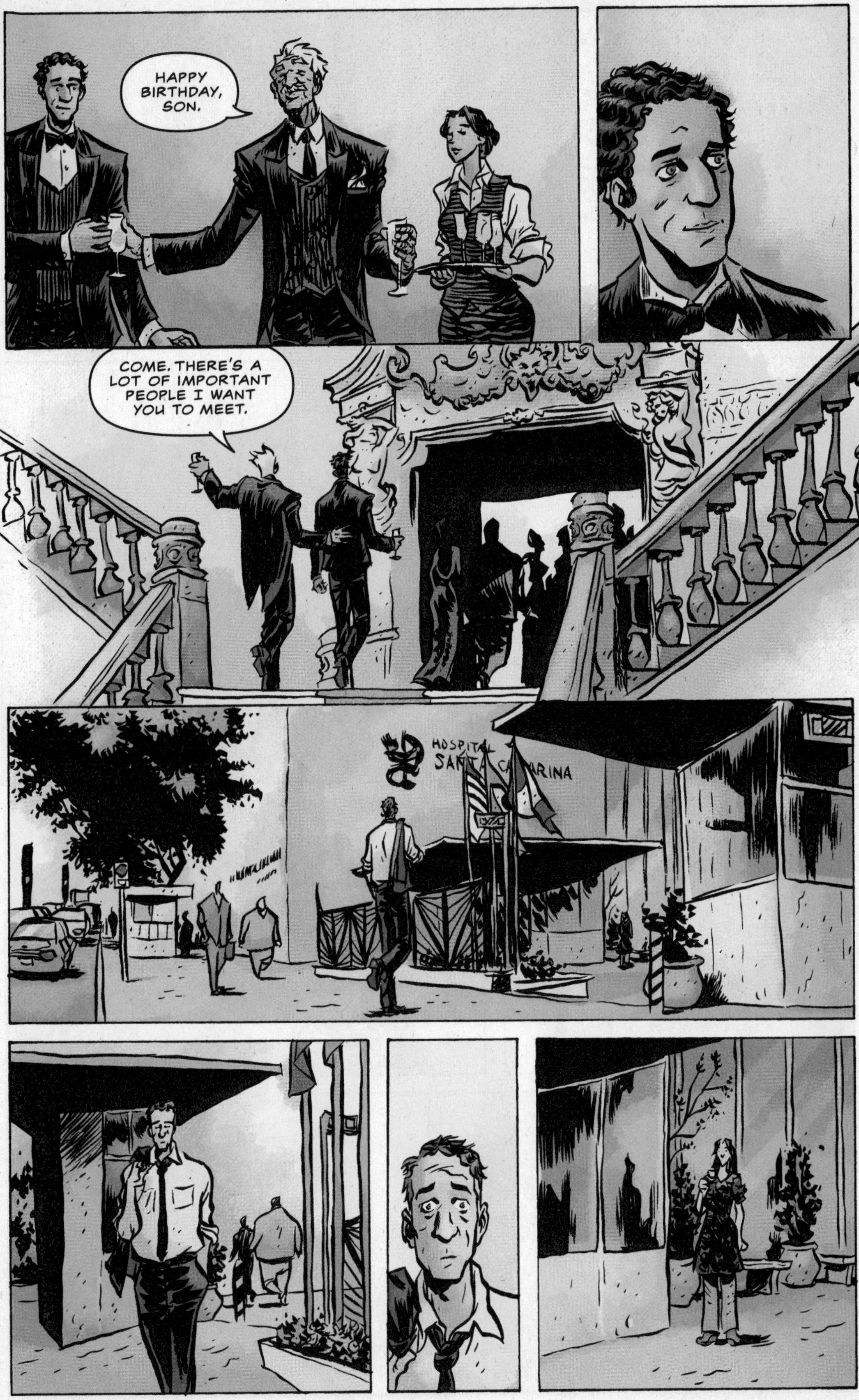
HAPPY BIRTHDAY, SON.
COME. THERE'S A LOT OF IMPORTANT PEOPLE I WANT YOU TO MEET.
HOSPITAL

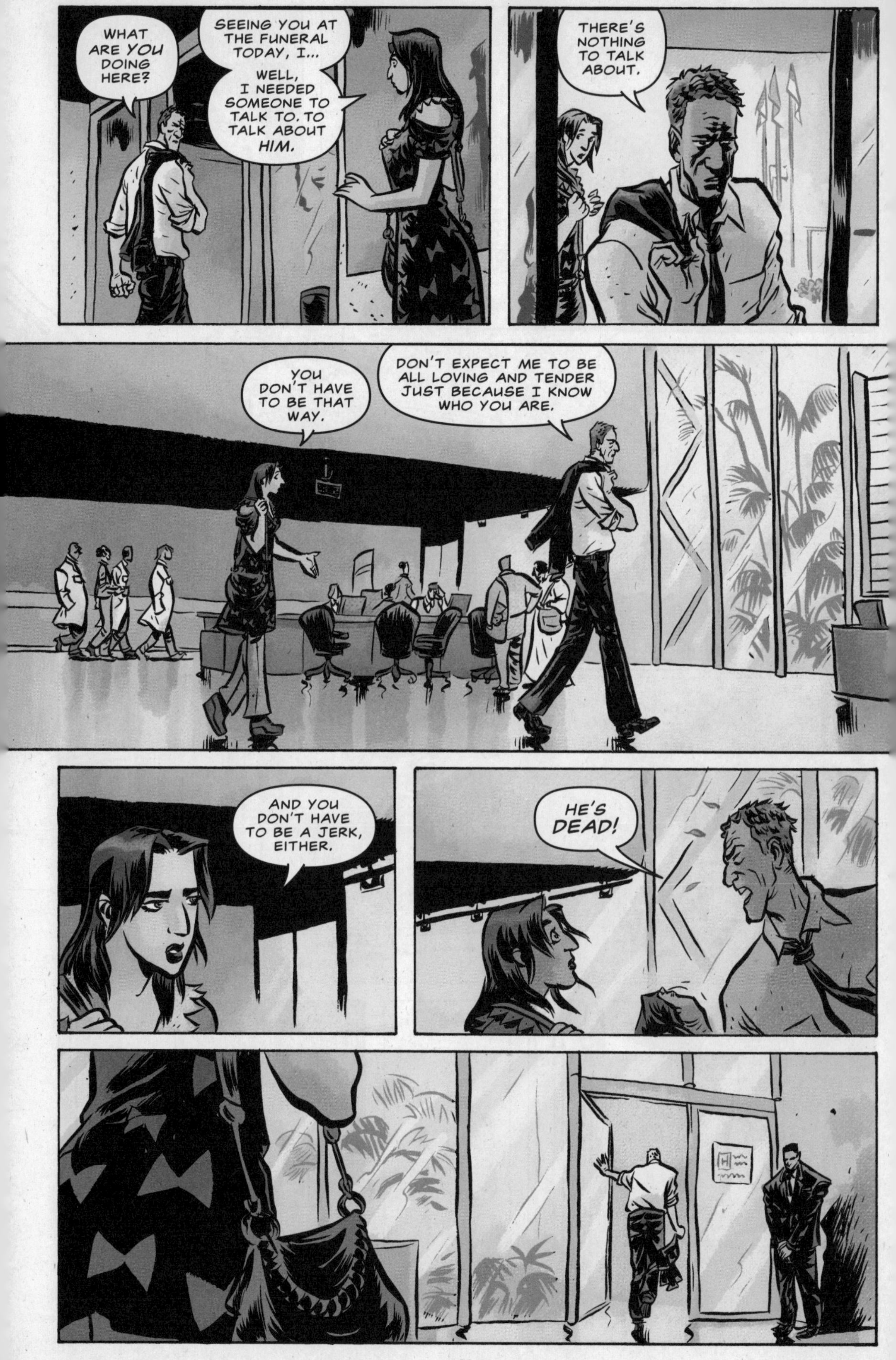
WHAT ARE YOU DOING HERE?
SEEING YOU AT THE FUNERAL TODAY, I...
WELL, I NEEDED SOMEONE TO TALK TO. TO TALK ABOUT HIM.
THERE'S NOTHING TO TALK ABOUT.
YOU DON'T HAVE TO BE THAT WAY.
DON'T EXPECT ME TO BE ALL LOVING AND TENDER JUST BECAUSE I KNOW WHO YOU ARE.
AND YOU DON'T HAVE TO BE A JERK, EITHER.
HE'S DEAD!

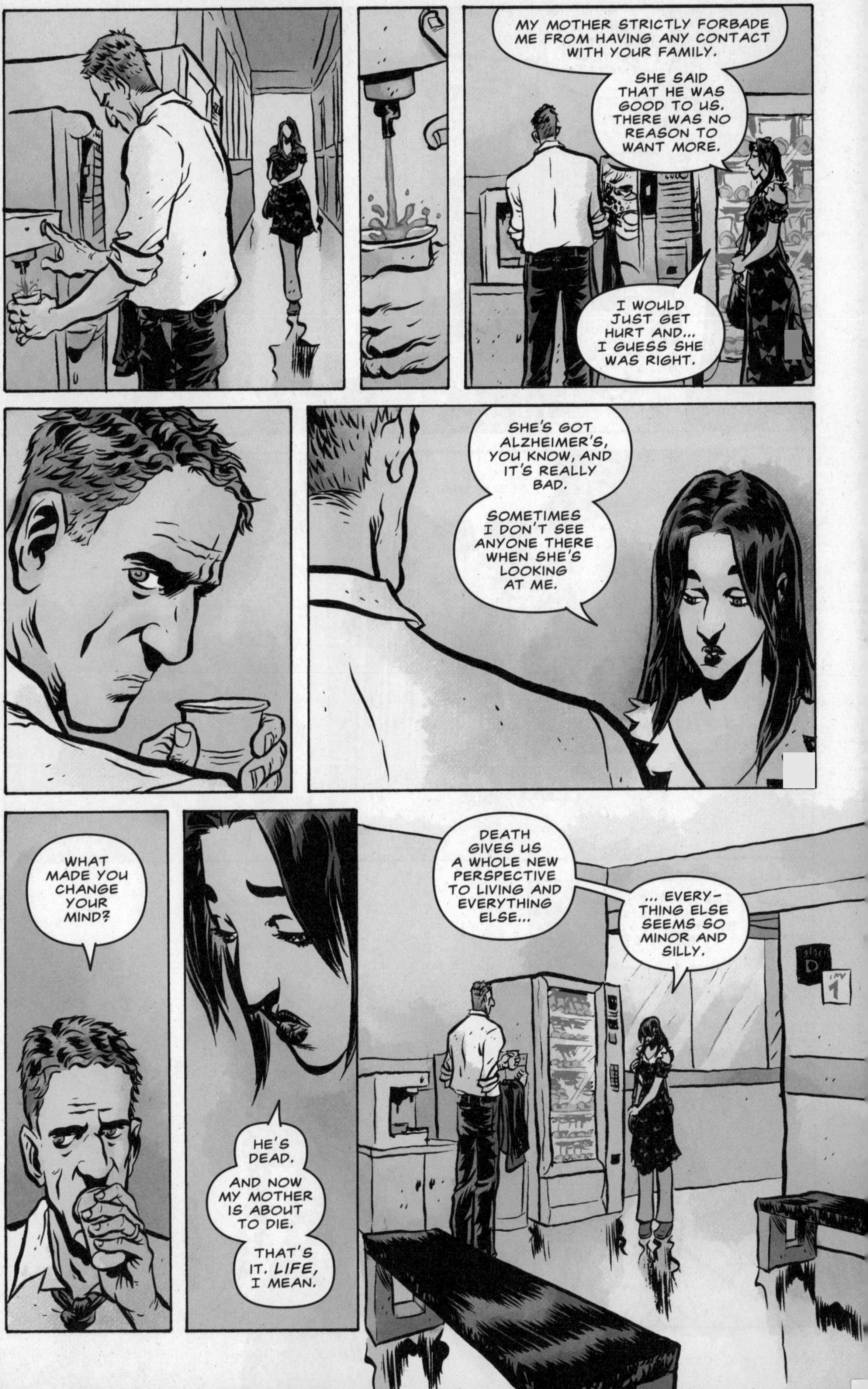
MY MOTHER STRICTLY FORBADE ME FROM HAVING ANY CONTACT WITH YOUR FAMILY.
SHE SAID THAT HE WAS GOOD TO US. THERE WAS NO REASON TO WANT MORE.
I WOULD JUST GET HURT AND... I GUESS SHE WAS RIGHT.
SHE'S GOT ALZHEIMER'S, YOU KNOW, AND IT'S REALLY BAD.
SOMETIMES I DON'T SEE ANYONE THERE WHEN SHE'S LOOKING AT ME.
WHAT MADE YOU CHANGE YOUR MIND?
HE'S DEAD.
AND NOW MY MOTHER IS ABOUT TO DIE.
THAT'S IT. LIFE, I MEAN.
DEATH GIVES US A WHOLE NEW PERSPECTIVE TO LIVING AND EVERYTHING ELSE...
... EVERY-THING ELSE SEEMS SO MINOR AND SILLY.

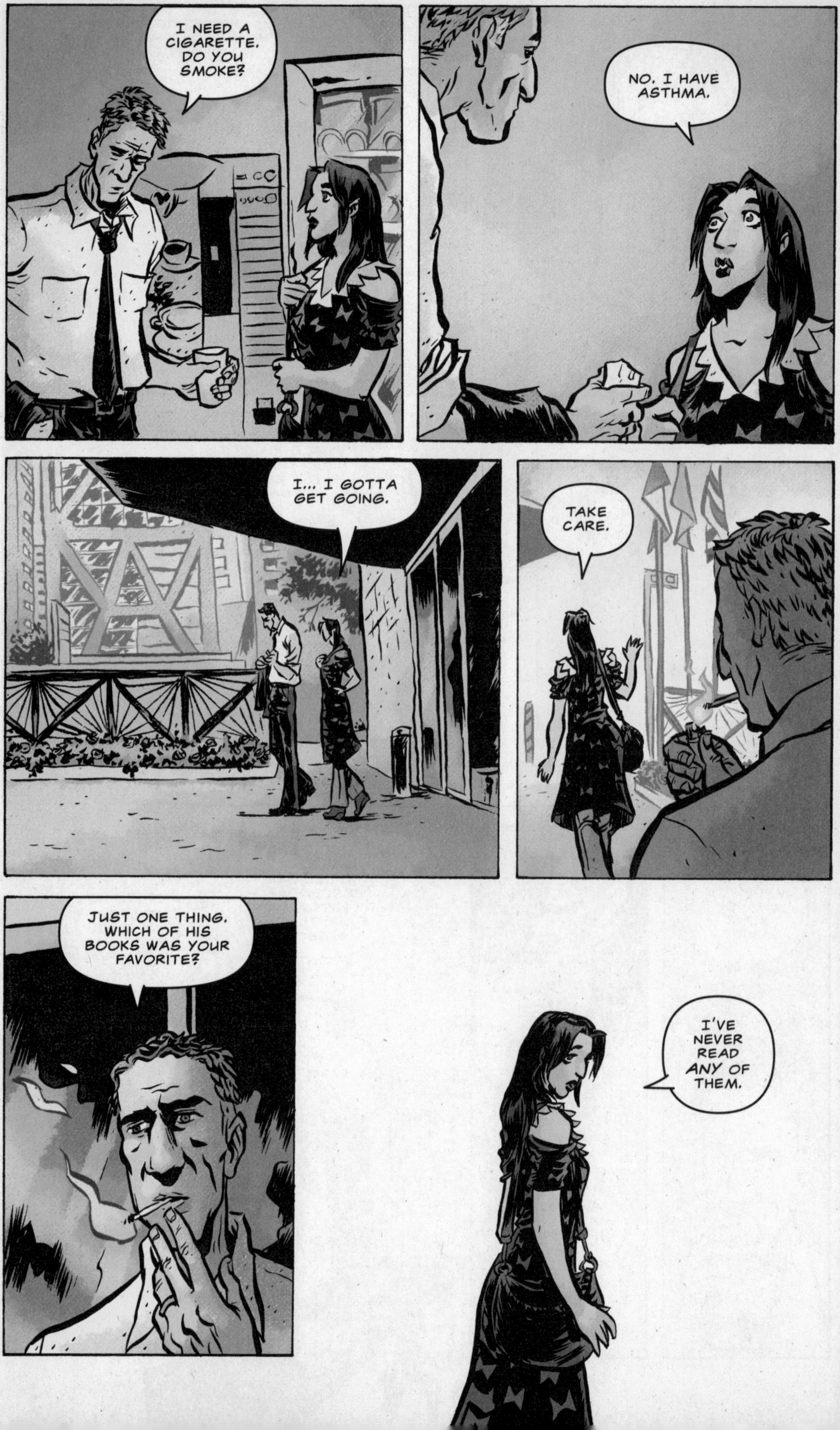
I NEED A CIGARETTE. DO YOU SMOKE?
NO. I HAVE ASTHMA.
I... I GOTTA GET GOING.
TAKE CARE.
JUST ONE THING. WHICH OF HIS BOOKS WAS YOUR FAVORITE?
I'VE NEVER READ ANY OF THEM.

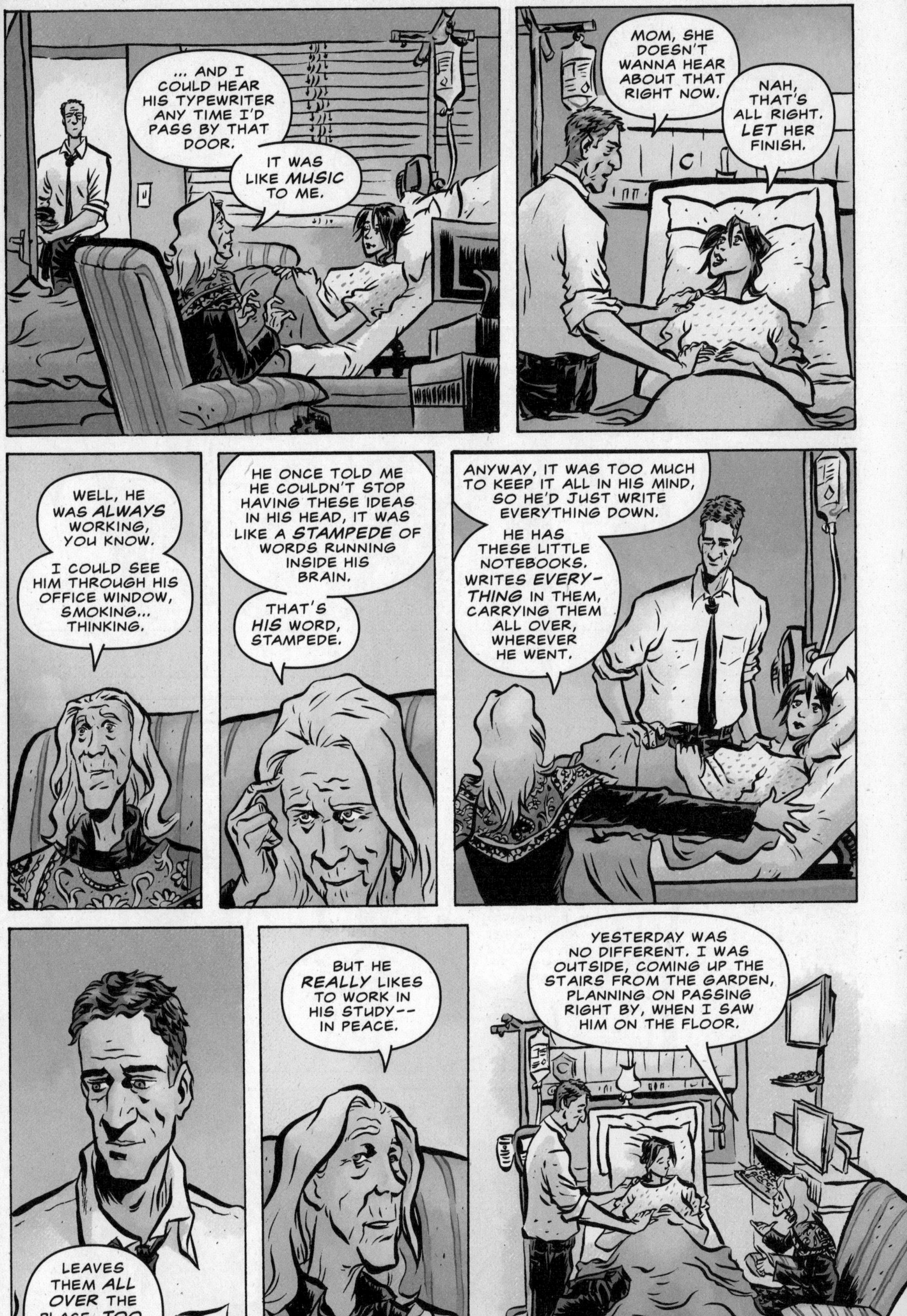
... AND I COULD HEAR HIS TYPEWRITER ANY TIME I'D PASS BY THAT DOOR.
IT WAS LIKE MUSIC TO ME.
MOM, SHE DOESN'T WANNA HEAR ABOUT THAT RIGHT NOW.
NAH, THAT'S ALL RIGHT. LET HER FINISH.
WELL, HE WAS ALWAYS WORKING, YOU KNOW.
I COULD SEE HIM THROUGH HIS OFFICE WINDOW, SMOKING... THINKING.
HE ONCE TOLD ME HE COULDN'T STOP HAVING THESE IDEAS IN HIS HEAD, IT WAS LIKE A STAMPEDE OF WORDS RUNNING INSIDE HIS BRAIN.
THAT'S HIS WORD, STAMPEDE.
ANYWAY, IT WAS TOO MUCH TO KEEP IT ALL IN HIS MIND, SO HE'D JUST WRITE EVERYTHING DOWN.
HE HAS THESE LITTLE NOTEBOOKS. WRITES EVERY-THING IN THEM, CARRYING THEM ALL OVER, WHEREVER HE WENT.
LEAVES THEM ALL OVER THE PLACE, TOO. THE HOUSE IS FULL OF THEM.
BUT HE REALLY LIKES TO WORK IN HIS STUDY-- IN PEACE.
YESTERDAY WAS NO DIFFERENT. I WAS OUTSIDE, COMING UP THE STAIRS FROM THE GARDEN, PLANNING ON PASSING RIGHT BY, WHEN I SAW HIM ON THE FLOOR.

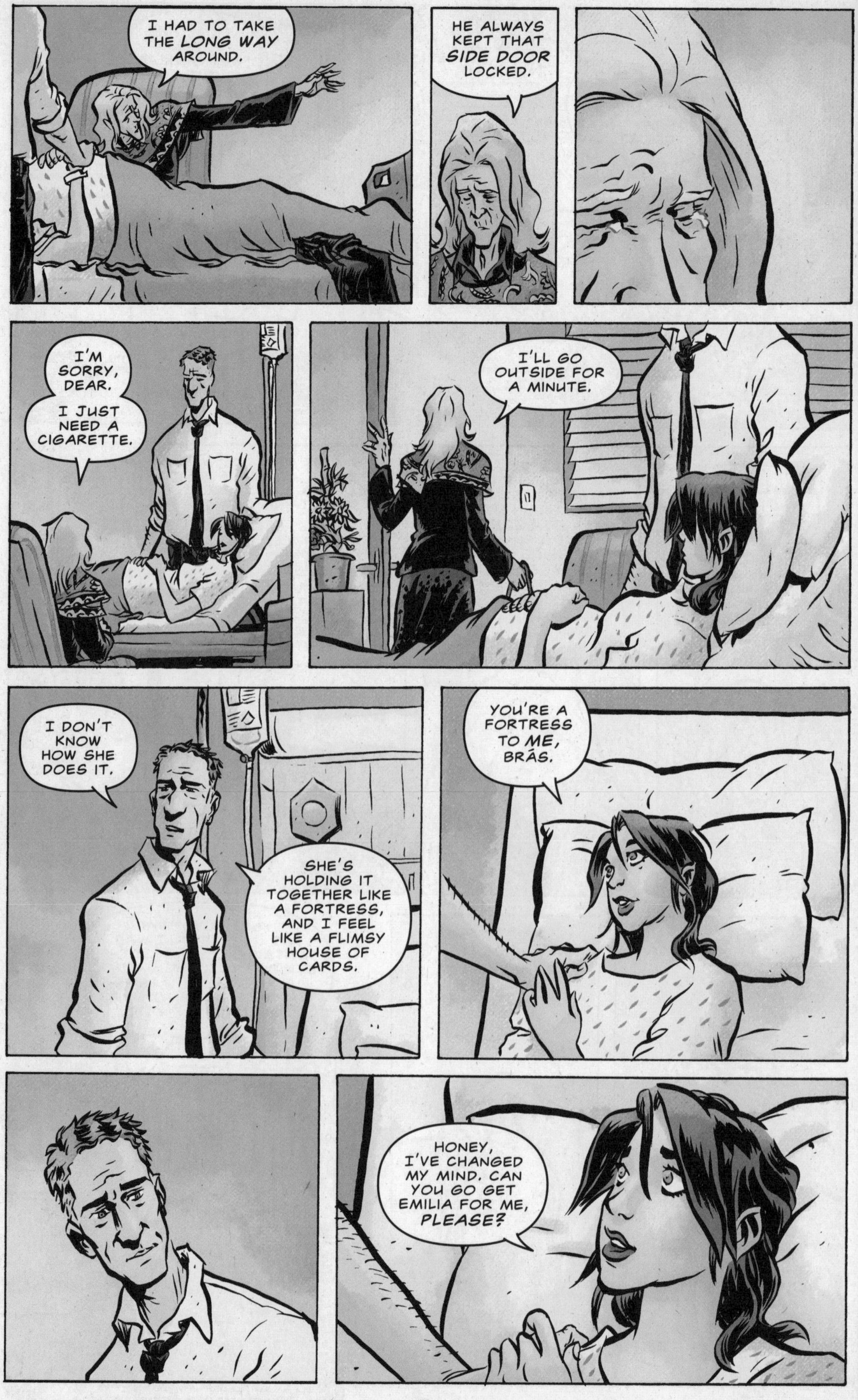
I HAD TO TAKE THE LONG WAY AROUND.
HE ALWAYS KEPT THAT SIDE DOOR LOCKED.
I'M SORRY, DEAR.
I JUST NEED A CIGARETTE.
I'LL GO OUTSIDE FOR A MINUTE.
I DON'T KNOW HOW SHE DOES IT.
SHE'S HOLDING IT TOGETHER LIKE A FORTRESS, AND I FEEL LIKE A FLIMSY HOUSE OF CARDS.
YOU'RE A FORTRESS TO ME, BRÁS.
HONEY, I'VE CHANGED MY MIND. CAN YOU GO GET EMILIA FOR ME, PLEASE?

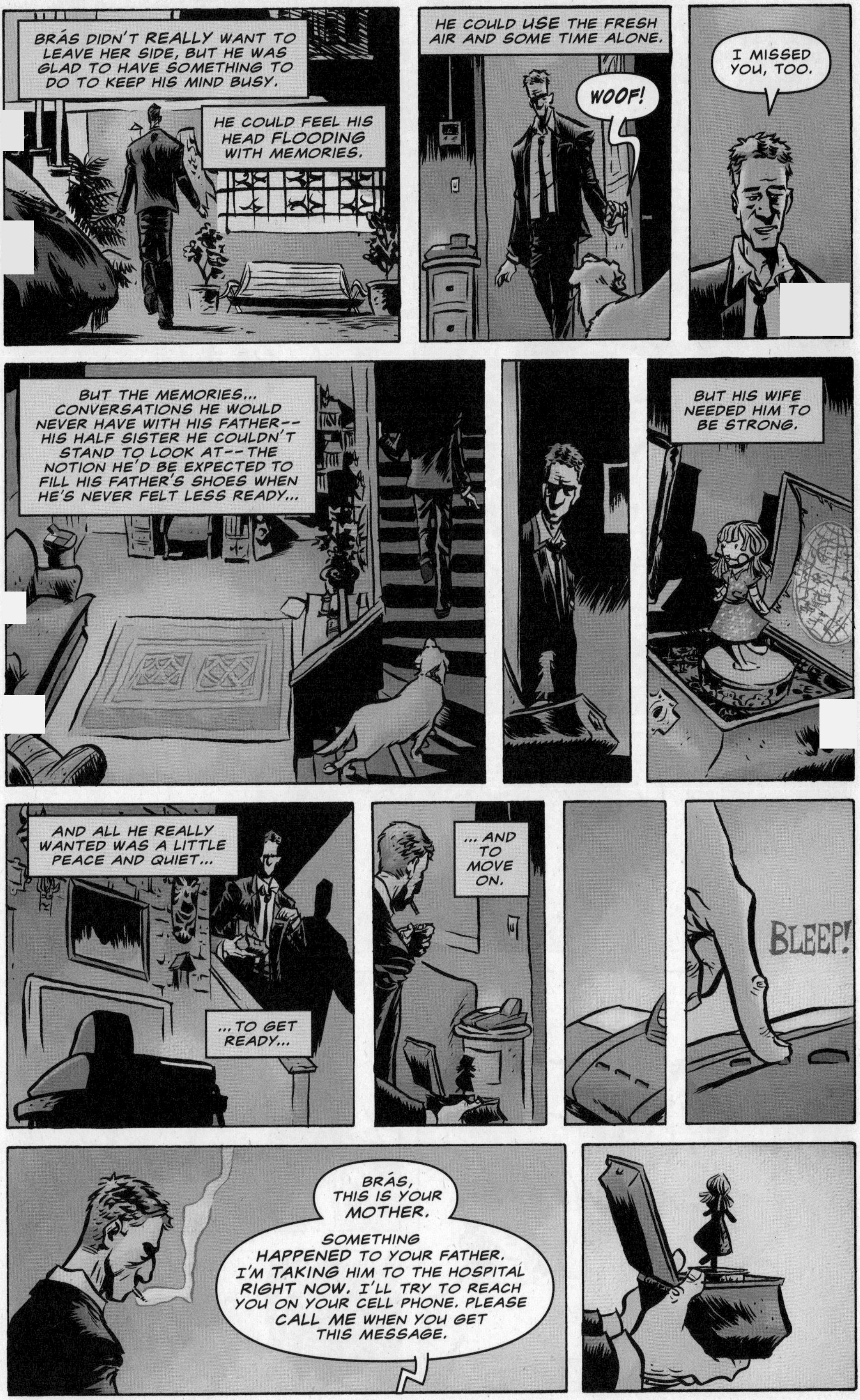
BRÁS DIDN'T REALLY WANT TO LEAVE HER SIDE, BUT HE WAS GLAD TO HAVE SOMETHING TO DO TO KEEP HIS MIND BUSY.
HE COULD FEEL HIS HEAD FLOODING WITH MEMORIES.
HE COULD USE THE FRESH AIR AND SOME TIME ALONE.
WOOF!
I MISSED YOU, TOO.
BUT THE MEMORIES... CONVERSATIONS HE WOULD NEVER HAVE WITH HIS FATHER-- HIS HALF SISTER HE COULDN'T STAND TO LOOK AT--THE NOTION HE'D BE EXPECTED TO FILL HIS FATHER'S SHOES WHEN HE'S NEVER FELT LESS READY...
BUT HIS WIFE NEEDED HIM TO BE STRONG.
AND ALL HE REALLY WANTED WAS A LITTLE PEACE AND QUIET...
...TO GET READY...
...AND TO MOVE ON.
BLEEP!
BRÁS, THIS IS YOUR MOTHER.
SOMETHING HAPPENED TO YOUR FATHER. I'M TAKING HIM TO THE HOSPITAL RIGHT NOW. I'LL TRY TO REACH YOU ON YOUR CELL PHONE. PLEASE CALL ME WHEN YOU GET THIS MESSAGE.

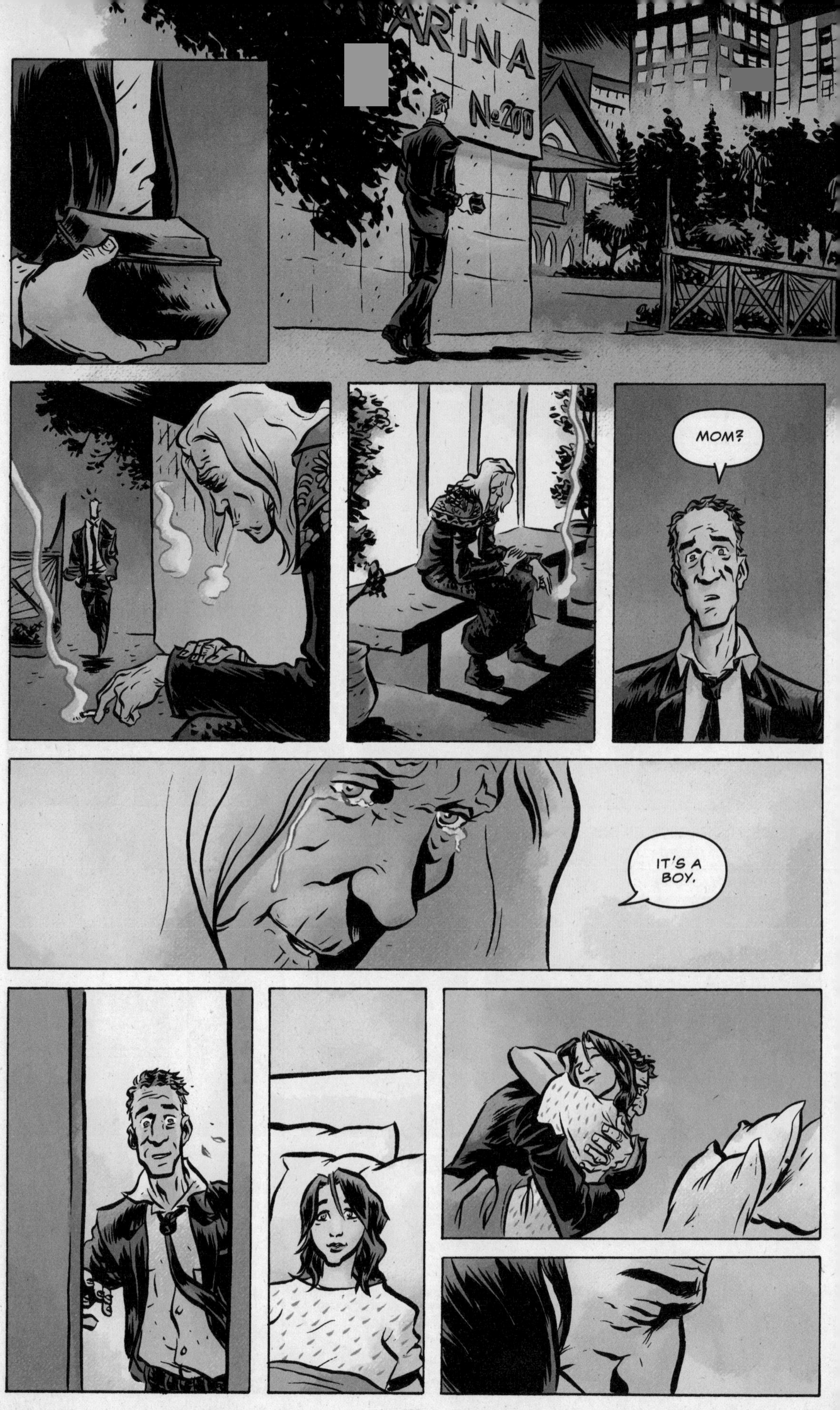
MOM?
IT'S A BOY.

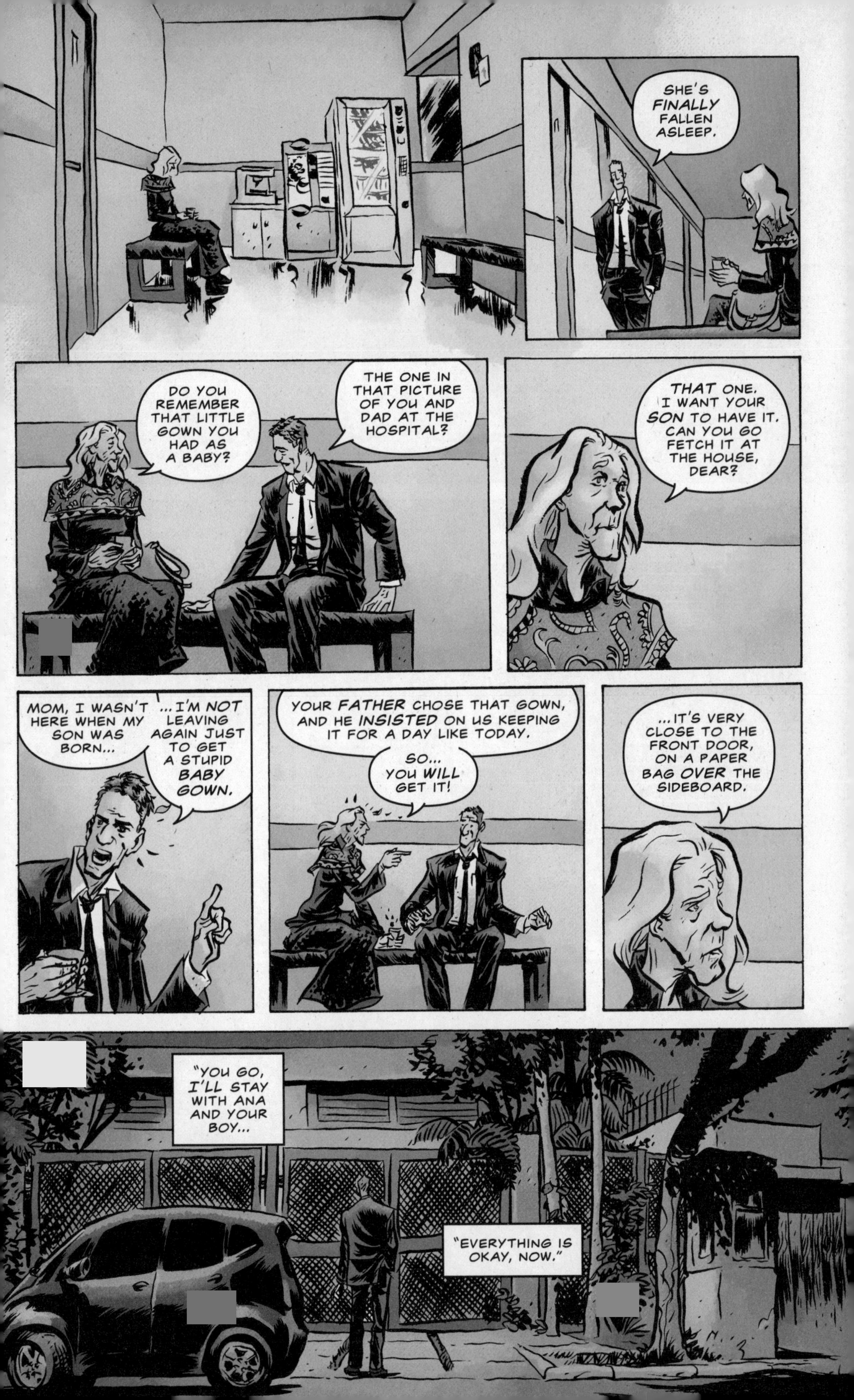
SHE'S FINALLY FALLEN ASLEEP.
DO YOU REMEMBER THAT LITTLE GOWN YOU HAD AS A BABY?
THE ONE IN THAT PICTURE OF YOU AND DAD AT THE HOSPITAL?
THAT ONE. I WANT YOUR SON TO HAVE IT. CAN YOU GO FETCH IT AT THE HOUSE, DEAR?
MOM, I WASN'T HERE WHEN MY SON WAS BORN...
...I'M NOT LEAVING AGAIN JUST TO GET A STUPID BABY GOWN.
YOUR FATHER CHOSE THAT GOWN, AND HE INSISTED ON US KEEPING IT FOR A DAY LIKE TODAY.
SO... YOU WILL GET IT!
...IT'S VERY CLOSE TO THE FRONT DOOR, ON A PAPER BAG OVER THE SIDEBOARD.
"YOU GO, I'LL STAY WITH ANA AND YOUR BOY...
"EVERYTHING IS OKAY, NOW."

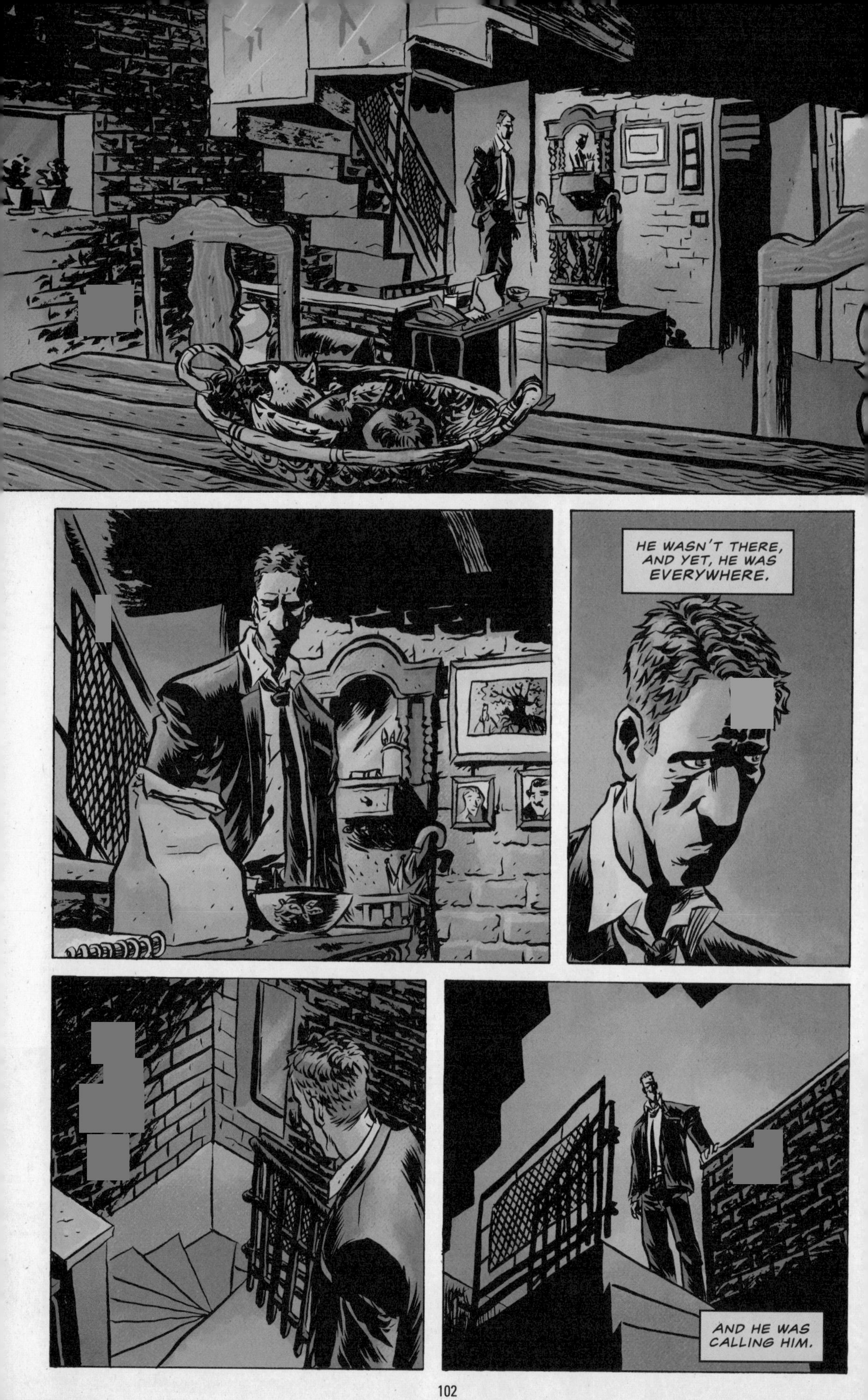
HE WASN'T THERE, AND YET, HE WAS EVERYWHERE.
AND HE WAS CALLING HIM.

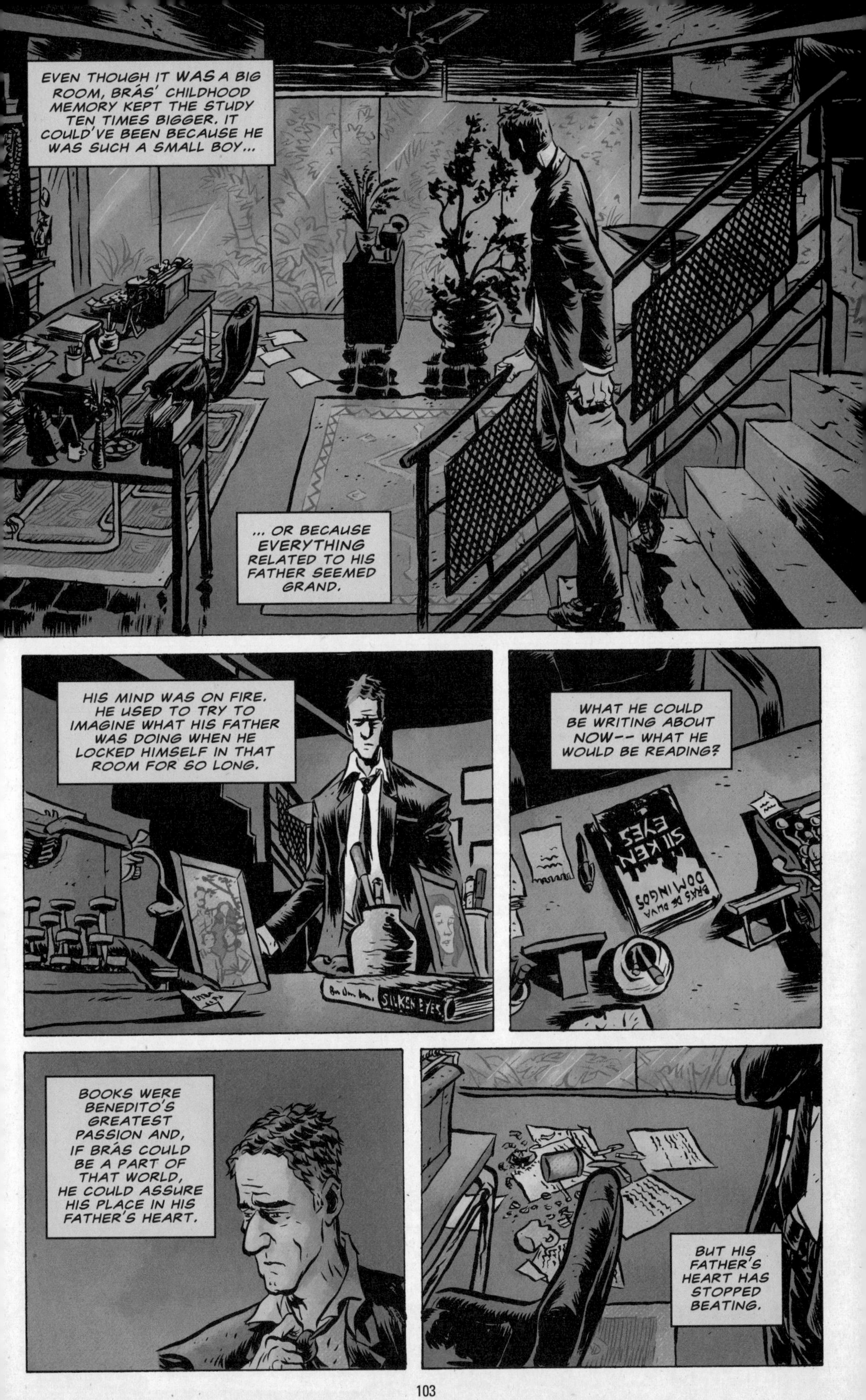
EVEN THOUGH IT WAS A BIG ROOM, BRÁS' CHILDHOOD MEMORY KEPT THE STUDY TEN TIMES BIGGER. IT COULD'VE BEEN BECAUSE HE WAS SUCH A SMALL BOY...
... OR BECAUSE EVERYTHING RELATED TO HIS FATHER SEEMED GRAND.
HIS MIND WAS ON FIRE. HE USED TO TRY TO IMAGINE WHAT HIS FATHER WAS DOING WHEN HE LOCKED HIMSELF IN THAT ROOM FOR SO LONG.
SILKEN EYES
WHAT HE COULD BE WRITING ABOUT NOW-- WHAT HE WOULD BE READING?
BOOKS WERE BENEDITO'S GREATEST PASSION AND, IF BRÁS COULD BE A PART OF THAT WORLD, HE COULD ASSURE HIS PLACE IN HIS FATHER'S HEART.
BUT HIS FATHER'S HEART HAS STOPPED BEATING.

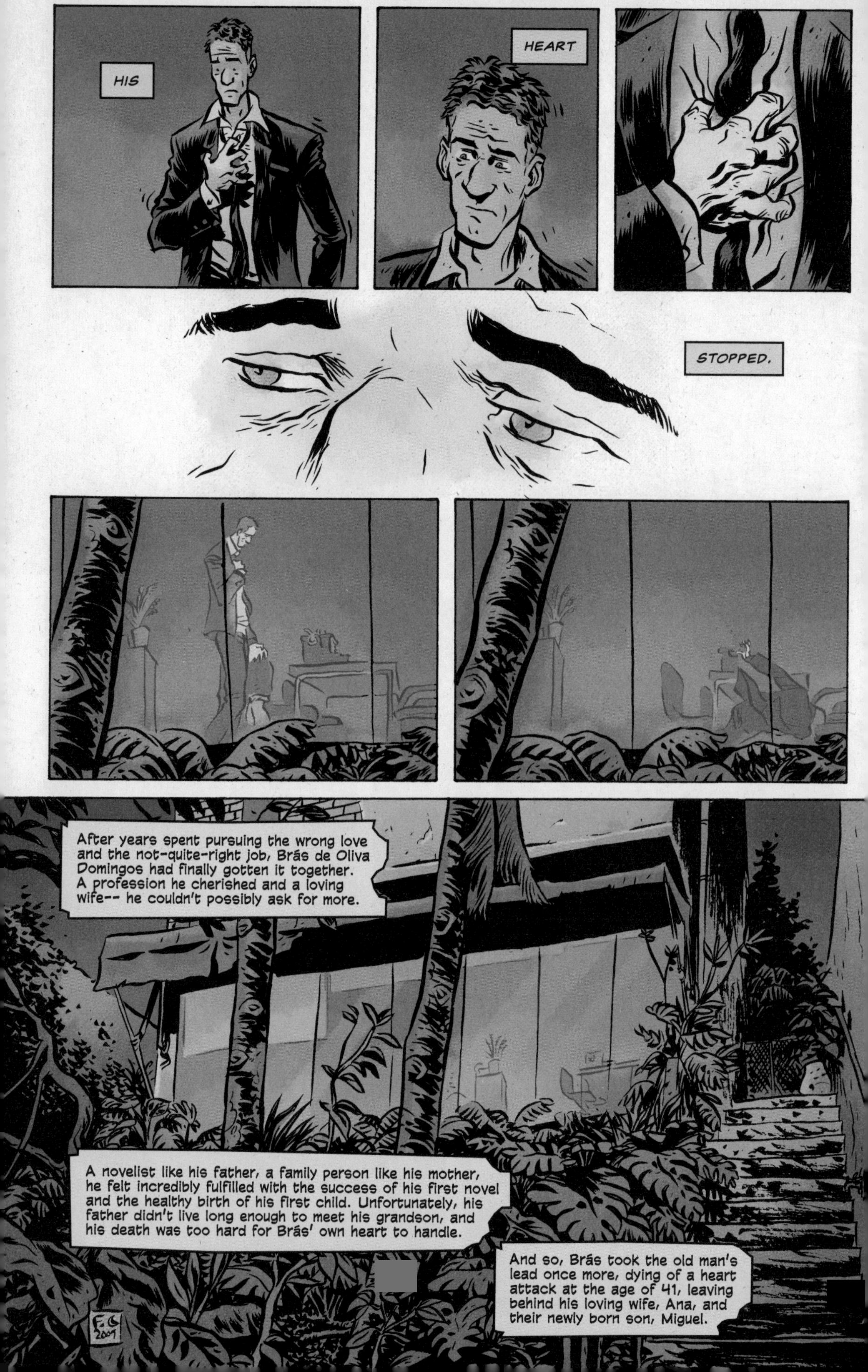
HIS
HEART
STOPPED.
After years spent pursuing the wrong love and the not-quite-right job, Brás de Oliva Domingos had finally gotten it together. A profession he cherished and a loving wife-- he couldn't possibly ask for more.
A novelist like his father, a family person like his mother, he felt incredibly fulfilled with the success of his first novel and the healthy birth of his first child. Unfortunately, his father didn't live long enough to meet his grandson, and his death was too hard for Brás' own heart to handle.
And so, Brás took the old man's lead once more, dying of a heart attack at the age of 41, leaving behind his loving wife, Ana, and their newly born son, Miguel.

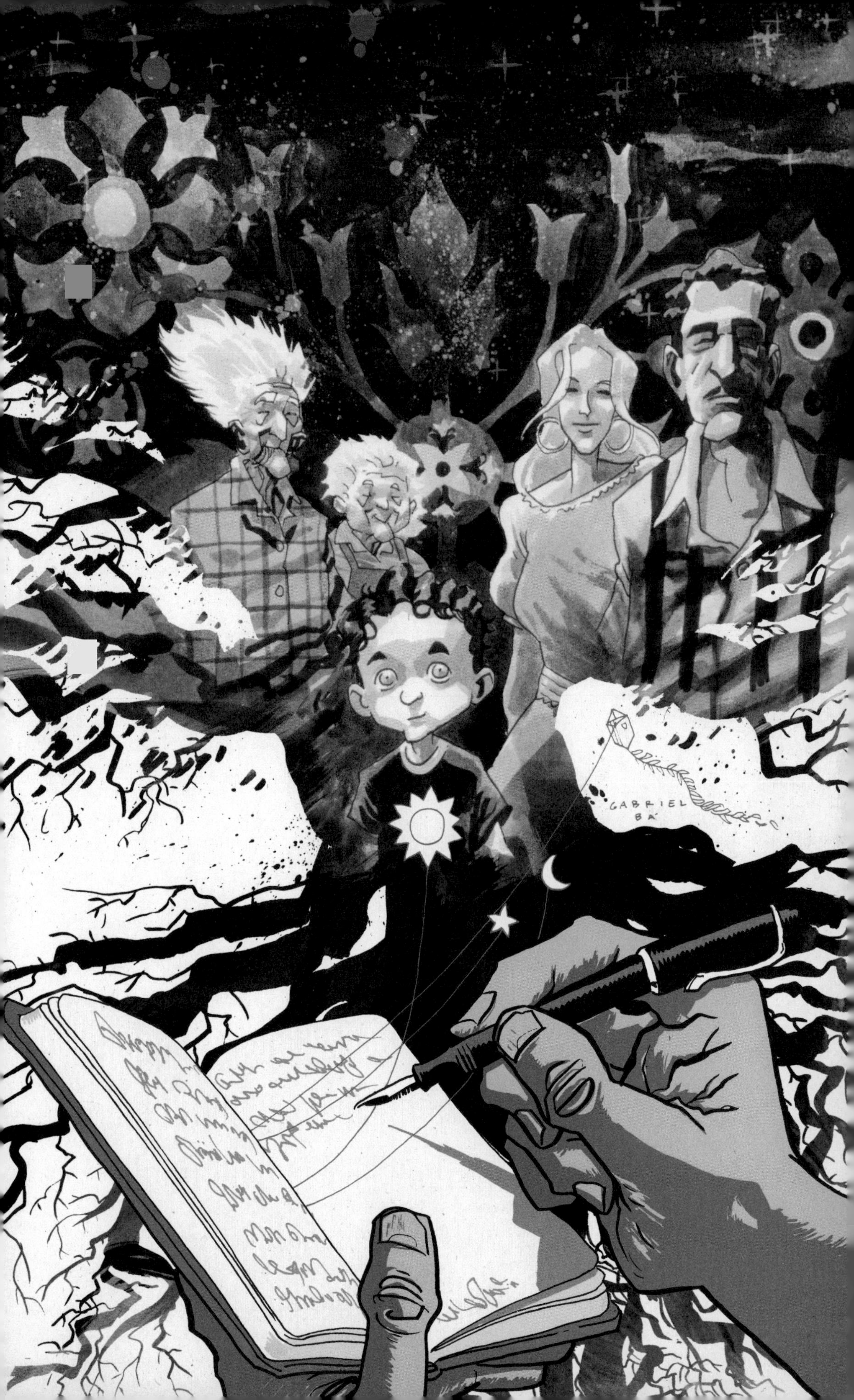
GABRIEL
BÁ

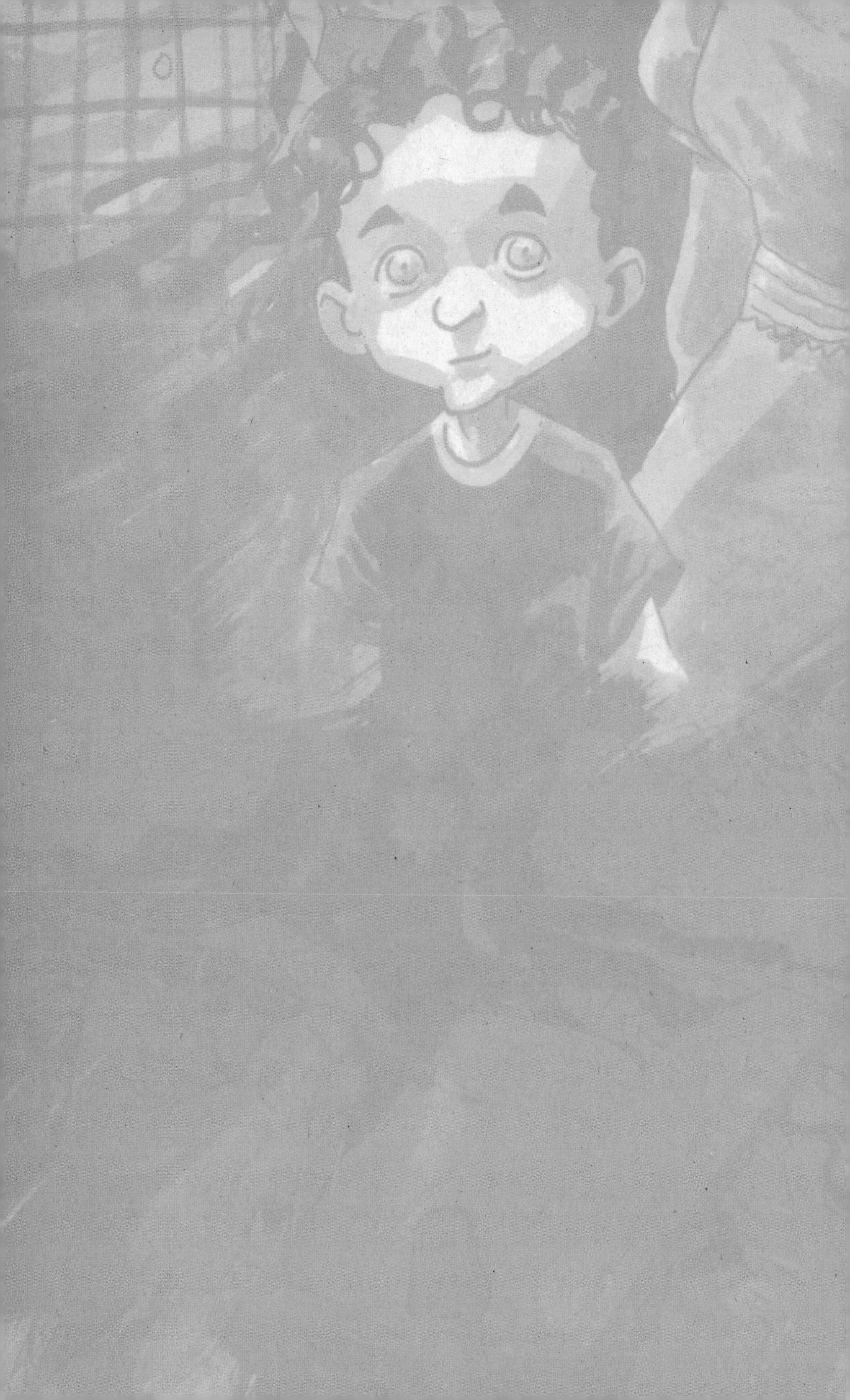

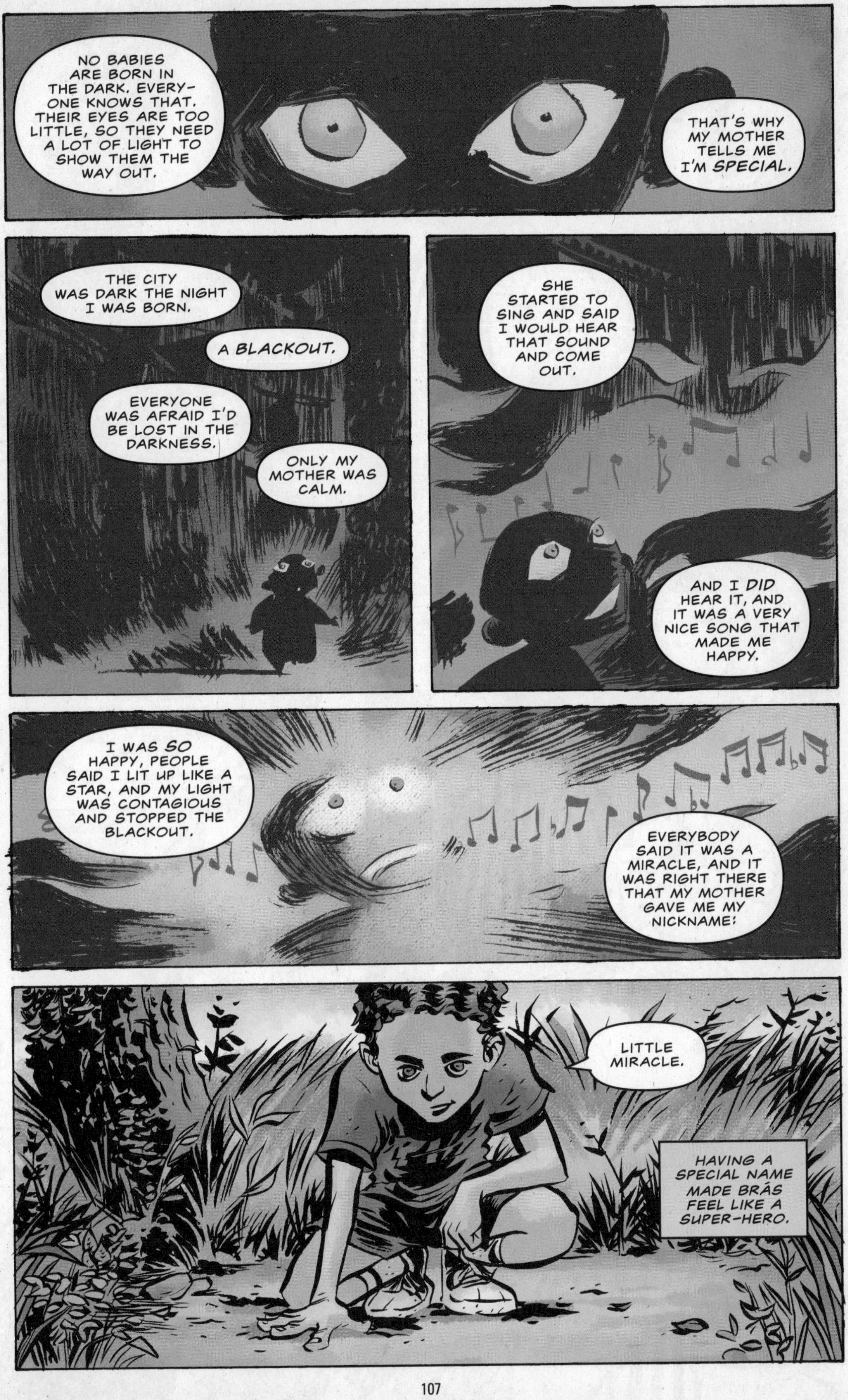
NO BABIES ARE BORN IN THE DARK. EVERY-ONE KNOWS THAT. THEIR EYES ARE TOO LITTLE, SO THEY NEED A LOT OF LIGHT TO SHOW THEM THE WAY OUT.
THAT'S WHY MY MOTHER TELLS ME I'M SPECIAL.
THE CITY WAS DARK THE NIGHT I WAS BORN.
A BLACKOUT.
EVERYONE WAS AFRAID I'D BE LOST IN THE DARKNESS.
ONLY MY MOTHER WAS CALM.
SHE STARTED TO SING AND SAID I WOULD HEAR THAT SOUND AND COME OUT.
AND I DID HEAR IT, AND IT WAS A VERY NICE SONG THAT MADE ME HAPPY.
I WAS SO HAPPY, PEOPLE SAID I LIT UP LIKE A STAR, AND MY LIGHT WAS CONTAGIOUS AND STOPPED THE BLACKOUT.
EVERYBODY SAID IT WAS A MIRACLE, AND IT WAS RIGHT THERE THAT MY MOTHER GAVE ME MY NICKNAME:
LITTLE MIRACLE.
HAVING A SPECIAL NAME MADE BRÁS FEEL LIKE A SUPER-HERO.

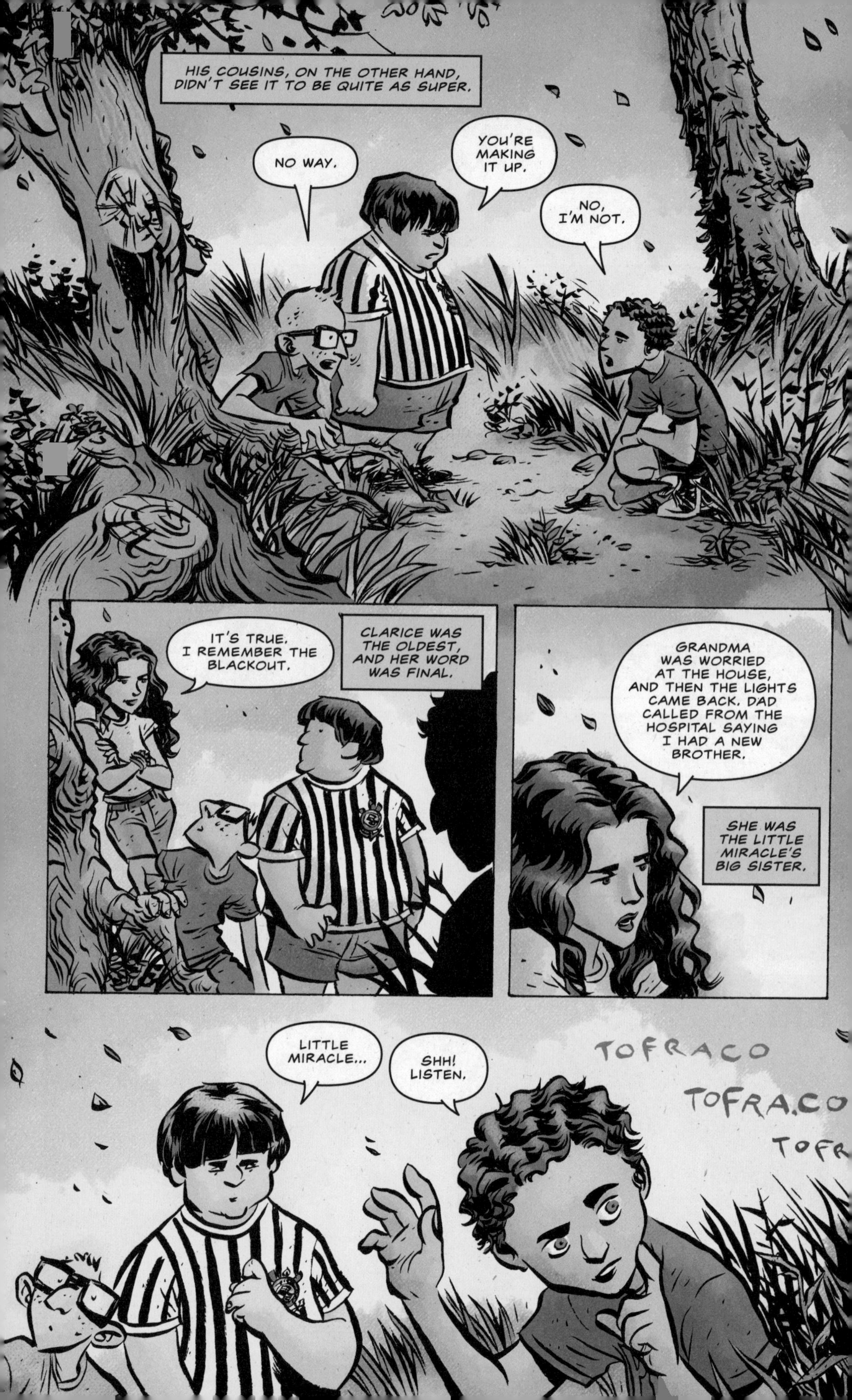
HIS COUSINS, ON THE OTHER HAND, DIDN'T SEE IT TO BE QUITE AS SUPER.
NO WAY.
YOU'RE MAKING IT UP.
NO, I'M NOT.
IT'S TRUE. I REMEMBER THE BLACKOUT.
CLARICE WAS THE OLDEST, AND HER WORD WAS FINAL.
GRANDMA WAS WORRIED AT THE HOUSE, AND THEN THE LIGHTS CAME BACK. DAD CALLED FROM THE HOSPITAL SAYING I HAD A NEW BROTHER.
SHE WAS THE LITTLE MIRACLE'S BIG SISTER.
LITTLE MIRACLE...
SHH! LISTEN.
TOFRACO
TOFRA.CO
TOFR

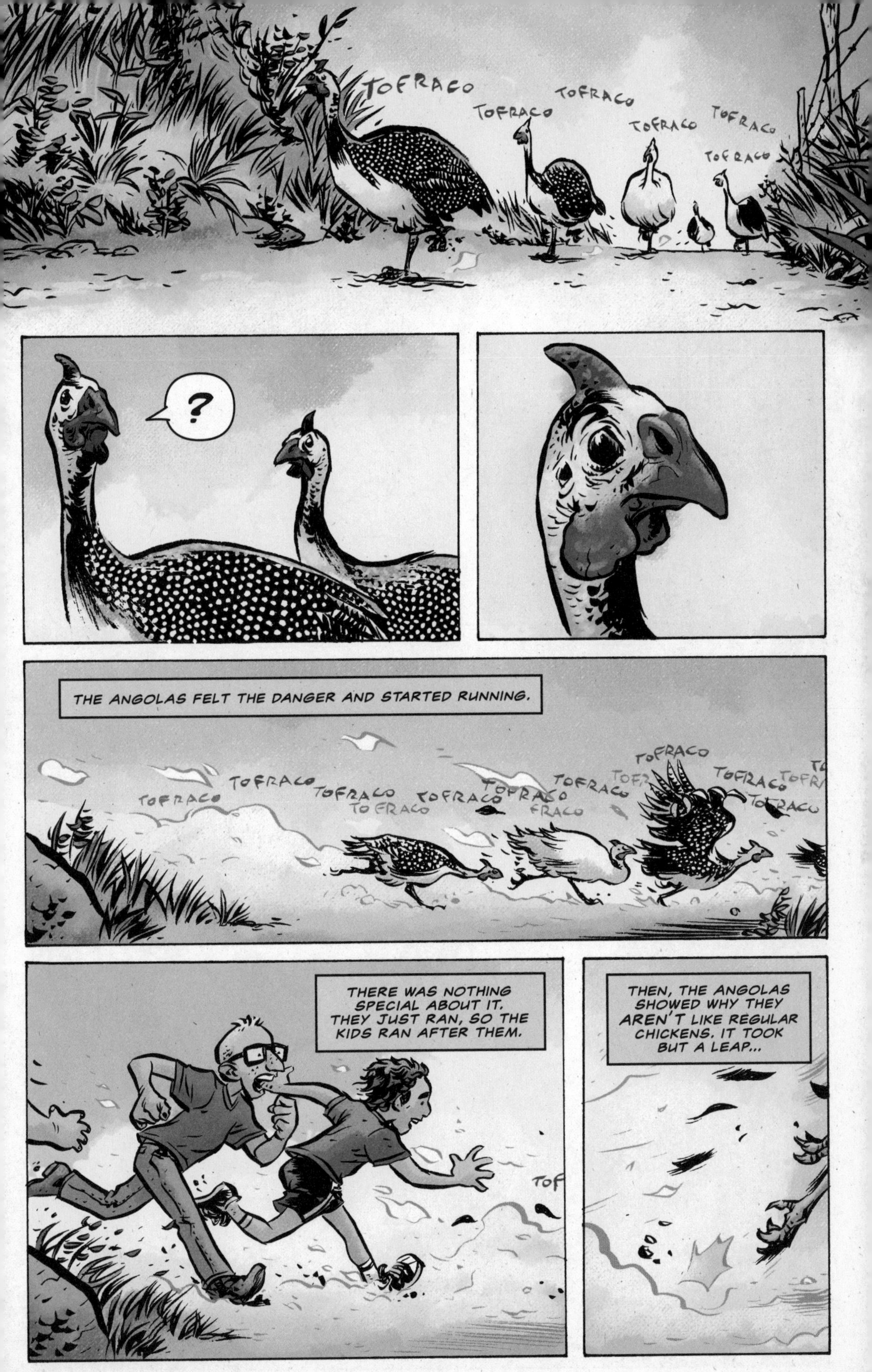
TOFRACO
TOFRACO
TOFRACO
TOFRACO
TOFRACO
TOFRACO
?
THE ANGOLAS FELT THE DANGER AND STARTED RUNNING.
TOFRACO
TOFRACO
TOFRACO
TOFRACO
TOFRACO
THERE WAS NOTHING SPECIAL ABOUT IT. THEY JUST RAN, SO THE KIDS RAN AFTER THEM.
THEN, THE ANGOLAS SHOWED WHY THEY AREN'T LIKE REGULAR CHICKENS. IT TOOK BUT A LEAP...

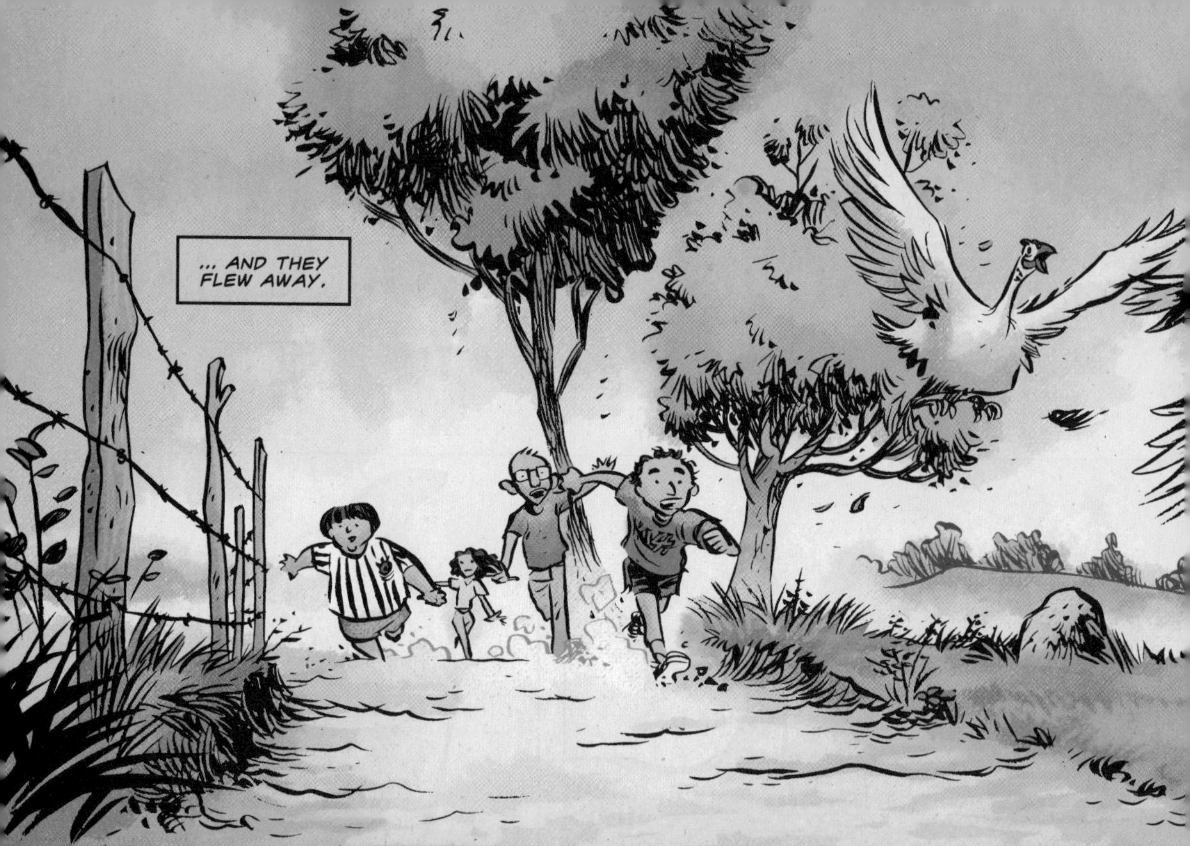
... AND THEY FLEW AWAY.

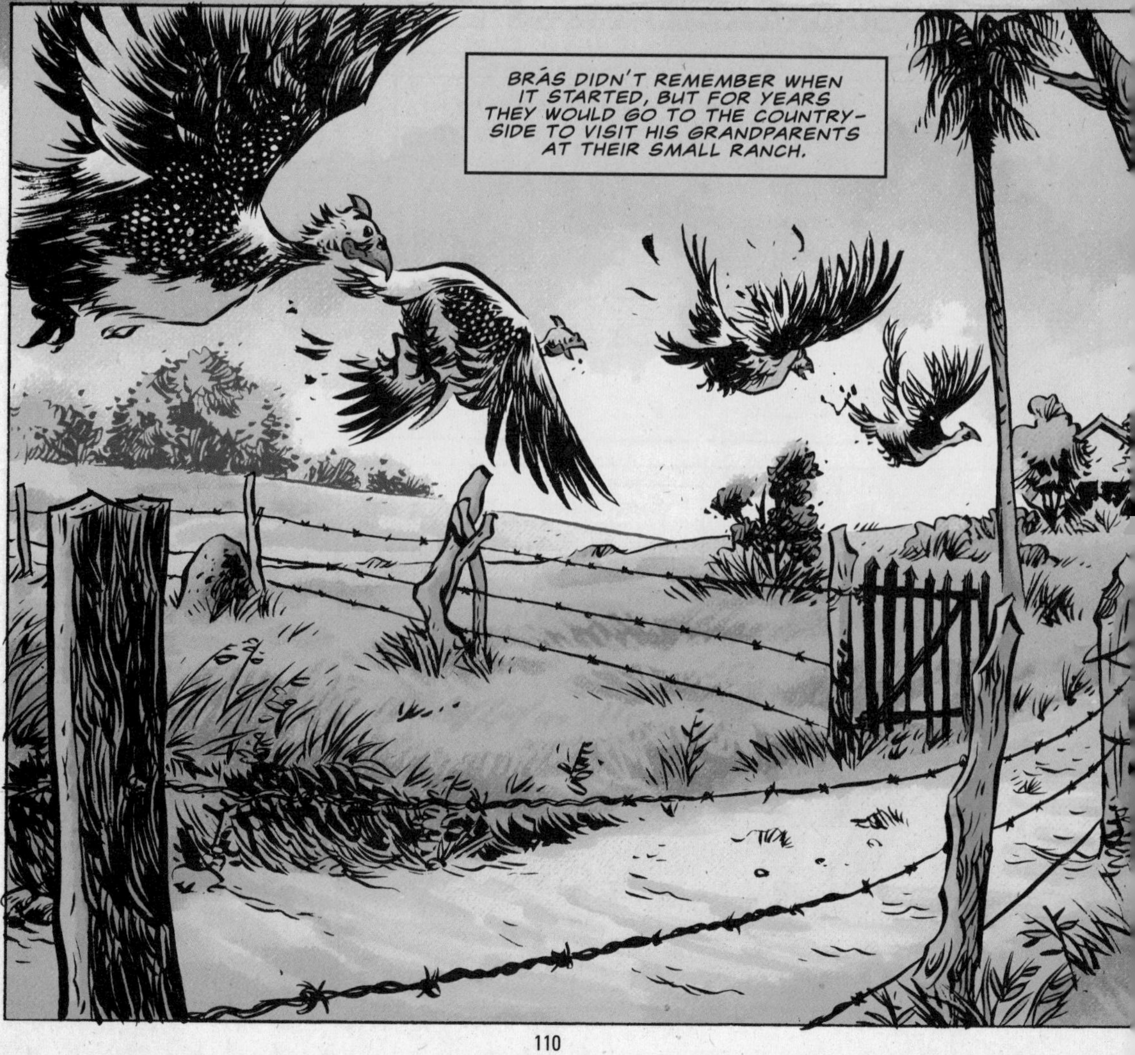
BRÁS DIDN'T REMEMBER WHEN IT STARTED, BUT FOR YEARS THEY WOULD GO TO THE COUNTRY-SIDE TO VISIT HIS GRANDPARENTS AT THEIR SMALL RANCH.

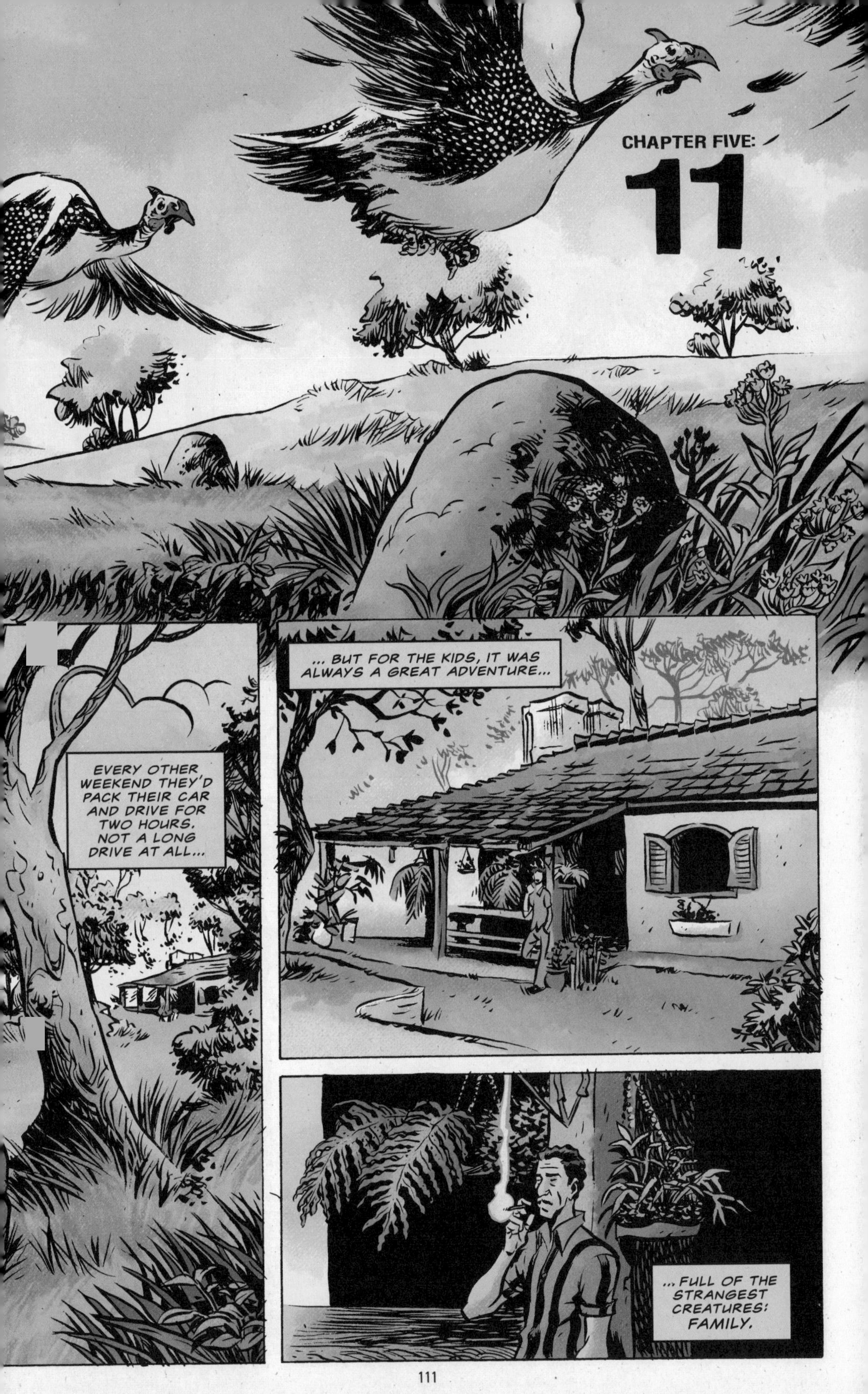
CHAPTER FIVE:
11
EVERY OTHER WEEKEND THEY'D PACK THEIR CAR AND DRIVE FOR TWO HOURS. NOT A LONG DRIVE AT ALL...
... BUT FOR THE KIDS, IT WAS ALWAYS A GREAT ADVENTURE...
...FULL OF THE STRANGEST CREATURES: FAMILY.

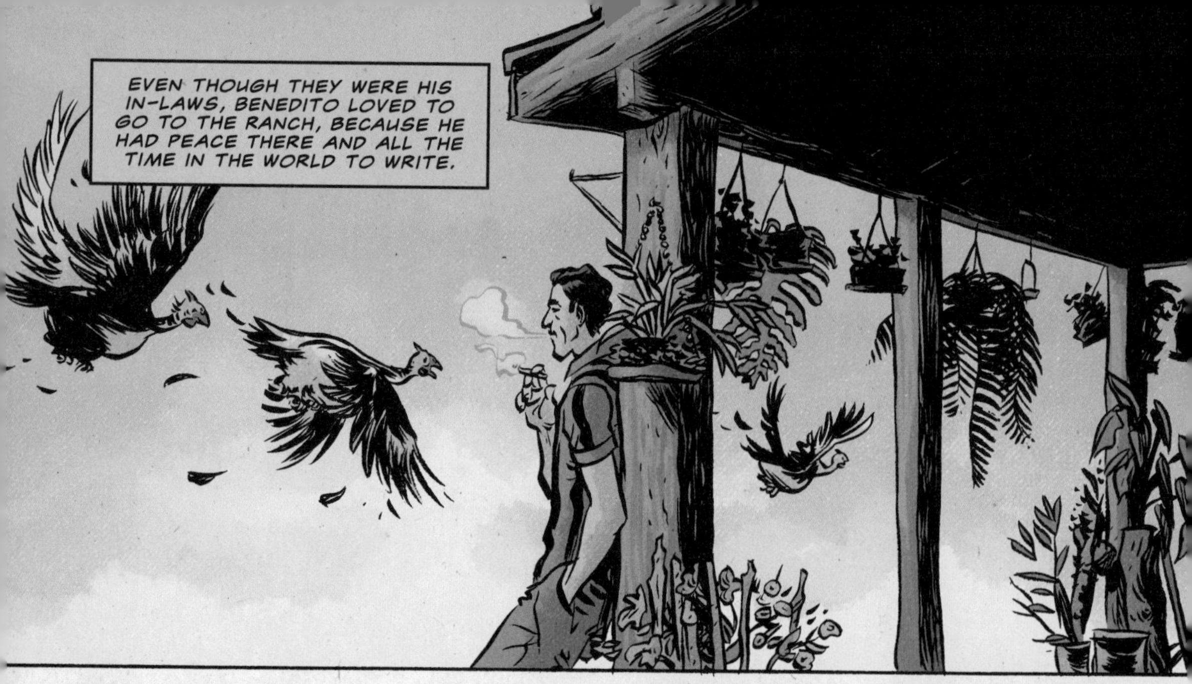
EVEN THOUGH THEY WERE HIS IN-LAWS, BENEDITO LOVED TO GO TO THE RANCH, BECAUSE HE HAD PEACE THERE AND ALL THE TIME IN THE WORLD TO WRITE.

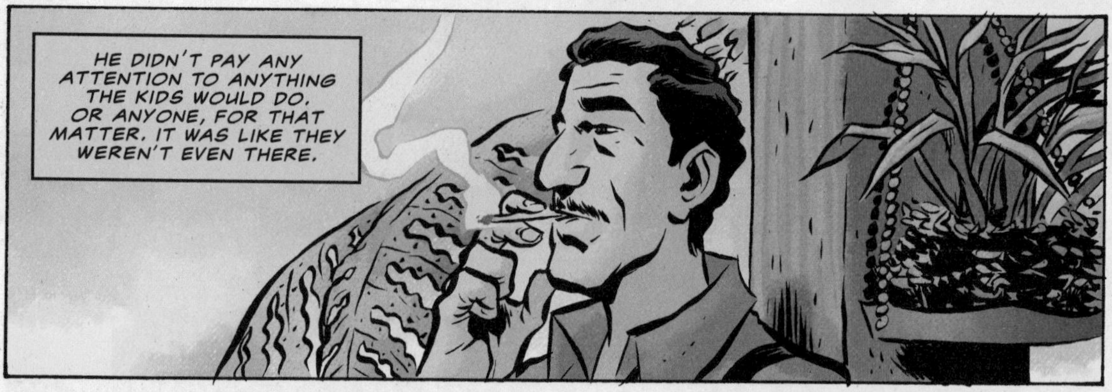
HE DIDN'T PAY ANY ATTENTION TO ANYTHING THE KIDS WOULD DO, OR ANYONE, FOR THAT MATTER. IT WAS LIKE THEY WEREN'T EVEN THERE.

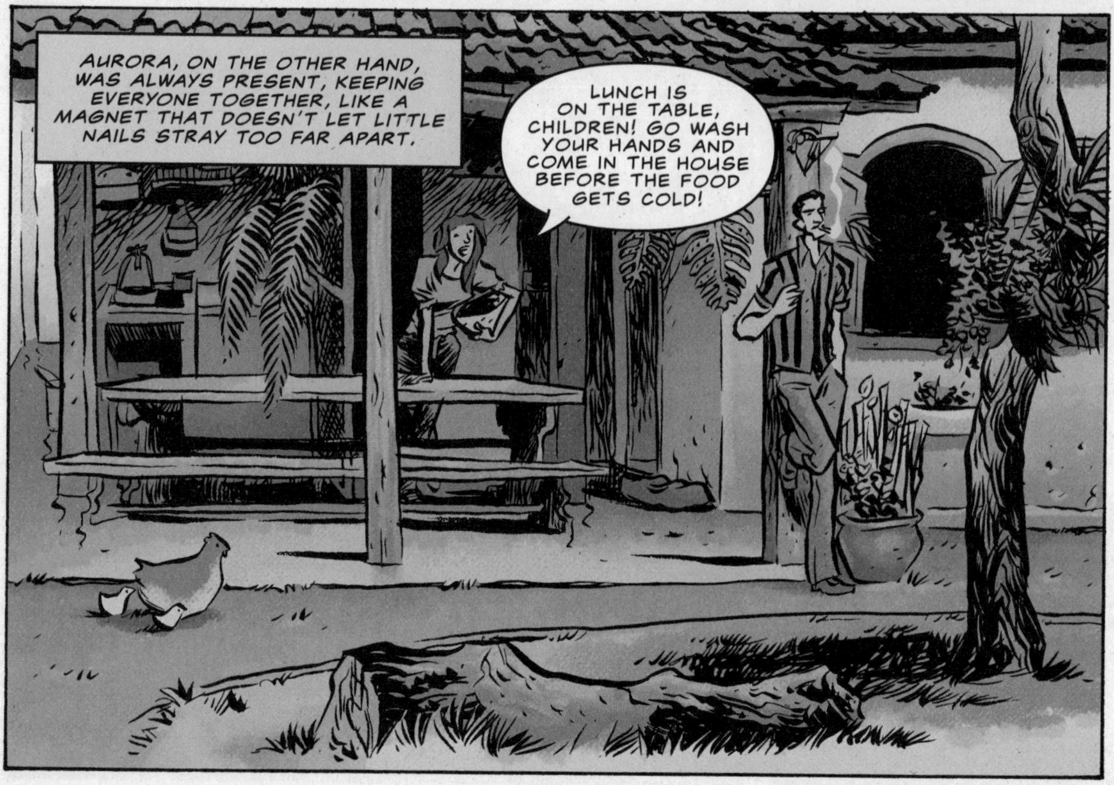
AURORA, ON THE OTHER HAND, WAS ALWAYS PRESENT, KEEPING EVERYONE TOGETHER, LIKE A MAGNET THAT DOESN'T LET LITTLE NAILS STRAY TOO FAR APART.
LUNCH IS ON THE TABLE, CHILDREN! GO WASH YOUR HANDS AND COME IN THE HOUSE BEFORE THE FOOD GETS COLD!

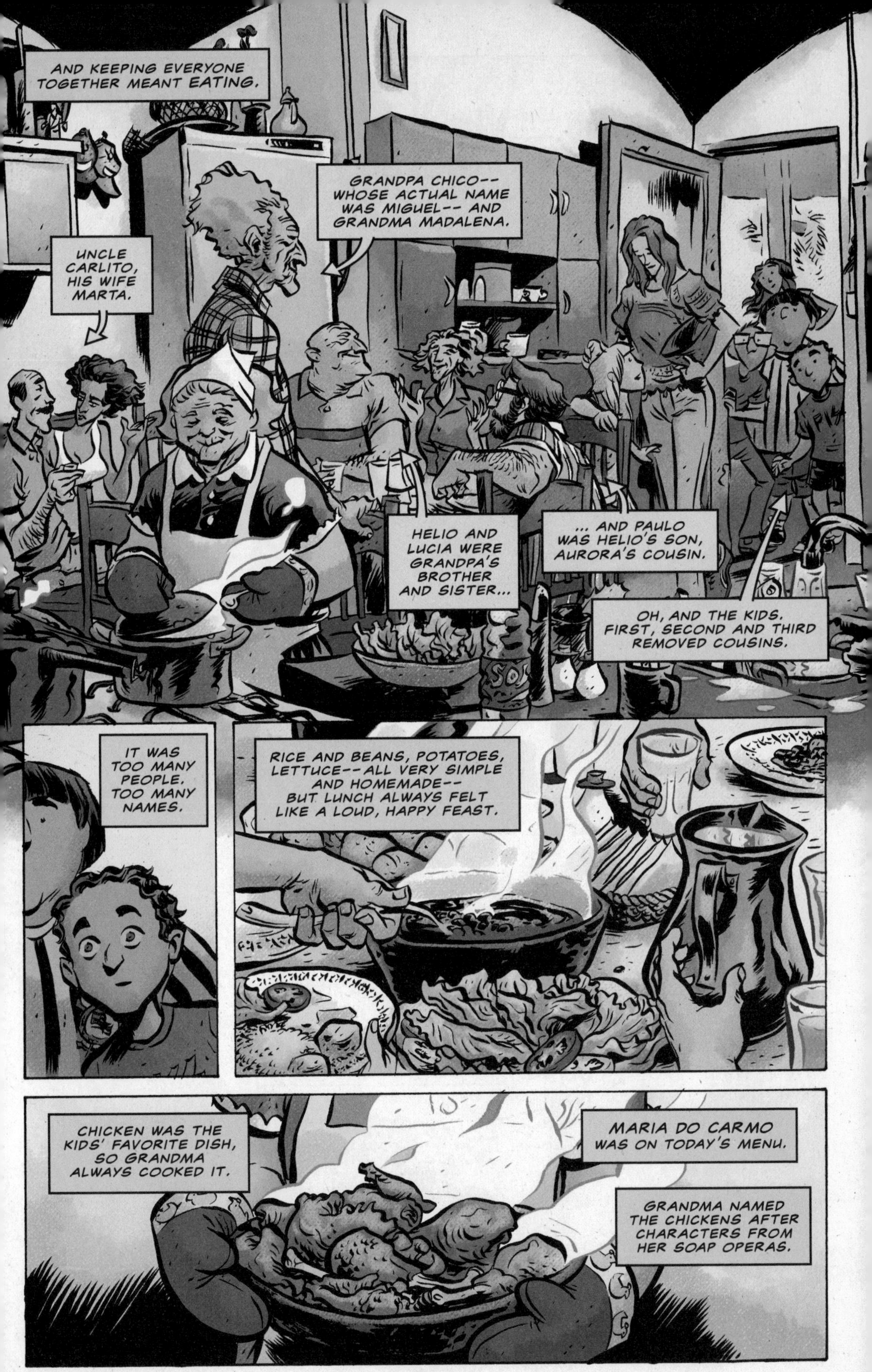
AND KEEPING EVERYONE TOGETHER MEANT EATING.
UNCLE CARLITO, HIS WIFE MARTA.
GRANDPA CHICO-- WHOSE ACTUAL NAME WAS MIGUEL-- AND GRANDMA MADALENA.
HELIO AND LUCIA WERE GRANDPA'S BROTHER AND SISTER...
... AND PAULO WAS HELIO'S SON, AURORA'S COUSIN.
OH, AND THE KIDS. FIRST, SECOND AND THIRD REMOVED COUSINS.
IT WAS TOO MANY PEOPLE. TOO MANY NAMES.
RICE AND BEANS, POTATOES, LETTUCE--ALL VERY SIMPLE AND HOMEMADE-- BUT LUNCH ALWAYS FELT LIKE A LOUD, HAPPY FEAST.
CHICKEN WAS THE KIDS' FAVORITE DISH, SO GRANDMA ALWAYS COOKED IT.
MARIA DO CARMO WAS ON TODAY'S MENU.
GRANDMA NAMED THE CHICKENS AFTER CHARACTERS FROM HER SOAP OPERAS.

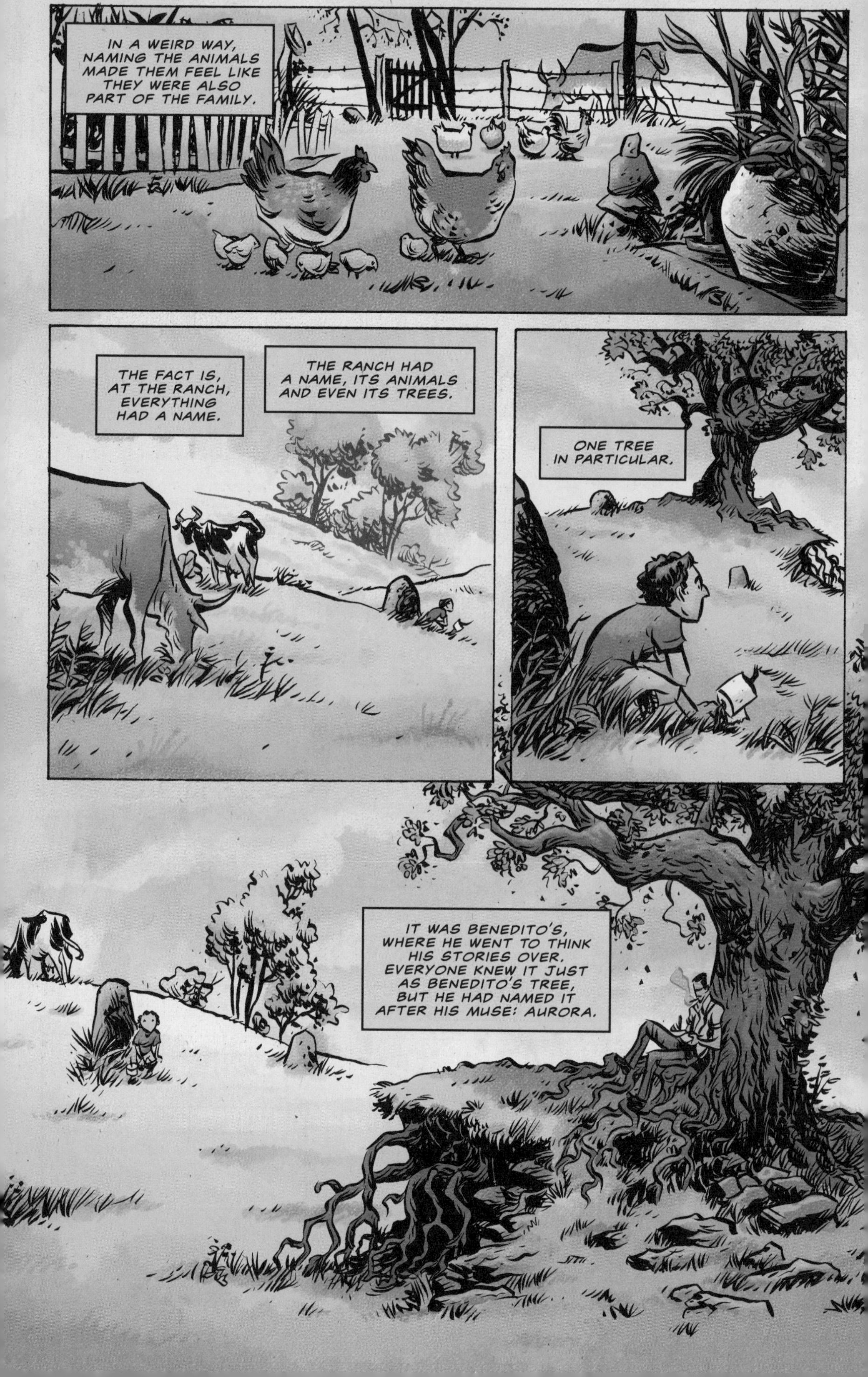
IN A WEIRD WAY, NAMING THE ANIMALS MADE THEM FEEL LIKE THEY WERE ALSO PART OF THE FAMILY.
THE FACT IS, AT THE RANCH, EVERYTHING HAD A NAME.
THE RANCH HAD A NAME, ITS ANIMALS AND EVEN ITS TREES.
ONE TREE IN PARTICULAR.
IT WAS BENEDITO'S, WHERE HE WENT TO THINK HIS STORIES OVER. EVERYONE KNEW IT JUST AS BENEDITO'S TREE, BUT HE HAD NAMED IT AFTER HIS MUSE: AURORA.

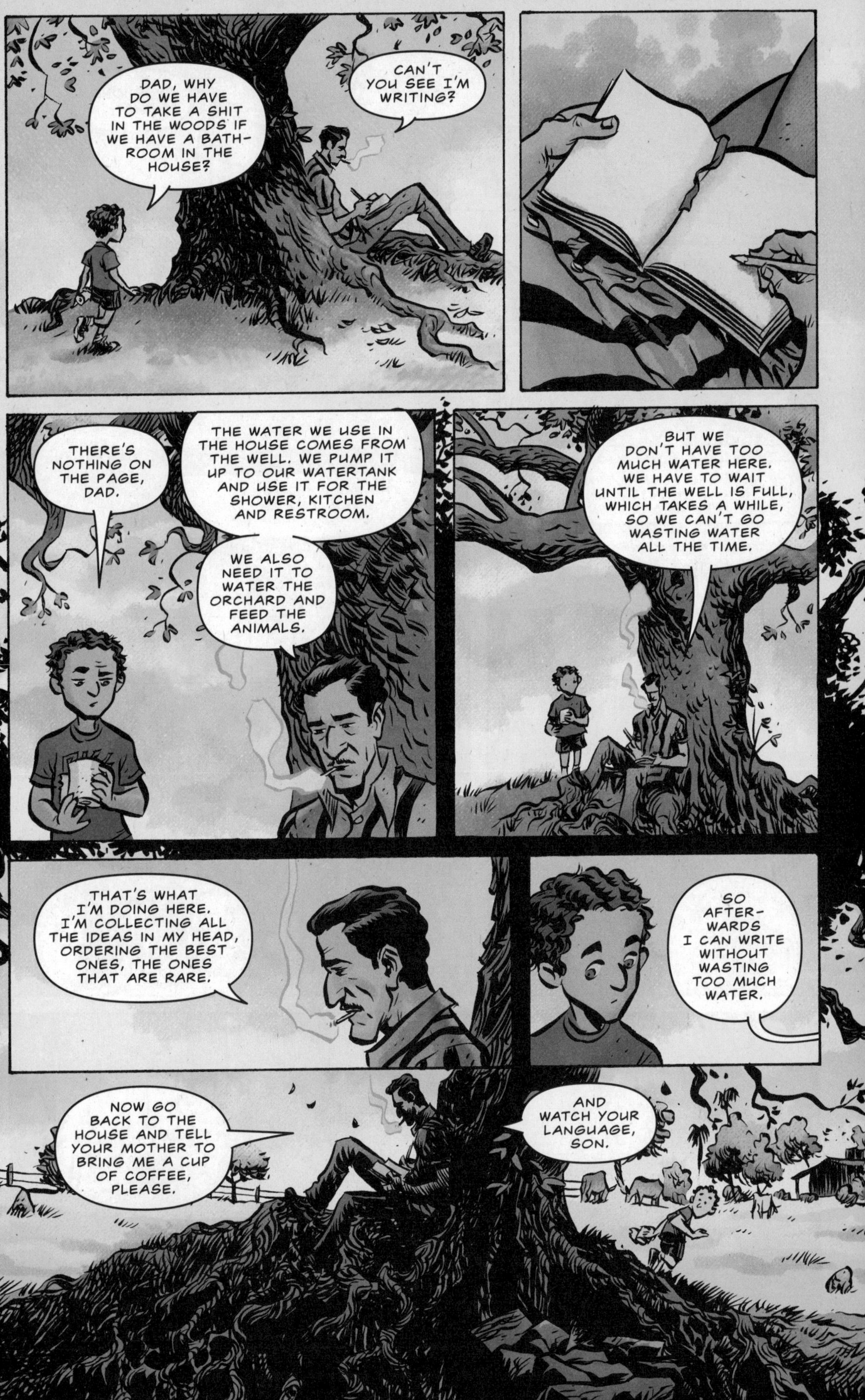
DAD, WHY DO WE HAVE TO TAKE A SHIT IN THE WOODS IF WE HAVE A BATHROOM IN THE HOUSE?
CAN'T YOU SEE I'M WRITING?
THERE'S NOTHING ON THE PAGE, DAD.
THE WATER WE USE IN THE HOUSE COMES FROM THE WELL. WE PUMP IT UP TO OUR WATERTANK AND USE IT FOR THE SHOWER, KITCHEN AND RESTROOM.
WE ALSO NEED IT TO WATER THE ORCHARD AND FEED THE ANIMALS.
BUT WE DON'T HAVE TOO MUCH WATER HERE. WE HAVE TO WAIT UNTIL THE WELL IS FULL, WHICH TAKES A WHILE, SO WE CAN'T GO WASTING WATER ALL THE TIME.
THAT'S WHAT I'M DOING HERE. I'M COLLECTING ALL THE IDEAS IN MY HEAD, ORDERING THE BEST ONES, THE ONES THAT ARE RARE.
SO AFTERWARDS I CAN WRITE WITHOUT WASTING TOO MUCH WATER.
NOW GO BACK TO THE HOUSE AND TELL YOUR MOTHER TO BRING ME A CUP OF COFFEE, PLEASE.
AND WATCH YOUR LANGUAGE, SON.

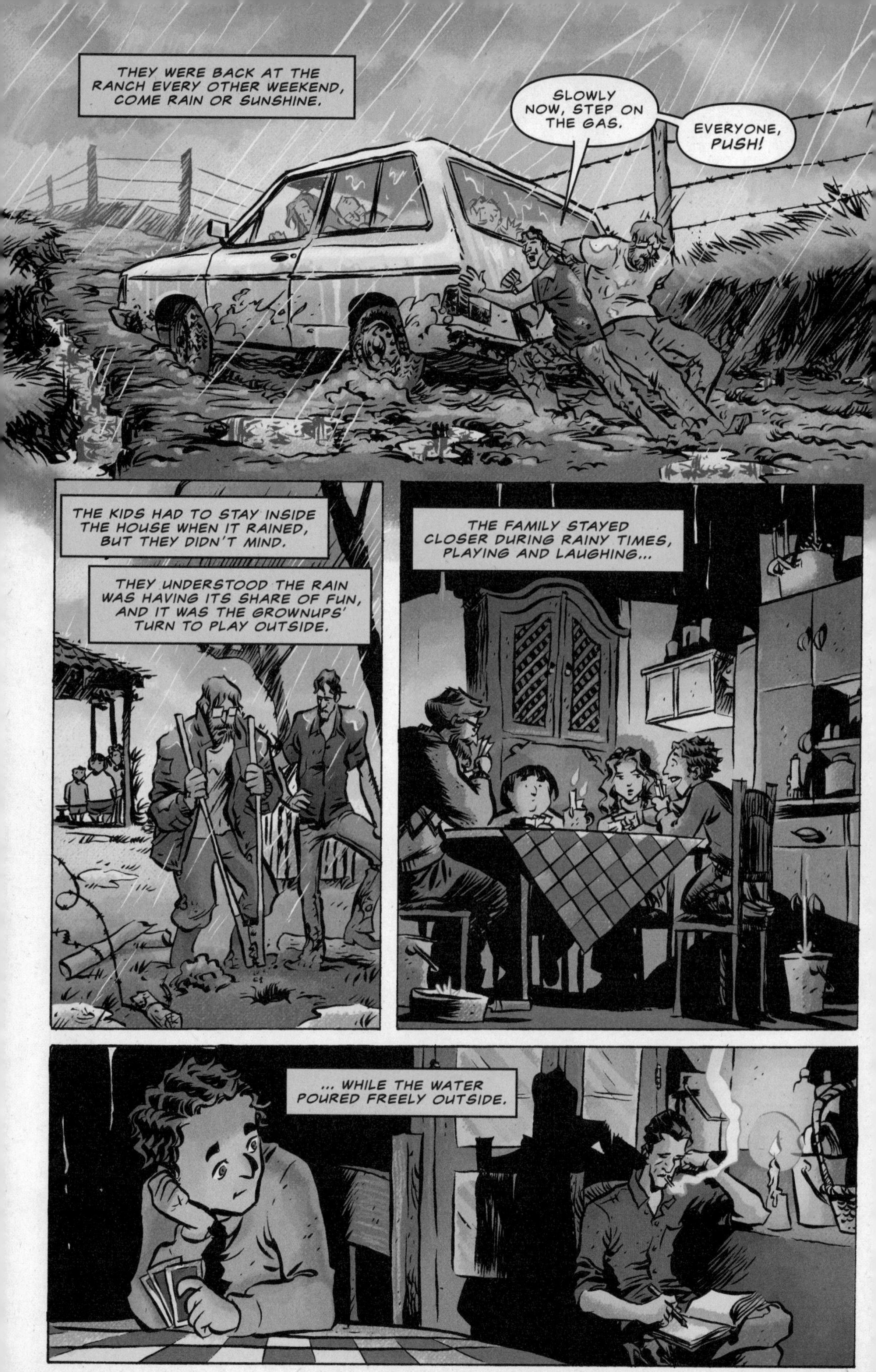
THEY WERE BACK AT THE RANCH EVERY OTHER WEEKEND, COME RAIN OR SUNSHINE.
SLOWLY NOW, STEP ON THE GAS.
EVERYONE, PUSH!
THE KIDS HAD TO STAY INSIDE THE HOUSE WHEN IT RAINED, BUT THEY DIDN'T MIND.
THEY UNDERSTOOD THE RAIN WAS HAVING ITS SHARE OF FUN, AND IT WAS THE GROWNUPS' TURN TO PLAY OUTSIDE.
THE FAMILY STAYED CLOSER DURING RAINY TIMES, PLAYING AND LAUGHING...
... WHILE THE WATER POURED FREELY OUTSIDE.

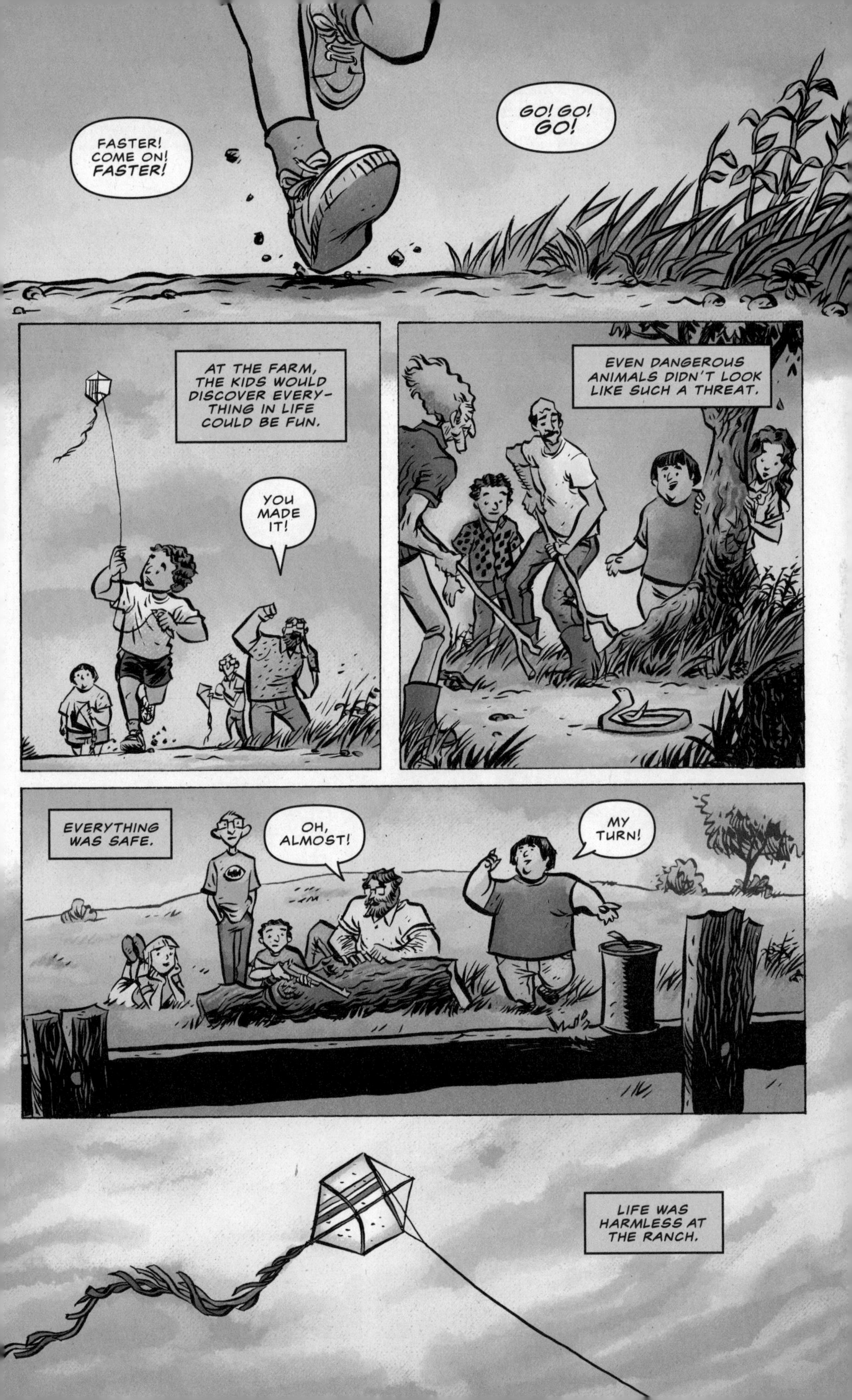
FASTER! COME ON! FASTER!
GO! GO! GO!
AT THE FARM, THE KIDS WOULD DISCOVER EVERY-THING IN LIFE COULD BE FUN.
YOU MADE IT!
EVEN DANGEROUS ANIMALS DIDN'T LOOK LIKE SUCH A THREAT.
EVERYTHING WAS SAFE.
OH, ALMOST!
MY TURN!
LIFE WAS HARMLESS AT THE RANCH.

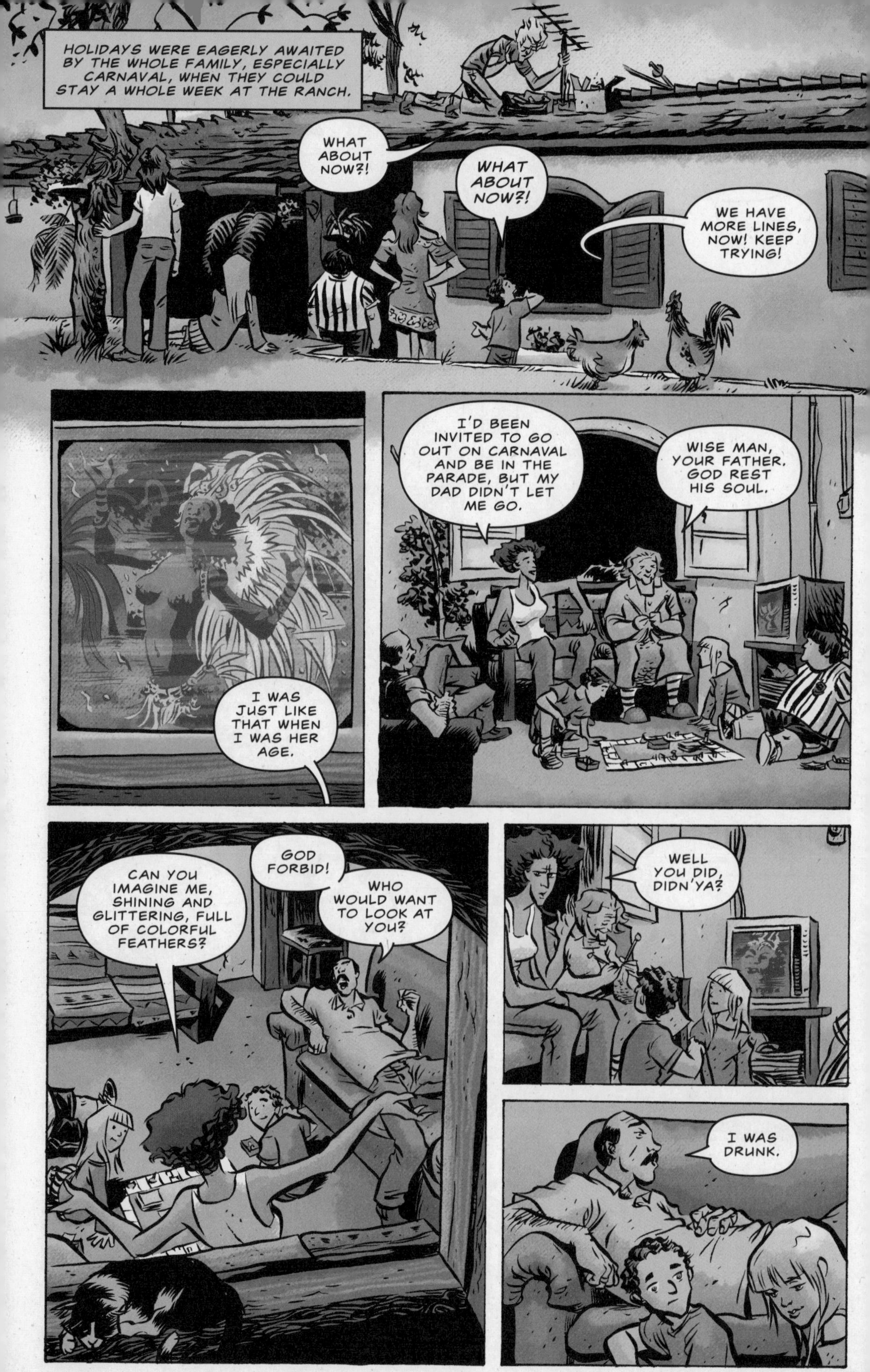
HOLIDAYS WERE EAGERLY AWAITED BY THE WHOLE FAMILY, ESPECIALLY CARNAVAL, WHEN THEY COULD STAY A WHOLE WEEK AT THE RANCH.
WHAT ABOUT NOW?!
WHAT ABOUT NOW?!
WE HAVE MORE LINES, NOW! KEEP TRYING!
I WAS JUST LIKE THAT WHEN I WAS HER AGE.
I'D BEEN INVITED TO GO OUT ON CARNAVAL AND BE IN THE PARADE, BUT MY DAD DIDN'T LET ME GO.
WISE MAN, YOUR FATHER. GOD REST HIS SOUL.
CAN YOU IMAGINE ME, SHINING AND GLITTERING, FULL OF COLORFUL FEATHERS?
GOD FORBID!
WHO WOULD WANT TO LOOK AT YOU?
WELL YOU DID, DIDN'YA?
I WAS DRUNK.

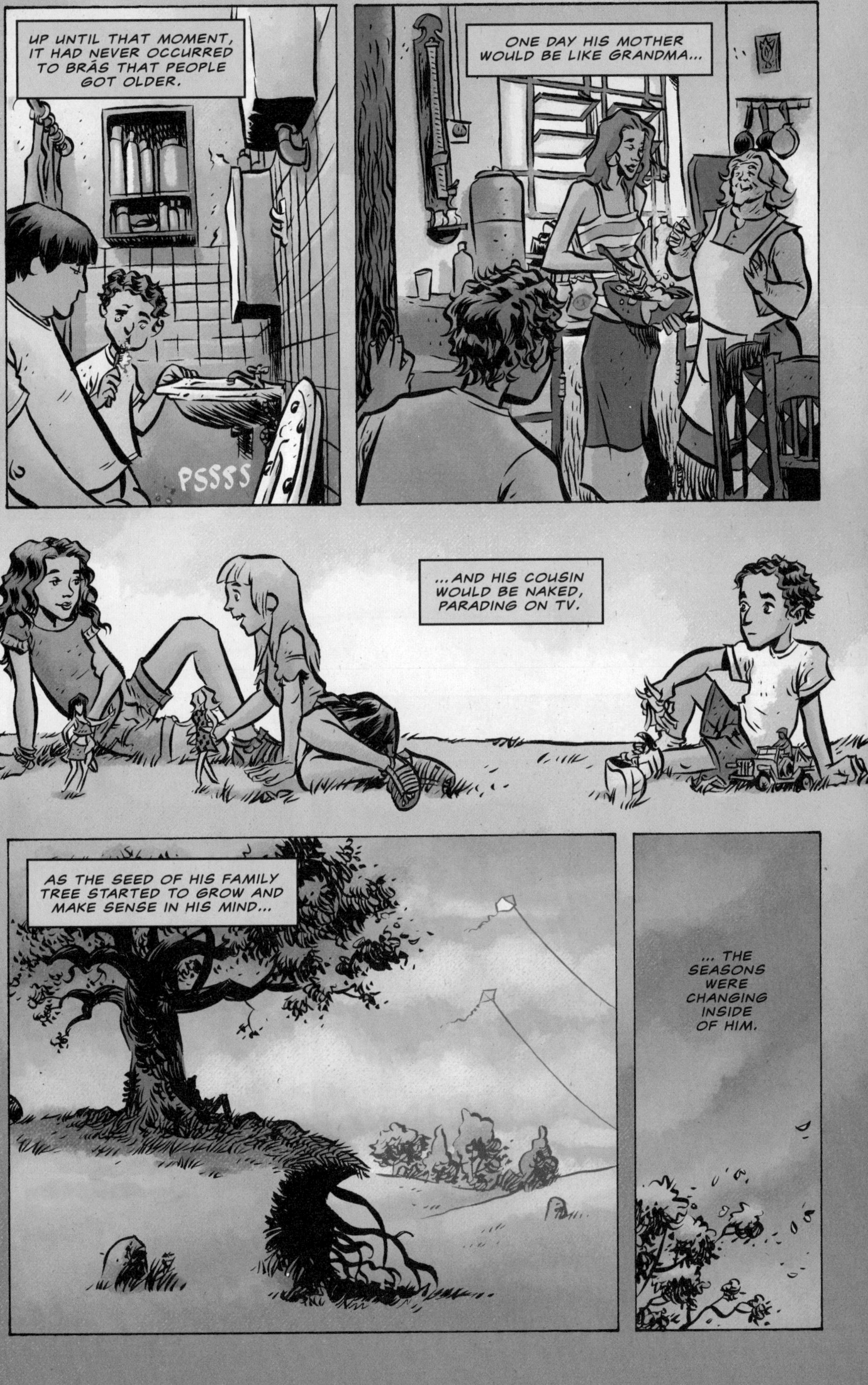
UP UNTIL THAT MOMENT, IT HAD NEVER OCCURRED TO BRÃS THAT PEOPLE GOT OLDER.
PSSSS
ONE DAY HIS MOTHER WOULD BE LIKE GRANDMA...
...AND HIS COUSIN WOULD BE NAKED, PARADING ON TV.
AS THE SEED OF HIS FAMILY TREE STARTED TO GROW AND MAKE SENSE IN HIS MIND...
... THE SEASONS WERE CHANGING INSIDE OF HIM.

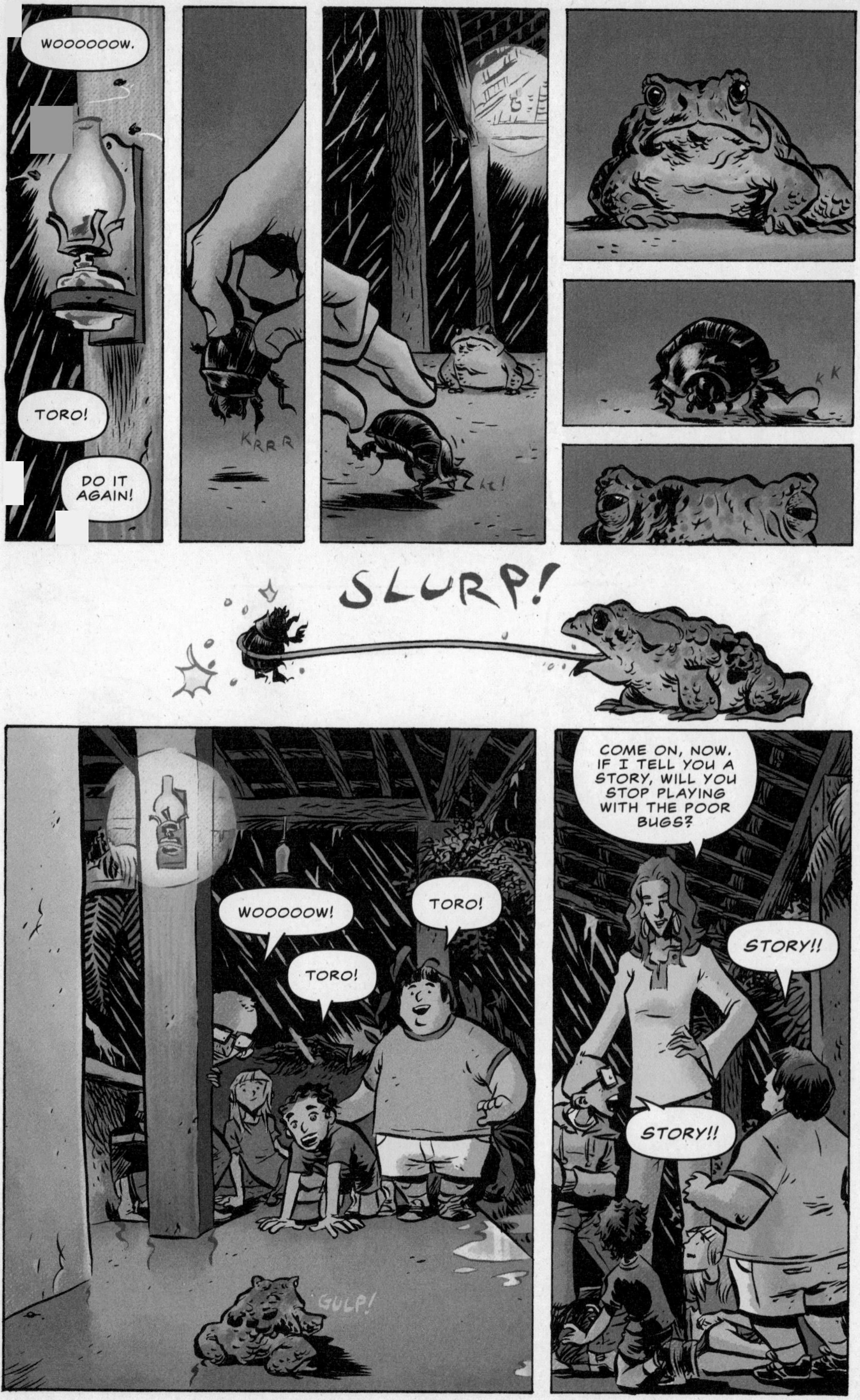
WOOOOOOW.
TORO!
DO IT AGAIN!
KRRR
KK
SLURP!
WOOOOOW!
TORO!
TORO!
GULP!
COME ON, NOW. IF I TELL YOU A STORY, WILL YOU STOP PLAYING WITH THE POOR BUGS?
STORY!!
STORY!!

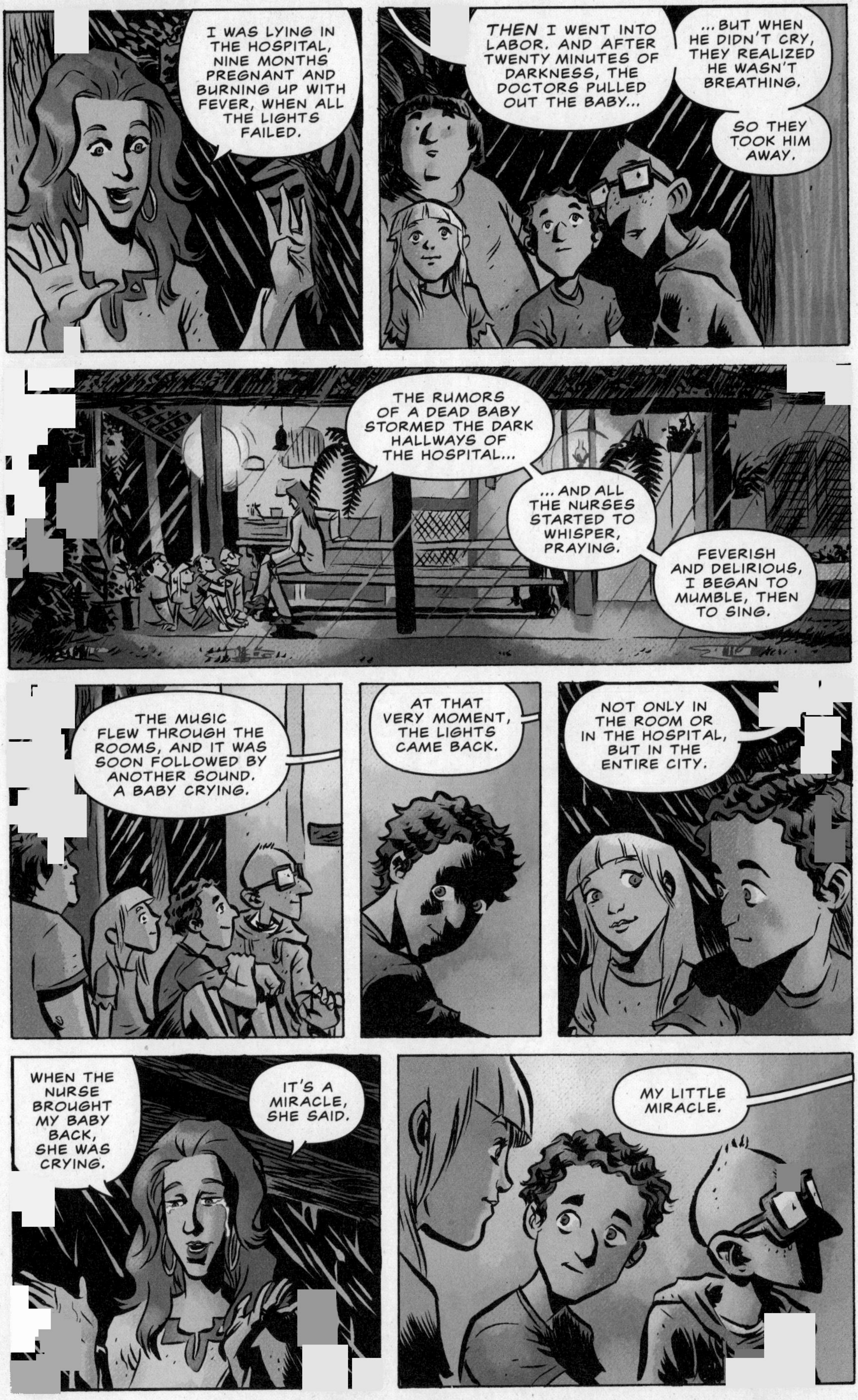
I WAS LYING IN THE HOSPITAL, NINE MONTHS PREGNANT AND BURNING UP WITH FEVER, WHEN ALL THE LIGHTS FAILED.
THEN I WENT INTO LABOR. AND AFTER TWENTY MINUTES OF DARKNESS, THE DOCTORS PULLED OUT THE BABY...
...BUT WHEN HE DIDN'T CRY, THEY REALIZED HE WASN'T BREATHING.
SO THEY TOOK HIM AWAY.
THE RUMORS OF A DEAD BABY STORMED THE DARK HALLWAYS OF THE HOSPITAL...
...AND ALL THE NURSES STARTED TO WHISPER, PRAYING.
FEVERISH AND DELIRIOUS, I BEGAN TO MUMBLE, THEN TO SING.
THE MUSIC FLEW THROUGH THE ROOMS, AND IT WAS SOON FOLLOWED BY ANOTHER SOUND. A BABY CRYING.
AT THAT VERY MOMENT, THE LIGHTS CAME BACK.
NOT ONLY IN THE ROOM OR IN THE HOSPITAL, BUT IN THE ENTIRE CITY.
WHEN THE NURSE BROUGHT MY BABY BACK, SHE WAS CRYING.
IT'S A MIRACLE, SHE SAID.
MY LITTLE MIRACLE.

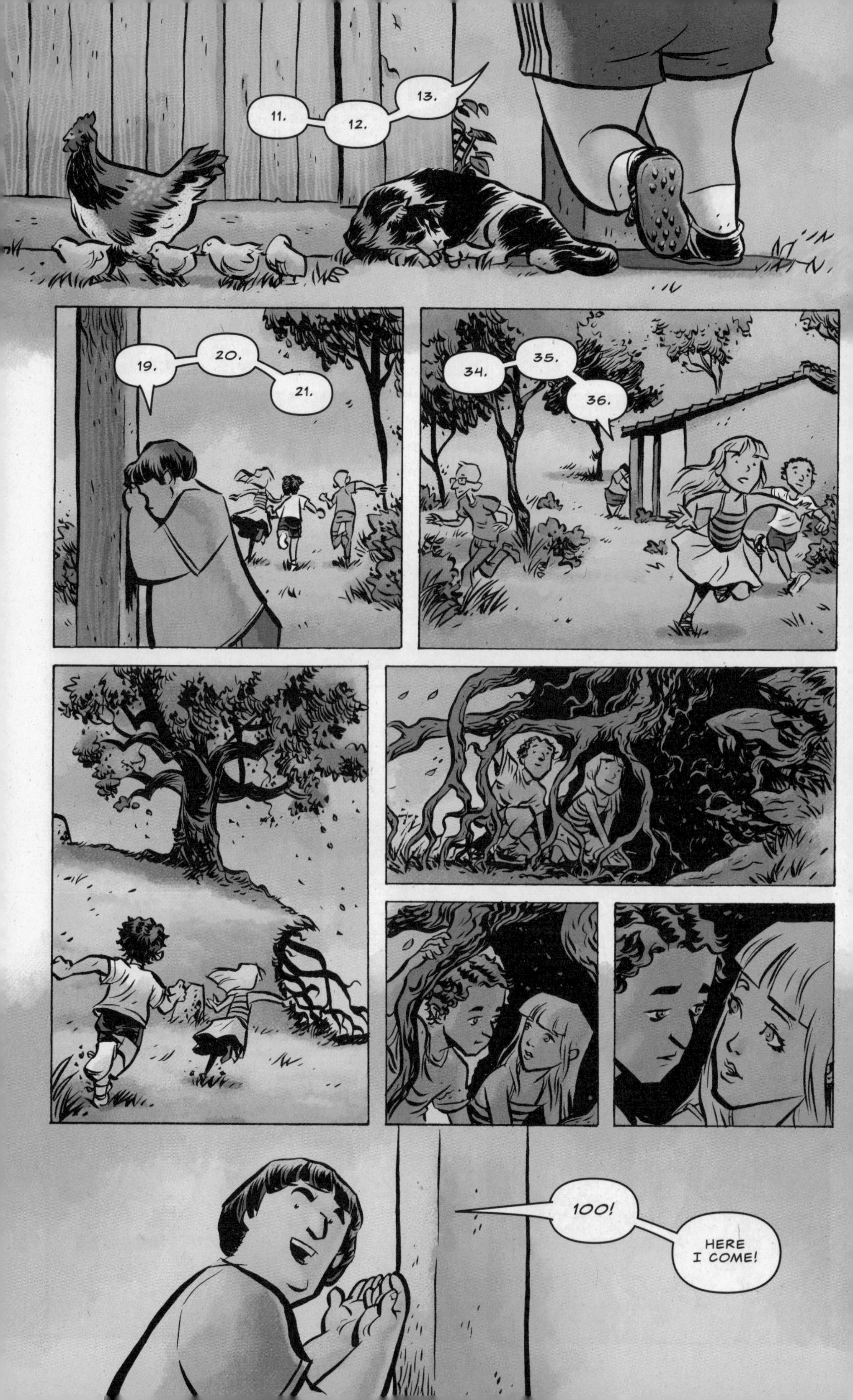
11.
12.
13.
19.
20.
21.
34.
35.
36.
100!
HERE I COME!

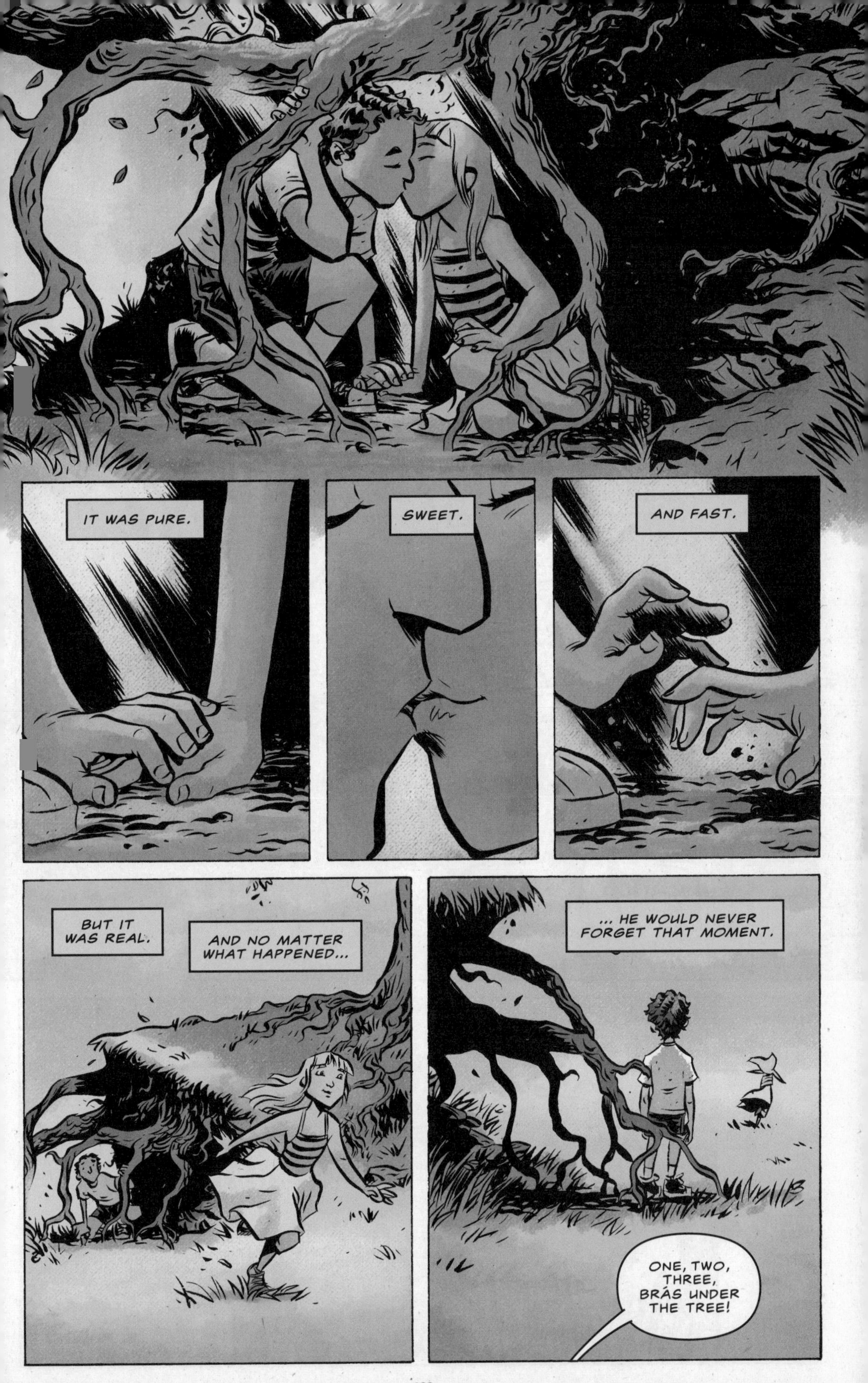
IT WAS PURE.
SWEET.
AND FAST.
BUT IT WAS REAL.
AND NO MATTER WHAT HAPPENED...
... HE WOULD NEVER FORGET THAT MOMENT.
ONE, TWO, THREE, BRÁS UNDER THE TREE!

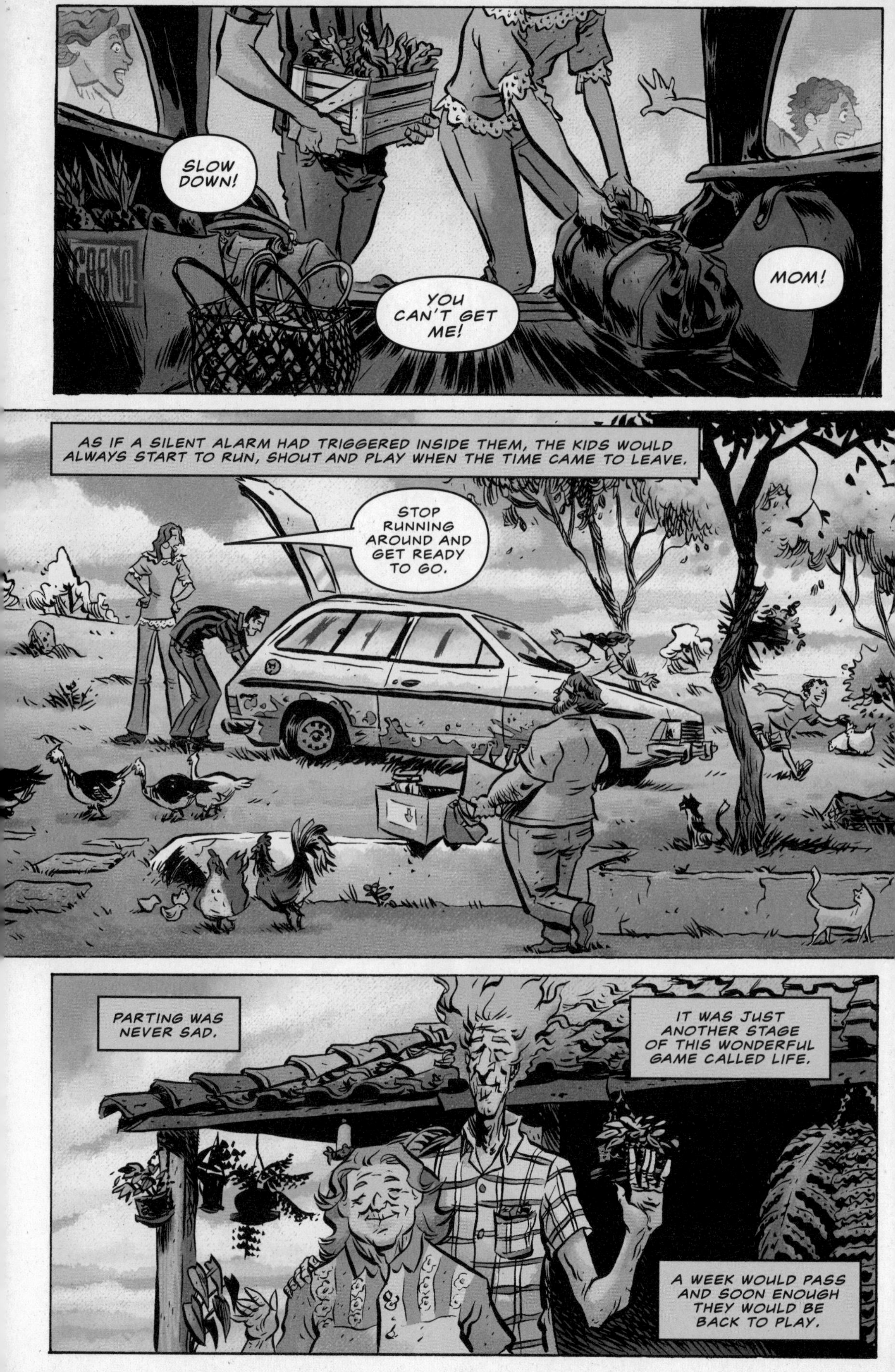
SLOW DOWN!
YOU CAN'T GET ME!
MOM!
AS IF A SILENT ALARM HAD TRIGGERED INSIDE THEM, THE KIDS WOULD ALWAYS START TO RUN, SHOUT AND PLAY WHEN THE TIME CAME TO LEAVE.
STOP RUNNING AROUND AND GET READY TO GO.
PARTING WAS NEVER SAD.
IT WAS JUST ANOTHER STAGE OF THIS WONDERFUL GAME CALLED LIFE.
A WEEK WOULD PASS AND SOON ENOUGH THEY WOULD BE BACK TO PLAY.

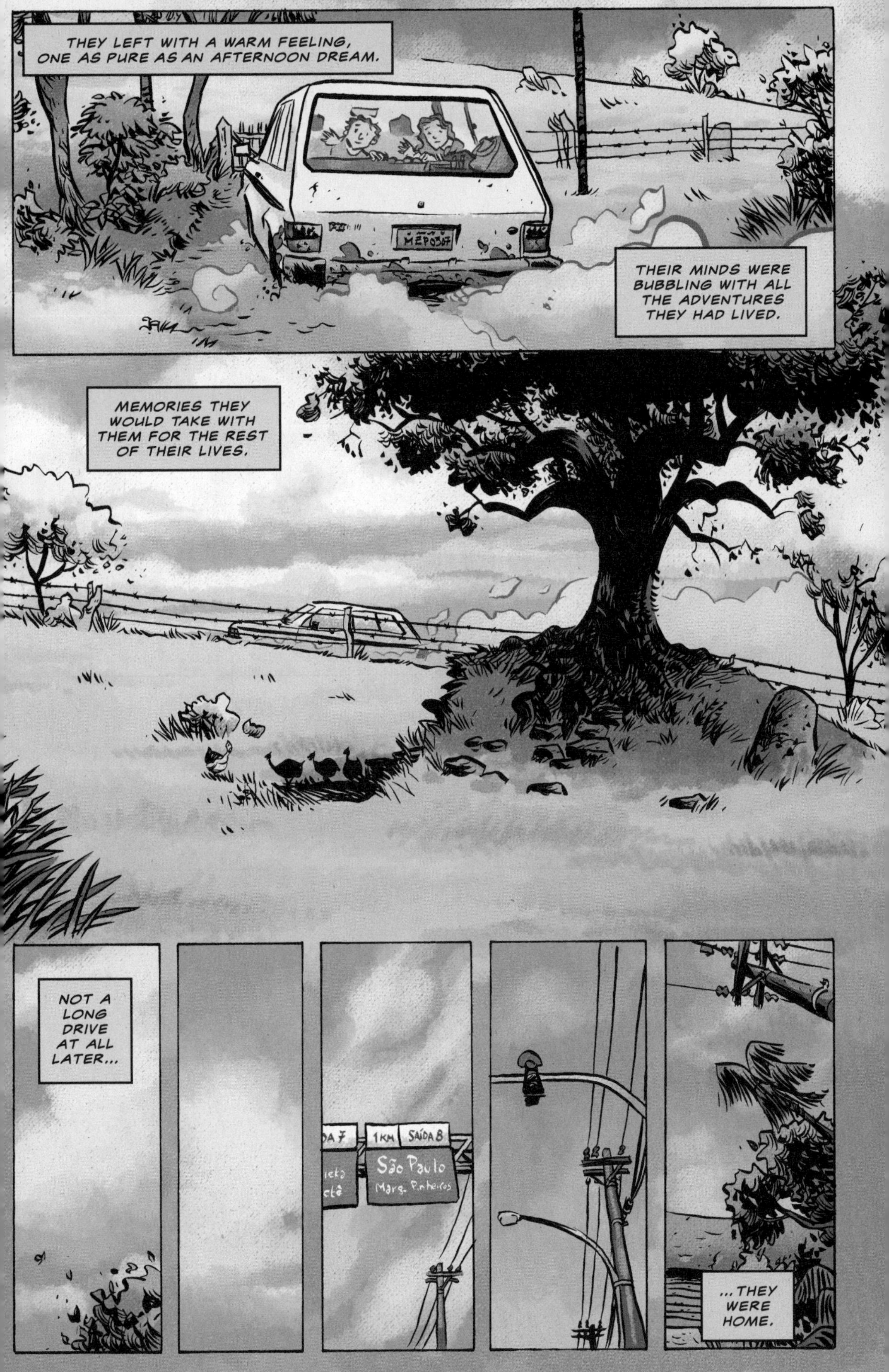
THEY LEFT WITH A WARM FEELING, ONE AS PURE AS AN AFTERNOON DREAM.
MEPO307
THEIR MINDS WERE BUBBLING WITH ALL THE ADVENTURES THEY HAD LIVED.
MEMORIES THEY WOULD TAKE WITH THEM FOR THE REST OF THEIR LIVES.
NOT A LONG DRIVE AT ALL LATER...
1KM SAÍDA 8
São Paulo
Marg. Pinheiros
...THEY WERE HOME.

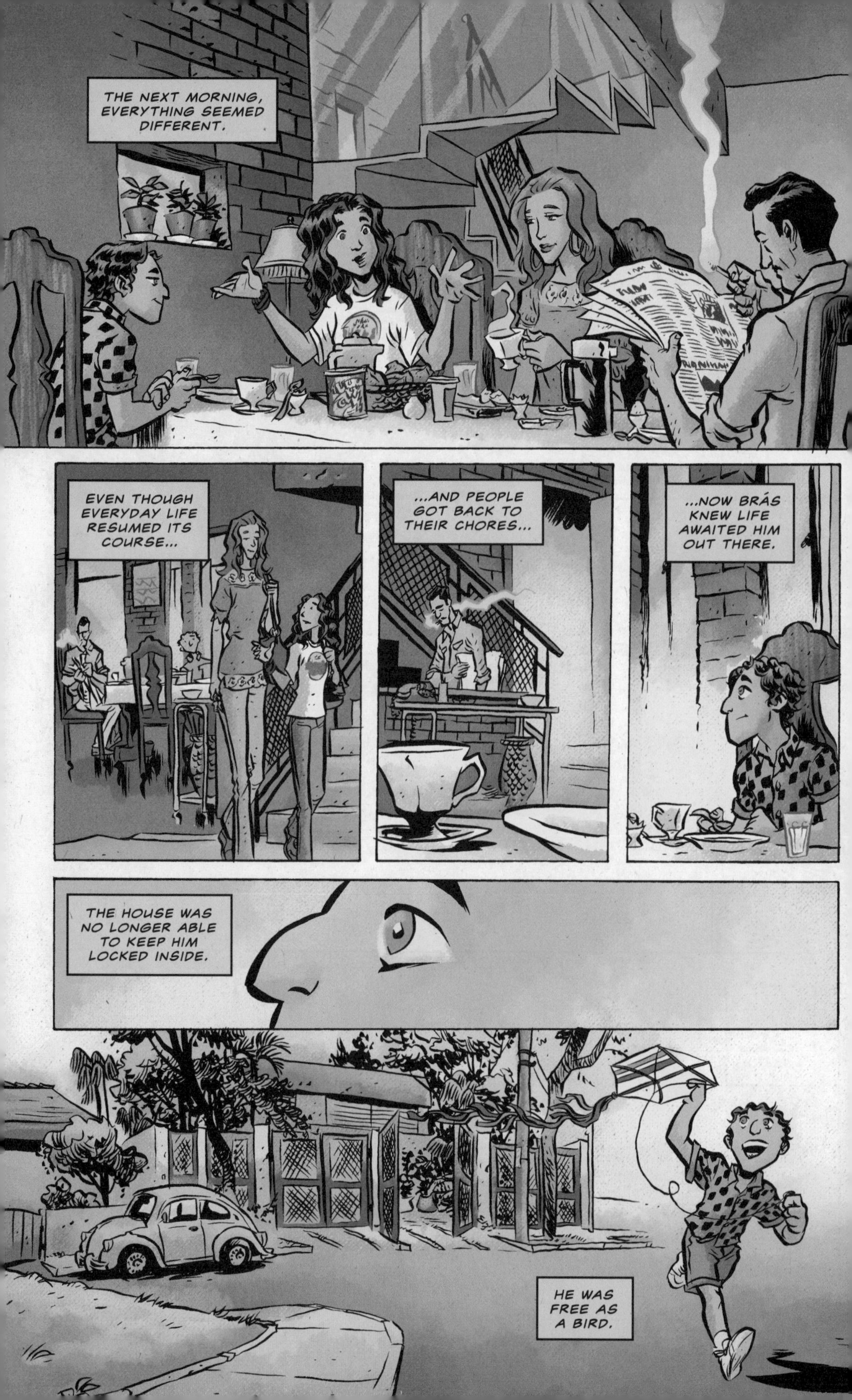
THE NEXT MORNING, EVERYTHING SEEMED DIFFERENT.
EVEN THOUGH EVERYDAY LIFE RESUMED ITS COURSE...
...AND PEOPLE GOT BACK TO THEIR CHORES...
...NOW BRÁS KNEW LIFE AWAITED HIM OUT THERE.
THE HOUSE WAS NO LONGER ABLE TO KEEP HIM LOCKED INSIDE.
HE WAS FREE AS A BIRD.

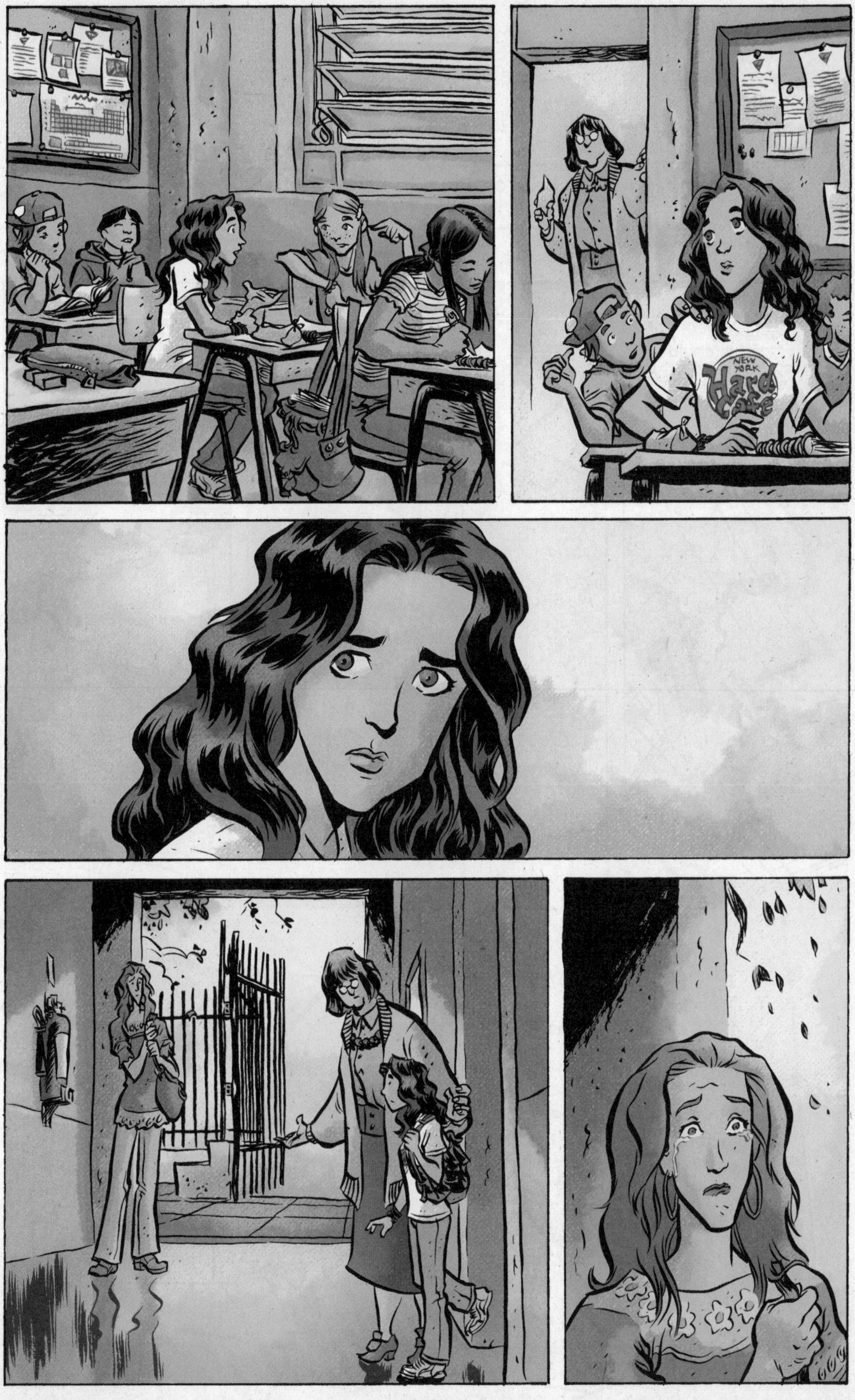
NEW YORK
Hard
Cafe

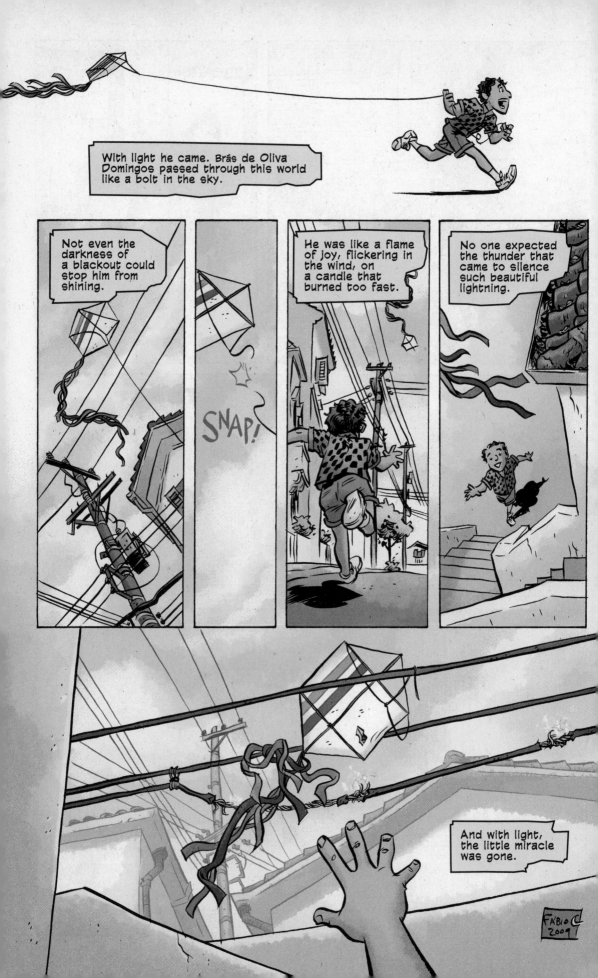

With light he came. Brás de Oliva Domingos passed through this world like a bolt in the sky.

Not even the darkness of a blackout could stop him from shining.

SNAP!

He was like a flame of joy, flickering in the wind, on a candle that burned too fast.

No one expected the thunder that came to silence such beautiful lightning.

And with light, the little miracle was gone.

FABIO
2009

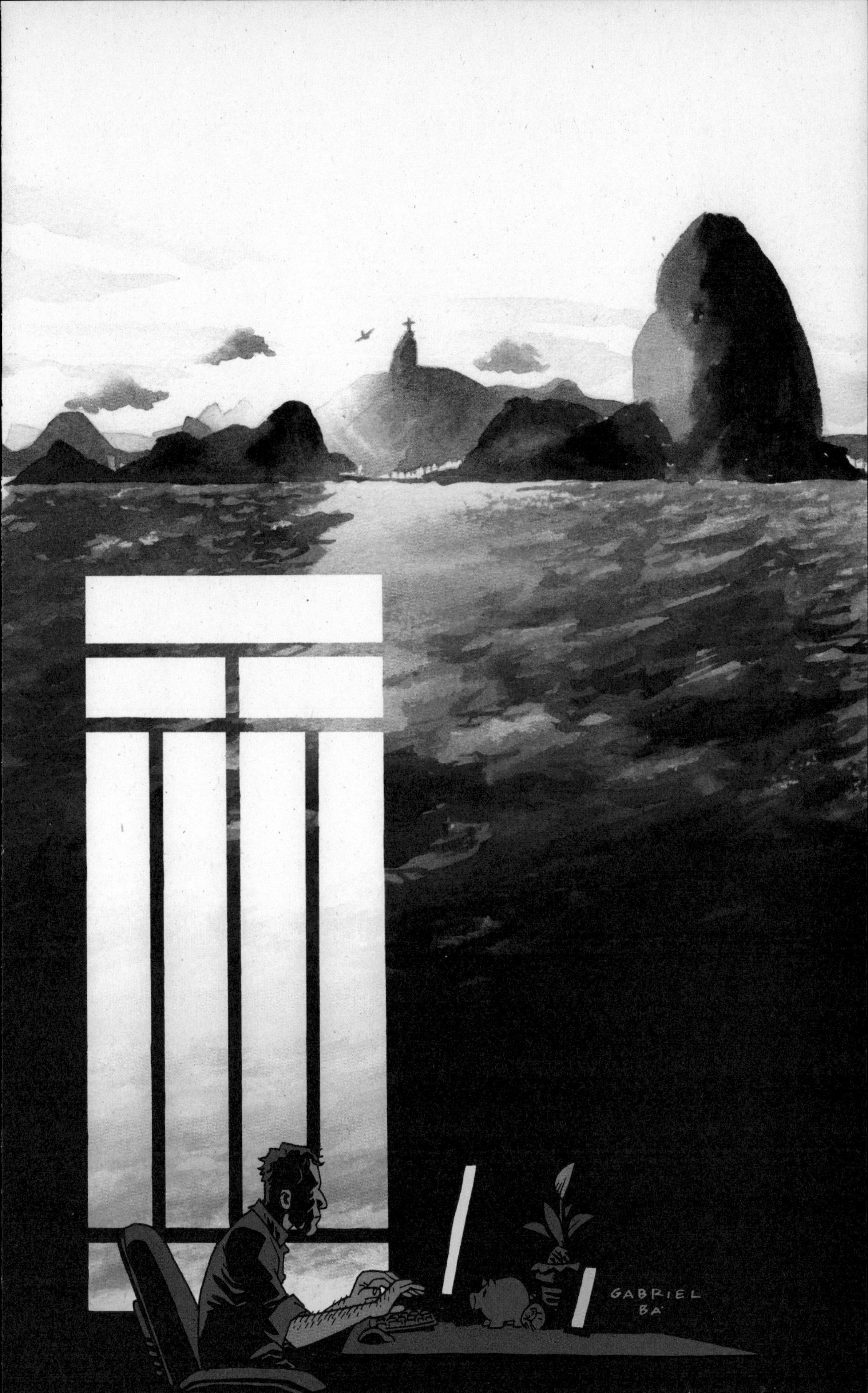
GABRIEL
BÁ

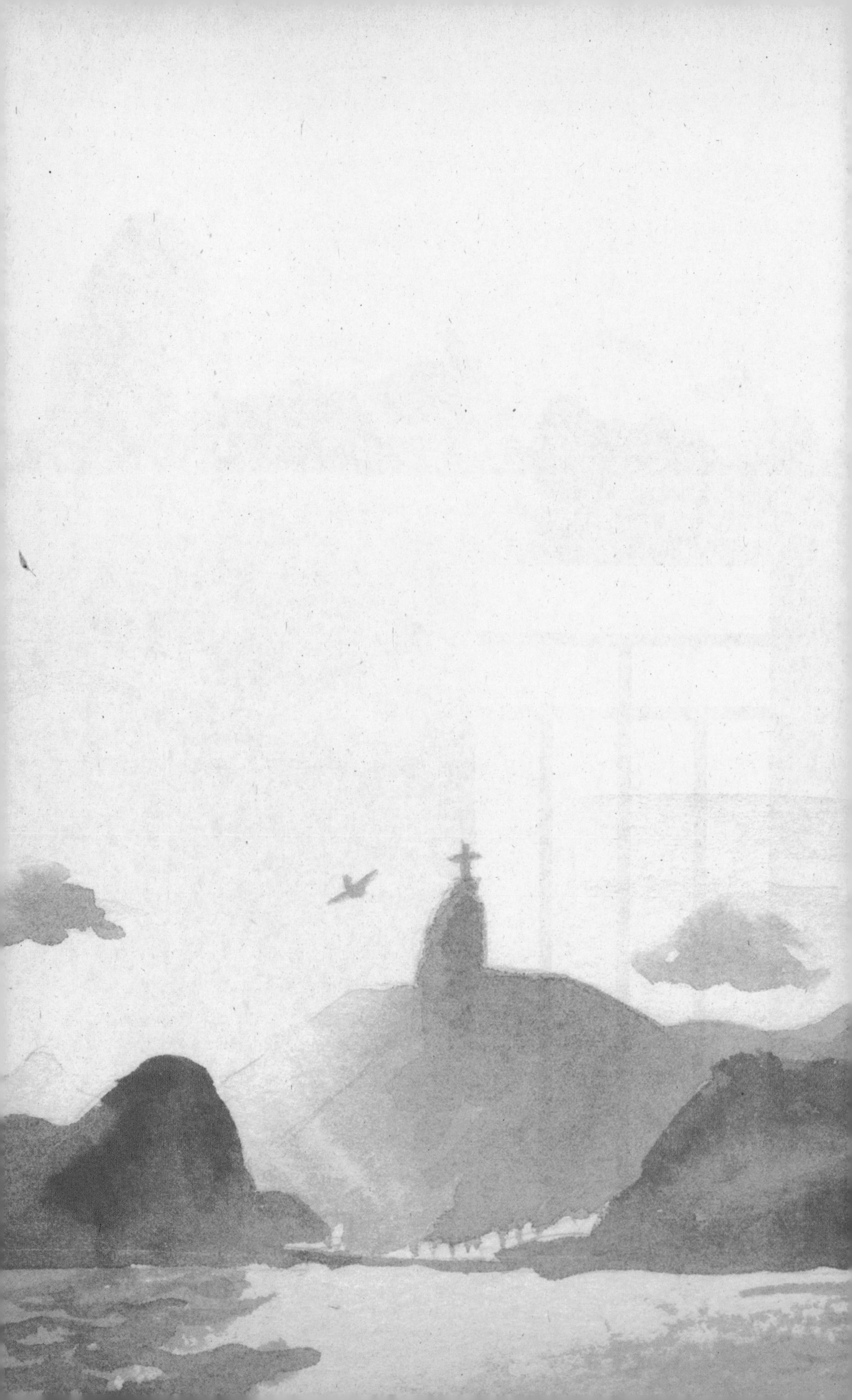

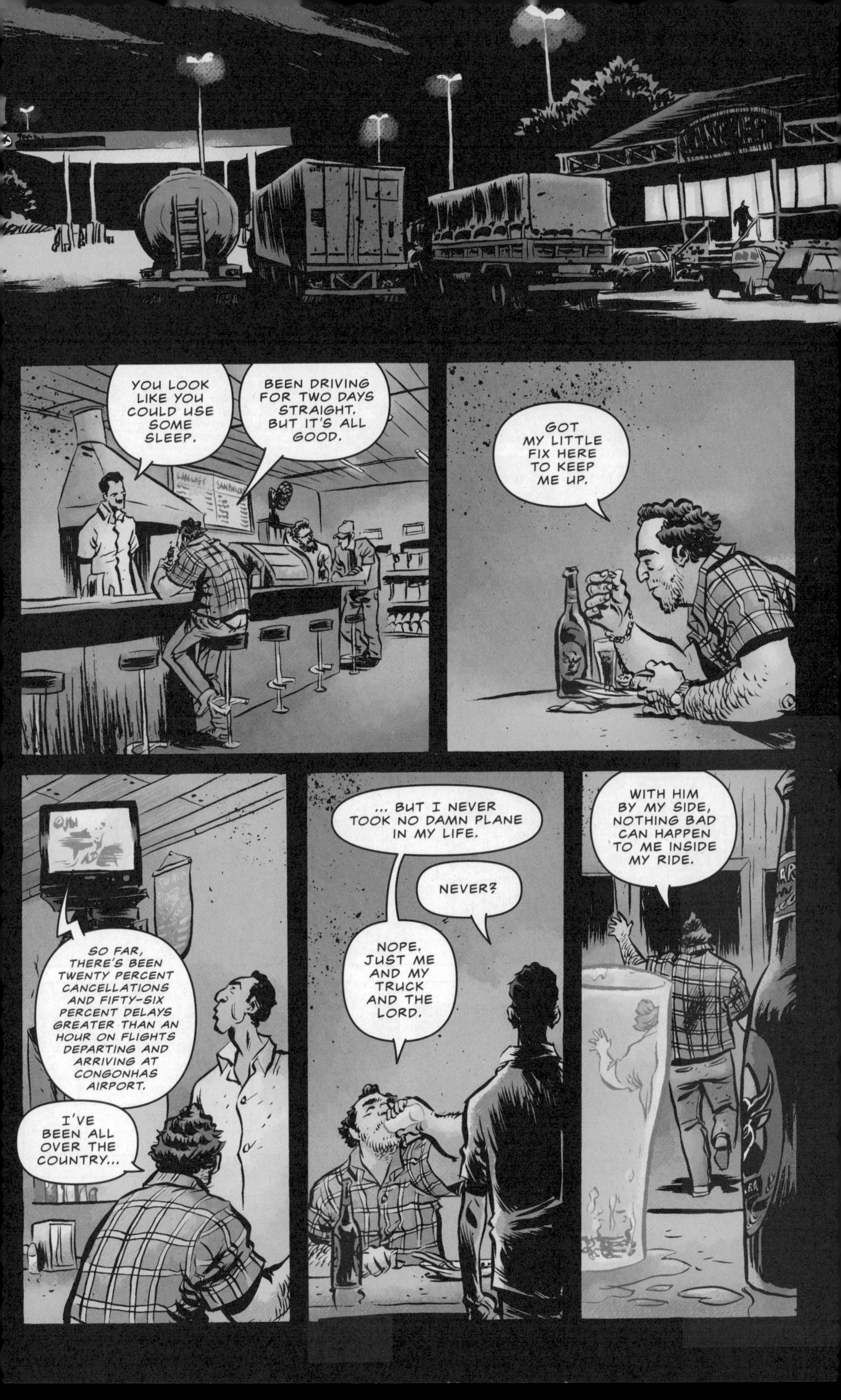
YOU LOOK LIKE YOU COULD USE SOME SLEEP.
BEEN DRIVING FOR TWO DAYS STRAIGHT. BUT IT'S ALL GOOD.
GOT MY LITTLE FIX HERE TO KEEP ME UP.
SO FAR, THERE'S BEEN TWENTY PERCENT CANCELLATIONS AND FIFTY-SIX PERCENT DELAYS GREATER THAN AN HOUR ON FLIGHTS DEPARTING AND ARRIVING AT CONGONHAS AIRPORT.
I'VE BEEN ALL OVER THE COUNTRY...
... BUT I NEVER TOOK NO DAMN PLANE IN MY LIFE.
NEVER?
NOPE. JUST ME AND MY TRUCK AND THE LORD.
WITH HIM BY MY SIDE, NOTHING BAD CAN HAPPEN TO ME INSIDE MY RIDE.

One month earlier...

CIA FLIGHT	VÔO	SAÍDA	DESTINO TO	PORTÃO GATE
06	4200	07:00	FLORIANÓPOLIS	2
06	1252	07:05	SALVADOR	10
TAM	3905	07:15	SÃO PAULO	6
ARIG	3251	07:25	CURITIBA	8
TAM	3024	07:30	BRASILIA	7
			SALVADOR	10
			ÃO PAULO	6

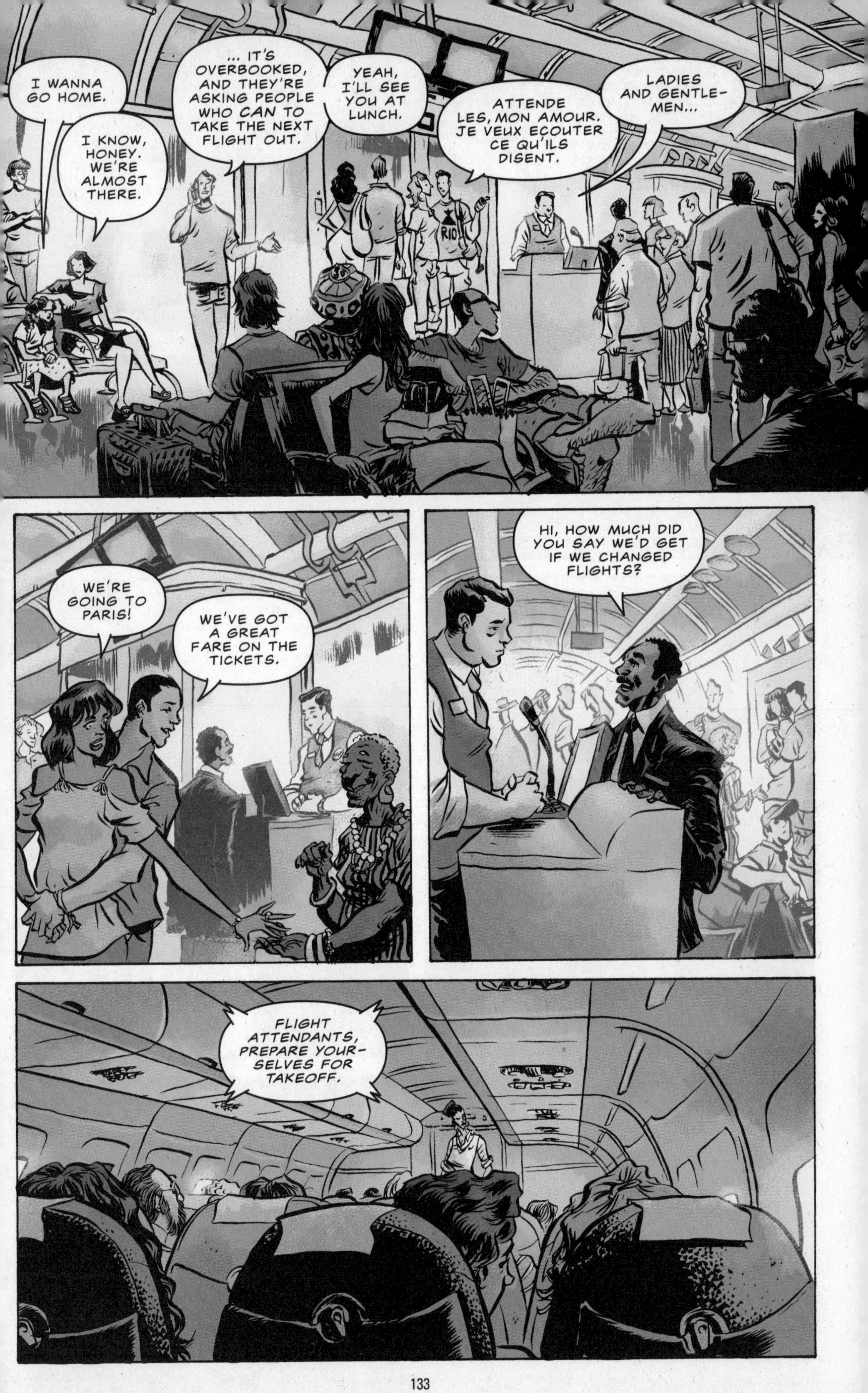
I WANNA GO HOME.
I KNOW, HONEY. WE'RE ALMOST THERE.
... IT'S OVERBOOKED, AND THEY'RE ASKING PEOPLE WHO CAN TO TAKE THE NEXT FLIGHT OUT.
YEAH, I'LL SEE YOU AT LUNCH.
ATTENDE LES, MON AMOUR. JE VEUX ECOUTER CE QU'ILS DISENT.
LADIES AND GENTLE-MEN...
RIO
WE'RE GOING TO PARIS!
WE'VE GOT A GREAT FARE ON THE TICKETS.
HI, HOW MUCH DID YOU SAY WE'D GET IF WE CHANGED FLIGHTS?
FLIGHT ATTENDANTS, PREPARE YOUR-SELVES FOR TAKEOFF.

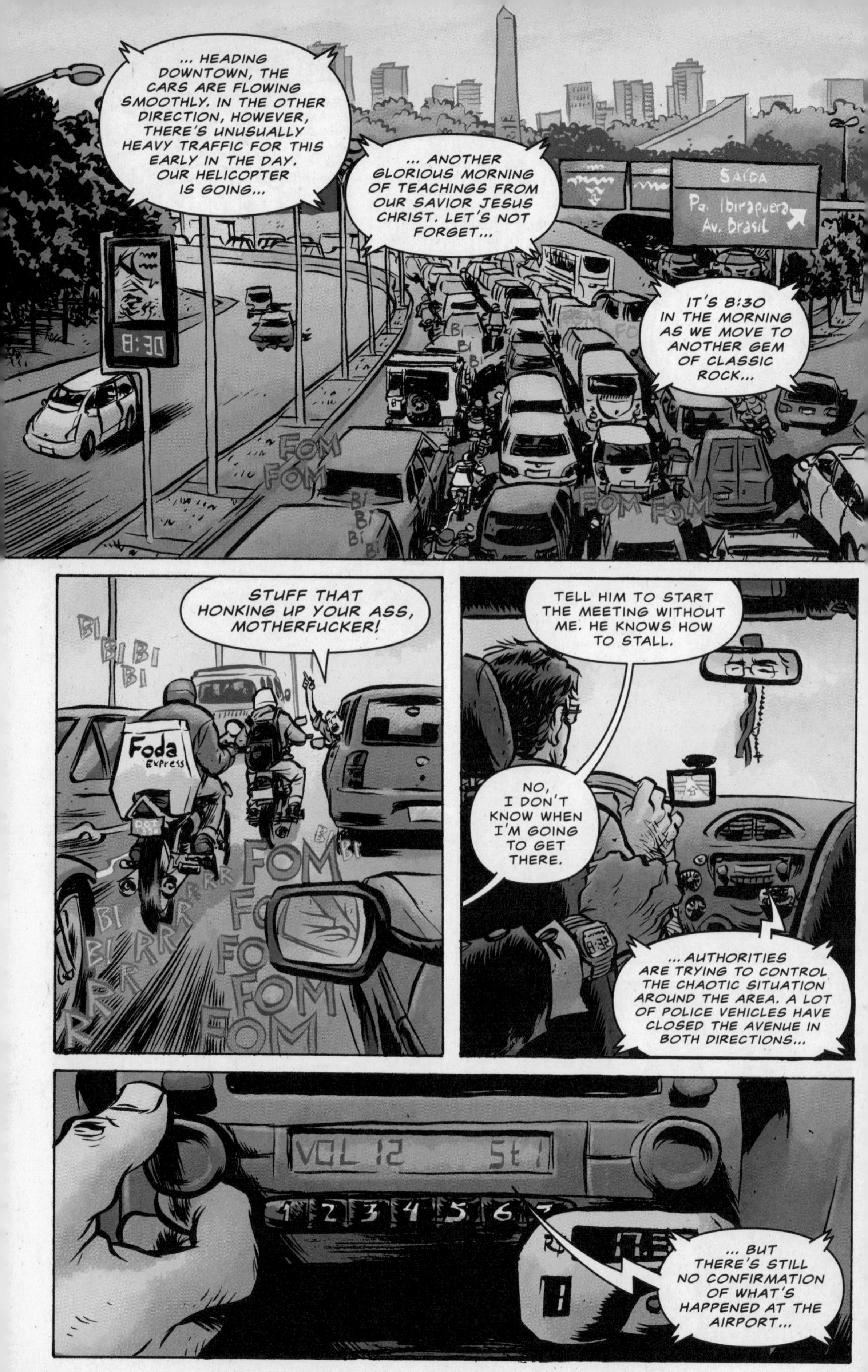
... HEADING DOWNTOWN, THE CARS ARE FLOWING SMOOTHLY. IN THE OTHER DIRECTION, HOWEVER, THERE'S UNUSUALLY HEAVY TRAFFIC FOR THIS EARLY IN THE DAY. OUR HELICOPTER IS GOING...
... ANOTHER GLORIOUS MORNING OF TEACHINGS FROM OUR SAVIOR JESUS CHRIST. LET'S NOT FORGET...
SAÍDA
Pq. Ibirapuera
Av. Brasil
8:30
IT'S 8:30 IN THE MORNING AS WE MOVE TO ANOTHER GEM OF CLASSIC ROCK...
FOM FOM
BI BI BI
FOM FOM
STUFF THAT HONKING UP YOUR ASS, MOTHERFUCKER!
BI BI BI BI
Foda Express
FOM FOM FOM FOM FOM
BI BI RRRR
TELL HIM TO START THE MEETING WITHOUT ME. HE KNOWS HOW TO STALL.
NO, I DON'T KNOW WHEN I'M GOING TO GET THERE.
8:32
...AUTHORITIES ARE TRYING TO CONTROL THE CHAOTIC SITUATION AROUND THE AREA. A LOT OF POLICE VEHICLES HAVE CLOSED THE AVENUE IN BOTH DIRECTIONS...
VOL 12 St 1
1 2 3 4 5 6
... BUT THERE'S STILL NO CONFIRMATION OF WHAT'S HAPPENED AT THE AIRPORT...

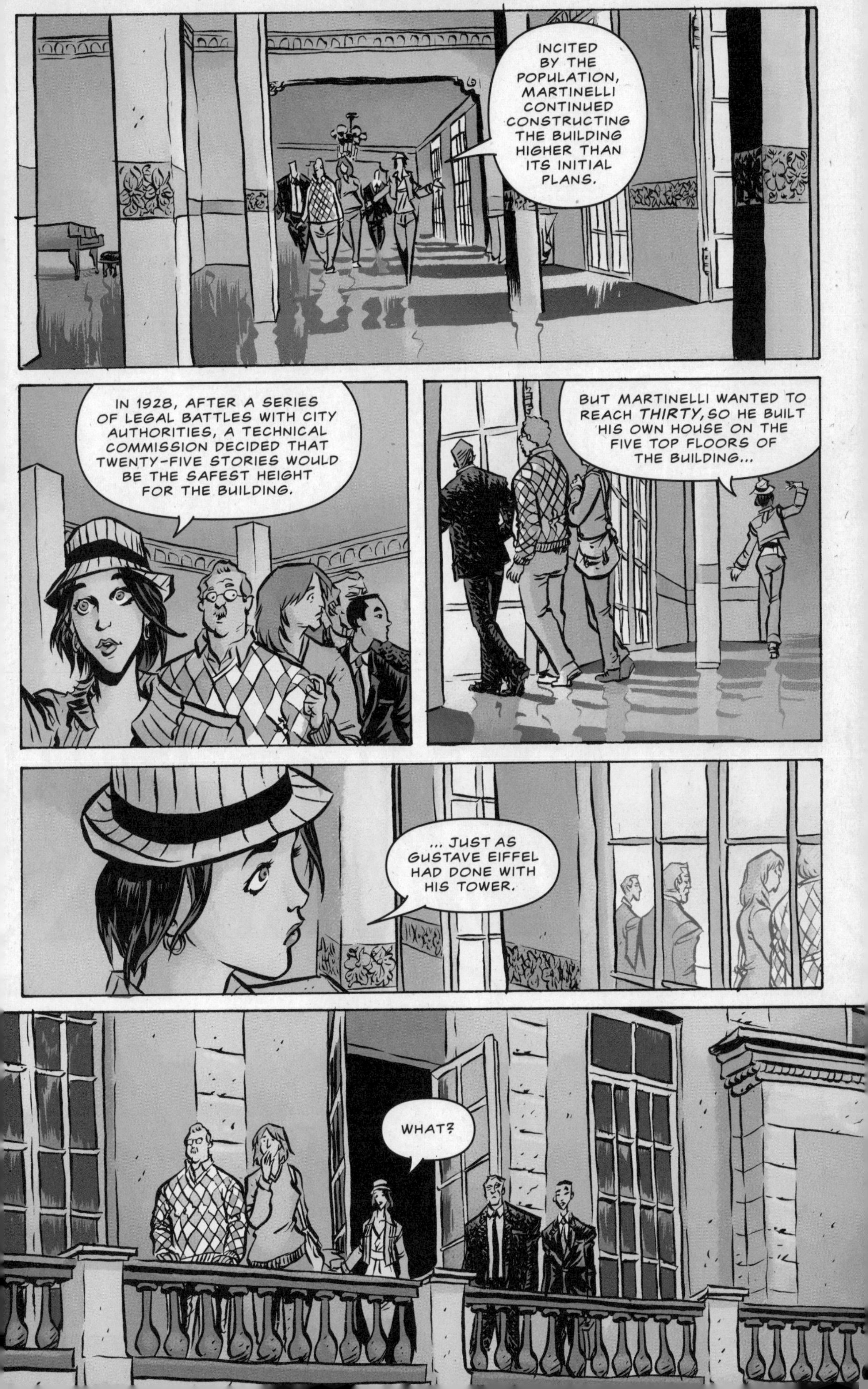
INCITED BY THE POPULATION, MARTINELLI CONTINUED CONSTRUCTING THE BUILDING HIGHER THAN ITS INITIAL PLANS.
IN 1928, AFTER A SERIES OF LEGAL BATTLES WITH CITY AUTHORITIES, A TECHNICAL COMMISSION DECIDED THAT TWENTY-FIVE STORIES WOULD BE THE SAFEST HEIGHT FOR THE BUILDING.
BUT MARTINELLI WANTED TO REACH *THIRTY*, SO HE BUILT HIS OWN HOUSE ON THE FIVE TOP FLOORS OF THE BUILDING...
... JUST AS GUSTAVE EIFFEL HAD DONE WITH HIS TOWER.
WHAT?

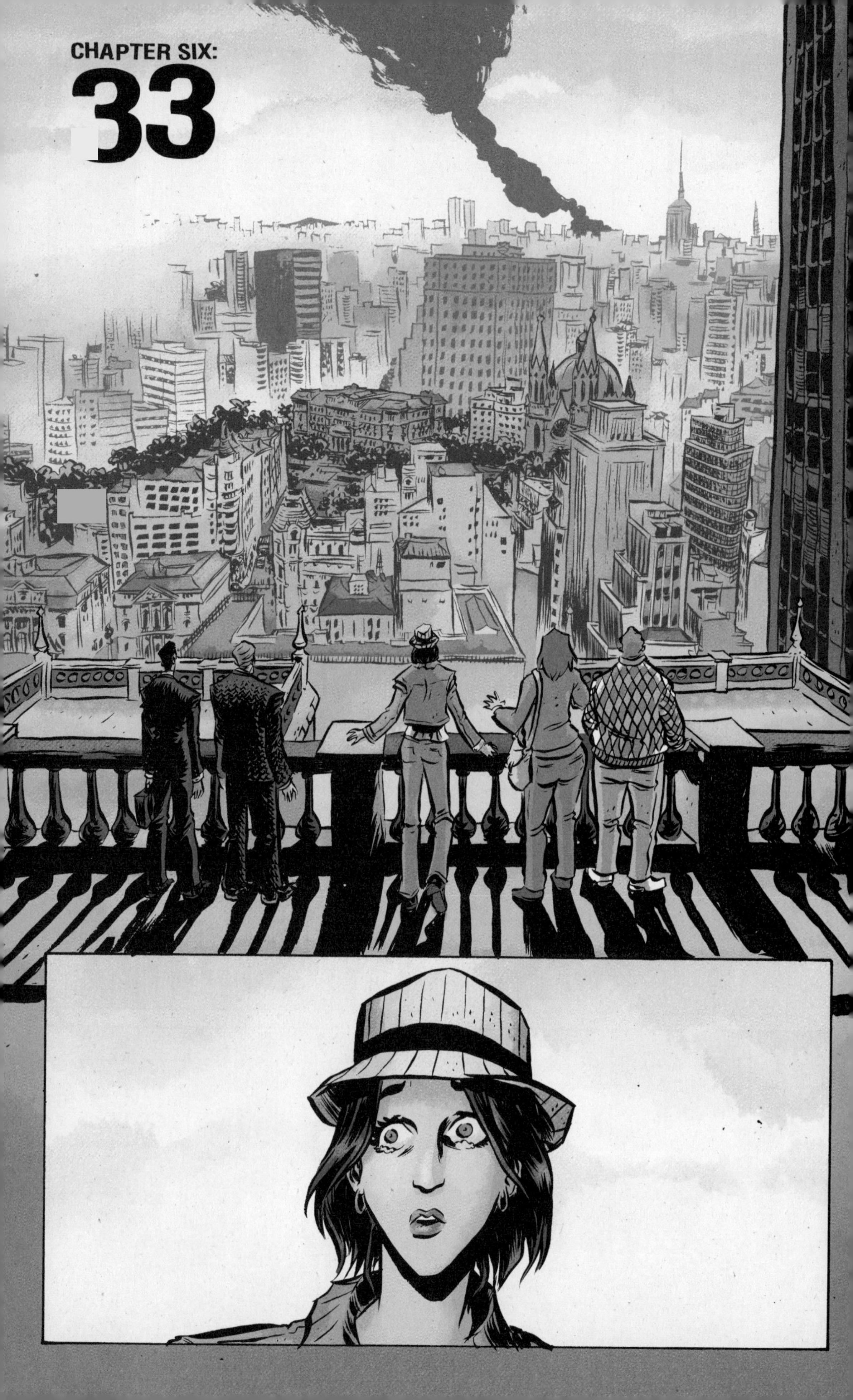
CHAPTER SIX:
33

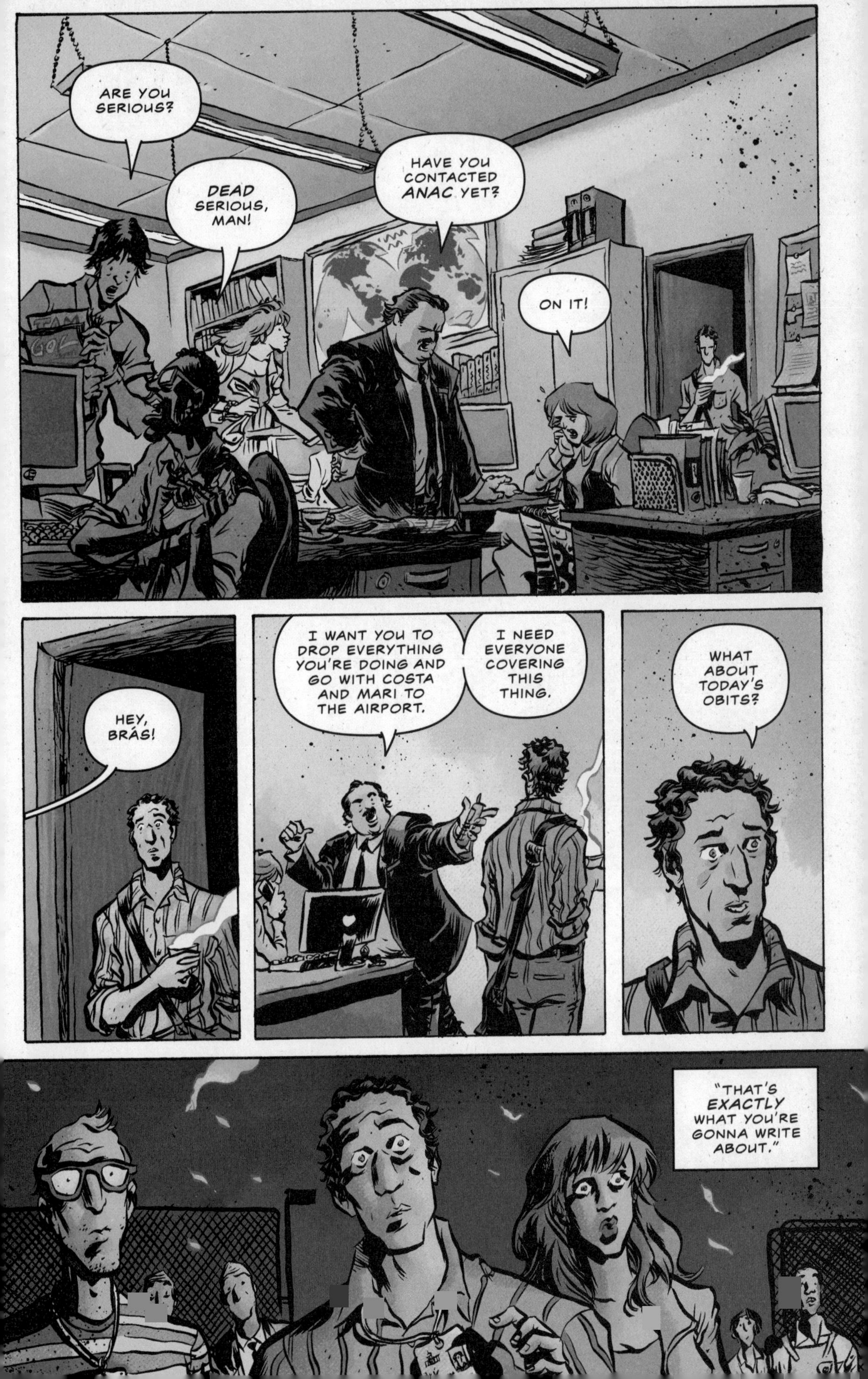
ARE YOU SERIOUS?
DEAD SERIOUS, MAN!
HAVE YOU CONTACTED ANAC YET?
ON IT!
HEY, BRÁS!
I WANT YOU TO DROP EVERYTHING YOU'RE DOING AND GO WITH COSTA AND MARI TO THE AIRPORT.
I NEED EVERYONE COVERING THIS THING.
WHAT ABOUT TODAY'S OBITS?
"THAT'S EXACTLY WHAT YOU'RE GONNA WRITE ABOUT."

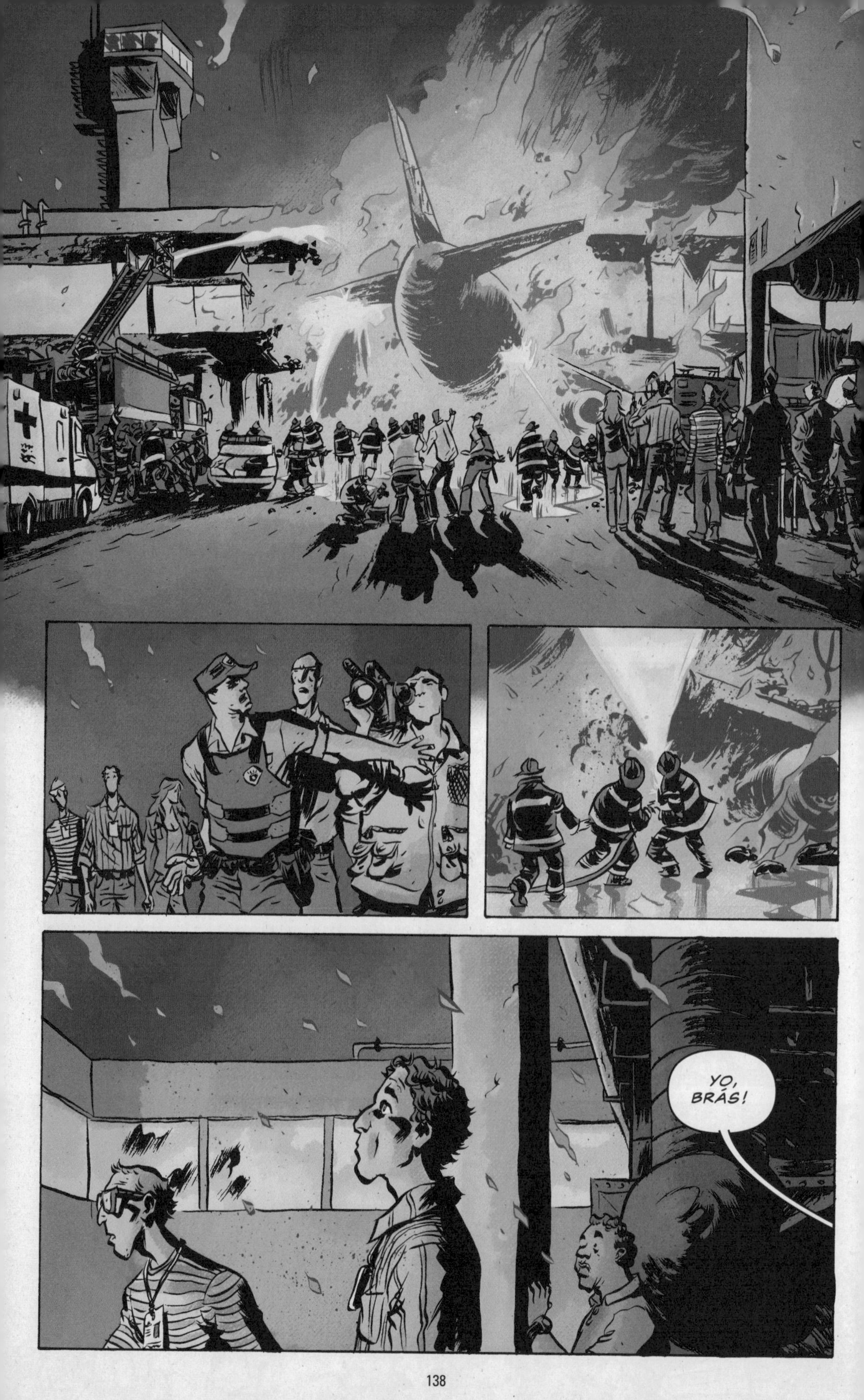
YO, BRÁS!

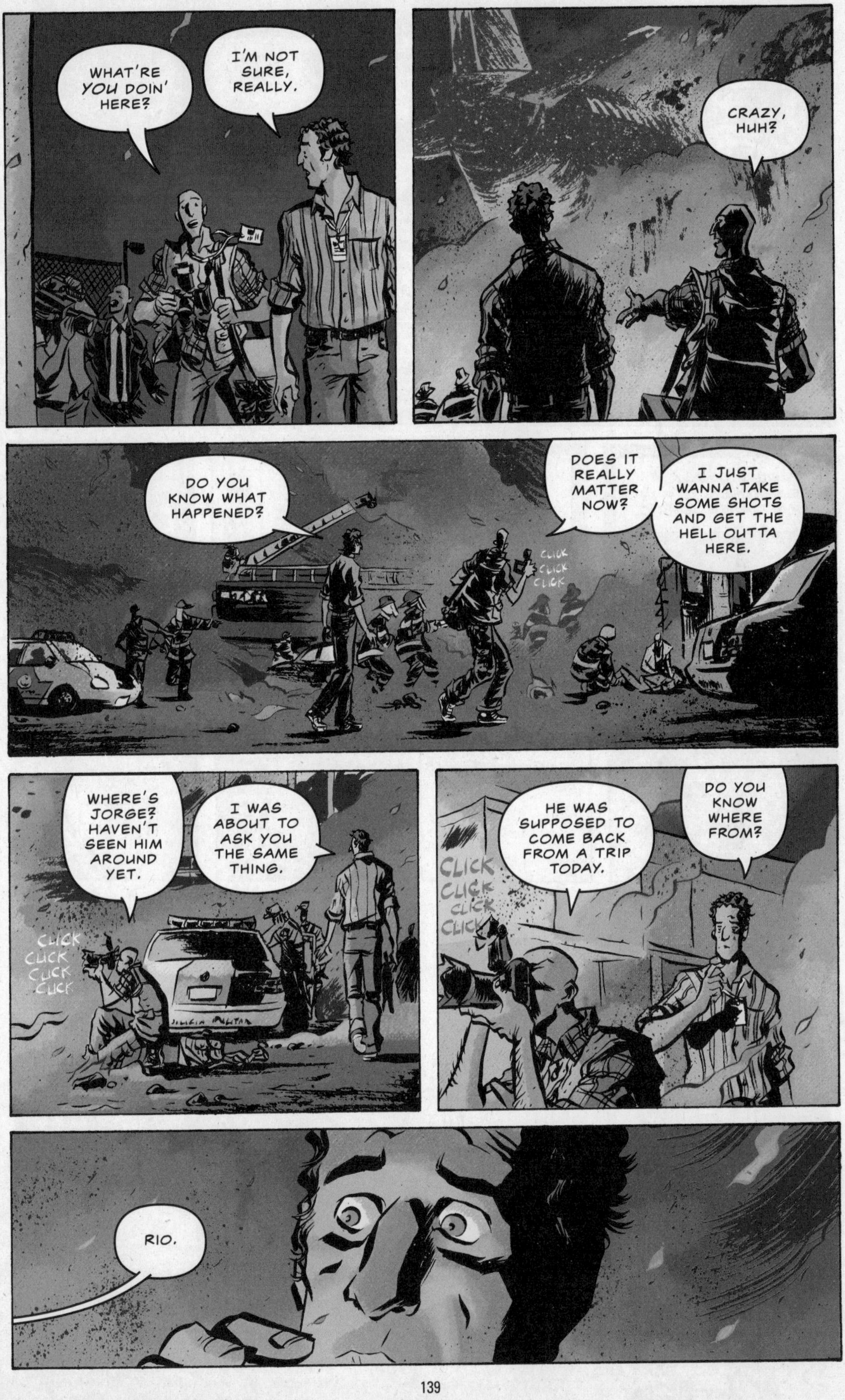
WHAT'RE YOU DOIN' HERE?
I'M NOT SURE, REALLY.
CRAZY, HUH?
DO YOU KNOW WHAT HAPPENED?
DOES IT REALLY MATTER NOW?
I JUST WANNA TAKE SOME SHOTS AND GET THE HELL OUTTA HERE.
CLICK CLICK CLICK
WHERE'S JORGE? HAVEN'T SEEN HIM AROUND YET.
I WAS ABOUT TO ASK YOU THE SAME THING.
CLICK CLICK CLICK CLICK
HE WAS SUPPOSED TO COME BACK FROM A TRIP TODAY.
DO YOU KNOW WHERE FROM?
CLICK CLICK CLICK CLICK
RIO.

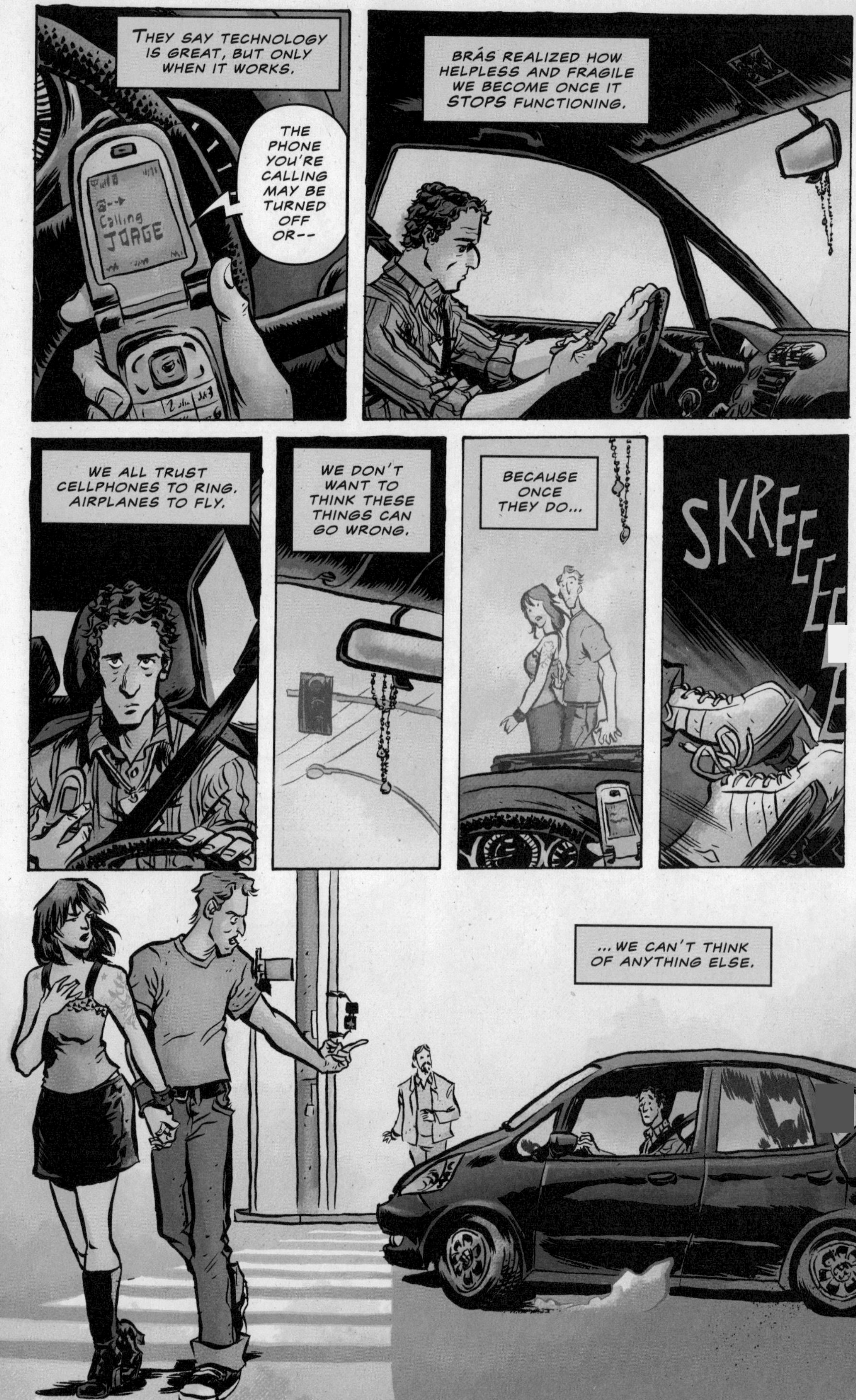
THEY SAY TECHNOLOGY IS GREAT, BUT ONLY WHEN IT WORKS.
Calling JORGE
THE PHONE YOU'RE CALLING MAY BE TURNED OFF OR--
BRÁS REALIZED HOW HELPLESS AND FRAGILE WE BECOME ONCE IT STOPS FUNCTIONING.
WE ALL TRUST CELLPHONES TO RING. AIRPLANES TO FLY.
WE DON'T WANT TO THINK THESE THINGS CAN GO WRONG.
BECAUSE ONCE THEY DO...
SKREEEEE
...WE CAN'T THINK OF ANYTHING ELSE.

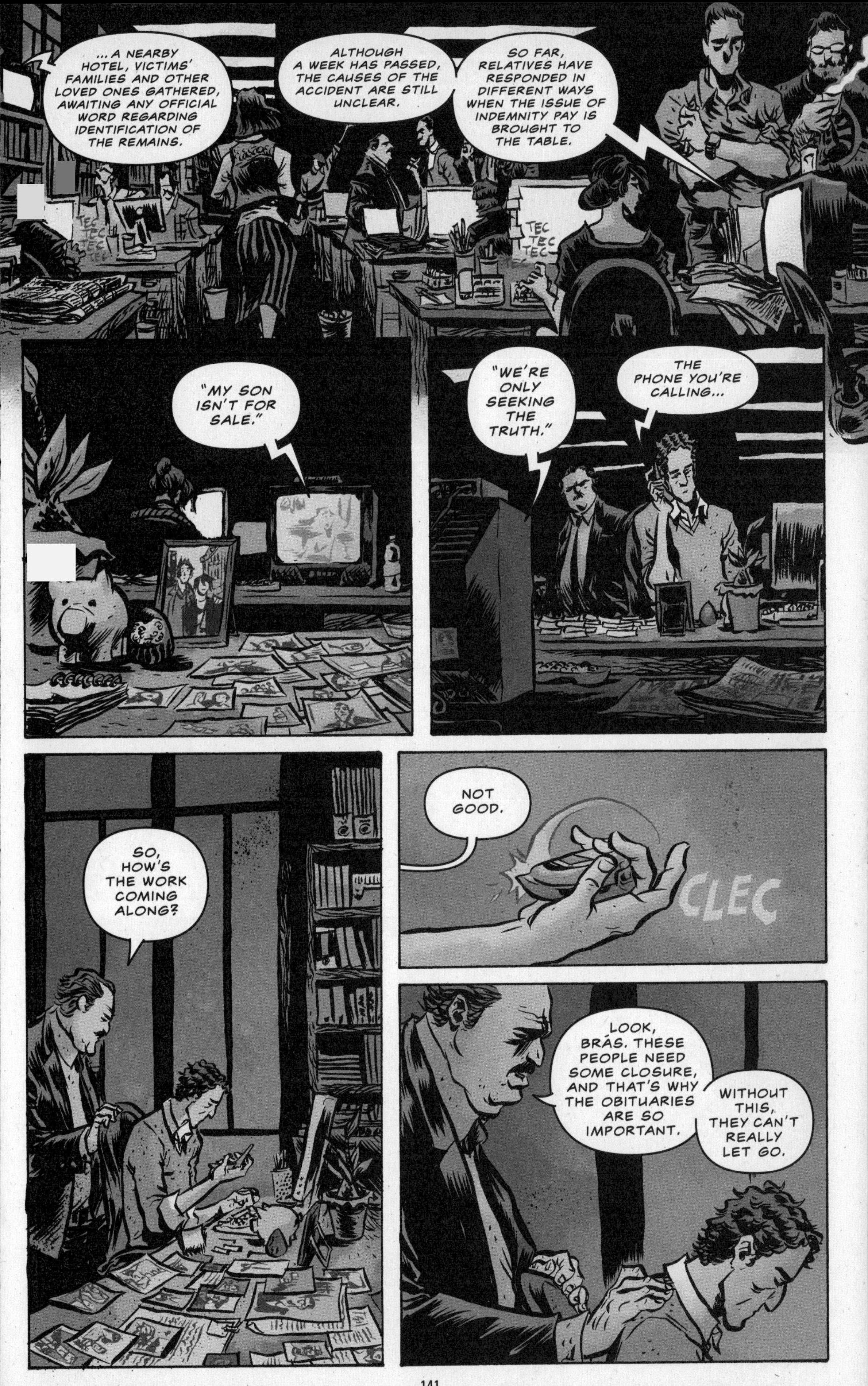
...A NEARBY HOTEL, VICTIMS' FAMILIES AND OTHER LOVED ONES GATHERED, AWAITING ANY OFFICIAL WORD REGARDING IDENTIFICATION OF THE REMAINS.
ALTHOUGH A WEEK HAS PASSED, THE CAUSES OF THE ACCIDENT ARE STILL UNCLEAR.
SO FAR, RELATIVES HAVE RESPONDED IN DIFFERENT WAYS WHEN THE ISSUE OF INDEMNITY PAY IS BROUGHT TO THE TABLE.
TEC TEC TEC TEC
TEC TEC TEC TEC
"MY SON ISN'T FOR SALE."
"WE'RE ONLY SEEKING THE TRUTH."
THE PHONE YOU'RE CALLING...
SO, HOW'S THE WORK COMING ALONG?
NOT GOOD.
CLEC
LOOK, BRÁS. THESE PEOPLE NEED SOME CLOSURE, AND THAT'S WHY THE OBITUARIES ARE SO IMPORTANT.
WITHOUT THIS, THEY CAN'T REALLY LET GO.

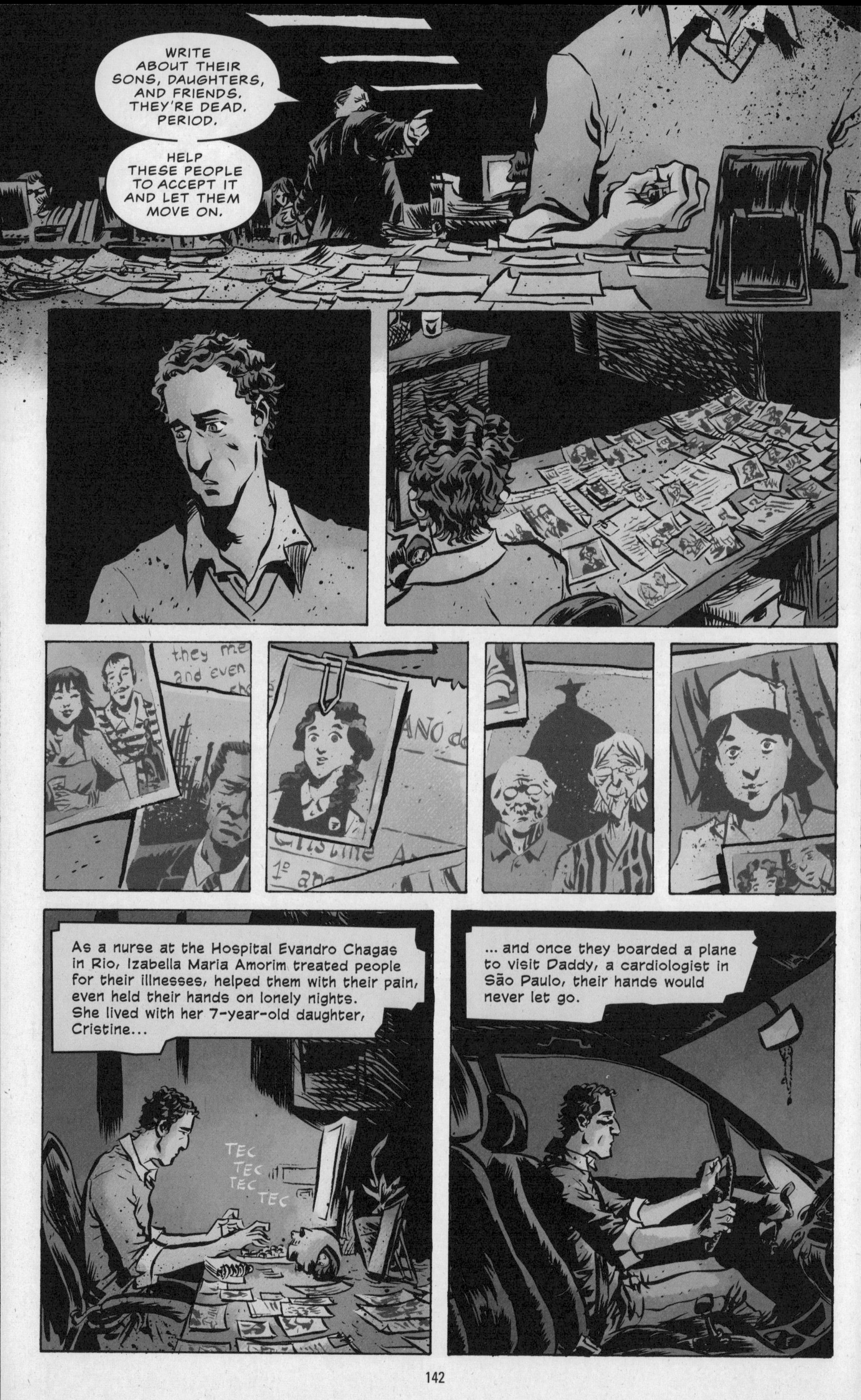

WRITE ABOUT THEIR SONS, DAUGHTERS, AND FRIENDS. THEY'RE DEAD. PERIOD.
HELP THESE PEOPLE TO ACCEPT IT AND LET THEM MOVE ON.
As a nurse at the Hospital Evandro Chagas in Rio, Izabella Maria Amorim treated people for their illnesses, helped them with their pain, even held their hands on lonely nights. She lived with her 7-year-old daughter, Cristine...
TEC TEC TEC TEC
... and once they boarded a plane to visit Daddy, a cardiologist in São Paulo, their hands would never let go.

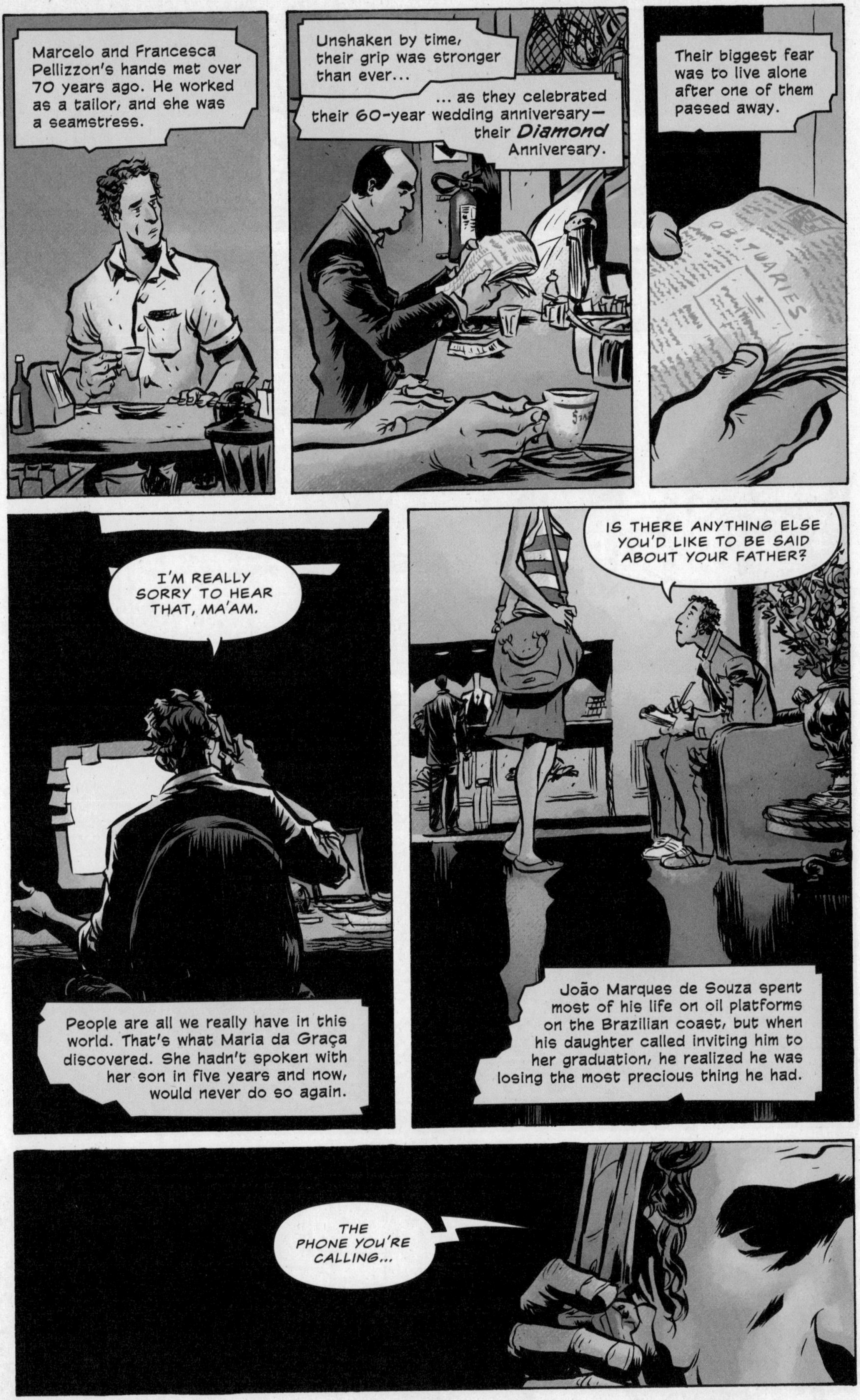
Marcelo and Francesca Pellizzon's hands met over 70 years ago. He worked as a tailor, and she was a seamstress.
Unshaken by time, their grip was stronger than ever...
... as they celebrated their 60-year wedding anniversary— their *Diamond* Anniversary.
Their biggest fear was to live alone after one of them passed away.
OBITUARIES
I'M REALLY SORRY TO HEAR THAT, MA'AM.
People are all we really have in this world. That's what Maria da Graça discovered. She hadn't spoken with her son in five years and now, would never do so again.
IS THERE ANYTHING ELSE YOU'D LIKE TO BE SAID ABOUT YOUR FATHER?
João Marques de Souza spent most of his life on oil platforms on the Brazilian coast, but when his daughter called inviting him to her graduation, he realized he was losing the most precious thing he had.
THE PHONE YOU'RE CALLING...

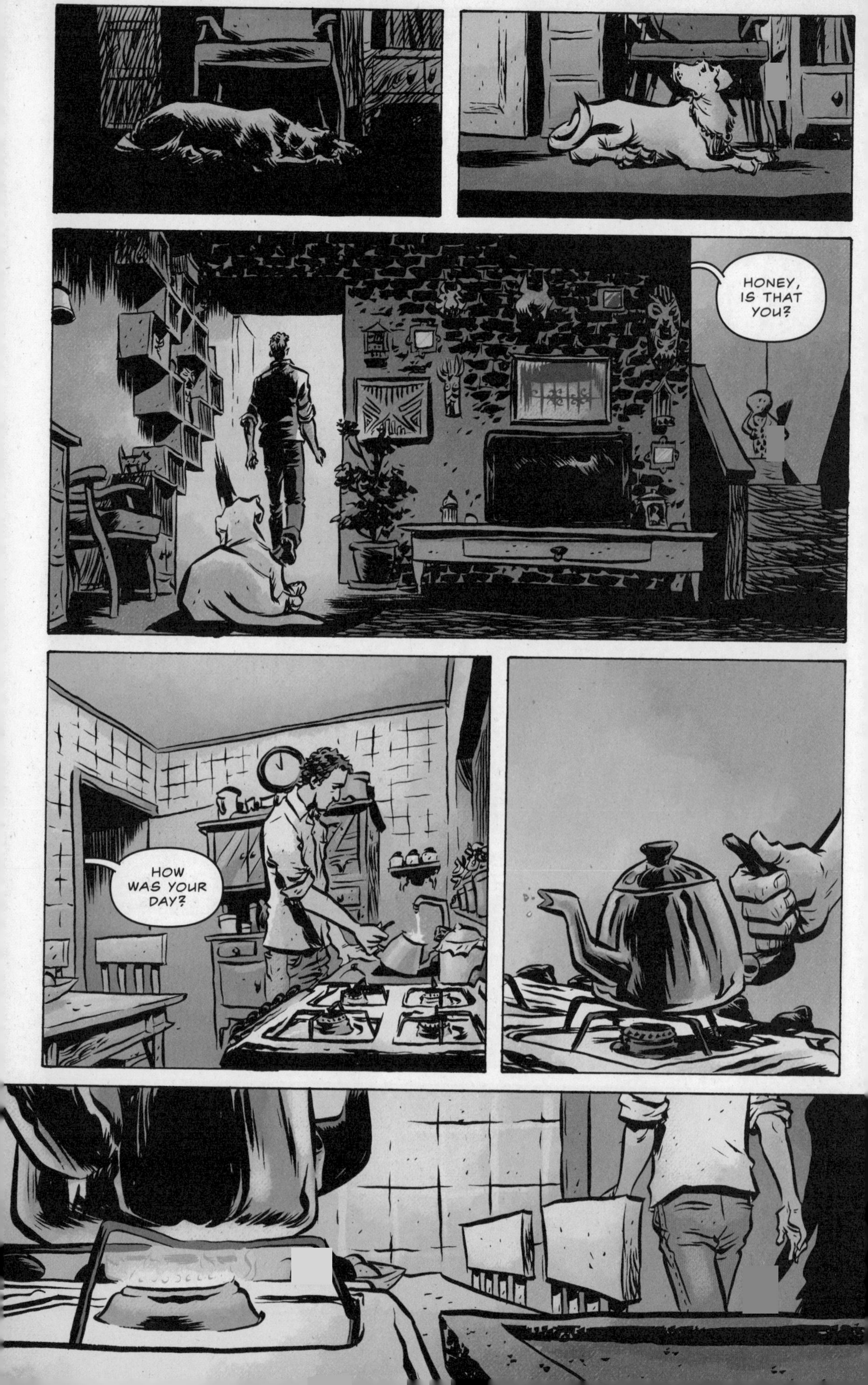
HONEY, IS THAT YOU?
HOW WAS YOUR DAY?

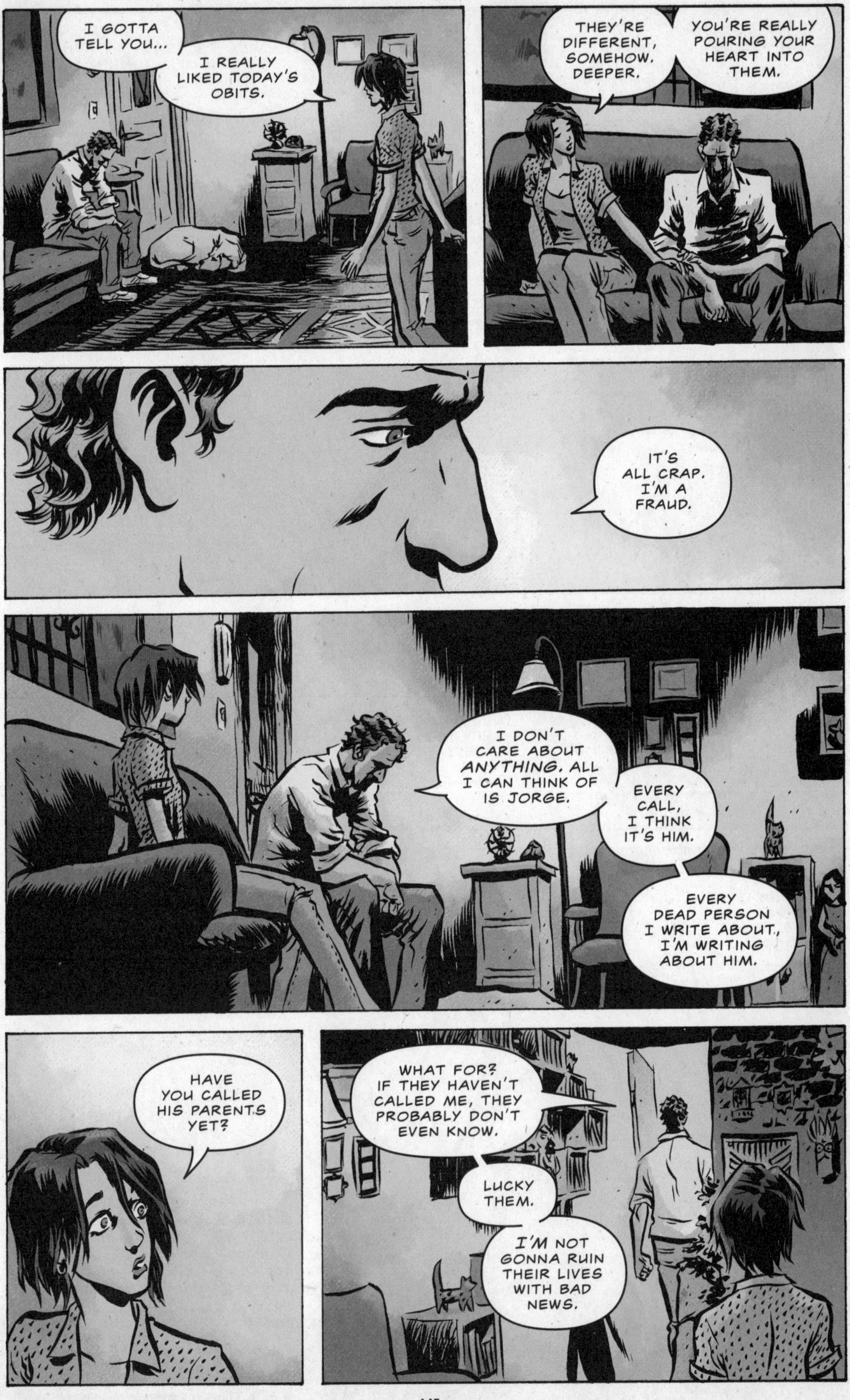
I GOTTA TELL YOU...
I REALLY LIKED TODAY'S OBITS.
THEY'RE DIFFERENT, SOMEHOW. DEEPER.
YOU'RE REALLY POURING YOUR HEART INTO THEM.
IT'S ALL CRAP. I'M A FRAUD.
I DON'T CARE ABOUT *ANYTHING*. ALL I CAN THINK OF IS JORGE.
EVERY CALL, I THINK IT'S HIM.
EVERY DEAD PERSON I WRITE ABOUT, I'M WRITING ABOUT HIM.
HAVE YOU CALLED HIS PARENTS YET?
WHAT FOR? IF THEY HAVEN'T CALLED ME, THEY PROBABLY DON'T EVEN KNOW.
LUCKY THEM.
I'M NOT GONNA RUIN THEIR LIVES WITH BAD NEWS.

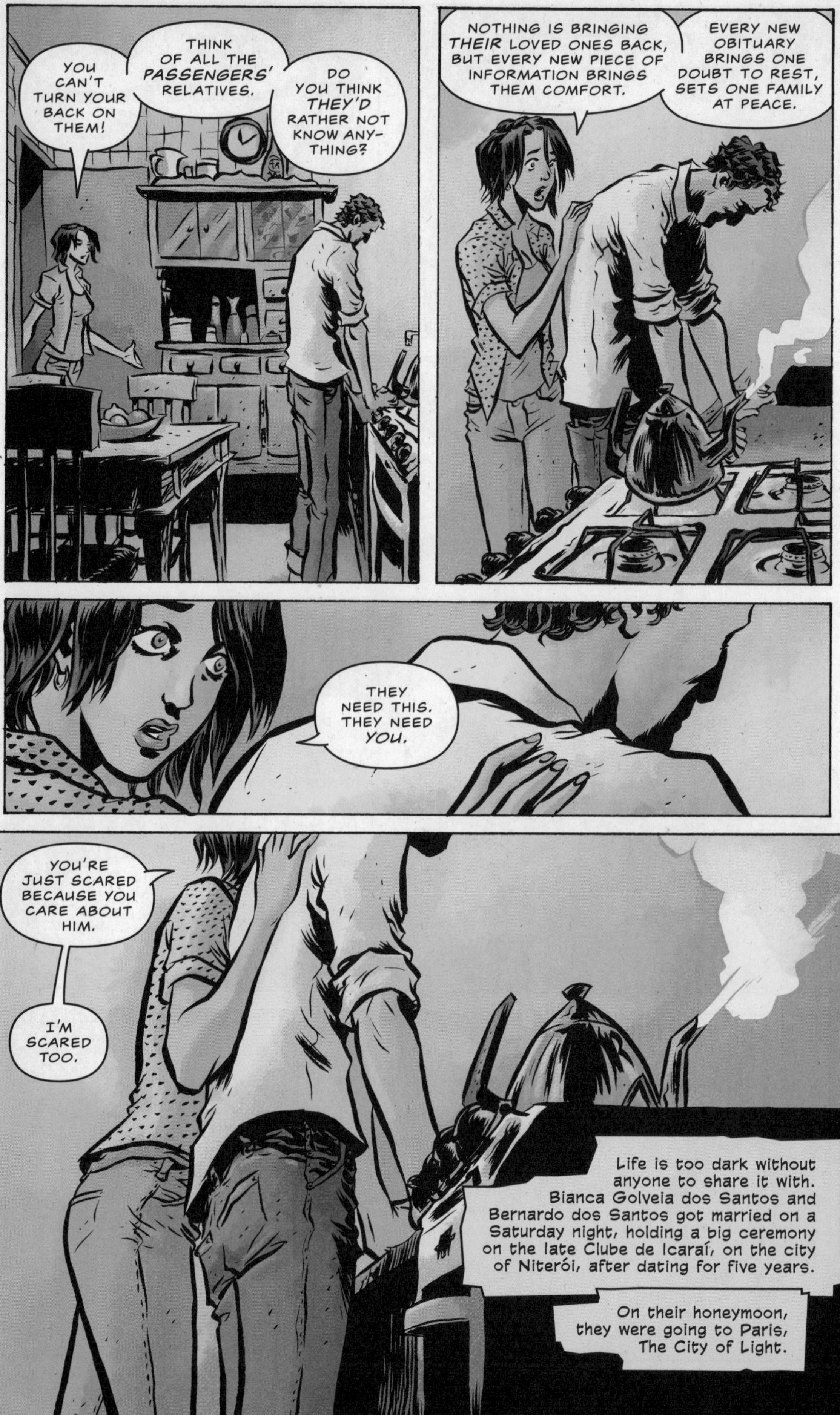

YOU CAN'T TURN YOUR BACK ON THEM!
THINK OF ALL THE PASSENGERS' RELATIVES.
DO YOU THINK THEY'D RATHER NOT KNOW ANY-THING?
NOTHING IS BRINGING THEIR LOVED ONES BACK, BUT EVERY NEW PIECE OF INFORMATION BRINGS THEM COMFORT.
EVERY NEW OBITUARY BRINGS ONE DOUBT TO REST, SETS ONE FAMILY AT PEACE.
THEY NEED THIS. THEY NEED YOU.
YOU'RE JUST SCARED BECAUSE YOU CARE ABOUT HIM.
I'M SCARED TOO.
Life is too dark without anyone to share it with. Bianca Golveia dos Santos and Bernardo dos Santos got married on a Saturday night, holding a big ceremony on the late Clube de Icaraí, on the city of Niterói, after dating for five years.
On their honeymoon, they were going to Paris, The City of Light.

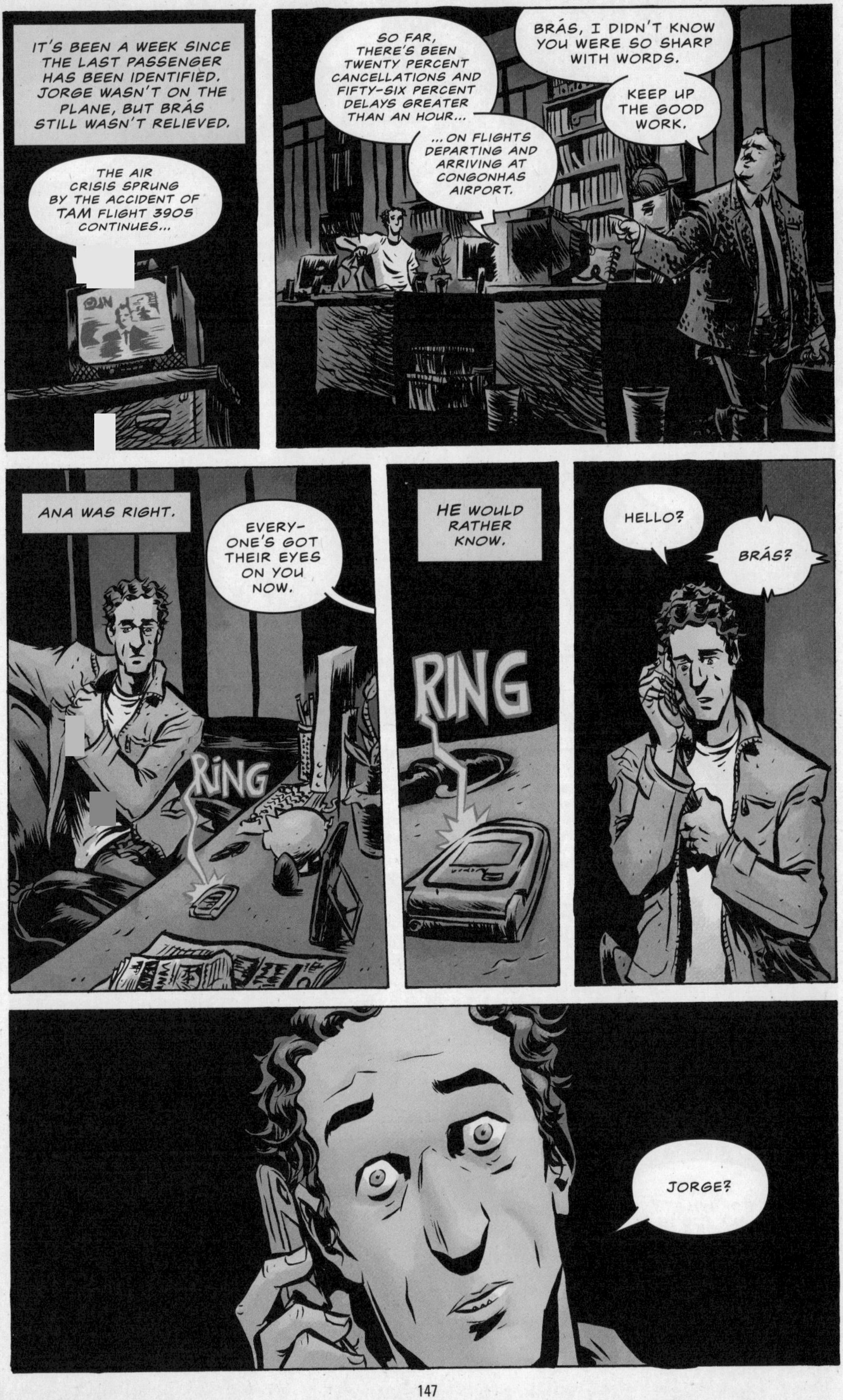
IT'S BEEN A WEEK SINCE THE LAST PASSENGER HAS BEEN IDENTIFIED. JORGE WASN'T ON THE PLANE, BUT BRÁS STILL WASN'T RELIEVED.
THE AIR CRISIS SPRUNG BY THE ACCIDENT OF TAM FLIGHT 3905 CONTINUES...
SO FAR, THERE'S BEEN TWENTY PERCENT CANCELLATIONS AND FIFTY-SIX PERCENT DELAYS GREATER THAN AN HOUR...
...ON FLIGHTS DEPARTING AND ARRIVING AT CONGONHAS AIRPORT.
BRÁS, I DIDN'T KNOW YOU WERE SO SHARP WITH WORDS.
KEEP UP THE GOOD WORK.
ANA WAS RIGHT.
EVERY-ONE'S GOT THEIR EYES ON YOU NOW.
RING
HE WOULD RATHER KNOW.
RING
HELLO?
BRÁS?
JORGE?

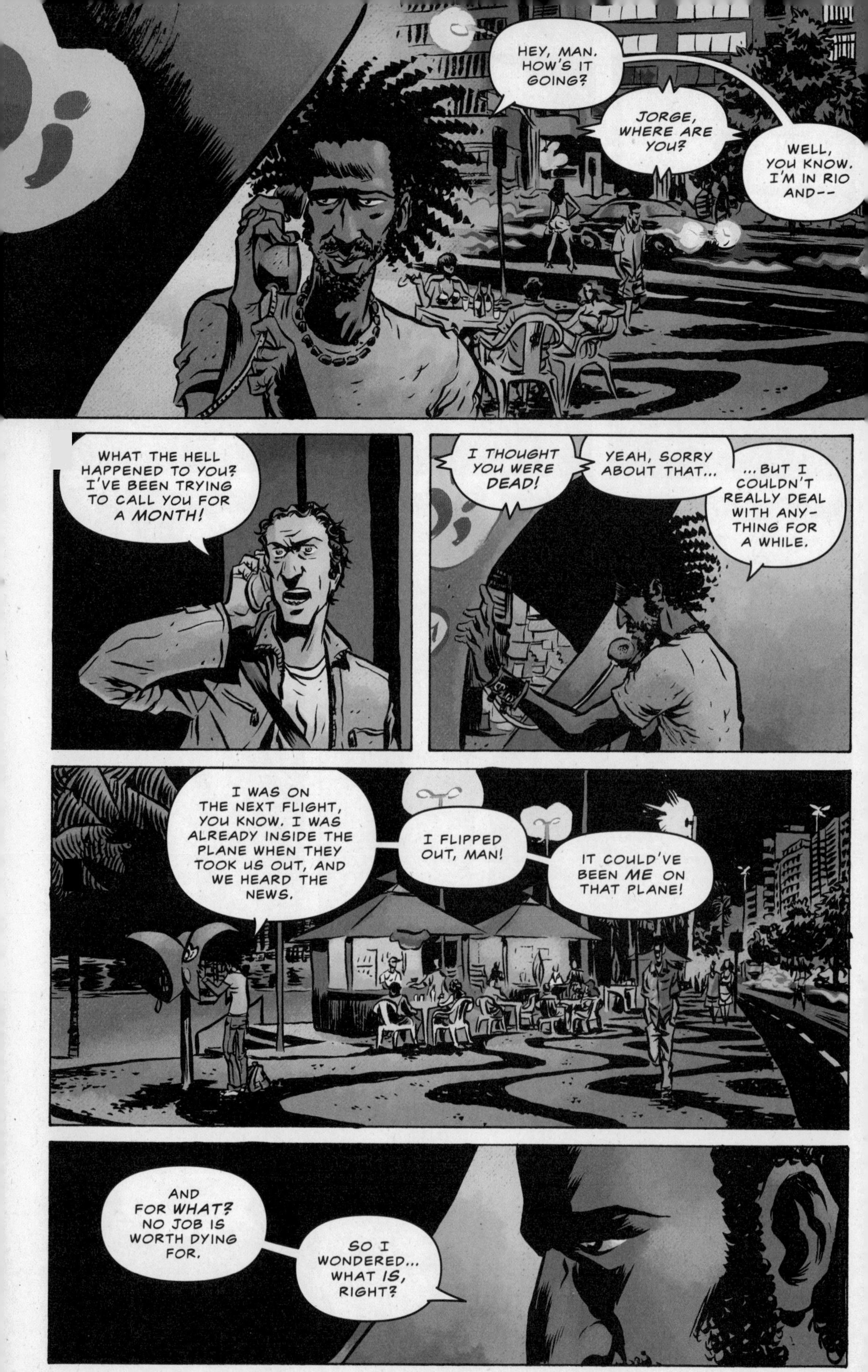
HEY, MAN. HOW'S IT GOING?
JORGE, WHERE ARE YOU?
WELL, YOU KNOW. I'M IN RIO AND--
WHAT THE HELL HAPPENED TO YOU? I'VE BEEN TRYING TO CALL YOU FOR A MONTH!
I THOUGHT YOU WERE DEAD!
YEAH, SORRY ABOUT THAT...
...BUT I COULDN'T REALLY DEAL WITH ANY-THING FOR A WHILE.
I WAS ON THE NEXT FLIGHT, YOU KNOW. I WAS ALREADY INSIDE THE PLANE WHEN THEY TOOK US OUT, AND WE HEARD THE NEWS.
I FLIPPED OUT, MAN!
IT COULD'VE BEEN ME ON THAT PLANE!
AND FOR WHAT? NO JOB IS WORTH DYING FOR.
SO I WONDERED... WHAT IS, RIGHT?

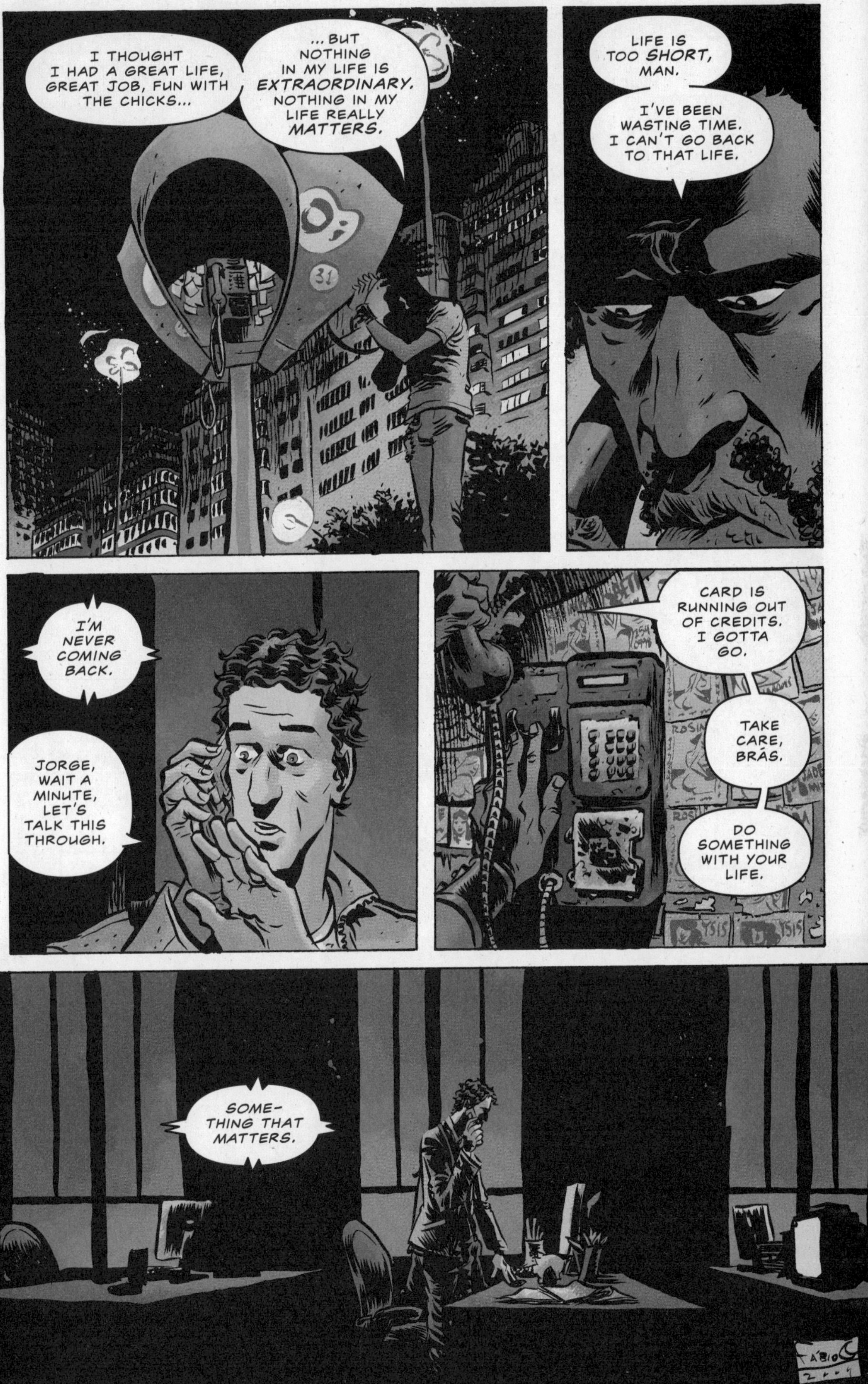
I THOUGHT I HAD A GREAT LIFE, GREAT JOB, FUN WITH THE CHICKS...
...BUT NOTHING IN MY LIFE IS EXTRAORDINARY. NOTHING IN MY LIFE REALLY MATTERS.
LIFE IS TOO SHORT, MAN.
I'VE BEEN WASTING TIME. I CAN'T GO BACK TO THAT LIFE.
I'M NEVER COMING BACK.
JORGE, WAIT A MINUTE, LET'S TALK THIS THROUGH.
CARD IS RUNNING OUT OF CREDITS. I GOTTA GO.
TAKE CARE, BRÁS.
DO SOMETHING WITH YOUR LIFE.
SOME-THING THAT MATTERS.

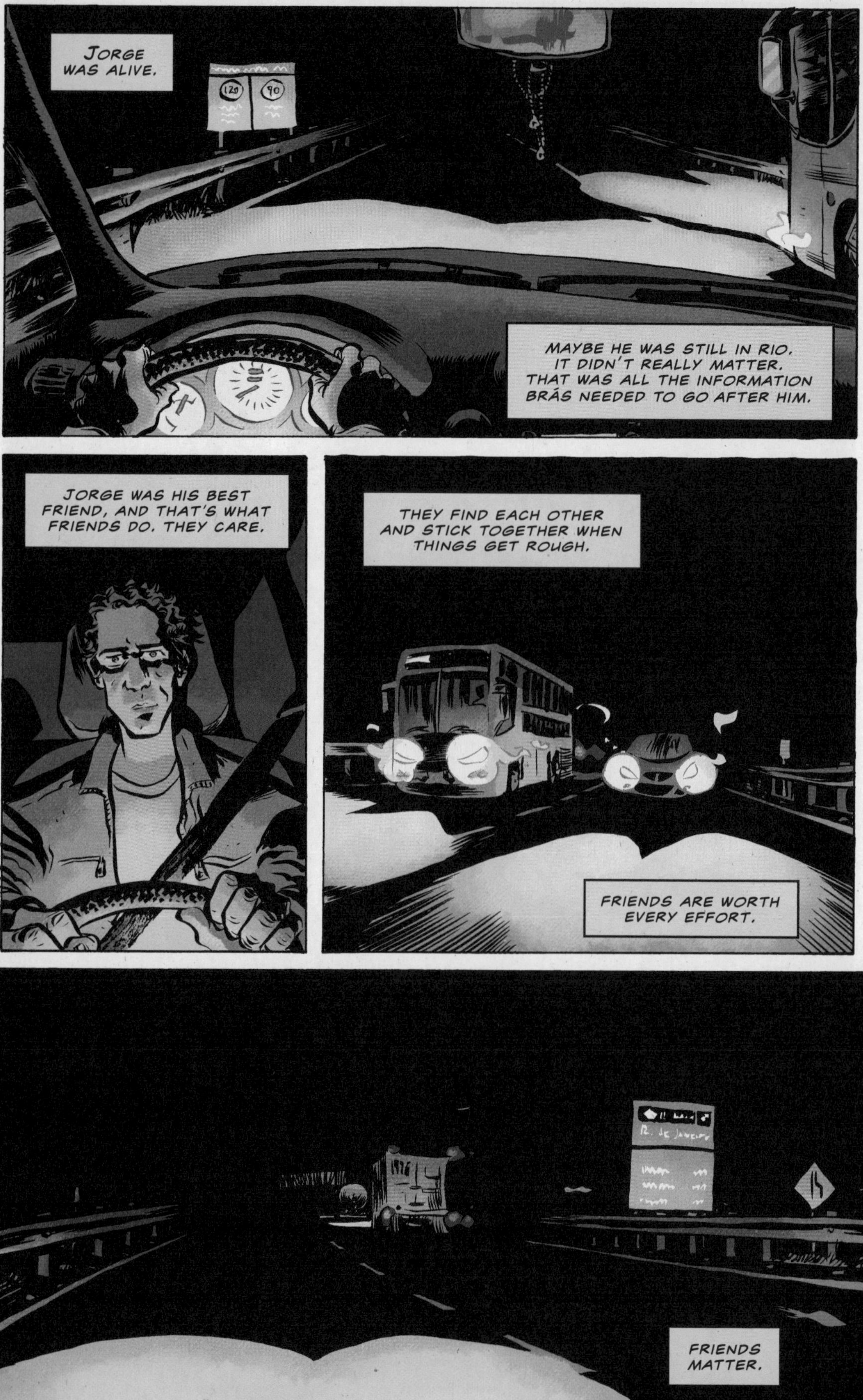
JORGE WAS ALIVE.
120
90
MAYBE HE WAS STILL IN RIO. IT DIDN'T REALLY MATTER. THAT WAS ALL THE INFORMATION BRÁS NEEDED TO GO AFTER HIM.
JORGE WAS HIS BEST FRIEND, AND THAT'S WHAT FRIENDS DO. THEY CARE.
THEY FIND EACH OTHER AND STICK TOGETHER WHEN THINGS GET ROUGH.
FRIENDS ARE WORTH EVERY EFFORT.
FRIENDS MATTER.

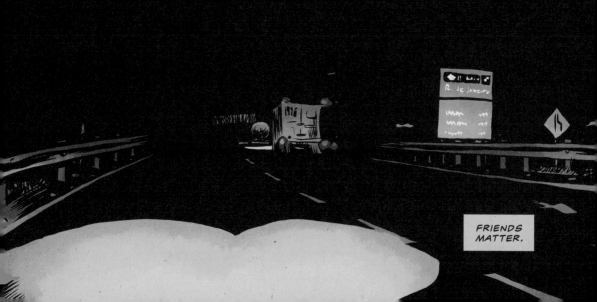

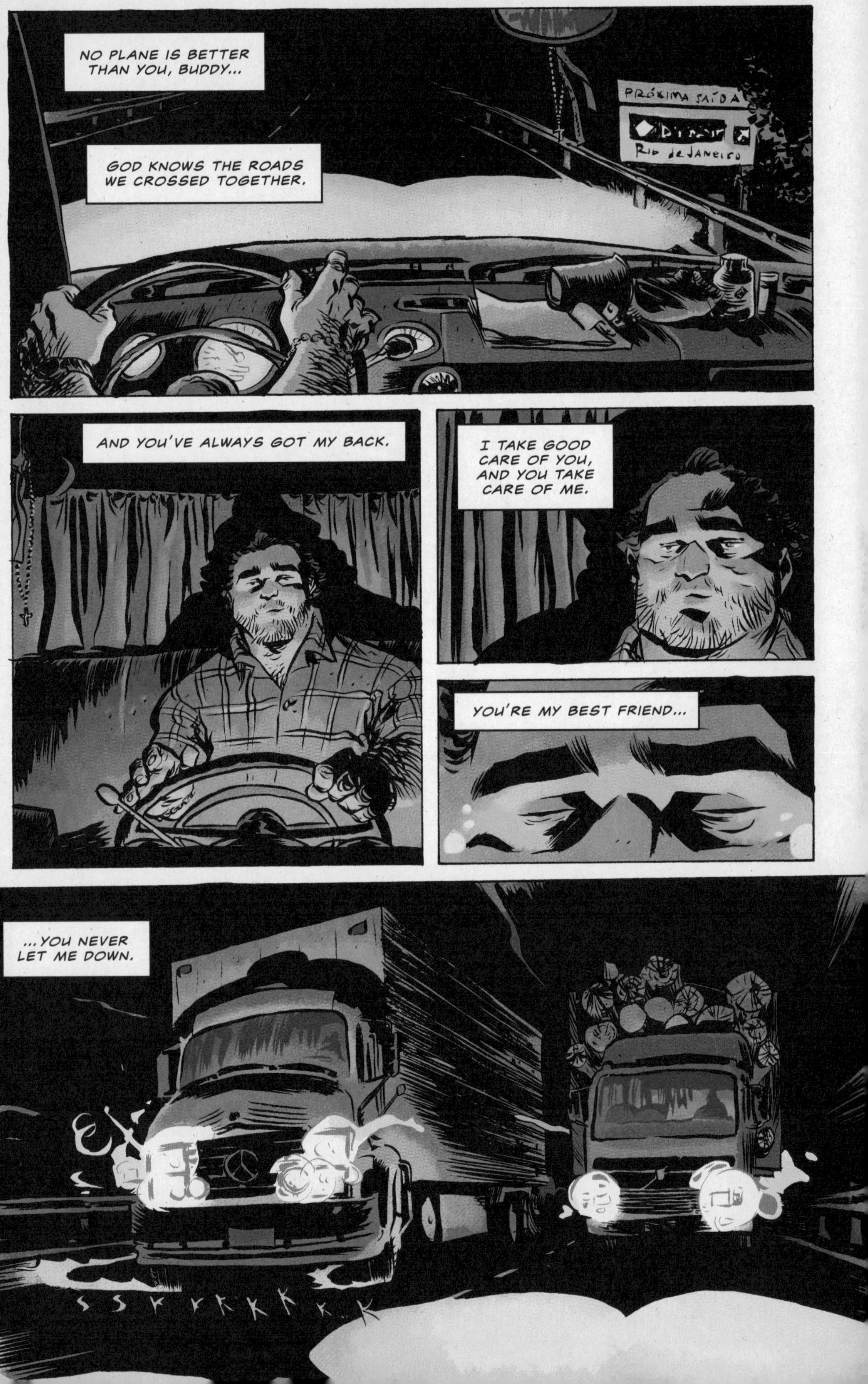
NO PLANE IS BETTER THAN YOU, BUDDY...
GOD KNOWS THE ROADS WE CROSSED TOGETHER.
PRÓXIMA SAÍDA
Rio de Janeiro
AND YOU'VE ALWAYS GOT MY BACK.
I TAKE GOOD CARE OF YOU, AND YOU TAKE CARE OF ME.
YOU'RE MY BEST FRIEND...
...YOU NEVER LET ME DOWN.
SSKKKKKKK

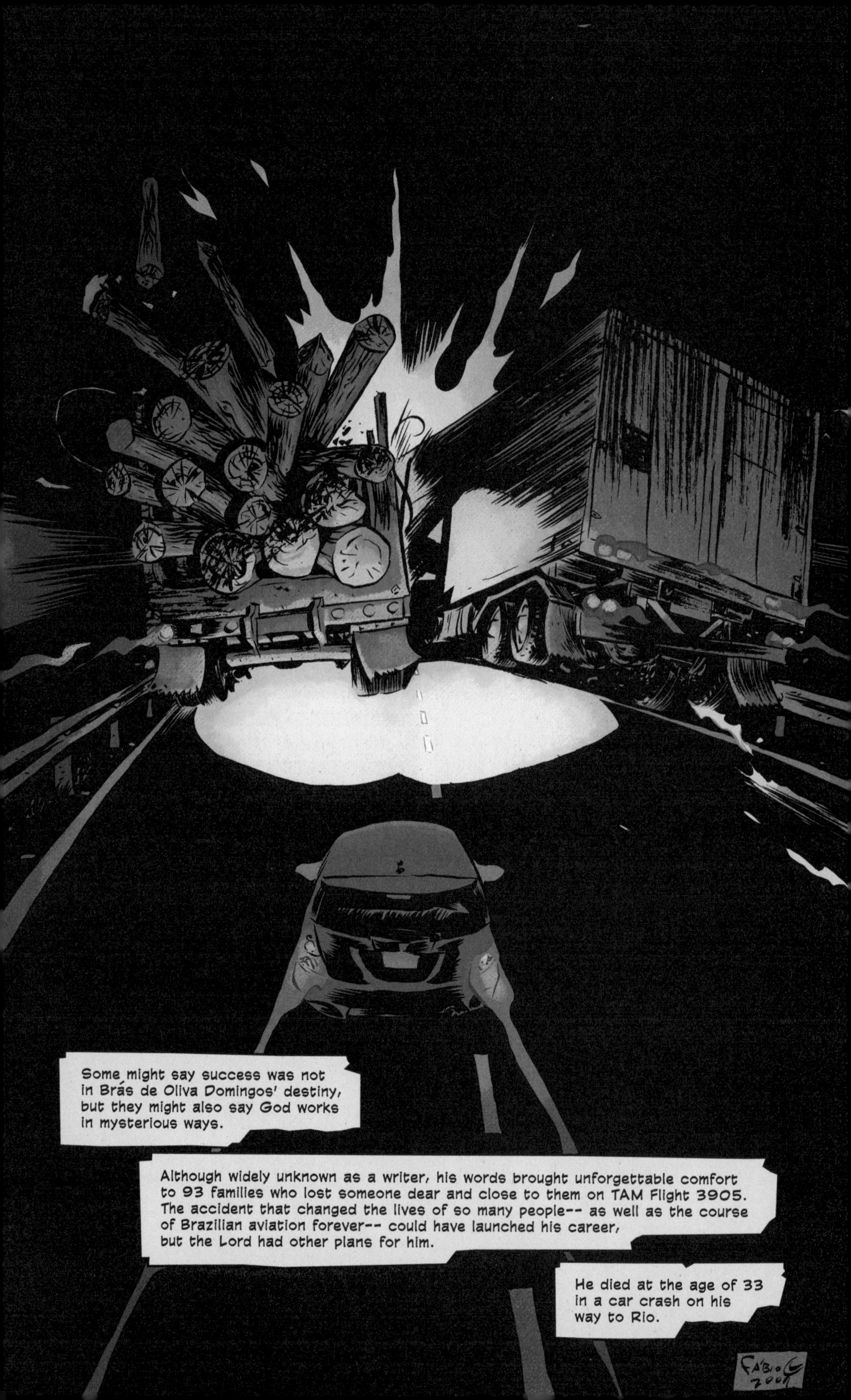
Some might say success was not in Brás de Oliva Domingos' destiny, but they might also say God works in mysterious ways.
Although widely unknown as a writer, his words brought unforgettable comfort to 93 families who lost someone dear and close to them on TAM Flight 3905. The accident that changed the lives of so many people-- as well as the course of Brazilian aviation forever-- could have launched his career, but the Lord had other plans for him.
He died at the age of 33 in a car crash on his way to Rio.

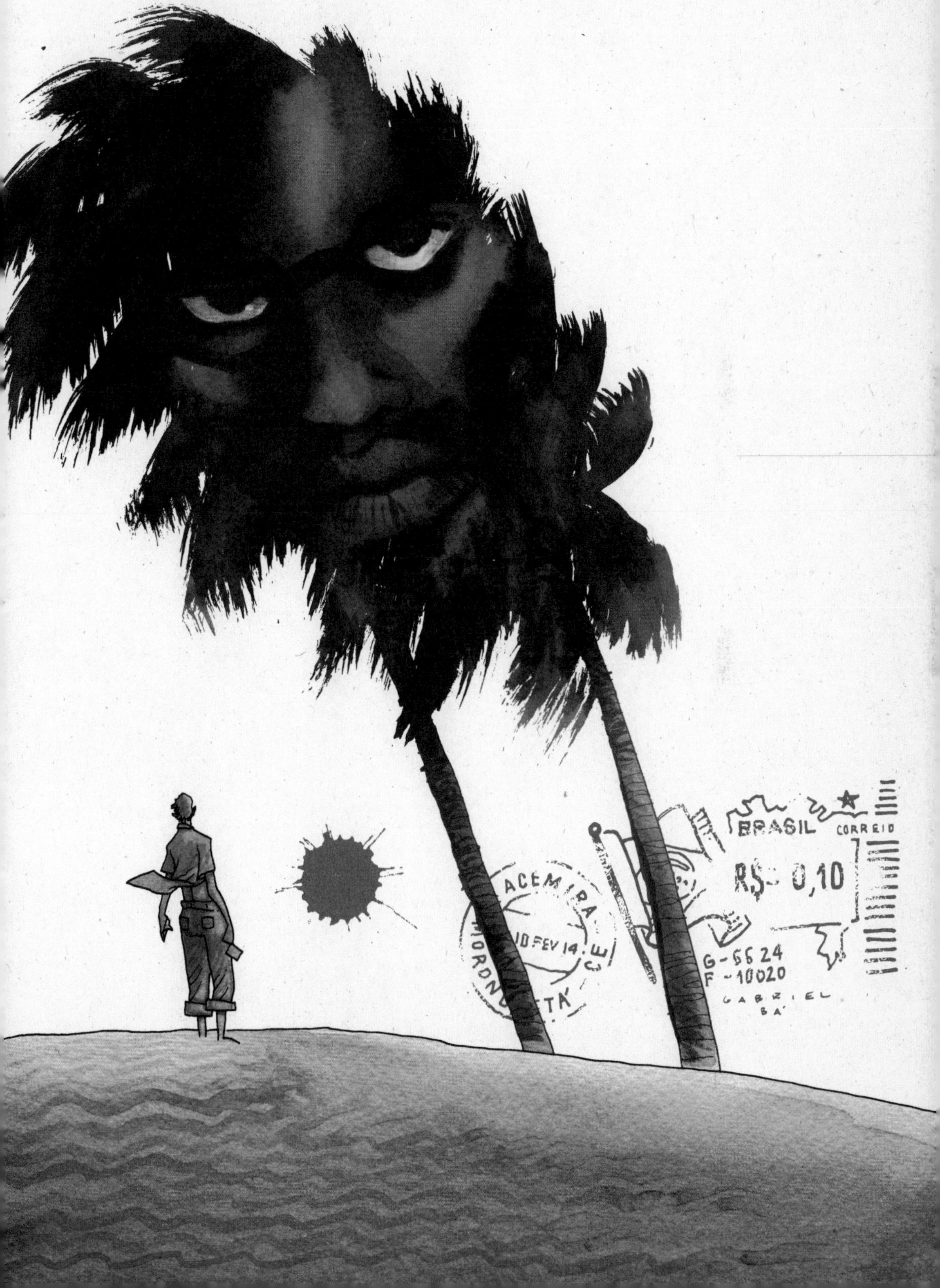
ACEMIRA
10 FEV 14
BRASIL
CORREIO
R$ 0,10
G-6624
F-10020
GABRIEL
BÁ

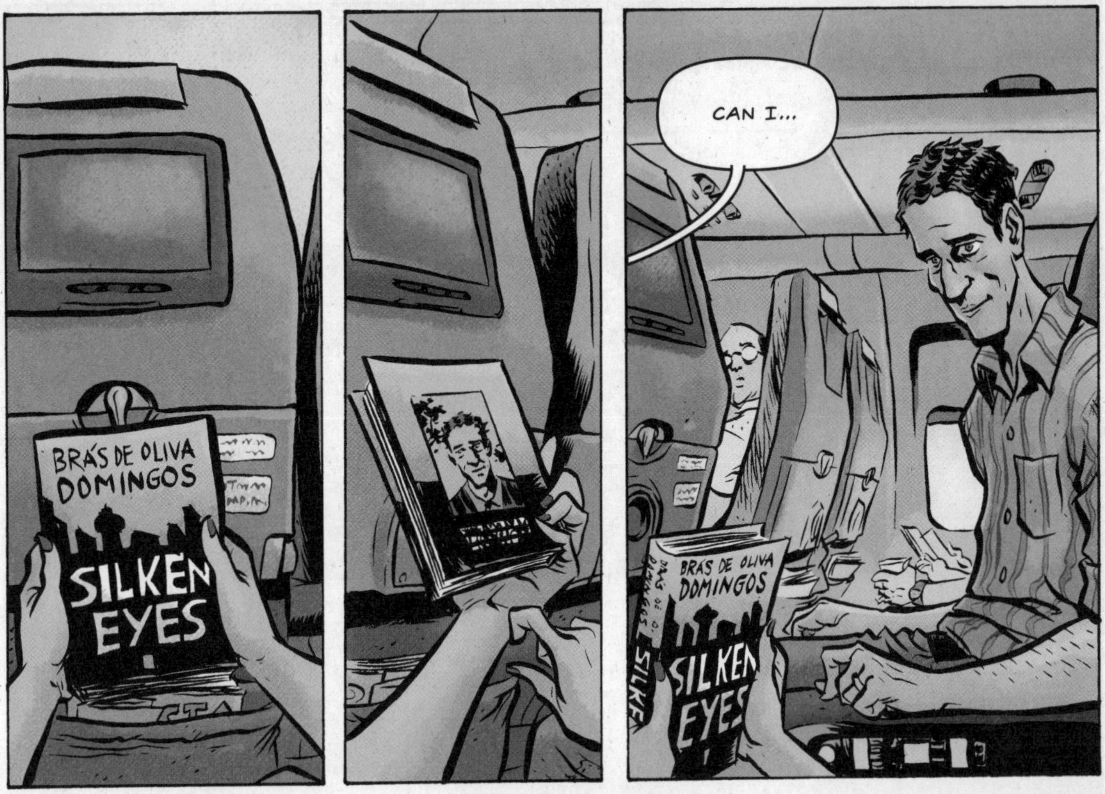
BRÁS DE OLIVA DOMINGOS
SILKEN EYES
CAN I...
BRÁS DE OLIVA DOMINGOS
SILKEN EYES
CAN I GET AN AUTO-GRAPH?

CHAPTER SEVEN:

38

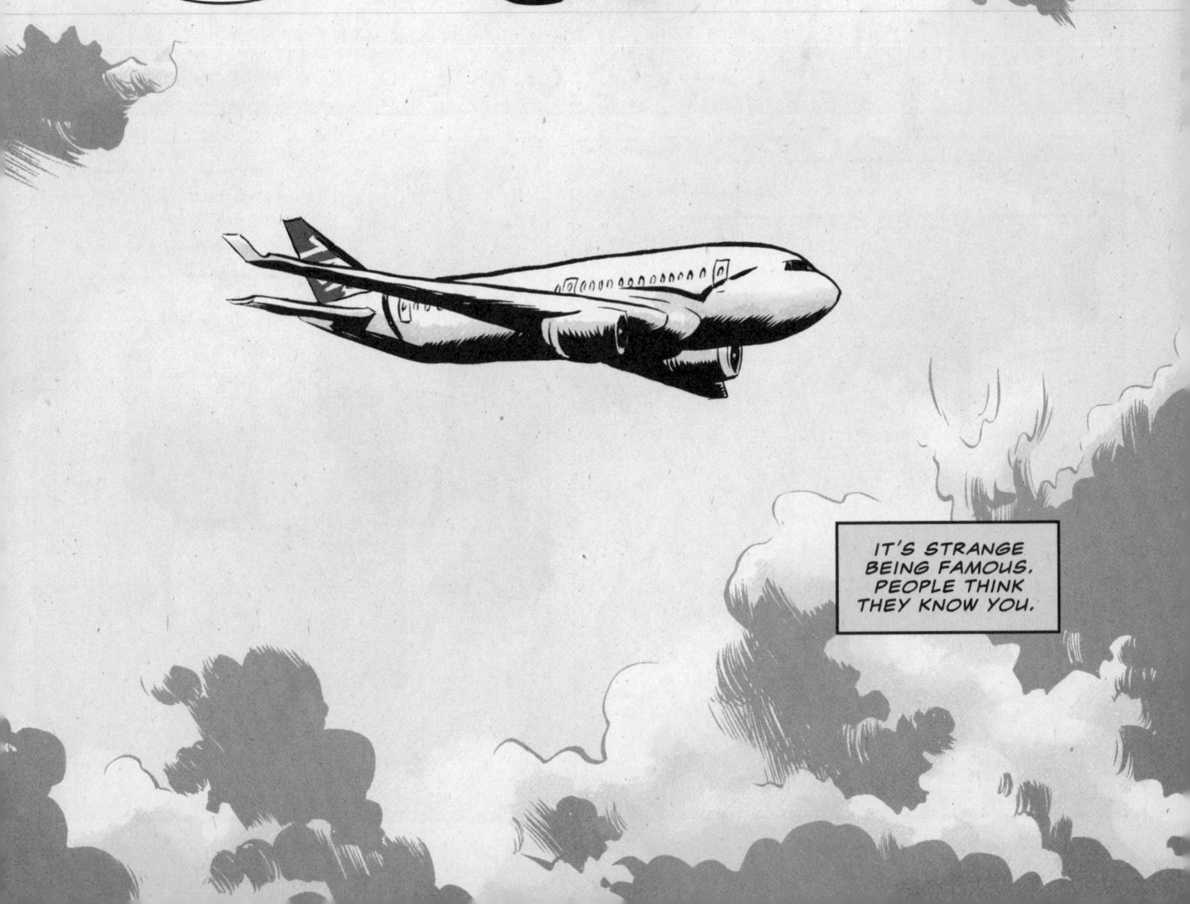
IT'S STRANGE BEING FAMOUS. PEOPLE THINK THEY KNOW YOU.

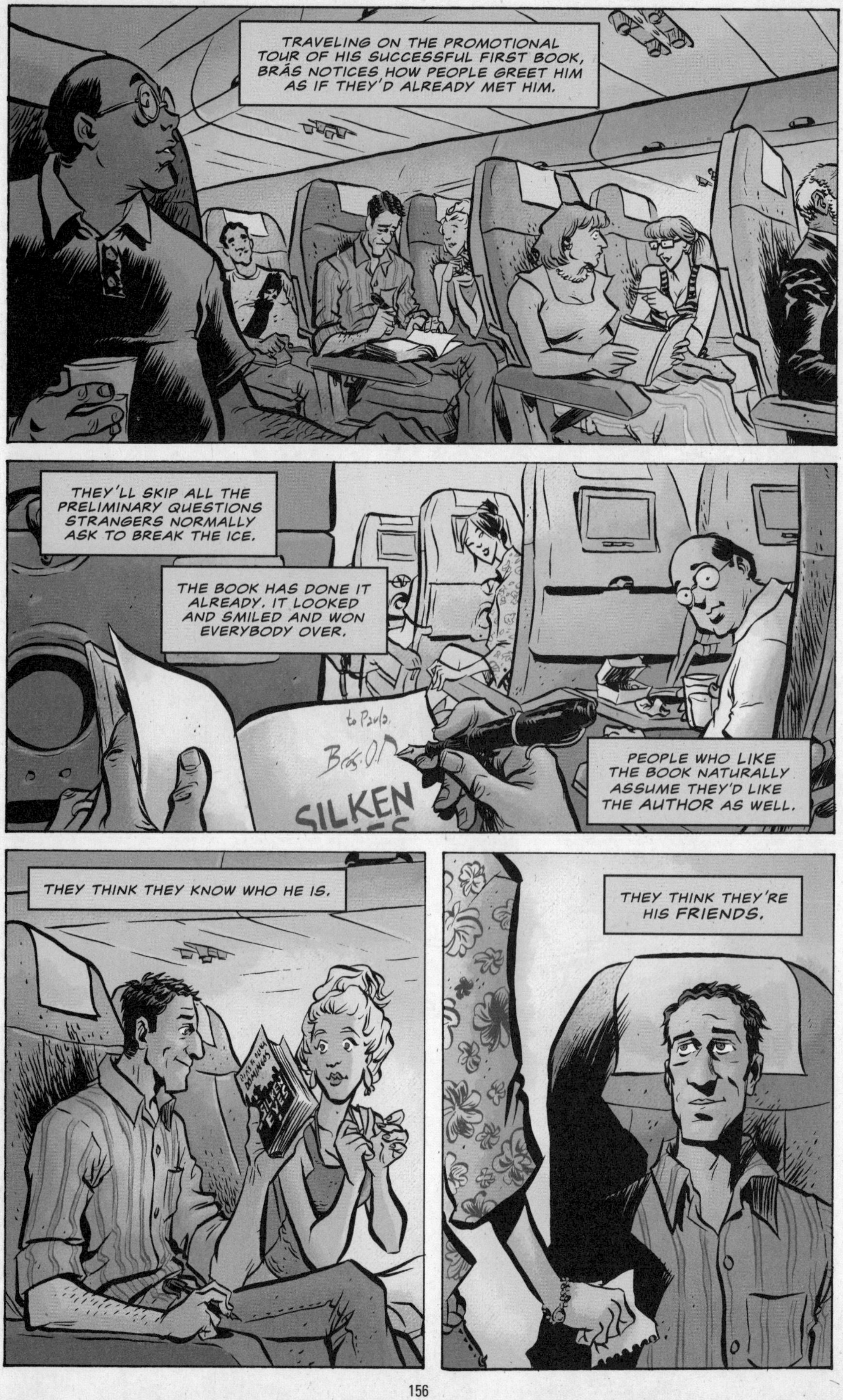
TRAVELING ON THE PROMOTIONAL TOUR OF HIS SUCCESSFUL FIRST BOOK, BRÁS NOTICES HOW PEOPLE GREET HIM AS IF THEY'D ALREADY MET HIM.
THEY'LL SKIP ALL THE PRELIMINARY QUESTIONS STRANGERS NORMALLY ASK TO BREAK THE ICE.
THE BOOK HAS DONE IT ALREADY. IT LOOKED AND SMILED AND WON EVERYBODY OVER.
SILKEN
PEOPLE WHO LIKE THE BOOK NATURALLY ASSUME THEY'D LIKE THE AUTHOR AS WELL.
THEY THINK THEY KNOW WHO HE IS.
THEY THINK THEY'RE HIS FRIENDS.

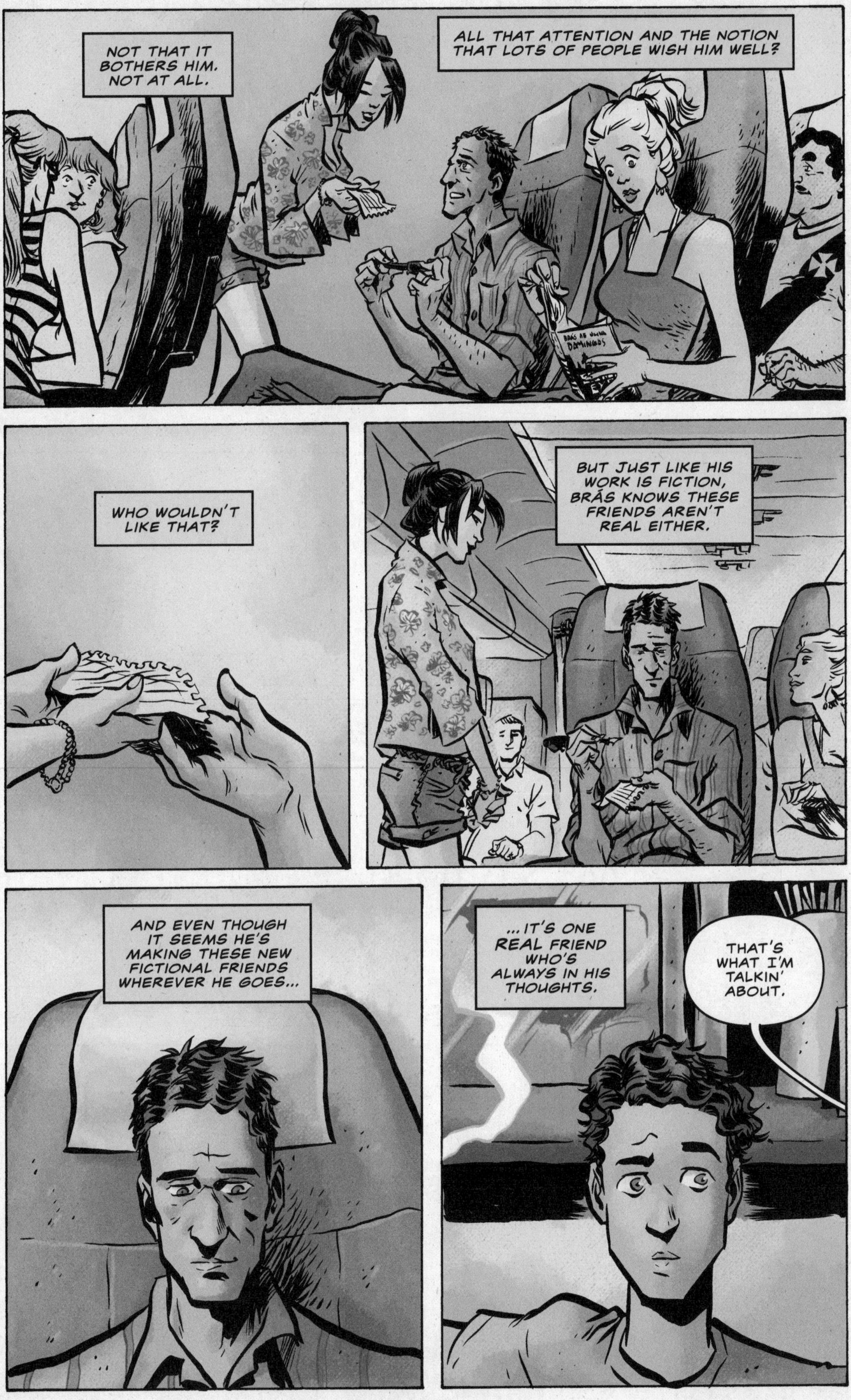
NOT THAT IT BOTHERS HIM. NOT AT ALL.
ALL THAT ATTENTION AND THE NOTION THAT LOTS OF PEOPLE WISH HIM WELL?
BRÁS DE OLIVA DOMINGOS
WHO WOULDN'T LIKE THAT?
BUT JUST LIKE HIS WORK IS FICTION, BRÁS KNOWS THESE FRIENDS AREN'T REAL EITHER.
AND EVEN THOUGH IT SEEMS HE'S MAKING THESE NEW FICTIONAL FRIENDS WHEREVER HE GOES...
...IT'S ONE REAL FRIEND WHO'S ALWAYS IN HIS THOUGHTS.
THAT'S WHAT I'M TALKIN' ABOUT.

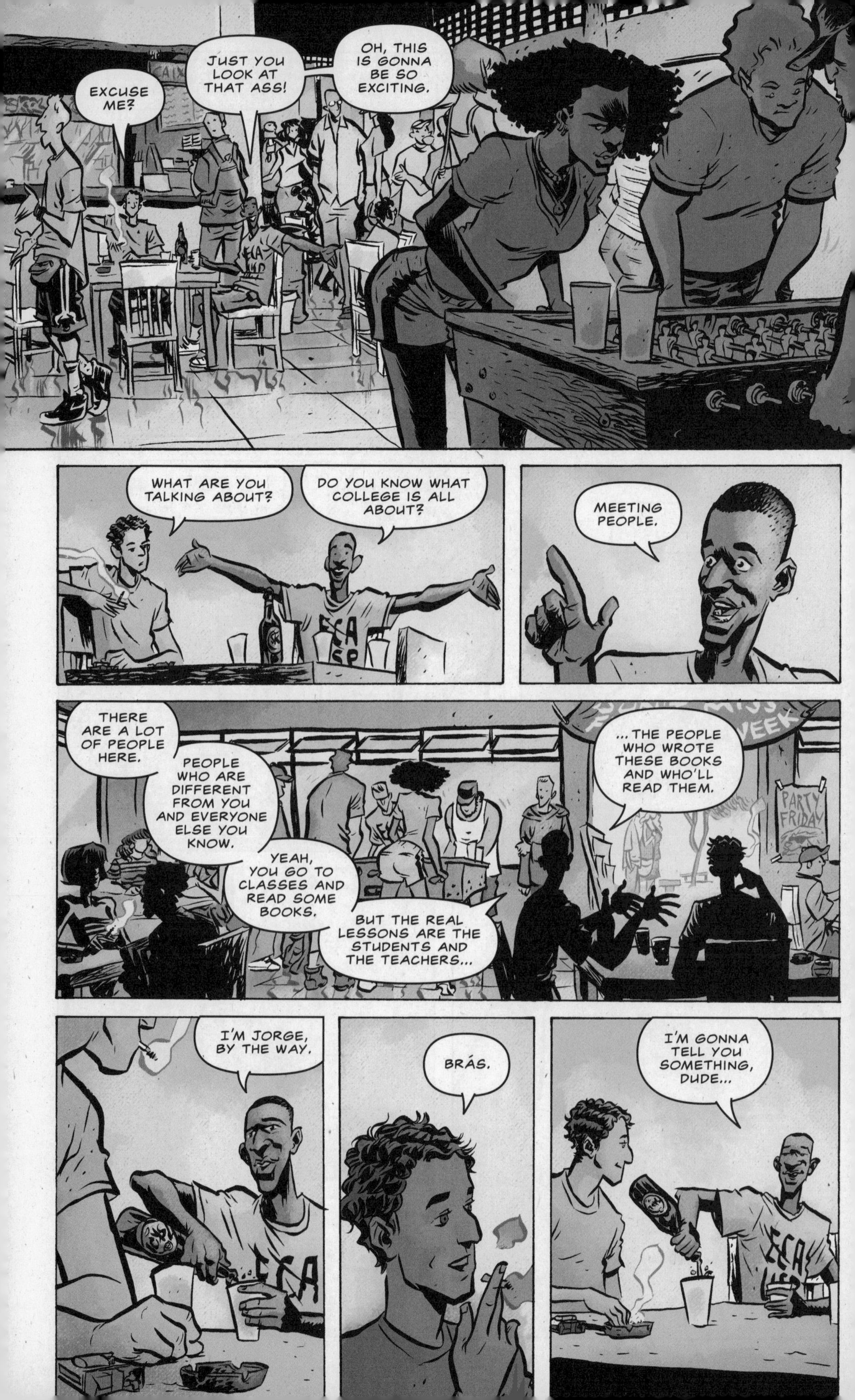
EXCUSE ME?
JUST YOU LOOK AT THAT ASS!
OH, THIS IS GONNA BE SO EXCITING.
WHAT ARE YOU TALKING ABOUT?
DO YOU KNOW WHAT COLLEGE IS ALL ABOUT?
MEETING PEOPLE.
THERE ARE A LOT OF PEOPLE HERE.
PEOPLE WHO ARE DIFFERENT FROM YOU AND EVERYONE ELSE YOU KNOW.
YEAH, YOU GO TO CLASSES AND READ SOME BOOKS.
BUT THE REAL LESSONS ARE THE STUDENTS AND THE TEACHERS...
...THE PEOPLE WHO WROTE THESE BOOKS AND WHO'LL READ THEM.
PARTY FRIDAY
I'M JORGE, BY THE WAY.
BRÁS.
I'M GONNA TELL YOU SOMETHING, DUDE...

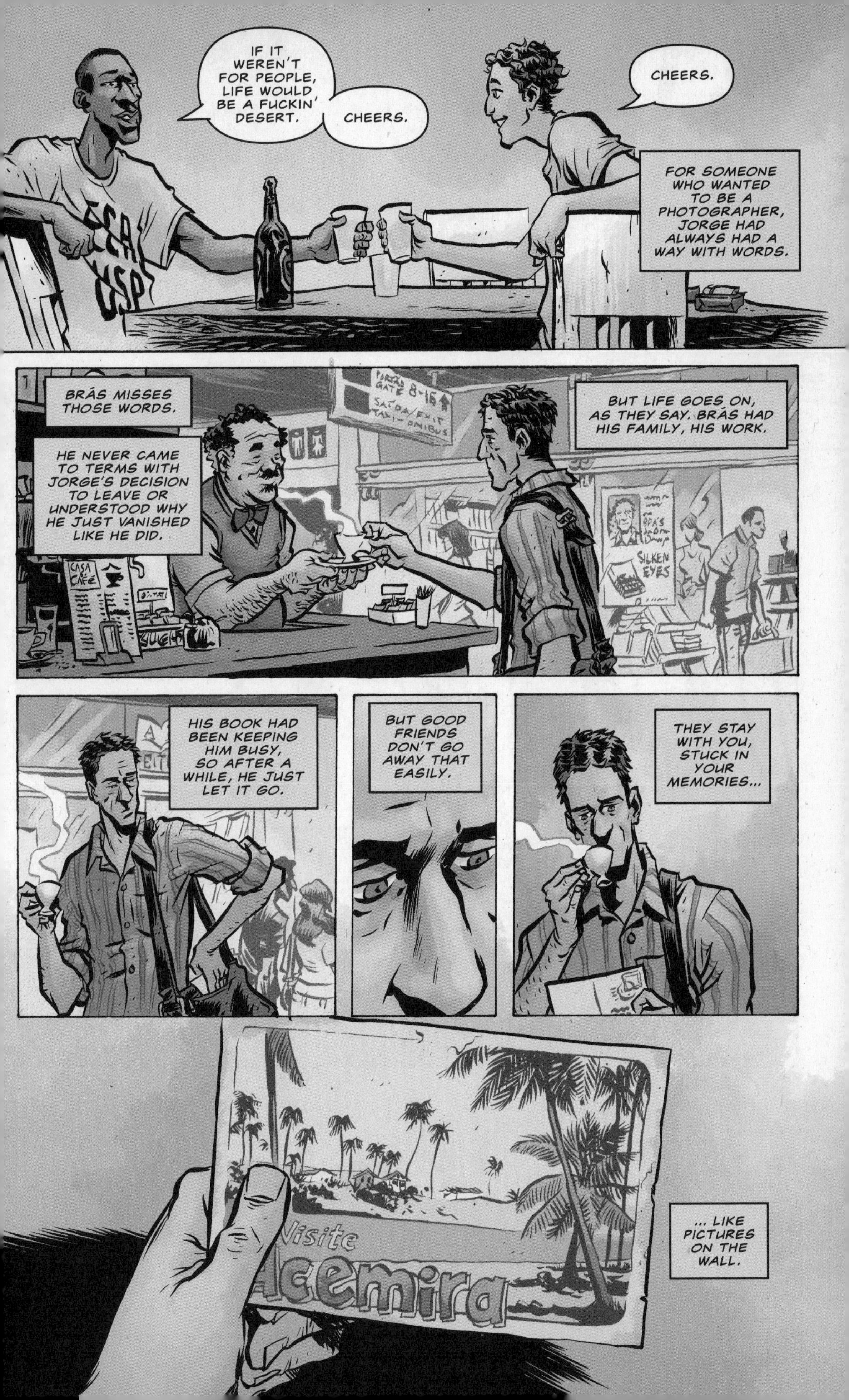
IF IT WEREN'T FOR PEOPLE, LIFE WOULD BE A FUCKIN' DESERT.
CHEERS.
CHEERS.
FOR SOMEONE WHO WANTED TO BE A PHOTOGRAPHER, JORGE HAD ALWAYS HAD A WAY WITH WORDS.
BRÁS MISSES THOSE WORDS.
HE NEVER CAME TO TERMS WITH JORGE'S DECISION TO LEAVE OR UNDERSTOOD WHY HE JUST VANISHED LIKE HE DID.
PORTÃO GATE 8-16
SAÍDA/EXIT
TAXI-ÔNIBUS
CASA CAFÉ
SILKEN EYES
BUT LIFE GOES ON, AS THEY SAY. BRÁS HAD HIS FAMILY, HIS WORK.
HIS BOOK HAD BEEN KEEPING HIM BUSY, SO AFTER A WHILE, HE JUST LET IT GO.
BUT GOOD FRIENDS DON'T GO AWAY THAT EASILY.
THEY STAY WITH YOU, STUCK IN YOUR MEMORIES...
Visite
Acemira
... LIKE PICTURES ON THE WALL.

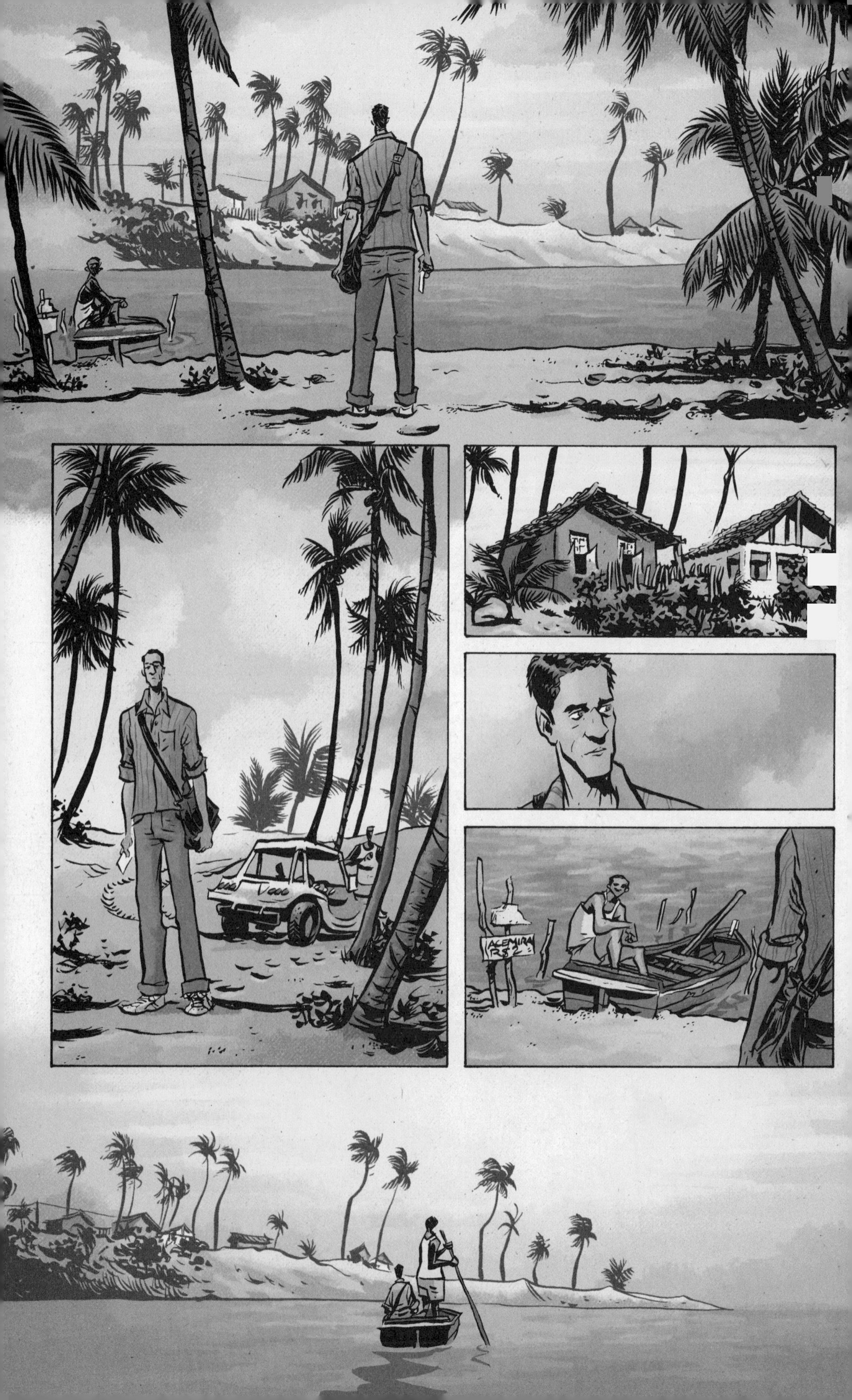
ACEMIRA
R$ 2

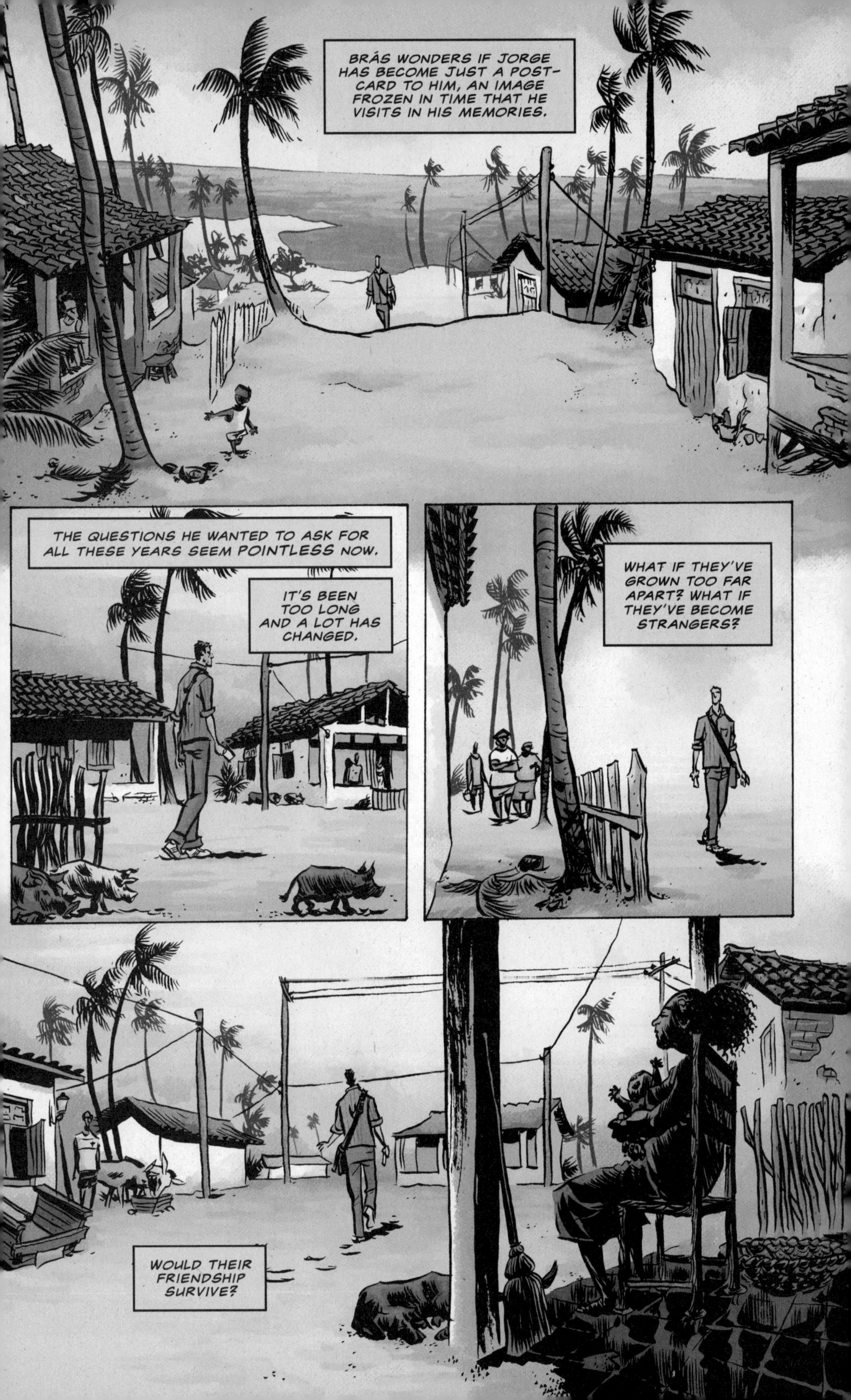
BRÁS WONDERS IF JORGE HAS BECOME JUST A POST-CARD TO HIM, AN IMAGE FROZEN IN TIME THAT HE VISITS IN HIS MEMORIES.
THE QUESTIONS HE WANTED TO ASK FOR ALL THESE YEARS SEEM POINTLESS NOW.
IT'S BEEN TOO LONG AND A LOT HAS CHANGED.
WHAT IF THEY'VE GROWN TOO FAR APART? WHAT IF THEY'VE BECOME STRANGERS?
WOULD THEIR FRIENDSHIP SURVIVE?

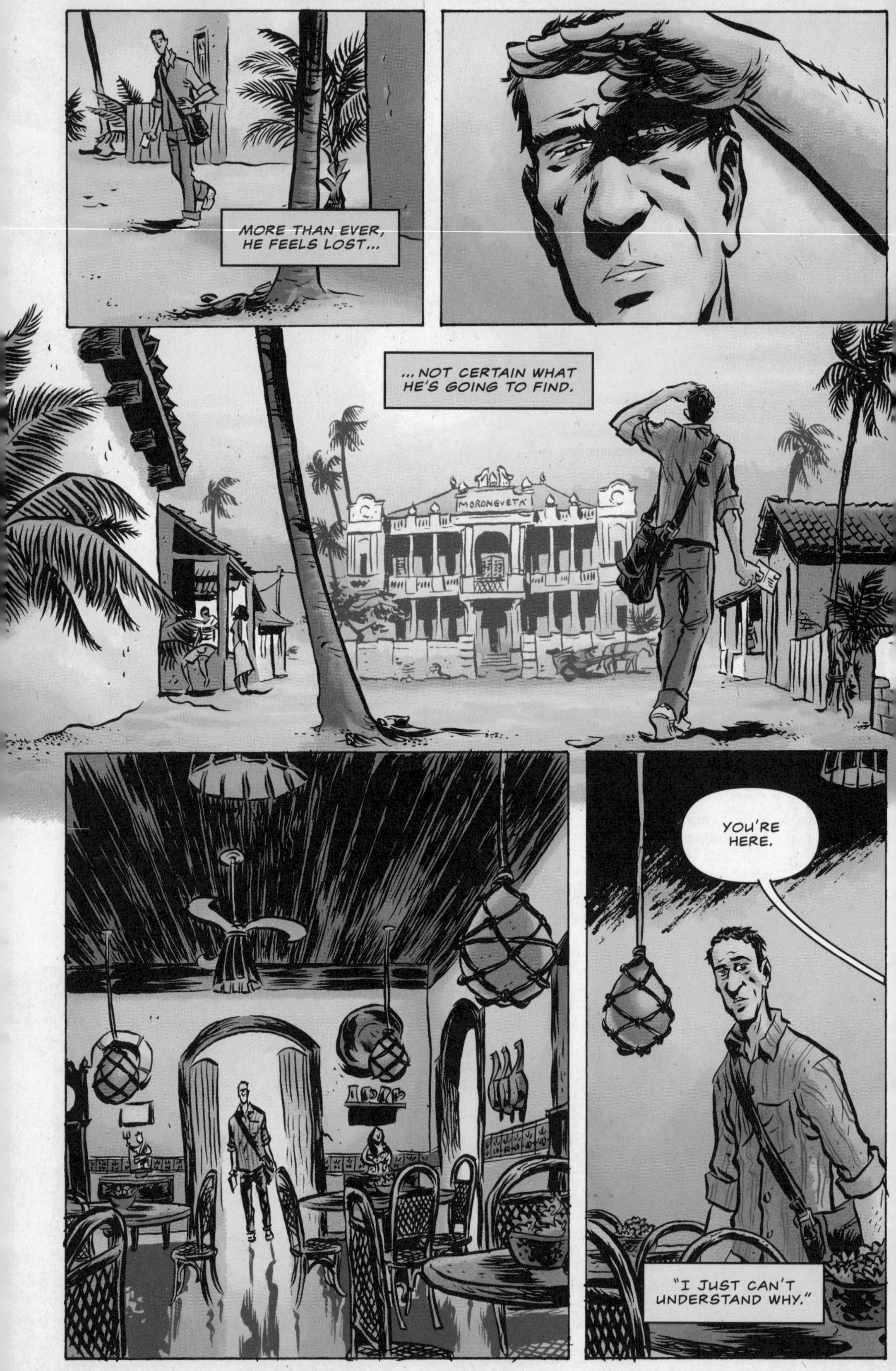

MORE THAN EVER, HE FEELS LOST...
...NOT CERTAIN WHAT HE'S GOING TO FIND.
MORONGVETA
YOU'RE HERE.
"I JUST CAN'T UNDERSTAND WHY."

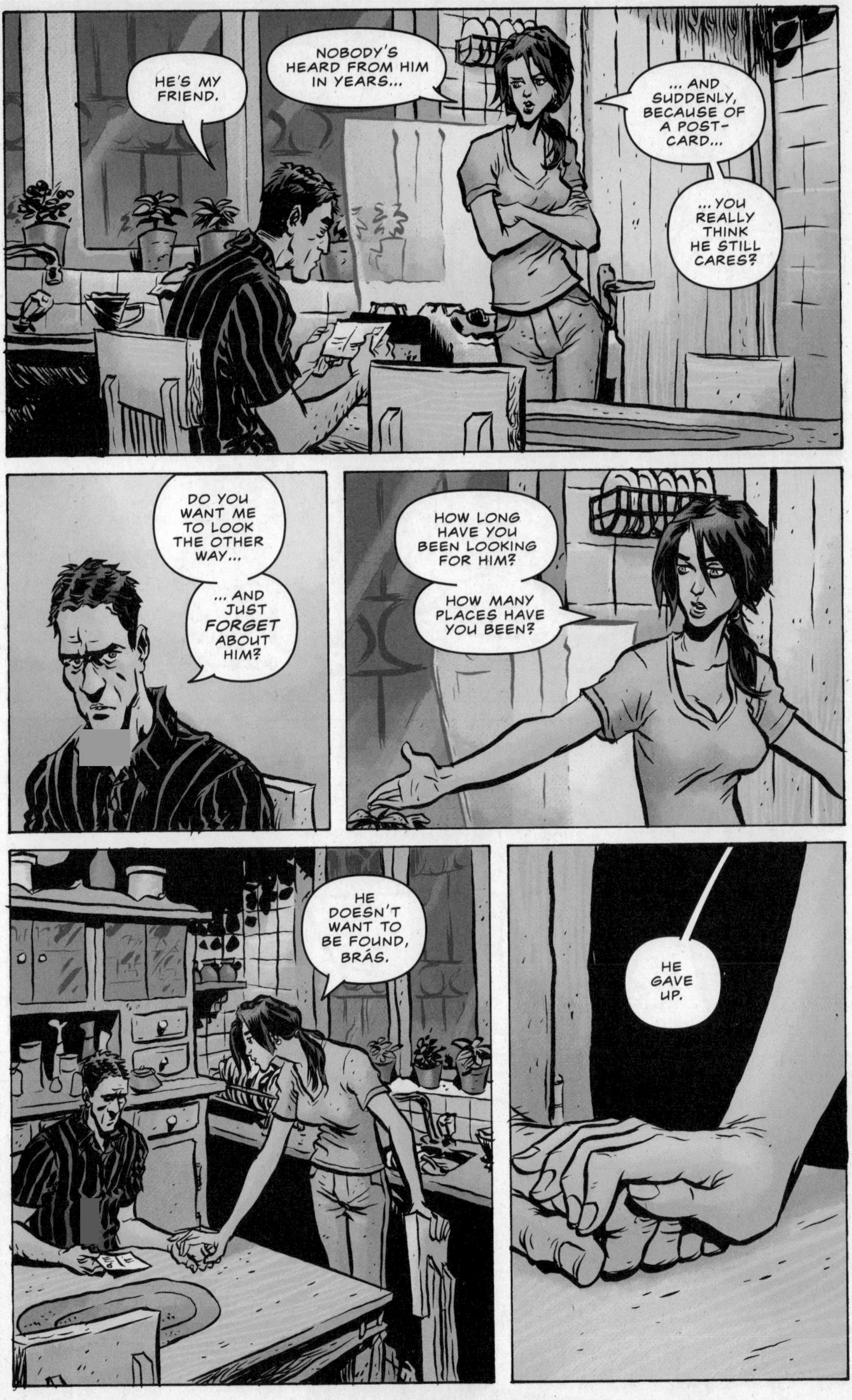
HE'S MY FRIEND.
NOBODY'S HEARD FROM HIM IN YEARS...
... AND SUDDENLY, BECAUSE OF A POST-CARD...
...YOU REALLY THINK HE STILL CARES?
DO YOU WANT ME TO LOOK THE OTHER WAY...
... AND JUST FORGET ABOUT HIM?
HOW LONG HAVE YOU BEEN LOOKING FOR HIM?
HOW MANY PLACES HAVE YOU BEEN?
HE DOESN'T WANT TO BE FOUND, BRÁS.
HE GAVE UP.

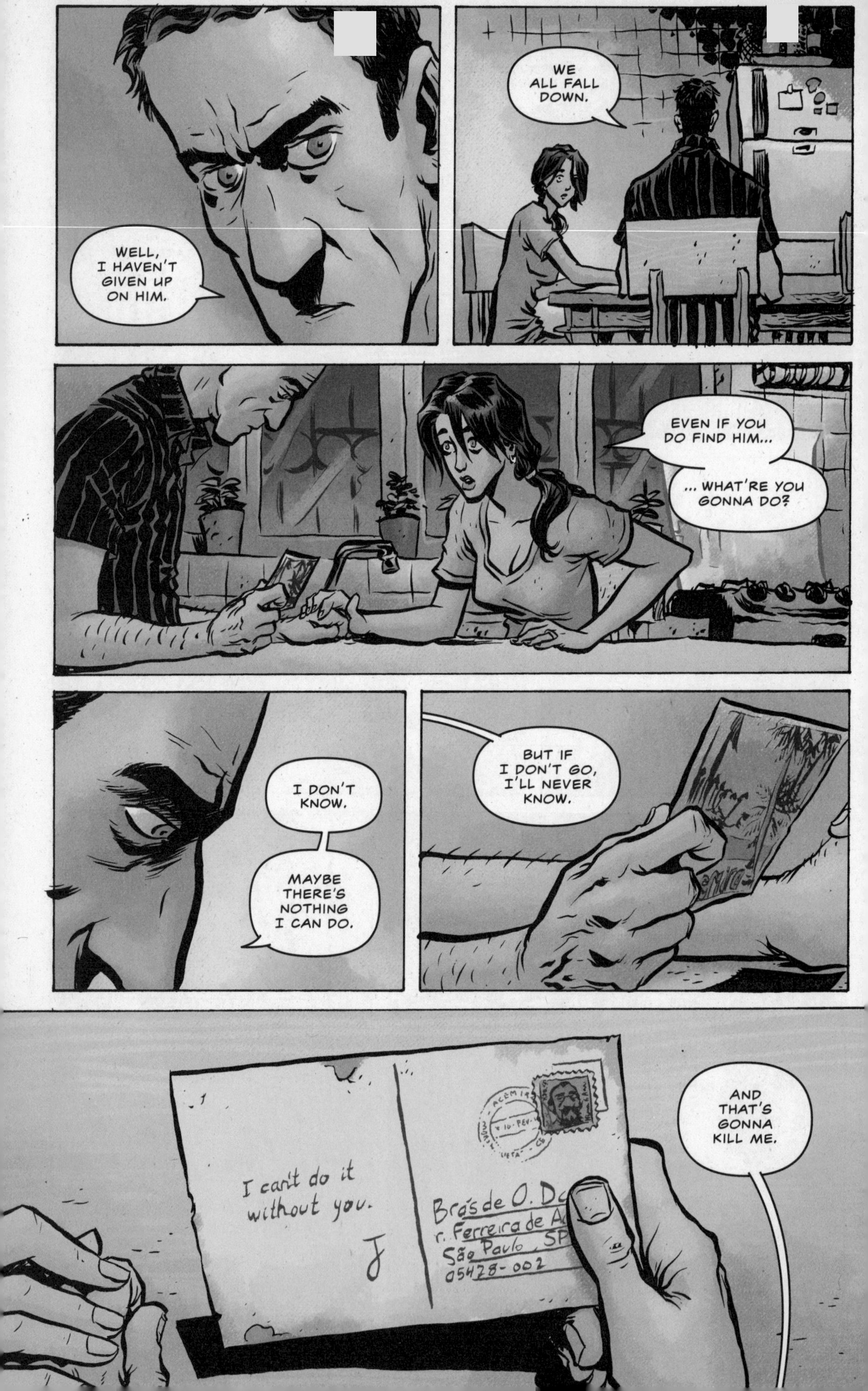
WELL, I HAVEN'T GIVEN UP ON HIM.
WE ALL FALL DOWN.
EVEN IF YOU DO FIND HIM...
... WHAT'RE YOU GONNA DO?
I DON'T KNOW.
MAYBE THERE'S NOTHING I CAN DO.
BUT IF I DON'T GO, I'LL NEVER KNOW.
I can't do it without you.
J
São Paulo, SP
05428-002
AND THAT'S GONNA KILL ME.

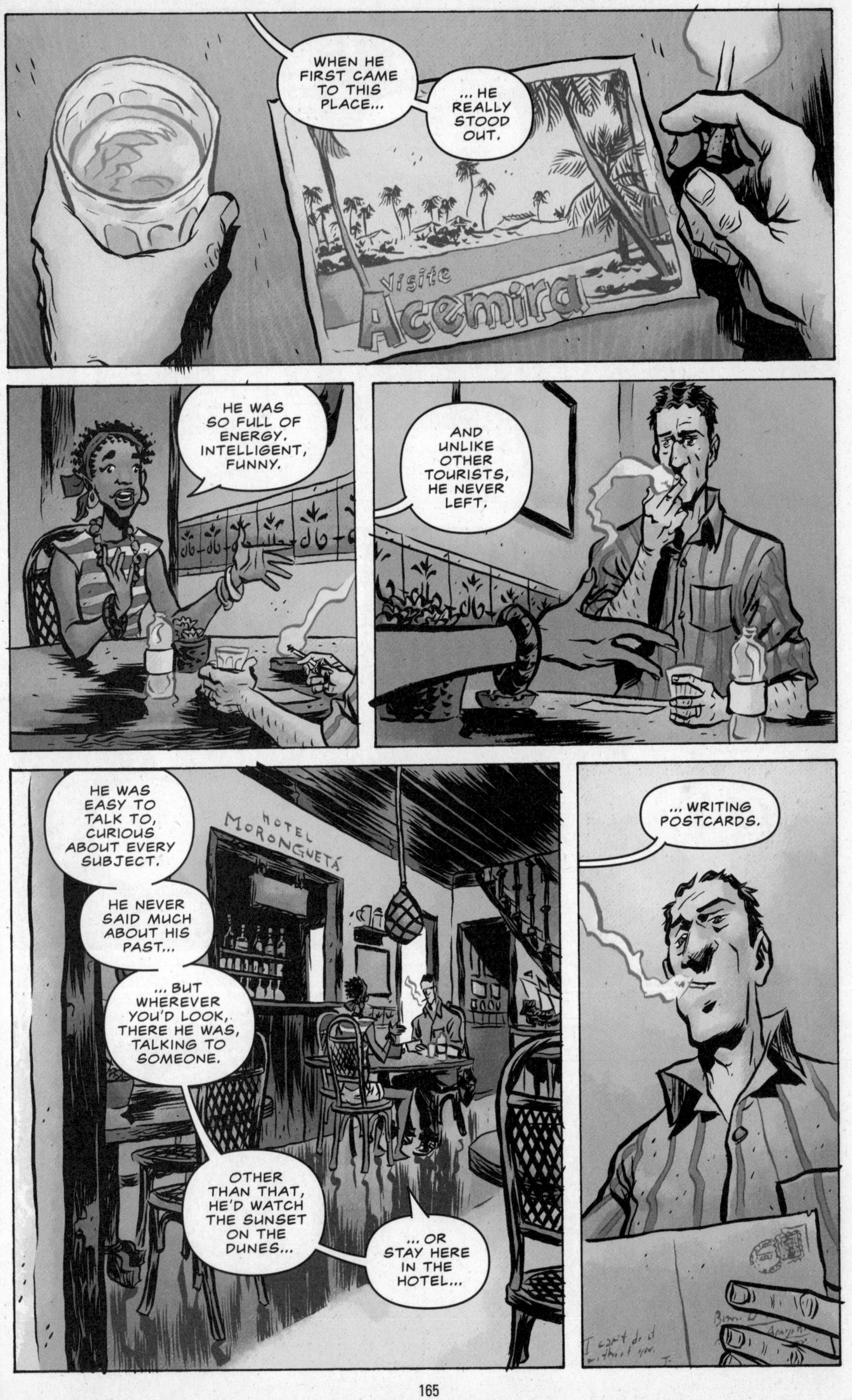
WHEN HE FIRST CAME TO THIS PLACE...
... HE REALLY STOOD OUT.
Visite
Acemira
HE WAS SO FULL OF ENERGY. INTELLIGENT, FUNNY.
AND UNLIKE OTHER TOURISTS, HE NEVER LEFT.
HE WAS EASY TO TALK TO, CURIOUS ABOUT EVERY SUBJECT.
HOTEL
MORONGUETÁ
HE NEVER SAID MUCH ABOUT HIS PAST...
... BUT WHEREVER YOU'D LOOK, THERE HE WAS, TALKING TO SOMEONE.
OTHER THAN THAT, HE'D WATCH THE SUNSET ON THE DUNES...
... OR STAY HERE IN THE HOTEL...
... WRITING POSTCARDS.

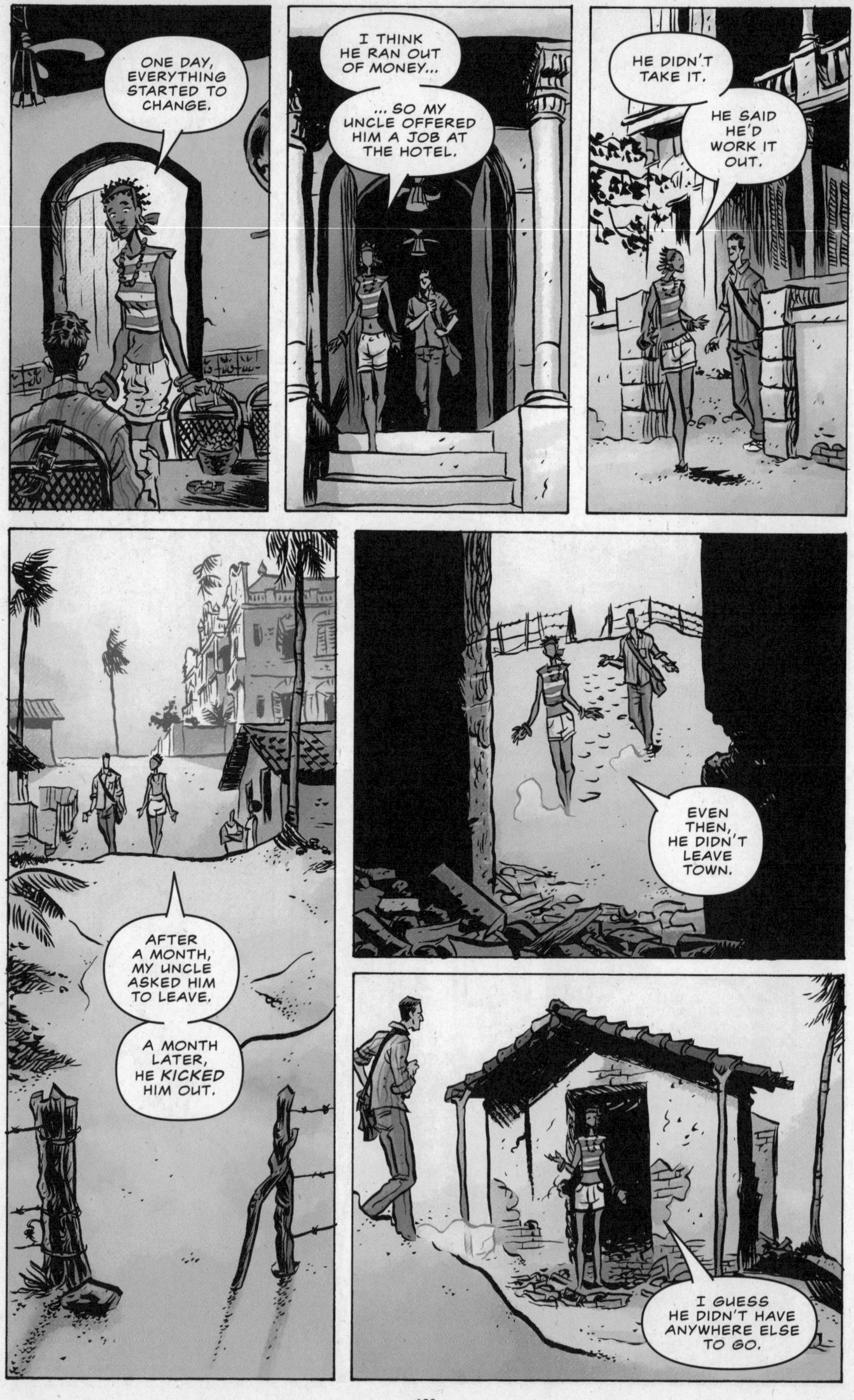
ONE DAY, EVERYTHING STARTED TO CHANGE.
I THINK HE RAN OUT OF MONEY...
... SO MY UNCLE OFFERED HIM A JOB AT THE HOTEL.
HE DIDN'T TAKE IT.
HE SAID HE'D WORK IT OUT.
AFTER A MONTH, MY UNCLE ASKED HIM TO LEAVE.
A MONTH LATER, HE *KICKED* HIM OUT.
EVEN THEN, HE DIDN'T LEAVE TOWN.
I GUESS HE DIDN'T HAVE ANYWHERE ELSE TO GO.

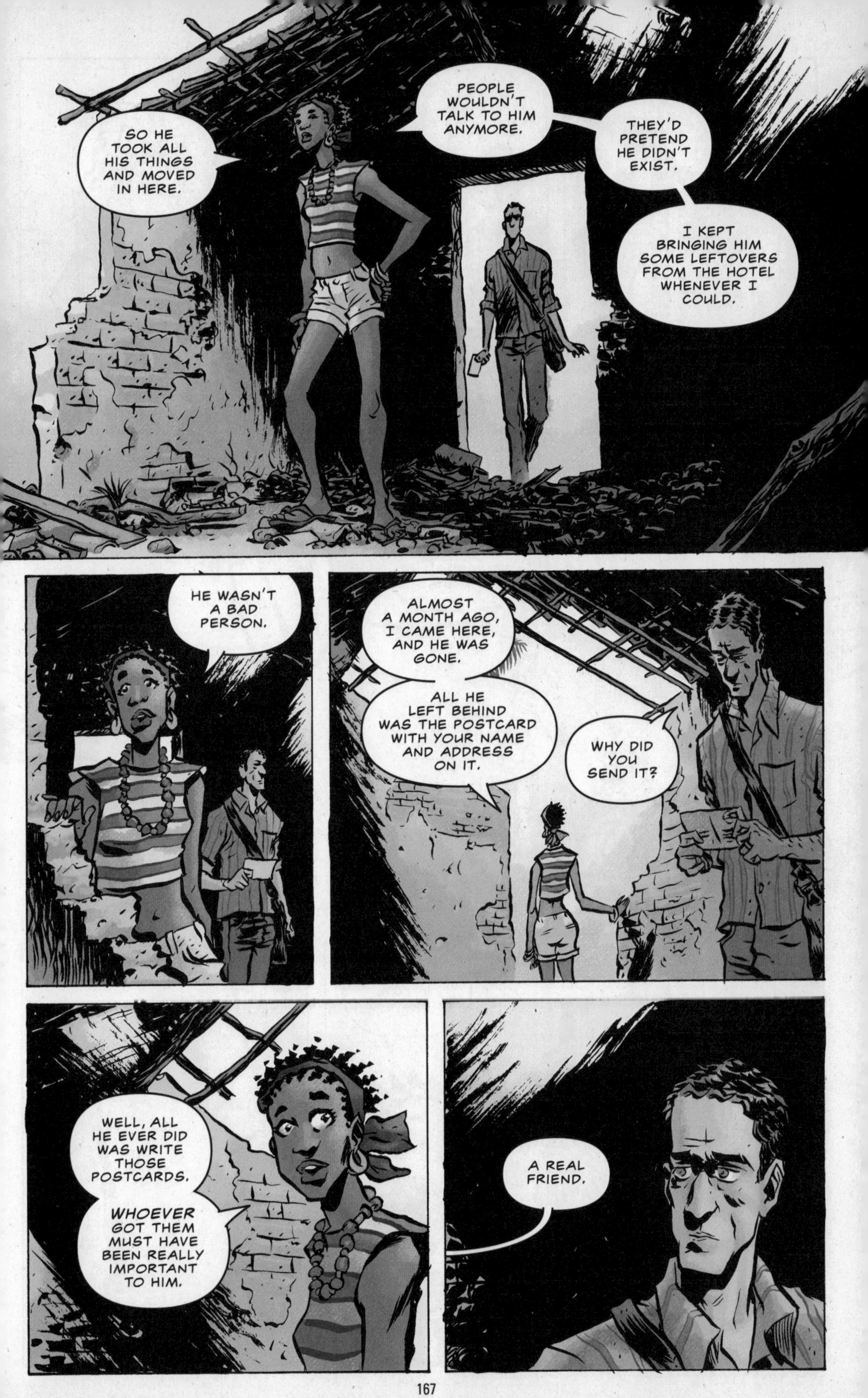

SO HE TOOK ALL HIS THINGS AND MOVED IN HERE.
PEOPLE WOULDN'T TALK TO HIM ANYMORE.
THEY'D PRETEND HE DIDN'T EXIST.
I KEPT BRINGING HIM SOME LEFTOVERS FROM THE HOTEL WHENEVER I COULD.
HE WASN'T A BAD PERSON.
ALMOST A MONTH AGO, I CAME HERE, AND HE WAS GONE.
ALL HE LEFT BEHIND WAS THE POSTCARD WITH YOUR NAME AND ADDRESS ON IT.
WHY DID YOU SEND IT?
WELL, ALL HE EVER DID WAS WRITE THOSE POSTCARDS.
WHOEVER GOT THEM MUST HAVE BEEN REALLY IMPORTANT TO HIM.
A REAL FRIEND.

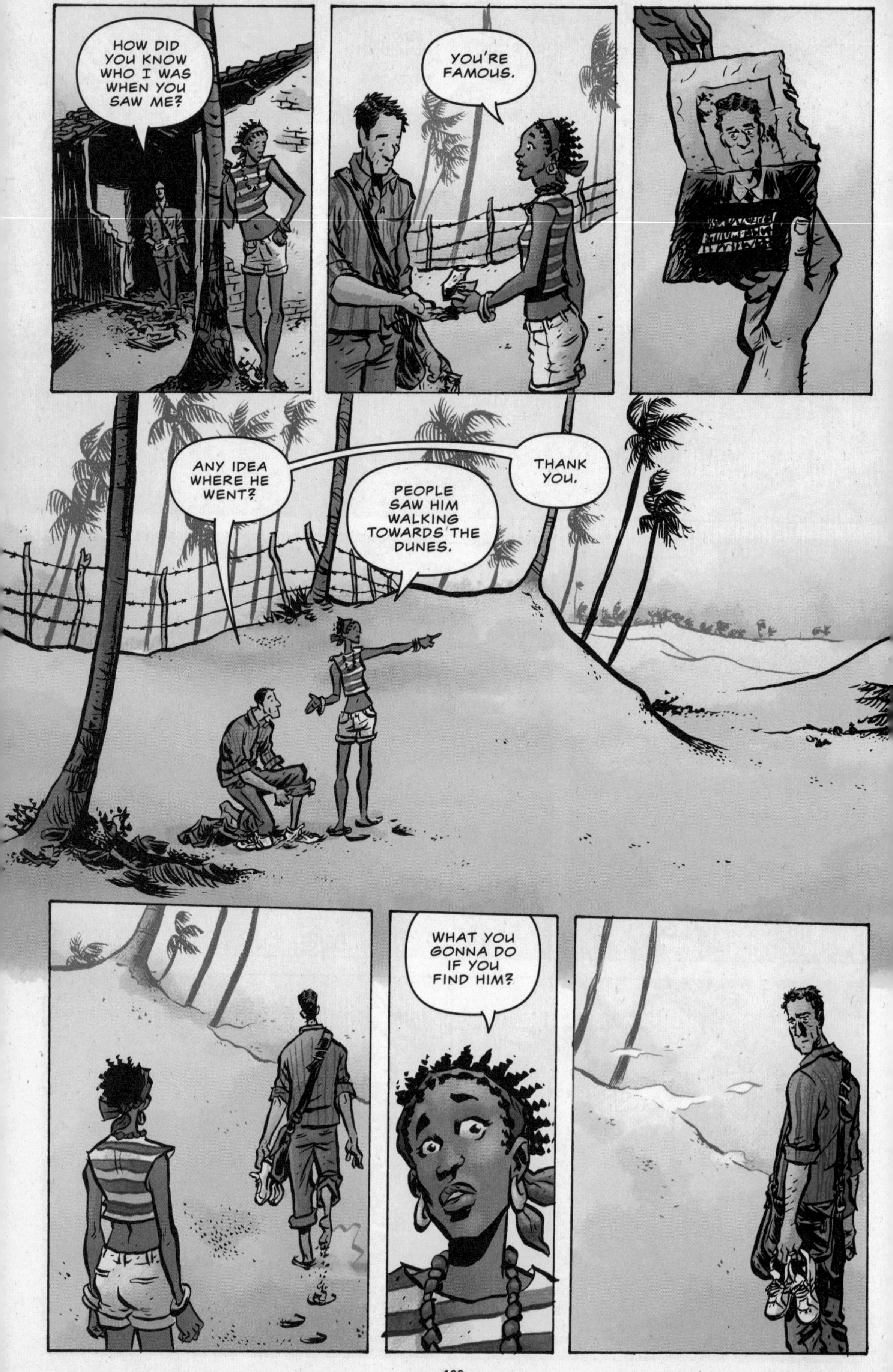
HOW DID YOU KNOW WHO I WAS WHEN YOU SAW ME?
YOU'RE FAMOUS.
ANY IDEA WHERE HE WENT?
PEOPLE SAW HIM WALKING TOWARDS THE DUNES.
THANK YOU.
WHAT YOU GONNA DO IF YOU FIND HIM?

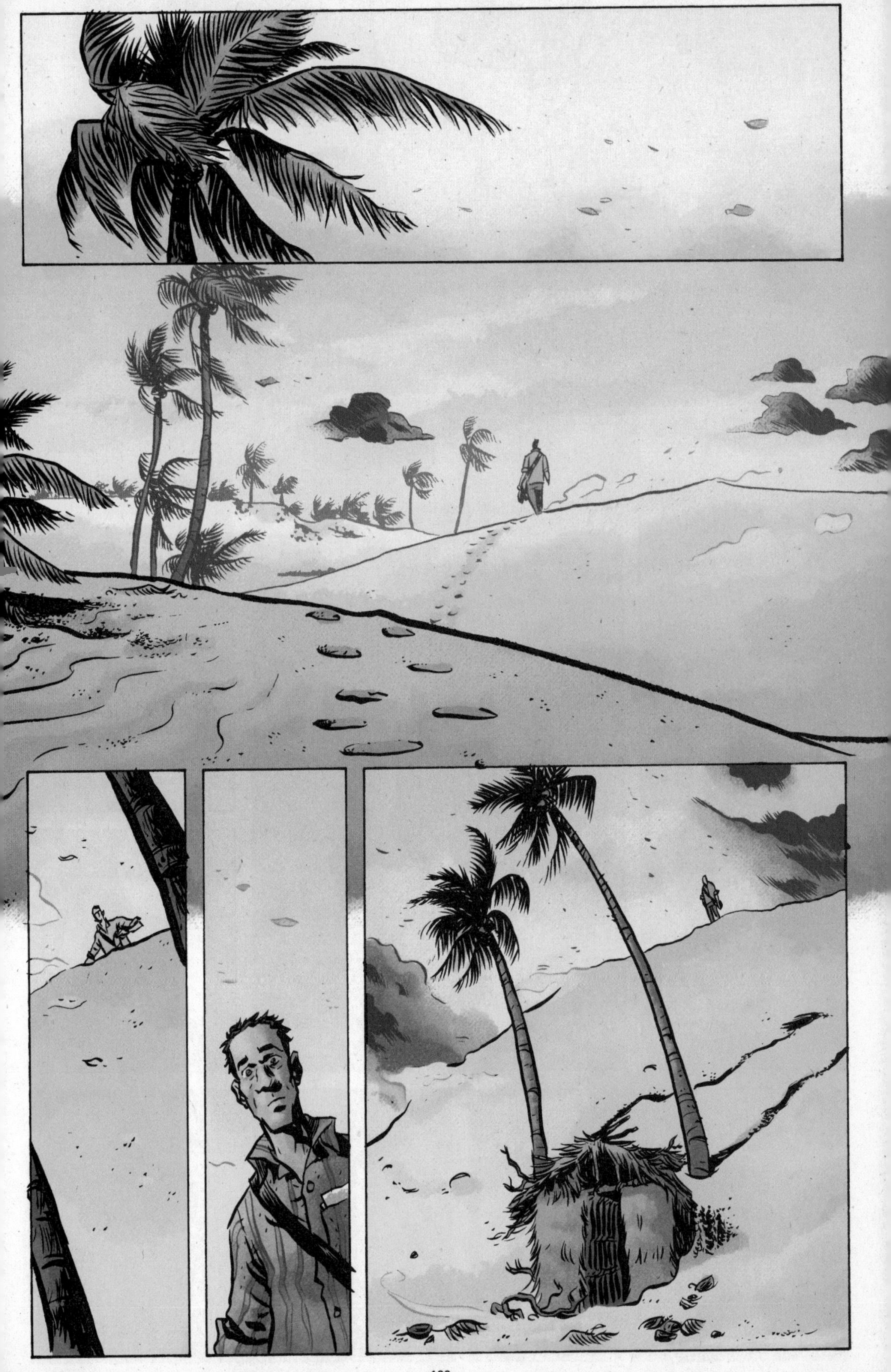

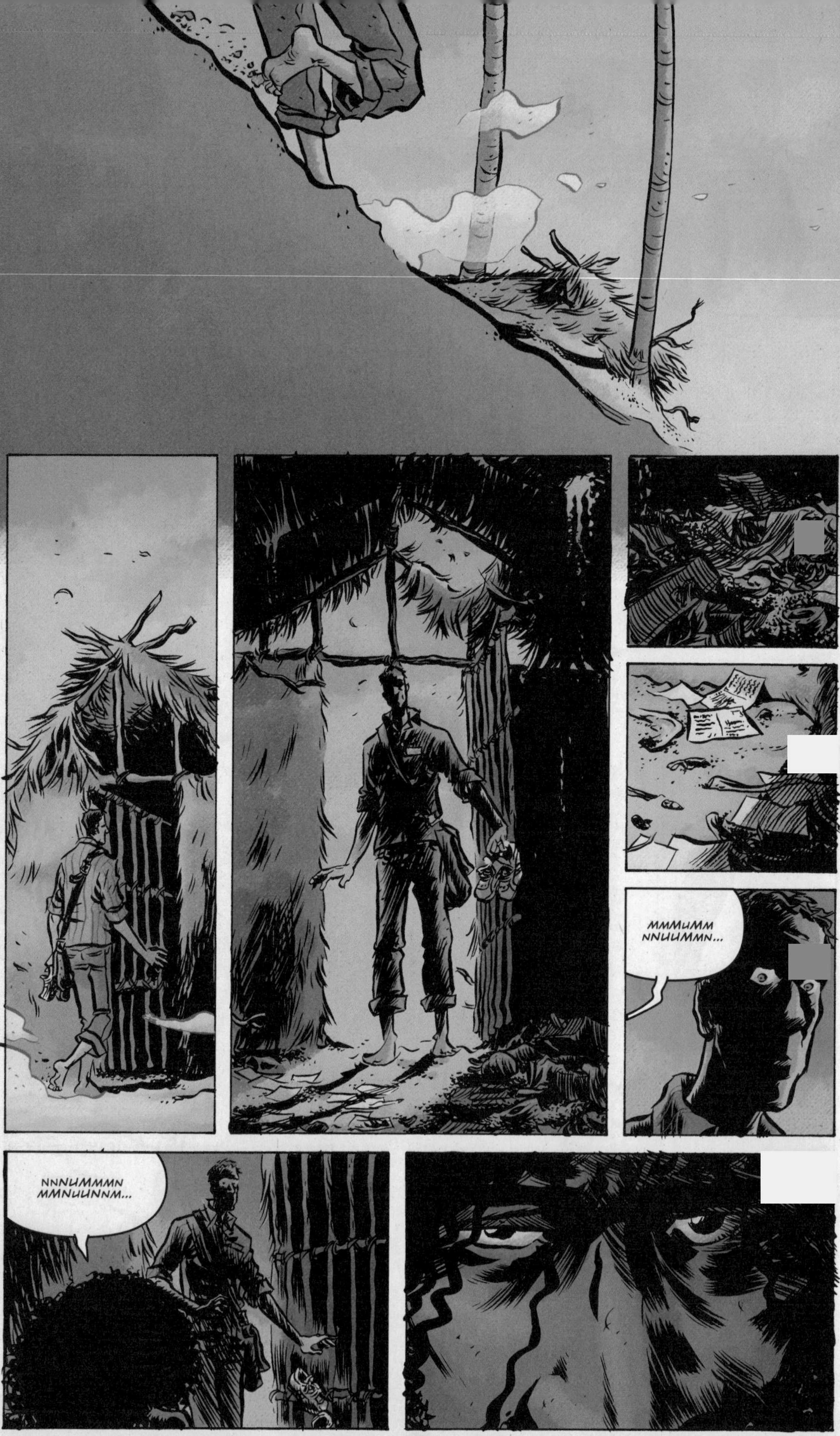
MMMUMM NNUUMMN...
NNNUMMMN MMNUUNNM...

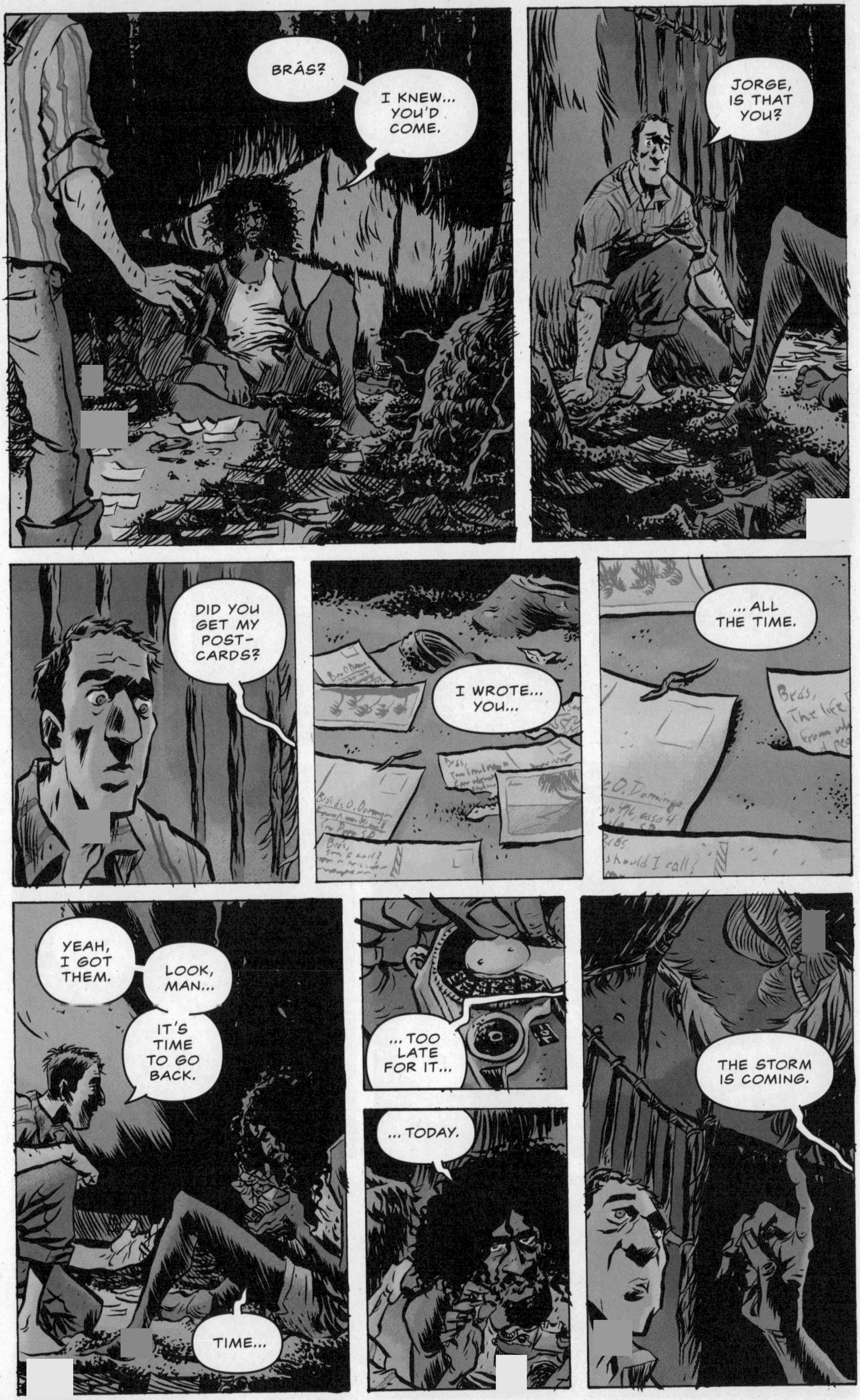
BRÁS?
I KNEW... YOU'D COME.
JORGE, IS THAT YOU?
DID YOU GET MY POST-CARDS?
I WROTE... YOU...
...ALL THE TIME.
YEAH, I GOT THEM.
LOOK, MAN...
IT'S TIME TO GO BACK.
TIME...
...TOO LATE FOR IT...
...TODAY.
THE STORM IS COMING.

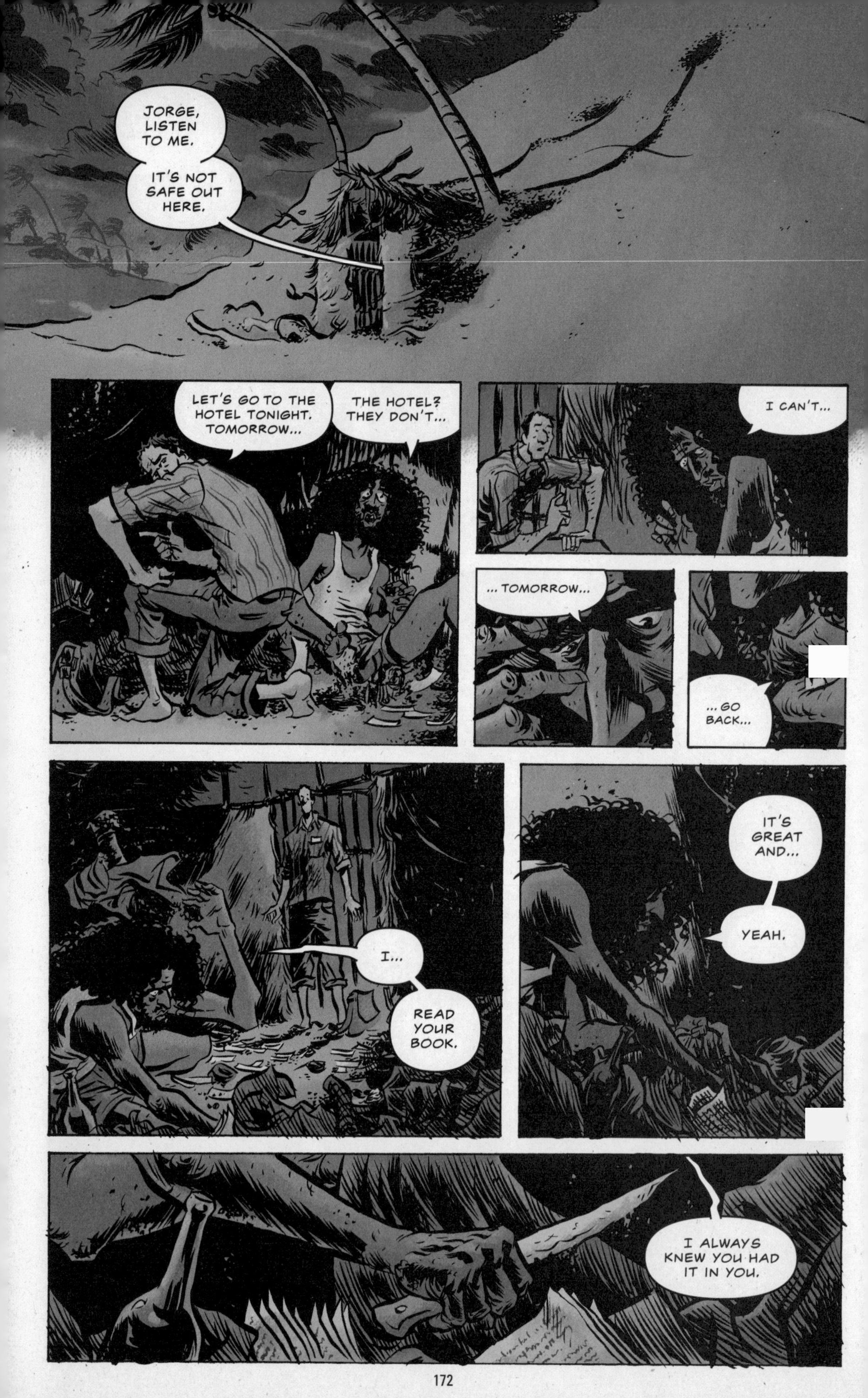
JORGE, LISTEN TO ME.
IT'S NOT SAFE OUT HERE.
LET'S GO TO THE HOTEL TONIGHT. TOMORROW...
THE HOTEL? THEY DON'T...
I CAN'T...
... TOMORROW...
... GO BACK...
I...
READ YOUR BOOK.
IT'S GREAT AND...
YEAH.
I ALWAYS KNEW YOU HAD IT IN YOU.

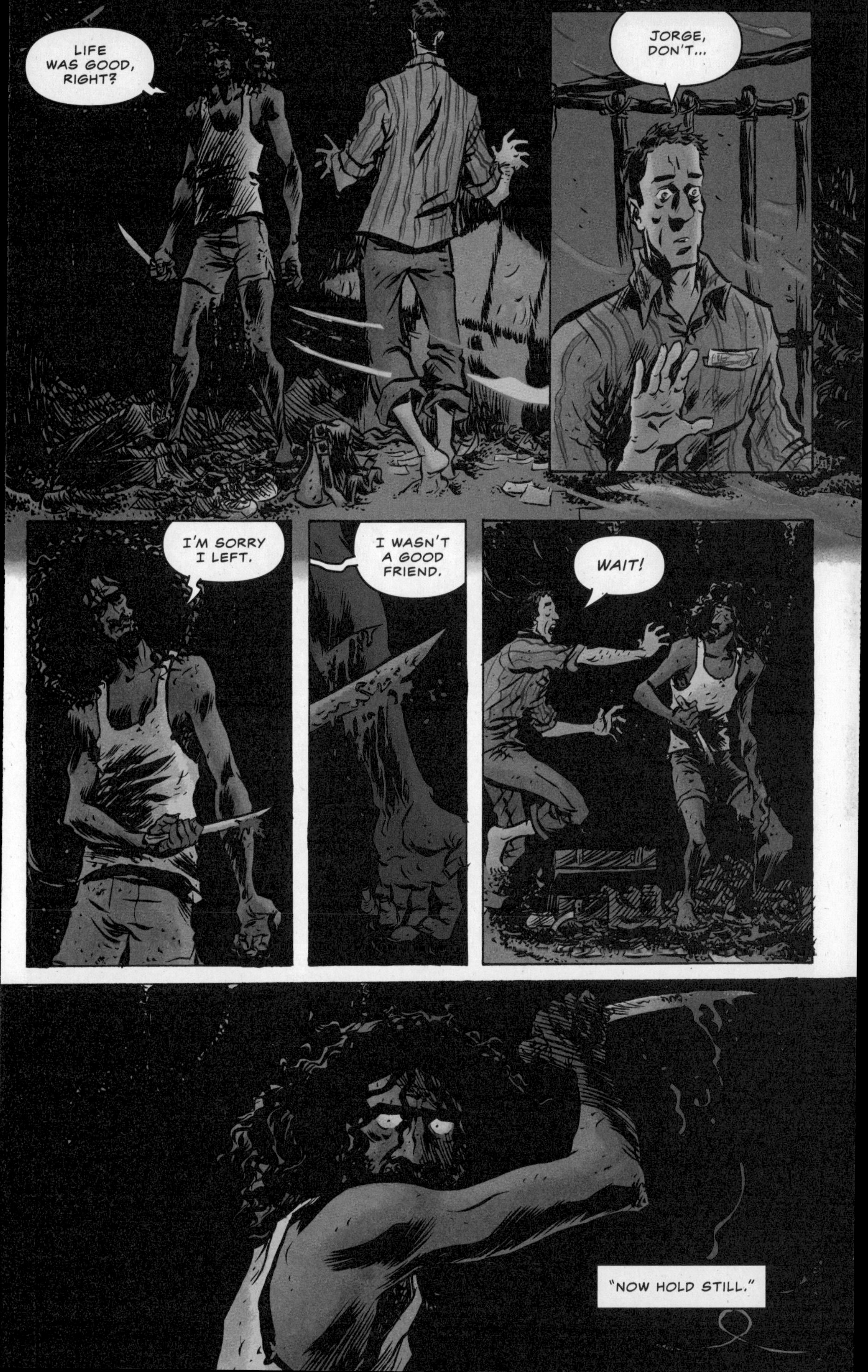
LIFE WAS GOOD, RIGHT?
JORGE, DON'T...
I'M SORRY I LEFT.
I WASN'T A GOOD FRIEND.
WAIT!
"NOW HOLD STILL."

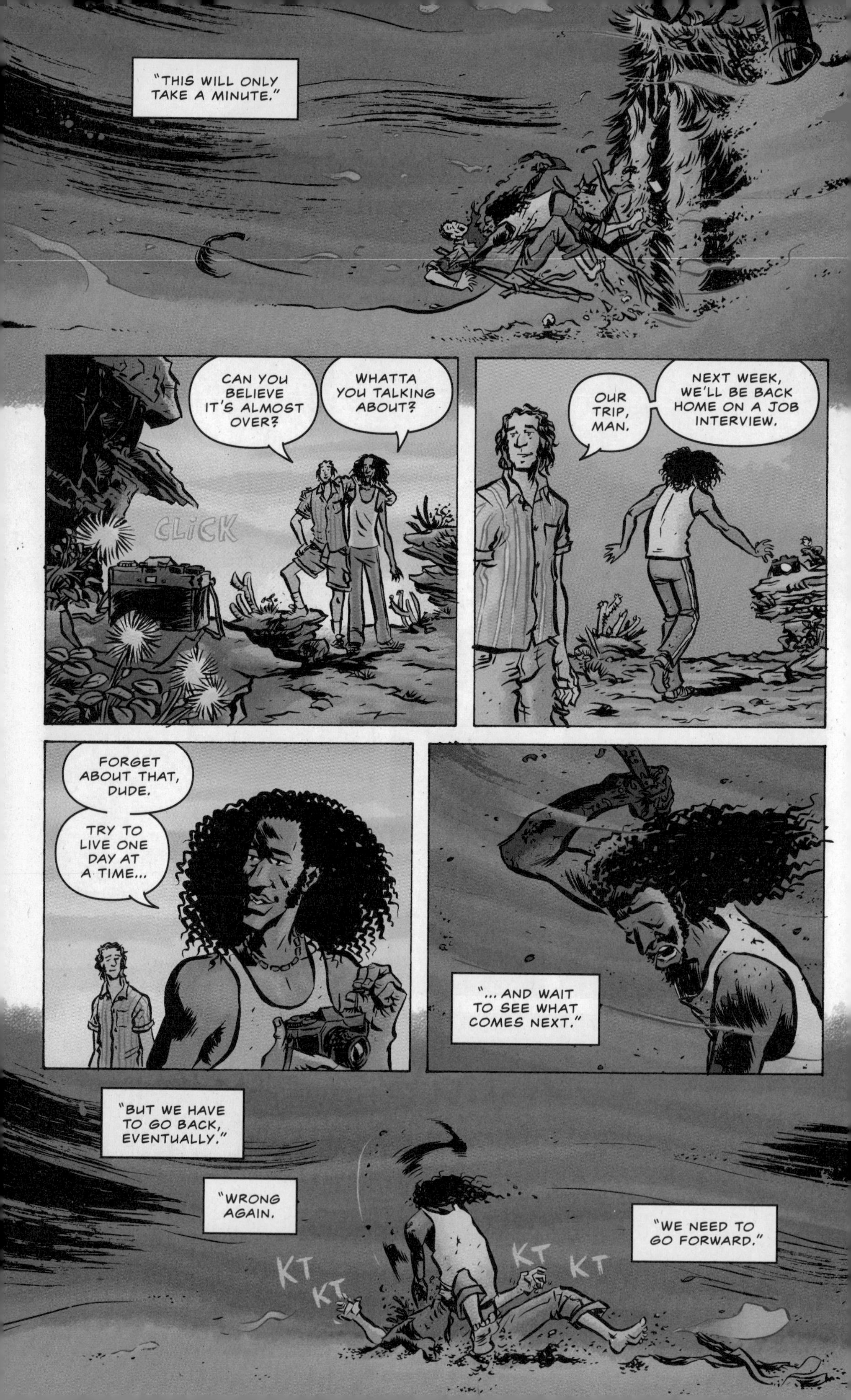
"THIS WILL ONLY TAKE A MINUTE."
CAN YOU BELIEVE IT'S ALMOST OVER?
WHATTA YOU TALKING ABOUT?
CLICK
OUR TRIP, MAN.
NEXT WEEK, WE'LL BE BACK HOME ON A JOB INTERVIEW.
FORGET ABOUT THAT, DUDE.
TRY TO LIVE ONE DAY AT A TIME...
"... AND WAIT TO SEE WHAT COMES NEXT."
"BUT WE HAVE TO GO BACK, EVENTUALLY."
"WRONG AGAIN.
"WE NEED TO GO FORWARD."
KT
KT
KT
KT

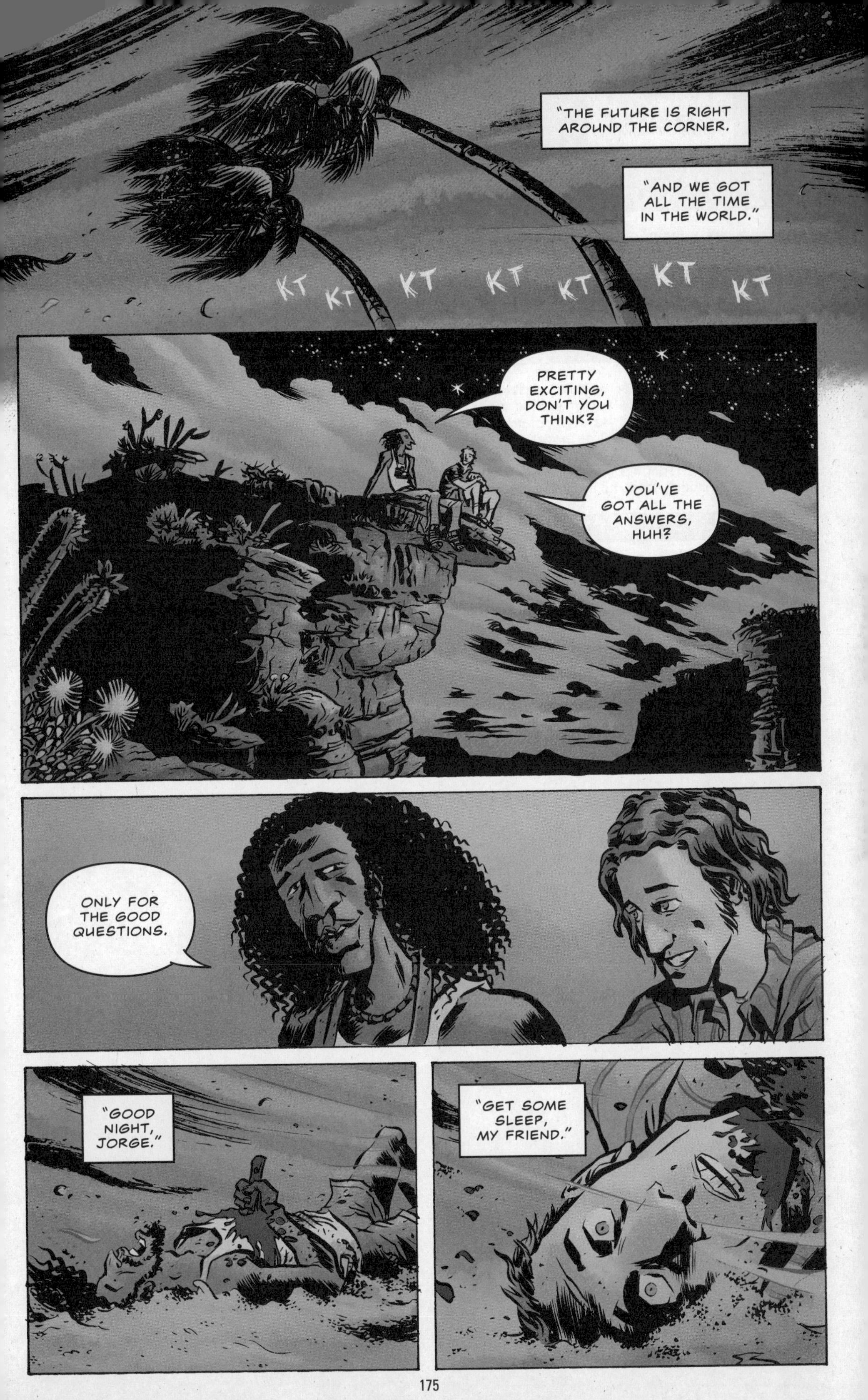
"THE FUTURE IS RIGHT AROUND THE CORNER.
"AND WE GOT ALL THE TIME IN THE WORLD."
KT KT KT KT KT KT KT
PRETTY EXCITING, DON'T YOU THINK?
YOU'VE GOT ALL THE ANSWERS, HUH?
ONLY FOR THE GOOD QUESTIONS.
"GOOD NIGHT, JORGE."
"GET SOME SLEEP, MY FRIEND."

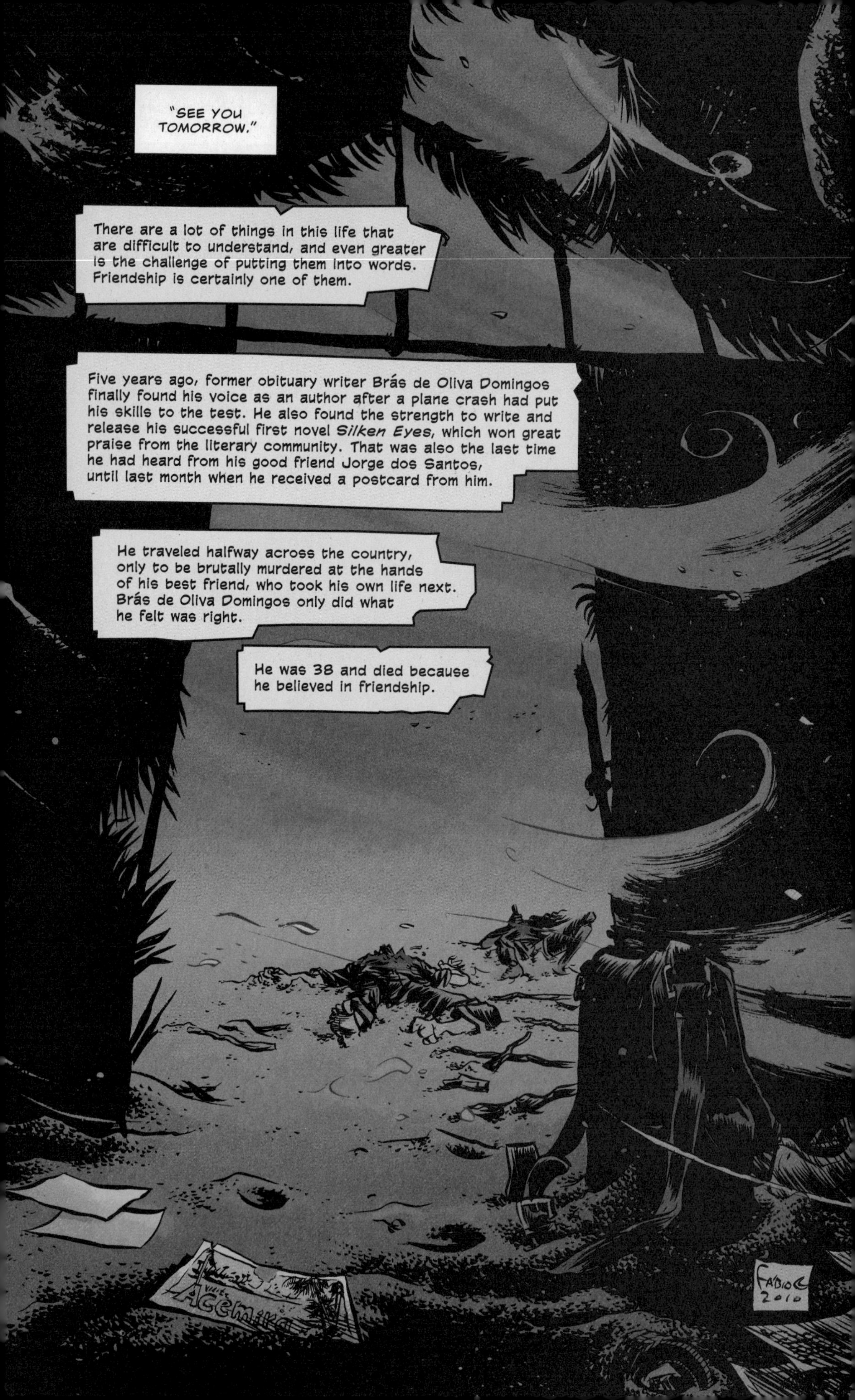
"SEE YOU TOMORROW."
There are a lot of things in this life that are difficult to understand, and even greater is the challenge of putting them into words. Friendship is certainly one of them.
Five years ago, former obituary writer Brás de Oliva Domingos finally found his voice as an author after a plane crash had put his skills to the test. He also found the strength to write and release his successful first novel *Silken Eyes*, which won great praise from the literary community. That was also the last time he had heard from his good friend Jorge dos Santos, until last month when he received a postcard from him.
He traveled halfway across the country, only to be brutally murdered at the hands of his best friend, who took his own life next. Brás de Oliva Domingos only did what he felt was right.
He was 38 and died because he believed in friendship.
FÁBIO G 2010

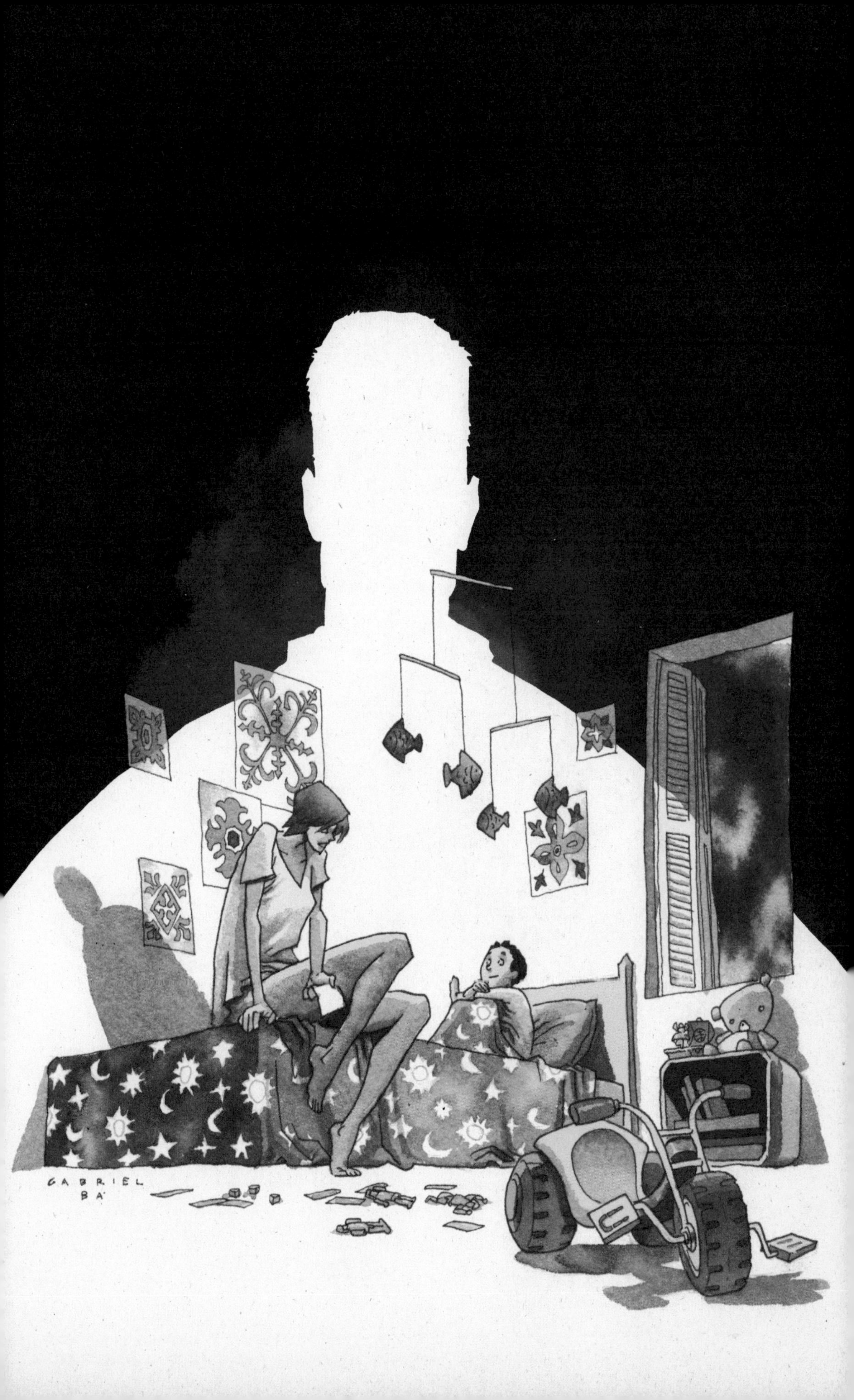
GABRIEL
BÁ

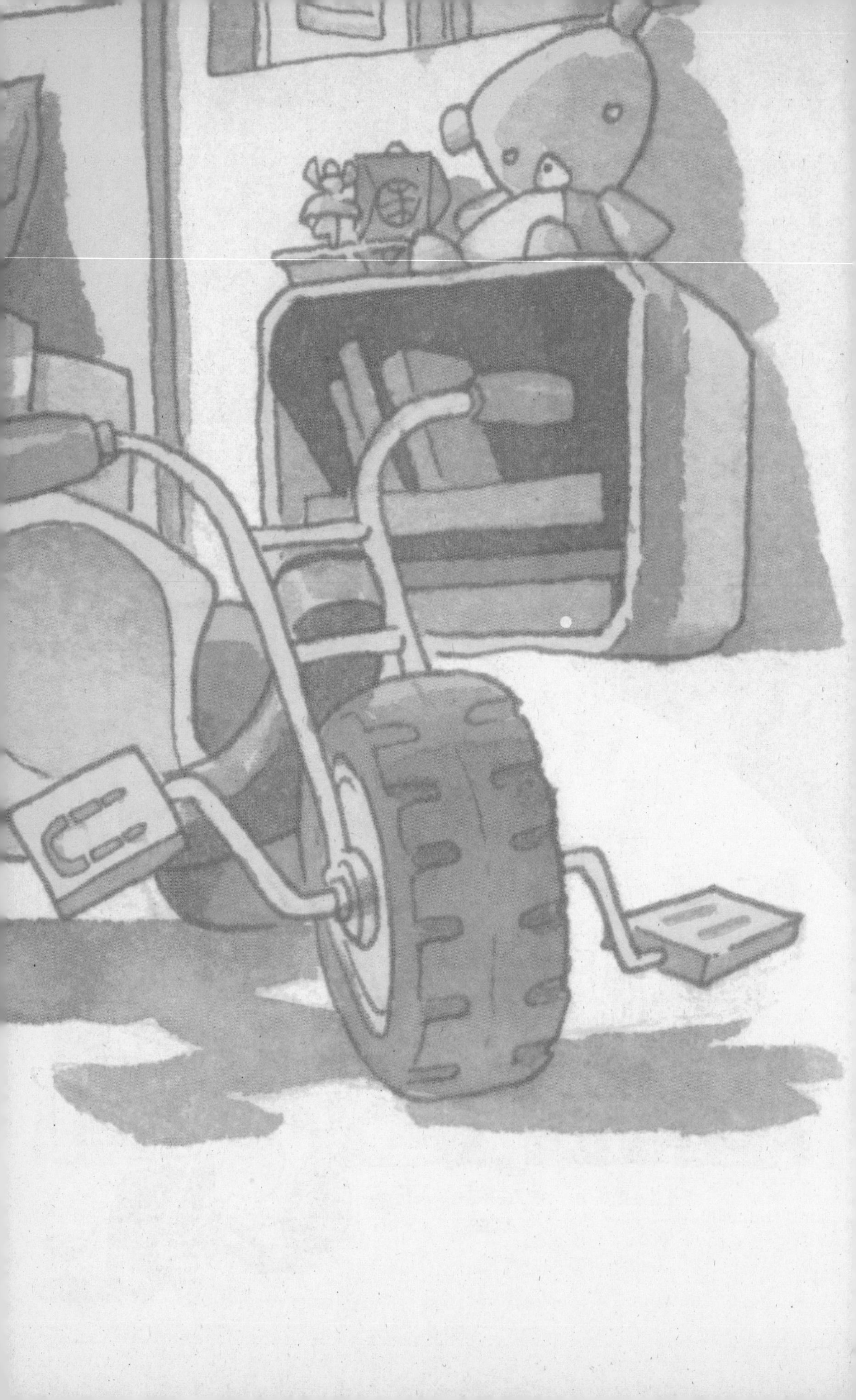

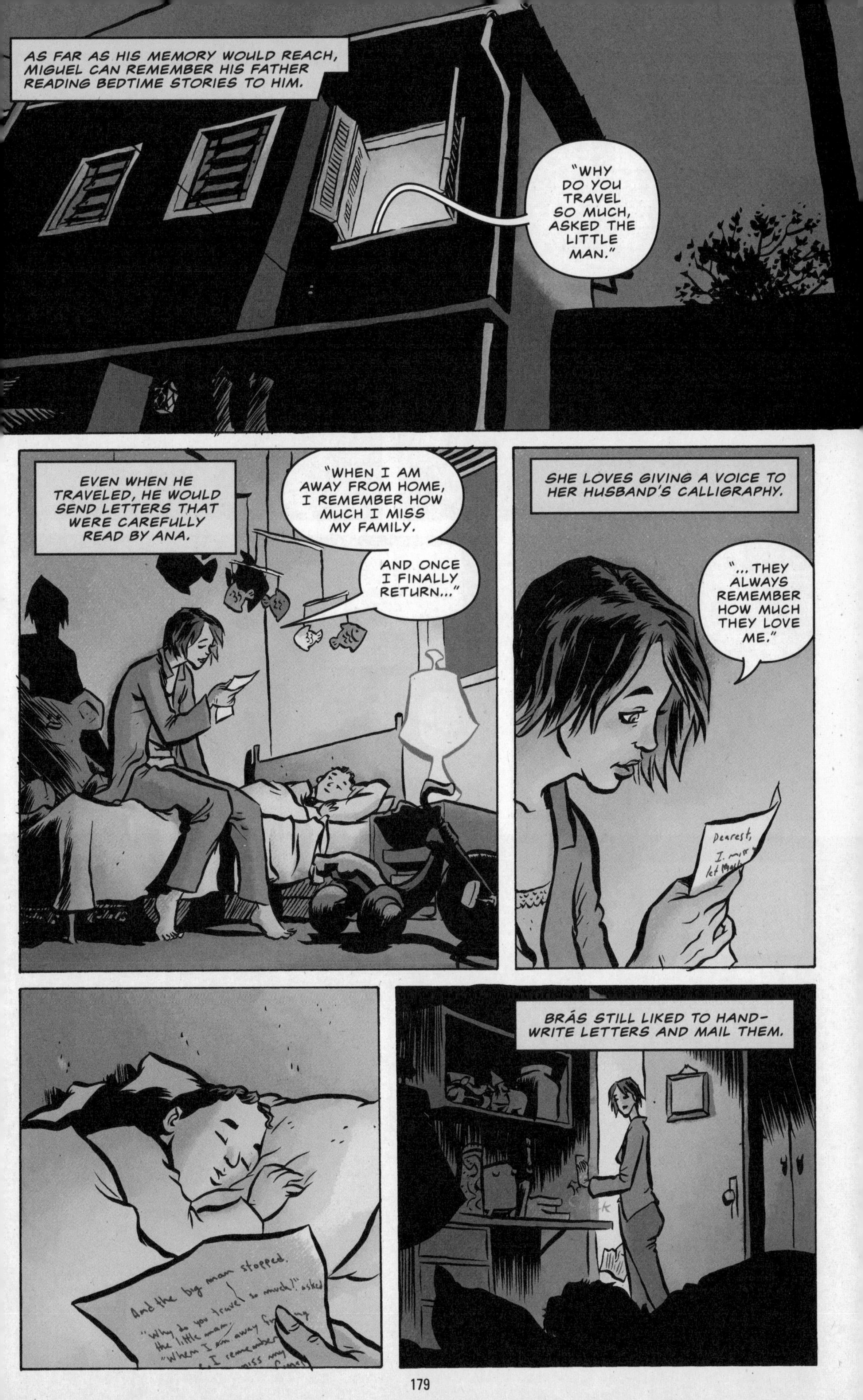

AS FAR AS HIS MEMORY WOULD REACH, MIGUEL CAN REMEMBER HIS FATHER READING BEDTIME STORIES TO HIM.
"WHY DO YOU TRAVEL SO MUCH, ASKED THE LITTLE MAN."
EVEN WHEN HE TRAVELED, HE WOULD SEND LETTERS THAT WERE CAREFULLY READ BY ANA.
"WHEN I AM AWAY FROM HOME, I REMEMBER HOW MUCH I MISS MY FAMILY.
AND ONCE I FINALLY RETURN..."
SHE LOVES GIVING A VOICE TO HER HUSBAND'S CALLIGRAPHY.
"...THEY ALWAYS REMEMBER HOW MUCH THEY LOVE ME."
Dearest,
And the big man stopped.
BRÁS STILL LIKED TO HAND-WRITE LETTERS AND MAIL THEM.

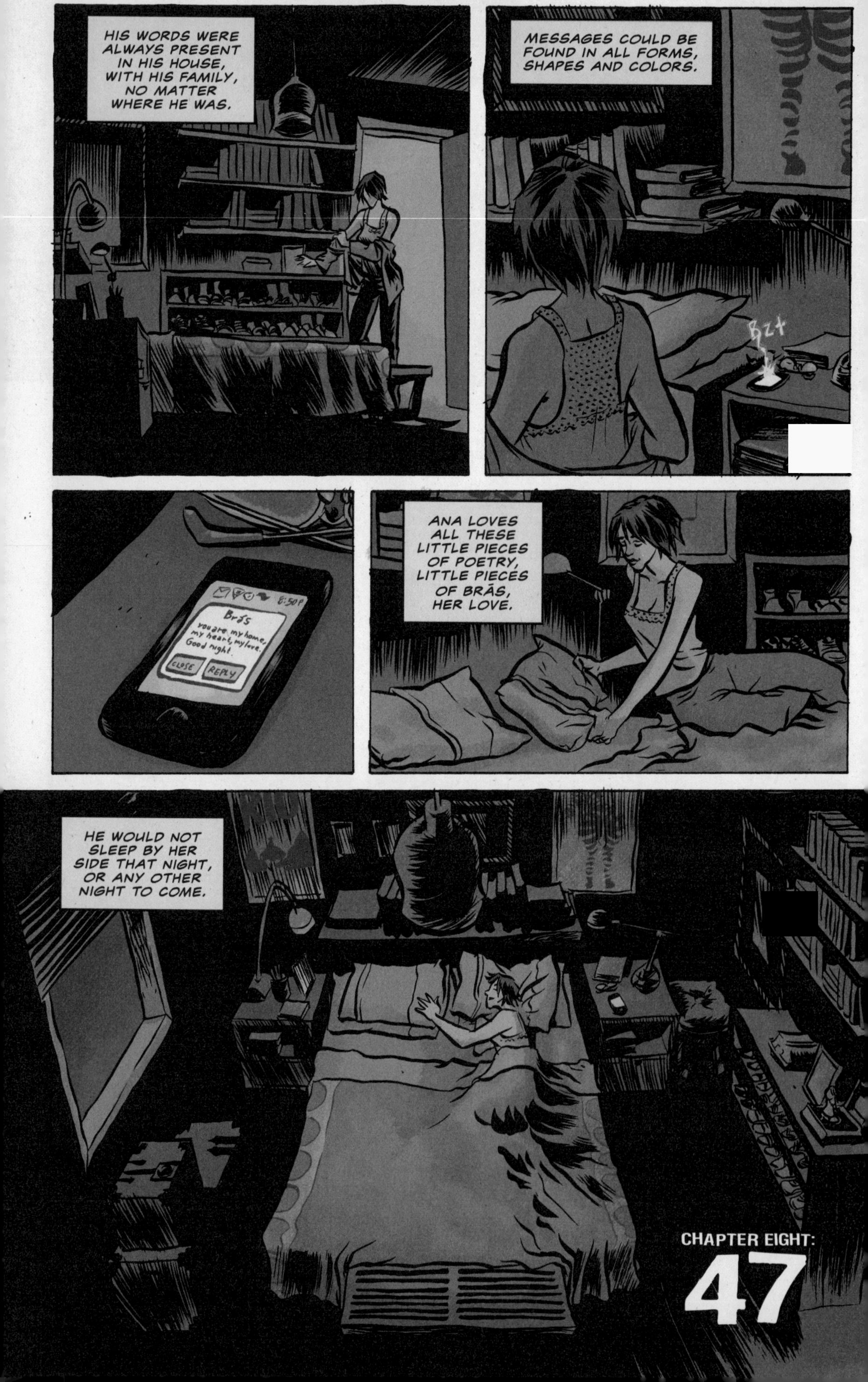
HIS WORDS WERE ALWAYS PRESENT IN HIS HOUSE, WITH HIS FAMILY, NO MATTER WHERE HE WAS.
MESSAGES COULD BE FOUND IN ALL FORMS, SHAPES AND COLORS.
Bzt
8:50P
Brās
you are my home, my heart, my love. Good night.
CLOSE
REPLY
ANA LOVES ALL THESE LITTLE PIECES OF POETRY, LITTLE PIECES OF BRĀS, HER LOVE.
HE WOULD NOT SLEEP BY HER SIDE THAT NIGHT, OR ANY OTHER NIGHT TO COME.
CHAPTER EIGHT:
47

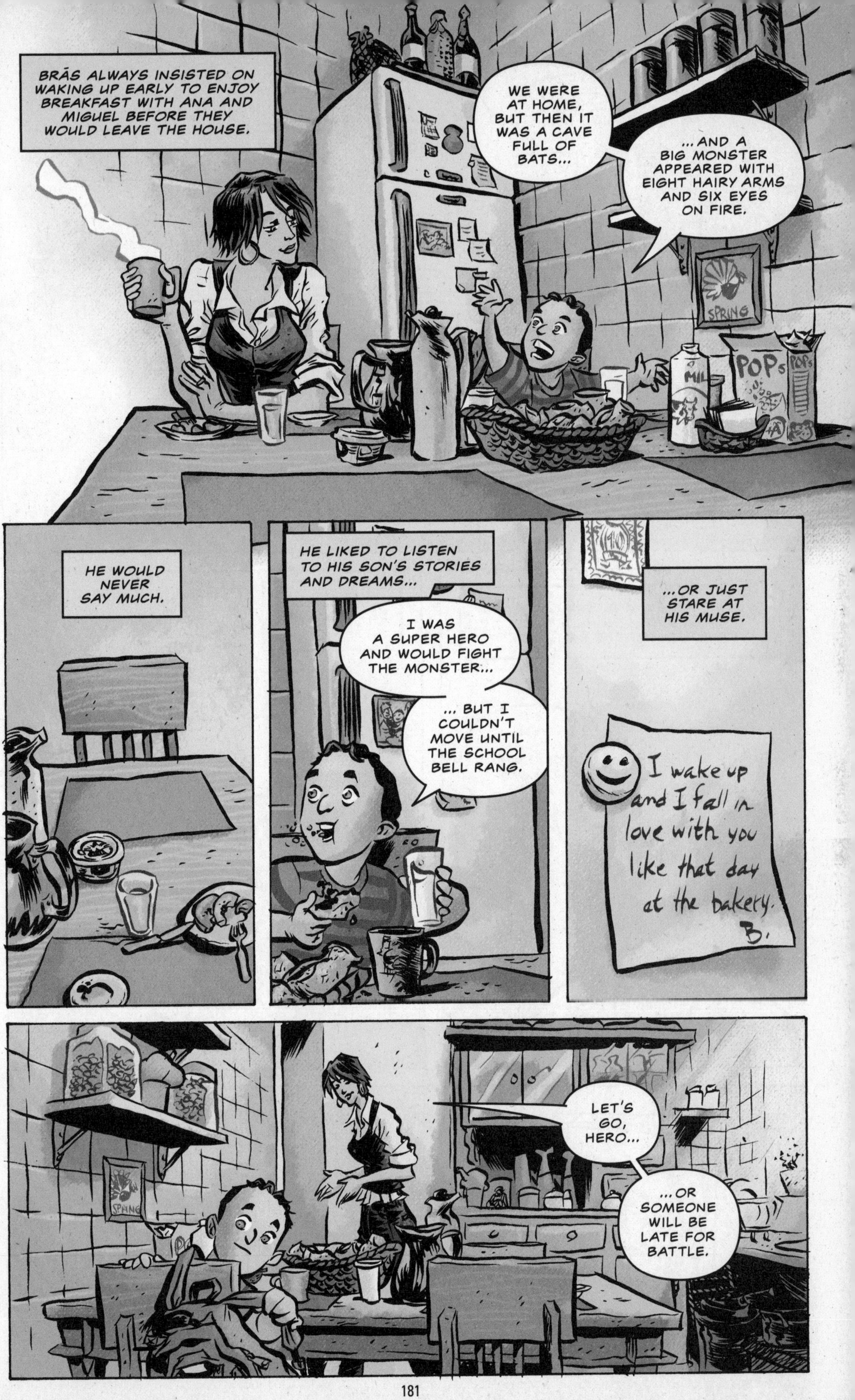
BRÁS ALWAYS INSISTED ON WAKING UP EARLY TO ENJOY BREAKFAST WITH ANA AND MIGUEL BEFORE THEY WOULD LEAVE THE HOUSE.
WE WERE AT HOME, BUT THEN IT WAS A CAVE FULL OF BATS...
...AND A BIG MONSTER APPEARED WITH EIGHT HAIRY ARMS AND SIX EYES ON FIRE.
SPRING
MILK
POPs
HE WOULD NEVER SAY MUCH.
HE LIKED TO LISTEN TO HIS SON'S STORIES AND DREAMS...
I WAS A SUPER HERO AND WOULD FIGHT THE MONSTER...
... BUT I COULDN'T MOVE UNTIL THE SCHOOL BELL RANG.
...OR JUST STARE AT HIS MUSE.
I wake up and I fall in love with you like that day at the bakery. B.
LET'S GO, HERO...
...OR SOMEONE WILL BE LATE FOR BATTLE.

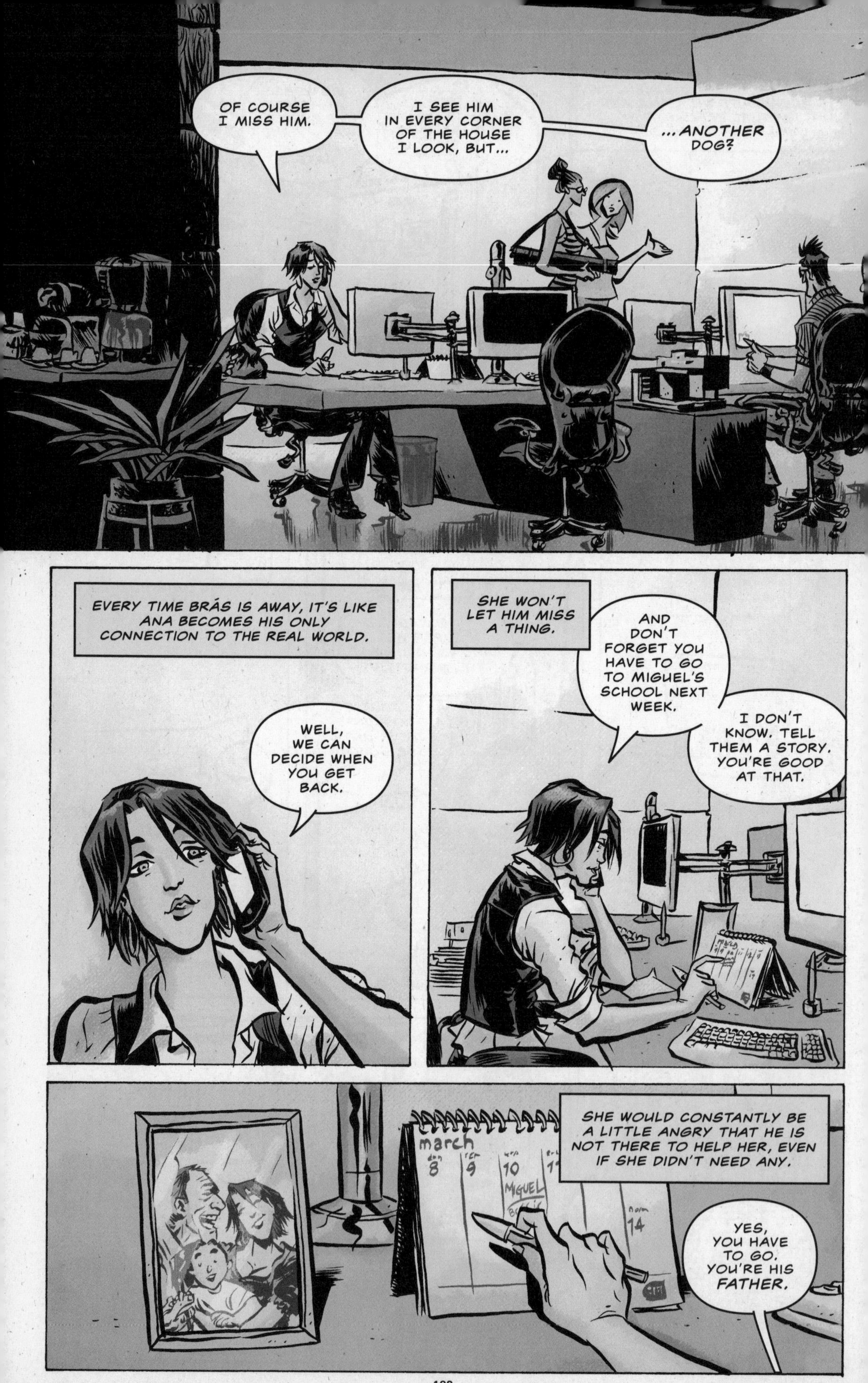
OF COURSE I MISS HIM.
I SEE HIM IN EVERY CORNER OF THE HOUSE I LOOK, BUT...
...ANOTHER DOG?
EVERY TIME BRÁS IS AWAY, IT'S LIKE ANA BECOMES HIS ONLY CONNECTION TO THE REAL WORLD.
WELL, WE CAN DECIDE WHEN YOU GET BACK.
SHE WON'T LET HIM MISS A THING.
AND DON'T FORGET YOU HAVE TO GO TO MIGUEL'S SCHOOL NEXT WEEK.
I DON'T KNOW. TELL THEM A STORY. YOU'RE GOOD AT THAT.
march
MIGUEL
SHE WOULD CONSTANTLY BE A LITTLE ANGRY THAT HE IS NOT THERE TO HELP HER, EVEN IF SHE DIDN'T NEED ANY.
YES, YOU HAVE TO GO. YOU'RE HIS FATHER.

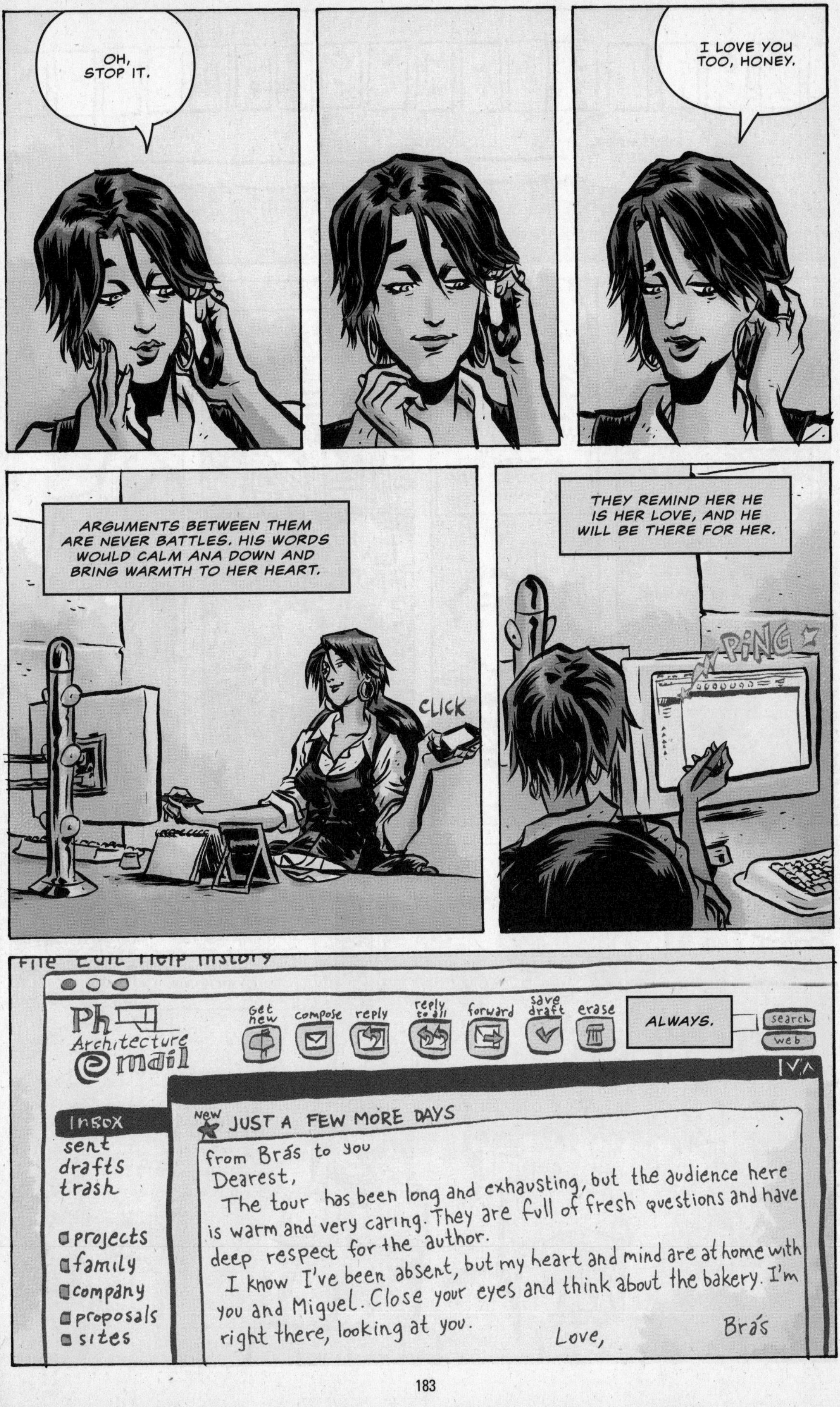
OH, STOP IT.
I LOVE YOU TOO, HONEY.
ARGUMENTS BETWEEN THEM ARE NEVER BATTLES. HIS WORDS WOULD CALM ANA DOWN AND BRING WARMTH TO HER HEART.
CLICK
THEY REMIND HER HE IS HER LOVE, AND HE WILL BE THERE FOR HER.
PING
File Edit Help History
Ph Architecture @mail
Get new
compose
reply
reply to all
forward
save draft
erase
ALWAYS.
search
web
Inbox
sent
drafts
trash
projects
family
company
proposals
sites
New
JUST A FEW MORE DAYS
from Brás to you
Dearest,
The tour has been long and exhausting, but the audience here is warm and very caring. They are full of fresh questions and have deep respect for the author.
I know I've been absent, but my heart and mind are at home with you and Miguel. Close your eyes and think about the bakery. I'm right there, looking at you.
Love, Brás

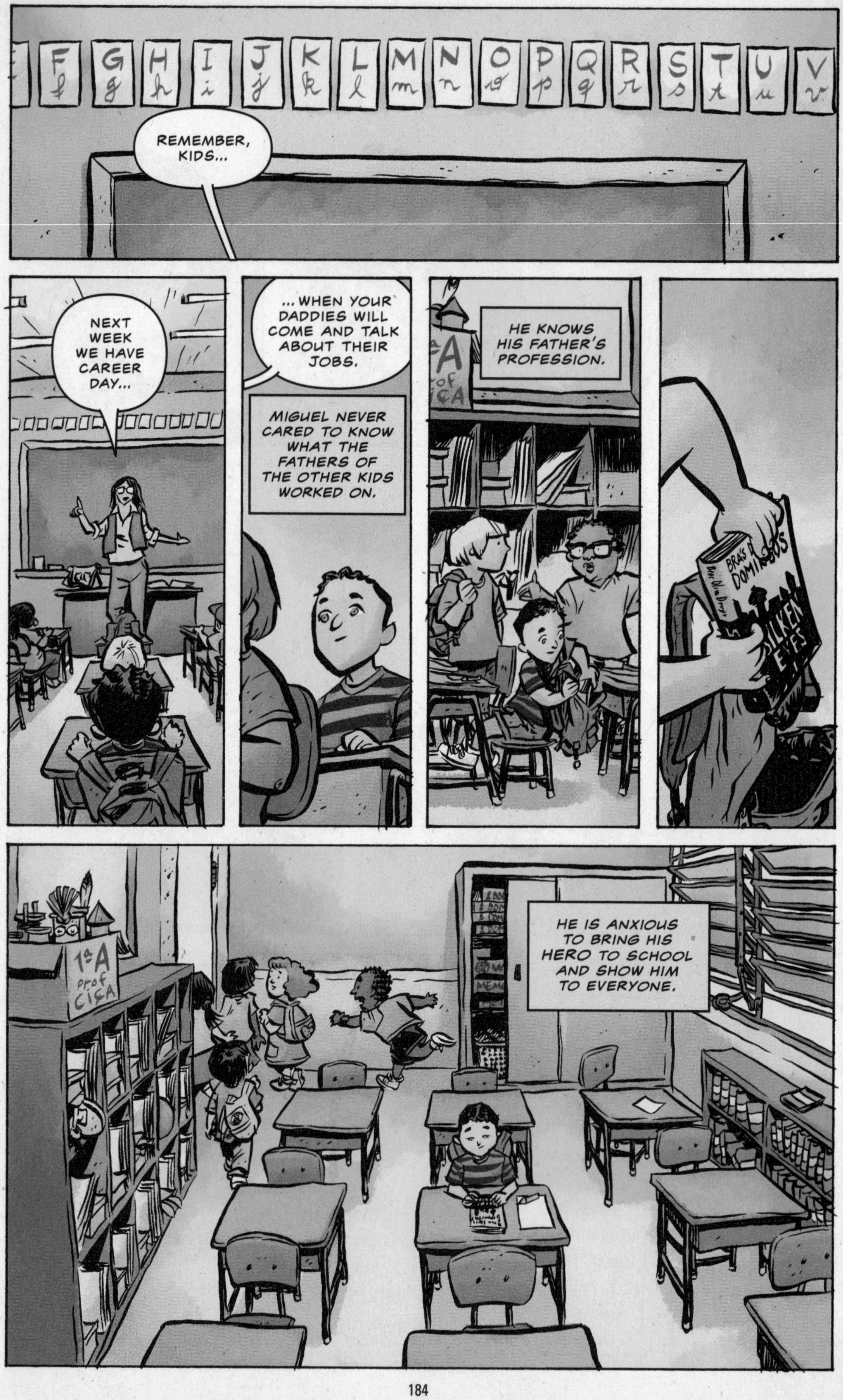
REMEMBER, KIDS...
NEXT WEEK WE HAVE CAREER DAY...
...WHEN YOUR DADDIES WILL COME AND TALK ABOUT THEIR JOBS.
MIGUEL NEVER CARED TO KNOW WHAT THE FATHERS OF THE OTHER KIDS WORKED ON.
HE KNOWS HIS FATHER'S PROFESSION.
1ª A prof CIÇA
HE IS ANXIOUS TO BRING HIS HERO TO SCHOOL AND SHOW HIM TO EVERYONE.

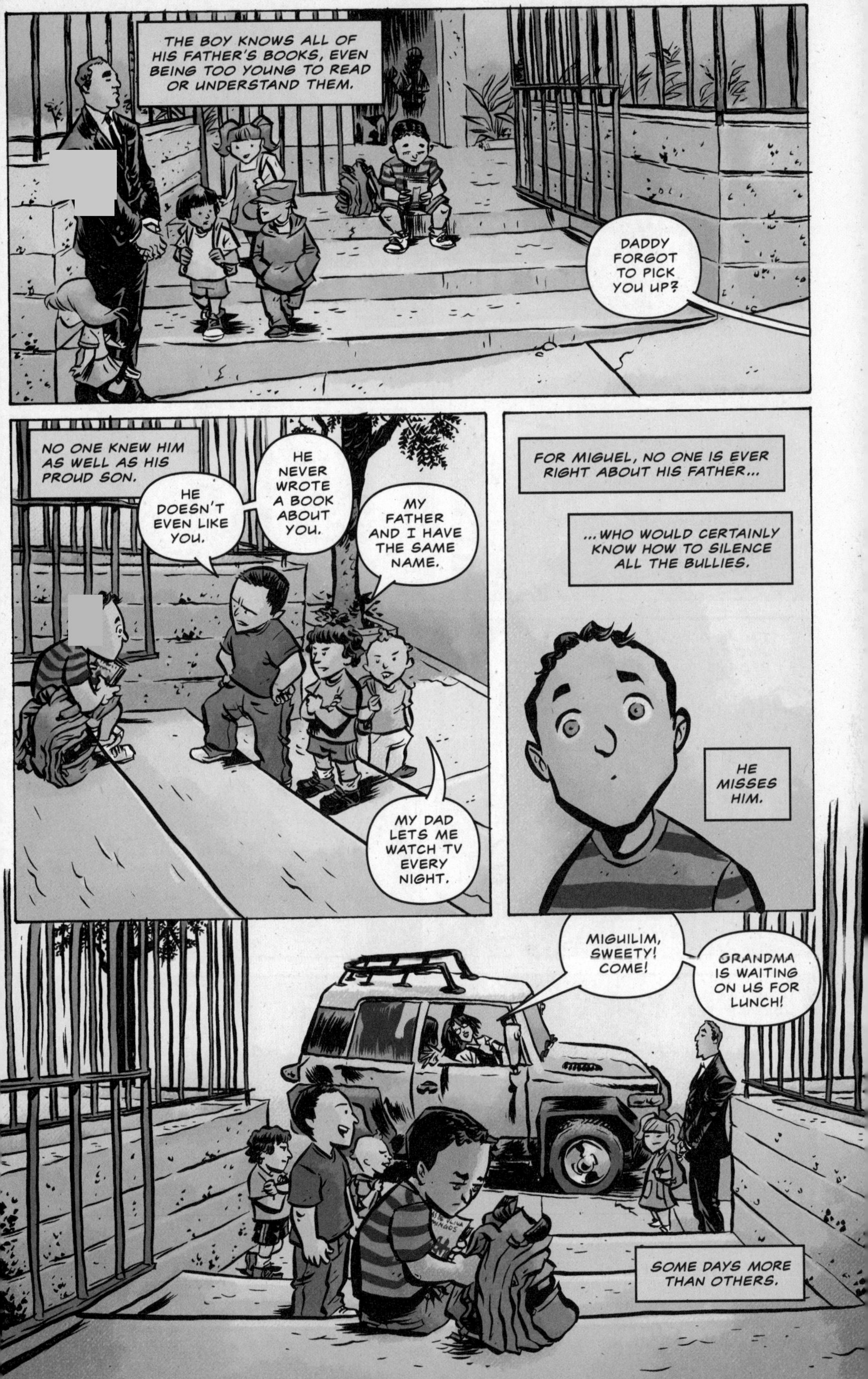
THE BOY KNOWS ALL OF HIS FATHER'S BOOKS, EVEN BEING TOO YOUNG TO READ OR UNDERSTAND THEM.
DADDY FORGOT TO PICK YOU UP?
NO ONE KNEW HIM AS WELL AS HIS PROUD SON.
HE DOESN'T EVEN LIKE YOU.
HE NEVER WROTE A BOOK ABOUT YOU.
MY FATHER AND I HAVE THE SAME NAME.
MY DAD LETS ME WATCH TV EVERY NIGHT.
FOR MIGUEL, NO ONE IS EVER RIGHT ABOUT HIS FATHER...
...WHO WOULD CERTAINLY KNOW HOW TO SILENCE ALL THE BULLIES.
HE MISSES HIM.
MIGUILIM, SWEETY! COME!
GRANDMA IS WAITING ON US FOR LUNCH!
SOME DAYS MORE THAN OTHERS.

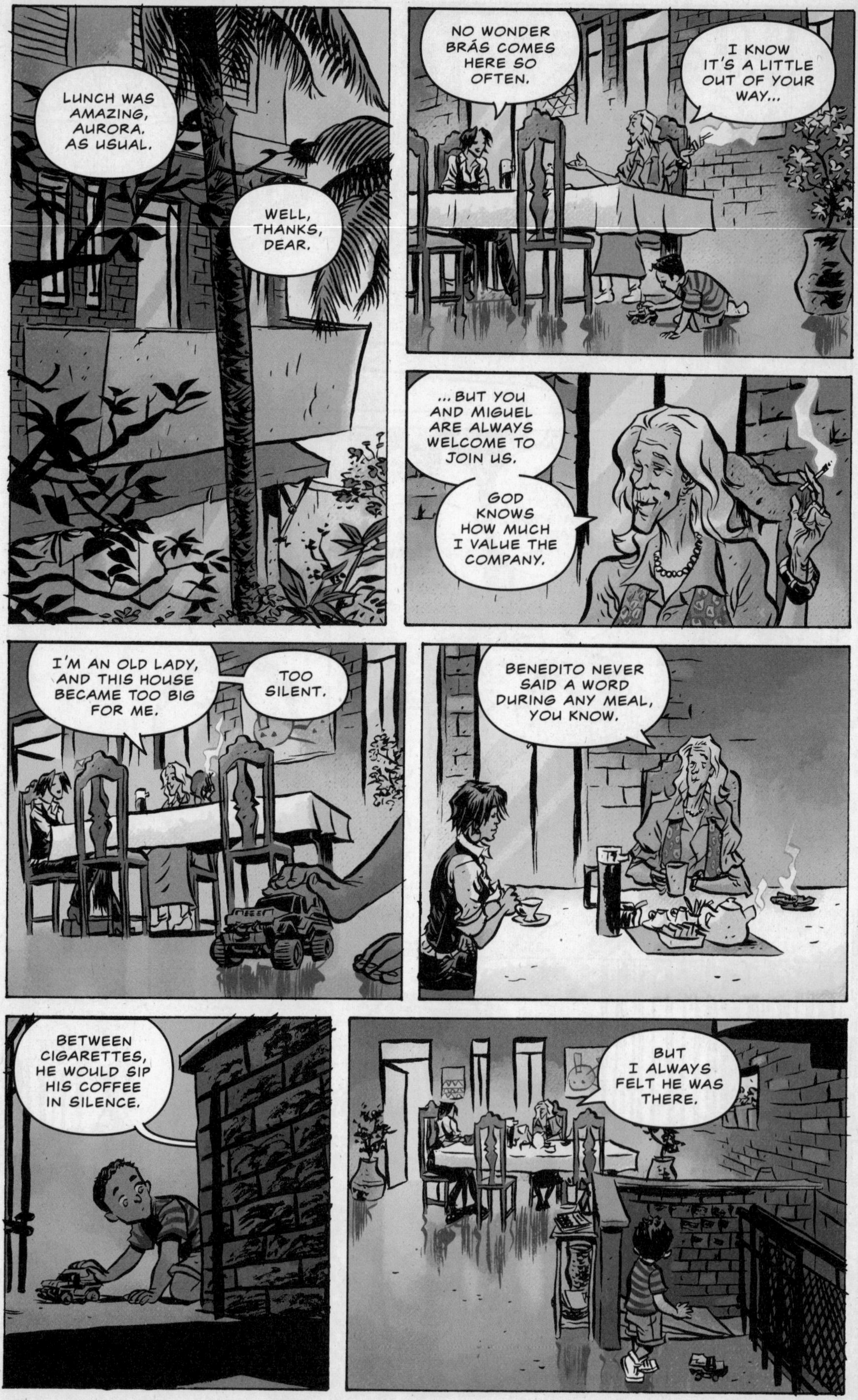
LUNCH WAS AMAZING, AURORA. AS USUAL.
WELL, THANKS, DEAR.
NO WONDER BRÁS COMES HERE SO OFTEN.
I KNOW IT'S A LITTLE OUT OF YOUR WAY...
...BUT YOU AND MIGUEL ARE ALWAYS WELCOME TO JOIN US.
GOD KNOWS HOW MUCH I VALUE THE COMPANY.
I'M AN OLD LADY, AND THIS HOUSE BECAME TOO BIG FOR ME.
TOO SILENT.
BENEDITO NEVER SAID A WORD DURING ANY MEAL, YOU KNOW.
BETWEEN CIGARETTES, HE WOULD SIP HIS COFFEE IN SILENCE.
BUT I ALWAYS FELT HE WAS THERE.

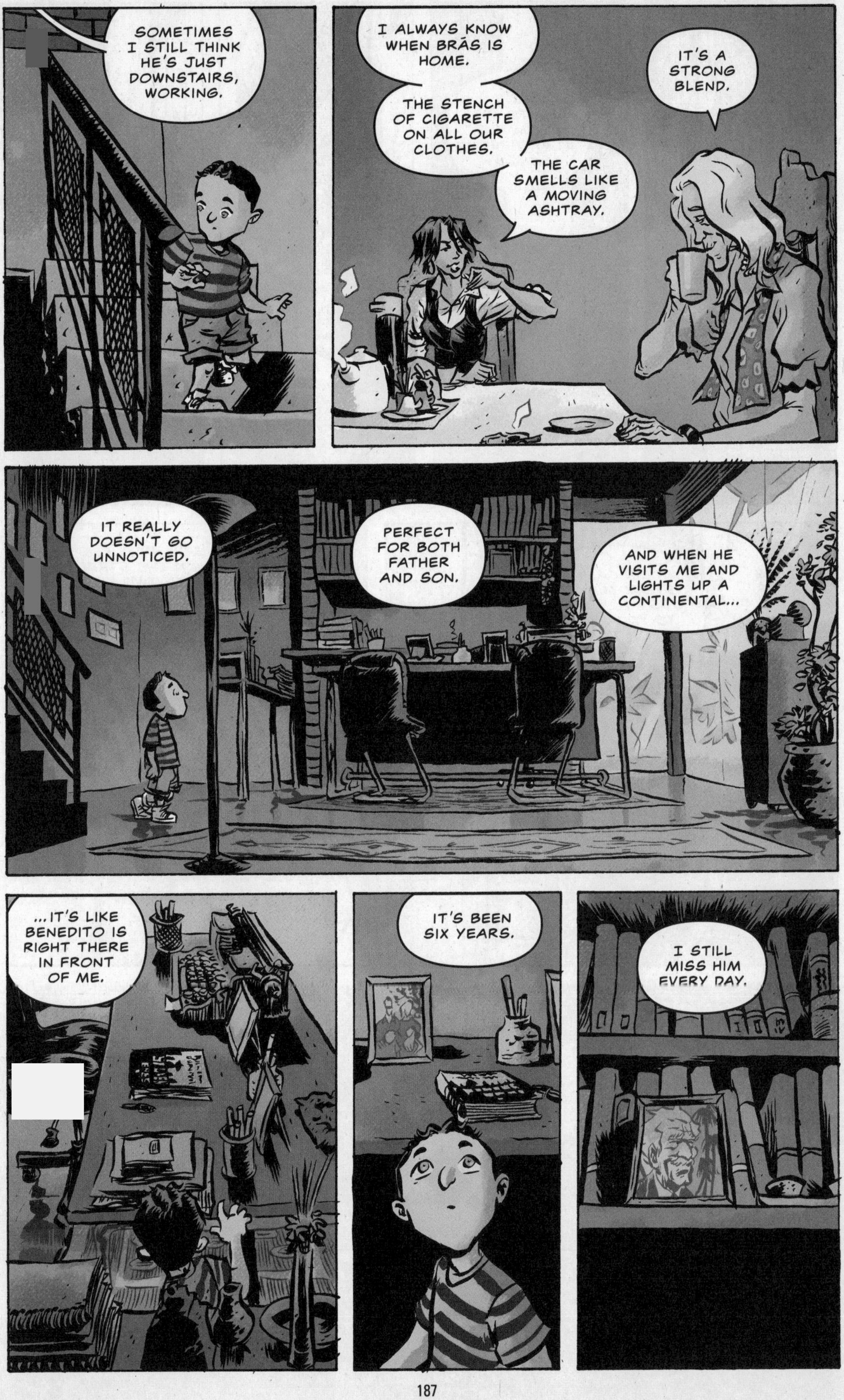
SOMETIMES I STILL THINK HE'S JUST DOWNSTAIRS, WORKING.
I ALWAYS KNOW WHEN BRÁS IS HOME.
THE STENCH OF CIGARETTE ON ALL OUR CLOTHES.
THE CAR SMELLS LIKE A MOVING ASHTRAY.
IT'S A STRONG BLEND.
IT REALLY DOESN'T GO UNNOTICED.
PERFECT FOR BOTH FATHER AND SON.
AND WHEN HE VISITS ME AND LIGHTS UP A CONTINENTAL...
...IT'S LIKE BENEDITO IS RIGHT THERE IN FRONT OF ME.
IT'S BEEN SIX YEARS.
I STILL MISS HIM EVERY DAY.

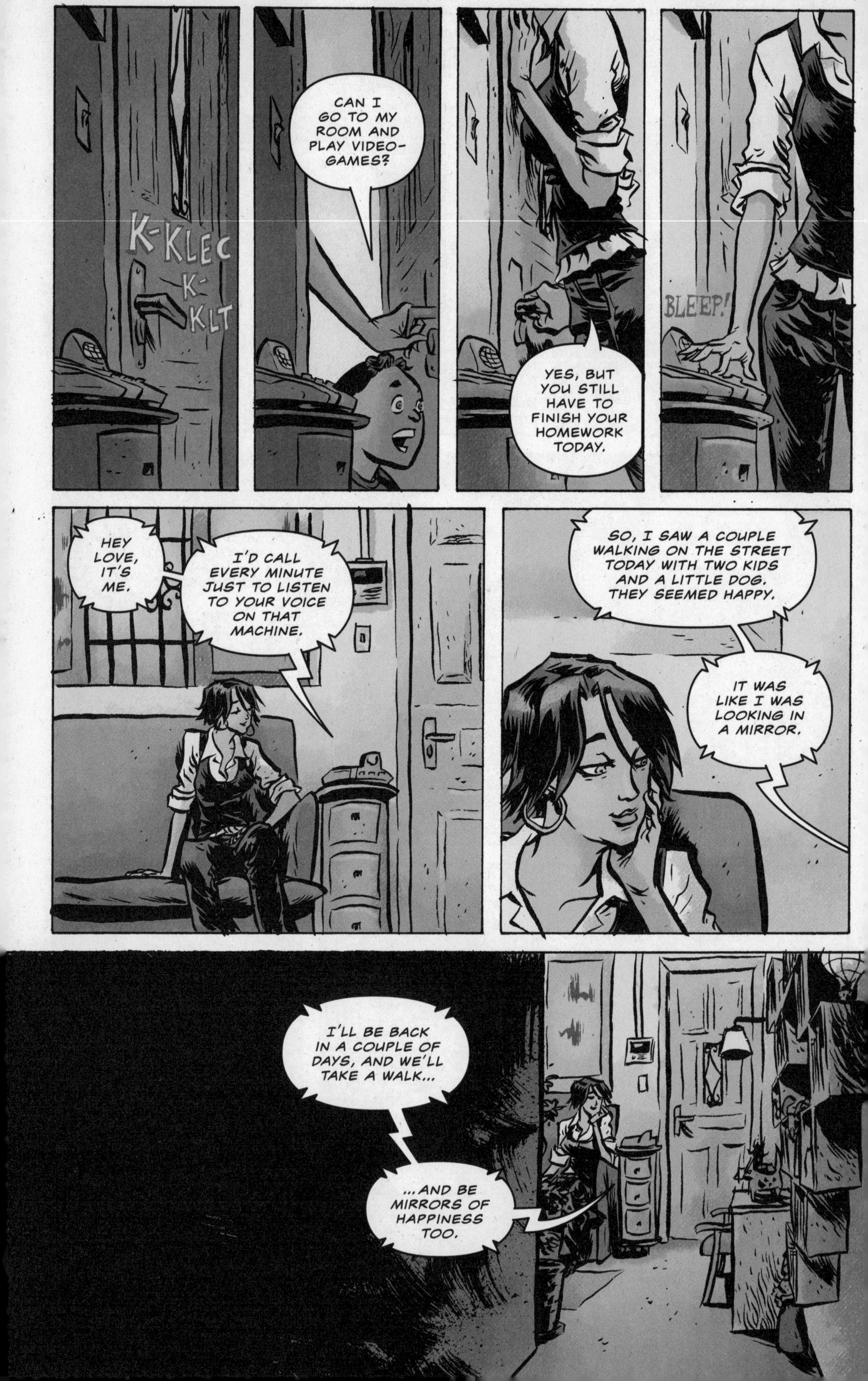
K-KLEC K-KLT
CAN I GO TO MY ROOM AND PLAY VIDEO-GAMES?
YES, BUT YOU STILL HAVE TO FINISH YOUR HOMEWORK TODAY.
BLEEP!
HEY LOVE, IT'S ME.
I'D CALL EVERY MINUTE JUST TO LISTEN TO YOUR VOICE ON THAT MACHINE.
SO, I SAW A COUPLE WALKING ON THE STREET TODAY WITH TWO KIDS AND A LITTLE DOG. THEY SEEMED HAPPY.
IT WAS LIKE I WAS LOOKING IN A MIRROR.
I'LL BE BACK IN A COUPLE OF DAYS, AND WE'LL TAKE A WALK...
...AND BE MIRRORS OF HAPPINESS TOO.

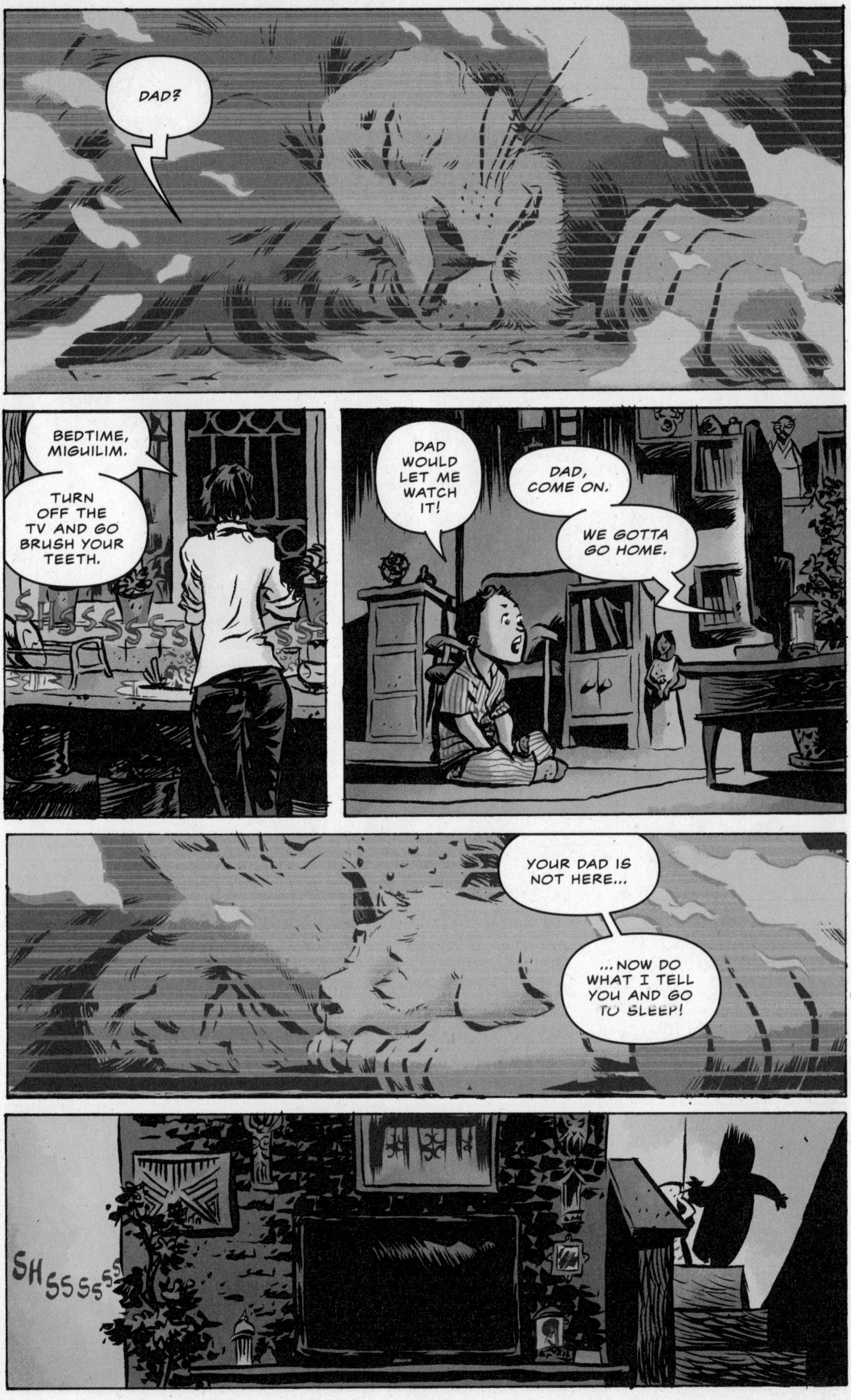
DAD?
BEDTIME, MIGUILIM.
TURN OFF THE TV AND GO BRUSH YOUR TEETH.
SHSSSSSS
DAD WOULD LET ME WATCH IT!
DAD, COME ON.
WE GOTTA GO HOME.
YOUR DAD IS NOT HERE...
...NOW DO WHAT I TELL YOU AND GO TO SLEEP!
SHSSSSSS

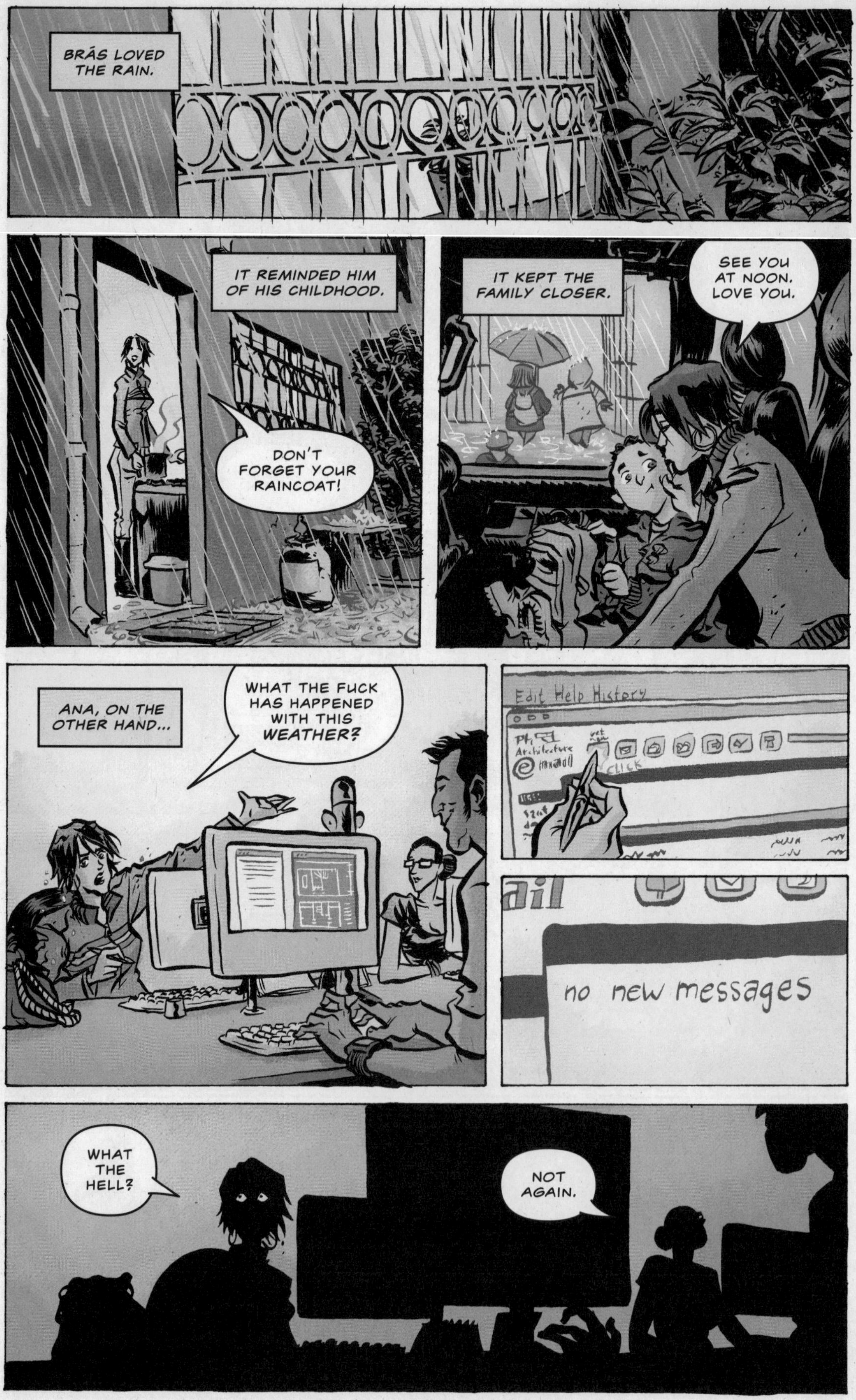
BRÁS LOVED THE RAIN.
IT REMINDED HIM OF HIS CHILDHOOD.
DON'T FORGET YOUR RAINCOAT!
IT KEPT THE FAMILY CLOSER.
SEE YOU AT NOON. LOVE YOU.
ANA, ON THE OTHER HAND...
WHAT THE FUCK HAS HAPPENED WITH THIS WEATHER?
Edit Help History
CLICK
no new messages
WHAT THE HELL?
NOT AGAIN.

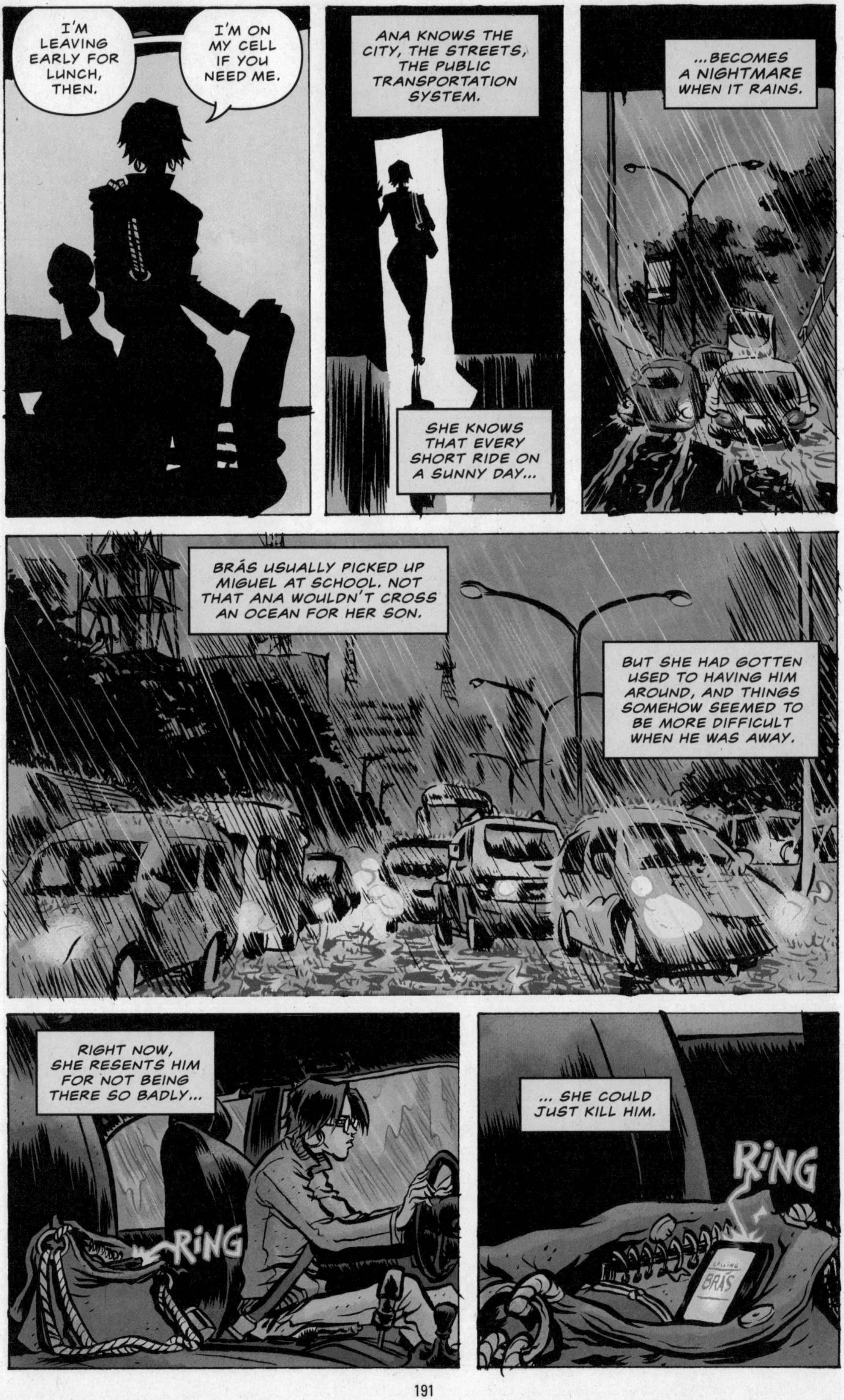
I'M LEAVING EARLY FOR LUNCH, THEN.
I'M ON MY CELL IF YOU NEED ME.
ANA KNOWS THE CITY, THE STREETS, THE PUBLIC TRANSPORTATION SYSTEM.
SHE KNOWS THAT EVERY SHORT RIDE ON A SUNNY DAY...
...BECOMES A NIGHTMARE WHEN IT RAINS.
BRÁS USUALLY PICKED UP MIGUEL AT SCHOOL. NOT THAT ANA WOULDN'T CROSS AN OCEAN FOR HER SON.
BUT SHE HAD GOTTEN USED TO HAVING HIM AROUND, AND THINGS SOMEHOW SEEMED TO BE MORE DIFFICULT WHEN HE WAS AWAY.
RIGHT NOW, SHE RESENTS HIM FOR NOT BEING THERE SO BADLY...
RING
... SHE COULD JUST KILL HIM.
RING
BRÁS

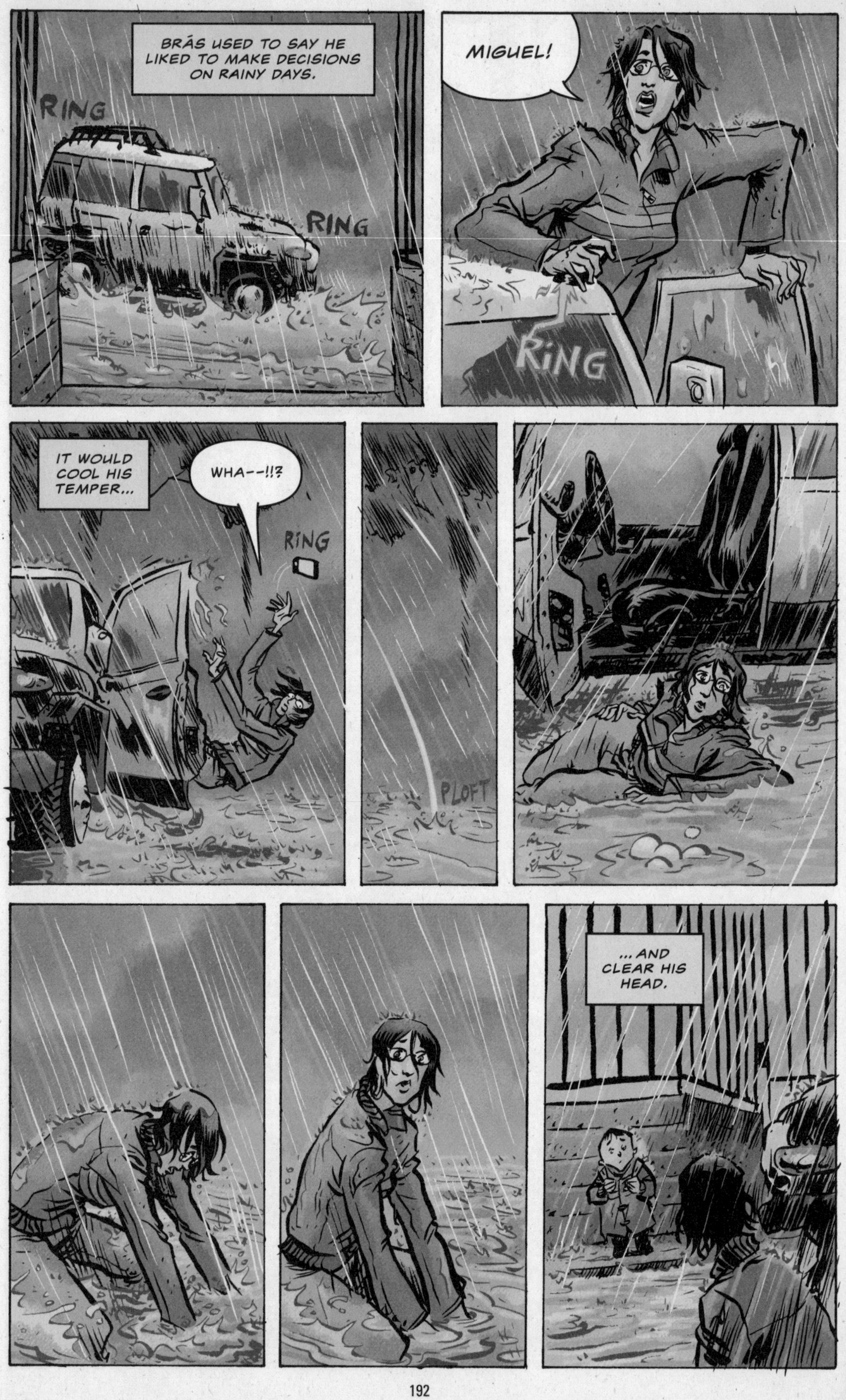
BRÁS USED TO SAY HE LIKED TO MAKE DECISIONS ON RAINY DAYS.
RING
RING
MIGUEL!
RING
IT WOULD COOL HIS TEMPER...
WHA--!!?
RING
PLOFT
...AND CLEAR HIS HEAD.

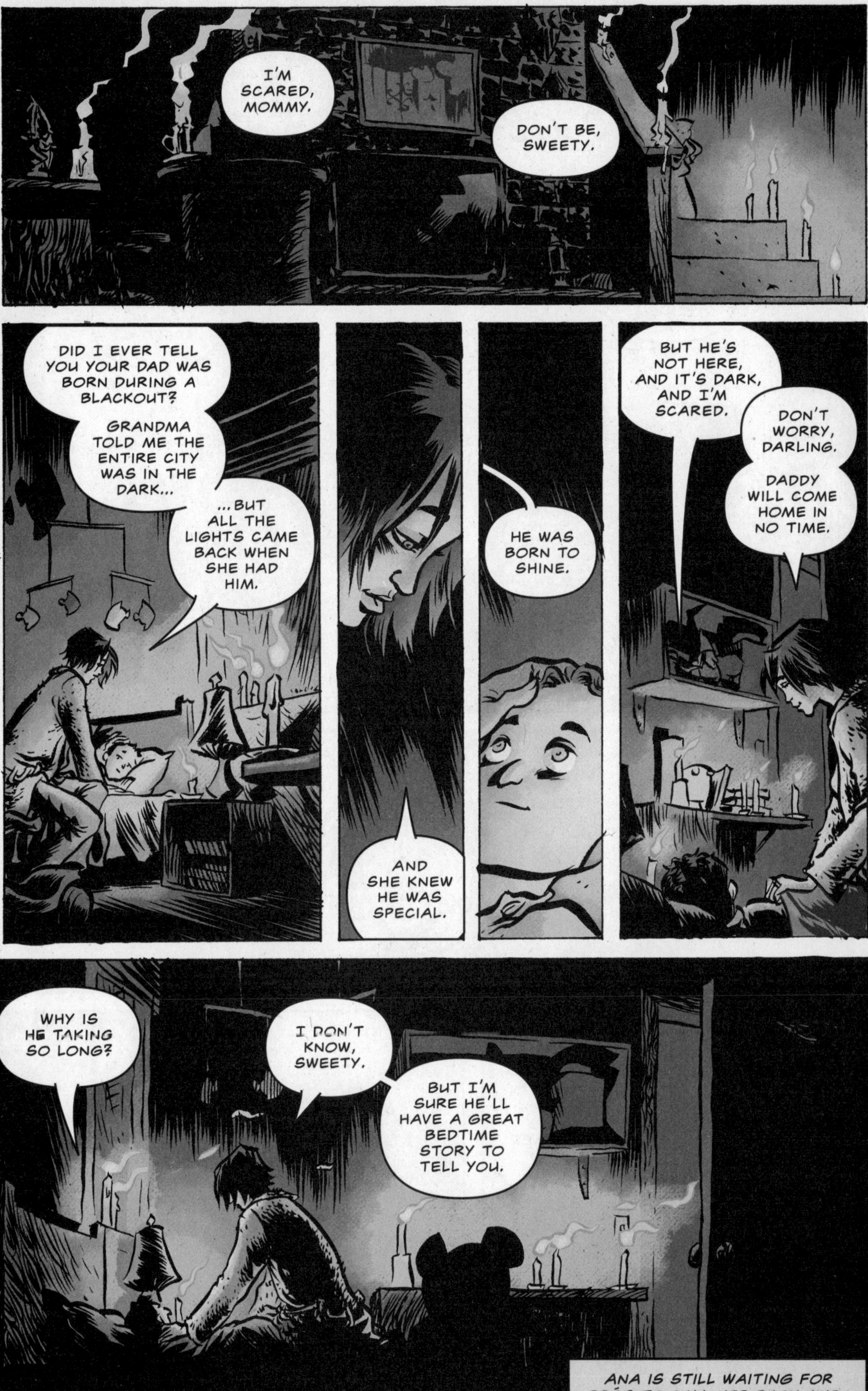
I'M SCARED, MOMMY.
DON'T BE, SWEETY.
DID I EVER TELL YOU YOUR DAD WAS BORN DURING A BLACKOUT?
GRANDMA TOLD ME THE ENTIRE CITY WAS IN THE DARK...
...BUT ALL THE LIGHTS CAME BACK WHEN SHE HAD HIM.
AND SHE KNEW HE WAS SPECIAL.
HE WAS BORN TO SHINE.
BUT HE'S NOT HERE, AND IT'S DARK, AND I'M SCARED.
DON'T WORRY, DARLING.
DADDY WILL COME HOME IN NO TIME.
WHY IS HE TAKING SO LONG?
I DON'T KNOW, SWEETY.
BUT I'M SURE HE'LL HAVE A GREAT BEDTIME STORY TO TELL YOU.
ANA IS STILL WAITING FOR BRÁS TO CALL HER BACK WHEN SHE FINALLY FALLS ASLEEP.

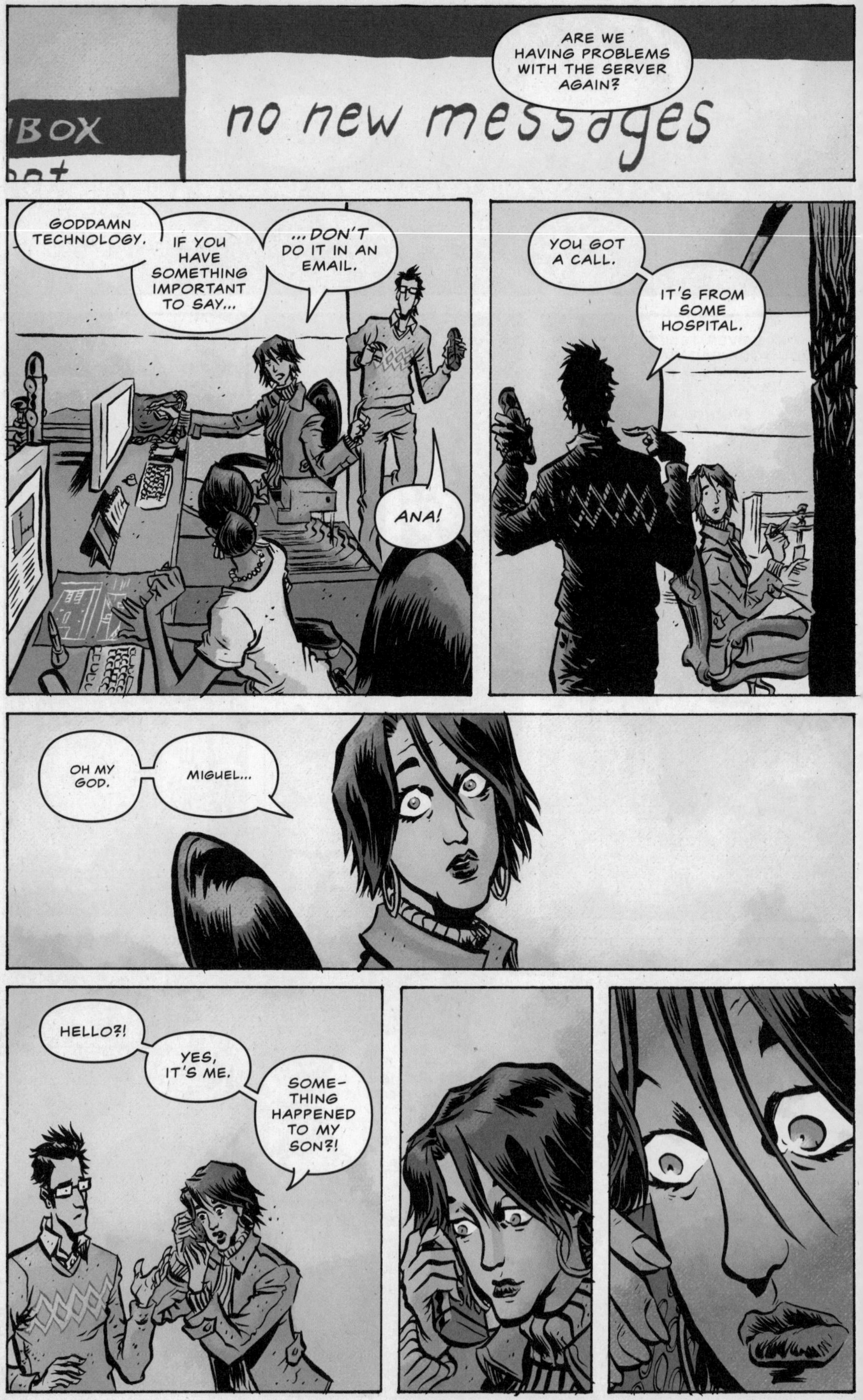
ARE WE HAVING PROBLEMS WITH THE SERVER AGAIN?
no new messages
GODDAMN TECHNOLOGY.
IF YOU HAVE SOMETHING IMPORTANT TO SAY...
...DON'T DO IT IN AN EMAIL.
ANA!
YOU GOT A CALL.
IT'S FROM SOME HOSPITAL.
OH MY GOD.
MIGUEL...
HELLO?!
YES, IT'S ME.
SOME-THING HAPPENED TO MY SON?!

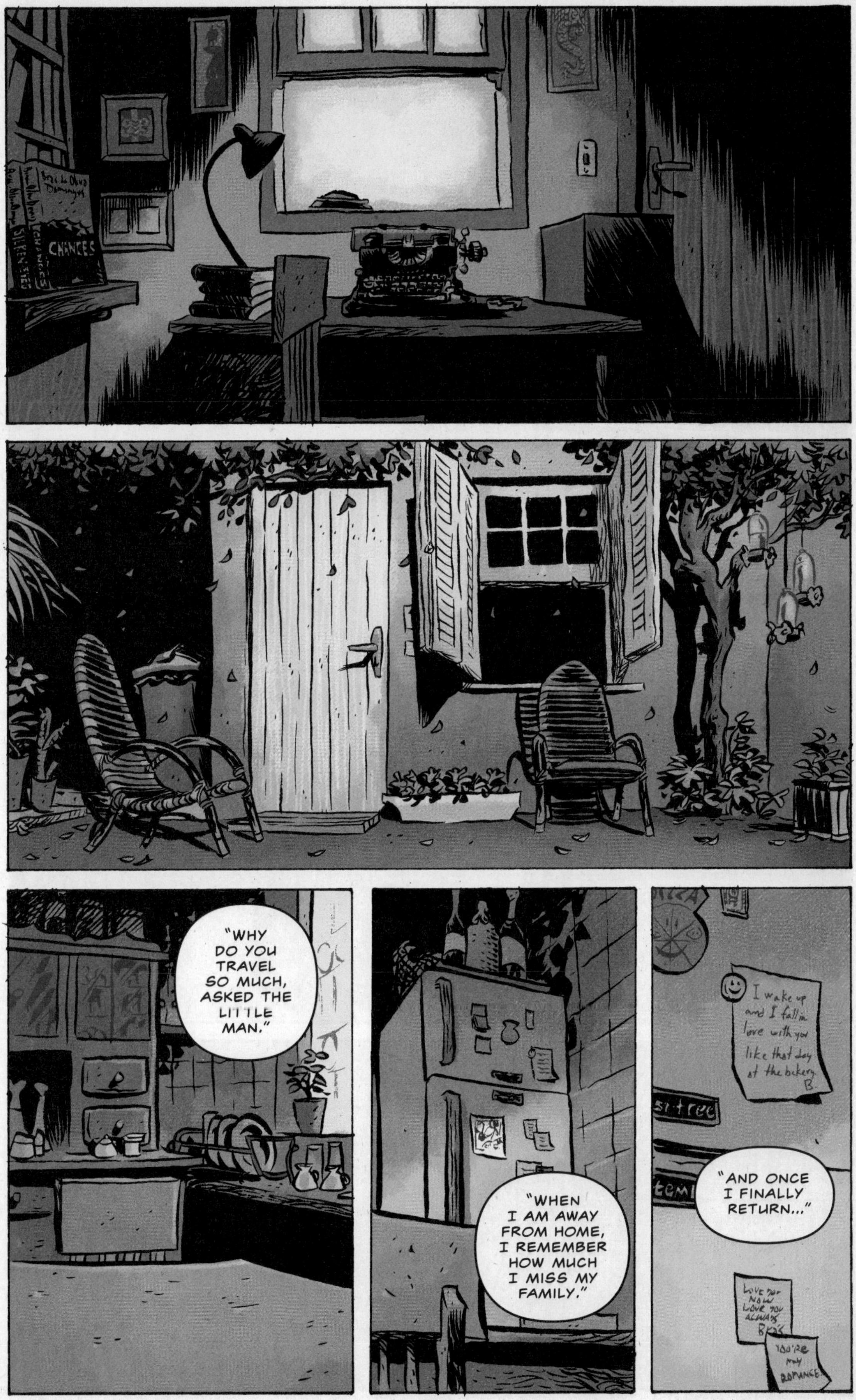
CHANCES
"WHY DO YOU TRAVEL SO MUCH, ASKED THE LITTLE MAN."
"WHEN I AM AWAY FROM HOME, I REMEMBER HOW MUCH I MISS MY FAMILY."
I wake up and I fall in love with you like that day at the bakery. B.
"AND ONCE I FINALLY RETURN..."
YOU'RE MY ROMANCE.

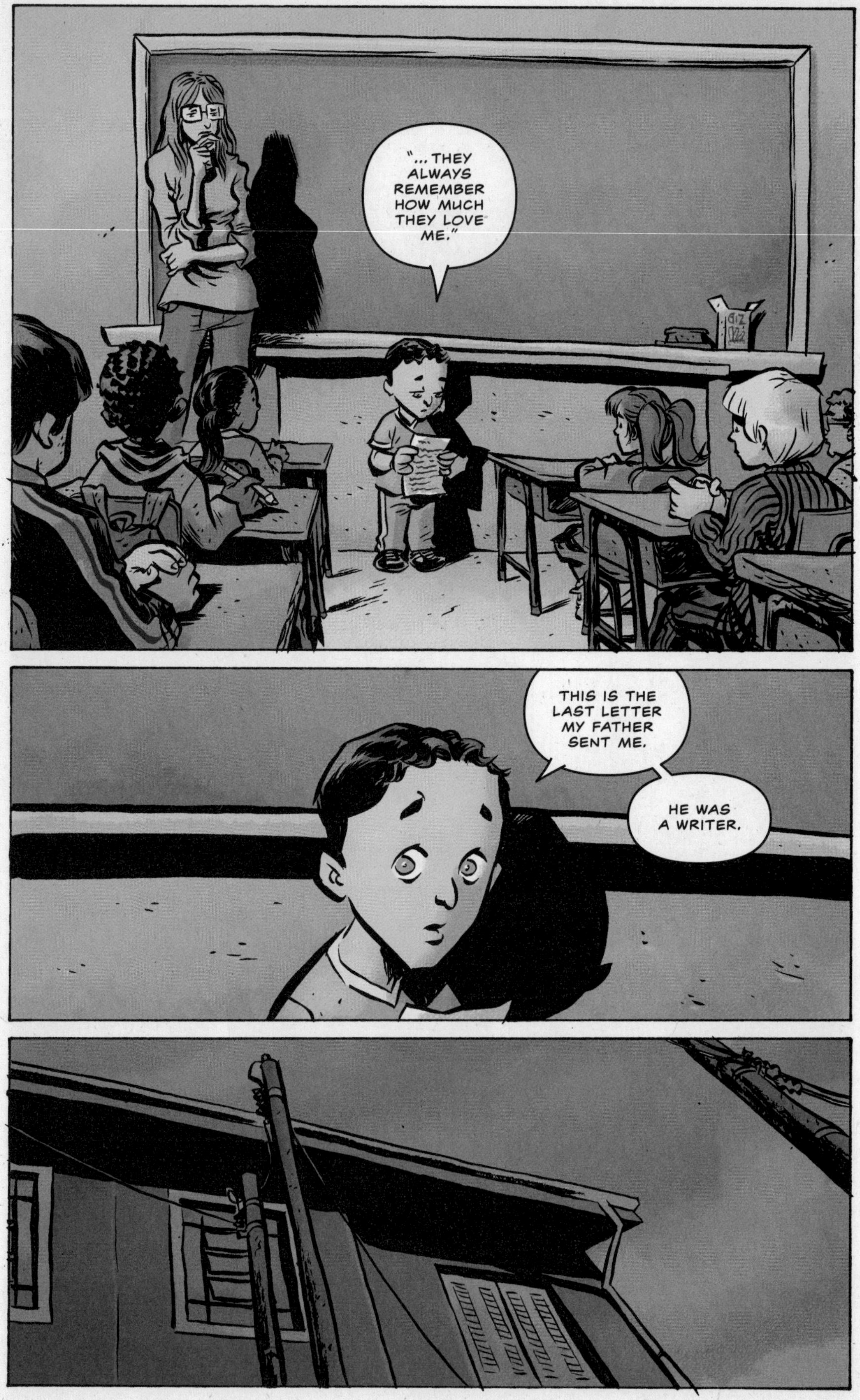
"...THEY ALWAYS REMEMBER HOW MUCH THEY LOVE ME."
THIS IS THE LAST LETTER MY FATHER SENT ME.
HE WAS A WRITER.

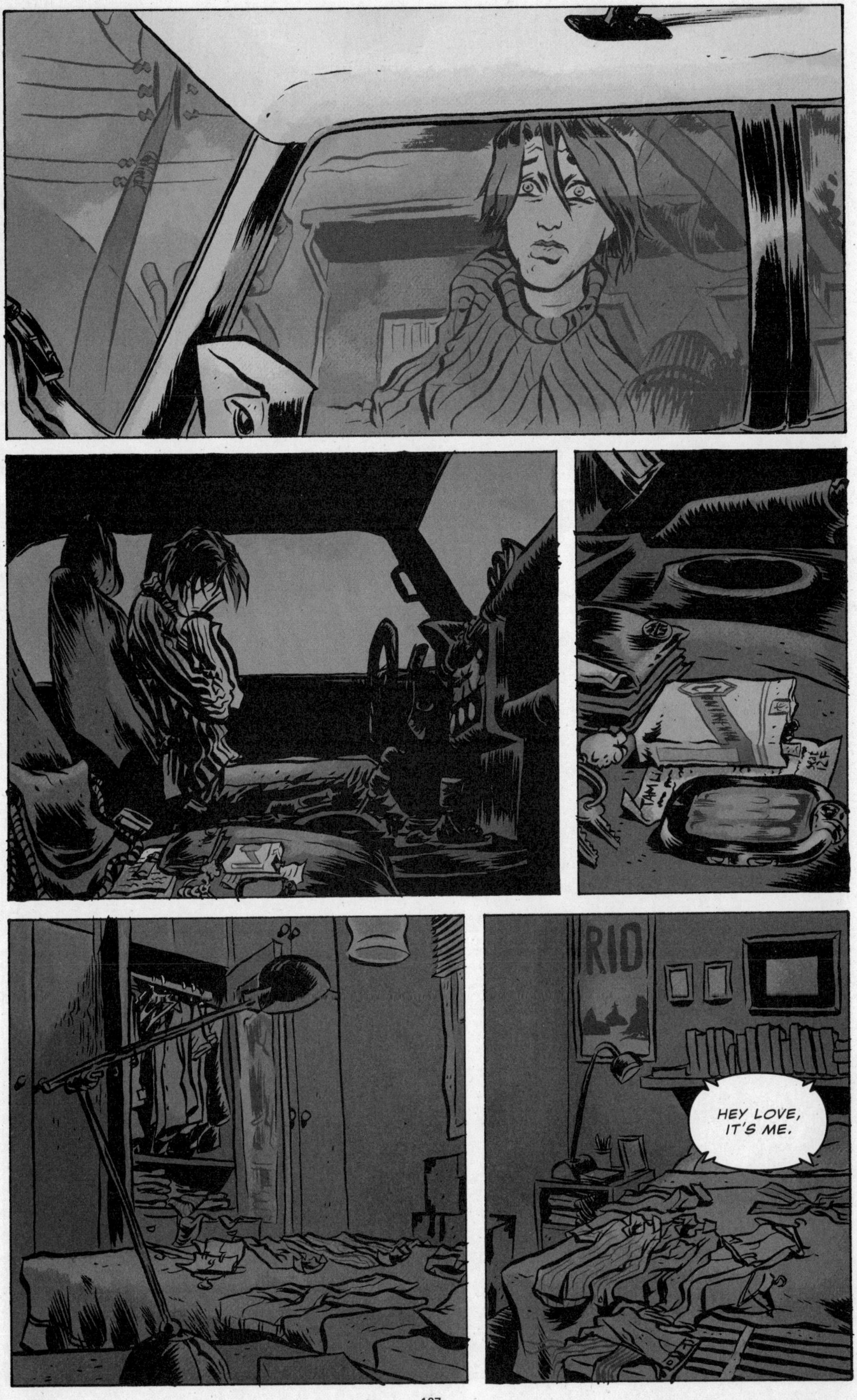
HEY LOVE,
IT'S ME.

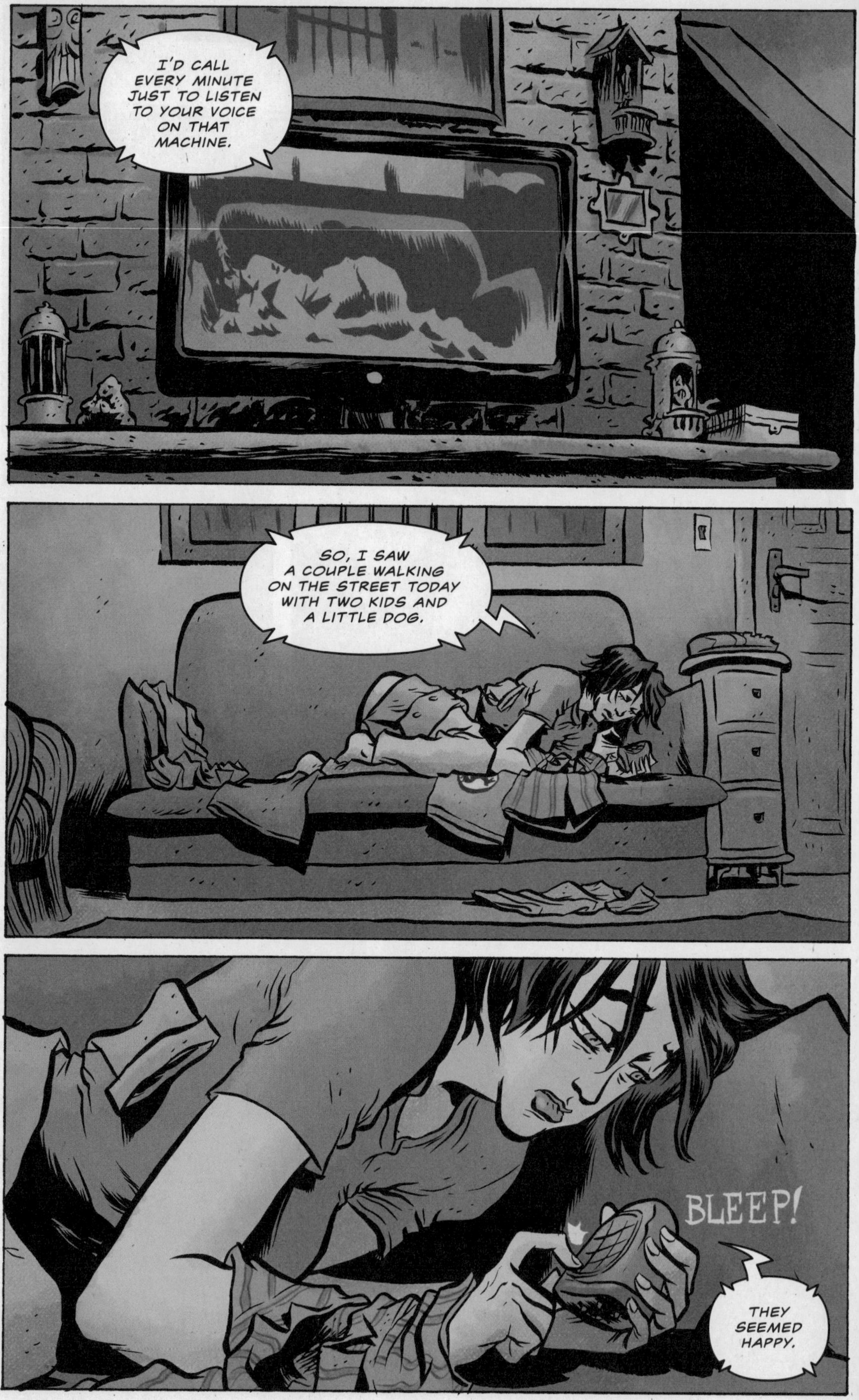
I'D CALL EVERY MINUTE JUST TO LISTEN TO YOUR VOICE ON THAT MACHINE.
SO, I SAW A COUPLE WALKING ON THE STREET TODAY WITH TWO KIDS AND A LITTLE DOG.
BLEEP!
THEY SEEMED HAPPY.

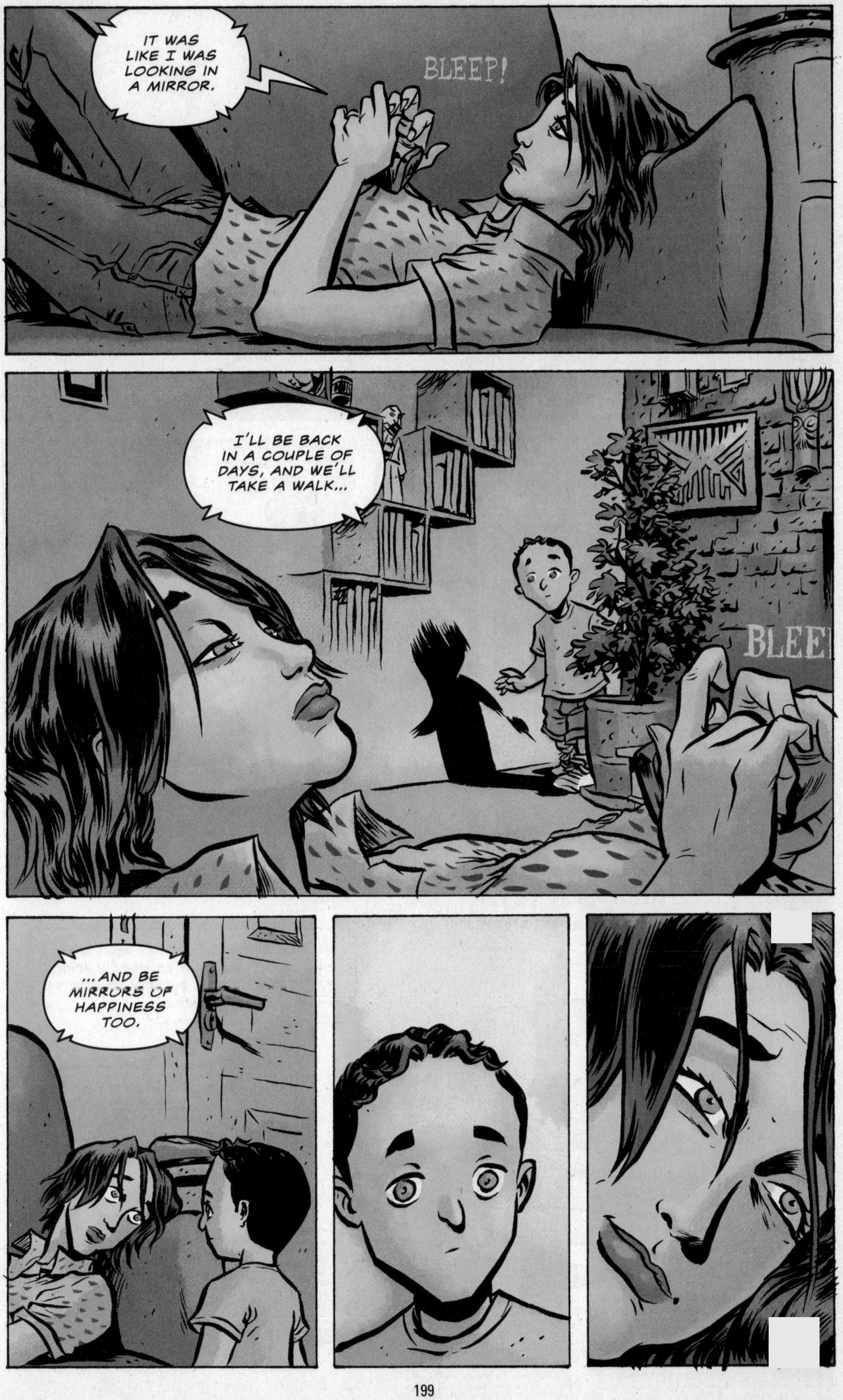
IT WAS LIKE I WAS LOOKING IN A MIRROR.
BLEEP!
I'LL BE BACK IN A COUPLE OF DAYS, AND WE'LL TAKE A WALK...
...AND BE MIRRORS OF HAPPINESS TOO.

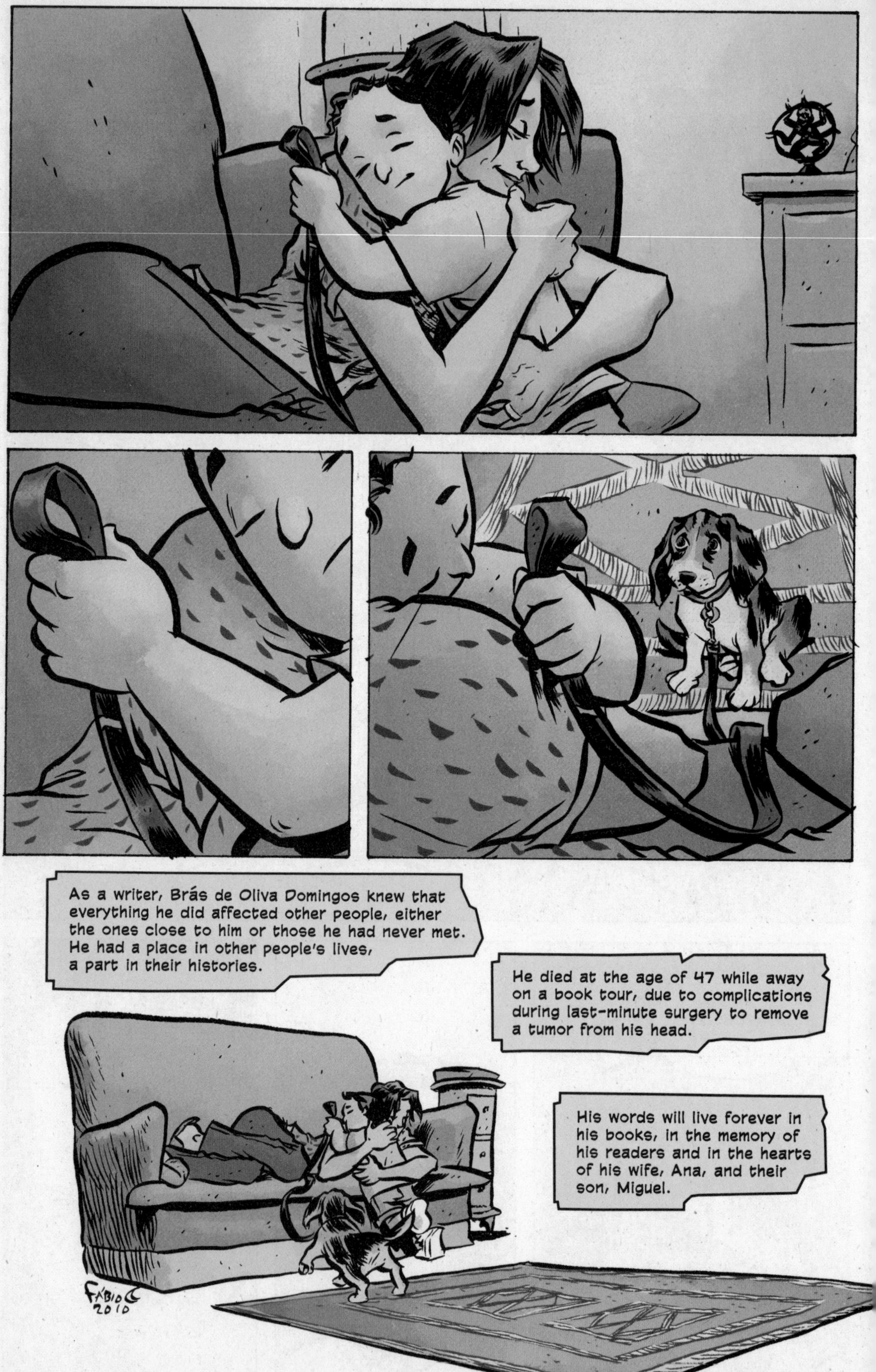
As a writer, Brás de Oliva Domingos knew that everything he did affected other people, either the ones close to him or those he had never met. He had a place in other people's lives, a part in their histories.
He died at the age of 47 while away on a book tour, due to complications during last-minute surgery to remove a tumor from his head.
His words will live forever in his books, in the memory of his readers and in the hearts of his wife, Ana, and their son, Miguel.
FÁBIO 2010

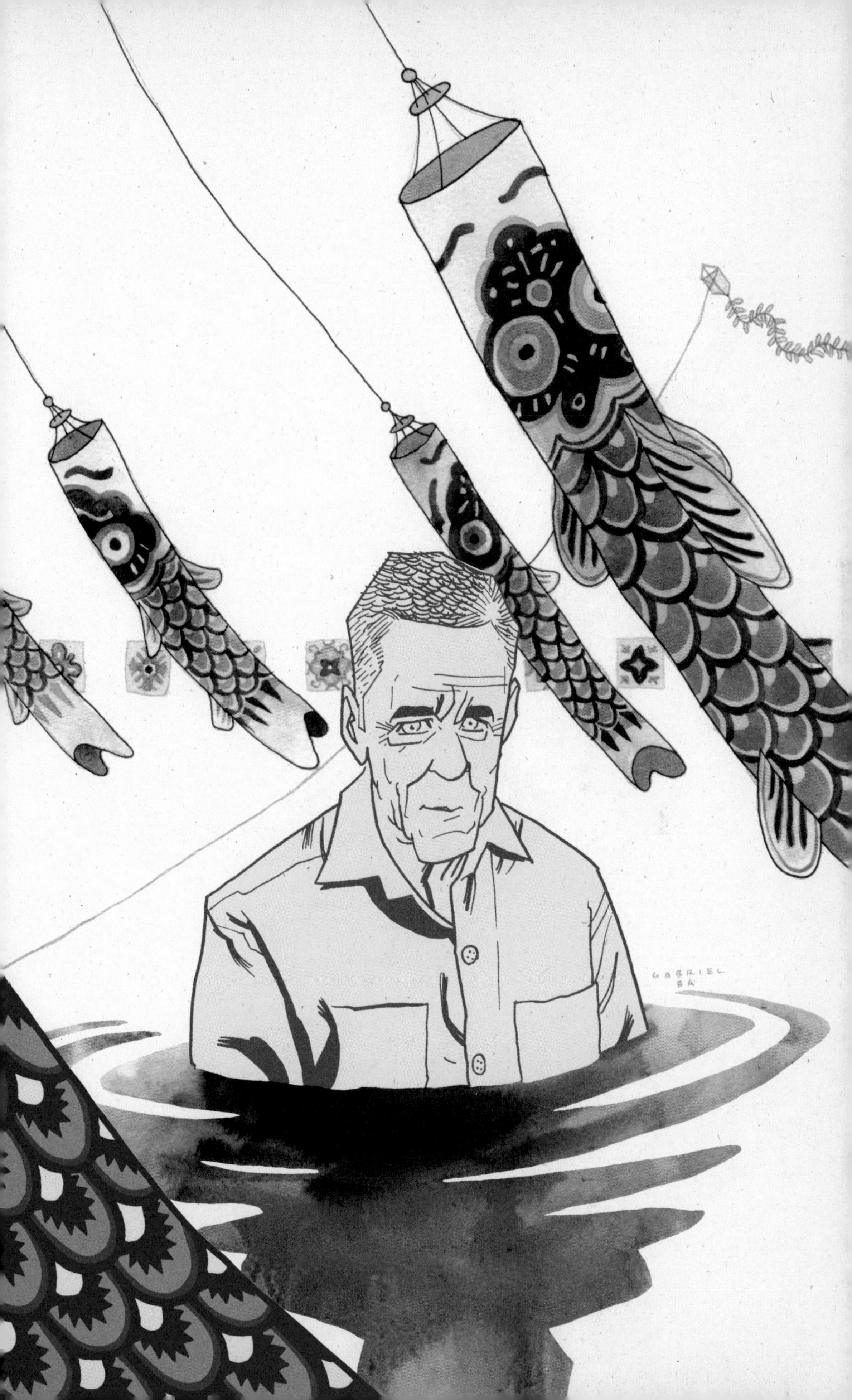
GABRIEL
BÁ

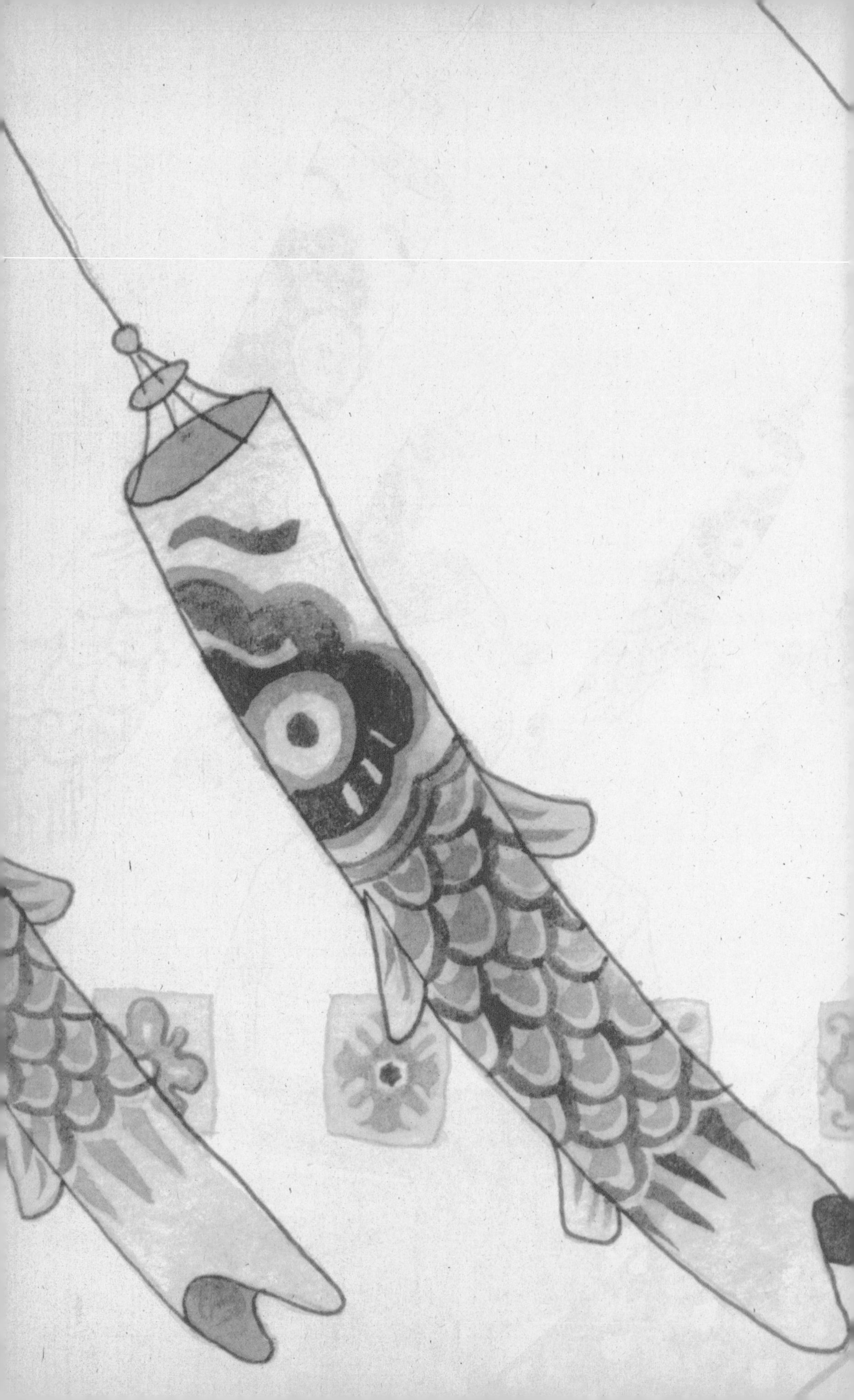

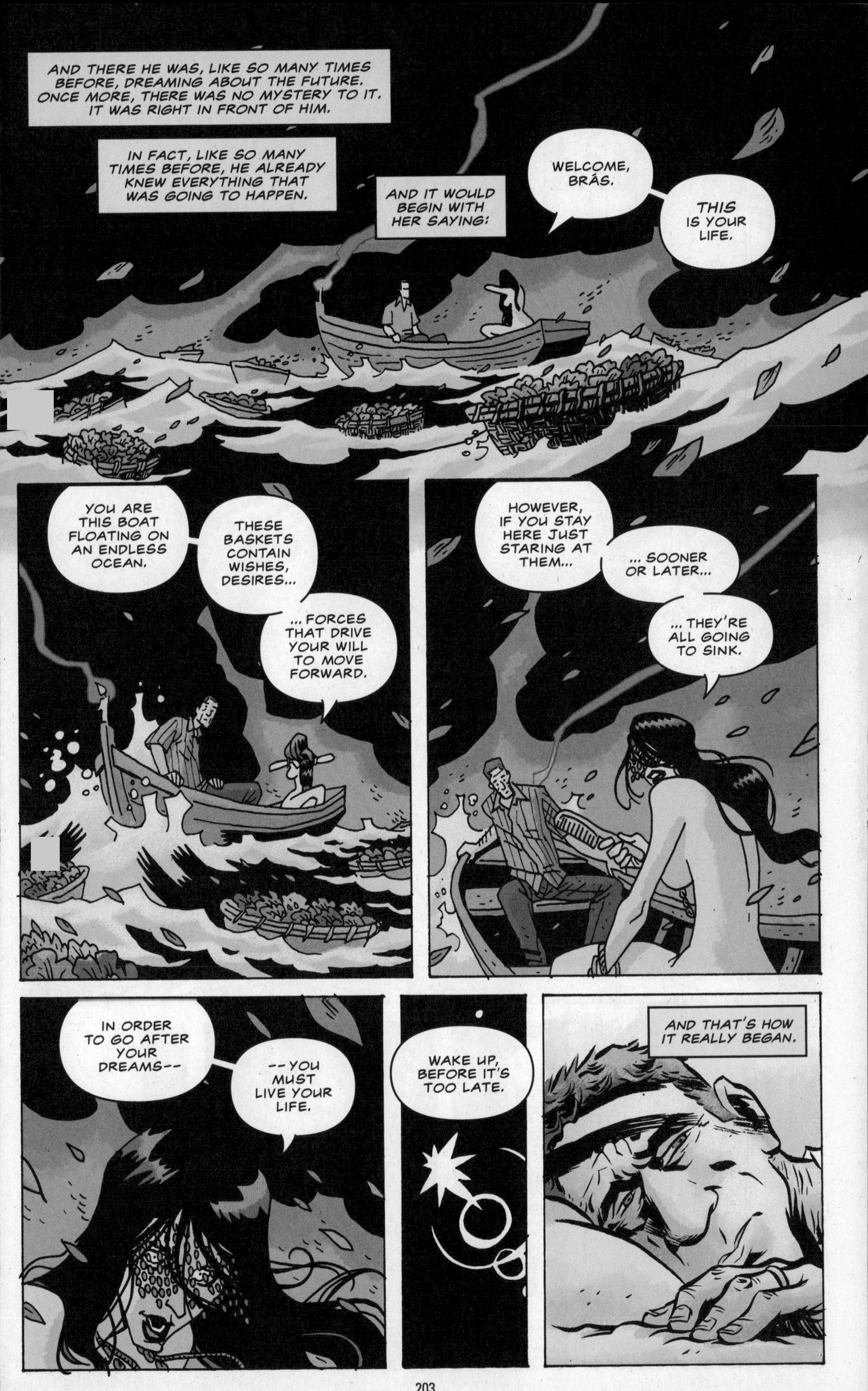
AND THERE HE WAS, LIKE SO MANY TIMES BEFORE, DREAMING ABOUT THE FUTURE. ONCE MORE, THERE WAS NO MYSTERY TO IT. IT WAS RIGHT IN FRONT OF HIM.
IN FACT, LIKE SO MANY TIMES BEFORE, HE ALREADY KNEW EVERYTHING THAT WAS GOING TO HAPPEN.
AND IT WOULD BEGIN WITH HER SAYING:
WELCOME, BRÁS.
THIS IS YOUR LIFE.
YOU ARE THIS BOAT FLOATING ON AN ENDLESS OCEAN.
THESE BASKETS CONTAIN WISHES, DESIRES...
... FORCES THAT DRIVE YOUR WILL TO MOVE FORWARD.
HOWEVER, IF YOU STAY HERE JUST STARING AT THEM...
... SOONER OR LATER...
... THEY'RE ALL GOING TO SINK.
IN ORDER TO GO AFTER YOUR DREAMS--
--YOU MUST LIVE YOUR LIFE.
WAKE UP, BEFORE IT'S TOO LATE.
AND THAT'S HOW IT REALLY BEGAN.

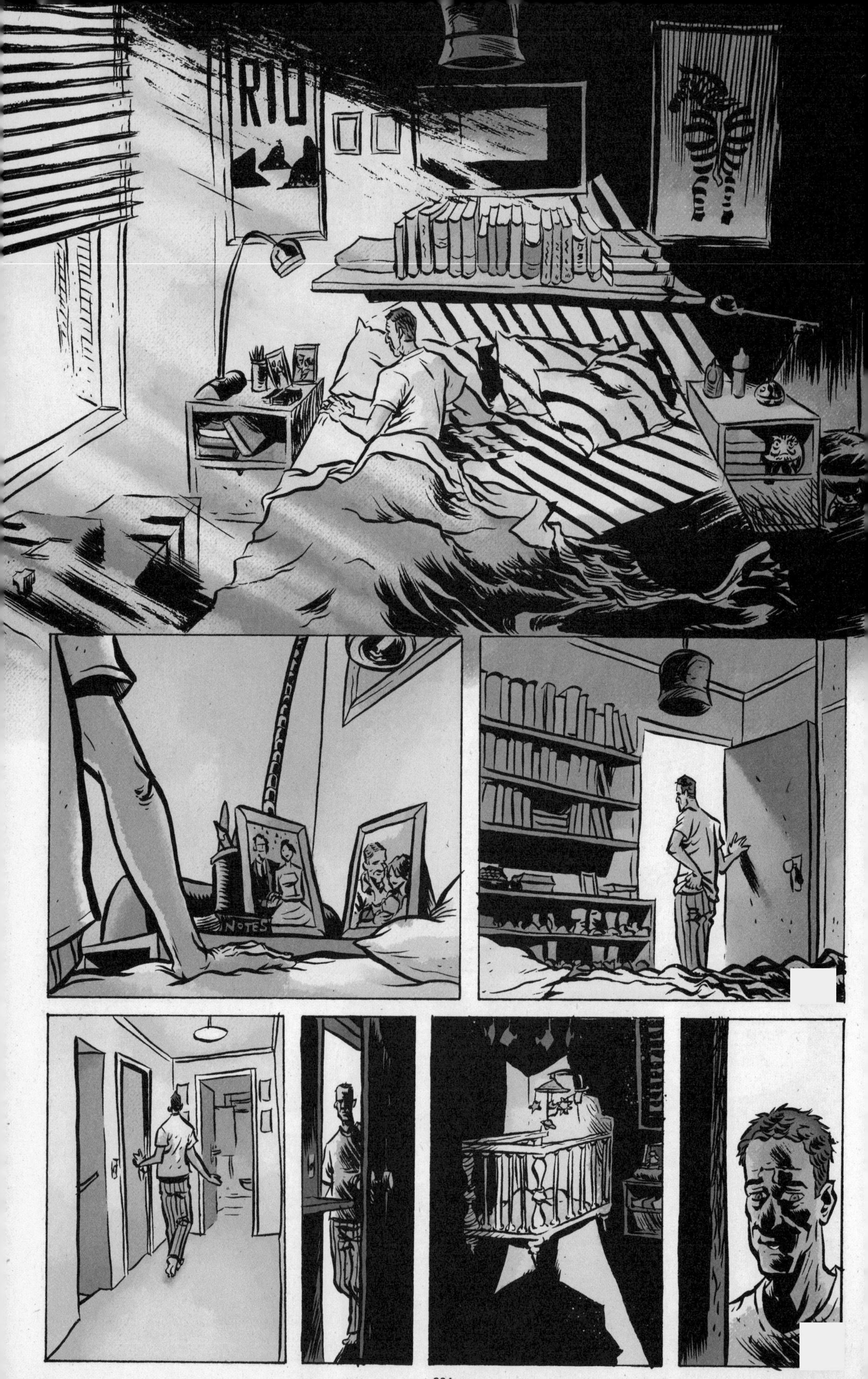
RIO
NOTES

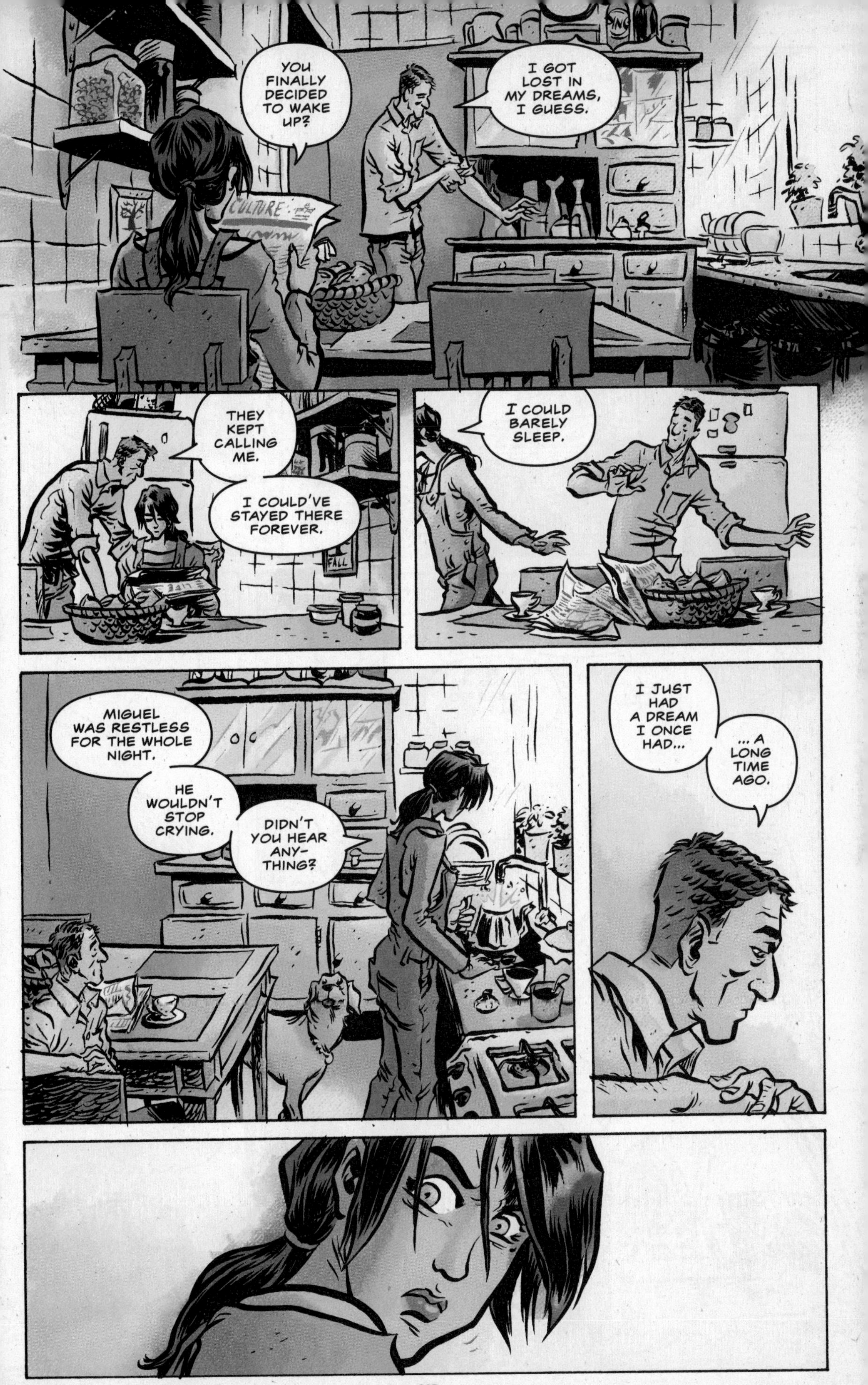
YOU FINALLY DECIDED TO WAKE UP?
I GOT LOST IN MY DREAMS, I GUESS.
CULTURE
THEY KEPT CALLING ME.
I COULD'VE STAYED THERE FOREVER.
I COULD BARELY SLEEP.
MIGUEL WAS RESTLESS FOR THE WHOLE NIGHT.
HE WOULDN'T STOP CRYING.
DIDN'T YOU HEAR ANY-THING?
I JUST HAD A DREAM I ONCE HAD...
... A LONG TIME AGO.

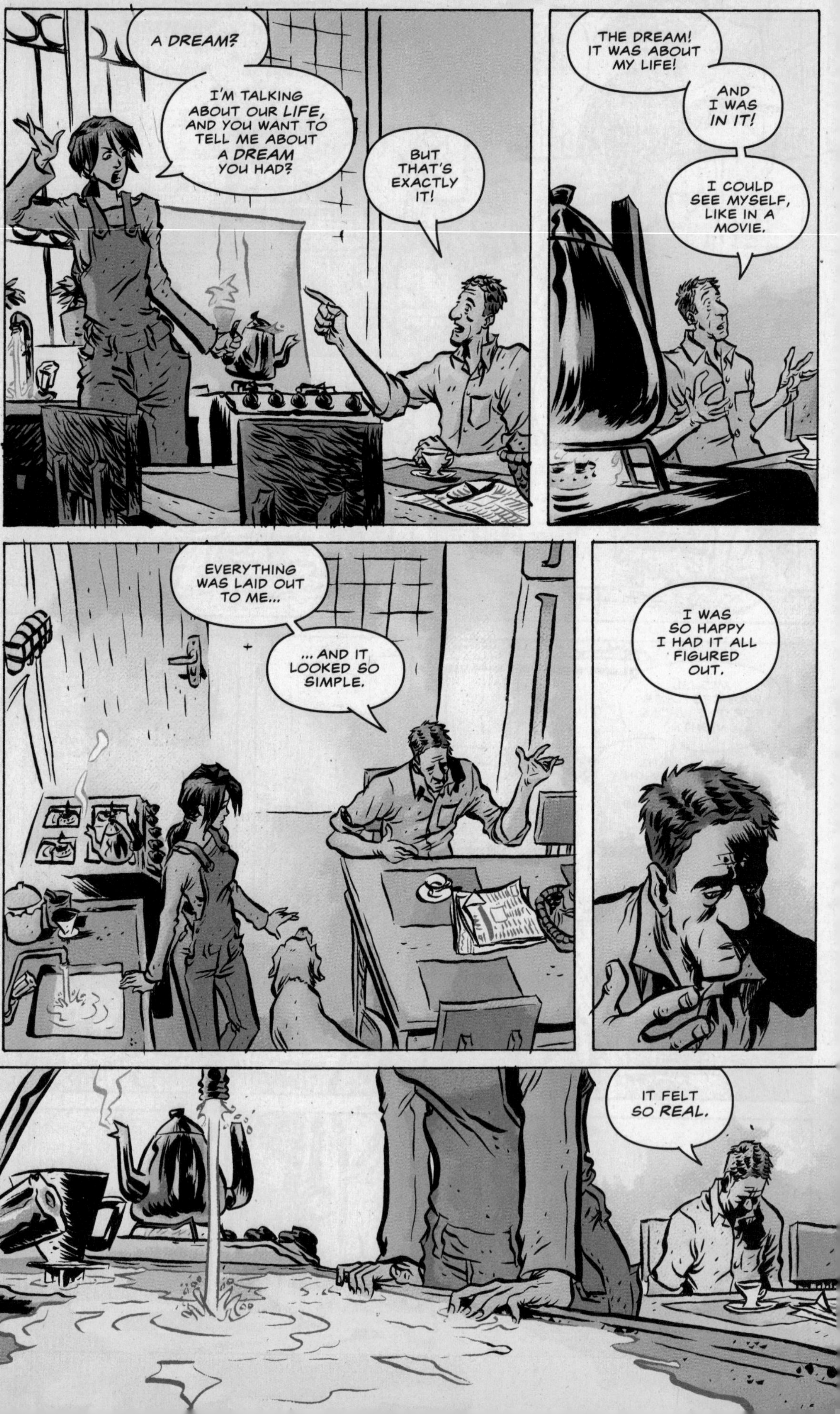
A DREAM?
I'M TALKING ABOUT OUR LIFE, AND YOU WANT TO TELL ME ABOUT A DREAM YOU HAD?
BUT THAT'S EXACTLY IT!
THE DREAM! IT WAS ABOUT MY LIFE!
AND I WAS IN IT!
I COULD SEE MYSELF, LIKE IN A MOVIE.
EVERYTHING WAS LAID OUT TO ME...
...AND IT LOOKED SO SIMPLE.
I WAS SO HAPPY I HAD IT ALL FIGURED OUT.
IT FELT SO REAL.

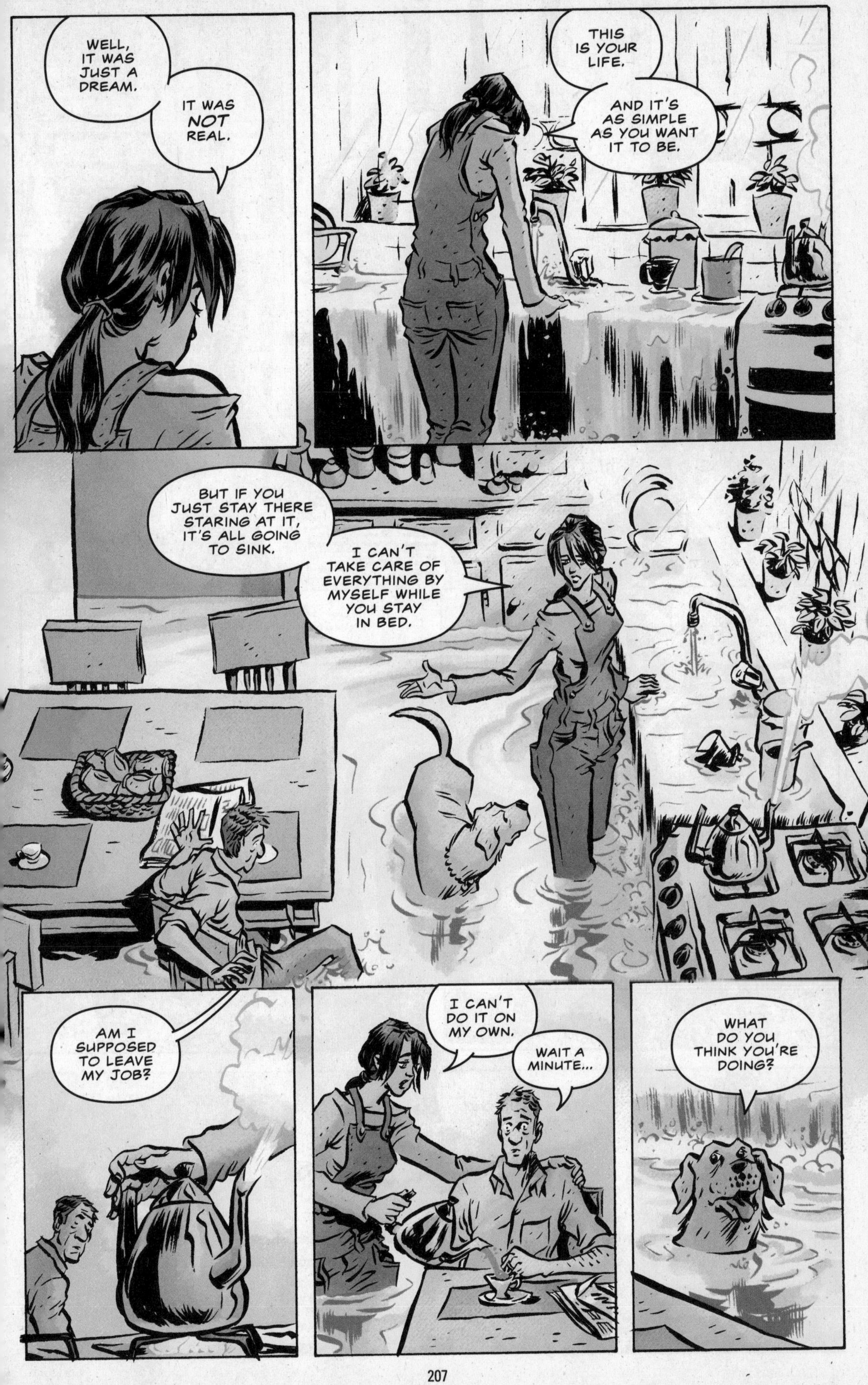
WELL, IT WAS JUST A DREAM.
IT WAS NOT REAL.
THIS IS YOUR LIFE.
AND IT'S AS SIMPLE AS YOU WANT IT TO BE.
BUT IF YOU JUST STAY THERE STARING AT IT, IT'S ALL GOING TO SINK.
I CAN'T TAKE CARE OF EVERYTHING BY MYSELF WHILE YOU STAY IN BED.
AM I SUPPOSED TO LEAVE MY JOB?
I CAN'T DO IT ON MY OWN.
WAIT A MINUTE...
WHAT DO YOU THINK YOU'RE DOING?

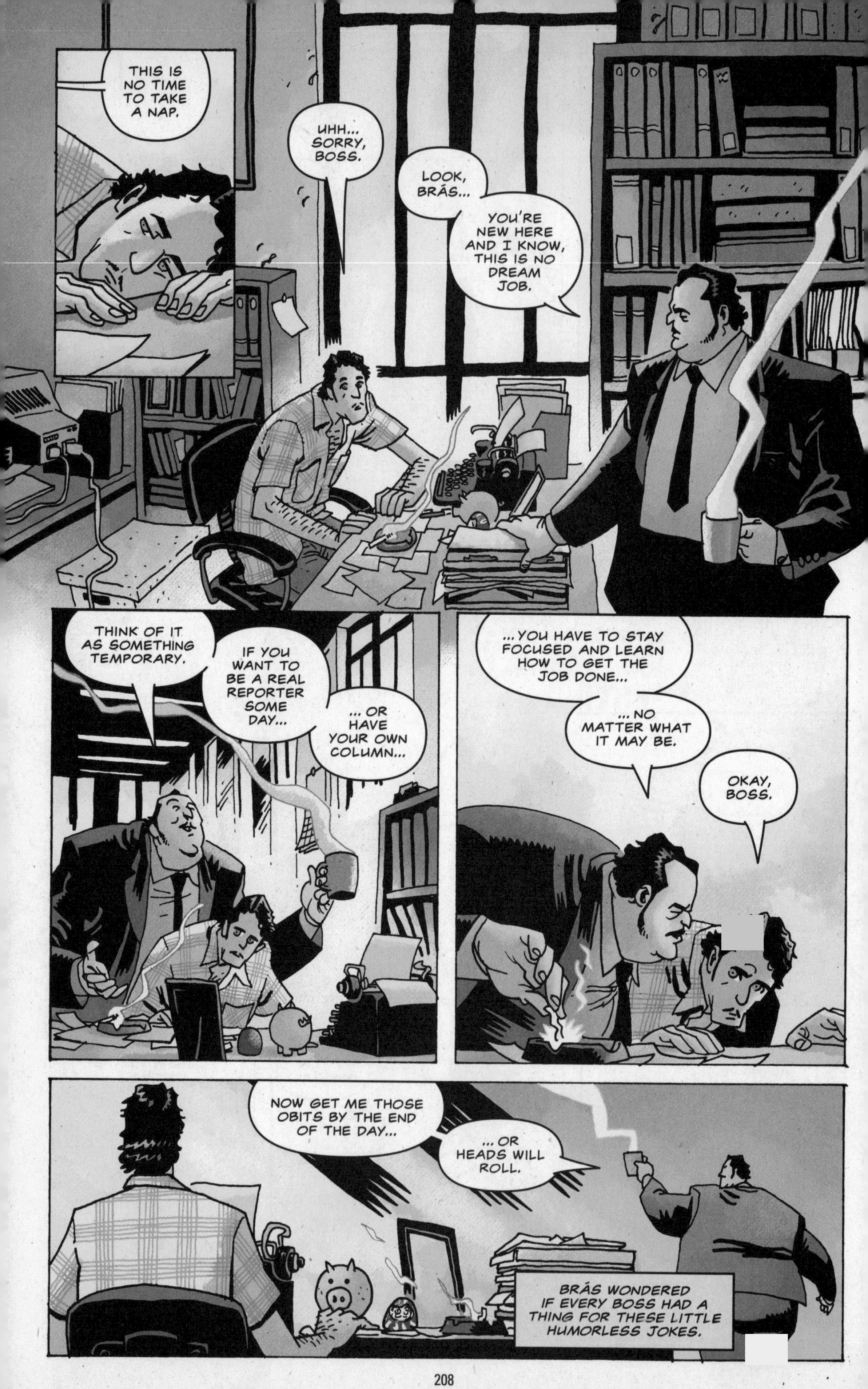
THIS IS NO TIME TO TAKE A NAP.
UHH... SORRY, BOSS.
LOOK, BRÁS...
YOU'RE NEW HERE AND I KNOW, THIS IS NO DREAM JOB.
THINK OF IT AS SOMETHING TEMPORARY.
IF YOU WANT TO BE A REAL REPORTER SOME DAY...
... OR HAVE YOUR OWN COLUMN...
... YOU HAVE TO STAY FOCUSED AND LEARN HOW TO GET THE JOB DONE...
... NO MATTER WHAT IT MAY BE.
OKAY, BOSS.
NOW GET ME THOSE OBITS BY THE END OF THE DAY...
... OR HEADS WILL ROLL.
BRÁS WONDERED IF EVERY BOSS HAD A THING FOR THESE LITTLE HUMORLESS JOKES.

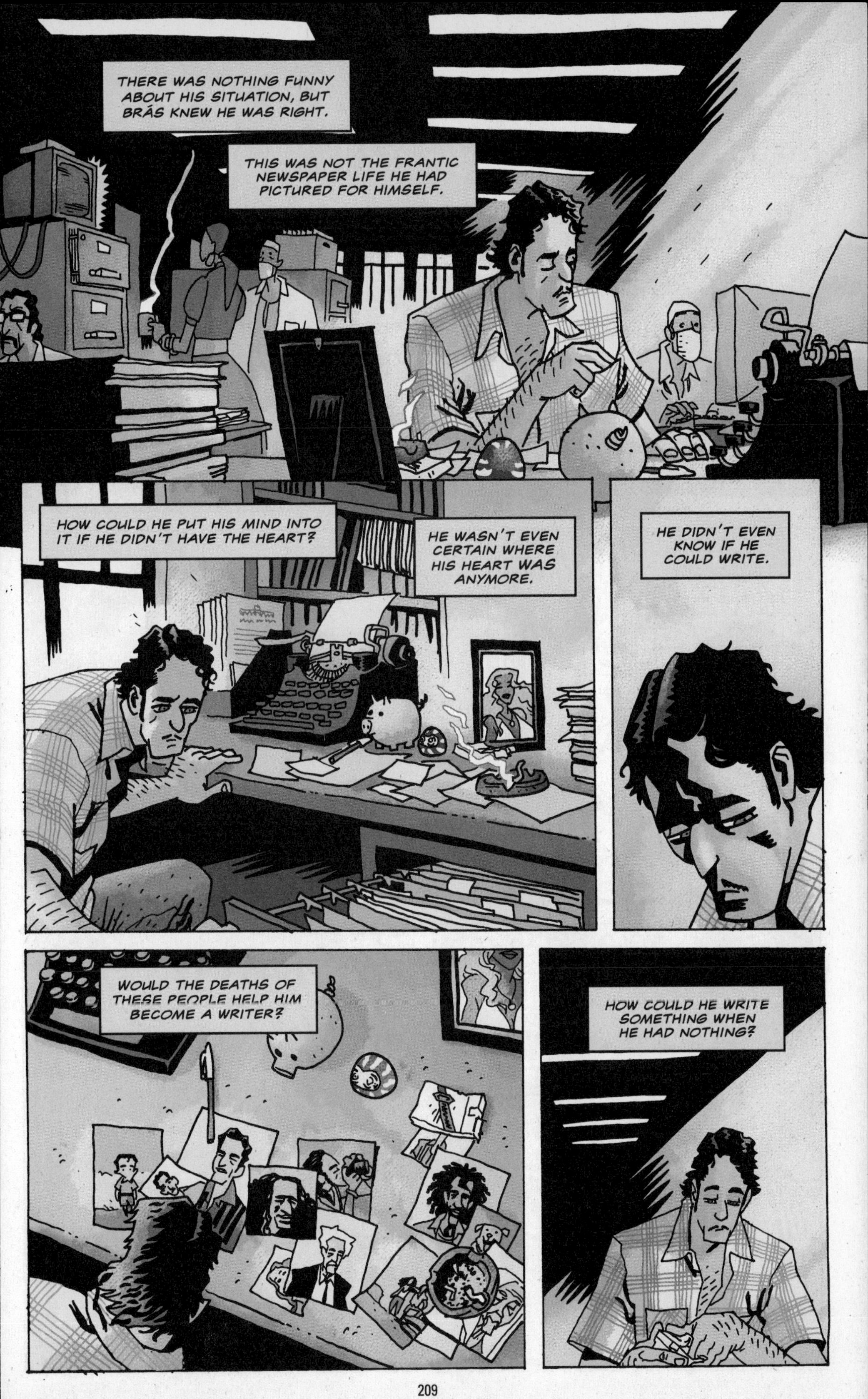
THERE WAS NOTHING FUNNY ABOUT HIS SITUATION, BUT BRÁS KNEW HE WAS RIGHT.
THIS WAS NOT THE FRANTIC NEWSPAPER LIFE HE HAD PICTURED FOR HIMSELF.
HOW COULD HE PUT HIS MIND INTO IT IF HE DIDN'T HAVE THE HEART?
HE WASN'T EVEN CERTAIN WHERE HIS HEART WAS ANYMORE.
HE DIDN'T EVEN KNOW IF HE COULD WRITE.
WOULD THE DEATHS OF THESE PEOPLE HELP HIM BECOME A WRITER?
HOW COULD HE WRITE SOMETHING WHEN HE HAD NOTHING?

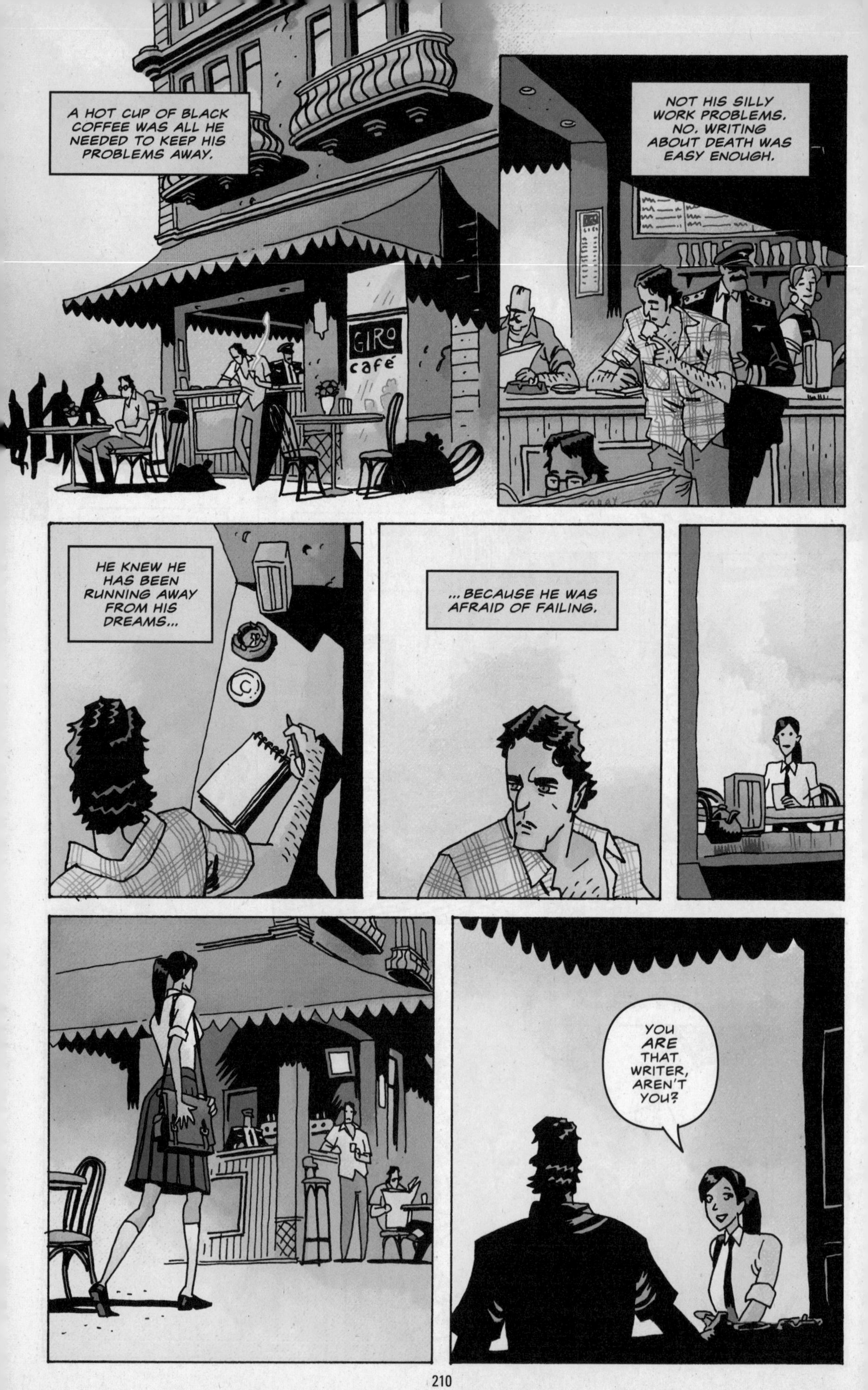
A HOT CUP OF BLACK COFFEE WAS ALL HE NEEDED TO KEEP HIS PROBLEMS AWAY.
GIRO
café
NOT HIS SILLY WORK PROBLEMS. NO. WRITING ABOUT DEATH WAS EASY ENOUGH.
HE KNEW HE HAS BEEN RUNNING AWAY FROM HIS DREAMS...
...BECAUSE HE WAS AFRAID OF FAILING.
YOU ARE THAT WRITER, AREN'T YOU?

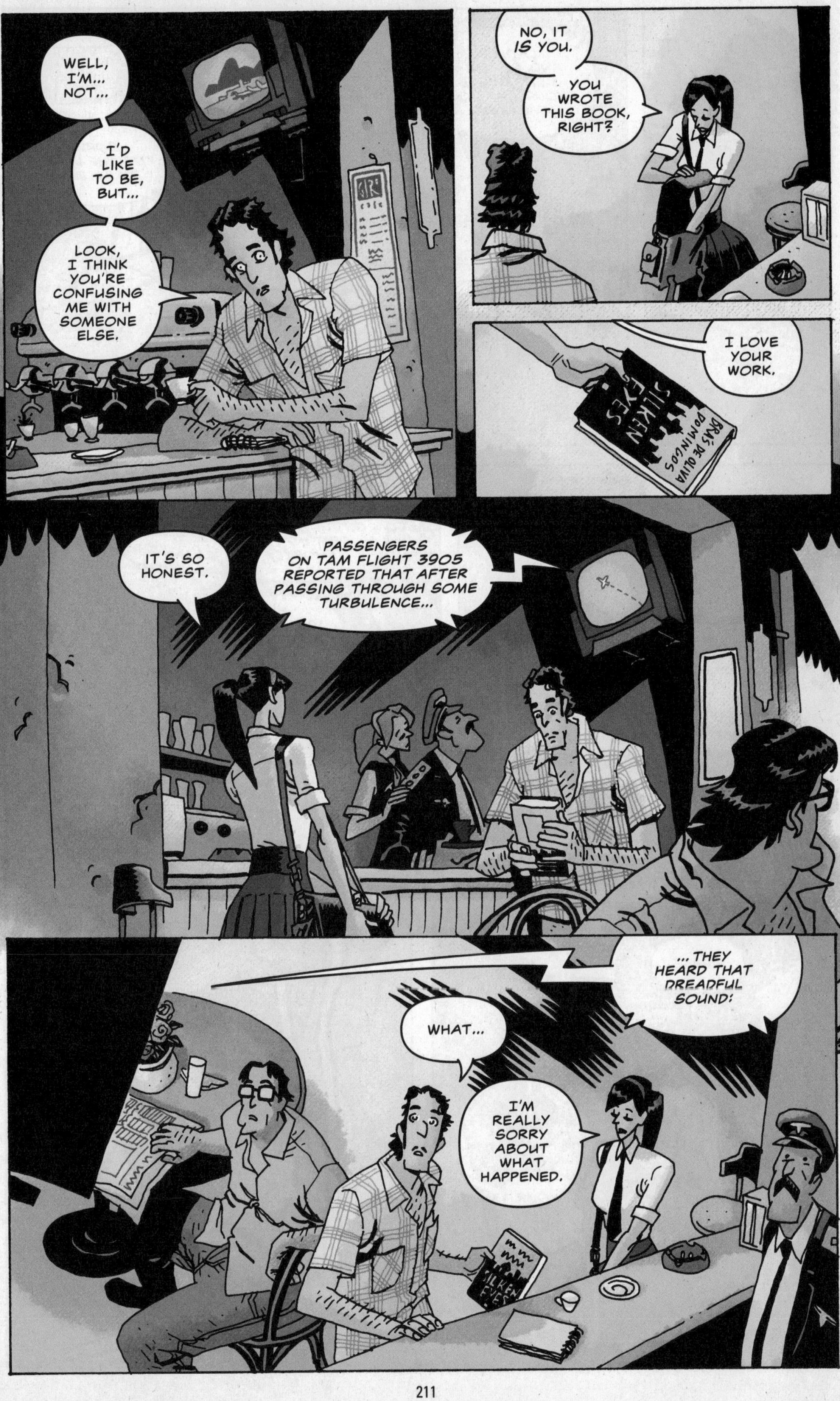
WELL, I'M... NOT...
I'D LIKE TO BE, BUT...
LOOK, I THINK YOU'RE CONFUSING ME WITH SOMEONE ELSE.
NO, IT IS YOU.
YOU WROTE THIS BOOK, RIGHT?
I LOVE YOUR WORK.
SILKEN EYES
BRÁS DE OLIVA DOMINGOS
IT'S SO HONEST.
PASSENGERS ON TAM FLIGHT 3905 REPORTED THAT AFTER PASSING THROUGH SOME TURBULENCE...
...THEY HEARD THAT DREADFUL SOUND:
WHAT...
I'M REALLY SORRY ABOUT WHAT HAPPENED.

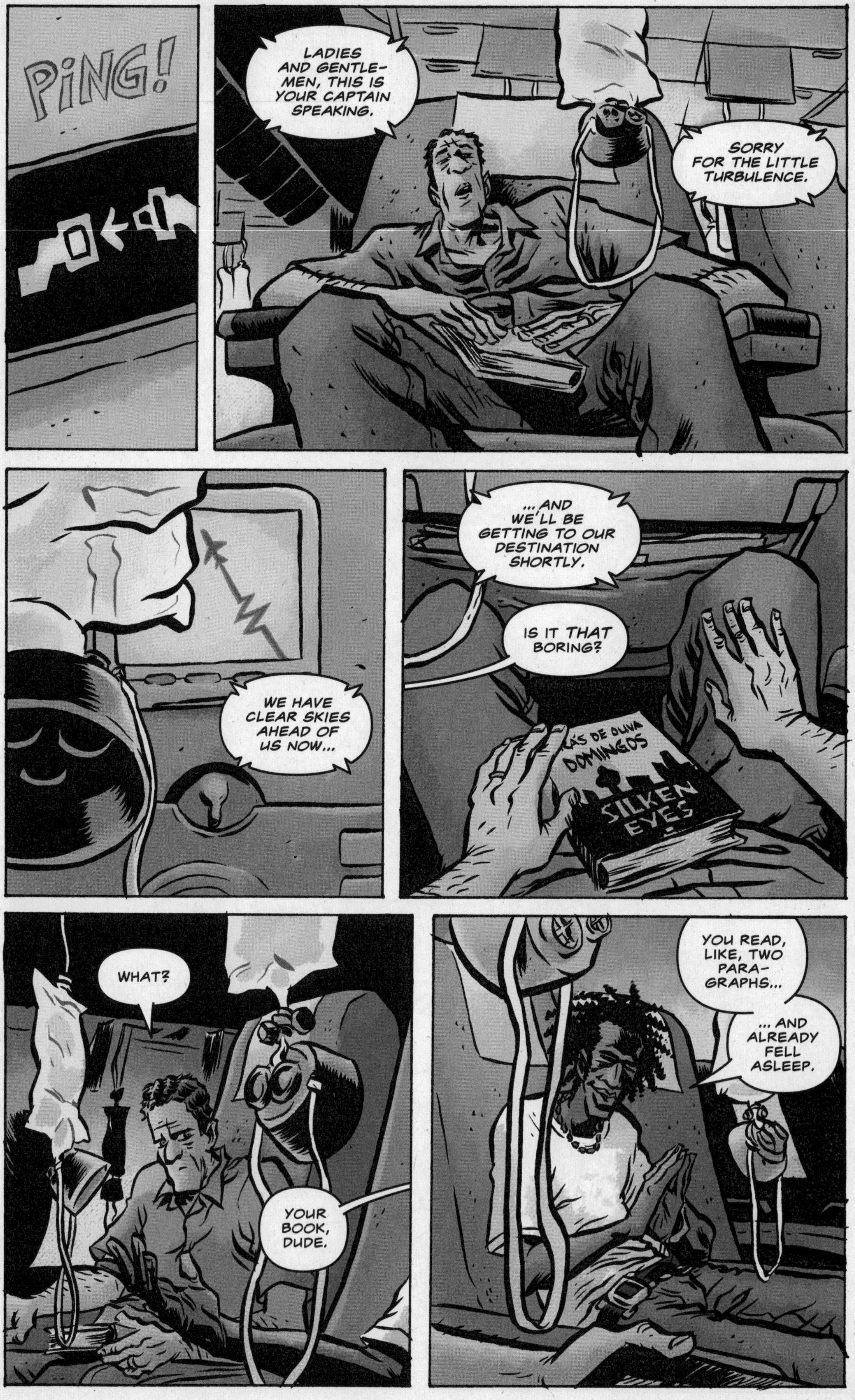
PiNG!
LADIES AND GENTLEMEN, THIS IS YOUR CAPTAIN SPEAKING.
SORRY FOR THE LITTLE TURBULENCE.
WE HAVE CLEAR SKIES AHEAD OF US NOW...
...AND WE'LL BE GETTING TO OUR DESTINATION SHORTLY.
IS IT THAT BORING?
DOMINGOS
SILKEN EYES
WHAT?
YOUR BOOK, DUDE.
YOU READ, LIKE, TWO PARAGRAPHS...
...AND ALREADY FELL ASLEEP.

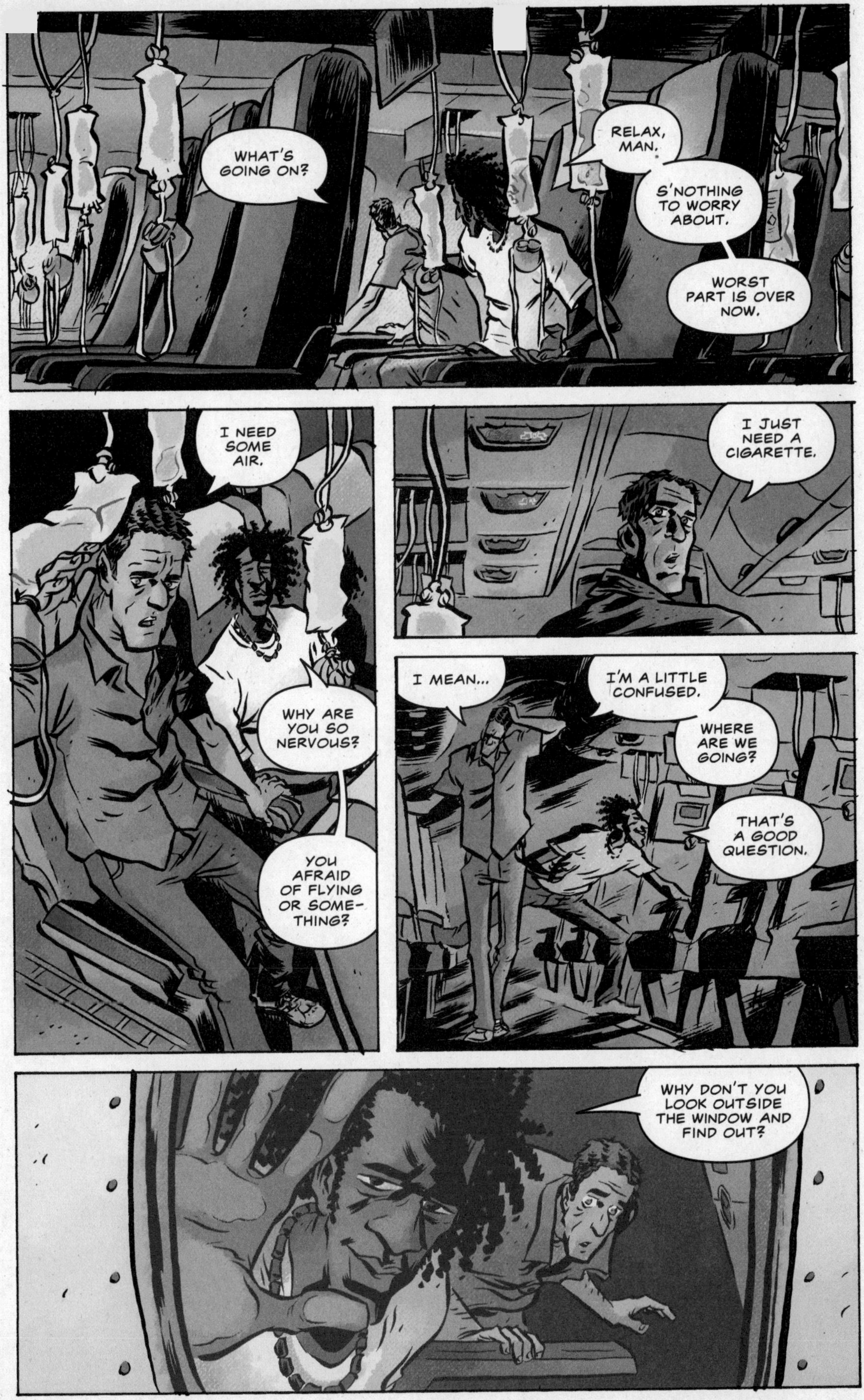
WHAT'S GOING ON?
RELAX, MAN.
S'NOTHING TO WORRY ABOUT.
WORST PART IS OVER NOW.
I NEED SOME AIR.
WHY ARE YOU SO NERVOUS?
YOU AFRAID OF FLYING OR SOME-THING?
I JUST NEED A CIGARETTE.
I MEAN...
I'M A LITTLE CONFUSED.
WHERE ARE WE GOING?
THAT'S A GOOD QUESTION.
WHY DON'T YOU LOOK OUTSIDE THE WINDOW AND FIND OUT?

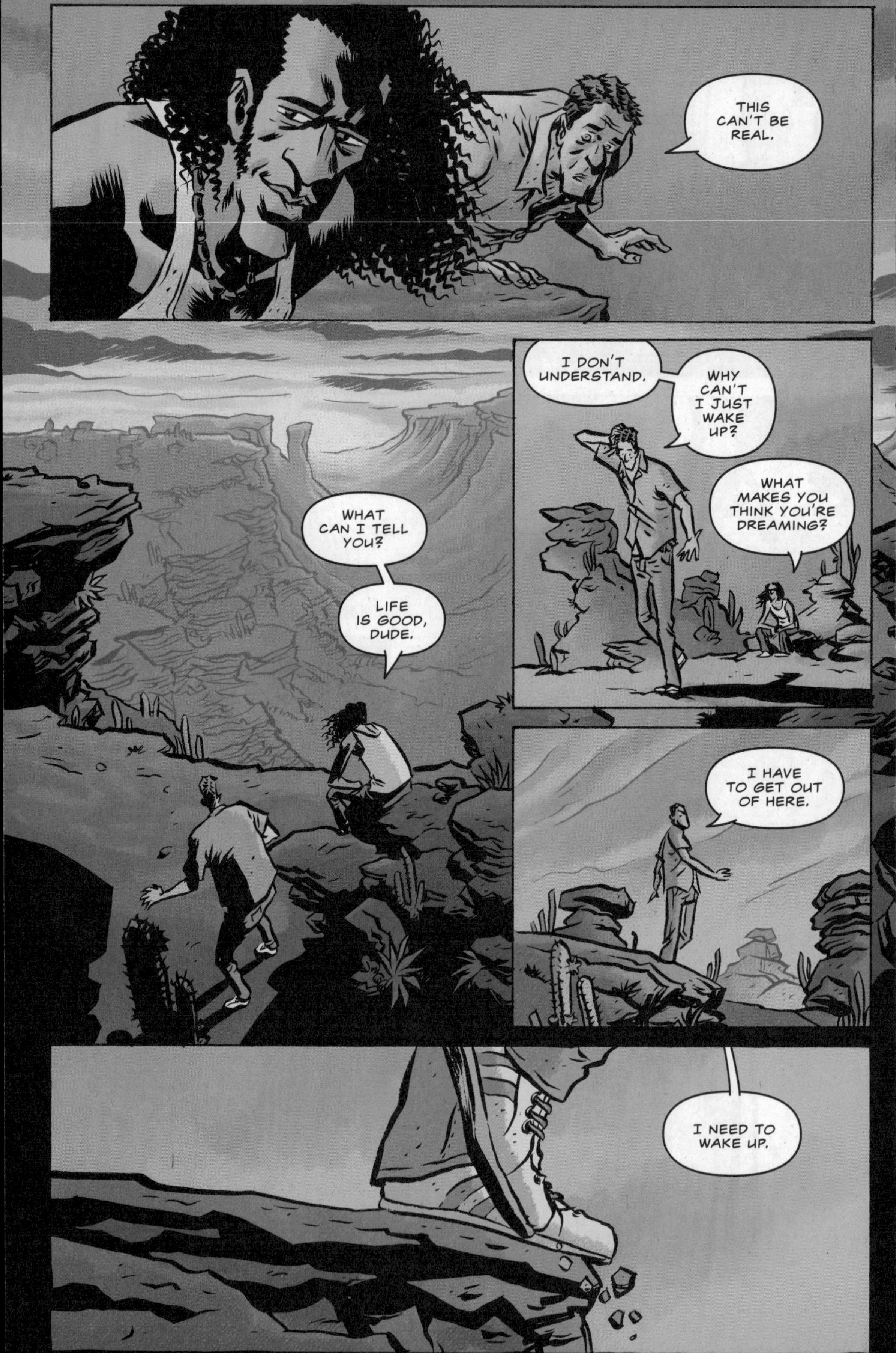
THIS CAN'T BE REAL.
WHAT CAN I TELL YOU?
LIFE IS GOOD, DUDE.
I DON'T UNDERSTAND.
WHY CAN'T I JUST WAKE UP?
WHAT MAKES YOU THINK YOU'RE DREAMING?
I HAVE TO GET OUT OF HERE.
I NEED TO WAKE UP.

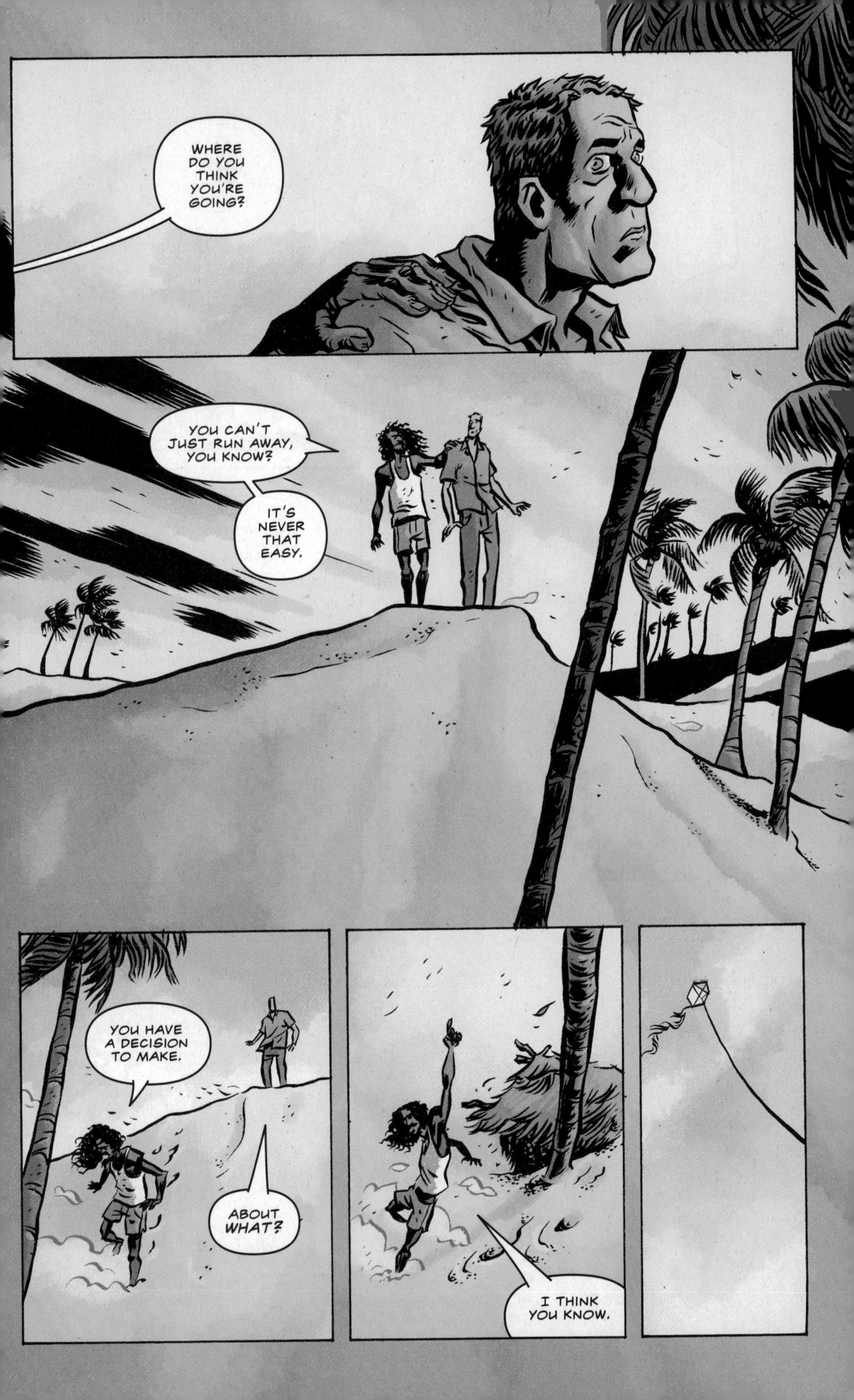
WHERE DO YOU THINK YOU'RE GOING?
YOU CAN'T JUST RUN AWAY, YOU KNOW?
IT'S NEVER THAT EASY.
YOU HAVE A DECISION TO MAKE.
ABOUT WHAT?
I THINK YOU KNOW.

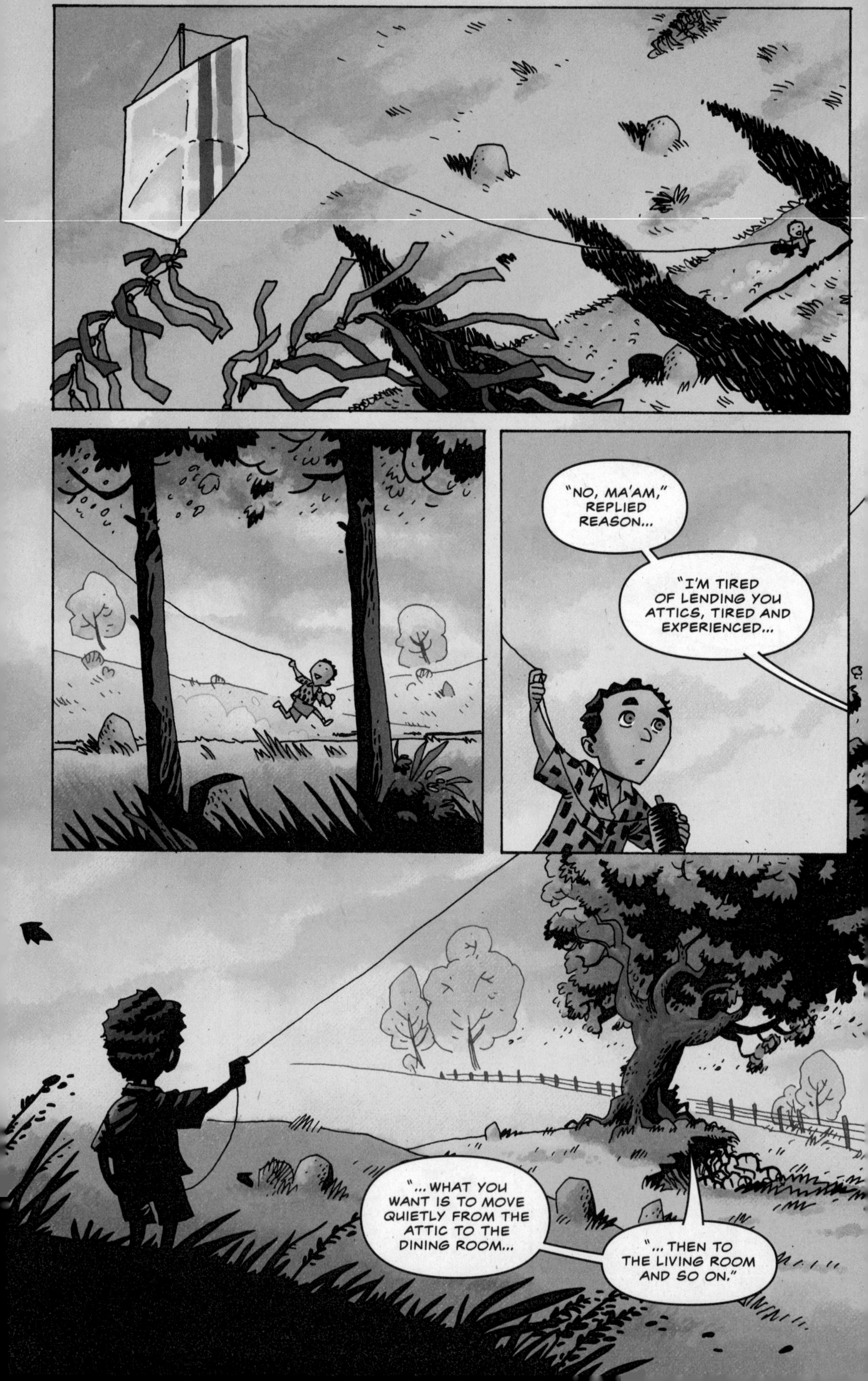
"NO, MA'AM," REPLIED REASON...
"I'M TIRED OF LENDING YOU ATTICS, TIRED AND EXPERIENCED...
"...WHAT YOU WANT IS TO MOVE QUIETLY FROM THE ATTIC TO THE DINING ROOM...
"...THEN TO THE LIVING ROOM AND SO ON."

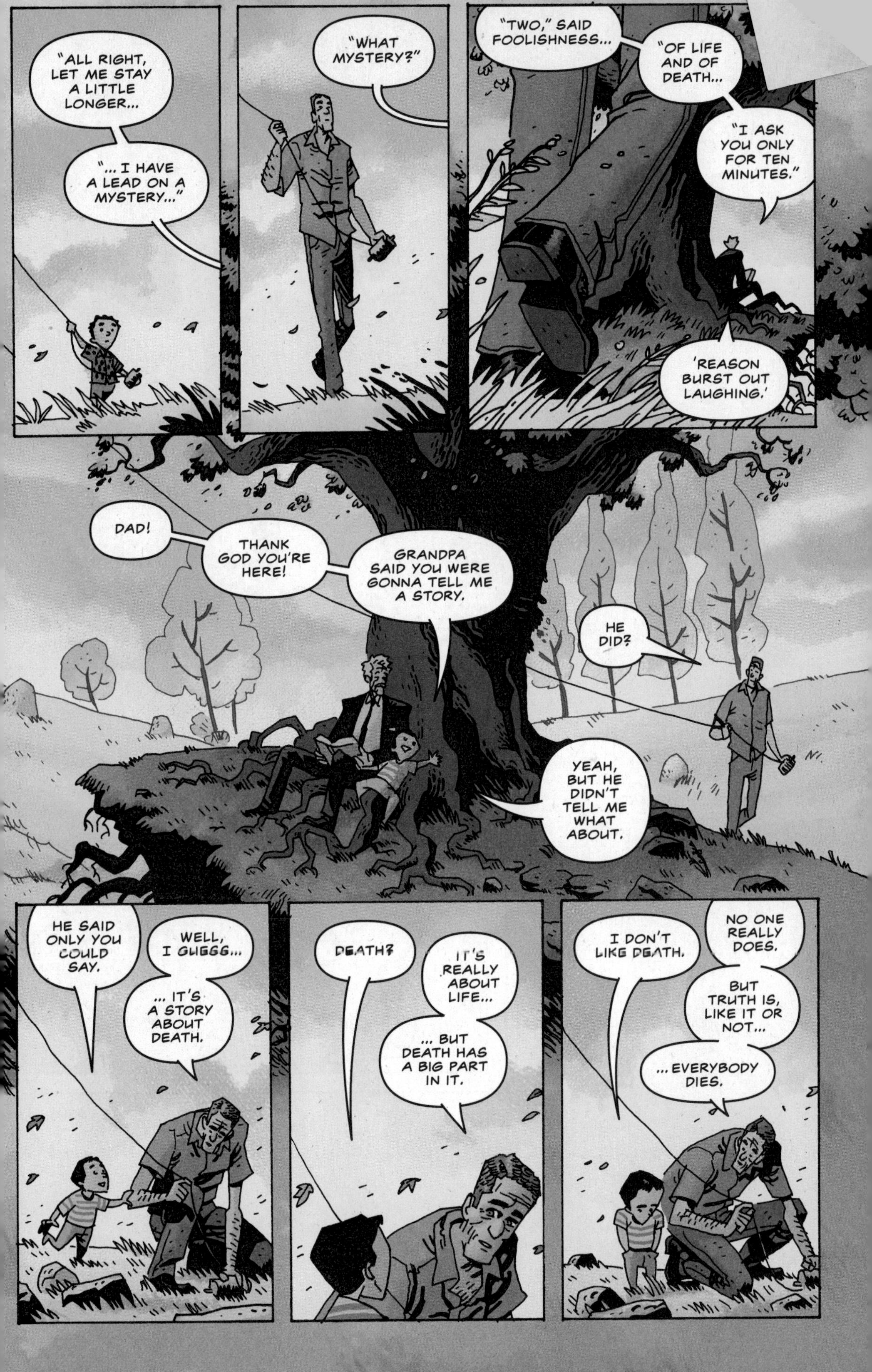
"ALL RIGHT, LET ME STAY A LITTLE LONGER...
"... I HAVE A LEAD ON A MYSTERY..."
"WHAT MYSTERY?"
"TWO," SAID FOOLISHNESS...
"OF LIFE AND OF DEATH...
"I ASK YOU ONLY FOR TEN MINUTES."
'REASON BURST OUT LAUGHING.'
DAD!
THANK GOD YOU'RE HERE!
GRANDPA SAID YOU WERE GONNA TELL ME A STORY.
HE DID?
YEAH, BUT HE DIDN'T TELL ME WHAT ABOUT.
HE SAID ONLY YOU COULD SAY.
WELL, I GUESS...
... IT'S A STORY ABOUT DEATH.
DEATH?
IT'S REALLY ABOUT LIFE...
... BUT DEATH HAS A BIG PART IN IT.
I DON'T LIKE DEATH.
NO ONE REALLY DOES.
BUT TRUTH IS, LIKE IT OR NOT...
... EVERYBODY DIES.

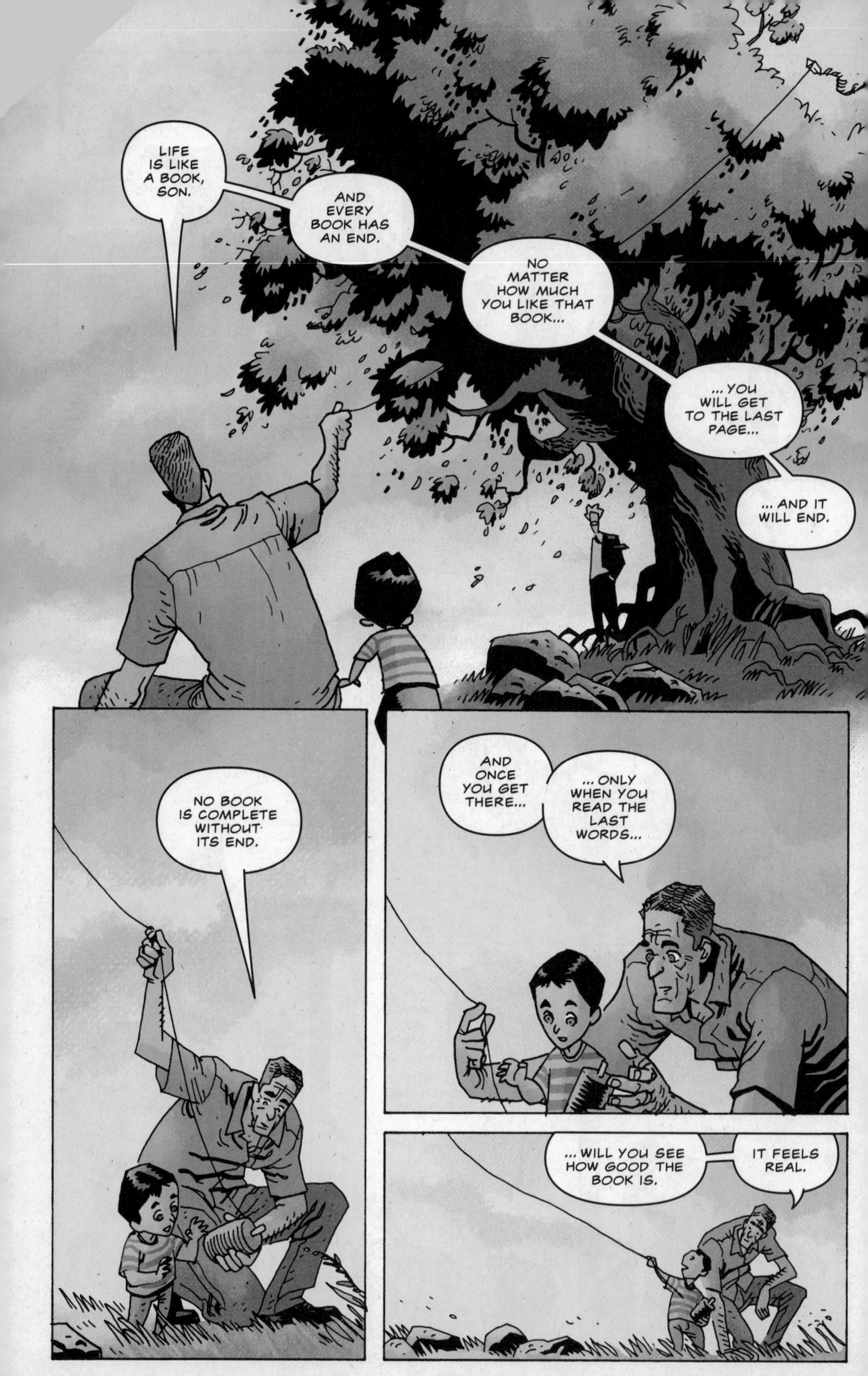
LIFE IS LIKE A BOOK, SON.
AND EVERY BOOK HAS AN END.
NO MATTER HOW MUCH YOU LIKE THAT BOOK...
...YOU WILL GET TO THE LAST PAGE...
...AND IT WILL END.
NO BOOK IS COMPLETE WITHOUT ITS END.
AND ONCE YOU GET THERE...
...ONLY WHEN YOU READ THE LAST WORDS...
...WILL YOU SEE HOW GOOD THE BOOK IS.
IT FEELS REAL.

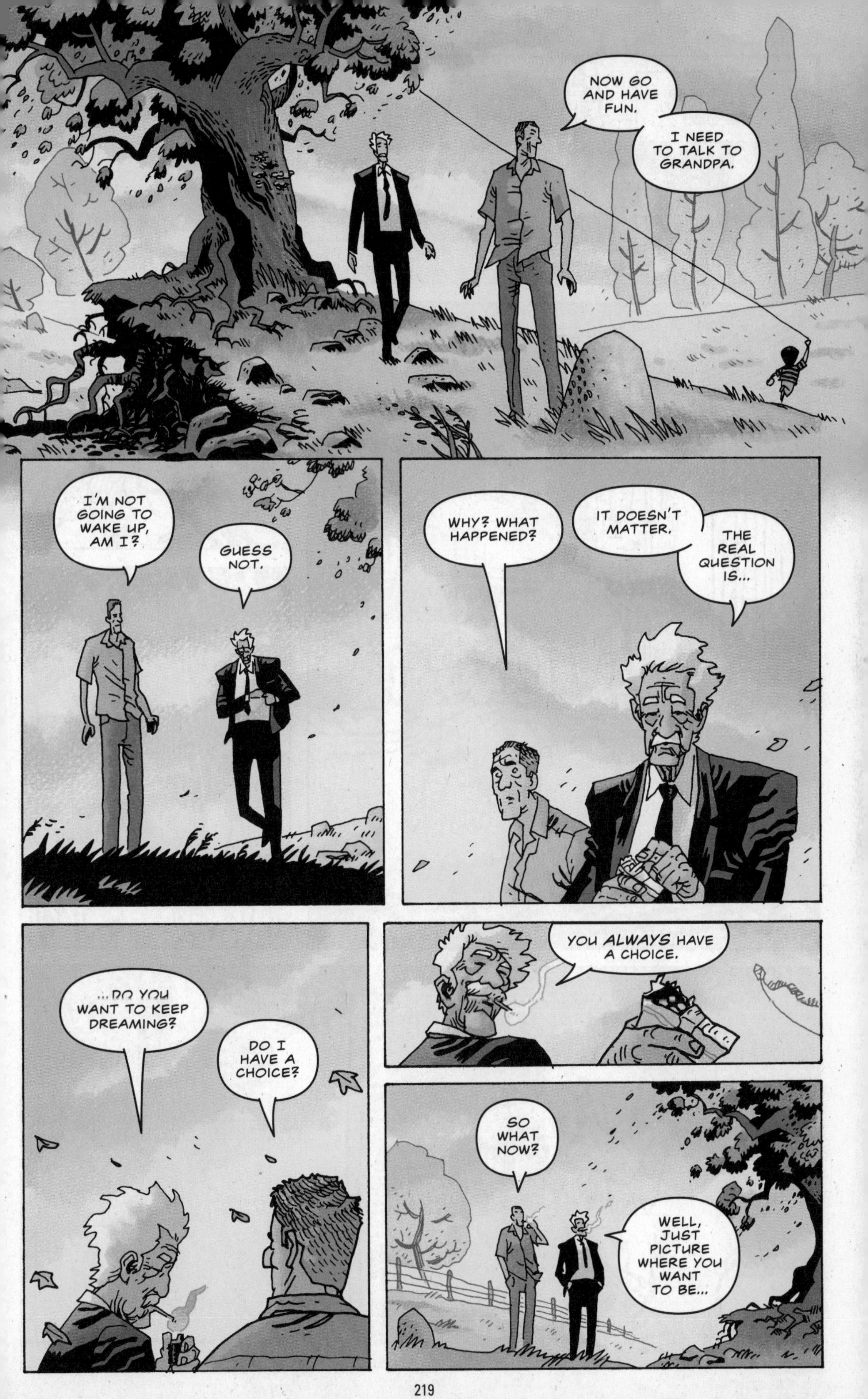
NOW GO AND HAVE FUN.
I NEED TO TALK TO GRANDPA.
I'M NOT GOING TO WAKE UP, AM I?
GUESS NOT.
WHY? WHAT HAPPENED?
IT DOESN'T MATTER.
THE REAL QUESTION IS...
...DO YOU WANT TO KEEP DREAMING?
DO I HAVE A CHOICE?
YOU *ALWAYS* HAVE A CHOICE.
SO WHAT NOW?
WELL, JUST PICTURE WHERE YOU WANT TO BE...

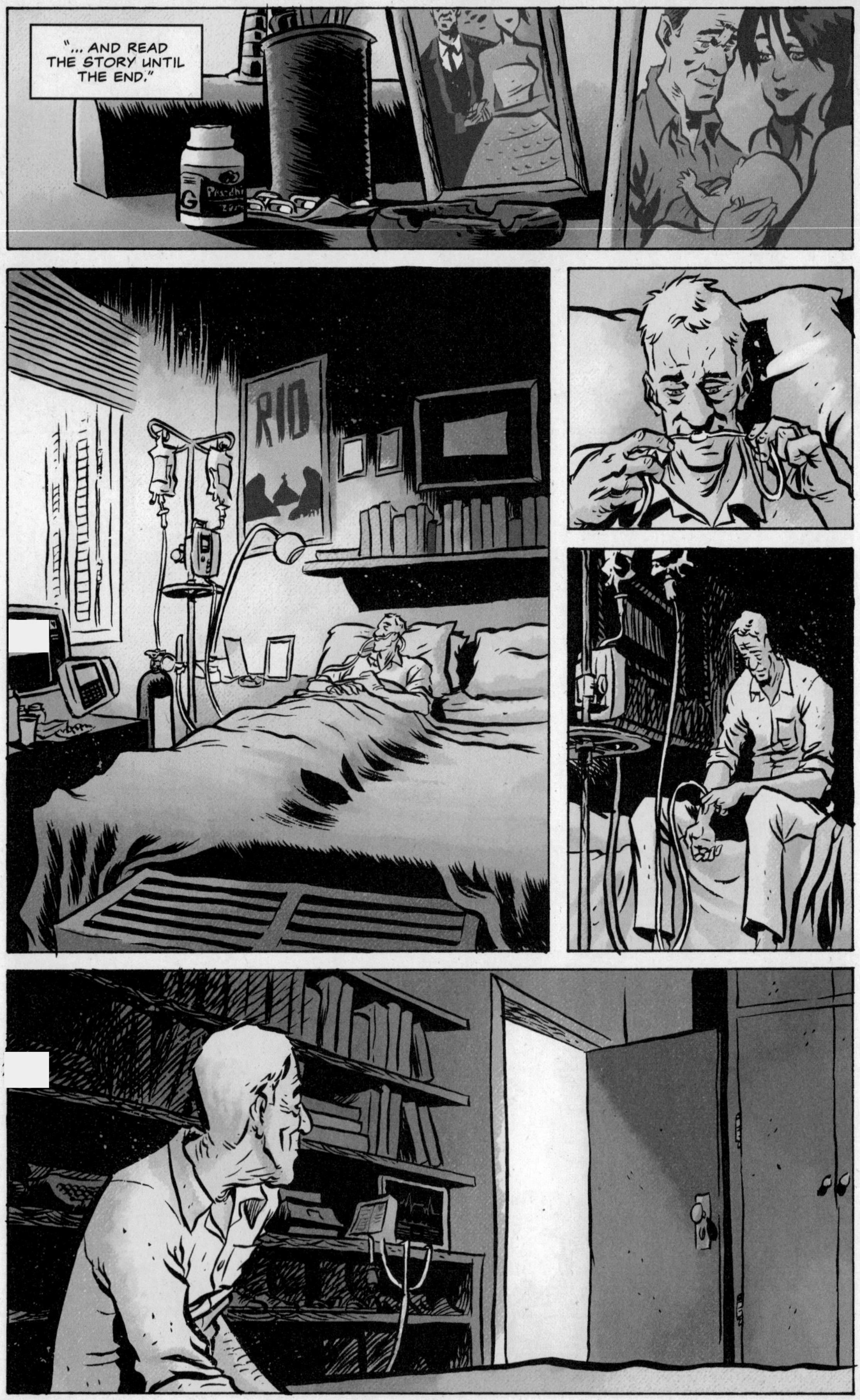
"... AND READ THE STORY UNTIL THE END."
RIO

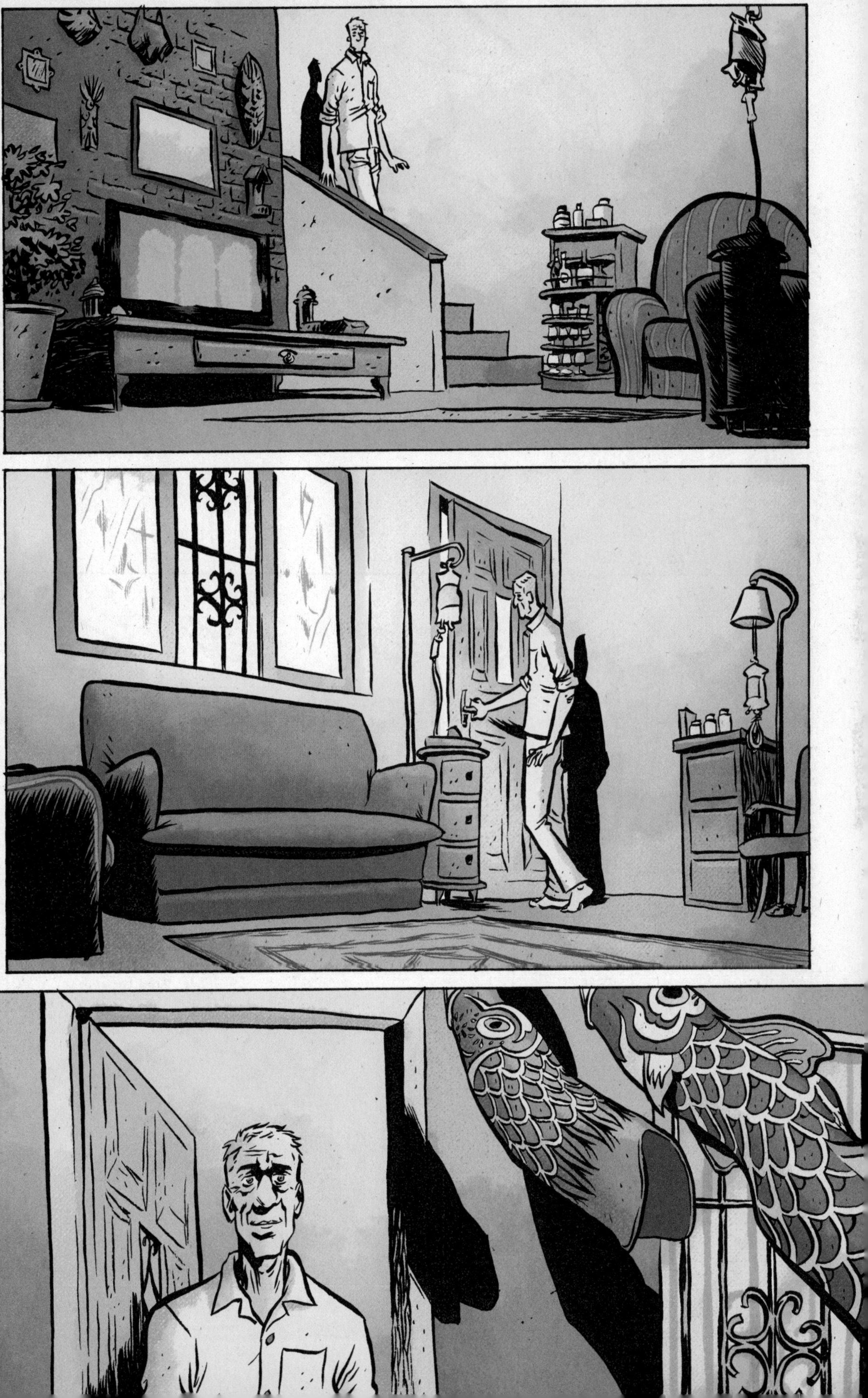

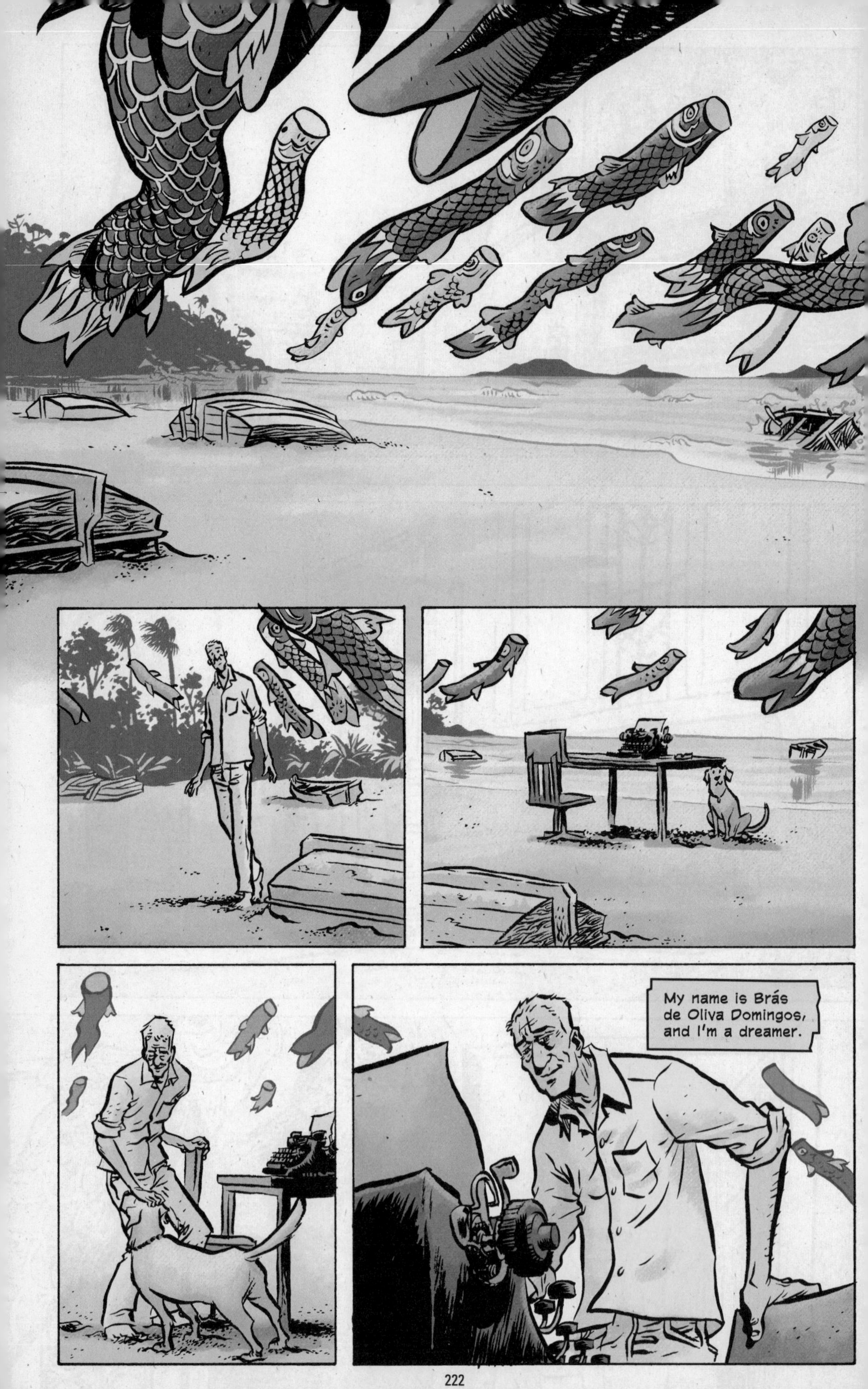
My name is Brás
de Oliva Domingos,
and I'm a dreamer.

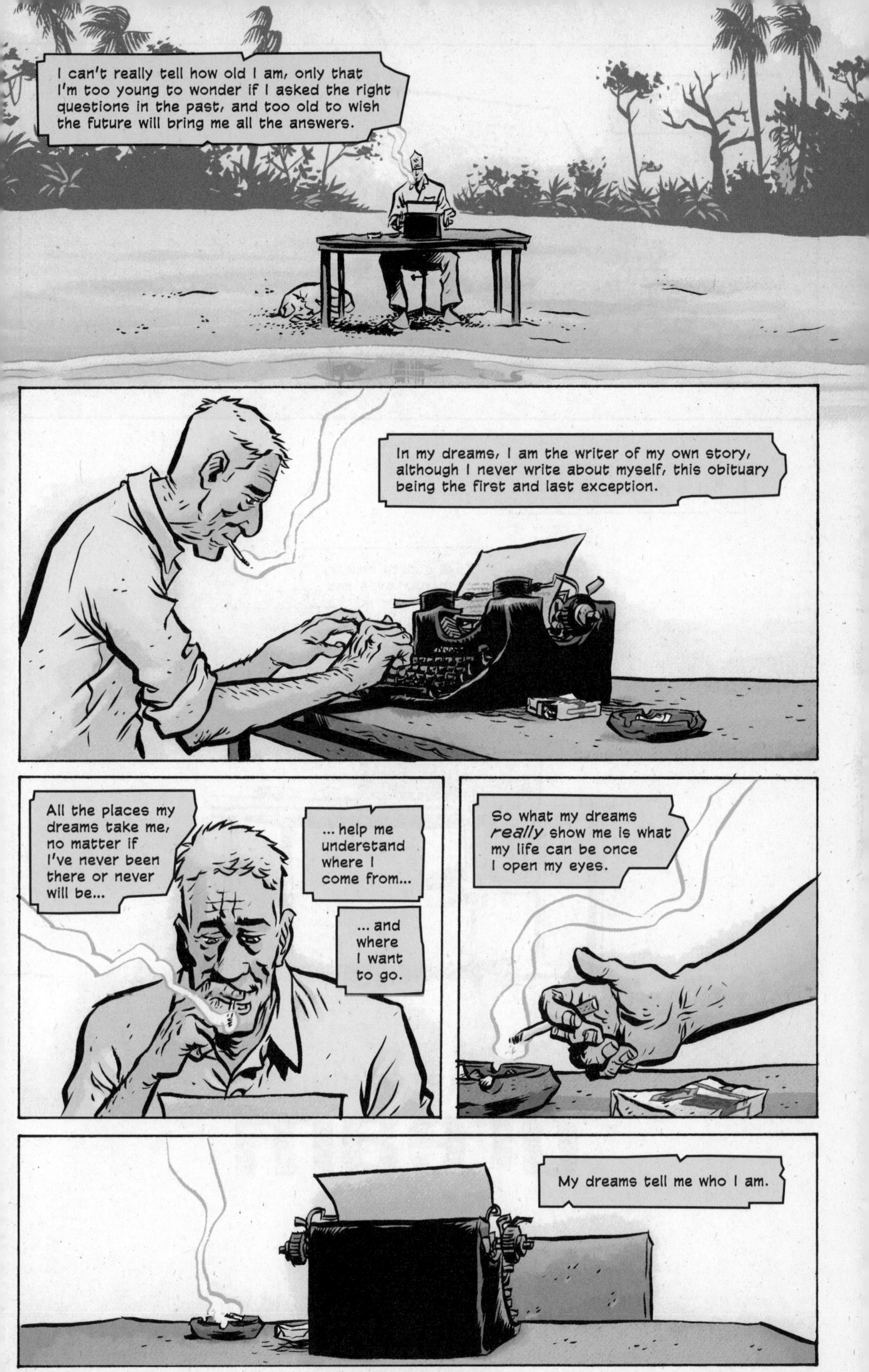
I can't really tell how old I am, only that I'm too young to wonder if I asked the right questions in the past, and too old to wish the future will bring me all the answers.
In my dreams, I am the writer of my own story, although I never write about myself, this obituary being the first and last exception.
All the places my dreams take me, no matter if I've never been there or never will be...
... help me understand where I come from...
... and where I want to go.
So what my dreams *really* show me is what my life can be once I open my eyes.
My dreams tell me who I am.

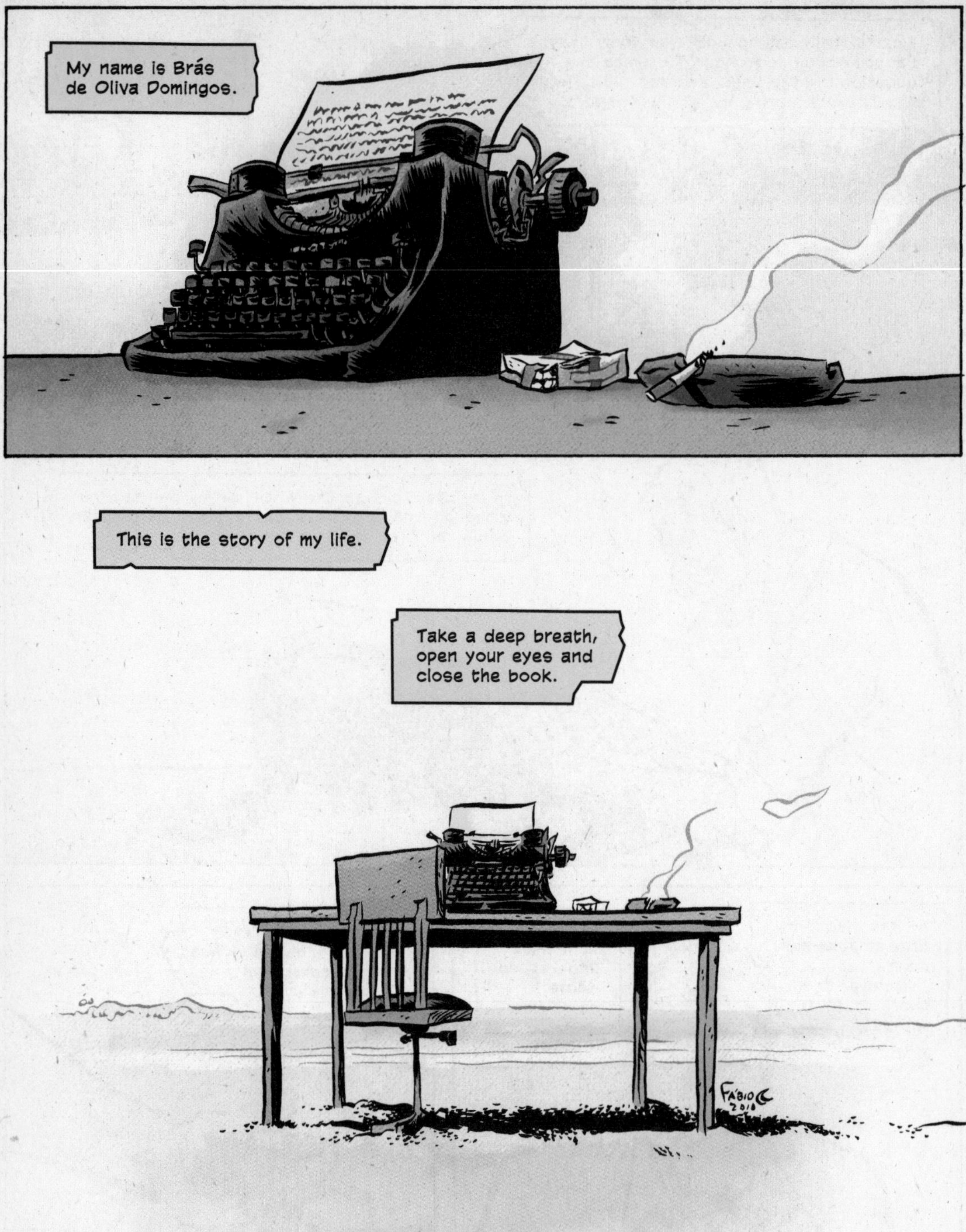
My name is Brás de Oliva Domingos.
This is the story of my life.
Take a deep breath, open your eyes and close the book.

CHAPTER NINE:
dream

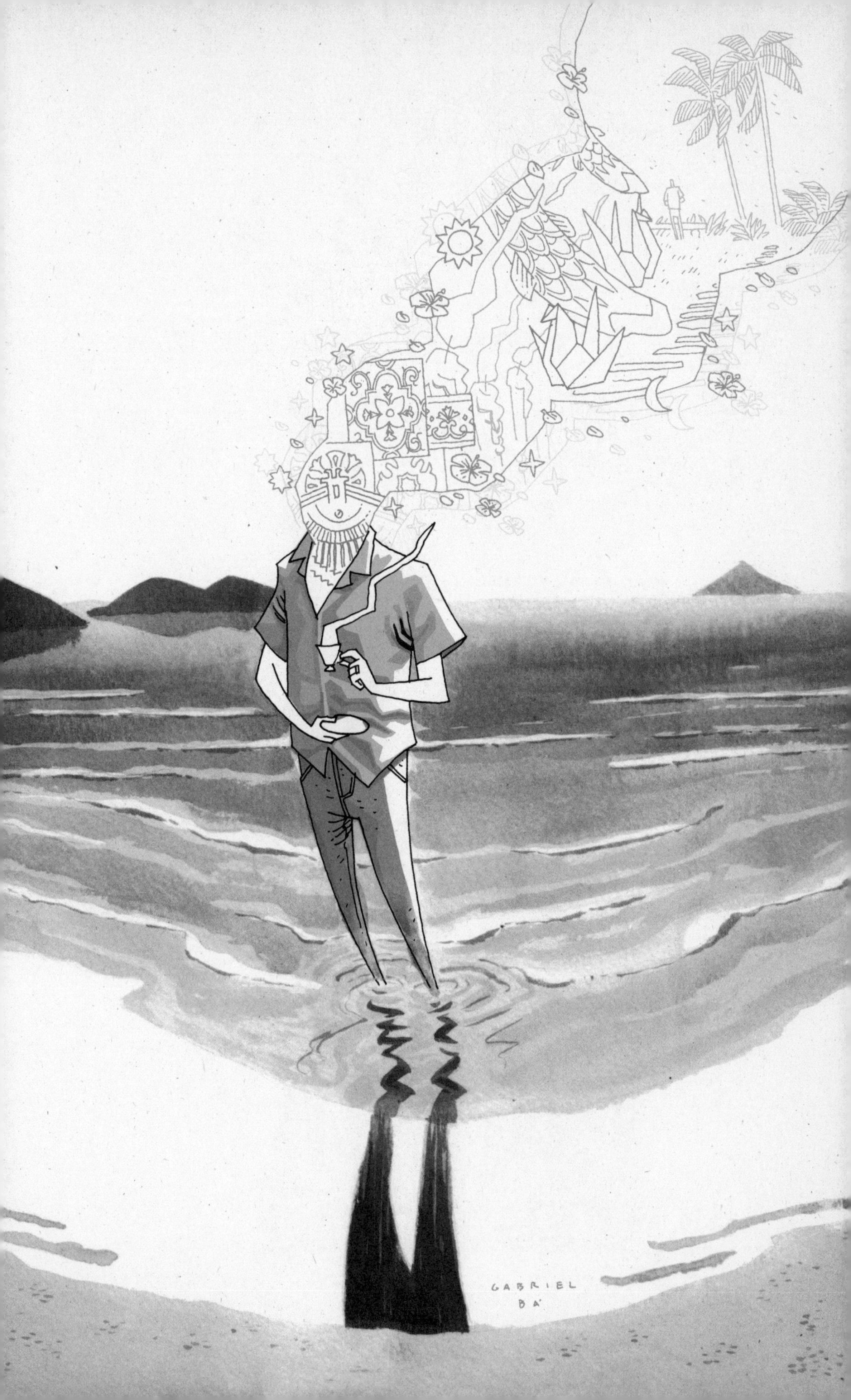
GABRIEL
BÁ

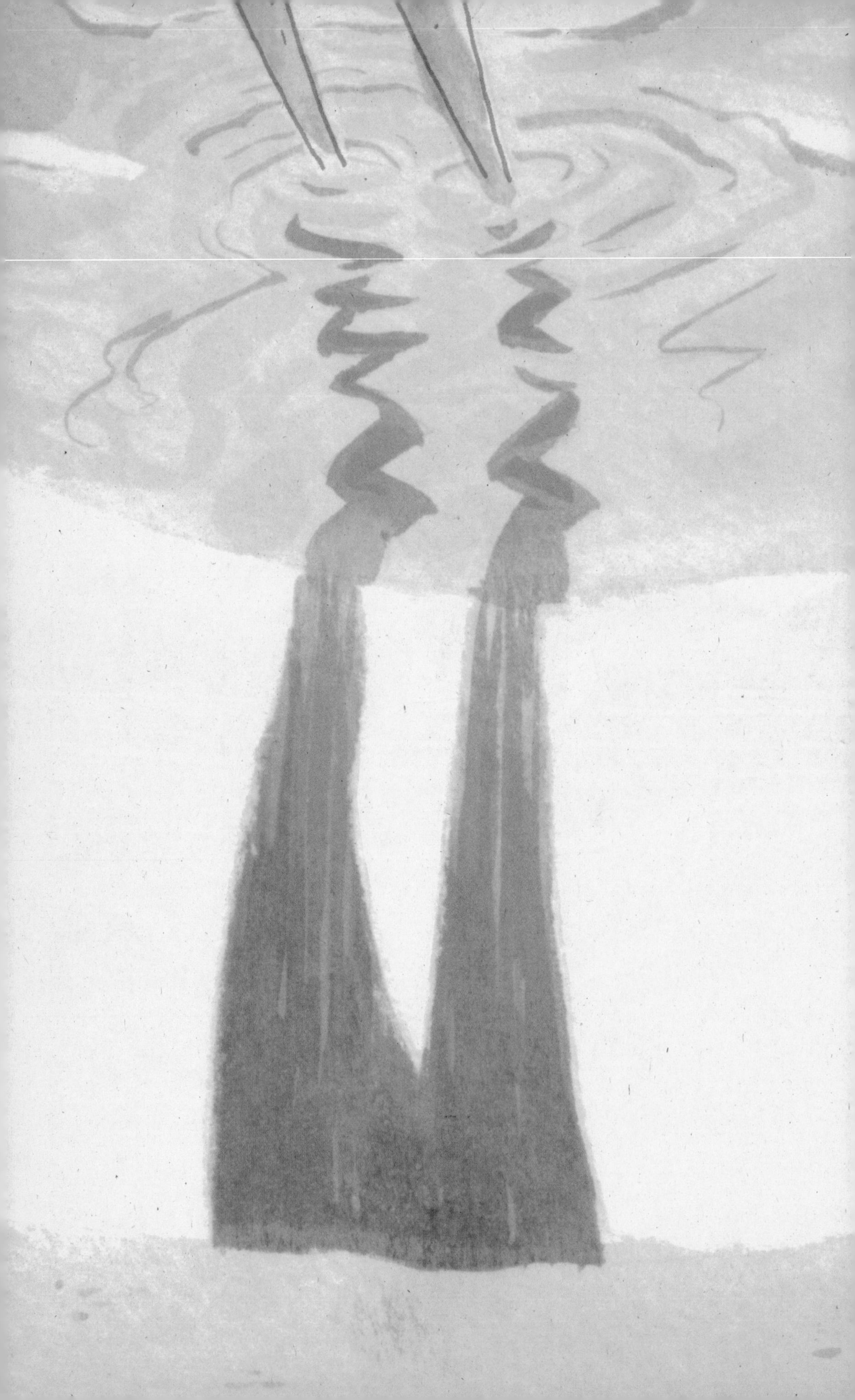

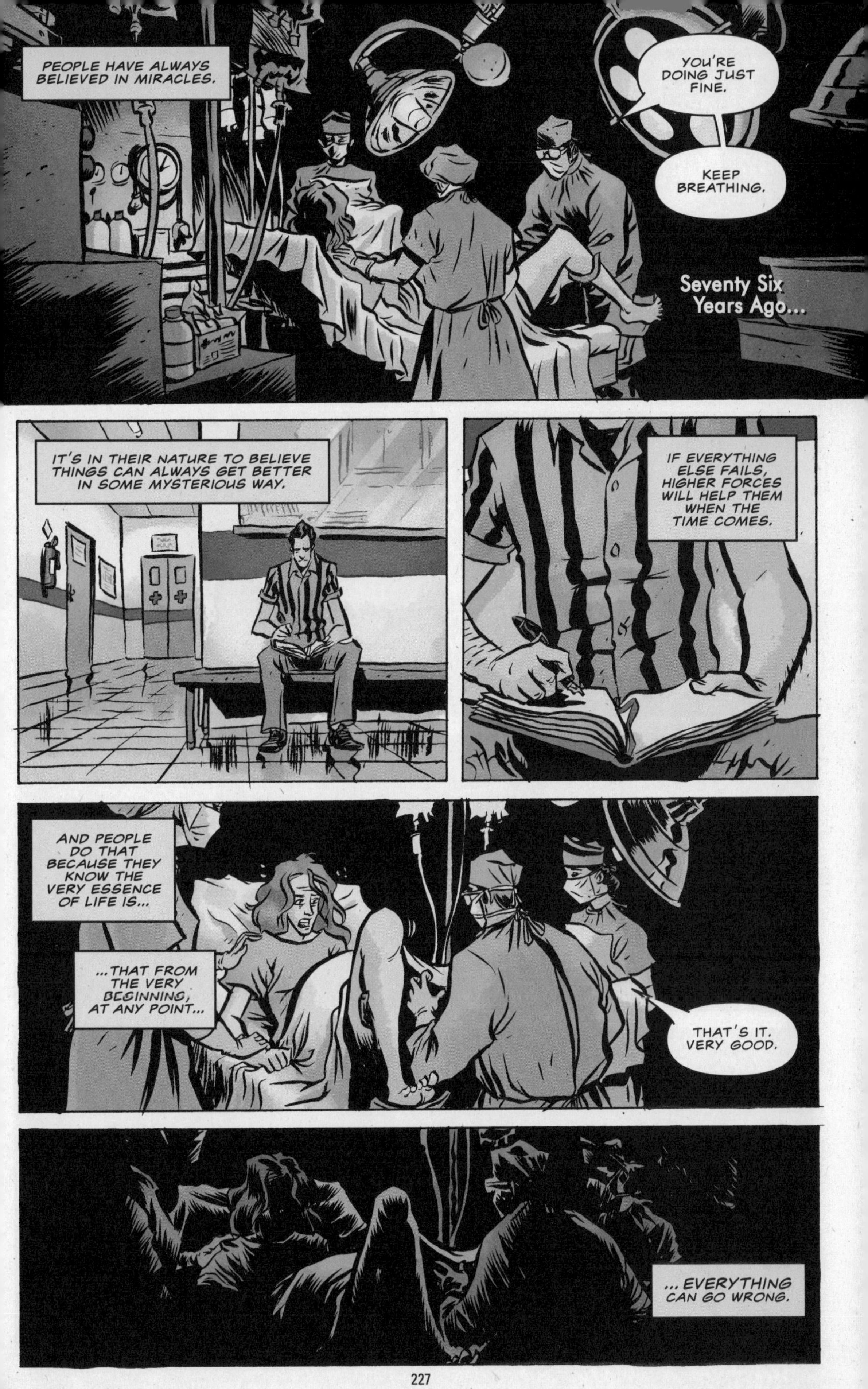
PEOPLE HAVE ALWAYS BELIEVED IN MIRACLES.
YOU'RE DOING JUST FINE.
KEEP BREATHING.
Seventy Six Years Ago...
IT'S IN THEIR NATURE TO BELIEVE THINGS CAN ALWAYS GET BETTER IN SOME MYSTERIOUS WAY.
IF EVERYTHING ELSE FAILS, HIGHER FORCES WILL HELP THEM WHEN THE TIME COMES.
AND PEOPLE DO THAT BECAUSE THEY KNOW THE VERY ESSENCE OF LIFE IS...
...THAT FROM THE VERY BEGINNING, AT ANY POINT...
THAT'S IT. VERY GOOD.
...EVERYTHING CAN GO WRONG.

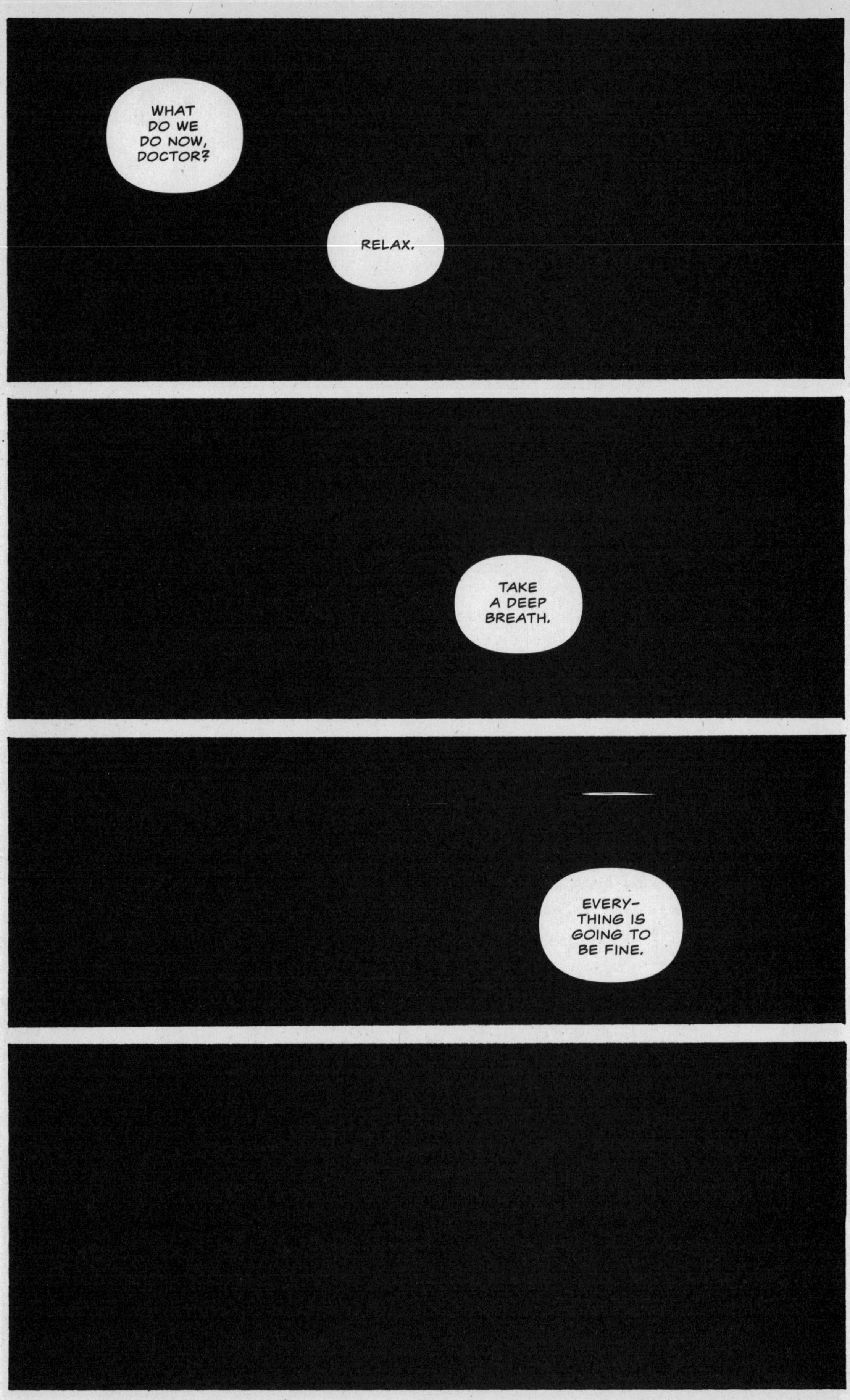
WHAT DO WE DO NOW, DOCTOR?
RELAX.
TAKE A DEEP BREATH.
EVERY-THING IS GOING TO BE FINE.

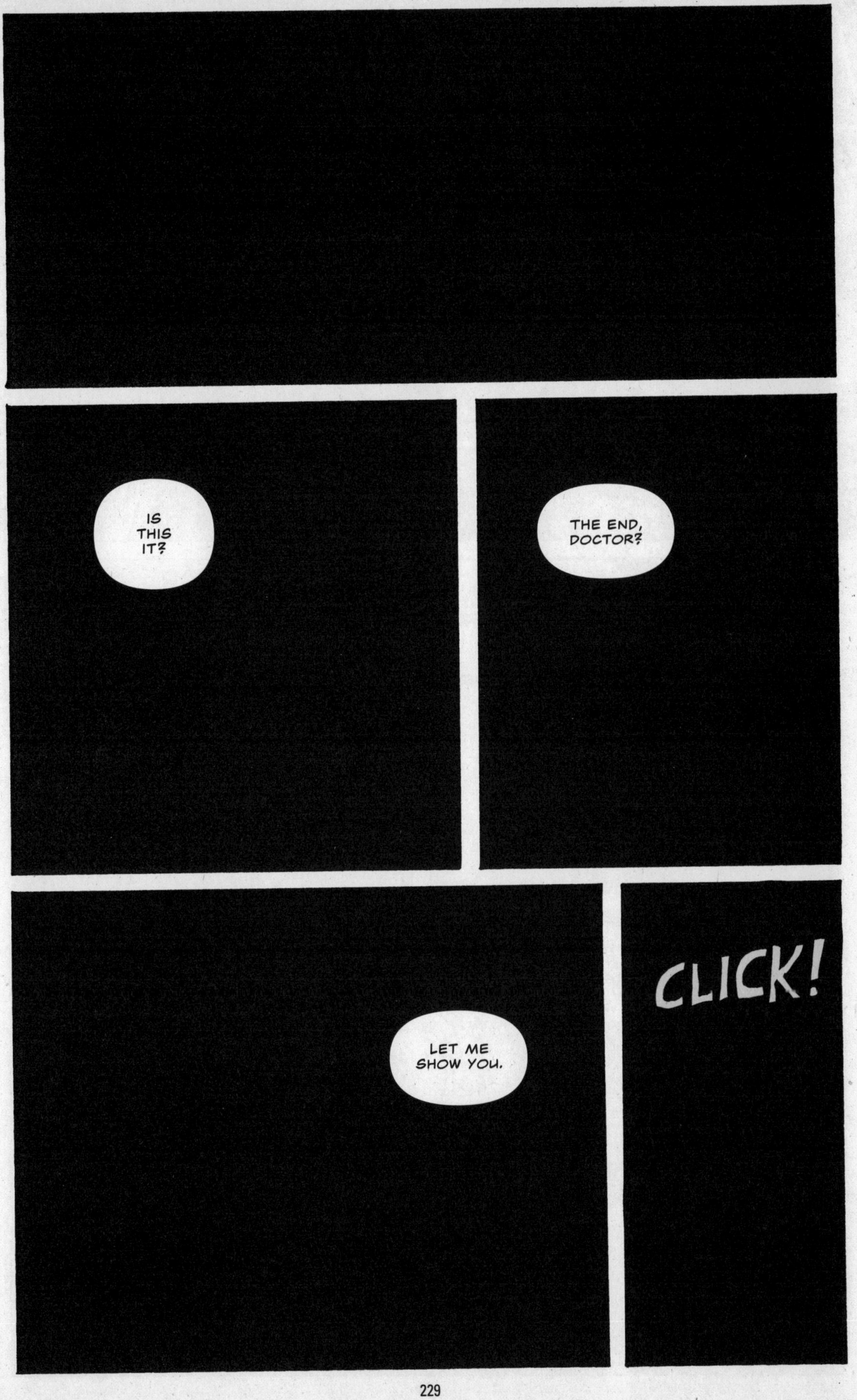
IS THIS IT?
THE END, DOCTOR?
LET ME SHOW YOU.
CLICK!

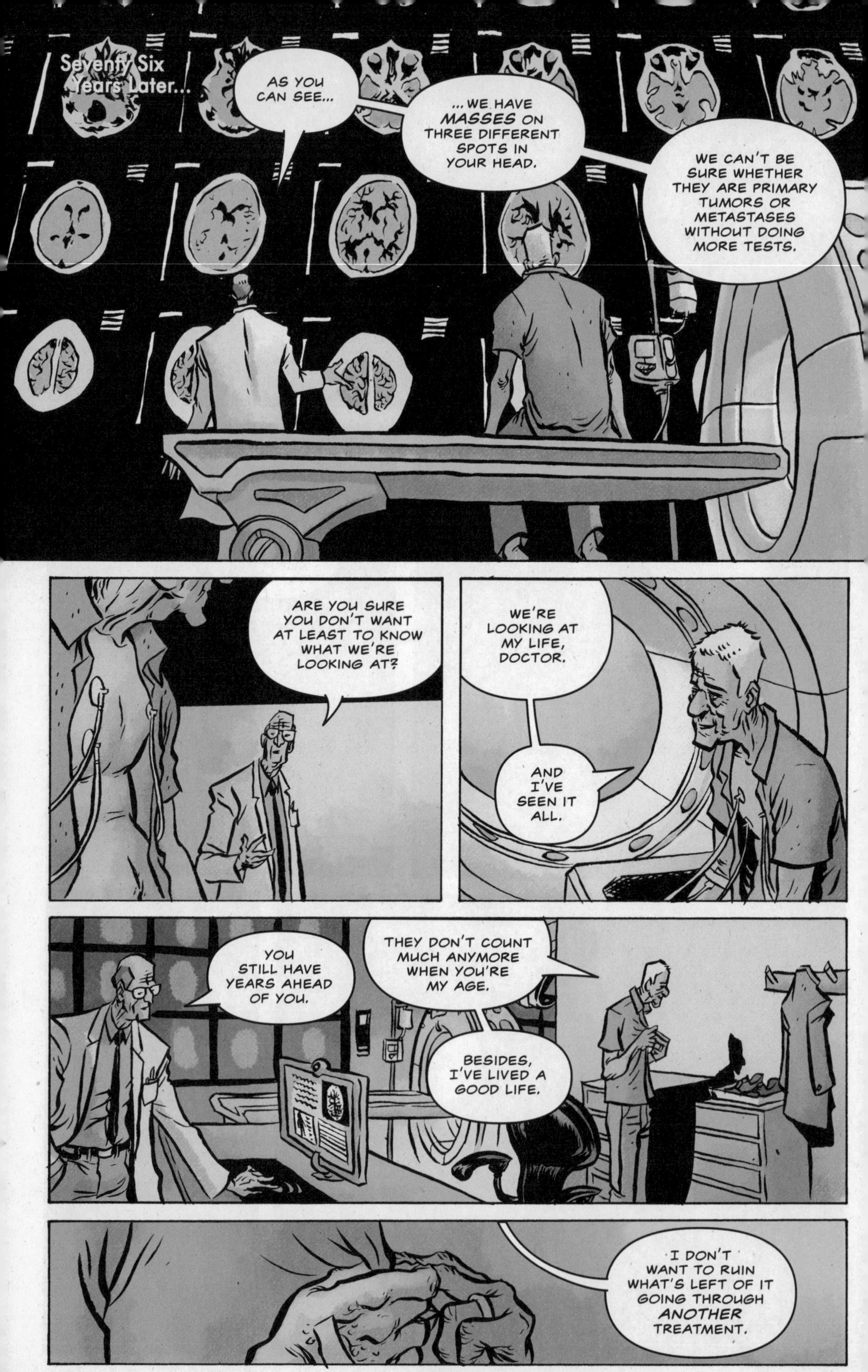
Seventy Six Years Later...
AS YOU CAN SEE...
...WE HAVE MASSES ON THREE DIFFERENT SPOTS IN YOUR HEAD.
WE CAN'T BE SURE WHETHER THEY ARE PRIMARY TUMORS OR METASTASES WITHOUT DOING MORE TESTS.
ARE YOU SURE YOU DON'T WANT AT LEAST TO KNOW WHAT WE'RE LOOKING AT?
WE'RE LOOKING AT MY LIFE, DOCTOR.
AND I'VE SEEN IT ALL.
YOU STILL HAVE YEARS AHEAD OF YOU.
THEY DON'T COUNT MUCH ANYMORE WHEN YOU'RE MY AGE.
BESIDES, I'VE LIVED A GOOD LIFE.
I DON'T WANT TO RUIN WHAT'S LEFT OF IT GOING THROUGH ANOTHER TREATMENT.

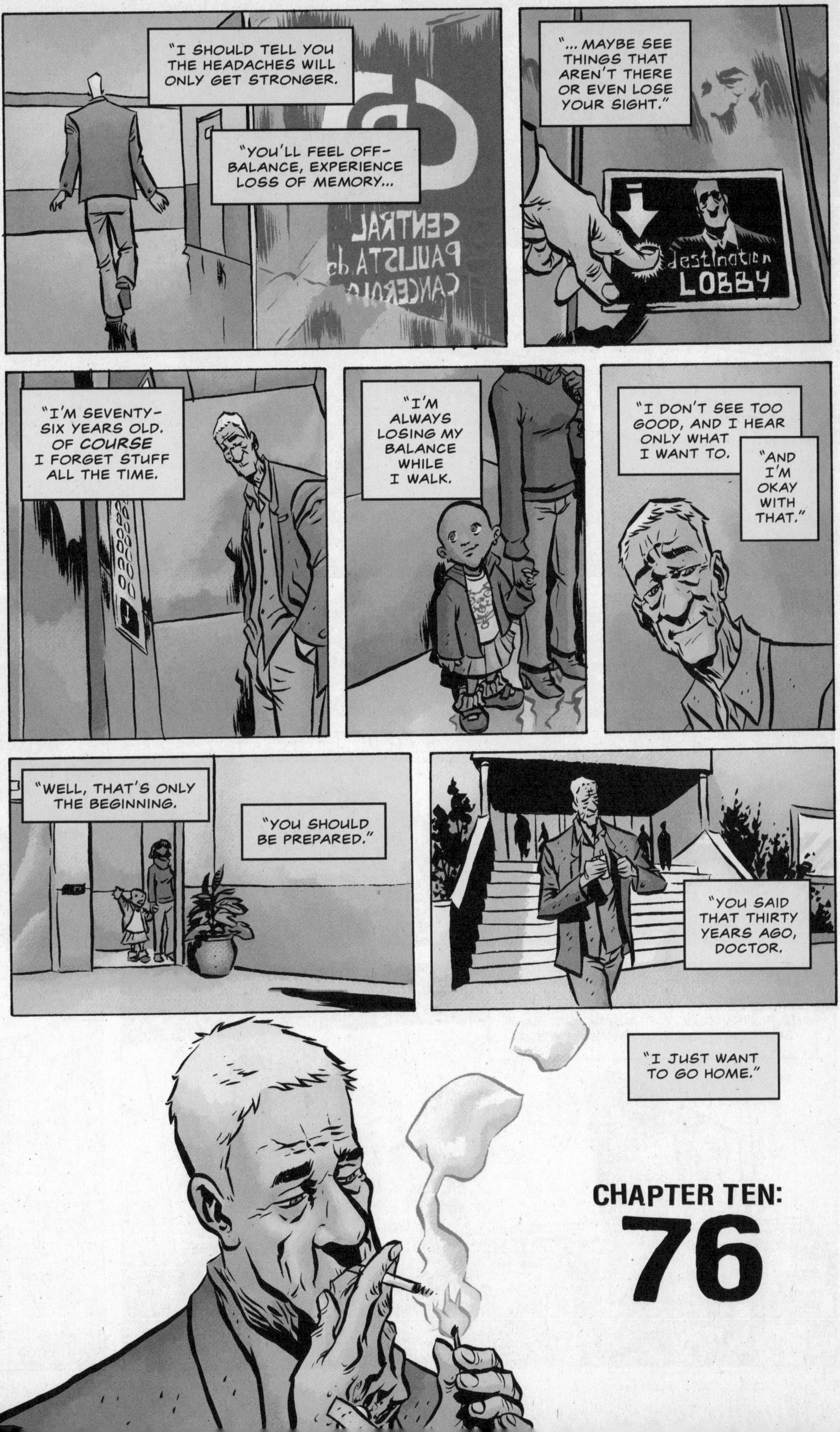
"I SHOULD TELL YOU THE HEADACHES WILL ONLY GET STRONGER.
"YOU'LL FEEL OFF-BALANCE, EXPERIENCE LOSS OF MEMORY...
CENTRAL PAULISTA do CANCEROLO
"... MAYBE SEE THINGS THAT AREN'T THERE OR EVEN LOSE YOUR SIGHT."
destination LOBBY
"I'M SEVENTY-SIX YEARS OLD. OF COURSE I FORGET STUFF ALL THE TIME.
"I'M ALWAYS LOSING MY BALANCE WHILE I WALK.
"I DON'T SEE TOO GOOD, AND I HEAR ONLY WHAT I WANT TO.
"AND I'M OKAY WITH THAT."
"WELL, THAT'S ONLY THE BEGINNING.
"YOU SHOULD BE PREPARED."
"YOU SAID THAT THIRTY YEARS AGO, DOCTOR.
"I JUST WANT TO GO HOME."
CHAPTER TEN:
76

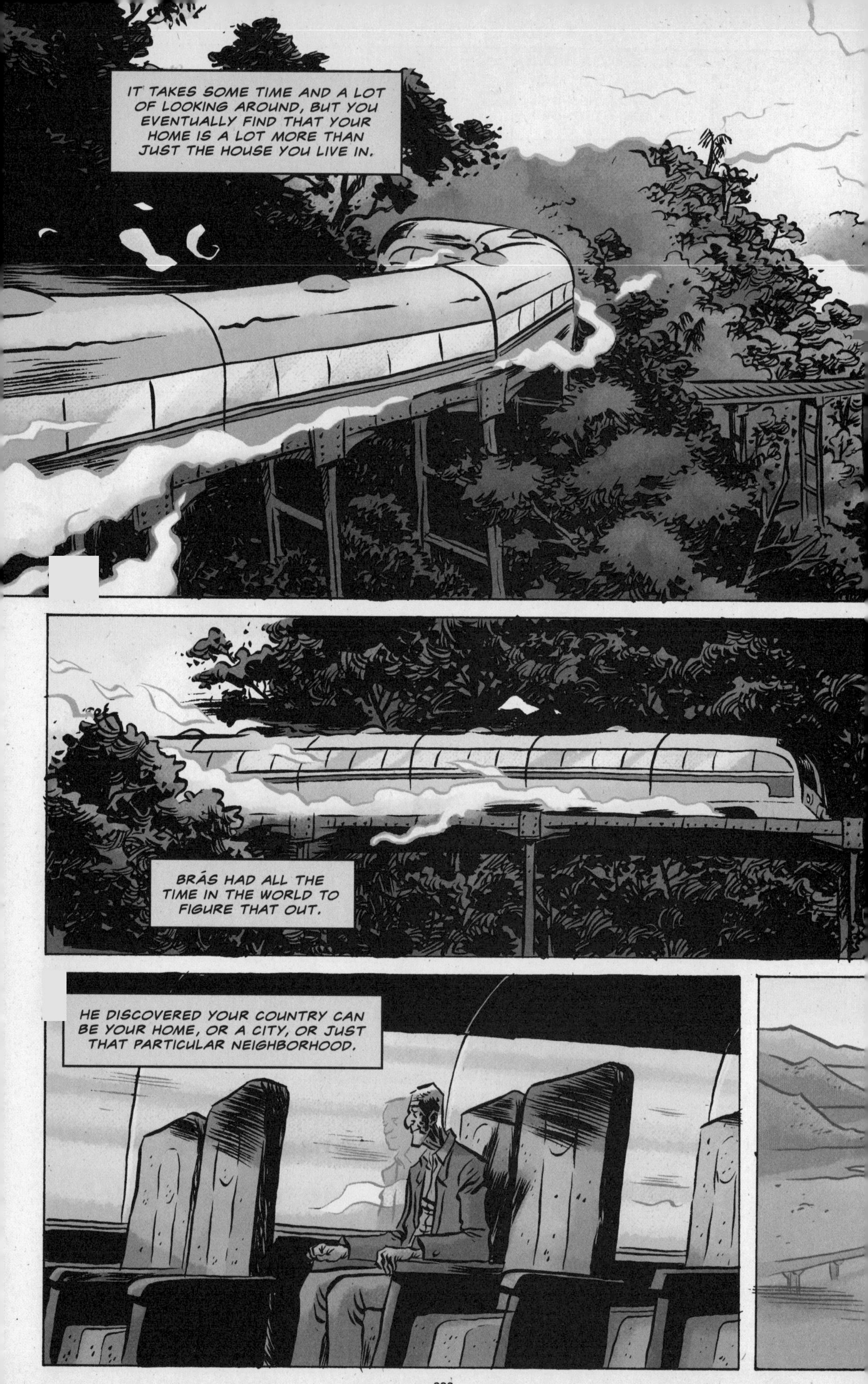
IT TAKES SOME TIME AND A LOT OF LOOKING AROUND, BUT YOU EVENTUALLY FIND THAT YOUR HOME IS A LOT MORE THAN JUST THE HOUSE YOU LIVE IN.
BRÁS HAD ALL THE TIME IN THE WORLD TO FIGURE THAT OUT.
HE DISCOVERED YOUR COUNTRY CAN BE YOUR HOME, OR A CITY, OR JUST THAT PARTICULAR NEIGHBORHOOD.

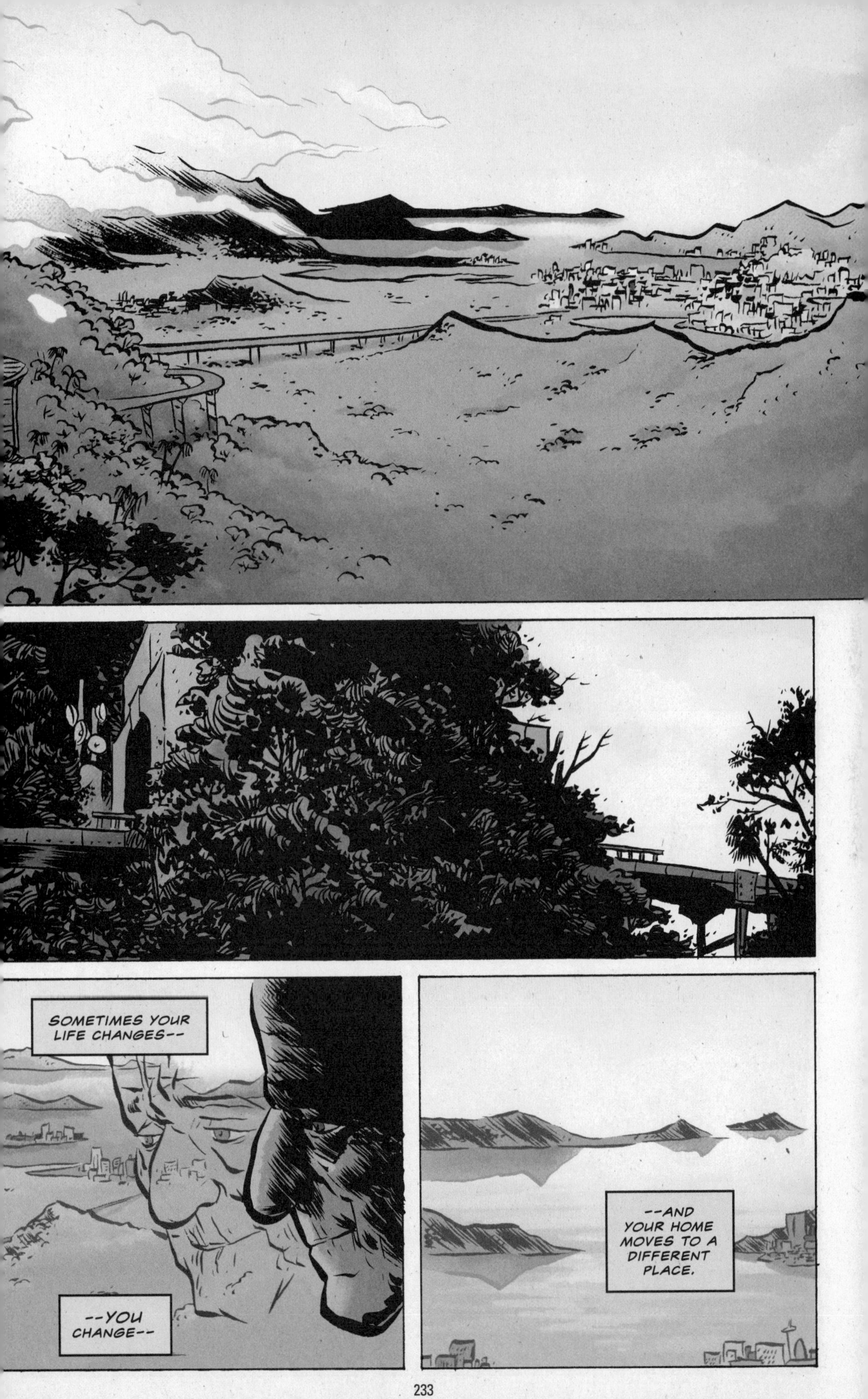
SOMETIMES YOUR LIFE CHANGES--
--YOU CHANGE--
--AND YOUR HOME MOVES TO A DIFFERENT PLACE.

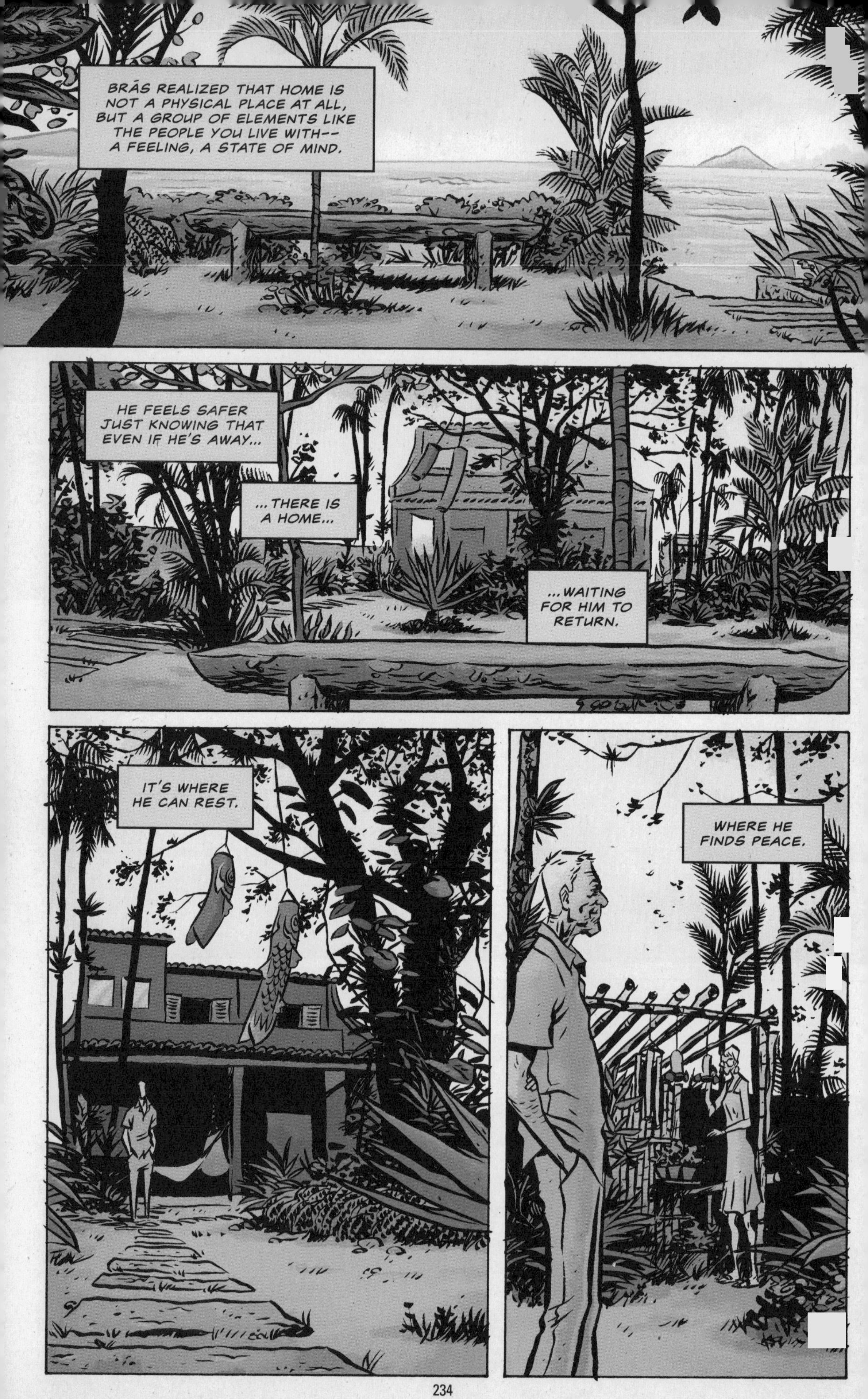
BRÁS REALIZED THAT HOME IS NOT A PHYSICAL PLACE AT ALL, BUT A GROUP OF ELEMENTS LIKE THE PEOPLE YOU LIVE WITH-- A FEELING, A STATE OF MIND.
HE FEELS SAFER JUST KNOWING THAT EVEN IF HE'S AWAY...
...THERE IS A HOME...
...WAITING FOR HIM TO RETURN.
IT'S WHERE HE CAN REST.
WHERE HE FINDS PEACE.

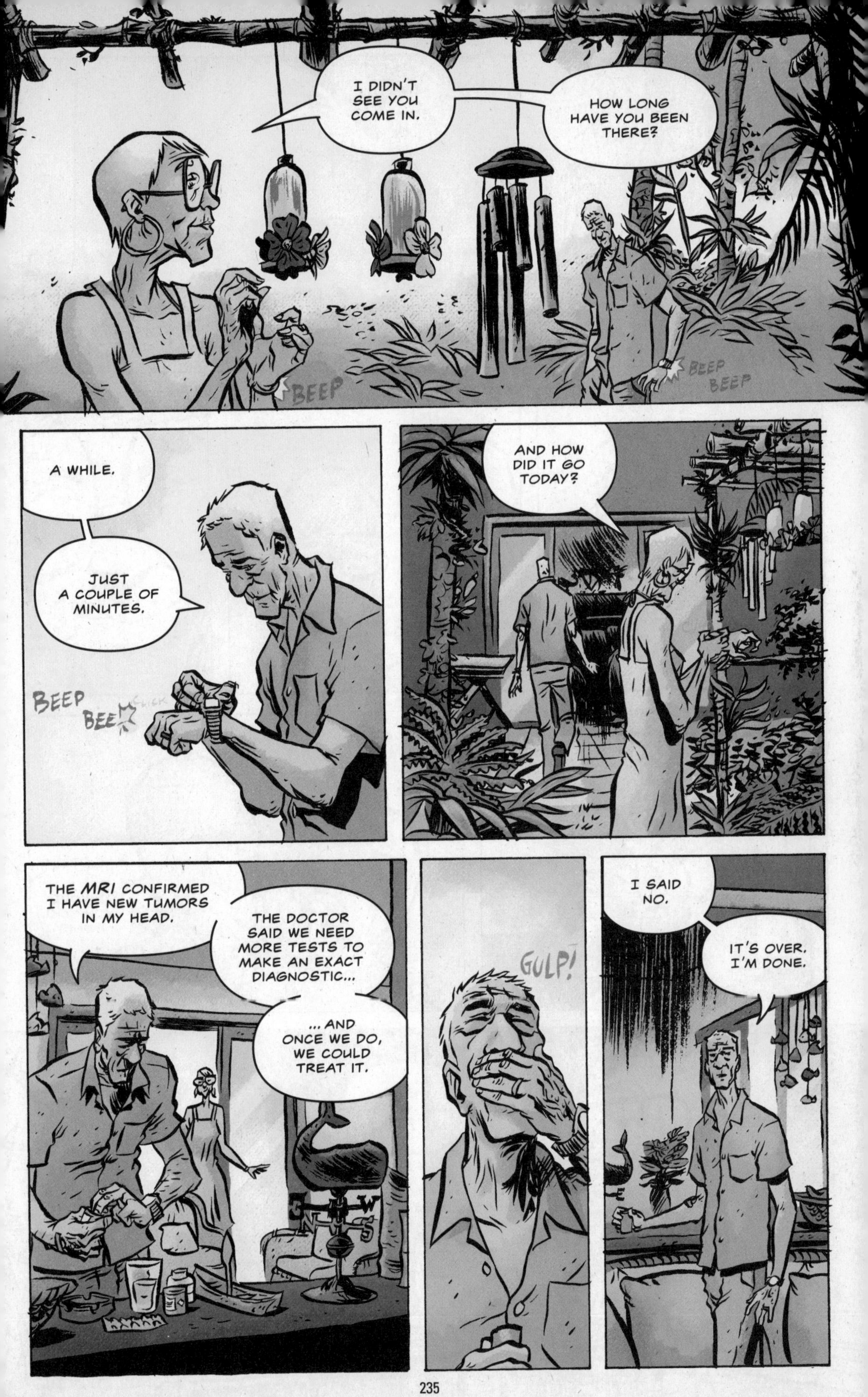
I DIDN'T SEE YOU COME IN.
HOW LONG HAVE YOU BEEN THERE?
BEEP
BEEP
BEEP
A WHILE.
JUST A COUPLE OF MINUTES.
BEEP
BEE
AND HOW DID IT GO TODAY?
THE MRI CONFIRMED I HAVE NEW TUMORS IN MY HEAD.
THE DOCTOR SAID WE NEED MORE TESTS TO MAKE AN EXACT DIAGNOSTIC...
... AND ONCE WE DO, WE COULD TREAT IT.
GULP!
I SAID NO.
IT'S OVER. I'M DONE.

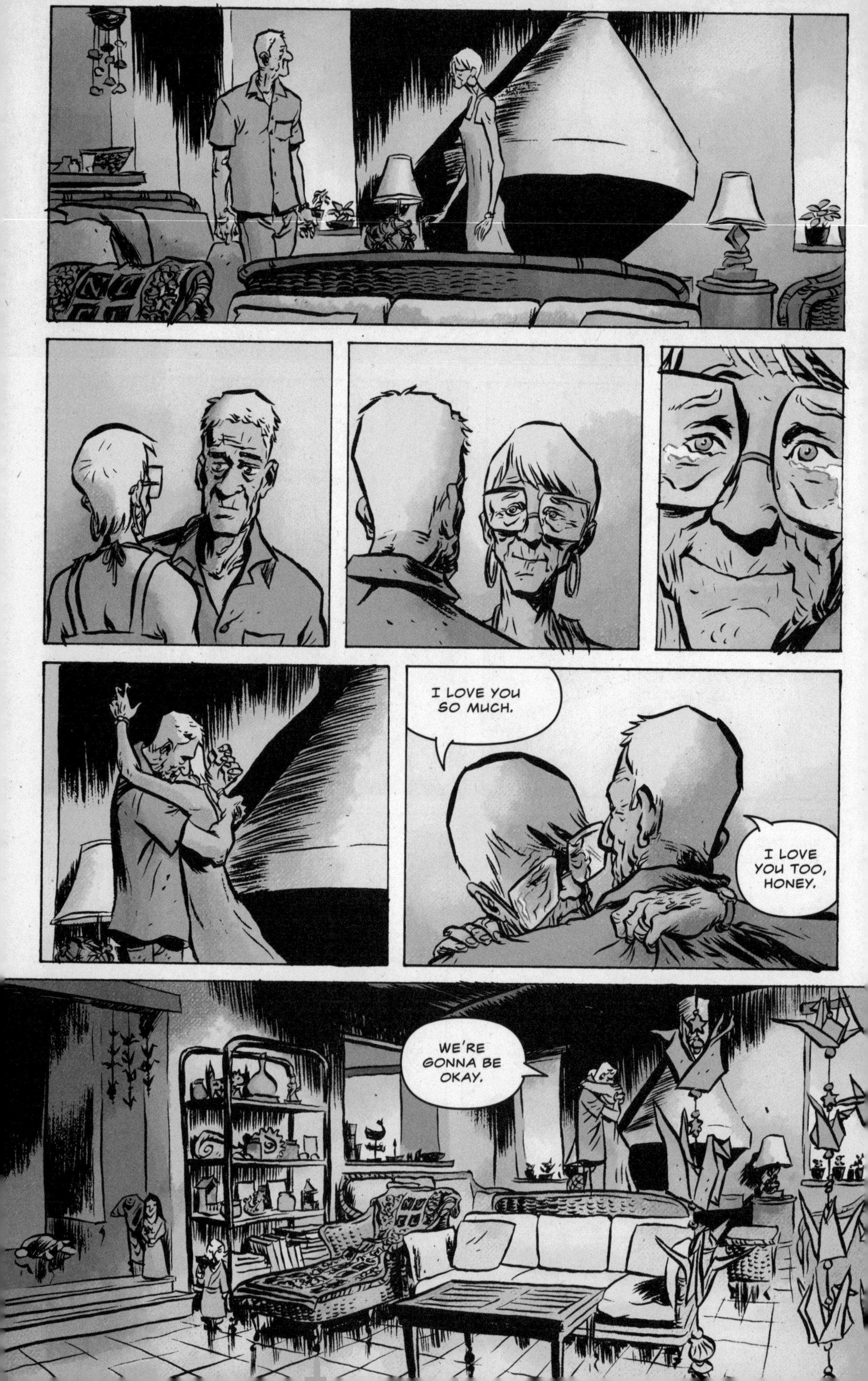
I LOVE YOU SO MUCH.
I LOVE YOU TOO, HONEY.
WE'RE GONNA BE OKAY.

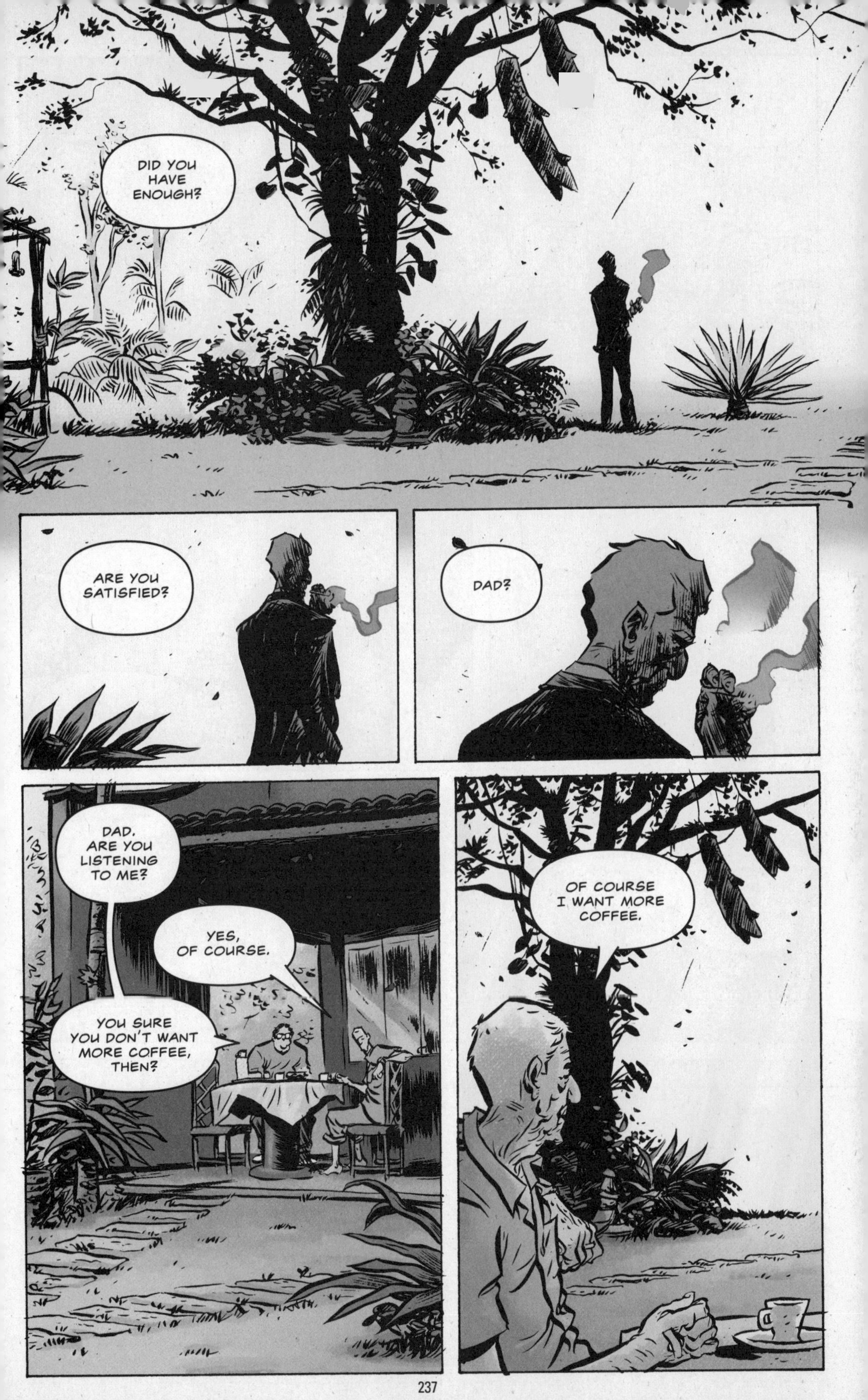
DID YOU HAVE ENOUGH?
ARE YOU SATISFIED?
DAD?
DAD. ARE YOU LISTENING TO ME?
YES, OF COURSE.
YOU SURE YOU DON'T WANT MORE COFFEE, THEN?
OF COURSE I WANT MORE COFFEE.

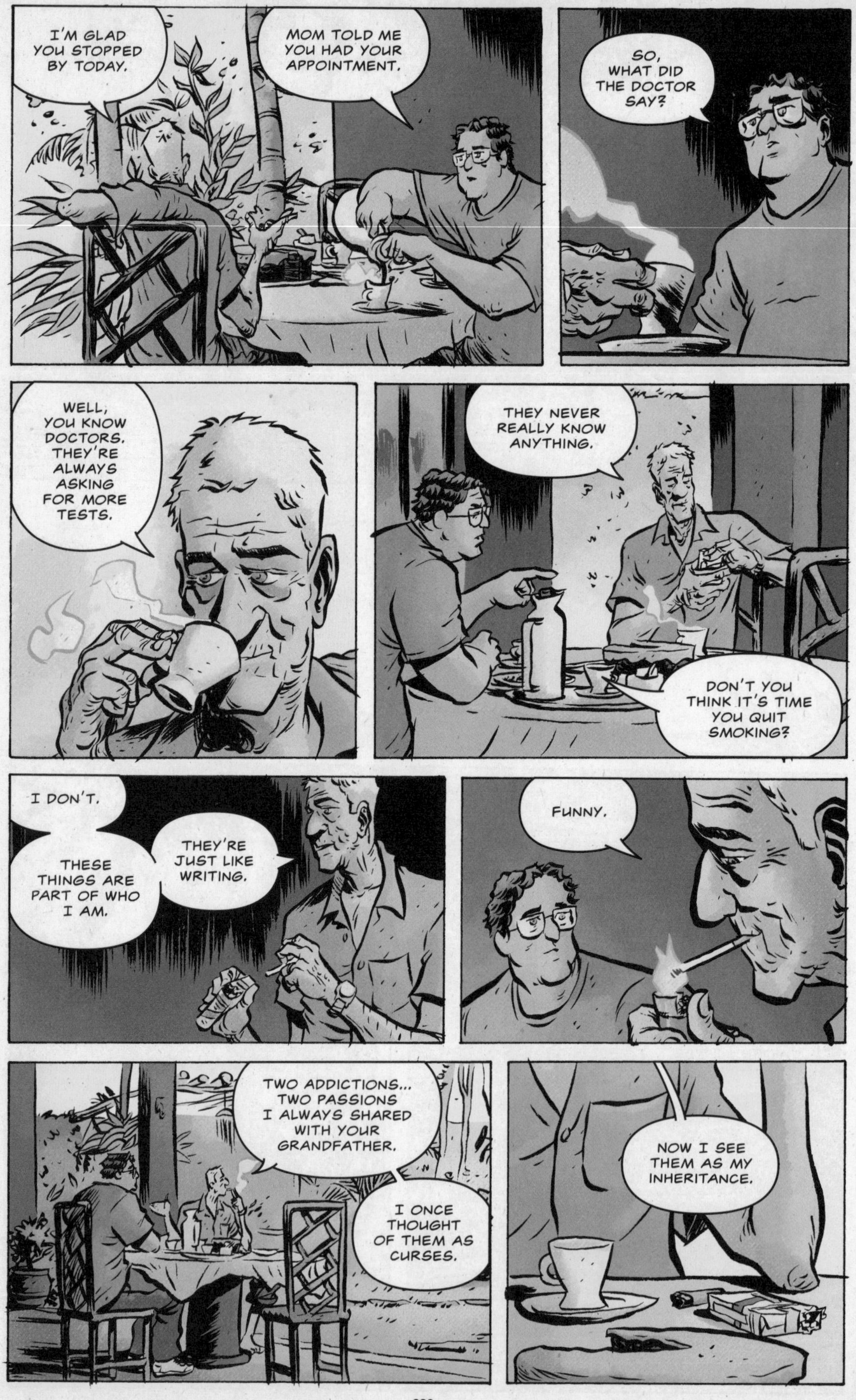
I'M GLAD YOU STOPPED BY TODAY.
MOM TOLD ME YOU HAD YOUR APPOINTMENT.
SO, WHAT DID THE DOCTOR SAY?
WELL, YOU KNOW DOCTORS. THEY'RE ALWAYS ASKING FOR MORE TESTS.
THEY NEVER REALLY KNOW ANYTHING.
DON'T YOU THINK IT'S TIME YOU QUIT SMOKING?
I DON'T.
THESE THINGS ARE PART OF WHO I AM.
THEY'RE JUST LIKE WRITING.
FUNNY.
TWO ADDICTIONS... TWO PASSIONS I ALWAYS SHARED WITH YOUR GRANDFATHER.
I ONCE THOUGHT OF THEM AS CURSES.
NOW I SEE THEM AS MY INHERITANCE.

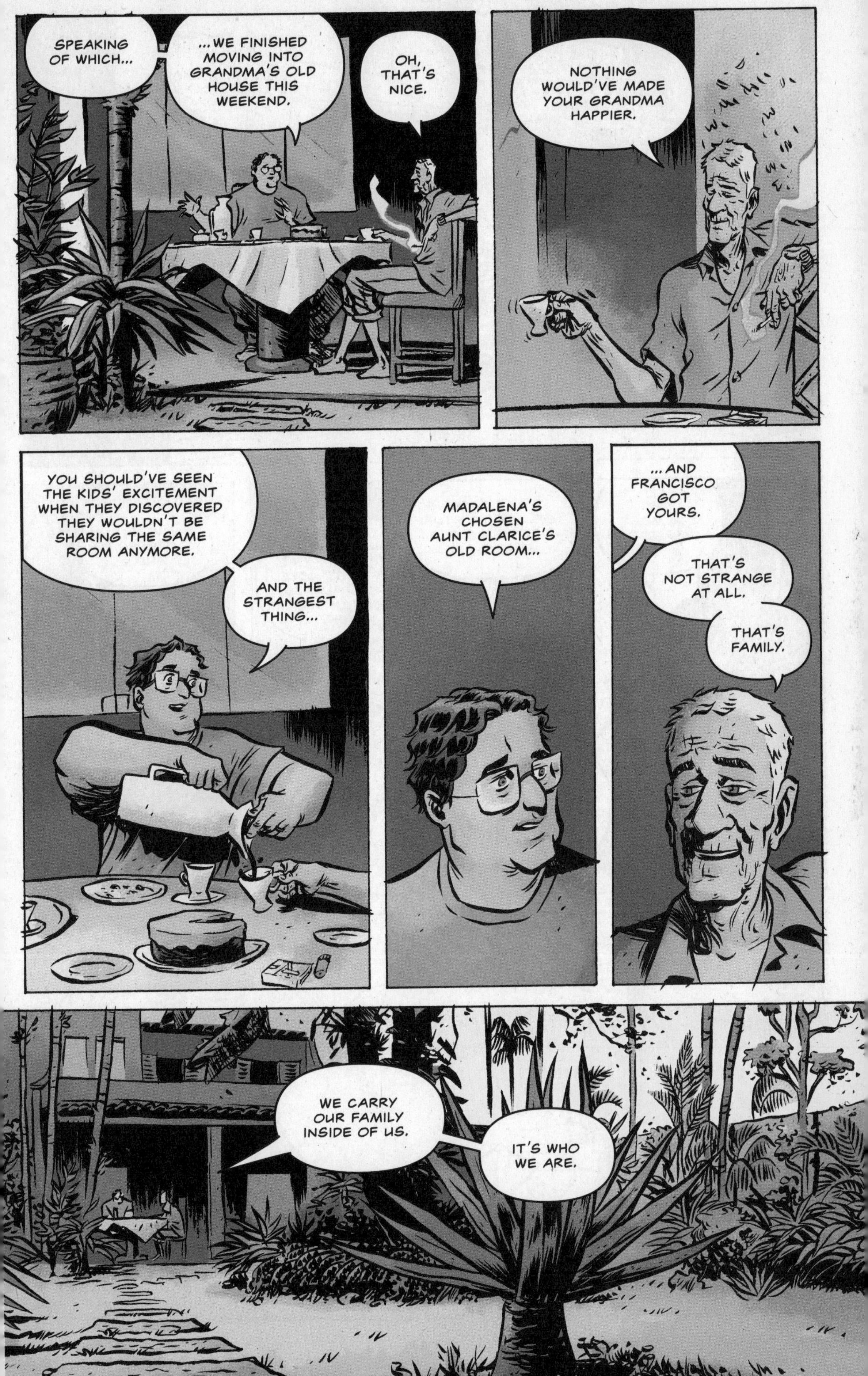
SPEAKING OF WHICH...
...WE FINISHED MOVING INTO GRANDMA'S OLD HOUSE THIS WEEKEND.
OH, THAT'S NICE.
NOTHING WOULD'VE MADE YOUR GRANDMA HAPPIER.
YOU SHOULD'VE SEEN THE KIDS' EXCITEMENT WHEN THEY DISCOVERED THEY WOULDN'T BE SHARING THE SAME ROOM ANYMORE.
AND THE STRANGEST THING...
MADALENA'S CHOSEN AUNT CLARICE'S OLD ROOM...
...AND FRANCISCO GOT YOURS.
THAT'S NOT STRANGE AT ALL.
THAT'S FAMILY.
WE CARRY OUR FAMILY INSIDE OF US.
IT'S WHO WE ARE.

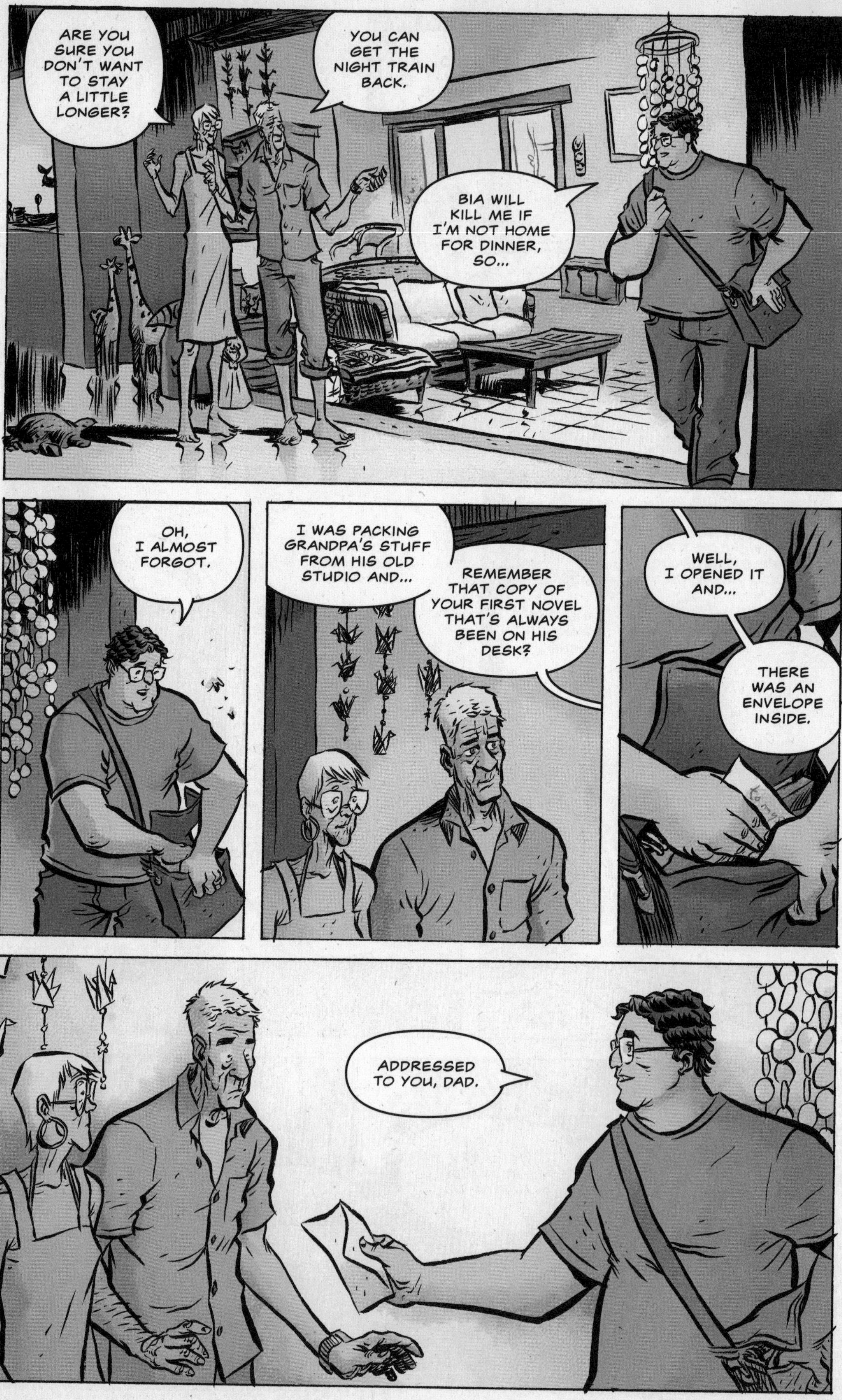
ARE YOU SURE YOU DON'T WANT TO STAY A LITTLE LONGER?
YOU CAN GET THE NIGHT TRAIN BACK.
BIA WILL KILL ME IF I'M NOT HOME FOR DINNER, SO...
OH, I ALMOST FORGOT.
I WAS PACKING GRANDPA'S STUFF FROM HIS OLD STUDIO AND...
REMEMBER THAT COPY OF YOUR FIRST NOVEL THAT'S ALWAYS BEEN ON HIS DESK?
WELL, I OPENED IT AND...
THERE WAS AN ENVELOPE INSIDE.
ADDRESSED TO YOU, DAD.

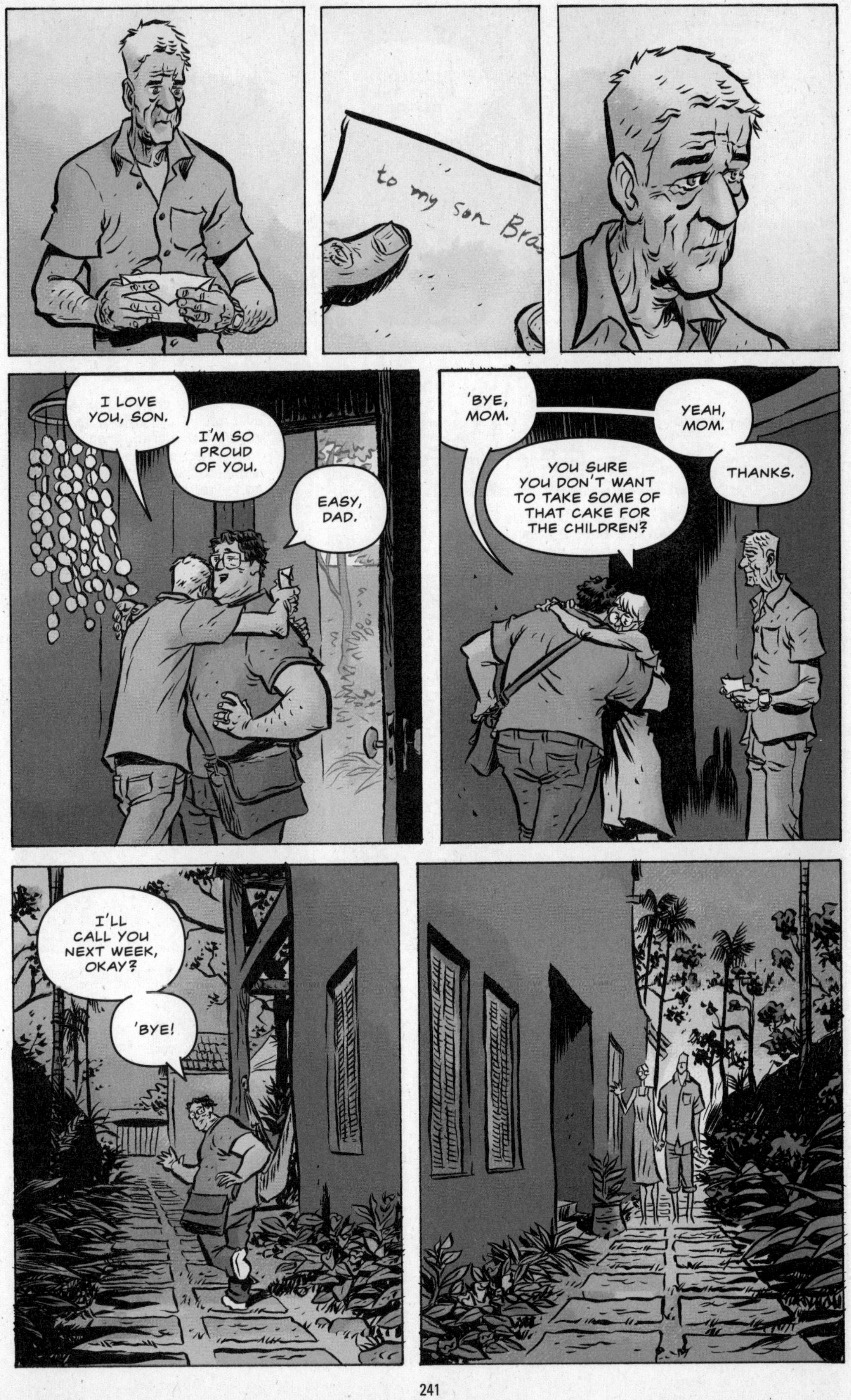
to my son Bra
I LOVE YOU, SON.
I'M SO PROUD OF YOU.
EASY, DAD.
'BYE, MOM.
YEAH, MOM.
YOU SURE YOU DON'T WANT TO TAKE SOME OF THAT CAKE FOR THE CHILDREN?
THANKS.
I'LL CALL YOU NEXT WEEK, OKAY?
'BYE!

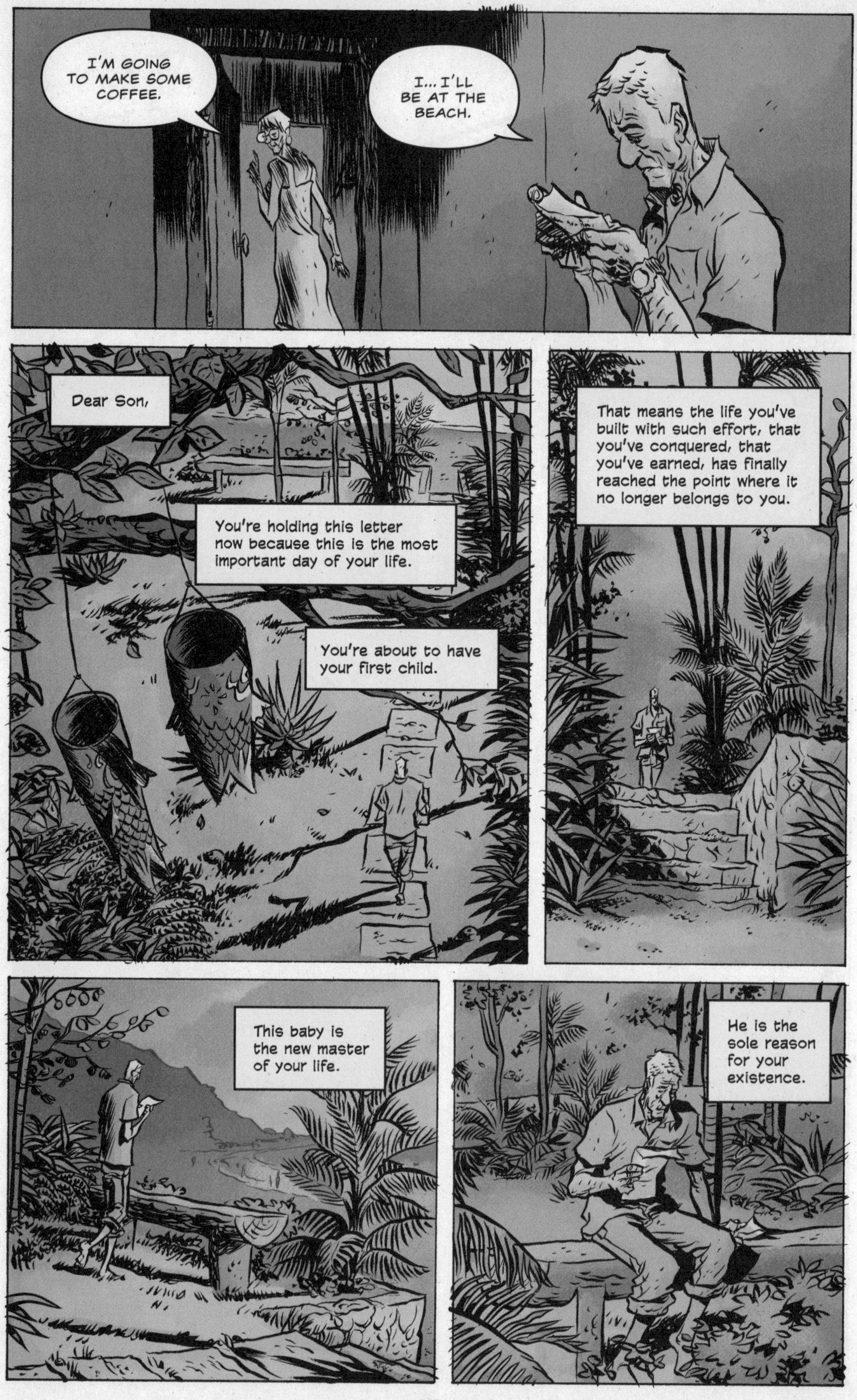
I'M GOING TO MAKE SOME COFFEE.
I... I'LL BE AT THE BEACH.
Dear Son,
You're holding this letter now because this is the most important day of your life.
You're about to have your first child.
That means the life you've built with such effort, that you've conquered, that you've earned, has finally reached the point where it no longer belongs to you.
This baby is the new master of your life.
He is the sole reason for your existence.

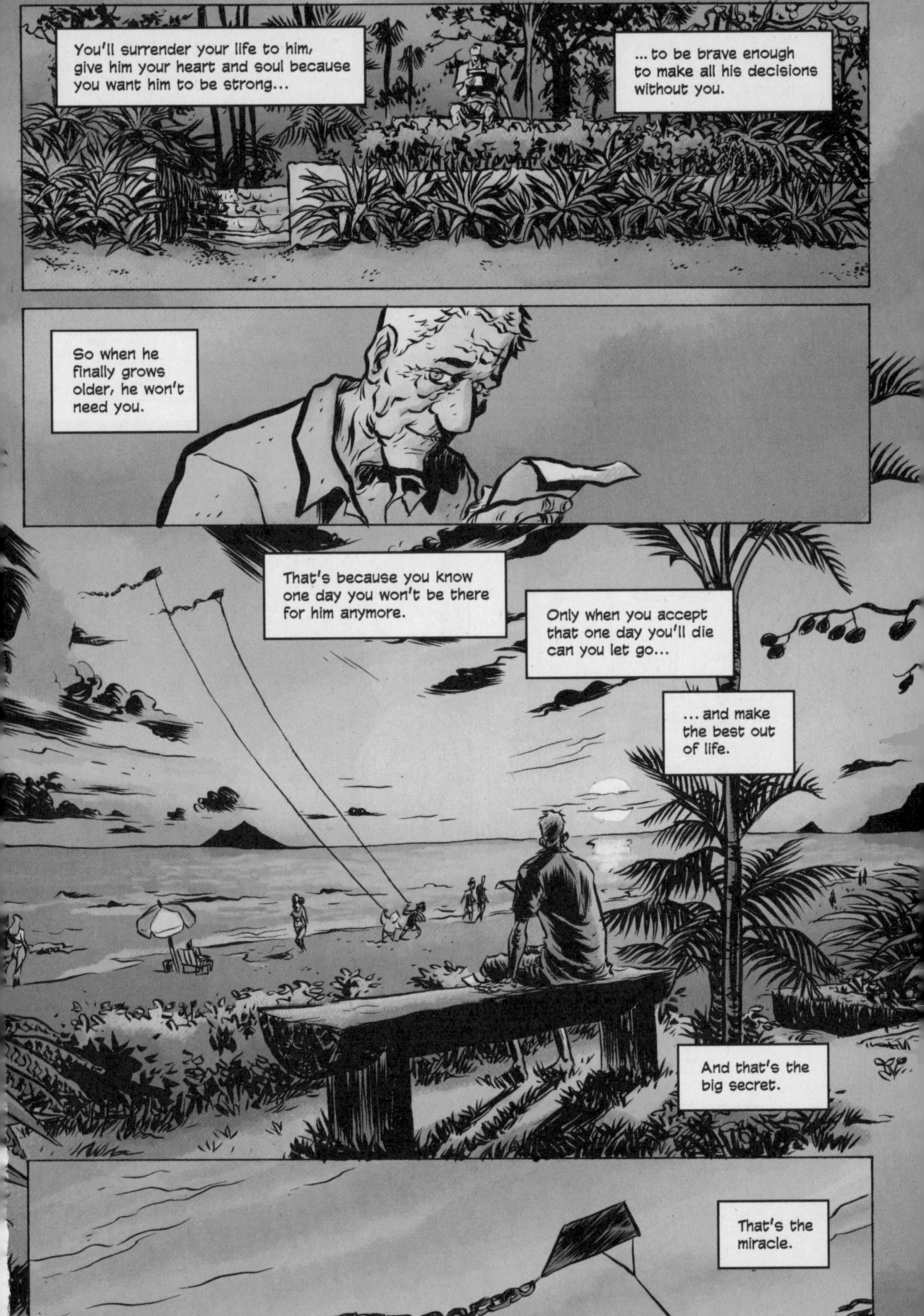
You'll surrender your life to him, give him your heart and soul because you want him to be strong...
...to be brave enough to make all his decisions without you.
So when he finally grows older, he won't need you.
That's because you know one day you won't be there for him anymore.
Only when you accept that one day you'll die can you let go...
...and make the best out of life.
And that's the big secret.
That's the miracle.

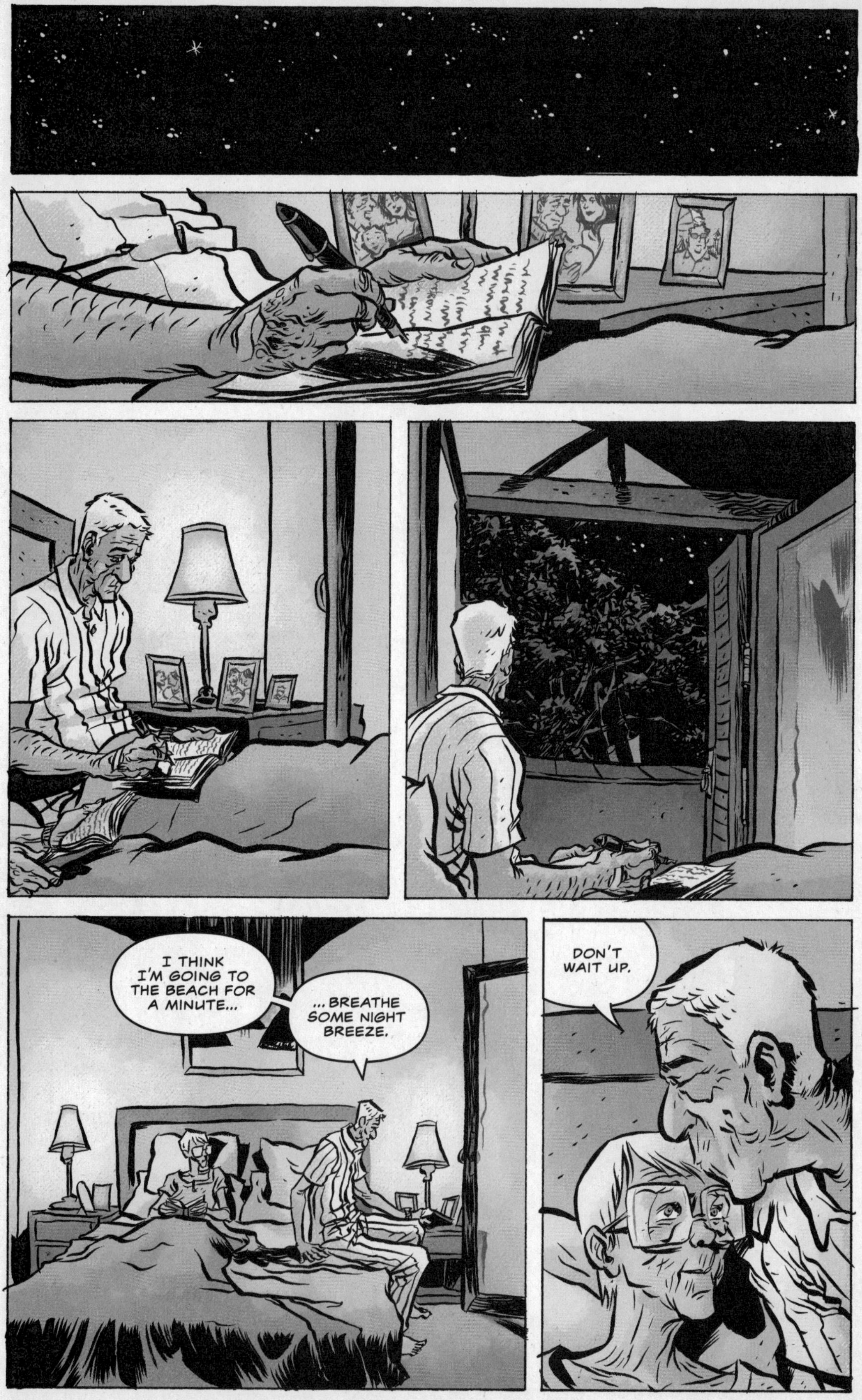

I THINK I'M GOING TO THE BEACH FOR A MINUTE...
...BREATHE SOME NIGHT BREEZE.
DON'T WAIT UP.

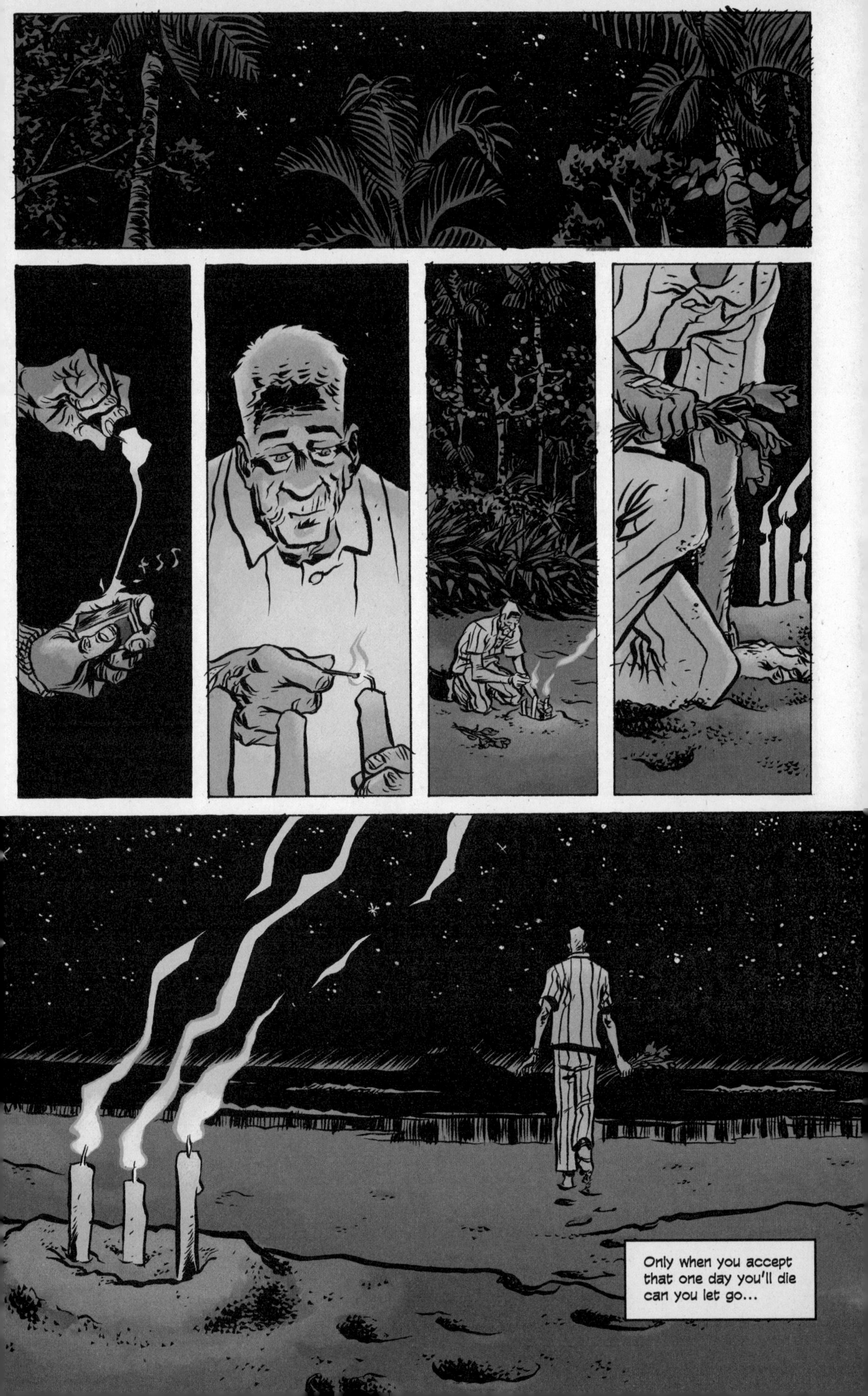
Only when you accept that one day you'll die can you let go...

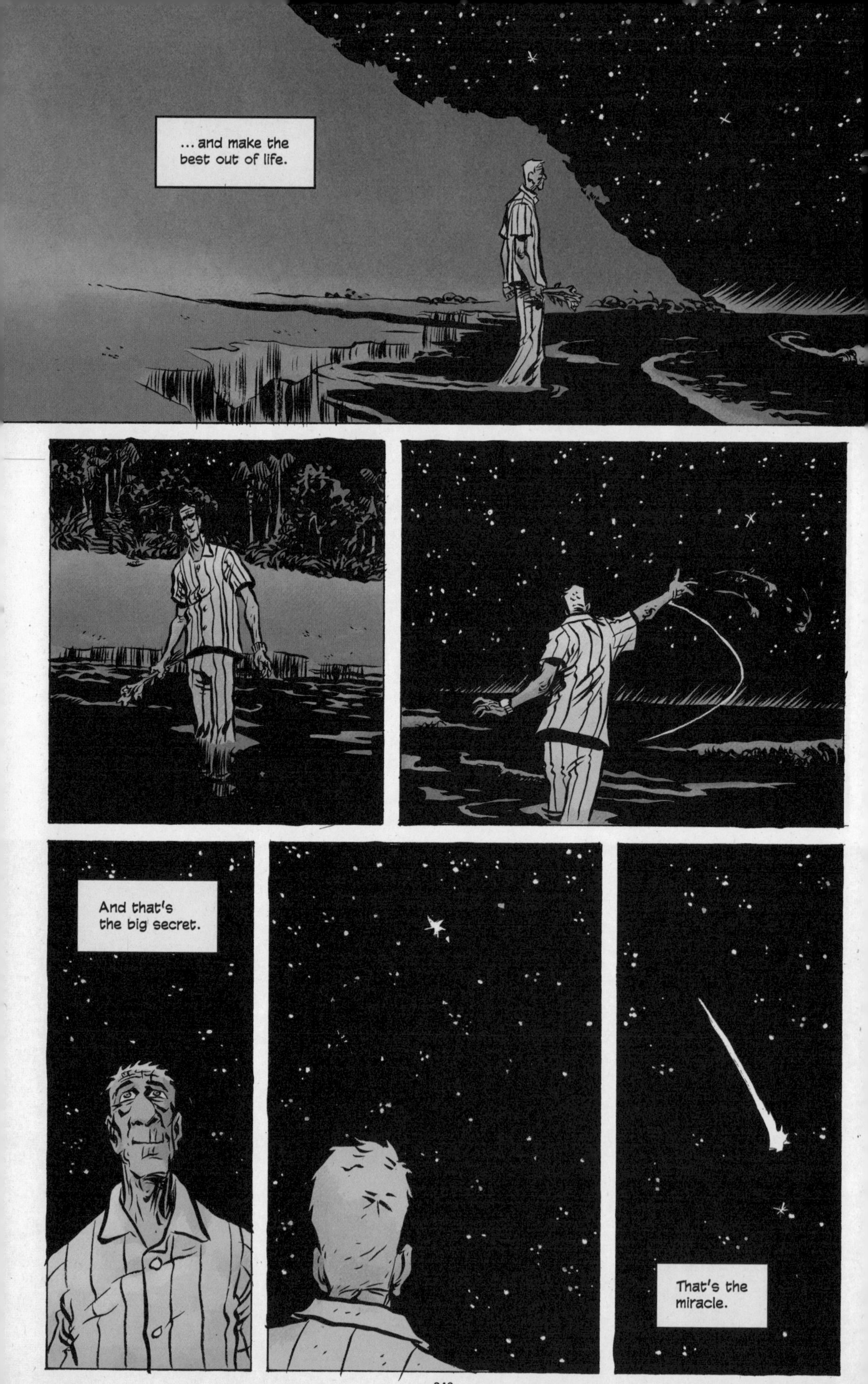
... and make the best out of life.
And that's the big secret.
That's the miracle.

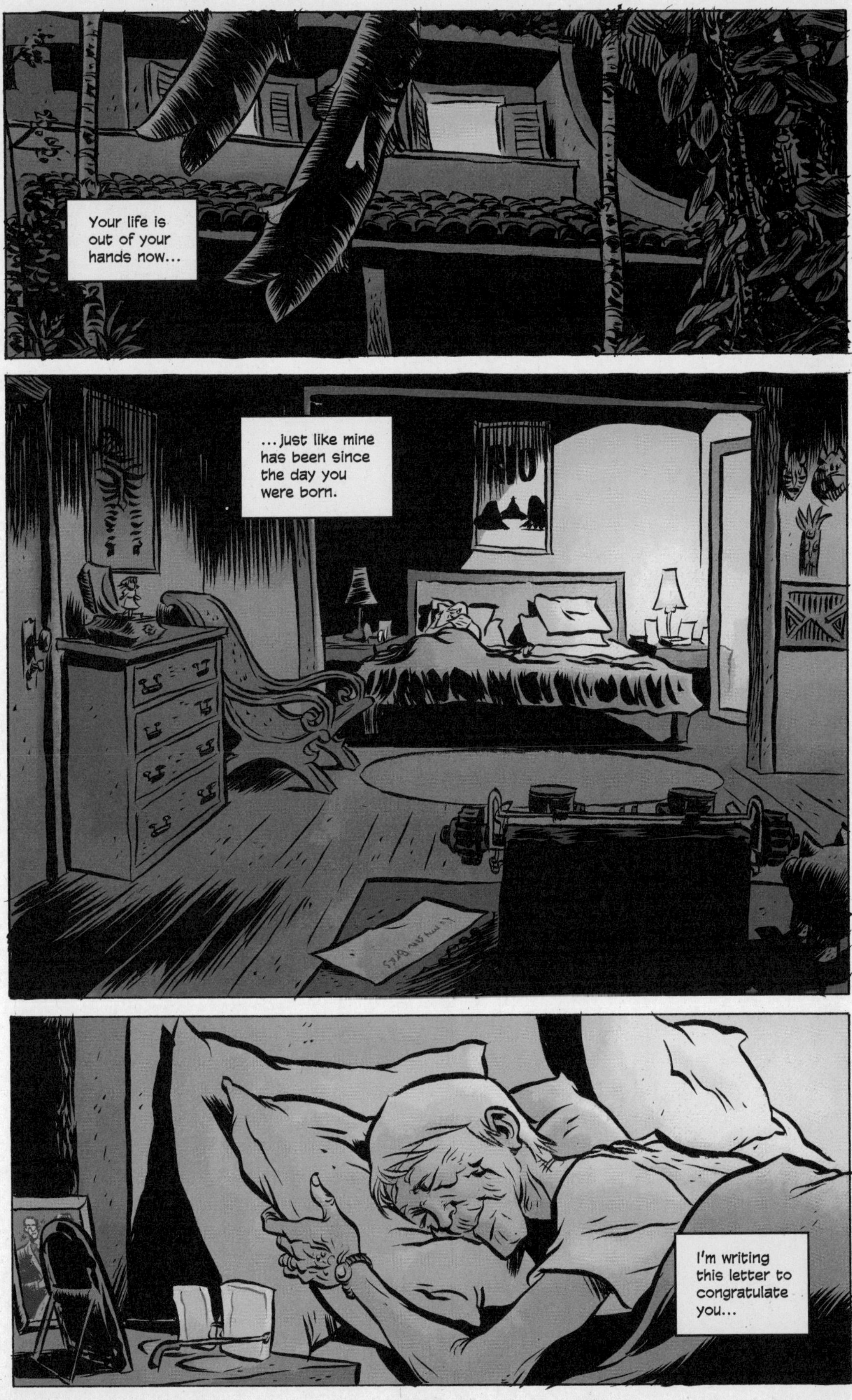
Your life is out of your hands now...
...just like mine has been since the day you were born.
I'm writing this letter to congratulate you...

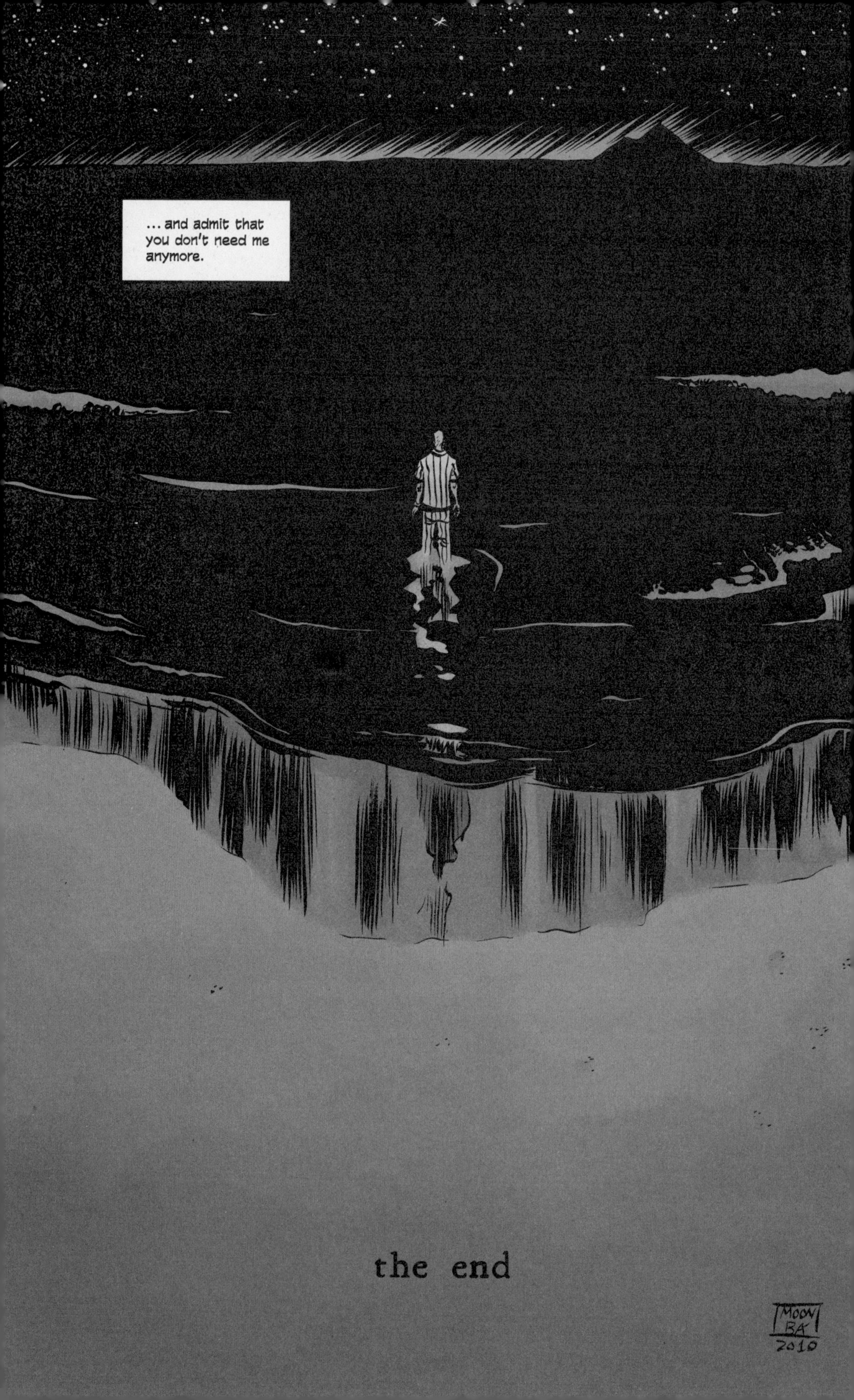
... and admit that you don't need me anymore.
the end
MOON BA 2010

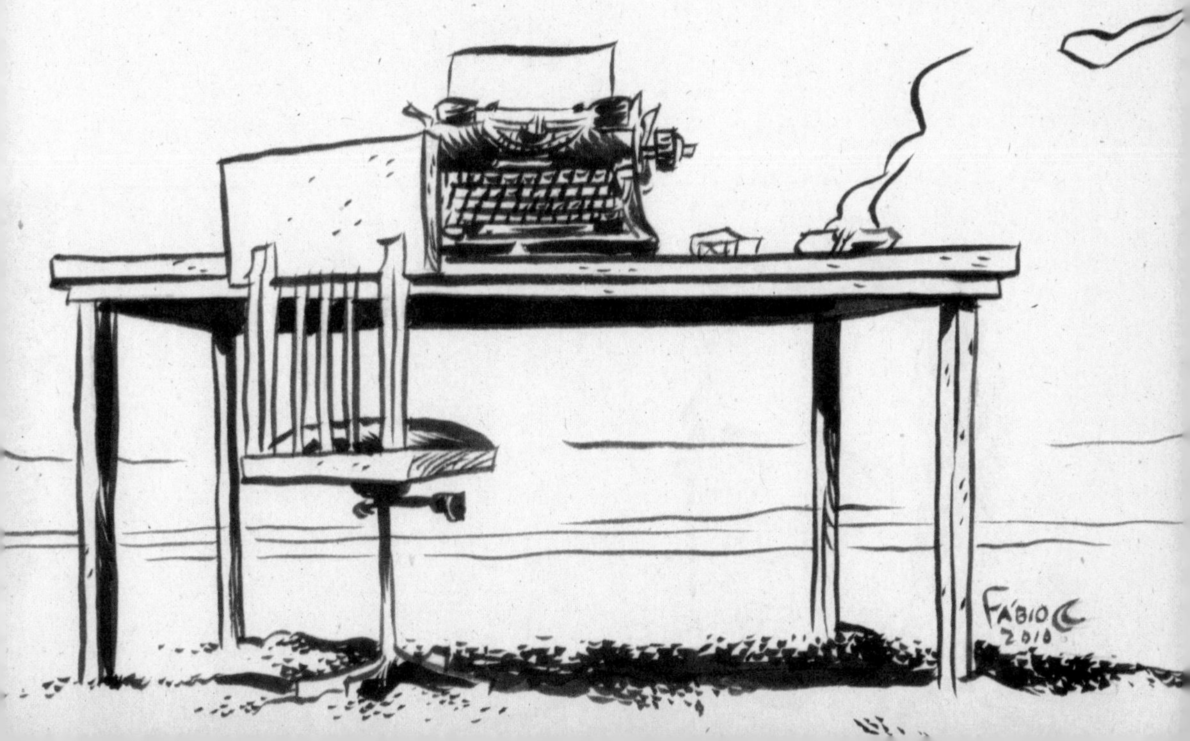
FÁBIO
2010

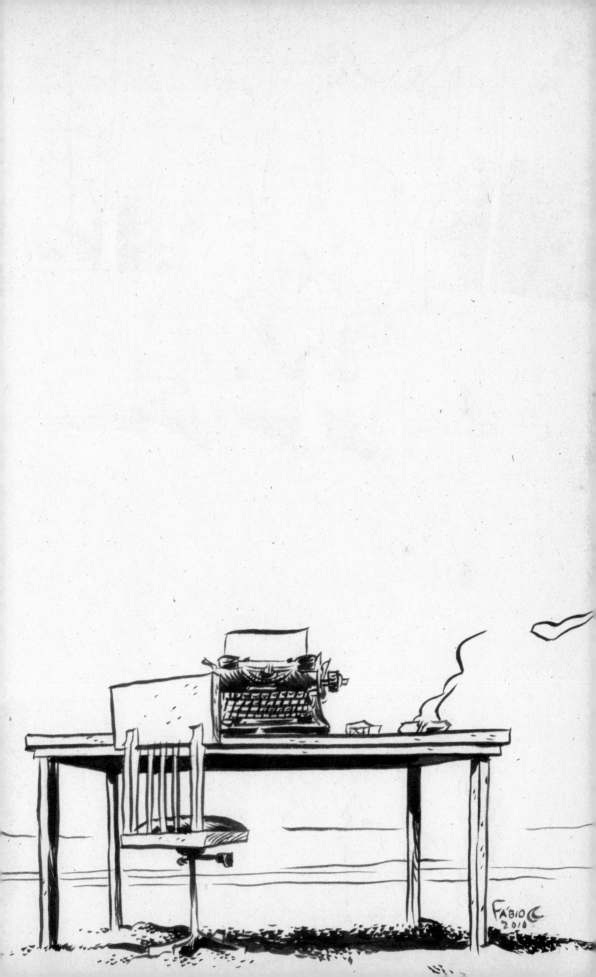

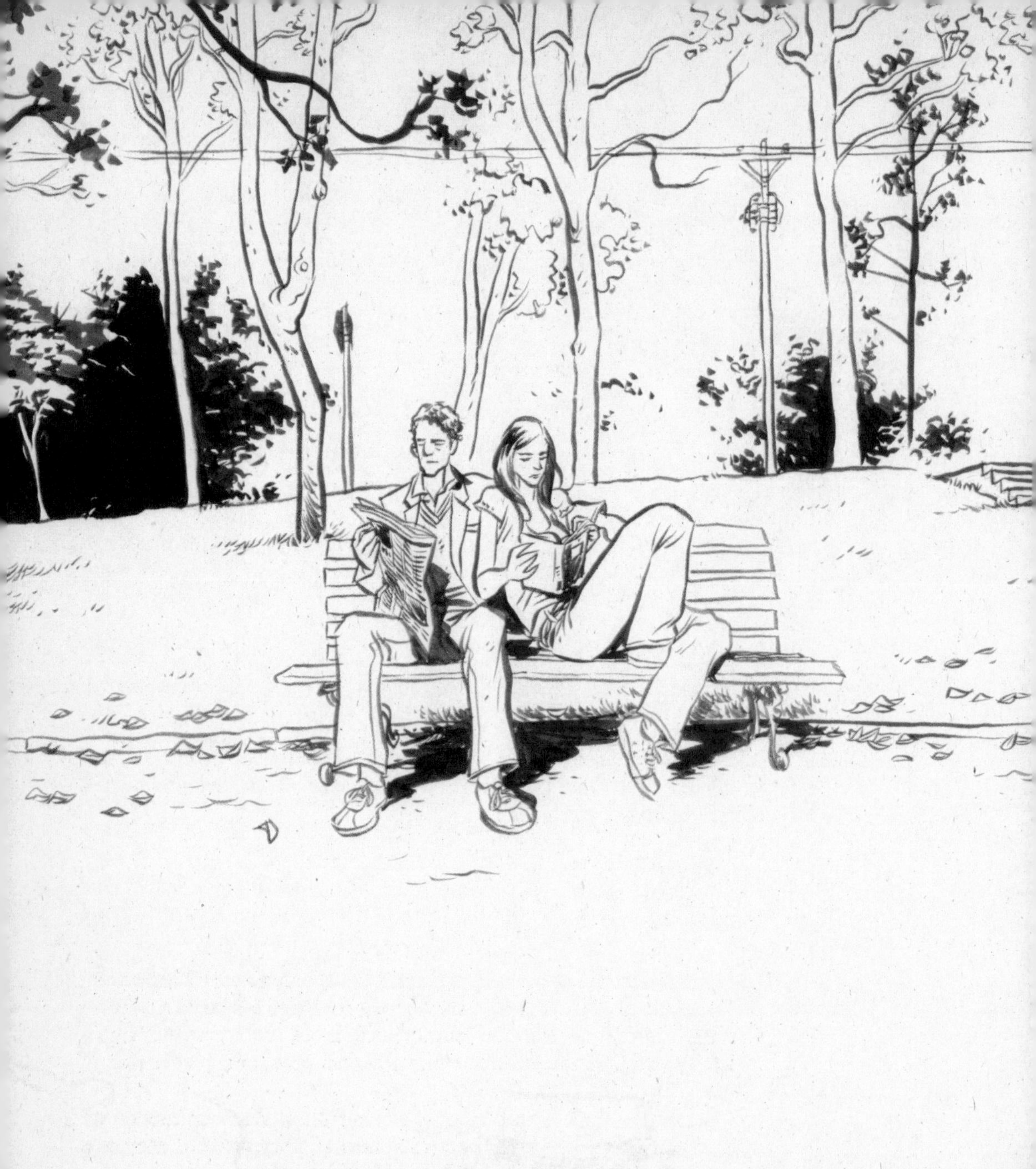

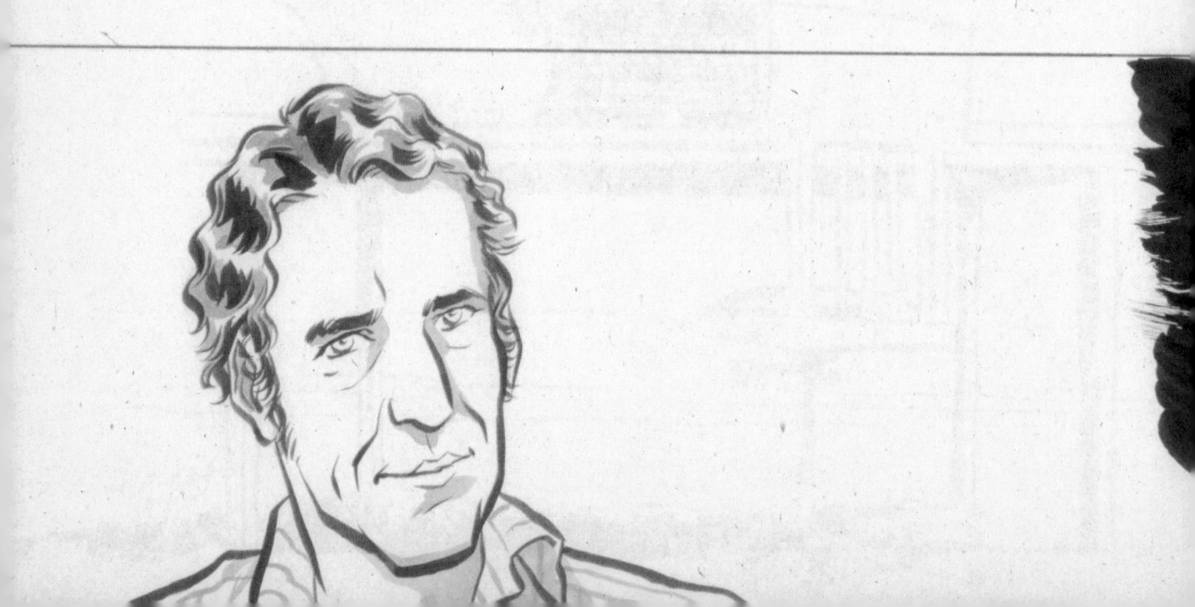

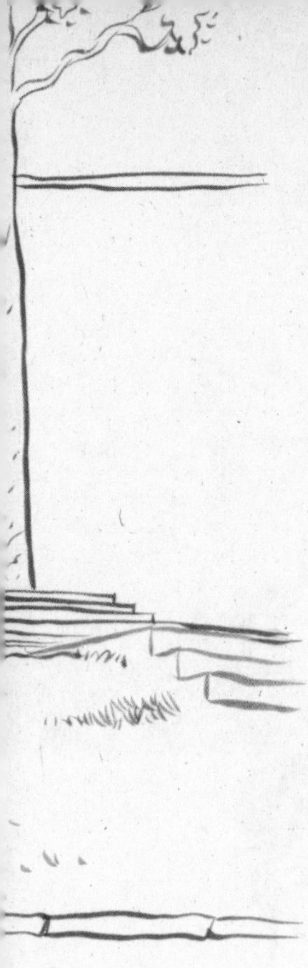

These were the first drawings I made to try to explain that, above all, this would be a story about quiet moments. It would be about what you can tell from somebody's eyes.

An exchange of looks.

A smile.

Many other sketches were made, and many sketchbooks were filled in order for us to take that trip until we came to that last page on the ocean. Every drawing was one step on our journey and, if we did everything right, hopefully you were able to follow our steps and come along for the ride.

We had made a plan. A road map we would follow. But soon enough we realized some days we would have to follow a different path, and some stories took a turn to unexpected places. Happy accidents.

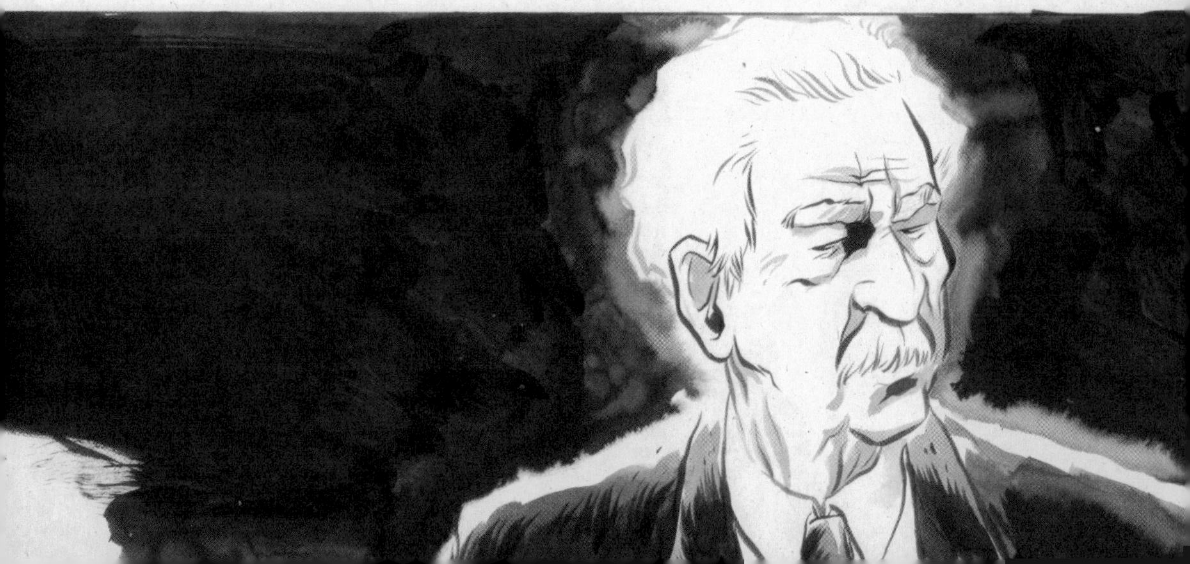

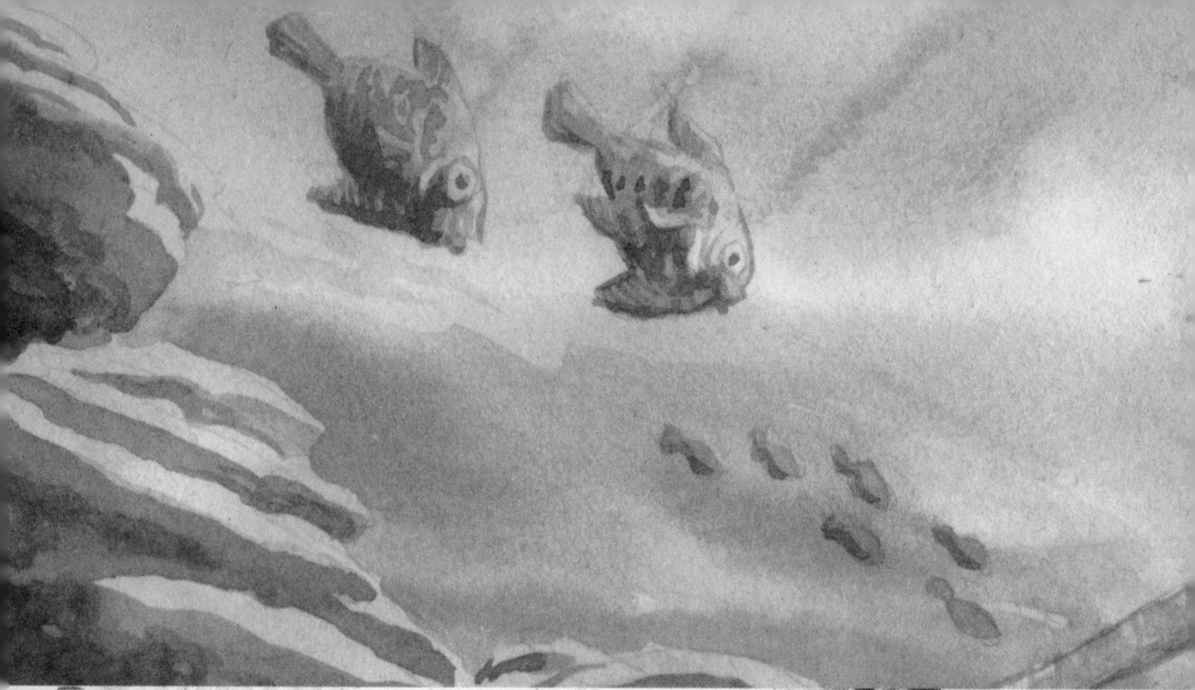
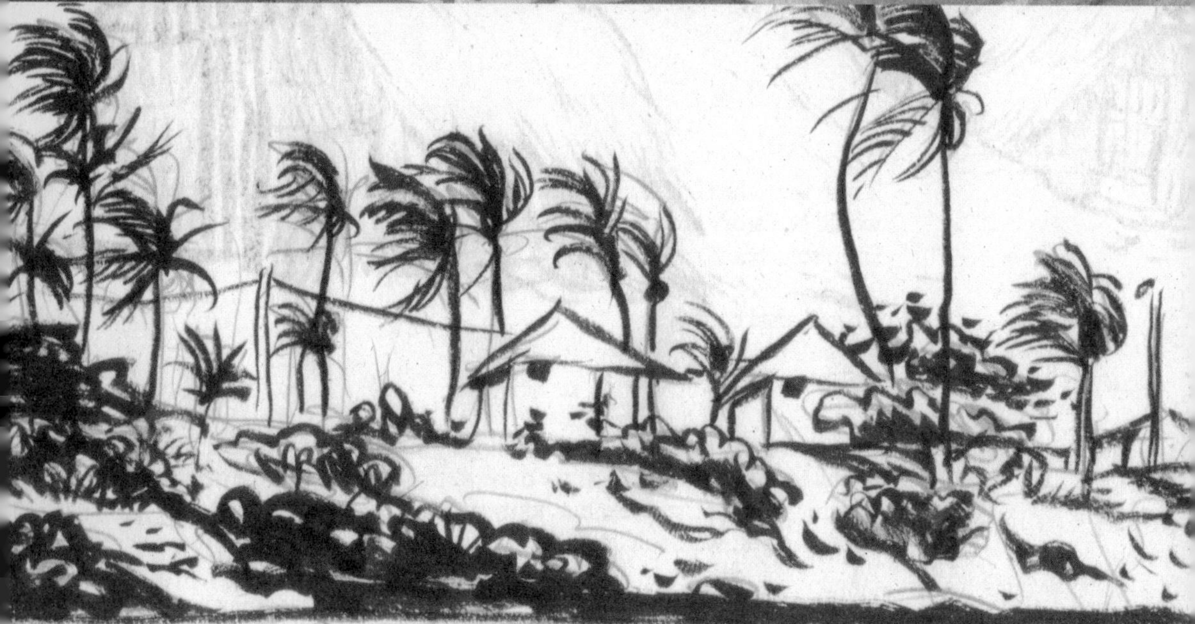
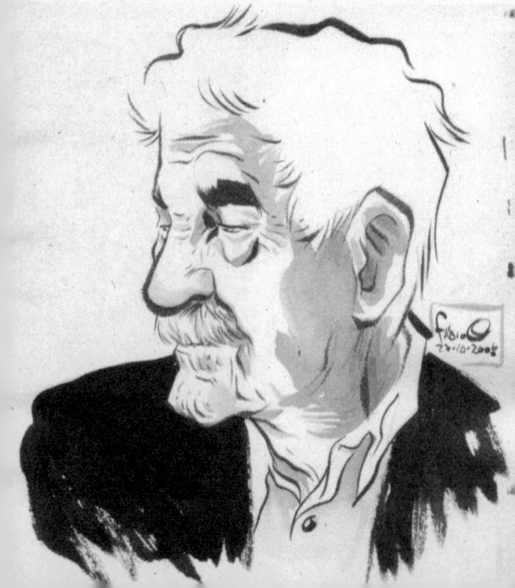
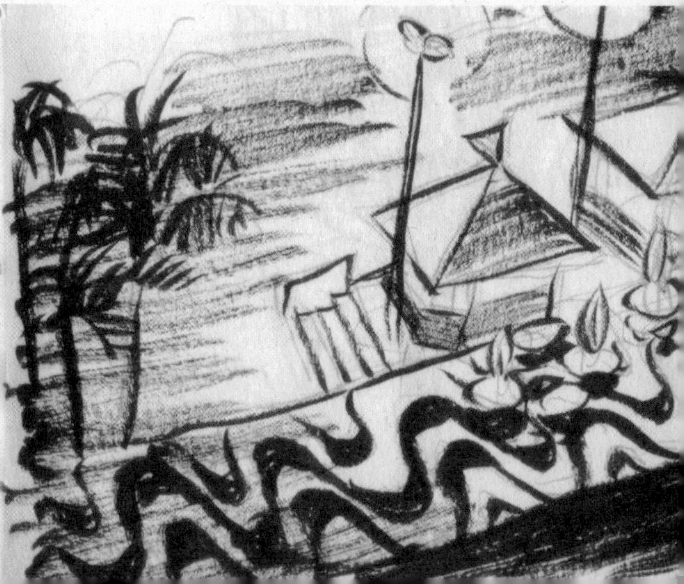

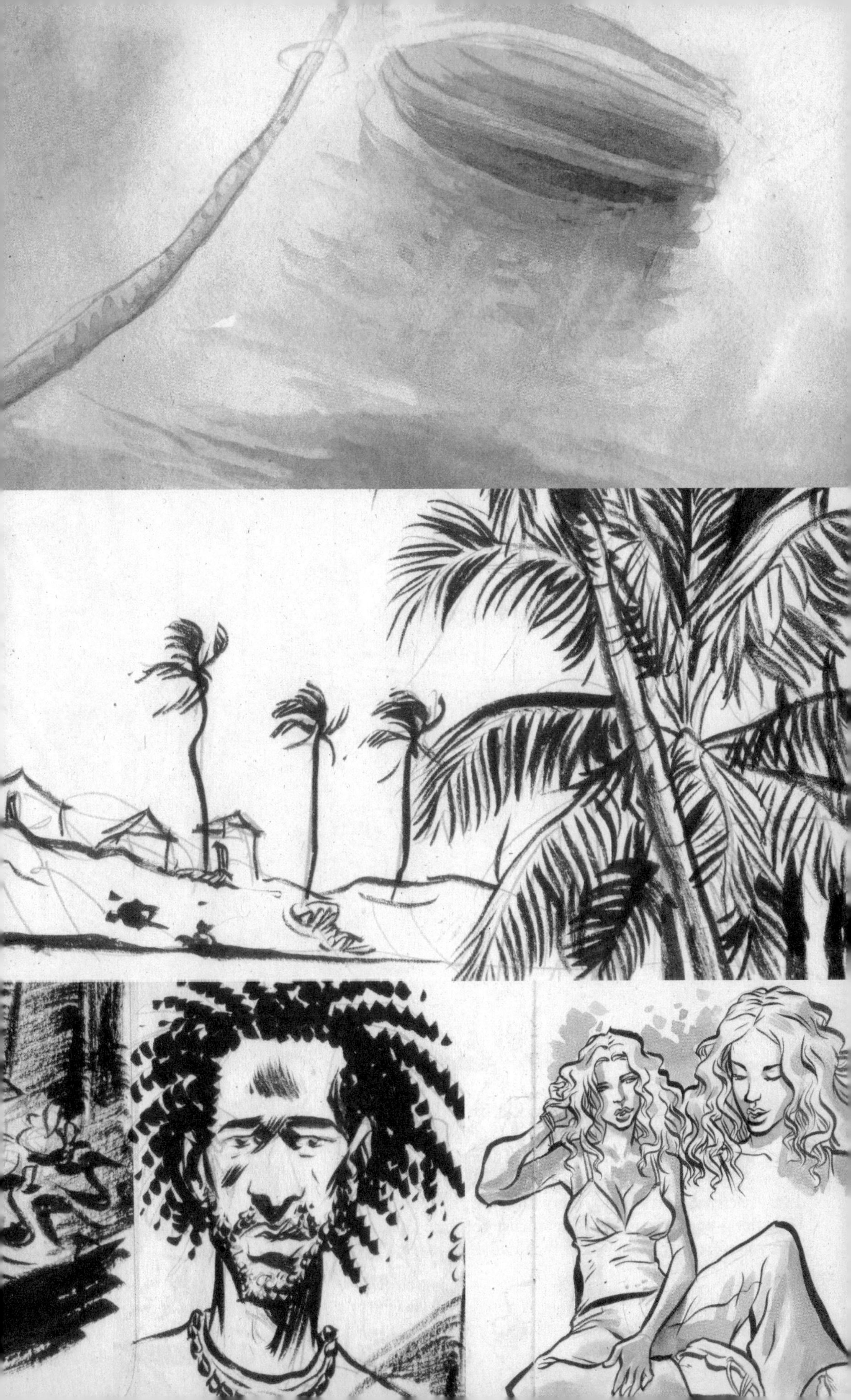

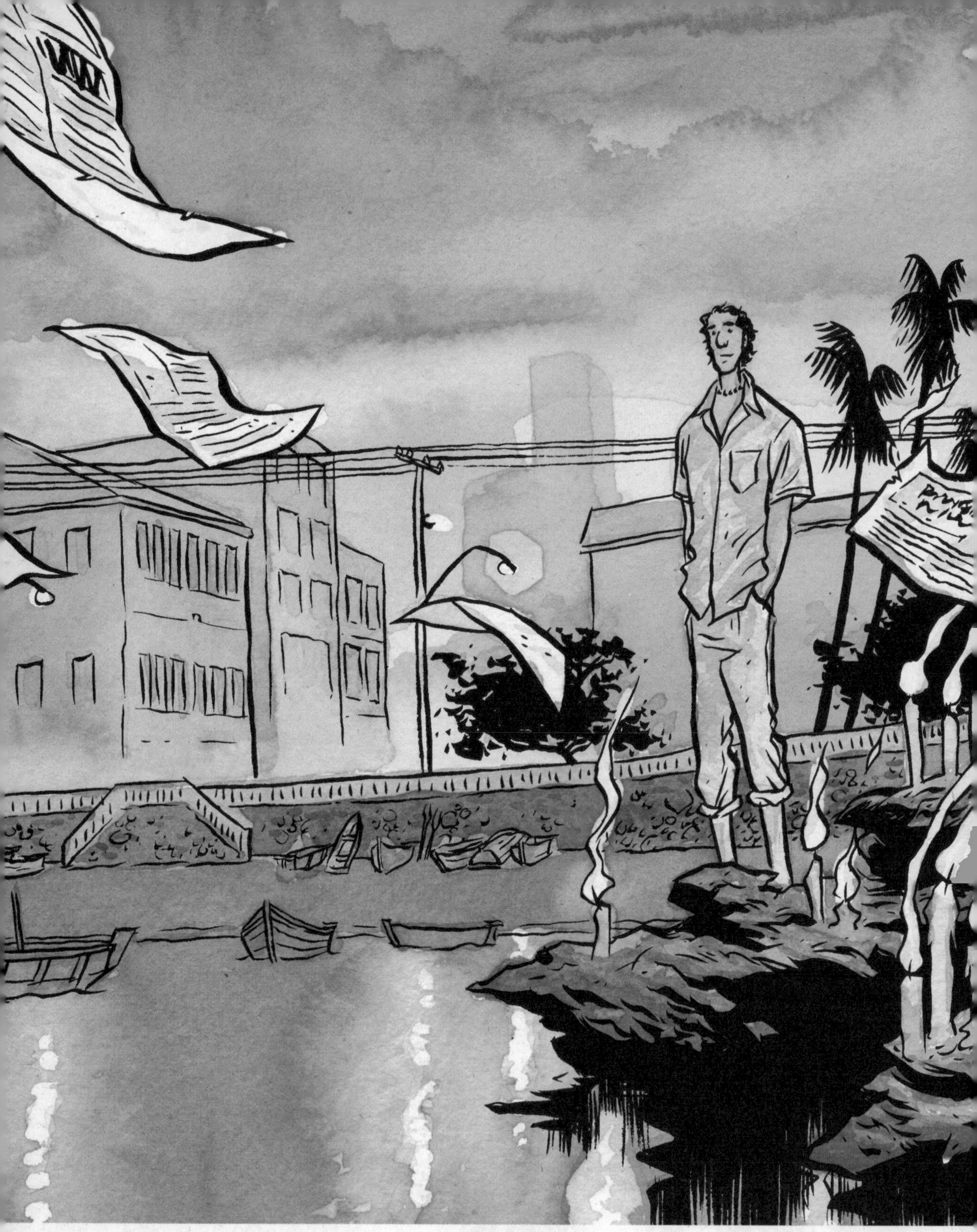

Firmly based on reality, the most difficult thing wasn't trying to create a world that would *look* real. No, the hardest thing was creating a world that would *feel* real.

Every reference, every photo, every color and every character, everything was made to try to reproduce feelings. A feeling that you were alive, happy, lonely, afraid or in love.

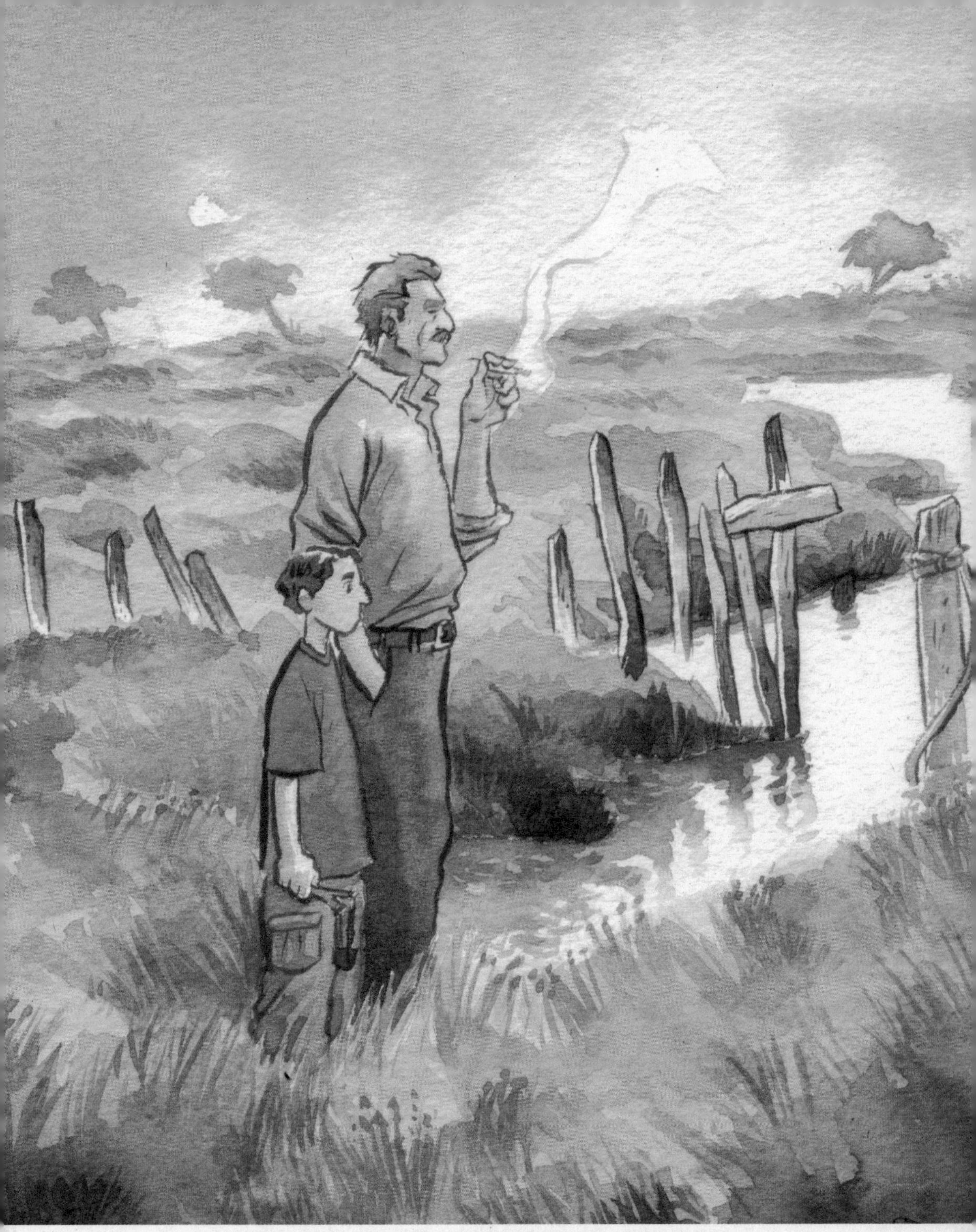

We wanted that feeling that life was happening right there, in front of every one of us, and we were living it.

And we did live it.

And sometimes we die to prove that we lived.

Fábio Moon
São Paulo, November 2010

Fábio Moon and Gabriel Bá are twin brothers, born in
São Paulo, Brazil, where they live until this day. They
have their friends there and their family; it's their home.

They have been telling stories in comic book form for almost
fifteen years, and their work has been published in France,
Italy, Spain, Greece, Japan, Germany, as well as in the U.S.
and Brazil. They like their coffee black, with no sugar, so
that the taste is strong and memorable. They believe stories
should taste equally strong and be just as memorable. They
work with a fresh pot that's always handy to make sure they
never forget that.